POLITICS IN FLORIDA

FOURTH EDITION

SUSAN A. MACMANUS
Distinguished University Professor
Director, USF-Nielsen Sunshine State Survey
University of South Florida

AUBREY JEWETT
Associate Professor
University of Central Florida

DAVID J. BONANZA
Research Analyst

THOMAS R. DYE
Emeritus McKenzie Professor of Government
Florida State University

RESEARCH ASSOCIATES
UNIVERSITY OF SOUTH FLORIDA
VICTORIA M. PEARCE
ALEXANDRA M. HOLLIDAY
ANTHONY CILLUFFO
GEORGIA PEVY

POLITICS IN FLORIDA

FOURTH EDITION

For information regarding permissions, call 941.922.2662

or contact us at our website:

www.peppertreepublishing.com or write to:

The Peppertree Press, LLC.,

Attention: Publisher

1269 First Street, Suite 7

Sarasota, Florida 34236

ISBN: 978-1-61493-381-6

Library of Congress Control Number: 2015913029

Printed August 2015

PREFACE

POLITICS IN FLORIDA highlights Florida's fast-ascension onto the national political stage and its emergence as one of the nation's premier battleground states. It shows how Florida has become the microcosm of America in the 21st century in its demographics, population make-up, and its politics. The state is at the forefront of the nation's changing political culture—an ever more mobile American people, an aging population, an ethnically and racially more diverse society, and an electorate ever more dependent on the media of mass communication. Most Florida voters come from someplace else. They have no deep roots in the state. They are aptly described as an "electorate of visitors." Even if they know the state capital is Tallahassee, not Miami, they are unlikely to know much about what goes on there.

POLITICS IN FLORIDA is an overview of government, politics, and public affairs in the Sunshine State with original research and analysis. If indeed we have a transient electorate in the state, the need for such a volume would appear to be especially pressing. The book is addressed primarily to the state's constant flow of new voters—retirees, immigrants, transplanted workers, professionals, and business people, as well as college students and younger people.

POLITICS IN FLORIDA is designed to be nonpartisan, informative, and descriptive. It summarizes the political culture of the state, prevailing public opinion, the state's constitution, political parties, power centers and interest groups, legislative affairs in Tallahassee, the roles of the governor and cabinet, the law enforcement and judicial systems, the financing of government, and city, county, and special district government in the state. It also provides brief summaries of key issues facing the state and the debates surrounding each: crime and corrections, education, social welfare, health care, the environment, growth management, economic development, and transportation.

SUSAN A. MACMANUS

AUBREY JEWETT

DAVID J. BONANZA

THOMAS R. DYE

ABOUT THE AUTHORS

SUSAN A. MACMANUS, a native of Pasco County, is a Distinguished University Professor in the Department of Government and International Affairs at the University of South Florida and Director of the USF-Nielsen Sunshine State Survey. She is the author of *Young v. Old: Generational Combat in the 21st Century* (Westview Press 1996), *Targeting Senior Voters: Campaign Outreach to Elders and Others With Special Needs,* (Rowman & Littlefield, 2000), and co-author with Thomas R. Dye of *Politics in States and Communities,* 15th ed. (Prentice-Hall, 2015). MacManus edited two books on redistricting in Florida: *Mapping Florida's Political Landscape: The Changing Art & Politics of Reapportionment & Redistricting* (Florida Institute of Government, 2002); *Reapportionment and Representation in Florida: A Historical Collection* (University of South Florida Innovation Institute, 1991). She co-edited (with Kevin Hill and Dario Moreno) and contributed to *Florida Politics: Ten Media Markets, One Powerful State* (Florida Institute of Government, 2004). With her mother Elizabeth Riegler MacManus, she co-authored *Citrus, Sawmills, Critters, & Crackers: Early Life in Lutz and Central Pasco County* (University of Tampa Press, 1998) and *Going, Going, Almost Gone: Lutz-Land O' Lakes Pioneers Share their Precious Memories* (University of Tampa Press, 2011). MacManus served as Chair of the Florida Elections Commission from 1999 to 2003 and is past president of the Florida Political Science Association, the Southern Political Science Association, and the Urban Politics Section of the American Political Science Association. She was a Fulbright Research Scholar at Yonsei University, Seoul, South Korea, 1988, and is a Florida Institute of Government Reubin O'D. Askew Fellow. MacManus is the long-time political analyst for WFLA-TV (Tampa's NBC affiliate), and the featured columnist for Sayfie Review—a popular Florida political website.

AUBREY JEWETT received his Ph.D. from Florida State University. He is currently Associate Professor of Political Science at the University of Central Florida (UCF). His main research and teaching interests are in American national, state and local politics with a special emphasis on Florida. In September 2002 Professor Jewett received the Leon Weaver Award for his study of ballot invalidation in Florida during the 2000 presidential election. He authored the chapter on central Florida politics in the edited volume *Florida Politics: Ten Media Markets, One Powerful State* and the chapter on Florida county government structure in the Florida Association of Counties' *Florida County Government Guide.* He is co-editor of the book *Political Rules of the Road: Representatives, Senators and Presidents Share Their Rules for Success in Congress, Politics, and Life.* Most recently, he published chapters in *Jigsaw Puzzle Politics* (evaluating the redistricting process in Florida in 2012) and *The Political Battle over Congressional Redistricting* (examining congressional redistricting in Florida). Professor Jewett has helped to bring in over $1 million of external funding to UCF. He has won multiple awards for teaching and advising excellence and professional service. Professor Jewett was also selected and served as an American Political Science Association Congressional Fellow. He supervised the department internship program for over ten years and placed over 1,400 University of Central Florida political science students at various local, state, and national sites.

DAVID J. BONANZA graduated from the University of South Florida with a Bachelor of Science summa cum laude in business economics. His professional experience includes analytical roles with Fortune 100 companies in the banking and telecommunications industries. His research focuses primarily on the interaction between economics and politics. He has coauthored chapters in Larry Sabato's *Pendulum Swing* (2011) and *The Year of Obama* (2009) and assisted with other publications, including a featured column for Sayfie Review.

THOMAS R. DYE, retired McKenzie Professor of Government at Florida State University, is now Professor Emeritus living in West Palm Beach. He is the author of *Politics in America*, 10th ed. (Prentice Hall, 2014); *Understanding Public Policy*, 14th ed. (Prentice Hall, 2012); *Who's Running America? The Obama Reign*, 8th ed. (Paradigm, 2014); *Politics in States and Communities* (co-author) 15th ed. (Prentice Hall, 2015), and numerous other books and articles on public affairs. He has served as president of the Southern Political Science Association and secretary of the American Political Science Association. He has received national awards from the Policy Studies Organization, the Southern Political Science Association, and the Florida Political Science Association. He was recognized as an Outstanding Alumnus of the College of Liberal Arts at Penn State University.

ACKNOWLEDGEMENTS

The authors wish to thank the many individuals who helped make the fourth edition a reality.

For the cover design: Cambry Lichtenberger, Marketing Assistant at the John Scott Dailey Florida Institute of Government at the University of South Florida.

For photographs: Sarasota County and Polk County governments, the Florida Department of State, State Library & Archives of Florida, and Dr. Susan A. MacManus.

For sharing invaluable research findings and graphics, the Collins Center For Public Policy, Inc., Enterprise Florida, the Florida Association of Counties, the Florida League of Cities, Inc., Florida TaxWatch, *Florida Trend* magazine, the James Madison Institute, Leadership Florida, The Nielsen Company, and two county supervisors of elections (Susan Gill, Citrus County; Brian Corley, Pasco County).

For editing and proofing, Barbara A. Langham.

We also want to thank the late J. Stanley Marshall, Founding Chairman of the James Madison Institute, a nonpartisan nonprofit research and educational organization chartered in 1987, for a grant supporting the first edition.

Finally, we are grateful to The John Scott Dailey Florida Institute of Government at the University of South Florida for publishing this book as part of its educational mission and to its Director Angela Crist and Robyn Odegard, Learning and Development Facilitator, for all their support.

Thanks are also due to Michele Dye, Communications and Marketing Director, Office of the Dean, College of Arts and Sciences, University of South Florida, for her work with USF student analysts on the USF-Nielsen Sunshine State Survey.

The data provided by each greatly enhance our understanding of Florida politics. However, the interpretations of the data are solely those of the authors.

CONTENTS

LIST OF TABLES

LIST OF FIGURES

Chapter 1. Politics in the Sunshine State

"Welcome to Florida, the nation's third largest state, where everyone is from someplace else!" Or almost everyone—nearly two-thirds of the state's residents were born outside the Sunshine State. Florida is more of a crowd than a community—a large and growing population of diverse people, spread over a thousand miles, few of whom have deep roots in the state. Over the years, the state has had an influx of retirees fleeing cold winters, Cubans fleeing Castro, Haitians fleeing poverty, Colombians, Venezuelans, Nicaraguans, and others from Latin America seeking economic opportunity or escaping political unrest, along with young workers seeking jobs, investors seeking opportunities, tourists seeking entertainment, and drug traffickers seeking markets. Florida has become a real "melting pot" of cultures. The transition has altered the state's politics and its economy.

The change since 1940 has been *dramatic*: "From one of the least appealing, most racially polarized, and poorest states to one of the most desired, most diverse, and most prosperous; from a state that had been anything but a bellwether of the nation to one that... is 'the whole deal, the real deal, a big deal.'" [1]While the state's population growth slowed somewhat during the Great Recession, it soon rebounded so that by 2014, it was again growing by about 300,000 people a year.[2]

FLORIDA: A CRITICAL BATTLEGROUND SWING STATE

Florida is a powerhouse in national-level politics.[3] By surpassing New York to become the third most populous state, it now has the third largest number of Electoral College votes (29)—tied with New York—which means it greatly impacts the outcome of presidential elections. Presidential and vice presidential candidates make frequent trips to Florida when campaigning for the White House. It is one of only a handful of states to consistently be labeled a key battleground from start to finish.

Florida is also among the most politically competitive states in the United States. There is only a slim percentage difference in the number of registered Democrats and Republicans. The proportion of Floridians who describe themselves as independents is sizable and growing. Statewide contests are won by both Democrats and Republicans and are often close, with independents usually being the real swing voters. The state's reputation as a "battleground state" is well-deserved.

The Sunshine State is a microcosm of the nation at large in its racial and ethnic composition—more so than any other large competitive state. According to the 2015 U.S. Census, African Americans comprise about 17 percent of the state's population, and Hispanics make up nearly 24 percent. (Hispanics may be of any race.) Comparable figures for the United States are blacks, 13.2 percent, and Hispanics, 17.1 percent. (See Table 1-2.) While Florida's Asian population is smaller than in the United States, it is growing at a faster pace than either the black or Hispanic populations.

The state's unique *voter* age profile—an almost equal percentage of younger and older voters—makes the state an ideal place to conduct polling and focus groups to design political ads that will be used nationally. Prior to the 2014 gubernatorial elections, 48 percent of all *registered* voters were younger than 50, while 52 percent were older than 50. (See Chapter 4.)

Finally, Florida is important politically because it is a big donor state—a real "cash cow." Each election cycle, Floridians contribute millions of dollars to candidates, political parties, political action committees (PACs), and 527s—independent soft-money groups, named for the IRS code under which they are regulated.[4] Only California, New York, the District of Columbia, and Texas routinely rank ahead of Florida in total campaign contributions. (See Chapter 4.)

What Shapes Florida's Politics?

Florida is home to the wealthy, the poor, and the middle class; NASCAR dads and soccer moms; younger and older voters; bleeding heart liberals, middle-of-the-road moderates, and right-wing conservatives; rural residents, suburbanites, and big city dwellers; and old-timers and newcomers (native-born and foreign-born).[5] Nearly every ethnic and racial group is represented among the state's voting population.

Florida politics and policies have largely been shaped by five key characteristics of the state's population:

1. Rapid population growth with heavy in- and out-migration.[6]
2. Multiple population centers and media markets.
3. Age diversity—a large elderly population, a growing young population, and lots of Baby Boomers.
4. Racial and ethnic diversity.
5. Changing employment patterns, reflecting shifts in the state's economy.

The result is a state political culture, fractured along geographic, racial, ethnic, age, and income lines, the absence of a sense of statewide community, and "a sense of rootlessness and restlessness" among voters.[7] With so many newcomers, many with lingering attachments to their home states or countries, political loyalties are fluid and changing. Many voters lack information or interest in statewide issues; they are more attentive to news about their city than about events in the State Capitol in Tallahassee. Indeed, Florida has been described as "an electorate of visitors."[8] Florida's current political culture reflects its historical development over 500 years. But the state's political culture is constantly in flux because of the state's ever-changing population. Political analysts often say that relying on yesterday's demographics to win today's election can be a formula for failure.

A large part of Florida's population has moved here from somewhere else, prompting analysts to describe Florida's politics as largely "imported" from other states and nations. The steady influx of newcomers constantly changes the state's political dynamics.

UP-CLOSE: A SHORT HISTORY OF FLORIDA

Written records about life in Florida began with the arrival of the Spanish explorer and adventurer, Juan Ponce de Léon, in 1513. Ponce de Léon called the place "La Florida" in honor of Pascua Florida, Spain's Easter-time Feast of Flowers. For the next 300 years, three major European powers struggled to control Florida as part of their larger strategy to control the "New World."

Statue of Juan Ponce de Léon in St. Augustine's Fountain of Youth Park.

The Struggle for Control

In 1562, the French Protestant, Jean Ribault, explored the area; two years later, fellow Frenchman, René de Goulaine Laudonnière, succeeded in establishing Fort Caroline at the mouth of the St. Johns River, near present-day Jacksonville.

These French ventures prompted Spain to accelerate its plans for colonization. Pedro Menéndez de Avilés hastened across the Atlantic, his sights set on creating a settlement. Menéndez arrived in 1565 at a place he called San Augustín (St. Augustine) and established the first permanent settlement in what is now the United States.

As late as 1600, Spain's power over what is now the southeastern United States was unquestioned. So, when the English came to America, they wisely planted their first colonies well to the north, in Jamestown, Virginia (1607), and Plymouth, Massachusetts (1620). But in 1702, swept up in European conflicts and angered, in particular, by Spain's policy of granting freedom to escaped slaves, South Carolinians and their Indian allies, led by Colonel James Moore, laid siege to Spanish Florida. They destroyed St. Augustine but failed to capture Castillo de San Marcos—the fort that guarded the city that still stands to this day. England's southernmost continental colony, Georgia, founded in 1733, brought Spain's adversaries even closer. Georgians attacked Florida in 1740 and besieged the Castillo for almost a month but failed to capture it.

Britain temporarily gained control of Florida in 1763, following the Seven Years' War (1756-63). Spain evacuated Florida, leaving the province virtually empty. At that time, St. Augustine was still a garrison town with fewer than 500 houses, and Pensacola was an even smaller military town. But Spain regained Florida with the 1783 settlement that ended the American Revolution. However, instead of becoming more Spanish during this "second Spanish period," the Floridas (Britain had divided the area into two provinces—East and West.) became more American. Finally, after several official and unofficial American military incursions into the territory, Spain ceded the Floridas to the United States in 1821.

Territorial Government

In 1818, one of those military operations brought General Andrew Jackson into western Florida for skirmishes with Florida's Indians, later labeled the First Seminole War. Jackson returned in 1821 to establish a new territorial government for the United States over what was an unspoiled, underdeveloped wilderness, occupied mainly by Indians, blacks, and Spaniards. Tallahassee was chosen as the capital city because it was halfway between the existing governmental seats of St. Augustine and Pensacola. By 1830, the territory boasted a population of 34,730, many of whom had come from Georgia, Virginia, and the Carolinas. Of this population, almost half were slaves.

Seminoles, already respected for their fighting abilities, won the admiration of professional soldiers for their bravery, fortitude, and ability to adapt to changing circumstances during the Second Seminole War (1835-42). That war, by far the most significant of the three conflicts between the Indians and the federal government in Florida, began when the Seminoles resisted removal across the Mississippi River to what is now Oklahoma. Jackson, who had become President, sought their removal through force, sacrificing the lives of countless Indians, soldiers, and citizens. But in the end, the issue remained in doubt. Some Indians migrated "voluntarily," some were captured and sent west under military guard, and others escaped into the Everglades, where they carved out a life away from contact with whites. One name that has remained familiar after more than a century is that of Osceola, a war leader of the Seminoles who would not leave his home. Seized under a flag of truce, he died in captivity in 1838. Today there are

Indian reservations at Immokalee, Hollywood, and Brighton (near the city of Okeechobee) and along the Big Cypress Swamp. In addition to the Seminole tribes, Florida also has a Miccosukee Indian population.

Statehood and Civil War

Florida became the 27th state of the United States in 1845, and William D. Moseley was elected Governor. Five years later, the population had increased to 87,445, including about 39,000 slaves and 1,000 free blacks. The slavery issue soon dominated the affairs of the new state. In the 1860 presidential election, Republican Abraham Lincoln received no Florida votes, and, shortly thereafter, a special convention drew up an ordinance of secession. Florida left the Union on January 10, 1861.

The Civil War followed. Florida was not ravaged as several other Southern states were. Indeed, no decisive battles were fought on Florida soil. Tallahassee was the only Southern capital east of the Mississippi River to avoid capture during the war, spared by Southern victories at Olustee (1864) and Natural Bridge (1865). After General Robert E. Lee's surrender in Virginia, Union troops occupied Tallahassee on May 10, 1865.

Railroads and Economic Growth

The final quarter of the 19th century brought economic developments that propelled Florida into the 20th century. Large-scale commercial agriculture, especially citrus growing and cattle ranching, became the state's most important economic activity. Industry, particularly cigar manufacturing, took root in the immigrant communities of the state. Railroad construction began on a scale undreamed of in antebellum Florida. Between the end of the Civil War and the beginning of World War I, the Florida Legislature offered free public land to railroad investors.

Perhaps the most fabled of Florida's railroad tycoons was Henry Flagler. As a partner to John D. Rockefeller in what would become the huge monopoly Standard Oil, Flagler amassed a fortune. In 1878, on the advice of a physician, Flagler brought his ailing wife (the first of three) to Jacksonville for the winter. That was as far as the rails would take him. Five years later, he returned to Florida, this time purchasing a rail link to St. Augustine. Convinced that he was not the only winter-weary Northerner who would enjoy the mild weather in Florida, Flagler began building a railroad and matching luxury hotels down the East Coast. In St. Augustine, he built the Moorish-style Ponce de Leon Hotel (now Flagler College) and the Alcazar. By 1894, the Florida East Coast Railroad reached Palm Beach, where Flagler built the largest wooden hotel in the world, the Royal Poinciana, and a palatial home, Whitehall, now a museum. With the additional enticement of land—8,000 acres given to him by the state for each mile of railroad he built south of Daytona—Flagler extended his railroad to Miami in 1896. Henry Plant, a rival of Flagler, brought a railroad down the Gulf Coast, opening it to development as Flagler pushed southward on the eastern coast of the state. In Tampa, Plant built a magnificent Moorish-style hotel with minarets, the Tampa Bay, which outshone Flagler's Ponce de Leon in St. Augustine. The Tampa Bay Hotel is now the University of Tampa. In nearby Bellaire, Plant built the Belleview, the largest wooden hotel in the world until Flagler outdid him with the Royal Poinciana. Plant's hotel, now called the Belleview Biltmore, is still a deluxe resort. Plant City is named after him.

Both agriculture and tourism benefited from railroad building. Citrus especially benefited because it became possible to pick oranges in South Florida, put them on a train heading north, and eat them in Baltimore, Philadelphia, or New York in less than a week.

20th Century Florida

By the end of World War I, land developers had descended upon the state. With the rise in popularity of the automobile, it became commonplace for people to vacation in Florida. Many tourists stayed on, and developers even sold land sight unseen to Northerners persuaded by fantasy advertisements. But the land bubble burst after 1925 when money and credit ran out and banks and investors abruptly ceased trusting developers. Although hurricanes received a measure of blame for wiping out the Florida boom, they were merely the final blow. By the time the Great Depression came to the rest of the nation in 1929, Floridians had already become accustomed to tightening their belts.

World War II reinvigorated Florida. The state became a training center for troops, sailors, and airmen of the United States and her allies. Highway and airport construction was accelerated so that, by the war's end, Florida had an up to date transportation network ready for use by its citizens and by the visitors who seemed to arrive in an endless caravan.

Economically and culturally, Florida witnessed several achievements that began after World War II and continued unabated into the 1980s: the move to Florida by major American corporations in increasing numbers; the completion of the interstate highway system throughout the state; construction of major international airports; an expansion of the state's universities and community colleges; the mushrooming of suburban housing; the introduction and proliferation of high technology; and the successful development of the NASA space program, punctuated by historic launches from Cape Canaveral, lunar landings, and the use of space shuttle craft.

Despite periodic setbacks caused by winter freezes, infestations of fruit flies, and outbreaks of citrus canker, the citrus industry remains vital to the state's economy. Bolstered by huge capital investments, tourism is thriving as never before in Florida, although it suffers during an economic downturn. Symbolic of the trend toward increasing sophistication in Florida's tourist industry, Walt Disney World and its affiliated EPCOT Center have annually attracted more visitors from across the country and around the world than Florida has residents

21st Century Florida

Florida entered the 21st century as the center of electoral controversy. Its reputation as the nation's biggest and most important swing state was solidified by the 2000 presidential election between George W. Bush and Al Gore—a race decided by 537 votes and ended by a U.S. Supreme Court ruling that recounting ballots in just a handful of counties was unconstitutional. While Florida underwent major electoral reforms, it remains the focal point for discussions of election reform—particularly in light of the diversity (race, language, and age) of its population.

The state's diversity, its reputation as the nation's bellwether, and the rise of 24-7 news coverage and social media have thrust major legal battles onto the national stage—parents' custody rights (the Elian Gonzalez case), right to die (the Terri Schiavo case), child abandonment/murder (the Casey Anthony case), and civil rights/social justice (George Zimmerman's shooting of Trayvon Martin).

In spite of a number of economic trouble spots early in the decade—the shrinking of the space program, eight major hurricanes hitting the state in two years, significant damages to the state's citrus industry by a disease known as greening, the collapse of the housing market during the Great Recession prompting the highest foreclosure and unemployment rates in the nation—by 2014, the state's economy had rebounded, with population growth being a major driver. U.S. Census Bureau statistics showed that six of the nation's 20 fastest growing metropolitan areas were in Florida. The growth came from population in-migration from other states and abroad—persons drawn to Florida by the usual amenities (sunshine, beaches, the environment, retirement) but also by jobs in the hospitality, trade, and construction fields. The emergence of a strong medical sector has also prompted the rise of medical tourism. The normalization of U.S. relations with Cuba, announced by President Barack Obama, on December 17, 2014, promises to have major impacts politically and economically on Florida during the second half of the 21st Century.

Source: *A Short History of Florida.* Tallahassee: Florida Department of State, 1997; the 21st Century Florida entry is by the authors[9].

GROWTH, CHANGE, AND ROOTLESSNESS

In 1940, Florida was a sparsely populated, humid, swampy collection of country towns, fishing villages, migrant labor camps, Indian settlements, sugar cane fields, and orange groves, with a few plush coastal resorts catering to wealthy winter guests.[10] There were fewer than two million residents, and the state ranked 27th in population. Political power rested in the northern tier of counties with the "pork choppers," who dominated the state legislature, the state's multiple executive offices, and the state's courts. Florida politics was white, conservative, segregationist, and one-party Democratic.[11]

Today Florida is the nation's third largest state, with nearly 20 million people. (See Figure 1-1.) More than three million people moved into the state between 1990 and 2000 alone—a growth rate of 23.5 percent. From 2000 to 2010, it was 17.6 percent. It was the fourth consecutive decade in which Florida's population grew by nearly three million residents (see Figure 1-1).[12] In fact, over the 60-year period from 1950 to 2010, the state's population grew 578 percent. The growing racial and ethnic diversity among Florida's residents has, in large part, been driven by in-migration from Latin America (Hispanics) and the Caribbean (blacks).

Figure 1-1. Florida's Population Growth: 1980 to 2035 (Projected)

Florida Population

1950	2,771,305
1960	4,951,560
1970	6,789,447
1980	9,746,961
1990	12,938,071
2000	15,982,824
2010	18,801,310
2020	21,149,697
2030	23,608,972
2040	25,603,577

Sources: Bureau of Economic and Business Research, "Florida Population: Census Summary 2010," April 2011.
Bureau of Economic and Business Research, "Projections of Florida Population by County, 2009–2035," March 2010.

Between 2000 and 2010, every county (except for Monroe and Pinellas) increased its population. (See Figure 1-2.) Four counties grew by more than 50 percent (Flagler, Sumter, Osceola, and St. Johns); another 20 grew at least 20 percent.

Figure 1-2. Population Growth Rate: 2000-2010

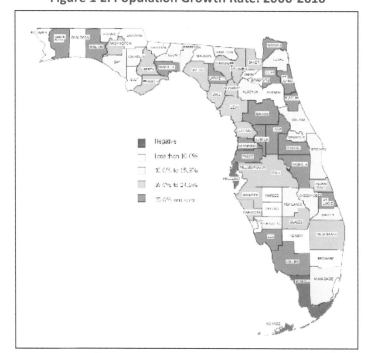

Source: Bureau of Economic and Business Research, "Florida Population:
Census Summary 2010," April 2011. Available at
http://www.bebr.ufl.edu/sites/default/files/population/Census_Summary_2010.pdf

The Population grew slightly faster in incorporated cities and towns (20 percent) than in unincorporated areas of the counties (16 percent). During the high growth decade, nine new cities and towns were formed.[13] Since 2010, there has been only one—Estero in Lee County (2014), although the Florida Legislature has granted voters in the community of Panacea (Wakulla County) the right to decide whether to incorporate (2015).

Great Recession Packs Powerful Punch

The growth rate for 2000-2010 masks the fact that 24 counties actually experienced population decline near the end of the decade. The Great Recession that began in 2007 led to "a declining housing market, substantial job losses, and a generally deteriorating economy."[14] (See Figure 1-3.) In areas hardest hit by the recession, more people were moving out than moving in (net out-migration). The construction industry took the biggest hit. (See Figure 1-4.)

Florida's highways are nearly at their peak capacity in high growth parts of the state.

Figure 1-3. The Great Recession that Began in 2007 Slowed Job and Population Growth

Unemployment in Florida and the U.S.
Recessions: 1981, 1990, 2001, 2007

Data for January of each year (seasonally adjusted).

United States ———— Florida

Source: Bureau of Labor Statistics, accessed April 30, 2015.
Available at http://www.bls.gov/eag/eag.fl.htm

Figure 1-4. The Great Recession: Job Losses Were Steepest in the Construction Industry
(The Housing Bubble Burst)

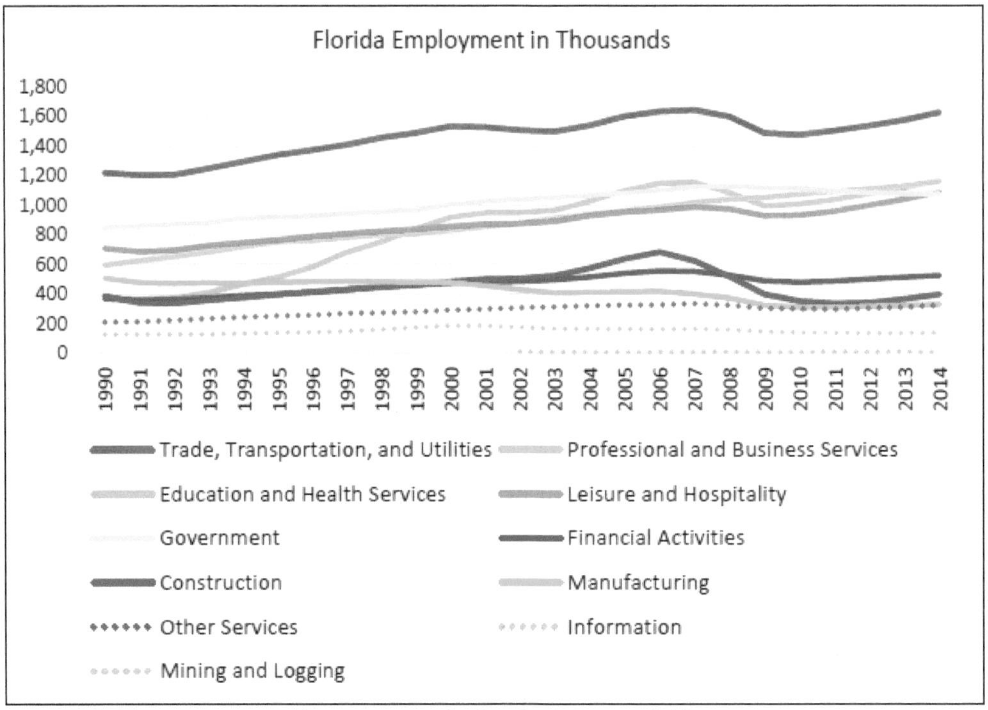

Florida Employment in Thousands

Legend:
- Trade, Transportation, and Utilities
- Professional and Business Services
- Education and Health Services
- Leisure and Hospitality
- Government
- Financial Activities
- Construction
- Manufacturing
- Other Services
- Information
- Mining and Logging

Source: *Florida Economy at a Glance*, Bureau of Labor Statistics. Available at
http://www.bls.gov/eag/eag.fl.htm.

Post-recession analyses by economists pointed out the strong correlation between population growth and the structure of the state's economy, primarily employment patterns:

"Low land costs, low taxes and inexpensive real estate helped attract scores of businesses to Florida over the past 50 years, creating an attractive employment picture across the state. Population growth itself served as an enormous catalyst for economic growth, creating thousands of jobs in construction and household and professional services. This historical dependence on continued population inflows also skewed Florida's economic base heavily toward industries tied to population growth, such as construction and real estate finance. Both immigrants from out of the country (especially from Mexico and Cuba) and in-migrants from other states rushed in to fill these job opportunities, fueling a virtuous cycle."[15]

The analysis underscored the importance of continuing to diversify the state's economy.

In spite of the downturn during the Great Recession, demographers continue to predict Florida will grow in the next decade, although perhaps not as fast. (Review Figure 1-1.) The state still has great appeal to people and businesses.

Population distribution has shifted from the Panhandle to Central and South Florida over the last century. (See Table 1-1.) The state's *centroid* (exact population center) was in Jefferson County in 1830 but, by 2010, was in southern Polk County.[16] (See Figure 1-5.) As a result, political power in Florida has shifted from the less-populated, rural North Florida counties to the urban centers in Central Florida (Orlando, Daytona, Titusville, and the Space Center), Southwest Florida (from the Tampa St. Petersburg Clearwater area to Sarasota, Fort Myers, and Naples), and Southeast Florida's "Gold Coast" (Palm Beach, Fort Lauderdale, and Miami). About 85 percent of Floridians live in urban areas within 10 miles of either coast.

More than 96 percent of Florida residents live in one of the state's metropolitan statistical areas—one of the highest metropolitanization rates in the nation.[17] The term "metropolitan statistical area " (MSA) is defined by the U.S. Census Bureau as containing a core urban population of 50,000 or more, including any counties that either contain the urban area or are adjacent to it and share strong socioeconomic ties, as measured by commuting for work purposes. (The demographic analysis of Florida MSAs that is presented in this text features only the top-ranked MSAs for each statistical category.)

Table 1 1. Florida's Largest and Smallest Counties

Largest Counties (Central, South)		Smallest Counties (North)	
Miami-Dade	2,613,692	Gulf	16,543
Broward	1,803,903	Dixie	16,356
Palm Beach	1,360,238	Union	15,647
Hillsborough	1,301,887	Jefferson	14,597
Orange	1,227,995	Calhoun	14,592
Pinellas	933,258	Hamilton	14,351
Duval	890,066	Glades	12,852
Lee	653,485	Franklin	11,794
Polk	623,174	Lafayette	8,696
Brevard	552,427	Liberty	8,668

Source: Bureau of Economic and Business Research, University of Florida, "Florida Estimates of Population 2014."

Figure 1-5. Florida's Population Centroid: 1830-2010

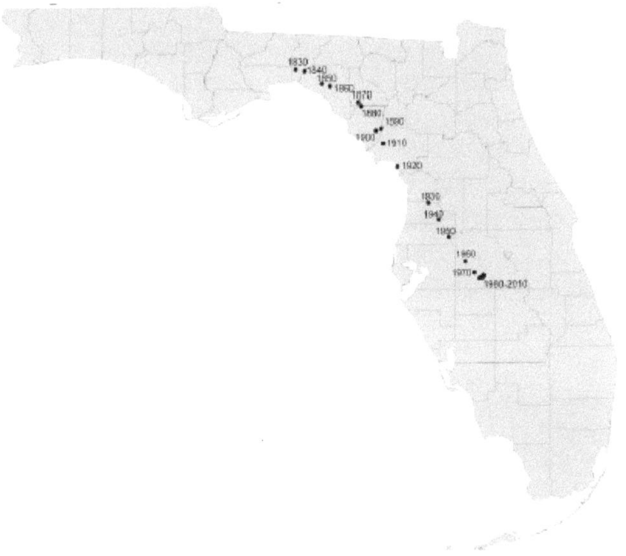

Source: "Florida's Population Center Migrates through History," Gainesville, FL: Bureau of Economic and Business Research, University of Florida, accessed April 2015.

Florida's population has clustered near its coasts.

Political Rootlessness

Florida's population makeup is constantly changing. Rapid population growth and heavy in- and out-migration have fostered a sense of political rootlessness among voters. Traditional party ties, as well as loyalties to particular political leaders, are left behind in hometowns, home states, and home countries. Florida's newcomers lack some of the traditional political anchors—lifelong church memberships, labor unions, long-established neighborhoods, and ties between family and friends—that may have served as sources of political allegiance in their city or country of origin.

Florida's newcomers are more open to political cues from the mass media—television (broadcast, cable), radio, social media, and newspapers. They are more persuadable; they drift from candidate to candidate with little lasting loyalty. Newcomers ensure that Florida always has an ample number of swing voters in elections—voters who can be influenced by slick television advertisements, snappy campaign slogans, and charismatic candidates. However, their turnout rates may be a bit lower than longer-term residents, at least until they get a better understanding of Florida politics, although, among newly naturalized citizens, turnout rates are often higher.

Growth Politics and Policy

Florida politics is synonymous with growth politics, which takes on a greatly different meaning during periods of high growth than during periods of population decline. In boom times, elected officials struggle to cope with the effects of rapid population increase, urbanization, and sprawl. While population growth usually translates into economic growth and increasing tax revenues (see Chapter 9), it also creates challenges in a number of policy areas, including crime and law enforcement, education, transportation, and the environment. Drug- and consumer-scam-related crime rates may increase in areas experiencing high growth (see Chapter 8). Pressures to build new schools, train and hire new teachers, and increase educational performance among a rapidly growing and diverse student population intensify (see Chapter 11). Congestion on Interstates 95, 75, 4, and 10, as well as on local roads increases citizens' demands for new or expanded roads and mass transit. Florida's water management districts must balance demands for water by farmers, developers, and homeowners, while addressing concerns about water quality and future availability (see Chapter 12). It is clear that, during high growth periods, Floridians often pressure politicians to restrict growth or, at least, to be smarter about it. The term "economic development" takes on a negative connotation and is seen as simply a code term for "pro-developer."

In contrast, "economic development" is viewed much more positively when the economy is bad and the state (or locality) is experiencing rising unemployment rates, business closures, and population out-migration. During those times, surveys show that citizens want government officials to enact policies that will bring new businesses (jobs) into the community, even if it means offering tax breaks to them—a policy that is often fought in boom times.[18]

Racial and Ethnic Diversity

Florida's political culture is arguably the most diverse of any state in the nation and is shaped by racial and ethnic diversity (see Table 1-2). Conservative, white, North Florida Democrats, while no longer dominant, still draw their political traditions from Dixie. But Democratic conservatives are now outnumbered by white Republican conservatives in the booming central and southern regions of the state. Black liberal Democrats, representing the state's 16.7 percent African-American population, occupy key offices in big cities and exercise statewide power through their Legislative Black Caucus.

Table 1-2. Florida's Racial and Ethnic Composition: A Comparison with the U.S.

Race	Percentage of Population	
	Florida 2015 (%)	U.S. 2015 (%)
White	78.1	77.7
Non-Hispanic White	56.4	62.6
Hispanic/Latino	23.6	17.1
African American	16.7	13.2
Asian	2.7	5.3
Native American	0.5	1.2
Pacific Islander	0.1	0.2
Two or more races	1.9	2.4

Source: U.S. Bureau of the Census, 2015 Census Estimates.
http://quickfacts.census.gov/qfd/states/12000.html

Hispanics constitute another 23.6 percent of the state's population and are more splintered in their partisan preferences. Cuban Americans are the largest Hispanic subgroup in Florida, although they are now outnumbered by non-Cuban Hispanics. Historically Cubans have identified with the Republican Party, although that is gradually changing. Colombians also lean Republican, while Mexicans, Venezuelans, and Dominicans strongly identify with the Democratic Party. The large Puerto Rican vote (concentrated in Central Florida) tends to be split between those who have moved to Florida from the Northeast (Democrats) and those who have in-migrated directly from the Island (independent swing voters).[19]

Asians, while still a small proportion of Florida's total population, are its fastest growing minority group. They are projected to comprise seven percent of the state's eligible voters by 2060.[20] Asian Americans, like Hispanics, are not monolithic in their languages, religions, cultures, or politics. The Census category "Asian" includes Chinese, Japanese, Koreans, Filipinos, Vietnamese, Asian Indians, Laotians, and Thais. A higher percentage of Asians than other racial or ethnic groups register as independents, although the immigration issue has pushed them more Democratic. They are concentrated in the state's large metropolitan areas—Fort Lauderdale, Orlando, and Jacksonville—and in smaller counties with a high concentration of knowledge-based jobs (universities, military installations).

Fractured Political Geography

Florida is also fragmented geographically. Eight hundred miles separate Pensacola from Key West. Media markets are widely divided, with different newspapers and television stations serving each major city.[21] An old adage of Florida politics is "The farther north you go, the farther south you get." The northern part of Florida reflects the politics of the traditional South, while South Florida reflects the political culture of many northern states—and Latin American countries.

The northern Panhandle still reflects the Democratic, Bible Belt politics of the Old South. Military installations, including Pensacola Naval Air Station and the sprawling Eglin Air Force Base, add to the area's conservative bent. The "Redneck Riviera" describes the white-sand beaches of the Gulf Coast, extending eastward from Pensacola to the "Big Bend," where the coastline curves southward. Pine trees, cotton fields, small towns, and large churches, both black and white, extend northward to the Alabama and Georgia borders. Tallahassee, the capital city, with many state employees, and Gainesville, with its university community, provide liberals with oases of support.

Jacksonville is a booming business center, combining insurance, international trade, and commercial development with the Mayport Naval Base and a Mayo Clinic. The city's consolidation with surrounding Duval County makes it the state's largest "city." Although Jacksonville was once a solidly Democratic area, Republicans have gained ground in recent years and now nearly equal Democrats in registration (41 vs. 36 percent respectively). The area still has a sizeable black population (30 percent). Since 1992, voters have elected a black Congresswoman, a black sheriff (1995), and a black mayor (2011)—all Democrats.

Florida's midsection—along the I-4 Corridor, linking Daytona Beach, Titusville, Orlando, and Disney World with Tampa, St. Petersburg, and Clearwater—is one of the most rapidly growing areas of the state. The

Tarpon Springs' thriving Greek community celebrates the Epiphany. Florida is home to a wide variety of ethnic, cultural, and religious groups.

"Space Coast," Orlando, and Disney World attract many working families, while Tampa, St. Petersburg, and Clearwater, as well as Pasco, Hernando, and Citrus counties to the north are home to many retirees who are extremely protective of Social Security, Medicare, and low taxes. The midsection is moderate to conservative, increasingly competitive for Republicans and Democrats, and home to many independent, or swing, voters. Younger voters moving to the area to take advantage of high-tech jobs, especially in the health care and financial services sectors, tend to register as independents.

The southwest Gulf Coast, from Sarasota and Bradenton to Naples and Fort Myers, is largely a resort and retirement area. Historically, these retirees came from Midwestern states like Michigan and Ohio and brought their Republican Party affiliation with them. More recently, there has been an influx of Democratic-voting retirees from the Northeast (New York, New Jersey, Massachusetts). These new arrivals have made several counties, including Pinellas and Sarasota, much more partisan-competitive.

But the heavily populated southeast region—downtown Miami and surrounding Miami-Dade County, Fort Lauderdale and Broward County communities, and Palm Beach County—is a polyglot of cultures. The region includes wealthy, upper-class WASP enclaves in Palm Beach; Jewish communities in Miami, Miami Beach, Hollywood, and Boca Raton;[22] African-American neighborhoods in Miami, Fort Lauderdale, and Riviera Beach; large Cuban-American communities in Miami and Hialeah; and rapidly growing Haitian communities in North Miami, Fort Lauderdale, and West Palm Beach. Large numbers of New Deal-generation seniors still live in retirement villages and condominiums, although the number is steadily declining due to generational replacement. They are reliable Democratic voters. The southeast region houses more native-born New Yorkers than Floridians. Historically, Palm Beach and Broward County usually gave Democratic candidates their largest vote margins in the state, while Miami-Dade County tended to divide its vote, with the Republican Cuban community balancing the liberal African American and Jewish Miami Beach vote. That, too, has changed. Miami-Dade has become a solidly Democratic voting county due to the increased in-migration of Democratic-leaning non-Cuban Hispanics and Afro-Caribbeans and a higher proportion of young Cubans voting Democratic.

Media Markets

It is difficult to develop a statewide sense of civic community in an area as large as Florida. The state is not dominated by a single major city in the fashion of New York and Illinois, or even by two major urban centers, such as California's Los Angeles and San Francisco. Nor do Floridians think of themselves as Floridians in the fashion of Texans. Rather, Floridians are more likely to look to city and regional newspaper and television stations for whatever sense of community they may develop.

Florida politics is fragmented along 10 media markets—separate population centers served by local television stations and daily newspapers (see Table 1-3). Aspiring statewide candidates must project a favorable image in each of these markets and often must develop different advertisements tailored to the political culture of each region. (See Figure 1-6.) Candidates running for statewide office must raise large sums of money to buy television, radio, and social media advertisements to increase their name recognition among Florida voters. Local newspapers are often the source of political stories that end up on regular news coverage of the campaign by TV and radio—also known as "free" or "earned" media coverage.

Figure 1-6. Voter Registration in Florida's Media Markets (Nov. 2014)

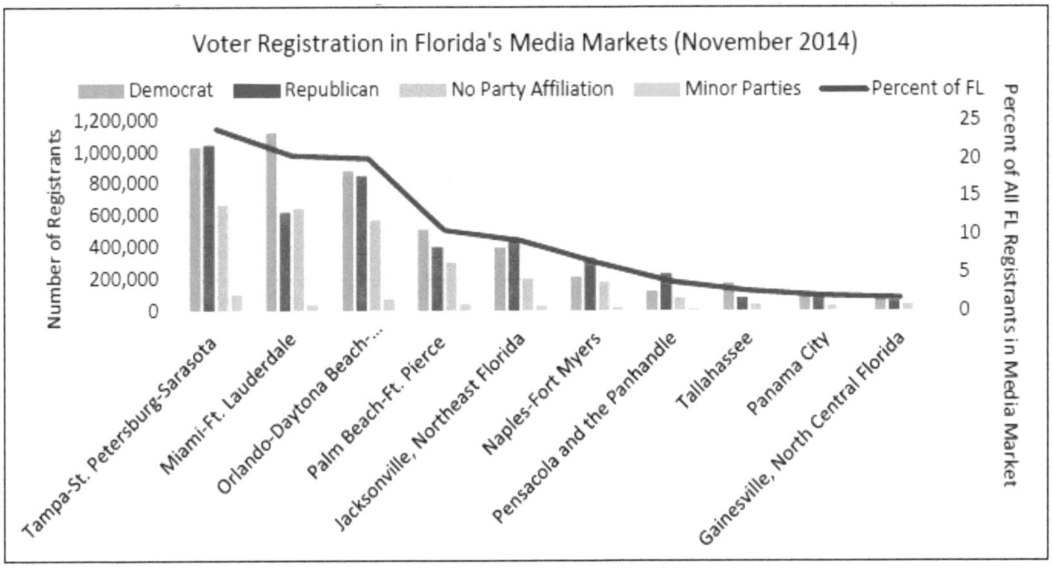

Source: Florida Division of Elections, Voter Registration Statistics. Available at
http://election.dos.state.fl.us/voter-registration/statistics/elections.shtml#2014.

Table 1-3. Florida's 10 Media Markets

Tampa-St. Petersburg-Sarasota
Counties: Citrus, Hardee, Hernando, Highlands, Hillsborough, Manatee, Pasco, Pinellas, Polk, Sarasota
Largest Daily Newspapers: *Tampa Tribune, St. Petersburg Times, Sarasota Herald Tribune, Bradenton Herald, Lakeland Ledger*
Miami-Fort Lauderdale
Counties: Broward, Miami-Dade, Monroe
Largest Daily Newspapers: *Miami Herald, Nuevo Herald, Sun-Sentinel*
Orlando-Daytona Beach-Melbourne
Counties: Brevard, Lake, Marion, Orange, Osceola, Seminole, Sumter, Volusia
Largest Daily Newspapers: *Orlando Sentinel, Daytona Beach News Journal, Florida Today*
Palm Beach-Fort Pierce
Counties: Indian River, Martin, Okeechobee, Palm Beach, St. Lucie
Largest Daily Newspapers: *Palm Beach Post, Fort Pierce Tribune*
Jacksonville, Northeast Florida
Counties: Baker, Bradford, Clay, Columbia, Duval, Flagler, Nassau, Putnam, St. Johns, Union
Largest Daily Newspapers: *Florida Times-Union*
Naples-Fort Myers
Counties: Charlotte, Collier, Desoto, Glades, Hendry, Lee
Largest Daily Newspapers: *Naples Daily News, Fort Myers News Press*
Pensacola and the Panhandle
Counties: Escambia, Okaloosa, Santa Rosa
Largest Daily Newspapers: *Pensacola News-Journal*
Tallahassee
Counties: Gadsden, Hamilton, Jefferson, Lafayette, Leon, Madison, Suwannee, Taylor, Wakulla
Largest Daily Newspapers: *Tallahassee Democrat*
Panama City
Counties: Bay, Calhoun, Franklin, Gulf, Holmes, Jackson, Liberty, Walton, Washington
Largest Daily Newspapers: *Panama City News Herald*
Gainesville, North Central Florida
Counties: Alachua, Dixie, Gilchrist, Levy
Largest Daily Newspapers: *Gainesville Sun, Ocala Star Banner*

Source: Kevin A. Hill, Susan A. MacManus, and Dario Moreno, *Florida's Politics: Ten Media Markets, One
Powerful State* Tallahassee, FL: Florida Institute of Government, 2004; updated by authors.

GENERATIONAL POLITICS IN FLORIDA

There is no better place to observe generational politics than in Florida. The makeup of its electorate shows it to be a much more age-diverse state than is commonly thought. Many Floridians (and non-Floridians) still believe that senior voters (65+) totally dominate Florida politics. That's simply not true, especially in presidential election years, when younger and older cohorts turn out at similar rates and make up larger shares of the electorate. However, the elderly, mostly white retirees, do tend to have a louder voice in Florida politics in elections held in non-presidential election years because of their sharply higher turnout rates.

"Generations carry with them the imprint of early political experiences... Most people's basic outlooks and orientations are set fairly early on in life." That is the conclusion of a major study of how age affects attitudes and voting behavior conducted by the Pew Research Center.[23] (The birth years of five generations of Americans are listed in Table 1-4, as are the major events and the presidents[24] often associated with the different generations.[25])

The Pew Research Center study found that those who came of age during the Truman and Eisenhower administrations (the Silent Generation) have fairly consistently voted for Republican candidates, while those who turned 18 under Bill Clinton, George W. Bush, and Barack Obama have almost always voted more Democratic. In Florida, the Millennials are the most solidly Democratic voting bloc, even though many register as independents. Seniors 65+ (oldest Baby Boomers, youngest Silent Generation) are the most Republican.

Table 1-4. Today's Living Generations and Their Early Political Experiences

Generation	Born	Age (2016)	Major Events	Presidents*
Greatest Generation/GI Generation	Before 1928	89+	World War II, The Great Depression, The New Deal	Franklin Delano Roosevelt
The Silent Generation	1928-1945	71-88	Postwar Happiness, Era of Conformity, Korean War	Harry Truman and Dwight Eisenhower
The Baby Boomers	1946-1964	52-70	Civil Rights Movement, 60s Youth Culture—Save the World Activism, Drugs, Free Love, Vietnam War	John F. Kennedy, Lyndon B. Johnson, Richard Nixon, Gerald Ford, and Jimmy Carter
Generation X	1965-1980	36-51	MTV, 24-hour news, latch-key kids, transition to computers, AIDS	Ronald Reagan, George H.W. Bush, and Bill Clinton
Millennials/Generation Y	After 1980	18 to 35**	9/11, Social Media, Iraq and Afghanistan conflicts, Great Recession, BP oil spill	George W. Bush and Barack Obama

Note: *President at the time a member of the generation turned 18 years of age.
**The youngest Millennials are in their teens. No chronological endpoint has been set for this group.

Source: "Millennials in Adulthood," Pew Research Center, March 5, 2014;
http://www.pewsocialtrends.org/2014/03/07/millennials-in-adulthood/sdt-next-america-03-07-2014-0-06/

Senior Voters

Florida ranks first among the 50 states in the percentage of residents older than 65. Seniors in Florida are about 19 percent of the total population. But that figure is deceptive; their true political power derives from their clout at the ballot box. They are high turnout voters who tend to vote in every election, not just presidential races. They also tend to vote a complete ballot—recording their preference in races from the top of the ballot all the way down to the bottom, and on the constitutional amendments.

At the Ballot Box

The voter turnout among seniors—persons 65 and older—regularly exceeds that of persons younger than 30 in Florida and in the United States at large.[26] The age gap is smaller in a presidential election. For example, in 2012, 18-29-year-olds were 17 percent of Florida's registered voters but made up 16 percent of the voters, whereas seniors 65 and older comprised 26 percent of the registrants but made up 24 percent of all who voted.

In 2014 (a gubernatorial election year), 18-29-year-olds made up 18 percent of the registrants but only 14 percent of all voters. In contrast, persons 65 and older were 26 percent of all registered voters but made up 25 percent of those who voted. The senior share of all voters more closely mirrored their share of total registrants (25 vs. 26 percent) than the younger cohort (14 vs. 18 percent)—indicative of a higher turnout rate among seniors than among Millennials.

Senior power in off-year local elections is even more impressive. The overall turnout rate in these local elections often falls below 25 percent, but the consistent voting habits of seniors can raise their percentage from 40 to 50 percent of these smaller off-year electorates. That is why local elected officials often target their campaigns more to older voters, with their higher turnout rate, who are frequently the deciding factor in any election.[27]

Age and Affluence

The elderly in Florida and elsewhere in the nation experience less poverty than the young. (See Chapter 11.) The poverty rate for persons older than 65 is well below the national average. This was not always true. As late as 1970, the poverty rate for the elderly was higher than the national average, but increasing Social Security benefits (indexed at or above the inflation rate), together with Medicare, lifted about 90 percent of the elderly out of poverty. Today, Florida has more than 4 million Social Security beneficiaries, equal to one-fifth of its population.

Florida is a much more age-diverse state than is commonly perceived. But older voters still have higher turnout rates than younger voters.

Wealth is the net worth of all one's possessions—home value minus mortgage, auto value minus loan, savings minus debts, and similar measures. The aged are more likely than younger people to own homes with paid-off mortgages. Medicare pays a large portion of their medical expenses, although the increasing cost of prescription drugs and the rising cost of living are sources of worry to many seniors. They no longer, or rarely, have expenses for child rearing and education. However, when the Great Recession hit Florida, many seniors found themselves having to financially help their adult children, as well as their grandchildren, as best they could.

Seniors' Party Affiliation

Florida's oldest seniors (85 and older) came of voting age during the high-water mark of Democratic ascendancy in America—the New Deal of Franklin D. Roosevelt and the nation's victory in World War II. These seniors are the strongest supporters of Social Security and Medicare, from which they receive direct benefits. At one time, most seniors viewed the Democratic Party as more protective of these programs than the Republican Party. But the gradual generational replacement of the staunchly Democratic Depression-era cohort with a more evenly divided younger-old cohort has created an increasingly partisan-divided, but slightly Republican-leaning, senior electorate. In Florida, 51 percent of seniors 65 and older supported George W. Bush in 2004; 53 percent voted for John McCain in 2008, and 58 percent cast their ballots for Romney in 2012.[28]

Seniors are more concerned than any other age group about crime and taxes. Older Floridians feel especially vulnerable to crime (see Chapter 8), and they support candidates who appear tough on crime, whether Republican or Democrat. Many Florida seniors live on fixed incomes and tend to oppose tax increases of all types, especially property taxes. Older Floridians are the most fiscally conservative age group in the state.

Senior Policy Agenda

The policy preferences of seniors heavily influence the policy agenda of Florida. Senior preferences have been summarized as "resistance to government taxing and spending programs lacking immediate benefits for aging people, and increasing demands for services benefiting principally the elderly population at the expense of younger persons."[29] The most important policy programs for seniors—Social Security and Medicare—are governed by Congress and administered by the federal Social Security Administration. But seniors look to Florida state and local governments to:

- Keep taxes low, especially property taxes, and prohibit state or local income taxation, since many seniors are on a fixed income.
- Increase spending for crime-fighting and prison-building, because older people are often the target of criminals. Elder scams are increasing.
- Improve the state's educational system—elementary, secondary, and higher education.
- Keep the economy strong. Seniors' concern for the economic future of their children and grandchildren has become a stronger voting cue since the recession of 2007.

Education in Florida is especially affected by the views of seniors. They are often the strongest supporters of education but the most vocal critics of the current system, primarily because they believe today's schools are not effective in producing students with adequate reading, writing, and math skills.

Young Voters

Typically, younger voters are more liberal and Democratic in their voting patterns. They make up a larger share of the electorate in presidential election years than in off-year state and local elections, although their share has fluctuated. The proportion of the electorate age 18-29 increased from 15 percent in 2000 to 17 percent in 2004, then fell back to 15 percent in 2008—the first Obama election—before inching up to 16 percent in 2012—Obama's second election. These fluctuations have been attributed to a wide variety of factors such as the degree of each party's targeting of the youth vote, the competitiveness of the race, media coverage, candidates' issue priorities and articulation, the path-breaking nature of a candidate, and candidate visits. Interestingly, in the 2008 presidential election, Florida's younger-voter share of the electorate lagged behind the national average (15 percent versus 18 percent). Some analysts speculated that some younger Florida voters took it for granted that Obama would win because polls had been showing that outcome for several months before the election.

Historically, turnout rates among younger voters fall off considerably from those in presidential election years, although they, too, fluctuate. Reasons for the sharp drop in turnout in mid-term elections typically include the following: less knowledge of state and local politics due to an overemphasis on national-level politics in high school; more frequent moves from one state or locality to another; and a lack of knowledge about how to change one's voter registration after a move. Highly negative campaigns also alienate younger voters more than they do older voters. Younger voters are often most interested in education (higher education), jobs, and the environment.

Baby Boomers

Baby Boomers are the largest portion of the Florida voting public. They are often called the "sandwich" generation—squeezed between the oldest and youngest cohorts—often having to care for both. As a voting bloc, they are more Republican than either of the other age groups. Financial concerns, health care, education, and moral issues often top their concerns: money because they know they are not saving enough for their own retirement, health care because affordable coverage is increasingly unavailable, and education and moral issues because they have children.

RELIGION AND POLITICS

Religion and politics have become more intertwined in recent years in Florida and elsewhere. Knowledge of a person's religious beliefs is often the key to understanding vote choices, particularly on highly divisive, often explosive, moral issues—from the right to die (the Terri Schiavo case) to abortion, the death penalty, bioethics, and gay marriage and adoptions. On such issues, a person's religious beliefs may be a stronger voting cue than one's political party affiliation. Such issues also prompt high voter turnout among those who feel strongly about them—on one side or the other.

Not surprisingly, the religious affiliations of Floridians are diverse. Half identify with a Protestant faith, 26 percent are Catholic, and 3 percent are Jewish. The remainder are of other faiths such as Jehovah's Witness, Muslim, Buddhist, Hindu, and Mormon, while 16 percent are unaffiliated with any religion.[30] Certain regions of the state have greater concentrations of religious affiliations than others. For example, the more liberal Jewish voters are heavily concentrated in South Florida and largely vote Democratic, whereas conservative Protestants are more prevalent in the Panhandle and tend to vote Republican.

Religious identification is also intertwined with country of origin. For example, Florida's Hispanic population is heavily Catholic, the Hindu and Buddhist faiths are more common among the state's Asians, and the Muslim religion is the choice of most residents of Arab descent. Regardless of one's religious preference, voter turnout is higher among persons who regularly attend a religious service.

RACIAL AND ETHNIC POLITICS IN FLORIDA

Florida is one of the most diverse states in the nation, ranking third in Hispanic population, 11th in African-American population, and 23rd in its Asian population. Traditionally, African Americans were the largest minority group in Florida. However, the Hispanic population in Florida has been growing sharply for the last half-century, while the African-American population has grown much more slowly. Hispanics surpassed African Americans as the state's largest minority group in the late 1990s (see Figure 1-7). Currently, Hispanics make up nearly 24 percent of Florida's population and African Americans almost 17 percent. Hispanics comprise a larger share of the metropolitan areas in South Florida, while blacks comprise a larger share of MSAs in North Florida (see Figures 1-8 and 1-9, respectively).

Figure 1-7. Racial and Ethnic Change in Florida: 1980-2010

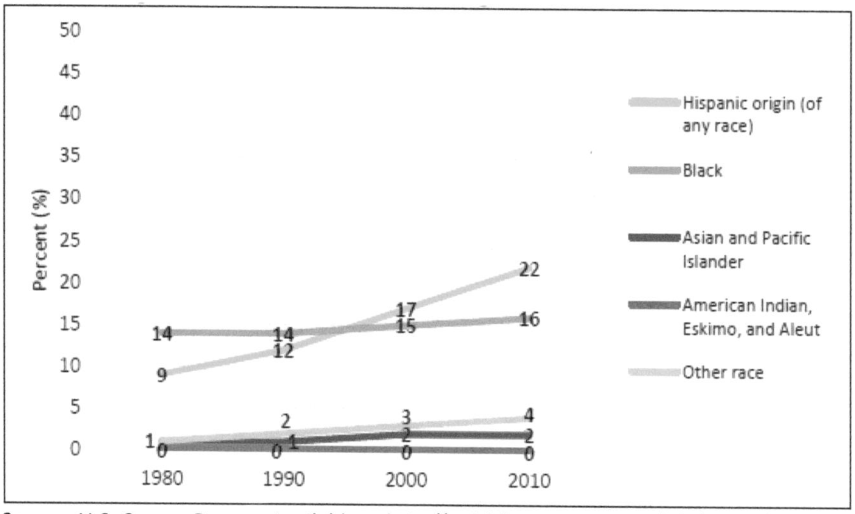

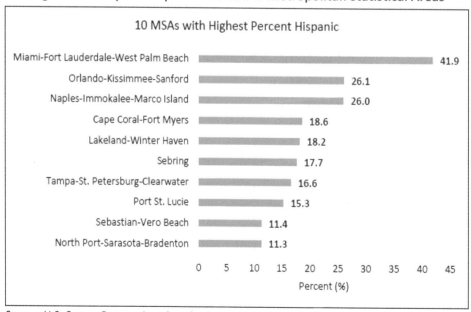

Source: U.S. Census Bureau. Available at http://quickfacts.census.gov/qfd/states/12000.html

Asian Americans now make up over three percent of the state's population. Their presence is greatest in the Gainesville (college area), Orlando, and Jacksonville MSAs. (See Figure 1-10.) Florida's "economic opportunity, house prices, education opportunities, and good weather" have been magnets for Asian Americans.[31]

Figure 1-8. Hispanic Population Share in Metropolitan Statistical Areas

Source: U.S. Census Bureau, American Community Survey, 2009-2013 (5-year estimates).

Figure 1-9. Black or African-American Population Share in Metropolitan Statistical Areas

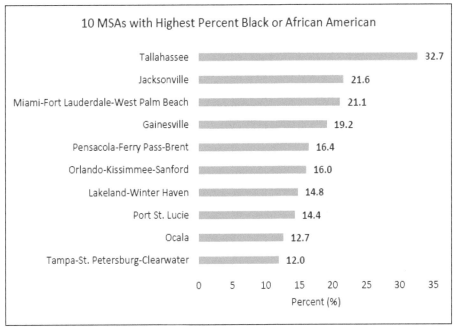

Source: U.S. Census Bureau, American Community Survey, 2009-2013 (5-year estimates).

Figure 1-10. Asian Population Share in Metropolitan Statistical Areas

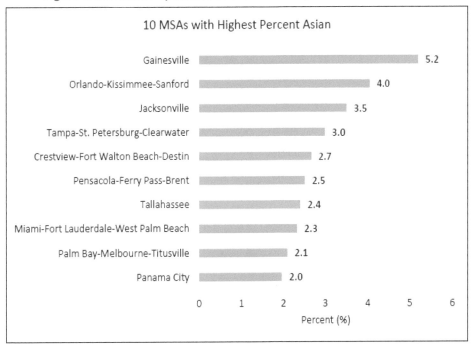

Source: U.S. Census Bureau, American Community Survey, 2009-2013 (5-year estimates).

The Sunshine State's Asian population is diverse, as evidenced by membership in the Asian American Federation of Florida. It includes "over 70 Bangladesh, Burmese, Cambodian, Chinese, Filipino, Indian, Iranian, Korean, Laotian, Taiwanese, Thai, Turkish, and Vietnamese organizations, businesses, and media."[32] As with "Hispanic," the "Asian" label creates an image of cohesiveness, when, in fact, the groups often differ culturally and politically.

Racial and Ethnic Political History

The political history of Florida has long been driven by racial and ethnic conflict. Seminole Indian wars, slavery and emancipation, Reconstruction, followed by segregation (see Up Close: Rosewood), the communist revolution in Cuba, and the Hispanic and Haitian migration to the state are all examples. Racial and ethnic politics continues to shape public affairs in Florida and may grow even more important in the next century, as the state's population continues to diversify. From 2000 to 2010, the state's Asian population grew the fastest (more than 70 percent), followed by the Hispanic (more than 57 percent) and black (more than 26 percent) populations.[33] By 2010, nearly one-fifth of Florida's residents were foreign-born—three-fourths of whom are from Latin America. (See Figure 1-11.)

Population size alone does not perfectly translate into the size of the electorate. For example, persons younger than 18 and non-citizens (53 percent of Florida's immigrants[34]) are ineligible to vote. Florida's Hispanic population has a larger share of both groups. (More than one-fourth of Hispanics, 26 percent, are younger than 18, compared to 20 percent of non-Hispanics.[35]) Taking both Florida's age and citizenship status into account, the Pew Hispanic Center estimates that just 48.3 percent of the state's Latino population is eligible to vote, compared to 63.5 percent of its black population and 79.8 percent of its white population.[36]

Figure 1-11. Region of Birth of Foreign-Born Floridians

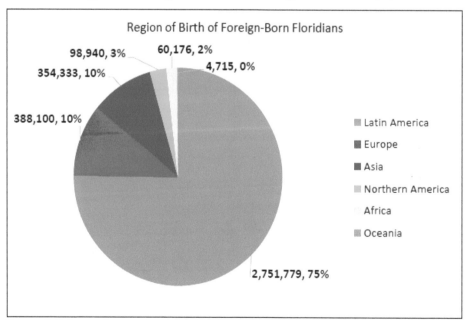

Source: U.S. Census Bureau, American Community Survey, 2010.

AFRICAN AND CARIBBEAN AMERICANS IN FLORIDA POLITICS

As late as 1900, nearly half of Florida's population (44 percent) was African American. Yet blacks in Florida and elsewhere in the South were socially and economically deprived and politically repressed. Thus, many blacks left the region seeking better opportunity in the North. During Reconstruction, immediately after the Civil War, blacks actively participated in the political life of the state. They served in the Florida Legislature, and Floridian Josiah T. Walls became the first African-American member of the U.S. House of Representatives in 1870. Virtually all black voters and officeholders of this era were Republicans. But, by 1900, white Democrats had recaptured all of the important offices. Democratic primaries became the only meaningful elections, and blacks were officially excluded by a rule requiring all primary voters to be white. Not until the U.S. Supreme Court outlawed the white primary in *Smith v. Allwright* (1944) were any blacks registered as Democrats in Florida.[37]

The Florida Legislature eliminated the poll tax in 1937, well before the 24th Amendment (1964) to the U.S. Constitution barred it throughout the nation. Black voting began to increase after World War II, especially in the state's larger cities. By the early 1950s, about one-third of the state's eligible blacks were registered to vote. But in many rural counties, threats, intimidation, and extralegal means still prevented blacks from registering or voting.

Led by civil rights activists Harry T. Moore, C.K. Steele, and others, black voting rose in the early 1960s. After the federal Voting Rights Act of 1965, black registration and voting increased dramatically, as the threat of federal intervention eliminated the last official obstacles at the local level. However, white in-migration to the state, combined with African-American out-migration, greatly diluted black voting strength. More recently, African-American political power has been somewhat lessened by the growing Hispanic population. Latinos are now the state's largest minority, although they are less cohesive than blacks in their voting patterns.

Democratic Party Loyalty

African Americans in Florida and elsewhere are the Democratic Party's most loyal voting bloc. Less than five percent of Florida's black voters identify themselves as Republicans. And, while about one-third identify themselves to pollsters as independent (mostly young blacks), few register as such to preserve their voting power in Democratic primary elections. Florida's closed primary law requires party registration as a prerequisite for voting in a party's primary under most circumstances (see Chapter 4). Black voters cast more than one-quarter of the total votes in statewide Democratic primary elections, and their ideological preference for liberals over conservatives plays a major role in the selection of Democratic candidates.

Republican Party gains among blacks, while small, have primarily been among those who are concerned about education (pro-voucher advocates), moral issues (gay marriage), business opportunities, taxes (small business owners), and national security. Two of the state's high profile black Republican officeholders were retired military officers—Lieutenant Governor Jennifer Carroll (Navy) and Congressman Allen West (Army).

Black Organizations

Traditionally, churches were the center of political—as well as social—activity in Florida's black communities. Black congregations relied heavily on their ministers for political, as well as spiritual, advice. The National Association for the Advancement of Colored People (NAACP), and its local and state affiliates, played the decisive role in challenging segregation in Florida and elsewhere. Prior to the historic U.S. Supreme Court decision of *Brown v. Board of Education of Topeka* in 1954,[38] only one state university was open to blacks—Florida Agricultural and Mechanical University (FAMU) in Tallahassee. Private Bethune-Cookman College in Daytona Beach, founded in 1923 by Mary McLeod Bethune, was also open to black students. Both institutions produced many of the state's early African-American professional, business, and political leaders. FAMU students took the lead in the civil rights protests, boycotts, and sit-ins of the early 1960s that led to the historic Civil Rights Act of 1964. Decades after closing the FAMU law school in Tallahassee and opening a law school across town at Florida State University when desegregation began in the late 1960s, the legislature opened a new FAMU law school in Orlando in 2002.

Black Political Clout

Real political clout for African Americans did not begin to develop in Florida until after the state was ordered by the federal courts to reapportion itself in the early 1960s.

Legislature

The first African American, Joe Lang Kershaw, was elected to the state legislature in 1968. He was followed in 1970 by the first black female legislator, Gwen Cherry, a Miami attorney and FAMU graduate. The first black state senators since Reconstruction were elected in 1982: Arnett E. Girardeau from Jacksonville and Carrie Meek from Miami. But the keys to black political power in the state were the adoption of single-member legislative districts in 1982 and federal court-ordered redistricting in 1992 (see Chapter 6).

Florida's African American and Caribbean black activists encourage their communities to vote.

Today, black representation in the Florida State Legislature is proportional to the black percentage of the state's population[39] (see Chapter 6). The Black Legislative Caucus has proven its effectiveness on issues of special importance to minorities (see the section on Rosewood that follows). African Americans hold more elected offices in Florida, at all levels, than ever before, several hundred, according to the Washington-based Joint Center for Political Studies.

Supreme Court

Governor Reubin Askew (D) appointed Joseph Hatchett to the Florida Supreme Court in 1975, and Hatchett became the first African American to win a statewide office (not just in Florida, but in the South), when he won a contentious, racially charged election to keep the seat in 1976. (In 1976, Floridians also changed the law so that future Supreme Court justices were only subject to a retention vote to keep them in office or turn them out.) Governor Bob Graham (D) appointed Leander Shaw in 1983. Shaw would later become Florida's first black Chief Justice. Lawton Chiles (D) and Jeb Bush (R) placed the first African-American woman on the Florida Supreme Court, Peggy Quince, in a rare joint appointment in 1998. And Governor Charlie Crist (R) appointed James E. C. Perry in 2009.

Governor and Cabinet

Bids by African Americans to win gubernatorial and Cabinet posts in the post-Reconstruction period have mostly failed. Doug Jamerson lost his 1996 electoral bid to remain as Commissioner of Education, after appointment to the vacant seat by Governor Lawton Chiles in 1994. Daryl L. Jones, a state senator from South Florida, finished third in the 2002 Democratic gubernatorial primary. However, he may have pulled enough votes from Janet Reno to help provide the slim margin of victory for Bill McBride. In 2006, Democratic gubernatorial candidate Jim Davis selected Jones as his running mate. Had the Davis-Jones ticket won, Jones would have been the state's first African American to be elected statewide to a non-judicial post. But that honor went to Republican Jennifer Carroll, a former state legislator from Jacksonville, who was elected Lieutenant Governor in 2010 as the running mate of Governor Rick Scott.

Congress

Black representation in Congress began to increase after the redrawing of district lines in 1992 (required redistricting). In that year, three districts (two in South Florida and one in Jacksonville) were crafted specifically with the intent to maximize the opportunity for black representation in the congressional delegation to comply with the federal Voting Rights Act. Three black Democrats were elected from those districts (Carrie Meek, Alcee Hastings, and Corrine Brown).[40] The 2002 redistricting process left these three districts largely intact, although Congresswoman Carrie Meek retired and was replaced in 2002 by her son Kendrick Meek, who served four terms in Congress before running unsuccessfully for the U.S. Senate in 2010. He was replaced by former state senator Frederica Wilson.

By 2011, there were four African-American members of Congress from Florida—three from Southeast Florida (two Democrats, Alcee Hastings and Frederica Wilson; one Republican, Allen West) and one from Jacksonville (Democrat Corrine Brown). Carrie Meek and Corrine Brown were the state's first African-American women elected to Congress (1992). Allen West, elected in 2010, was the first black Republican since Reconstruction chosen to represent Florida in Congress. West, strongly supported by Tea Party activists, defeated a white Democrat, the incumbent, in a district that was 87 percent white, but lost in 2012—a victim of the redistricting process. (His district was made less Republican so he ran for another and narrowly lost to Democrat Patrick Murphy by less than one percent.)

In 2012, all of Florida's congressional districts were drawn in what was a highly contentious redistricting process that ended up in court—multiple times.[41] At issue was whether the legislature had violated the law against partisan gerrymandering laid out in the Fair Districts amendment approved by state voters in 2010. There were also charges of racial gerrymandering—unnecessarily packing high proportions of black voters into some districts thereby making other districts whiter (bleaching). In the first case, a state circuit court judge ordered the legislature to redraw two of the state's 27 districts (District 5—Jacksonville and District 10—Orlando). The second suit, filed by a coalition of groups including the Florida League of Women Voters, challenged the first court ruling as too narrow and petitioned the Florida Supreme Court to order the adoption of an alternative map for all 27 districts—one that eliminated partisan gerrymandering.[42] (See Chapter 6 for a discussion of the redistricting process.)

New Black Power: The Arrival of Caribbean Blacks

Three countries send the most black Caribbean immigrants to the United States—Jamaica, Haiti, and Trinidad and Tobago.[43] In recent years, the number of blacks immigrating to Florida from Caribbean countries has increased. So, too, has their political power, especially in multi-racial South Florida. The Miami-Fort Lauderdale area is where the majority of black Caribbean immigrants in the United States reside. Haitians are more dominant in Miami-Dade County, Jamaicans in Broward County.[44] The growing presence of Caribbean blacks has occasionally put them at odds with U.S.-born black Floridians.[45] "Residential, as well as political strategies at the local level reveal that West Indians (Caribbean blacks) do not always match the Black American pattern."[46] It has prompted many to demand that the media refer to them as Caribbean Americans or Caribbean blacks, rather than African Americans. At the congressional level, a push is on to require the next U.S. Census form to have a checkbox to allow Caribbean nationals to identify their origins.

The number of Haitians immigrating to Florida in recent years has been sizeable. While it is difficult to estimate with any accuracy the size of the Haitian community in Florida, what is known is that Florida and New York are home to more than 70 percent of Haitian immigrants[47] The Haitian community is likely to continue to grow after President Barack Obama's announcement in 2014 that the U.S. Department of Homeland Security was speeding up its Haitian Family Reunification Parole Program "to more quickly unify Haitians who are here and their families who stayed behind."[48] Most have fled the abject poverty of their native land. The U.S. federal government considers most Haitian immigrants as economic rather than political refugees and, hence, not automatically entitled to political asylum. But efforts to turn back the tide of small rickety boats from Haiti have been generally unsuccessful. Large numbers of Haitian immigrants have gradually moved north from their original "Little Haiti" inner-city residential area of Miami along the I-95 Corridor into low-income housing in Broward and Palm Beach counties. There is also a fairly large Haitian community in the Orlando metropolitan area. Most Haitians are employed in low-wage, unskilled work in landscaping, restaurants, hospitals, nursing homes, and agriculture, although that is rapidly changing. Haitian Americans are gaining political clout as more become citizens.

A number of Haitian Americans have been elected to the state legislature and to city and county offices in Miami-Dade and Broward counties. Phillip Brutus (D) was elected to the Florida House of Representatives in 2000. In 2002, Brutus was joined by another Haitian state legislator, his ex-wife Yolly Roberson (D). Since then, a number of other Haitians in the South Florida area have been elected to offices at the state and local levels.[49] Political party matters less than national ancestry when it comes to voting. In 2001, Joe Celestin, a Republican, was elected mayor of the City of North Miami, despite the fact that 87 percent of the Haitian voters were registered Democrats.[50] Celestin became the second-ever Haitian-American mayor in the United States. The first was Philippe Derose, elected mayor of the Village of El Portal (Miami-Dade County) in 2000.

South Florida is home to the second largest Jamaican population outside Jamaica—heavily concentrated in Miami-Dade, Broward, and Palm Beach counties.[51] Political turmoil in Jamaica in the 1970s prompted many to leave their country. As with Haitians, Jamaican-born blacks have successfully entered the political arena. Democrat Hazelle Rogers from Broward County was the first legislator born in Jamaica to be elected to the state House (2008). A number of other Jamaicans have been elected to local office in Broward County, including Jamaican national Samuel Brown, who was elected mayor of Lauderdale Lakes in 1998.

In 2003, Jennifer Carroll (R-Jacksonville), born in Trinidad, became the first black from that Caribbean country to be elected to the state House of Representatives, and then in 2010 as Lieutenant Governor.

Other black legislators from South Florida have strong ties to the Bahamas, which is technically not part of the Caribbean. Edward Bullard from Miami was the first legislator born in the Bahamas (Nassau). He was elected to the Florida House in 2000.

UP-CLOSE: ROSEWOOD

Successful efforts to gain compensation for the victims of the Rosewood Massacre show the power of the Black Legislative Caucus. For many years, rumors had circulated in North Florida about a massacre of hundreds of blacks and the destruction of a small North Florida village called Rosewood. An early, somewhat sketchy story had been published by investigative reporter Gary Moore of the *St. Petersburg Times*, and the story was reported by CBS's Ed Bradley on *60 Minutes* on December 13, 1983. Eventually, the story captured the attention of attorney Steve Hanlon of the Community Service Team (the *pro bono* public services division) of Holland & Knight, Florida's largest and most prestigious law firm. He committed himself and his firm to the imposing task of winning compensation for the survivors and their descendants against the State of Florida. He argued that the state "knew about the slaughter" at the time but did nothing to protect the victims' lives and property.

With keen political insight, Hanlon chose to contact the Republican leader of the Cuban Legislative Caucus, Representative Miguel DeGrandy, and the Democratic leader of the Black Legislative Caucus, Representative Al Lawson, and ask that they become bipartisan co-sponsors of a compensation bill. After the bill's introduction in 1993, Democratic House Speaker Bolley L. ("Bo") Johnson commissioned a study by a team of university historians to develop "a full accounting and investigation into the incident." The report, 93 double-spaced pages and more than 400 additional pages of appendices, including verbatim transcriptions of interviews conducted by the team, reported the following facts.[52]

Rosewood: A Historical Account

In 1923, Rosewood, Florida, was located in western Levy County in Central Florida, nine miles west of the coastal town of Cedar Key. At that time, Rosewood had an African-American population of about 350, with thriving churches and black-owned and operated stores and businesses. But Rosewood's community life was shattered on the morning of January 1, 1923, when Fannie Taylor, a white woman and resident of nearby Sumner, claimed she was attacked by a black man in her home. Whether she had been raped has never been determined, but whites believed that a black escaped convict, Jesse Hunter, was responsible. Later that afternoon, a white mob targeted another black man, 45-year-old Sam Carter, whom they tortured and killed in an effort to obtain information about Hunter's whereabouts. Carter's mutilated body was strung up on display within the town of Rosewood as a warning to the black community.

The next day, a rumor circulated among the white crowd gathering in nearby Sumner that a black man, Sylvester Carrier, was hiding Hunter in his family home. An armed mob of whites approached the Carriers' large, two-story frame house, but Carrier was armed and ready. He shot two invaders as they broke into his mother's home, killing both men instantly. Surrounding the house, whites riddled it with rifle and shotgun fire. As adults and children huddled in the upstairs bedrooms under mattresses for protection, a shotgun blast killed Carrier's mother. The shooting continued for more than an hour. Four white men were wounded. The white mob returned to Sumner to rearm and regroup, but not before torching one of the town's churches and several empty houses.

The idea that blacks in Rosewood had taken up arms spread fear and anger among whites throughout North Florida. More than 200 armed whites descended on Rosewood by horseback, wagon, and Model T to seek retribution. As homes burned, most of the town's people fled into the swamps. Although the homes of all black residents in Rosewood were destroyed, the homes of two white families remained untouched, including that of John Wright, who lived in Rosewood and operated a general store. He offered a refuge for a number of black children in his home, and, for weeks after the riot, acted as a liaison to blacks hiding in the swamps, providing them with food.[53] Black residents were also assisted by two white train conductors, brothers John and William Bryce. As their train left Rosewood, it moved slowly up the tracks, blowing its horn as a signal to women and children hiding in the woods. The survivors of the riot who escaped on the train were taken in by Gainesville's black community until family members could be located. The actual number of dead and wounded at Rosewood is difficult to determine, but no arrests were ever made in the Rosewood murders.

Ruins of a burned African-American home in Rosewood, Florida.

In the Legislature

The report by the historians was critical to the success of the compensation bill, but it did not silence opposition in the legislature. Indeed, at several points in the bill's legislative journey, prospects for its passage appeared bleak. When DeGrandy and Lawson began to lobby the bill at the beginning of the 1994 session, many lawmakers declined to meet with the sponsors on the grounds that the bill was too politically charged to risk supporting. Florida legislators were getting hundreds of calls about Rosewood, and the majority of them were negative. Key support came, however, from the House Republican leader, Sandra Mortham. She pledged her support for the bill and, more importantly, agreed that the Republican Party would not take a position on the issue. (In 1994, Mortham was elected Florida's Secretary of State, the first woman to hold the office, thereby indicating that the political consequences of voting for Rosewood were minimal.)

In a series of compromises to secure passage of the bill, Lawson was forced to reduce the monetary compensation awards and to drop the second and third generations of Rosewood families as recipients. One week before the close of session, Lawson called the members of the Legislative Black Caucus to a lunch with Governor Lawton Chiles. Lawson bluntly threatened Chiles with deserting him on his health care package unless he got some help on Rosewood. The lunch nearly came to an abrupt end when Representative Cynthia Chestnut suggested that the black lawmakers walk out. But Lieutenant Governor Buddy MacKay suggested that they say grace again and told the group, "We're all friends here." Chiles and MacKay agreed that the executive branch would do whatever it could. The meeting had the desired result. With political leverage applied by the Governor, Lawson garnered the necessary votes to move the bill out of committee.

When the bill reached the House floor, amendments were voted down by wide margins. With the Rosewood families looking down from the gallery, the final Rosewood compensation bill passed the Florida House by a vote of 71 to 40. On April 8, 1994, the Florida Senate voted 24 to 16 to send the bill to Governor Lawton Chiles for his signature. On May 4, 1994, in a ceremony held at Florida's old historic Capitol with the Rosewood families present, Governor Chiles stated, "For more than seven decades a shadow of shame fell across the State of Florida. The long silence has been broken and the shadow has been lifted."

HISPANIC POLITICS: CUBAN AND NON-CUBAN

Nearly half, 48 percent, of the state's Hispanics live in Miami-Dade and Broward counties.[54] Among Florida's 10 largest cities, the 2010 Census shows Hialeah with the largest Hispanic population (95 percent), followed by Miami (70 percent), Pembroke Pines (41 percent), Orlando (25 percent), and Tampa (23 percent).[55] The composition of the Latino population in each city varies considerably, a fact that makes Hispanic outreach challenging to candidates. It is important to remember that the broad label "Hispanic" masks important cultural, religious, and *political* differences among Cubans, Puerto Ricans, Mexicans, Dominicans, Nicaraguans, Venezuelans, Salvadorians, Guatemalans, and Hispanics with roots in other Latino countries.

For many years, Cuban Americans were the largest, most politically powerful Hispanic group in Florida, particularly in South Florida and the Tampa area. Cubans still dominate political office-holding, due to their numbers, concentration, and shared agenda, but other Hispanic groups are gaining power. More recently, immigrants from other Central and South American countries, such as Mexico, the Dominican Republic, Colombia, Venezuela, and Nicaragua have swelled the ranks of non-Cuban Hispanics in the state, even in South Florida. Nonetheless, Cubans are still the largest group statewide and in the Miami-Fort Lauderdale-Pompano Beach MSA. Puerto Ricans are now the second largest group statewide and largest Hispanic group in both the Orlando and Tampa areas. (Mexicans are the third largest Hispanic group in Florida but they are more geographically dispersed and wield less political clout). These two areas comprise the I-4 Corridor, which is considered the swing part of the state. This makes it imperative that both Democrats and Republicans have strategic campaign outreach efforts aimed at Central Florida's Puerto Rican communities. Puerto Ricans lean Democratic but are considered "in play" by both parties. When the 2010 Census figures were released and Florida was awarded two more congressional seats, some speculated that the Hispanic gains

Reaching Hispanic voters is important to both Democrats and Republicans running for office.

in Central Florida might "lead to at least one new Latino-majority congressional district in the center of the state," and possibly one other in South Florida.[56] Ultimately a 40 percent Hispanic district was created in Central Florida—the Orlando area.

The Growing Hispanic Vote

Hispanics now routinely make up a slightly larger share of those who vote than blacks, with the exception of the 2006 and 2014 midterm elections.[57] In the two most recent presidential contests, exit polls showed that Hispanics outnumbered black voters: 2008 (Obama vs. McCain—Hispanics, 14 percent, blacks, 13 percent); and 2012 (Obama vs. Romney—Hispanics, 17 percent and blacks, 12 percent). But in the 2014 midterm race, the black share of the electorate was 14 percent compared to 13 percent for Hispanics.

The Hispanic vote is far from monolithic. The label "Hispanic" includes persons from many different countries of heritage with varying cultural, religious, and political backgrounds. Political analysts typically divide Florida's Hispanic voters into two categories—Cuban and non-Cuban. According to the 2012 exit poll, Cubans made up six percent of all Florida voters, non-Cuban Hispanics nine percent. The exit poll showed heavy support for Obama among non-Cuban Hispanics and more divided support among Cubans—reflecting the growing tendency of younger Cubans to vote Democratic.

Hispanics tend to vote less strictly along party lines and somewhat more cohesively (ethnic solidarity) when a Latino candidate is running (for example, Republican Mel Martinez for U.S. Senate in 2004; Republican Marco Rubio for U.S. Senate in 2010). Party loyalty is also weaker among Hispanics than among African Americans. A Broward County survey found that just 48 percent of Hispanic Republicans "almost always" support their party; among Hispanic Democrats, it was 36 percent.[58] The same research found that ethnic solidarity is more important to foreign-born than to U.S.-born Hispanics.[59]

Hispanic Migration

The Spanish were the first Europeans to colonize Florida, and parts of the state have historically reflected a Latin culture. Shortly after the Civil War, Cuban and Spanish cigar makers established a thriving community in Key West. Later, a Spanish industrialist, Martinez Ybor, expanded cigar production near Tampa in a

Immigration is a complex issue in Florida, with its large and growing Hispanic population.

community that became known as Ybor City. Tampa quickly became the nation's leading center for cigar making.

Cuba achieved independence from Spain in 1898, the same year that the City of Miami was incorporated. Miami soon became closely linked to neighboring Havana across the narrow Florida straits. Refugees from unstable politics in Cuba arrived in Miami throughout the 1940s and 1950s. Even before Fidel Castro's revolution in 1959, the Little Havana neighborhood of Miami had developed.

But it was Castro's revolutionary embrace of communism after 1959 that permanently changed Florida. Over the next four decades, nearly one million Cubans fled their homeland for the United States, and most of them settled in the Miami area. The earliest Cuban exiles were primarily business and professional people and their families whose assets and homes were seized by the Castro government. They were joined a short time later by others who had initially supported Castro but were quickly disillusioned by his abandonment of democracy and embrace of communism and the Soviet Union. In the Cuban Adjustment Act of 1966, the U.S. government recognized Cuban exiles as political refugees and allowed them to enter without quotas and with permanent resident alien status. The 1980 Mariel Boatlift brought an additional 257,000 Cuban exiles to Florida, some of whom were expelled from prisons by the Castro regime.

The Cubans fleeing Castro initially identified themselves with the perceived strong anti-communist position of the national Republican Party. Their business, professional, and financial backgrounds reinforced their Republicanism. The established Cuban-American leadership remains Republican today. But the influence of older anti-communist Cuban exile leaders is waning as younger Cuban Americans assume more community leadership positions. And, of course, Fidel Castro will not live forever. When he is gone, a powerful source of unity for Cuban Republicans will be removed.

The early Cuban exiles were well educated, professionally trained, and experienced in business. They quickly revitalized the economy of Miami, which had deteriorated into a seedy retirement and tourist town. Today, Cuban Americans collectively have more education, better jobs, and higher incomes than many other ethnic minorities in the United States. In recent years, additional migration from Central and South America has greatly increased the Hispanic population in South and Central Florida (see Figure 1-12) and made the areas considerably more diverse politically. However, Cuban Americans are still more successful at electing their own to Congress and to the state legislature than are the state's non-Cuban Hispanics, although non-Cuban Hispanics have made more inroads into the legislature than into Congress.

Hispanic Political Influence

Historically, Cubans have been able to secure more political influence than other Hispanic groups for several reasons. First, they are a larger group that is more geographically concentrated. Second, they are more cohesive—sharing similar policy goals and partisan (Republican) attitudes especially on policies related to Cuba and Fidel Castro, although that is changing. Generational differences are emerging. Younger Cuban Americans are far more likely to be Democrats or independents than their elders. Third, a higher proportion of Cubans are citizens and eligible to vote. Their naturalization rates are higher than those of non-Cuban Hispanic immigrants.

The political clout of Puerto Ricans has grown as well, as a consequence of big influxes into Central Florida (Orange and Osceola counties) and the fact that they are already U.S. citizens. They lean Democratic but are considered more up for grabs politically, thanks to new arrivals directly from the Island who arrive here without strong partisan attachments.

While Hispanic political influence has increased over the decades, Hispanic membership in the Florida Legislature does not yet match the Hispanic population percentage for two major reasons: (1) a larger percent of Hispanics are younger and not eligible to vote, and (2) a number of Hispanics are still not citizens and thus are ineligible to vote. However, by 2014, the percentage of Hispanics in the state legislature (16 percent) nearly equaled the Hispanic *eligible* voter percentage (17 percent).

Florida Legislature

Hispanics were elected to the Florida Legislature much earlier than blacks. The first Hispanic to serve in the Florida Legislature was actually a Cuban American from Key West, Fernando Figueredo—elected in 1885. There were 33 more Hispanics that served in the legislature prior to 1967—when the U.S. Supreme Court in *Swann v. Adams* ordered Florida's legislative districts in each chamber to be drawn using the one-person, one-vote standard. The standard had been established in *Baker v. Carr* (1962), and then extended to state legislatures in *Reynolds v. Sims* (1964). But Florida had failed to implement the prior Supreme Court rulings, prompting the *Swann* order. Most analyses of increases in minority representation begin with the mid-1960s, with the advent of equally sized districts—reflecting the one-person, one-vote principle.

Most of the Hispanics serving in the Florida Legislature have been Cuban Americans, although one of the earliest Hispanic legislators who served in both the pre- and post-1967 period was Frederick Charles Usina (D) from St. Augustine whose family roots tracked back to 13th century Spain. Another non-Cuban Hispanic who served pre-and-post 1967 was Puerto Rican Democrat Maurice Ferré from Miami. He was elected to the state House in 1967—and later became the nation's first Puerto Rican-born mayor of a large city (Miami). Cuban-American influence in the Florida Legislature increased, especially after redistricting in 1982, 1992, and 2002.

Republican Roberto Casas became the first Cuban-American legislator in the Florida House in 57 years when he won a special election in 1982. Republican Ileana Ros-Lehtinen, who emigrated from Havana to Miami in 1960 at the age of 8, was the first female Cuban-American legislator. She, too, was elected to the House in 1982 and moved up to the Senate in 1986. Republicans Casas and Javier Souto were the first Cuban males to be elected to the Senate (1988). In 1994, Cuban-American Annie Betancourt from South Florida became the first female Cuban Democrat to win a seat in the House. Republican Marco Rubio became Florida's first Cuban-American Speaker of the House in 2006—a visible sign of the growing clout of Cuban Americans in state politics.

Figure 1-12. Florida's Hispanic or Latino Population 2010

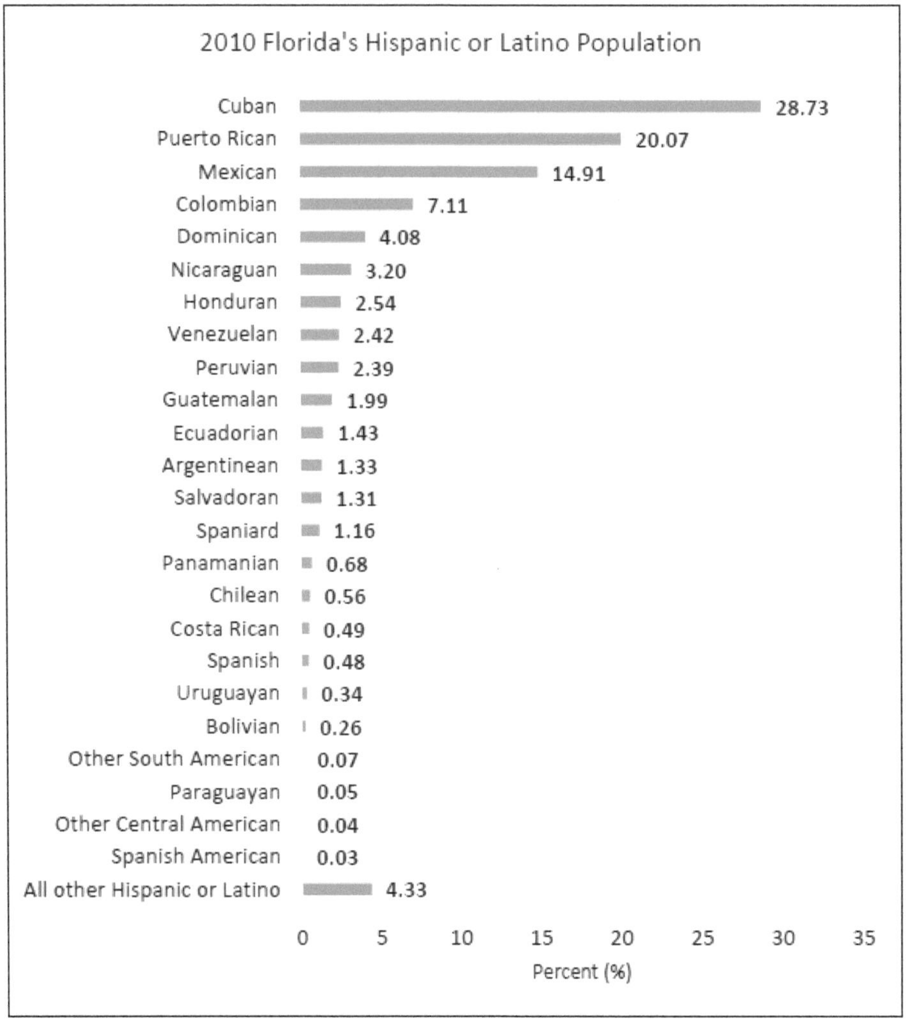

2010 Florida's Hispanic or Latino Population

Group	Percent
Cuban	28.73
Puerto Rican	20.07
Mexican	14.91
Colombian	7.11
Dominican	4.08
Nicaraguan	3.20
Honduran	2.54
Venezuelan	2.42
Peruvian	2.39
Guatemalan	1.99
Ecuadorian	1.43
Argentinean	1.33
Salvadoran	1.31
Spaniard	1.16
Panamanian	0.68
Chilean	0.56
Costa Rican	0.49
Spanish	0.48
Uruguayan	0.34
Bolivian	0.26
Other South American	0.07
Paraguayan	0.05
Other Central American	0.04
Spanish American	0.03
All other Hispanic or Latino	4.33

Percent (%)

Source: U.S. Census, 2010. Includes all Hispanics, not just foreign-born.

Among non-Cubans, it was not until 2002 that the first Republican Puerto Rican, John Quiñones from Orlando, was elected to the House. Democrat Darren Soto was the first Puerto Rican elected to the Senate (2012). Susan Bucher, Democrat from West Palm Beach, became the first Mexican-American House member in 1994. Other non-Cuban Hispanic House member "firsts" were Colombian Juan Carlos Zapata (R) elected in 2002, Nicaraguan Ana Rivas Logan (R) elected in 2010, and Ricardo Rangel of Ecuadorian descent (D) elected in 2012.

Congress

When the legendary Congressman Claude Pepper died in 1989, then-state senator Ileana Ros-Lehtinen won the special election for his vacant seat in the U.S. House of Representatives, becoming the first Hispanic in Congress from Florida in 166 years. (Joseph Marion Hernandez, who served from 1822 to 1823, was the first.) Ros-Lehtinen was the first Cuban American and the first Hispanic woman to serve in Congress.[60] The replacement of the aged liberal Democrat Pepper with a youthful Republican woman marked a historic shift in Miami and Florida politics.

Lincoln Diaz-Balart became the second Cuban-born but first Cuban American male from Florida to win a congressional seat in 1992 in a district created to elect a Hispanic. A third Hispanic seat was created in South Florida during the 2002 redistricting, and Mario Diaz-Balart joined his brother Lincoln in Congress.[61] A fourth congressional district with a sizable Hispanic population was drawn in 2012 in Central Florida. Much to the dismay of Hispanic political leaders, the seat was won by a white Democrat—liberal firebrand Alan Grayson.

Hispanic victories in statewide U.S. Senate contests have come later than state legislative wins. It was not until 2004, when Cuban-born Mel Martinez (R) beat Betty Castor (D) in a tight race to become the first Cuban American elected to the U.S. Senate. In 2010, Marco Rubio (R) handily defeated Democrat Kendrick Meek and independent Charlie Crist to fill the seat vacated by Martinez, who decided not to run for re-election. Rubio's decision to run for the Republican nomination for president in 2016 left the seat open again. Another Cuban American, Lieutenant Governor Carlos López-Cantera, was encouraged by Rubio to seek the seat.

Governor

In 1988 Bob Martinez (R) made history by being the first Hispanic elected governor of Florida. Once the Democratic mayor of Tampa, Martinez had switched to the Republican Party before running for governor.

Florida Supreme Court

Raoul G. Cantero III became the state's first Hispanic Supreme Court justice when Governor Jeb Bush (R) appointed him to the bench in 2002. Cantero is the grandson of Fulgencio Batista, the former Cuban dictator who was overthrown by Fidel Castro. Cantero resigned in 2008, citing family reasons (young children too far from their extended family). In January 2009, Governor Charlie Crist (R) appointed Cuban-American Jorge Labarga to the vacant seat. Labarga became the state's first Hispanic Chief Justice in 2014.

Big Gains

The number of Latino elected officials in Florida rose from 72 in 1996 to 158 in 2010—an increase of 119 percent![62]—and the number keeps climbing. Many of these gains have come at the local level. As local Hispanic populations have grown, more Latinos are running for local-level offices (mayoral posts and seats on county commissions, city councils, school boards, and judgeships). Often a chance for a Hispanic candidate to make history by winning increases Latino turnout and prompts interracial coalitions.

Hispanic Voter Turnout

Cuban Americans turn out to vote at higher rates than do non-Cuban Hispanics. There are a number of reasons for this, with non-citizenship status being near the top of the list. Unlike other Hispanic immigrants, Cubans who flee Cuba are given automatic asylum and a path to citizenship if they reach dry land (known as the "wet foot dry foot" policy).[63] Puerto Ricans, as U.S. citizens, also have an advantage over other Hispanic groups when it comes to voting eligibility. Language barriers may also present an obstacle to full participation, although ballots are available in Spanish in 10 counties with sizeable non-English speaking Hispanic populations.[64] Finally, many immigrants from Latin America come from countries where voting was discouraged, or even dangerous, because of political turmoil, so they may not be as interested in politics. However, once immigrants decide to become citizens, their voter turnout rates often exceed those of second- and third-generation immigrants.

Interethnic Cooperation and Conflict

African-American and Hispanic legislators have, at times, worked together to achieve common political goals related to immigration, civil rights, urban issues, and redistricting.[65] For instance, members of the Cuban and African-American legislative caucuses co-sponsored the Rosewood compensation bill and joined together in the fight to achieve minority access districts for the state legislature and for Congress. They also filed a federal lawsuit to change the Dade County Commission from at-large to single-member districts in 1993.[66]

In the state's large multi-ethnic metropolitan areas, interethnic competition is more common. Differences in economic status, religious background, ideology, culture, and language often make it nearly impossible for the two minority groups to avoid conflict. The antagonistic relationship is "due to strong ethnic bonds and the clash of cultures."[67] Competition for jobs and political power can be fierce, even violent. The black riots that broke out in Miami in 1980, 1982, and 1989 were attributed in part to resentment against Cuban refugees who were seen as taking away black-held jobs.[68]

Fights for political power can generate racially polarized voting. The 1996 Miami mayoral race was a good example. Regardless of the fact that African Americans are generally Democrats and Cuban Americans Republicans, surveys showed that 95 percent of Democratic-leaning black voters supported black *Republican* Arthur Teele, while 92 percent of Republican-leaning Hispanic voters supported the Cuban *Democrat* Alex Penelas.[69] The fight for local political offices and key appointments continues to evoke the most conflict between blacks and Latinos[70] in diverse metropolitan areas of the state—most notably South and Central Florida.

Interethnic conflict is not limited to blacks versus Hispanics. It can easily arise between other racial and ethnic groups in communities where one or both feel locked out of the political arena.[71] In Florida, immigration has been the catalyst for such animosity, particularly during economic downturns. But sometimes conflicts can occur *within* racial or ethnic groups on the basis of country of origin, such as a recent gang war between two groups of Afro-Caribbean youth (Haitian vs. Jamaican) in South Florida. Similarly, until recently, there were marked differences of opinion between Cuban and non-Cuban Hispanics about removing trade and travel barriers with Cuba.

Asian Americans in Florida

The Asian-American population in Florida is relatively small, but it is growing faster than any other major minority group.[72] In just a three-year period (2010-2013), it had climbed from 2.4 percent of Florida's population to 3.2 percent.[73] The Asian-Indian population is the largest, followed by Filipinos.

In general, Asians have a higher-than-average tendency to register as independents. Although they voted heavily Democratic in the 2012 presidential race, they are still regarded as "a highly persuadable—and growing—part of the electorate."[74] In the past, their turnout rates have lagged behind those of other minorities—a pattern that is partially attributable to ineffective outreach to Asian Americans by both political parties. The languages and cultural diversity of Asians (see Figure 1-13) have made it difficult to target these voters and to conduct polls accurately reflecting their political views and policy priorities.

Figure 1-13. Florida's Asian Population 2010

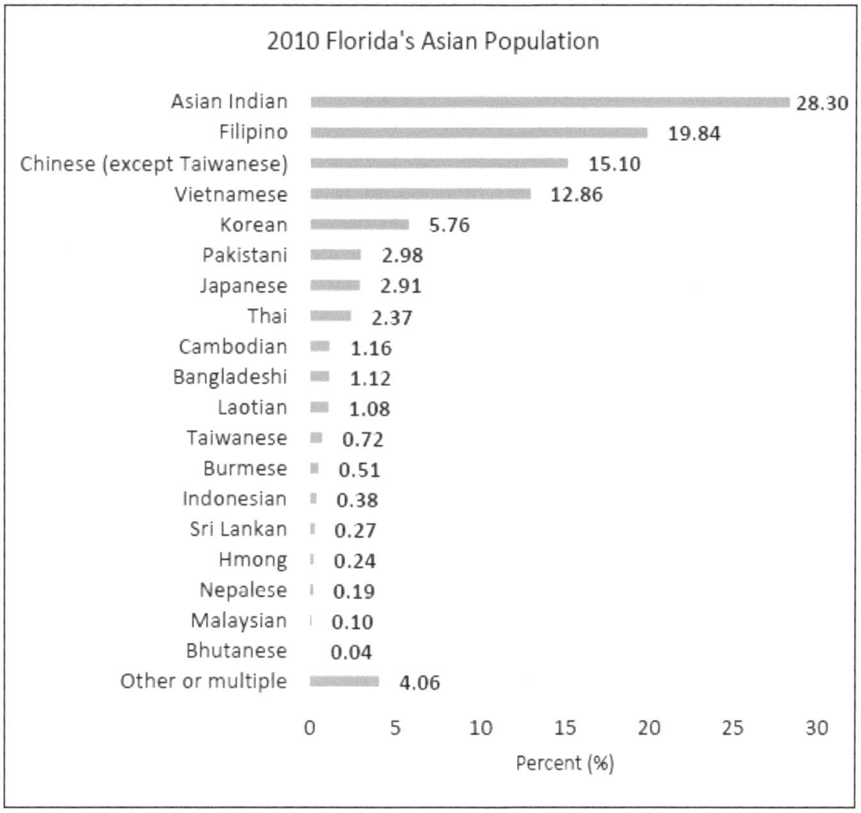

2010 Florida's Asian Population

Group	Percent
Asian Indian	28.30
Filipino	19.84
Chinese (except Taiwanese)	15.10
Vietnamese	12.86
Korean	5.76
Pakistani	2.98
Japanese	2.91
Thai	2.37
Cambodian	1.16
Bangladeshi	1.12
Laotian	1.08
Taiwanese	0.72
Burmese	0.51
Indonesian	0.38
Sri Lankan	0.27
Hmong	0.24
Nepalese	0.19
Malaysian	0.10
Bhutanese	0.04
Other or multiple	4.06

Percent (%)

Source: U.S. Census Bureau 2010. Includes all Asians, not just foreign-born.

Because Asian Americans make up a small portion of the voting public in most parts of the state, when they seek elective office they must attract crossover votes from whites, blacks, and Hispanics to win. Each of Florida's first Asians to be elected to state office were from diverse South Florida. Eddie Gong (D) from Miami-Dade County was elected to the Florida House in 1962, then to the Senate in 1966. In 1992, Mimi McAndrews (D) from Palm Beach County was the first Asian-American female elected to the state House. Gong is of Chinese descent, McAndrews, Korean.

As the Asian population has grown, the number of groups representing their interests has increased significantly. More than 50 different Asian-focused groups are active in Florida ranging from the Asian Coalition of Tallahassee, the Asian Pacific American Bar Association of South Florida, the Bangladesh American Chamber of Commerce Florida, the Big Bend Filipino-American Association, and the Gulfcoast Chinese American Association to the Florida Association of Physicians of Indian Origin, Inc., the Hong Kong Association of Florida, the Japan-America Society of Northwest Florida, and the Naples Asian Professionals Association. There is even the National Asian American PAC-FL headquartered in Jacksonville. NAAPAC is a national nonpartisan cyberspace political organization. Its stated mission is to win equal justice and opportunity for all Asian and Pacific Americans.[75]

At the local level, various ethnic groups have formed subgroups within both major parties. These include the Asian American Republican Club in Miami-Dade County, the Bangladeshi-American Democratic Club of Boca Raton, and the Panhandle Asian Republican Women Network. Activist organizations such as the Organization of Chinese Americas (OCA) of South Florida, part of a national organization, are working to advance social, political, and economic well-being of Asian and Pacific Americans. In 2010, the OCA joined with the nonprofit Asian American Federation of Florida to urge residents of Asian heritage to participate in the Census.

NATIVE AMERICANS IN FLORIDA POLITICS

More than 91,000 Floridians self-identify as Native Americans—the 10th highest among the states.[76] However, only about 4,000 of these people are members of one of Florida's federally recognized tribes—the Seminole or Miccosukee. Both tribes have their own culture, history, and identity. Members of the Seminole and Miccosukee tribes are citizens of the United States, Florida, and their tribes. They have all the rights of any other U.S. citizen. The tribes have powers of self-government on their reservations and are legally considered "dependent domestic governments." (See Table 1-5.)

The modern Seminole Tribe of Florida became a recognized political body in 1957 and the Miccosukee in 1962. The Seminoles have six reservations in the state, held in federal trust status by the U.S. government (Hollywood, Big Cypress, Brighton, Immokalee, Fort Pierce, and Tampa) with more than 3,300 registered members.[77]

There are about 700 Miccosukees registered with the tribe, that has four reservations—one on the Tamiami Trail in the Everglades National Park, one on Alligator Alley, and two at Krome Avenue and U.S. 41. Congress established the Miccosukee Reserved Area in 1998, giving tribe members permanent rights to the area. Previously, the Miccosukee had received a special permit to live on the land from the National Park Service.

Today relatively few of Florida's Native-American people live on the Seminole and Miccosukee reservations. Nonetheless, they keep alive some traditional ways, including ceremonial rites, clothing, and folk art—while, at the same time, engaging in a variety of modern economic enterprises.[78] Many place names in Florida derive from Seminole and Miccosukee languages—for example, Tallahassee, Okeechobee, Okaloosa, Kissimmee, and Wakulla.

The tribes are considered sovereign by the U.S. government, with laws and regulations concerning the tribes passed by Congress and administered by the U.S. Department of the Interior. The Governor's Council on Indian Affairs, created in 1974 by Governor Reubin Askew, strives to resolve issues concerning the tribes and the State of Florida. Members are appointed by the governor with the advice and consent of the two tribes. The chairs of the two tribes serve as co-chairs of the council.

The tribes have their own governing structures on their respective reservations. For example, the Seminole Tribe of Florida has its own constitution. The Tribal Council is the chief governing body. It is composed of a chairman, a vice-chairman, and council representatives from each reservation. Various programs and activities are administered by the Tribal Council (as described on their website):[79] "The council administers the Seminole Police Department, the Human Resources programs, the tribal gaming enterprises (see Chapter 9), citrus groves, the Billie Swamp Safari, the Ah-Tah-Thi-Ki Museum, and the majority of the tribe's cigarette-related enterprises. The Seminole Tribe of Florida's Legal Services Department administers a public defender's office, Water Resource Management, and the Utilities Department."

Table 1-5. What Is the Legal Status of American Indians and Indian Tribes?

Question	Answer
Who is an American Indian?	An Indian is a person who is of some degree Indian blood and is recognized as an Indian by a tribe and/or the United States. No single federal or tribal criterion establishes a person's identity as an Indian. Government agencies use differing criteria to determine eligibility for programs and services. Tribes also have varying eligibility criteria for membership. It is important to distinguish between the ethnological term "Indian" and the political/legal term "Indian." The protections and services provided by the United States for tribal members flow, not from an individual's status as an American Indian in an ethnological sense, but because the person is a member of a tribe recognized by the United States and with which the United States has a special trust relationship.
Are American Indians citizens?	American Indians are citizens of the United States and of the states in which they reside. They are also citizens of their tribes, according to the criteria established by each tribe.
Do American Indians have the right to vote?	American Indians have the same right to vote as all U.S. citizens. American Indians may vote in state and local elections, as well as in tribal elections. Just as federal, state, and local governments have the sovereign right to establish voter eligibility criteria, each tribe has the right to decide its voter eligibility criteria for tribal elections.
Do American Indians have the right to hold political office?	American Indians have the same rights as all citizens to hold public office. In this century, American Indian men and women have held elected and appointed offices at all levels of local, state, and federal government.
What is the legal status of American Indian tribes?	Article 1, Section 8 of the Constitution of the United States vests the Congress with the authority to engage in relations with the tribes. When the governmental authority of tribes was first challenged in the 1830s, Chief Justice John Marshall articulated a fundamental principle that has guided the evolution of federal Indian law: Tribes retain certain inherent powers of self-government as "domestic dependent nations."
What is the relationship between the U.S. Government and American Indian tribes?	The relationship between the tribes and the United States is one of a government to a government. This principle has shaped the history of dealings between the federal government and the tribes.
What does the term "federally recognized tribe" mean?	"Recognition" is a legal term meaning that the United States recognizes a government-to-government relationship with a tribe and that a tribe exists politically in a "domestic dependent nation" status. Federally recognized tribes possess certain inherent powers of self-government and entitlement to certain federal benefits, services, and protections because of the special trust relationship.
How are tribes organized?	Tribes have the inherent right to operate under their own governmental systems. Many have adopted constitutions, while others operate under articles of association or other bodies of law, and some still have traditional systems of government. The chief executive of a tribe is generally called tribal chairperson, principal chief, governor, or president. A tribal council or legislature often performs the legislative function for a tribe, although some tribes require a referendum of the membership to enact laws. Additionally, a significant number of tribes have created tribal court systems.
What is a reservation?	Reservations are territories reserved as permanent tribal homelands. Some were created through treaties, others by statutes or executive orders.

Source: U.S. Department of Justice. About Native Americans. Available at http://www.justice.gov/otj/nafaqs.htm.

The tribe does not have its own court system (judicial branch). "Legal and criminal matters not resolved on the community level are referred to the proper state or federal authorities." However, several disputes have arisen between the tribe and state and local authorities. The disputes have been jurisdictional battles centering on who has the right to prosecute tribe members, the economic development of property near their reservations (perceived as threatening wetlands, wildlife, and water resources on the reservation), and the type of gambling allowed in reservation casinos.

Seminole Tribe of Florida Reservations

The smaller Miccosukee Tribe is governed by the Miccosukee General Council, of which all tribe members 18 years of age or older are members. Council members elect five officers (chairman, assistant chairman, treasurer, secretary, and lawmaker) for four-year terms. The responsibilities of the General Council consist of development and management of resources and the day-to-day business activities of the tribe, including those involving membership, government, law and order, education, welfare, recreation, and fiscal disbursement. This group is also known as the Business Council.[80] The tribe owns and operates a restaurant, gift shop, general store, service station, and Indian Village on its Tamiami Trail Reservation.

On its Krome Avenue Reservation are an Indian gaming facility and a tobacco shop. On the Alligator Alley Reservation are a full-service gas station and service plaza.

While no Native Americans have been elected to state offices, the tribes have become big contributors to gubernatorial and state legislative campaigns. Their primary interests are in protecting their highly lucrative gaming industry, which generates more than $2 billion annually, and the Everglades. The Seminoles signed a compact with the State of Florida in 2010, allowing them to expand the types of gambling offered on the reservation casinos in return for giving a guaranteed sum to the state annually from the profits (see Chapter 9). The compact was up for renewal in 2015 but encountered competition from big casino owners in Vegas who wanted to eliminate the Seminole Tribe's gaming business monopoly—specifically card games like blackjack. The tribe spent an unprecedented amount of money running pro-Seminole compact ads in key TV markets around the state. They were joined in their fight by tourism-oriented firms like Disney opposed to allowing Las Vegas-style-casino resorts in the state under the guise of "destination tourism."

Politically, Florida's Native Americans are not politically cohesive. An analysis of registration data shows they are somewhat divided in their party preferences, although leaning slightly more Democratic. However, one-fourth register as independents. It is difficult to detect their voting patterns because they make up too small a share of the state's population to be included in polls.

Up-Close: Seminole Indians—What's in a Name?

Seminole History

The name "Seminole" is believed to be derived from the Spanish "Cimarron," used to refer to runaways. Seminoles came together as refugees from various southeastern tribes, primarily Creeks, who were forcibly displaced by whites. Fugitive slaves also fled to the swamp lands of Florida. Pressure from white settlers to claim land in North Florida and to recover escaped slaves brought a volunteer army under the command of Andrew Jackson to Florida in 1818. A series of bloody Seminole wars ensued. Most of the Seminoles were eventually forced to relocate to Oklahoma, but some escaped to the relative safety of the Everglades. After the Third Seminole War in 1858, Chief Billy Bowlegs accepted federal money to move west. Only a few hundred Seminoles remained in the Everglades and Big Cypress Swamp. For the next 100 years Seminoles managed to survive in the Everglades, keeping many traditions and customs alive, until officially recognized as tribes in the 1950s and 1960s.[81]

Florida State University's Chief Osceola rides Renegade at FSU football games. The university's use of "Seminoles" and "Chief Osceola" has received the blessing of the Seminole Tribe of Florida.

What's in a Name?

The Seminole Tribe of Florida has a close relationship with Florida State University. In early August 2005, the NCAA announced a policy to ban the use of American Indian nicknames and mascots deemed "hostile or abusive" on team uniforms or other clothing in any NCAA tournament. Eighteen schools across the country were singled out, including Florida State University. FSU President T. K. Wetherell immediately responded: "That the NCAA would now label our close bond with the Seminole people as culturally 'hostile and abusive' is both outrageous and insulting . . . . [Florida State] University will forever be associated with the unconquered spirit of the Seminole Tribe of Florida."[82] The state legislature and the governor also expressed their displeasure with the NCAA, calling the ruling insulting. Florida State challenged the ruling, pointing out that the Seminole Tribe of Florida officially sanctions the use of the nickname "Seminoles" and the mascot "Chief Osceola." In addition, they clarified that the Seminole Nation of Oklahoma had not taken an official position on the subject – earlier reports had suggested the Oklahoma tribe backed the NCAA position, but it was actually just the opinion of one member of the tribe. By late August, the NCAA removed Florida State from the list of schools cited as having "hostile or abusive" nicknames or imagery, acknowledging that there was a unique relationship between the tribe and the school. After the ruling, Chief Max Osceola, chief and general council president of the Seminole Tribe of Florida, said that it was an "honor" to be associated with Florida State University.[83]

Seminole Tribe Flag   ### Miccosukee Tribe Flag

   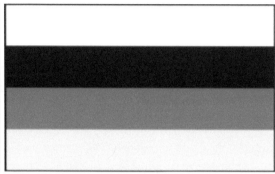

The Seminole Tribe of Florida flag features the four traditional colors of the Seminole and Miccosukee people. The central seal, with its fire and open, palm-thatched hut, called a chickee, represents the tribal council.

A Miccosukee belief holds that life spins in a circle, starting in the east and moving to the north, west, and south. The colors of the Miccosukee flag represent these four points of the compass. East is represented by yellow, north by red, west by black, and south by white. The Miccosukee Tribe adopted this flag in 1962.

THE LESBIAN, GAY, BISEXUAL, AND TRANSGENDER (LGBT) COMMUNITY IN FLORIDA POLITICS

A 2012 Gallup survey showed that LGBT adults make up 3.5 percent of Florida's adult population—ranking it 22nd among all states. A later Gallup survey of the 50 largest U.S. metropolitan areas reported these percentages: Jacksonville (4.3), Miami-Fort Lauderdale-West Palm Beach (4.2), Orlando-Kissimmee-Sanford (4.1), and Tampa-St. Petersburg-Clearwater (4.1). (The highest percentage was in the San Francisco-Oakland-Hayward MSA—6.2).[84]

In an analysis of the level of equality in more than 350 cities nationwide, four Florida cities—Wilton Manors, St. Petersburg, Orlando, and Miami Beach—received perfect scores. Among the factors included in the calculation of the Index by the Human Rights Campaign (a gay rights organization) are "the number of openly gay elected officials, partnership benefits, anti-discrimination laws, and law enforcement actions toward hate crimes."[85] Increasingly, localities are marketing to LGBT communities across the country as an economic strategy. For example, gay tourism has become a big business in certain parts of Florida. And discrimination against LGBT persons can hurt businesses to the tune of more than $360 million a year due to employee turnover, productivity losses, and lawsuits, according to a study by the Equality Means Business coalition.[86]

In Florida, as in other states, the LGBT community has become a stronger, although not monolithic, political force. Historically the Democratic Party has been more supportive of LGBT lifestyles, but both parties have political activist groups focused on the issues of lesbian, gay, bisexual, and transgender persons—the Stonewall Democrats and the Log Cabin Republicans. Each has local chapters in the state's urban population centers.

The number of openly gay elected officials is on the upswing as more have sought office and voter opinions have become more accepting. In 2010, it was estimated that there were 20-25 openly gay elected officials in Florida. By early 2014, the number had jumped to more than 30.[87] It was not until 2012, however, that the first openly gay state legislators were elected. David Richardson (D-Miami Beach) and Joe Saunders

(D-Orlando) were both elected to the Florida House of Representatives. Up to that point, Florida was the biggest state in the nation to have never voted in an openly gay state legislator.

The earliest successes of LGBT candidates actually came at the local government level. For example, the City of Wilton Manors elected its first gay commissioner in 1988. By 2000, the commission was the nation's second gay-majority governing body. The City of Orlando elected its first lesbian to the commission in 2000. St. Petersburg elected its first gay city council member in 2008. Four years later, it, too, had become a gay-majority council. Transgender candidates have had a tougher time winning, although several have run for office. Gina Duncan unsuccessfully sought a seat on the Orange County Commission in 2012, although she did receive 40 percent of the vote against a two-term incumbent.

Both statewide and local candidates benefit from LGBT activist organizations such as national Gay & Lesbian Victory Fund, Equality Florida, the National Center for Lesbian Rights, the ACLU of Florida, SAVE—a Miami group, and Freedom to Marry. Since 1991, the Fund has been helping candidates get elected to local, state, and federal offices through endorsements, fellowships, and candidate training seminars. (The Fund's Leadership Institute has provided training for prospective candidates in Fort Lauderdale.[88]) Equality Florida, founded in 1997, is the state's largest civil rights organization dedicated to securing full equality for Florida's LGBT community by lobbying, grassroots organizing, and coalition building. The organization has been active in promoting candidates and in pushing issues such as gay adoption, marriage equality, and safety for LGBT students, who are often targets of bullying in schools.[89]

Same-sex marriage in Florida was initially banned in 1997 when the Florida Legislature enacted the Florida Defense of Marriage Act (codified at Fla. Stat. § 741.212 [1997]). Then in 2008, Florida voters approved a constitutional amendment that banned both same-sex marriage and civil unions. Federal court rulings, however, made same sex-marriages legal in the state in January 2015. By that time, polls showed that nearly 57 percent of Floridians

Supporters of a bill to repeal Florida's ban on adoption by gay couples held a large rally at the State Capitol early in the 2009 legislative session.

supported same-sex marriage. That same year, a law was passed legalizing gay adoptions.

Despite the LGBT civil rights movement's growth, there is still strong opposition to its policy preferences among some Floridians, largely based on religious beliefs. For others, economic issues are more pressing than moral issues.

FLORIDA'S ECONOMY AND ITS POLITICAL IMPACT

Perhaps nothing—short of scandal—gives elected officials the jitters like a poor economy. Rising unemployment, tighter budgets, stock market declines, school closings, and lower incomes create a sense of doom. Angered and afraid, voters take it out on whoever happens to be running the government. The opposite scenario, says the common wisdom, tends to produce complacency. Voters return incumbents to their posts or do not even bother to go to the polls.

The reality is that no economy stays static for long. Demographic shifts, technological innovations, natural disasters, consumer preferences, and other events, subtle and cataclysmic, change the economy and perceptions of prosperity. Successful politicians seize the mood of the electorate and go with the flow.

Florida's Changing Economy

If Florida were a country, it would rank as the world's 19th largest economy.[90] Florida's economy is large— more than $800 billion.[91] (See Figure 1-14.) In 2013, its Gross Domestic Product (GDP), the broadest measure of economic output at the state level, accounted for about 4.8 percent of the nation's total GDP.

While Florida's economic growth roughly matched that of the United States in the late 1900s, the recession of the 2000s took Floridians on a roller coaster ride scarier than the ones found at the state's amusement parks. Real estate prices in Florida rose rapidly as the housing bubble grew, and, when it burst, home prices and the

The Great Recession of 2007 forced many Floridians out of their homes.

state's economy fell hard. To make matters worse, the bursting of the housing bubble stifled population growth, an important historical catalyst of the state's growth.

With the exception of the tourism industry, which is relatively immune to downturns in the *state* economy and was one of a handful of industries that actually added jobs during the recession, construction and many other industries took a major hit.[92] (Review Figure 1-4.) (The tourism industry is more sensitive to the *national* economy, which was not as severely affected by the housing bubble and subsequent burst.[93]) Immediately after the recession, the state struggled to get back on its feet. Eventually, the recovery accelerated, and the state's economic outlook improved.

Figure 1-14. Real GDP (Gross Domestic Product) in Millions of Dollars

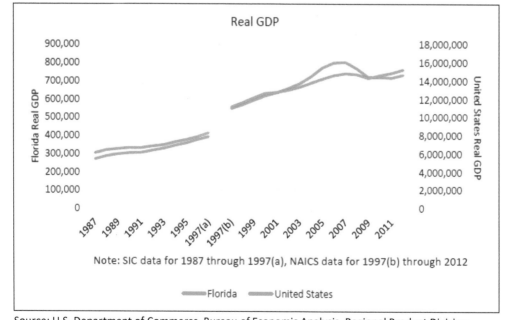

Source: U.S. Department of Commerce, Bureau of Economic Analysis, Regional Product Division.

Waves of Challenges Inspire Diversification

Early on, Florida's economy was driven by agriculture. Although the state's farms feature a range of fruits, vegetables, and livestock, the most notable produce is citrus. Florida's soil and climate are particularly hospitable to citrus trees, and farmers in Central Florida first started growing citrus crops commercially in the 19th century.[94] Florida trails only Brazil in production of oranges and produces the most grapefruit in the world. Indian River County is famous for its grapefruit. But citrus greening is threatening to destroy the state's citrus industry. Greening is spread by a disease-infected insect, the Asian citrus psyllid. Both the federal and state governments are spending millions to find a way to eradicate greening.

The Great Freeze of the 1890s, citrus canker and other diseases, and other environmental factors have occasionally resulted in difficult years for Florida citrus farmers. Fortunately, the development of the railroad system that began in the late 1800s opened the state to the tourism industry, which gradually added to the predominately agricultural economy of the state. As the tourism industry has grown, other events, including more natural disasters, reminded Floridians of the importance of not relying so heavily on a small group of industries.

Tourism has also been vulnerable to economic risks over the years. Spikes in gas prices discourage vacationers, the Gulf oil spill soiled the pristine beaches of the Panhandle, and, perhaps most significantly, hurricanes threaten not only residents but tourists as well. In response to devastation caused by hurricanes in recent decades, state leaders have employed economic development tools to facilitate further diversification of Florida's economy.

More recently, the Great Recession of the 2000s taught Floridians the importance of not relying so heavily on population growth to stimulate the economy. Florida is developing a healthier mix of jobs, many of which are in high paying fields like life sciences, which are gaining traction in the state.[95] As another example, financial services firms that traditionally employed Floridians in back-office roles, are now moving some of their front-office operations to the state. (See Figure 1-15 and Table 1-6.)

Figure 1-15. Map of Florida's Economic Regions

Source: "Florida Communities," Enterprise Florida (2015). Available at http://www.enterpriseflorida.com/data-center/florida-communities/.

Making Florida a Great Place to Do Business

Florida governments engage in economic development to encourage businesses to operate in the state, which is an easy sell for several reasons. The state represents an opportunity for businesses to innovate with the help of a technically skilled labor force, trade with other companies from around the world, and keep more of the money they make.

The economic development efforts have coincided with the growing footprint of high-tech industry in Florida, including health care, defense, transportation, professional services, and aerospace. Domestic and foreign investment in research and development and funding for research done within Florida's university system are key to sustaining the growth in these industries that demand innovation and a highly educated workforce.

Florida's low cost of living and lack of state personal income tax allow residents to enjoy a standard of living that, for the majority living near the coast, means close proximity to beaches and entertainment that people in other states can enjoy only while vacationing. This appeal is important to companies that choose to operate or even headquarter in Florida. The state is home to a large, skilled labor force, and the private sector has a low unionization rate.

Table 1-6. Sample of Major Employers in Florida's Economic Regions

Northwest	Staff	East Central	Staff
U.S. Dept. of the Air Force	16,000	Adventist Health System/Sunbelt	13,000
Landrum Prof Employer Services Inc.	11,000	United Space Alliance LLC	8,000
Fla Dept. Environmental Protection	4,600	Florida Hospital Medical Ctr.	7,200
Tallahassee Memor. Healthcare Inc.	2,750	Orlando Health Inc.	6,000
City of Tallahassee	2,633	Travelers Home & Mar. Insur. Co.	5,999
North Central		**South Central**	
University of Florida	12,000	Naes Corporation	2,100
N. Florida/S. Georgia VA Health	4,800	United States Sugar Corp.	1,400
Monroe Regional Health System	2,500	Adventist Health System/Sunbelt	1,200
Shands Teaching Hosp. Clinics Inc.	2,500	Florida Hospital Heartland	900
Fla. Dept. Children & Families	1,800	A Duda & Sons Inc.	500
Northeast		**Southeast**	
Baptist Health Sys. Foundation Inc.	8,000	American Airlines Inc.	9,000
Mayo Clinic	5,214	Baptist Health South Florida	7,169
Blue Cross Blue Shield Fla Inc.	5,000	Regal Springs Trading Co.	6,412
World Medical Govt. Solutions LLC	4,133	Miami Dade College	6,000
United States Dept. of Navy	4,000	C & W Fish Co. Inc.	4,925
Tampa Bay		**Southwest**	
Diversified Maintenance Sys. LLC	100,000	Softserve USA Inc.	1,800
FedEx Freight Corporation	8,800	Naples Community Hospital Inc.	1,780
Administrate Concept Inc.	7,000	Drs. Osteopathic Med. Ctr. Inc.	1,530
Raymond James & Associates Inc.	5,000	County of Collier	1,400
Tech Data Corporation	3,200	County of Lee	1,400

Note: Some employers have several entries in the data set, possibly due to multiple locations within a single region. In those cases, each entry is treated as a separate item for this list.

Source: "Community Search," Enterprise Florida (2015). Available at http://www.enterpriseflorida.com/data-center/florida-communities/community-search/.

Florida's geographic location (proximity to Latin America and the Caribbean), strategic ports in Miami and along the coast, and multimodal transportation infrastructure make it one of the premier North American hubs for international trade.

For each of the years from 2012 to 2015, the Tax Foundation ranked Florida fifth in the United States in its State Business Tax Climate Index, which accounts for corporate, individual income, sales, unemployment insurance, and property taxes.[96] The growing list of companies that have chosen to operate or headquarter in Florida demonstrates the state's attractiveness to businesses. (See Figure 1-16.)

Figure 1-16. Corporate and Regional/Hemispheric Headquarters Located in Florida

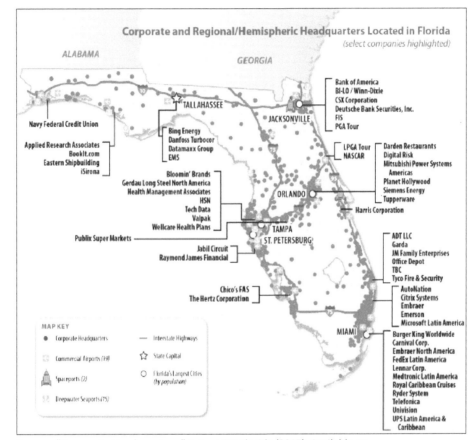

Source: "Corporate Headquarters," Enterprise Florida (2015). Available at
http://www.enterpriseflorida.com/wp-content/uploads/brief-headquarters-florida.pdf.

Post-Recession: Reserved Optimism

As Baby Boomers retire, many of them will likely consider moving to milder climates like the one in Florida, which positions the economy to benefit from another wave of population growth. A popular destination is South Florida, where metropolitan areas like Miami have grown in the wake of the Great Recession. However, as the economic recovery speeds up and real estate prices rebound, Floridians are wary of another housing bubble.

While high paying jobs in Florida's growing tech industries are improving the outlook for many, the fact remains that much of the tourism industry is supported by characteristically low-wage employment. Also, business owners are faced with ever-rising employee health care costs and fear that the situation will worsen, which will likely contribute to a continued reduction in work hours or, worse, a shift to part-time employment to mitigate skyrocketing health care costs.

The construction industry has been among the slowest to recover. While cash buyers (investors) take advantage of low prices, those sales may soon decline as real estate prices recover. If that happens, experts fear that residents may not be financially ready or able to obtain financing to replace the investors. [97]

Floridians have been gradually relieved by a recovering economy that has gained momentum in the decade following the Great Recession, at least partially due to an influx of high-tech and other employers attracted by low taxes and other factors. However, it remains to be seen whether a suppression of tax revenues may cause harm in the long run by constraining public investment in infrastructure and, perhaps more importantly, educating the workforce.

Employment: Jobs as a Key Political Issue

The link between the economy and politics is strong, as evidenced in the 2010 and 2014 gubernatorial elections. At the time of the 2010 election, Florida's home foreclosure rate ranked second among the states, and its unemployment rate, fourth. Not surprisingly, turnout and support for Republican Rick Scott was higher among Floridians living in rural counties where unemployment rates were higher (the Panhandle because of the BP oil spill) and in suburban counties with higher-than-average home foreclosure and unemployment rates. Scott ran on a fiscally conservative platform with an emphasis on job creation and lower taxes. Turnout in Democratic-leaning urban areas was lower, especially in South Florida. There the economy was stronger, in large part due to the strength of the international trade and tourism sectors.

In Scott's 2014 race against Democrat Charlie Crist, the Governor stuck to the same message—"Jobs, Jobs, Jobs"—but for slightly different reasons. Polls were showing that voters were not convinced the Great Recession was really over and they were worried about the future of the nation's economy. Many were still working part-time rather than full-time or at jobs that paid less than the ones they had lost in the depths of the recession, or simply could still not find work. Support for Scott was highest (58 percent) among voters who said they were somewhat or very worried about the future of the economy. And just as in 2010, Scott won a majority of the votes cast by citizens living in suburban, rural, and small city areas—where economic concerns still dominated. Citizens do "vote their pocketbooks."

GEOGRAPHICAL FACTS

Florida has unique geographical characteristics:

- Total area - 58,560 square miles
- Total land area - 54,136 square miles
- Total water area - 4,424 square miles
- Rank among states in total area - 22nd
- Length north and south - 447 miles (St. Marys River to Key West)
- Width east and west - 361 miles (Atlantic Ocean to Perdido River)
- Distance from Pensacola to Key West - 792 miles (by road)
- Highest natural point - 345 feet
- Geographic center - 12 miles northwest of Brooksville, Hernando County
- Coastline - 1,197 statute miles
- Tidal shoreline (general) - 2,276 statute   miles
- Beaches - 663 miles
- Longest river - St. Johns, 273 miles
- Largest lake - Lake Okeechobee, 700 square miles
- Largest county - Palm Beach, 2,578 square miles
- Smallest county - Union, 245 square miles
- Number of lakes (greater than 10 acres) - about 7,700
- Number of first-magnitude springs – 33
- Number of islands (greater than 10 acres) - about 4,500

Source: Florida Department of State, http://dos.myflorida.com/florida-facts/quick-facts/.

ONLINE SOURCES FOR DATA AND INFORMATION UPDATES

Bureau of Economic and Business Research: Populations Studies and Projections

The BEBR has information on Florida's current population numbers, growth, county size, distribution, and future projections for the state of Florida.
http://www.bebr.ufl.edu/population

Bureau of Labor Statistics

The BLS releases data statistics for all 50 states, and the U.S. economy as a whole. This information includes employment, unemployment, and labor force statistics. Specific data statistics for the state of Florida can be found here.
http://www.bls.gov/eag/eag.fl.htm

U.S. Department of Commerce, Bureau of Economic Analysis

The BEA releases data statistics from national, international, regional, and industry standpoints, including GDP (per capita and real), income, trade, and investment.
http://bea.gov/

U.S. Bureau of the Census

The Bureau of the Census has census records from every 10 years, until 2010. The census includes data such as population, race, education, family structure, and income. Specific data includes racial and ethnic compositions, MSA statistics, and population by race, region of birth, etc.

http://www.census.gov/

U.S. Bureau of the Census: American Community Survey

The American Community Survey, conducted by the Census Bureau, provides updated statistics every year (population, age, race, family structure, income, etc.) and includes helpful data comparison tables in order to compare national and state statistics, or two or more categories.
http://www.census.gov/acs/www/data_documentation/data_main/

Florida Division of Elections: Voter Registration Statistics

The Florida Division of Elections site includes voter registration statistics from 1994 to 2014. These statistics include data from both the primary, general, and special elections, as well as data about party, race, and county. Specific data includes registration numbers by party, region, race, etc.
http://election.dos.state.fl.us/voter-registration/statistics/elections.shtml

Enterprise Florida

Enterprise Florida releases data on Florida communities, industries, trade, economy, and accolades, as well as international trade. Specific data includes information on corporate headquarters, major employers, and economic regions in Florida.
http://www.enterpriseflorida.com/data-center/

U.S. Department of Justice: About Native Americans

This site includes information about the history and rights of Native Americans, and their relationship to U.S. government at the local, state, and federal level.
http://www.justice.gov/otj/nafaqs.htm

Chapter 2. The Florida Constitution

Constitutions govern governments. Contrary to popular opinion, they are not dull, unimportant, antiquated documents. They are frequently the center of intense, hard-fought, multimillion-dollar political battles over everything from school vouchers, medical malpractice, and parental notification of a minor's abortion to slot machines and the constitutional amendment process itself. In Florida, proposed constitutional amendments often get almost as much attention as presidential or gubernatorial elections.[1]

Constitutions establish the structure and organization of government; they describe the powers of various branches of government; and they set forth the rules by which laws are to be made. But most important, constitutions limit the powers of government and protect the rights of citizens. The true meaning of "constitutionalism" is *limited* government. And Americans, perhaps more than any other people in the world, are devoted to the idea of limiting governmental power through written constitutional guarantees of individual rights.

All 50 states have written constitutions, but the U.S. Constitution is the supreme law of the nation. State constitutions are legally subordinate to the U.S. Constitution and the laws of the United States. The U.S. Constitution mentions state constitutions only once, and it does so to assert the supremacy of the U.S. Constitution and the laws and treaties of the United States. Article VI states:

> This Constitution, and the Laws of the United States which shall be made in Pursuance thereof; and all Treaties made, or which shall be made, under the Authority of the United States, shall be the supreme Law of the Land; and the Judges in every State shall be bound thereby, any Thing in the Constitution or Laws of any State to the Contrary notwithstanding.

Constitutions are derived from the people themselves. The Preamble to the Florida Constitution states, "We, the people of the State of Florida . . . do ordain and establish this constitution." Florida's current Constitution was approved by the voters of the state in 1968, and all amendments to it must be approved by the voters. It is the foundation of the government of the state. It tells officials of the state, as well as its counties, cities, and school districts, what they can and cannot do. All laws enacted by the state legislature, and all actions by the governor, state agencies, state courts, and local governments, must conform to the state Constitution.

Florida's Constitution takes precedence over Florida statutes—laws passed by the legislature and signed by the governor. The Florida statutes cover 48 major topics (called Titles) totaling more than 1,000 Chapters.[2] Florida statutes take precedence over the Florida Administrative Code—state governmental agencies' interpretations of the statutes. The Florida Administrative Code covers 72 Chapters.[3] Florida statutes also take precedence over county and municipal ordinances.[4]

Interpretations, applications, and resolution of conflicts regarding Florida's Constitution, laws, administrative code, and local ordinances are the province of the Florida court system. The decisions of the Florida Supreme Court up to 1997 are compiled in 695 volumes of *West's Florida Cases in Southern Reporter,* 2nd series. Subsequent decisions are available online from several sites.[5] One can even listen to oral arguments before the Florida Supreme Court online.[6]

"WE THE PEOPLE OF THE STATE OF FLORIDA"

Like many other states, Florida has a very lengthy state constitution. Including history notes, it has grown to over 52,000 words. By comparison, the U.S. Constitution contains only about 8,700 words. State constitutions, including Florida's, tend to be longer because they address many specific policy areas not covered in the U.S. Constitution and because they tend to be easier to amend than the U.S. Constitution.

The Florida Constitution establishes the state's legislative, executive, and judicial branches of government and its counties, municipalities, and school districts. It also establishes policy on a great many topics, from a three day waiting period on the purchase of handguns to the allocation of the state's gas tax revenues to county governments. The Constitution has been officially rewritten six times.[7] (See Up-Close: Florida's Six Constitutions.) The current Constitution was drafted by a Constitutional Revision Commission and ratified by the voters in 1968. Amendments have been added to this document in nearly every statewide general election since then.

The Florida Constitution resembles other state constitutions in its general organization: a declaration of rights; articles establishing the legislative, executive, and judicial branches of state government; followed by articles on elections, finance and taxation, local government, education, and "miscellaneous"; and ending with amendment procedures (see below). But among the more distinctive features of the Florida Constitution are:

- A guarantee of the *right of privacy*, "to be let alone and free from government intrusion." The Florida Supreme Court has interpreted this provision to protect the right to abortion in the state, independent of any right under the U.S. Constitution.
- A *balanced-budget provision*, officially described as a prohibition on annual "revenue shortfalls." In the event that revenues fall short of appropriations, the governor and Cabinet are obliged to make "all necessary reductions in the state budget in order to comply."
- A *plural executive branch*, consisting of the governor and three separately elected Cabinet officers (see Chapter 7), and a *legislature* consisting of a House of Representatives with 120 members elected from single-member districts for two-year terms and a Senate with 40 members elected from single-member districts for four-year terms. (See Chapter 6.)
- A *prohibition on personal income taxes* and taxes on estates and inheritances.
- A *"sunshine" provision* that guarantees the right of citizens to examine public records and attend meetings of state and local government bodies.
- *Term limits* for all elected state officials, including the governor, Cabinet officers, and state legislators.
- *Tax limitations*, including a limit on the growth of annual property tax assessments to 3 percent or the inflation rate, whichever is lower; a limit on the growth rate in state revenues to no more than the growth rate in Florida personal income; and a requirement that any new constitutionally imposed tax must be approved by two-thirds of the voters.

When Constitutional Principles Clash—Privacy versus Sunshine

Both the right to privacy and the right to access public records (government in the sunshine) are guaranteed by the Florida Constitution and are considered fundamentally important. But sometimes the right to privacy conflicts with the right to open government. A high profile example of this public v. private conflict occurred over the release of famed NASCAR driver Dale Earnhardt's autopsy photos. Dale Earnhardt was killed February 18, 2001 on the last lap of the Daytona 500 race—the fourth driver to die of a skull fracture that year. Several newspapers requested the driver's autopsy photos as part of their investigation and coverage of the accident. After winning a court order stopping the release of the photos, Earnhardt's wife and son successfully got a court order to prohibit the release of the photos. They then personally appealed to the governor and the Florida Legislature for more permanent protection. The family was aided in their fight by 14,000 Earnhardt fans from across the country that sent e-mails in support of their privacy request. With little debate, the legislature quickly made it a felony to release autopsy photos without the approval of a judge. Governor Jeb Bush (R) quickly signed the Family Protection Act into law in late March, barely one month after the accident, stating that the speed with which the legislature had acted was "a tribute to the speed of Dale Earnhardt."[8]

Several newspapers and web sites filed suit to gain access to the photos and to overturn the law. Their complaint was that the statute was overly-broad, ill-conceived, and bad public policy. They argued that autopsy photos had always been open for inspection and that public access in the past had been vital to solving crimes and evaluating decisions made by medical examiners. The papers claimed they would only examine, not publish, the photos to avoid invading the Earnhardt's right to privacy. They argued that a public good would be served by their inspection of the autopsy photos which could lead to findings that could force NASCAR to take more precautions to protect drivers from serious injury or death in future races. Finally, they argued that the law should not apply retroactively to requests that had been made before the law was passed. In the end, the right to privacy prevailed. A Fifth District Court decision left the records sealed and declared the law constitutional. The Florida Supreme Court declined to review the decision.[9] Lawmakers voted to continue the "Earnhardt" law in 2006 with little controversy.

It is the role of the Supreme Court to interpret the Constitution and apply it to the current situation. But it is the role of the citizens to change the state Constitution either by rewriting it or amending it. Florida has had six different Constitutions in its history (see Up-Close: Florida's Six Constitutions) and they can be viewed at *www.floridamemory.com*.

"Constitutionalizing" Policy Preferences

The Florida Constitution not only specifies organizations and processes of government and guarantees basic individual liberties; it also undertakes to decide many specific policy questions. Unlike the U.S. Constitution, the Florida Constitution contains numerous policy mandates on topics as diverse as tax rates, lotteries, and exemptions from taxation, civil service, gun control, fishing, and English as the official state language.

Why does the Constitution include so much legislative detail? Reformers contend that a constitution should be brief and explicit; it should set forth general principles of governance rather than specific policies that should be left to elected officials. But citizens often distrust their elected officials to do what is right or think they are dragging their feet on an important issue. Either situation may prompt citizens to begin a petition drive to put a policy proposal (constitutional amendment) directly on the ballot for voter approval, thereby bypassing the state legislature. This, in effect, is an example of how various citizen and interest groups seek to "constitutionalize" their particular policy preferences rather than rely on the normal legislative process.

Placing so many policy decisions in the Constitution itself not only lengthens the document but also encourages even more amendments to be put before the electorate. In nearly every state election, there are multiple constitutional amendment proposals on the ballot. Voters readily acknowledge they often have little knowledge of what the amendment proposals really mean. (See Figure 2-1.)

UP-CLOSE: FLORIDA'S SIX CONSTITUTIONS

Constitution of 1838

This territorial Constitution, required by Congress before it would consider statehood for Florida, established a governing system much like the federal and other state governments. It set up three branches of government with a fairly weak governor limited to one four-year term. It strongly affirmed the system of slavery, prohibiting any legislation to emancipate slaves and authorizing legislation to prevent free blacks from entering Florida. Among its unusual features was its denial of many public offices to bank officers, clergymen, and anyone who had participated in a duel. The prohibition on duelists remained until the ratification of the 1968 Constitution. Under this territorial Constitution, Florida was granted statehood in 1845.

The Secretary of State and the Florida Supreme Court justices stand by the original 1838 Constitution on the opening day of the 2004 legislative session.

Constitution of 1861

In most respects, this Constitution copied the provisions of the 1838 Constitution but tied Florida to the Confederate States of America. Because civil war loomed, the militia provisions took on a new importance. This Constitution was not submitted to the electorate for ratification as the convention of 1860 had been empowered by the legislature to make binding changes to the 1838 Constitution.

Constitution of 1865

Shortly after the Civil War ended, President Andrew Johnson appointed a provisional governor with instructions to convene a Constitutional Convention. The convention met and adopted a new constitution but it never took effect. Congress rejected President Johnson's plan to return Florida and the other former Confederate states to the union. Instead Congress divided the South into five military districts, each under the command of a general. Although it acknowledged the abolition of slavery, it restricted jury service and even witness testimony to whites only (unless the victim was black) and denied newly freed blacks (as well as women) the right to vote.

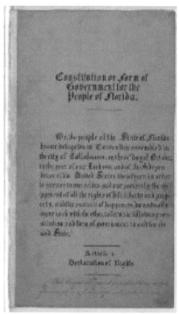

Constitution of 1868

This Constitution reflected the turbulence of Reconstruction and military occupation and was referred to by many Floridians as the "Carpetbag" Constitution. A constitutional convention was convened with delegates selected in an election supervised by the military. However, the delegates split into a number of factions and none could establish a quorum. Ultimately, the general overseeing the Third Military District chose the delegates who wrote this Constitution. It extended voting and other rights to all males, even allocating a seat in the state Senate and House to Seminole Indians. It centralized authority with the governor, providing that county officials would be appointed by him, not elected locally. It also required a system of public schools, a state prison, and institutions for the mentally ill and the blind and deaf. It also mandated that taxes be uniform and protected the homestead of a debtor from forced sale.

The 1865 Constitution adopted by a Constitutional Convention never took effect. It was preempted by Congress' dividing the South into military districts after the Civil War.

Constitution of 1885

The Constitution of 1885 imposed checks on what were considered the abuses of Reconstruction governments to weaken executive authority. An elected Cabinet and elected county officials positions were established, elected state official's salaries were reduced, and the governor was limited to one term. The Constitution authorized a poll tax (which lasted until 1937) that served to deny poor blacks, and many poor whites, the right to vote. While the 1885 Constitution was Florida's longest lived, it was also the most amended, growing to more than 50,000 words by 1968, compared to 8,700 words for the U.S. Constitution. There were 212 amendments proposed and 149 adopted by voters in those years. By the 1960s, dozens of amendments were proposed in each session of the legislature.

Constitution of 1968

Technically, the current Florida Constitution is a revision of the 1885 Constitution. It was initially drafted by a Constitutional Revision Commission established by the legislature in 1965. The commission's recommendations were revised and passed by the legislature in July 1968 and approved by the voters of the state in November of that year.

OUTLINE OF THE FLORIDA CONSTITUTION

A summary of Florida's Constitution is provided below.[10]

Preamble, 1968 Constitution

"We, the people of the State of Florida, being grateful to Almighty God for our constitutional liberty, in order to secure its benefits, perfect our government, insure domestic tranquility, maintain public order, and guarantee equal civil and political rights to all, do ordain and establish this constitution."

Article I-Declaration of Rights

This is Florida's Bill of Rights. It establishes equal protection under the law, religious freedom, freedom of speech, press and assembly, the right to bear arms, due process, the right of habeas corpus and pretrial release, the rights of the accused, and the right to access the courts and to a trial by jury. It also prohibits unreasonable searches and seizures, bills of attainder and ex post facto laws, imprisonment for debt except in cases of fraud, prosecution of a capital crime without presentment or indictment by a grand jury, excessive punishments, and administrative penalties. Some additional rights include the right to work, the rights of crime victims, the right to privacy, the right of access to public records and open meetings, a "Taxpayers' Bill of Rights" and a claimant's right to fair compensation. An amendment defining legal marriage in Florida as only between one man and one woman is also found here, although it was later negated by a federal court ruling.

Article II-General Provisions

The general provisions article establishes state boundaries, designates three branches of government, authorizes a state seal and flag, and designates Tallahassee as the state capital. Other less traditional provisions include a code of ethics for state and local government officers and employees, designation of English as the official language of Florida, and a requirement that state policy "conserve and protect its natural resources and scenic beauty" with laws to abate water, air, and noise pollution.

Article III-Legislature

Florida's legislature has a House and Senate, with house members elected for two years and senators for four years. Article III sets up the process for bill passage, veto, and veto override and it prohibits certain special laws. The article mandates the establishment of a civil service system, lays out the process for impeachment and for legislative reapportionment every ten years, and sets standards for redistricting legislative and congressional seats. It also requires an annual state budget and planning process that includes a budget stabilization fund (or "rainy day" fund) to cover revenue shortages caused by economic downturns.

Article IV-Executive

The executive branch in Florida consists of the offices of governor and lieutenant governor as well as Florida's unique Cabinet, which up until 2002 included an elected secretary of state, attorney general, comptroller, treasurer, commissioner of agriculture, and commissioner of education. Because of constitutional amendments, the elected Cabinet was reduced from six to three members: attorney general, chief financial officer (combining the comptroller and treasurer) and commissioner of agriculture. The secretary of state and commissioner of education are now appointed positions. Article IV establishes the qualifications, sets four-year terms of office, and lays out duties of the governor and Cabinet. For instance, the governor must faithfully execute the laws and may call out the militia, fill vacancies in state and county offices, suspend any state officer, and with the approval of the Cabinet grant clemency. The article authorizes up to 25 executive departments, each supervised by the governor or lieutenant governor, an individual Cabinet member, or both the governor and Cabinet. While it leaves the number and functions of executive departments to statutory law, it requires there will be a Fish and Wildlife Conservation Commission, Department of Veteran Affairs, and Department of Elder Affairs.

Article V-Judiciary

The judicial branch is divided into four levels of state courts, each with its own jurisdiction: county courts, circuit courts, district courts of appeal, and the Supreme Court. Article V specifies nonpartisan election of county judges for four-year terms and circuit judges for six-year terms. It dictates that the appointment of Supreme Court justices and district courts of appeal judges be done by the governor from a list prepared by the Judicial Nominating Commission. Voters then decide in general elections whether to retain them for succeeding six year terms. The article also creates a Judicial Qualifications Commission to investigate charges of judicial misconduct and recommend disciplinary action to the Florida Supreme Court. It gives the high court the jurisdiction to regulate admission of persons to the practice of law in the state. It also provides for the election of clerks of circuit courts, state's attorneys, and public defenders.

Article VI-Suffrage and Election

Article VI spells out dates of general elections, lists qualifications to vote, disqualifies convicted felons and the mentally incompetent, provides the form of an oath administered to persons registering to vote, and leaves to statutory law the details of special elections and referenda. It limits the governor, lieutenant governor, Cabinet members, state senators and representatives to no more than eight consecutive years in office. (A few years ago, the term limits provision was used in an effort to impose term limits on Florida's U.S. Representatives (8 consecutive years in office) and U.S. Senators (12 years). However, the U.S. Supreme Court ruled that *states'* imposition of terms limits on members of Congress was unconstitutional.) The suffrage and elections article also sets the date for general elections (the first Tuesday after the first Monday in November of even-numbered years) and establishes a system of voluntary public campaign financing for elective state-wide races. And, since 1998, the article requires that primary elections be open to all registered voters if all candidates in the primary are from the same party and the winner will have no opposition in the general election. Under other circumstances the primaries are closed, allowing only voters registered with that party to participate.

Article VII-Finance and Taxation

In Florida, all taxes and appropriations must be provided by the legislature, and most bond issues must be approved by voters. Article VII limits the authority to borrow, and it specifies taxing authority and exemptions. It limits annual increases in state revenues to the rate of personal income growth. It restricts increases in assessment of homes to either three percent a year or the rate of increase in consumer prices, whichever is lower and makes accumulated assessment savings portable when homeowners move. Article VII prohibits a state personal income tax, limits inheritance taxes, and establishes rules governing local government taxing, spending, and borrowing. It authorizes a homestead exemption of up to $50,000 and additional property tax exemptions for disabled veterans over 65, surviving spouses of veterans and first responders, and low income seniors. Limits on property tax assessments for conservation land, improvements made for energy conservation and wind protection, and working waterfront property are also spelled out.

Article VIII-Local Government

The state has the authority to create, abolish, or change counties and municipalities. Article VIII also specifies their powers, and requires that county officials must include county commissioners and five constitutional officers—a clerk of courts, sheriff, tax appraiser, tax collector, and supervisor of elections.

Article IX-Education

This provision provides authority to establish by statute a "uniform, efficient, safe, secure and high quality system of free public schools," institutions of higher learning, and other public education programs as needed. The Board of Education supervises this system. The Board historically consisted of the governor and the six Cabinet members, with day-to-day oversight in the hands of the elected Commissioner of Education. Since January 2003, the Board has been composed of seven members appointed by the governor to staggered four-year terms with the Commissioner of Education appointed by the Board. The article specifies one school district per county although county residents may vote to combine their school district with one or more contiguous counties. It establishes a school board of at least five members elected in nonpartisan elections to staggered four-year terms to oversee each district. It also mandates a superintendent, either elected to a four-year term or appointed by the school board, to oversee day-to-day operations of each district.

Article X-Miscellaneous

The miscellaneous section seems to grow every election cycle as it is a popular place for interest groups to place their preferred initiatives (constitutional amendments). Currently this Article includes 28 sections wide-ranging in their focus. Subjects range from the granting of authority for a state militia, protection from court seizure of a person's home, restrictions on the use of eminent domain, creation of the state lottery, public ownership of lands under all navigable waters, a limit on saltwater net fishing, the establishment of an Everglades Trust Fund, and a mandate to build a high speed ground transportation system (repealed in 2004) to a prohibition against smoking in most workplaces, a limitation on cruel confinement of pigs during pregnancy, required parental notification of a minor's desire to receive an abortion, authorization of slot machines in Broward and Miami-Dade after a local referendum (approved in Broward but not in Miami-Dade), creation of a Florida minimum wage, establishment of a patient's right to know about adverse medical incidents at a health care provider, removal of a physician's license to practice if found guilty of three or more incidents of medical malpractice, a requirement to spend 15 percent of the Florida tobacco settlement on programs to reduce youth smoking, and a mandate to dedicate 33 percent of the excise tax on documents for water and land conservation.

The Florida Constitution devotes one entire article (IX) to Education, one of the most important and expensive functions of government.

Article XI-Amendments

All changes to the Florida Constitution must be ratified in a general election by a super-majority—60 percent—up from the simple majority required prior to 2006. In addition, a two-thirds vote (as opposed to 60 percent) is needed to approve an amendment proposing to impose a new state tax or fee (like a personal income tax). The article provides five ways to propose amendments to Florida's Constitution (see "Getting an Amendment on the Ballot" later in the next section).

Article XII-Schedule

These twenty-five sections provide for an orderly transition from the 1885 Constitution to the present one and provide details on the implementation and timing of subsequent amendments.

AMENDING THE CONSTITUTION

Inasmuch as the Constitution derives from the people themselves, it can only be amended by popular vote ("government of, by, and for the people"). Amendments require a "yes" vote of a supermajority of those voting on it in a statewide general election. Proposals to institute new types of taxes require a two-thirds vote. (An emergency provision allows the state legislature by an extraordinary three-fourths vote of each chamber to call a special election to approve a proposed amendment.) General elections are held regularly in November of even-numbered years.

Since 1970, Floridians have voted on 165 proposed amendments to the Florida Constitution. They passed about 72 percent of them (119 of the 165). Over the years, passage rates have fluctuated. Between 2002 and 2006, the passage rate was the highest as Floridians voted "yes" on 23 out of 24 proposed amendments (96 percent). Since that time, only 12 out of 27 (44 percent) were approved. The decline in passage rates is due, in part, to the 2006 change requiring that a proposed amendment get the approval of 60 percent of the voters who voted on the proposal. In addition, several of the proposals that failed were confusing and highly controversial. (See Appendix A for a complete list of constitutional amendment proposals that Floridians voted on over the last three decades.)

Florida's Uniqueness

Florida's amendment activity in recent years has gone counter to that observed in the rest of the nation in four ways.[11] First, amendment activity in Florida is increasing, not declining. Second, citizen-initiated amendments are more common in Florida than elsewhere. Third, Florida has had more success in passing citizen initiatives than the 23 other states with citizen initiative processes in place. Fourth, Florida has a lower roll-off, or drop-off, rate. (The *roll off rate* is the percentage of voters who vote in races at the top of the ballot, such as president or governor, but who do not vote on amendments that typically appear at the bottom of the ballot.)

Issues can be just as important to voters as candidates. Both parties often use amendments as Get-Out-The-Vote tools.

Getting an Amendment on the Ballot

Proposed amendments can be put on the general election ballot for voter approval in five ways:

1. By the Florida Legislature; a joint resolution must pass each house by a three-fifths vote.
2. By direct citizen initiative; a petition must be signed by at least 8 percent of the number of votes cast in Florida in the most recent presidential election.
3. By a Constitutional Revision Commission, a 37-member body comprised of both public officials and private citizens that meets every 20 years.[12]
4. By the Florida Tax and Budget Reform Commission that meets every 20 years.
5. By a constitutional convention that can only be convened by voter petition and approved by majority vote in a general election (unlikely ever to be used).

State law determines the format that must be used to collect signatures to place a constitutional amendment on the ballot for citizen approval.

Generally, proposals put on the ballot by the Constitutional Revision Commission and the Tax and Budget Reform Commission are called *revisions*. Those put on the ballot by the state legislature or via citizen petitions are called *amendments*. However, in the public's mind, they are all amendments.

Legislative Proposal

Proposal of an amendment by the state legislature is the most common way to change the Florida Constitution. Since 1970, the Florida Legislature has placed 107 constitutional amendments on the ballot. Florida voters approved 79—a passage rate of 74 percent. For some 30 years, starting in 1978, Floridians tended to approve most of the legislative proposals. The passage rate averaged almost 90 percent. But once the 60 percent threshold for passage was put in place (2008), Floridians have actually rejected more legislative proposals than they have accepted. They have voted down 12 out of 18—a 66 percent *rejection* rate. The higher threshold for passage plus the more controversial nature of the amendments proposed by the Republican-dominated legislature help explain the change in direction.

Since legislative proposals are done through joint resolution, the governor does not have the ability to veto proposals as he would if they were done in the form of a bill. Because they require a three-fifths vote in each chamber as opposed to a simple majority, the proposals that emerge from this process tend to have greater appeal. (That is not necessarily the case when one party holds a very large majority in both chambers and does not need the support of minority party legislators for passage.) The legislature often weighs expected public reaction to their proposals when making decisions about what to put on the ballot. In 2006, legislators voted to remove an amendment from the ballot before the election that they had voted to place on the ballot the previous year. They originally were going to ask voters to lengthen legislative term limits, but decided not to because polls showed strong support among Floridians for the existing limits.

The Court and Legislature Clash over Amendments

While Florida's Supreme Court must review constitutional amendments proposed by citizens via the direct initiative process, it does not automatically review legislative proposals. However, private individuals or groups may bring a lawsuit to remove a proposal from the ballot that was put there by the legislature or even to invalidate an amendment that has actually passed.

Since 1978, eight legislative proposals have been removed from the ballot by the Florida Supreme Court. Five of these removals have occurred since 2008—three in one election year—2010. Earlier proposals removed from the ballot dealt with lobbying regulations, tort reform, and sales tax exemptions. The more recent removals covered federal health care insurance purchasing mandates, redistricting standards, and property tax exemptions and limitations (two proposals). In each case, the amendments themselves or their ballot summaries were declared confusing, misleading, or incomplete by the Supreme Court. At least one legislatively proposed amendment has been invalidated by the Florida Supreme Court *after* the people voted for it. In 1998, Florida voters approved an amendment intended to preserve the state's death penalty in case the U.S. Supreme Court deemed the electric chair cruel or unusual punishment. Two years later, the Court ruled that the amendment title and ballot summary presented to the voters lacked detail and were inaccurate.

Legislative Response to the Courts

The legislative majority typically resents having its legislative proposals removed or revoked and believes the Florida Supreme Court should not interfere with its ability to place constitutional changes before the voters. In several cases, the legislature has simply rewritten its proposal and put the issue back before the voters. In 2002, after the Court had revoked the death penalty preservation vote for having an inaccurate summary, the legislature put a "corrected" version back on the ballot. This time, it included a very lengthy 339 word "summary" that basically restated the entire amendment. Again, voters approved it. When the Supreme Court removed a proposal in September 2007 to reduce property taxes and increase property tax exemptions, the legislature called a special session the next month and got the rewritten proposal back on the ballot in time for the January 2008 presidential preference election, where it passed easily.

The Court's propensity to remove legislative proposals from the ballot (three removals in one year) incensed Republican legislators. In 2011, Republican leaders in the Florida House proposed legislation to split the Florida Supreme Court into a civil and a criminal division which would have created Republican appointed majorities on both new courts. They also proposed granting the legislature the power to approve future gubernatorial nominees to the Court. While the legislation did not pass, it was widely perceived as a warning to the Florida Supreme Court to show more restraint when reviewing constitutional proposals made by the legislature. That same year, the legislature did pass a 2011 law allowing the attorney general to rewrite any ballot title or summary of a legislative proposal removed by the Court over concerns with either. Opponents sued to have the law overturned but the court ruled it was legal since it dealt only with changing the description of the proposal and not changing the actual proposal itself. When the Court removed a legislative proposal titled Religious Freedom later that year for having a misleading summary, the description was reworded by the attorney general and appeared on the 2012 ballot. (It was subsequently defeated by the voters.[13])

Initiative and Referendum

Florida's citizens enjoy the power of the constitutional *initiative*, the power to place a state constitutional amendment on the ballot by petition, and *referendum*, the power to approve or disapprove of a constitutional amendment or other policy question by majority vote. At the state level, most referenda pertain to changing the state Constitution. Local referenda where local governments put local policy questions before the voters are much more common. However, occasionally the state legislature seeks public input in the form of a *non-binding referendum*—a vote that shows public opinion on an issue but that does not legally require action. In 2010, over 70 percent of Floridians voted "yes" on a non-binding referendum placed on the ballot by the legislature asking whether the U.S. Constitution should be amended to require the federal government to pass a balanced budget without raising taxes.

Many individuals and groups have tried to propose a constitutional initiative. However, the process to craft a petition and gain the required number of signatures is quite detailed and fairly difficult. Interested citizens must form a political committee and follow all formatting requirements for the petition. The state's Division of Elections can legally reject a petition solely because it is not formatted according to the rules.[14] The state's attorney general must review it and the Florida Supreme Court must decide whether or not to put a petition-driven constitutional amendment on the ballot.

The Florida Supreme Court must affirm that an amendment proposed by initiative is clearly written and deals only with a single subject. Since 1972 (when Florida voters approved constitutional initiatives) 22 of the 55 initiative petitions that achieved the required number of signatures for review were removed from the ballot by the Florida Supreme Court for violating the single subject requirement or for being unclear. In 2006, the Florida Supreme Court struck an initiative from the ballot that would have set up a bi-partisan committee to redistrict legislative and congressional seats because it violated the single subject rule *and* was unclear.

Initiative Signature Requirements and Ballot Successes

To get a proposed amendment on the ballot, signatures must be collected from a minimum of eight percent of the total number of Florida voters who cast their ballot in the most recent presidential election (over 8.5 million in 2012). Thus, to get a proposed amendment on the 2016 ballot via the petition (initiative) route, 683,149 signatures by valid registered voters are needed. The total number must include signatures from at least one half of the state's 27 congressional districts. Signatures must be submitted for verification by county supervisors of elections at least nine months before an election. The political committee collecting the signatures must pay for the verification process. In reality, most initiative drives need to collect more than the minimum required signatures because many signatures turn out to be invalid, mostly from persons who are not registered to vote. (Access websites listed at the end of the chapter for more detailed information on this process.)

Regardless of the difficulties, many committees have formed and sought signatures for their petitions since Florida voters approved constitutional initiatives in 1972. Hundreds of petition drives have been undertaken by more than 100 different political committees. (Groups can conduct more than one constitutional amendment petition drive.) For 2016, about 30 petitions were circulating in the state, sponsored by a wide variety of groups ranging from People United for Medical Marijuana, J.A.I.L. 4 Judges, and Justice – 2 – Jesus, to Floridians for Solar Choice, and "Right Now" is the Time to Legalize Recreational Marijuana Committee.

Since 1972, the overall success rate of *initiatives*, as measured by passing the Florida Supreme Court review and having voters ratify the change, is only 47 percent (26 out of 55). However, once on the ballot, initiatives have a passage rate of almost 80 percent (26 out of 33). Prior to 2002, the passage rate was about 67 percent but then Floridians started voting "Yes" on nearly every amendment. Since 2002, 16 out of 18 of the proposed initiatives passed. Of the two that failed, one (Amendment 2 in 2014 that would have legalized medical marijuana) received 58 percent of the vote—just short of the requisite 60 percent. The other (Amendment 4 in 2010) would have required local voter approval for all changes to the local comprehensive growth plan—a very controversial proposal.

Constitutional Revision Commission

The Florida Constitution provides for the formation of a Constitutional Revision Commission (CRC) every twenty years "to examine the constitution of the state." The commission is authorized to hold hearings and place its recommended constitutional amendments directly on the ballot for voter approval. The commission's 37 members include the attorney general, fifteen citizens chosen by the governor, nine appointed by the Speaker of the House, nine by the President of the Senate, and three by the Chief Justice of the Florida Supreme Court. The next Constitutional Revision Commission will meet in 2018.

In 2014, Amendment 2 would have legalized medical marijuana but fell short of receiving the required 60 percent vote. Supporters planned to try again in 2016.

Rejection and Acceptance of CRC Proposals

The first CRC failed in its efforts to streamline Florida government, eliminate several of the separately elected Cabinet officers, and strengthen the governorship. Indeed, voters rejected the commission's entire package of eight amendments in 1978. Yet when the legislature submitted a proposal to the voters in 1980 to eliminate the commission provision from the Constitution, it was defeated.

By contrast, the 1998 Constitutional Revision Commission placed nine recommendations on the ballot; voters approved eight. Among the changes accepted were restructuring and reducing the size of the Cabinet, requiring the conservation of natural resources, granting a local option for how to select judges, and establishing a waiting period to purchase firearms. Other changes included clarifying that the Florida Declaration of Rights includes protection for both males and females and removing gender specific references throughout the Florida Constitution, equalizing ballot access rules for major and minor political parties, and including a host of "miscellaneous matters and technical revisions." The only proposed amendment that failed would have allowed more local government property to be exempt from taxation. Overall, Florida voters have approved 8 of 17 revisions put forth by the two CRCs for a passage rate of 47 percent.

Explaining the Difference in CRC Passage Rates

There are several possible explanations for why the public rejected all the CRC's proposed amendments in 1978, and then approved eight of nine in 1998 (including several amendments quite similar to those rejected in 1978).[15] By 1998, the electorate had changed. There was far less citizen animosity toward government than in the post-Vietnam and Watergate 1970s. The state's population had grown and become considerably more diverse. The makeup of the 1998 CRC itself was more diverse than the 1978 CRC in terms of party, race, and gender. The 1998 CRC was more open in its deliberations. It held numerous hearings throughout the state soliciting citizen input. And in 1998, there were no highly unpopular amendment proposals on the ballot with the CRC proposals. (In 1978, an extremely unpopular initiative to legalize casino gambling appeared on the ballot with the eight CRC proposals and may have contributed to voter hostility toward *all* of the amendments up for approval.)

Taxation and Budget Reform Commission (TRBC)

Voters approved a legislative proposal to create a Taxation and Budget Reform Commission (TBRC) in 1988 specifically to review state taxes and the state budget and suggest constitutional changes to improve them. It first met in 1990 and proposed several constitutional revisions which were put on the 1992 general election ballot. The commission was originally supposed to meet every 10 years, but Florida voters approved a change for it to meet only every 20 years. So the second TBRC met and proposed amendments in 2008 and the next one will meet in 2028. The commission's 25 voting members cannot be members of the legislature. Eleven members are to be selected by the governor, seven chosen by the Speaker of the Florida House of Representatives, and seven picked by the President of the Florida Senate.

TBRC Proposals and Success Rate

The success rate for TBRC proposals voted on by the public is 75 percent – 3 out of 4 in both 1992 and 2008. In 1992 voters approved the establishment of a Taxpayers Bill of Rights, a provision to improve accountability and public review of the state's budget including a 72-hour review period before final passage, and a new tax law dealing with ad valorem (property) taxes on government leases. The only proposal that failed would have authorized local governments to levy a one-cent sales tax with local voter approval. In 2008 voters approved TBRC proposals related to cutting property taxes: requiring working waterfront property to be assessed at its present usage and not as higher value land; mandating that improvements made to homes to make them more wind resistant or energy efficient not result in increased assessment; and granting exemptions and lower assessments for conservation land. Again, the one proposal that might have increased taxes was defeated. It would have created a local option to levy a tax to fund community colleges with local voter approval.

The TBRC had originally proposed seven revisions for 2008, but after lawsuits were filed, the Florida Supreme Court removed three of them from the ballot declaring that they had confusing ballot summaries and/or that their subject matter went far beyond the TBRC's limited mission of tax and budget reform. These proposals suggested eliminating property taxes for school funding and replacing them with general revenue, removing the Florida Constitutional prohibition on state dollars going directly or indirectly to sectarian institutions, and allowing public school funding of private school alternatives to public school programs. (The last two would have paved the way for a voucher system for K-12 education that could have included private religious schools.)

Constitutional Convention

The Florida Constitution provides for the calling of a constitutional convention to revise or replace the entire Constitution, but it is unlikely that such a convention will ever be called. Calling a convention requires a petition filed by 15 percent of the number of voters in the last presidential election (versus only 8 percent for a constitutional amendment). Then the voters must approve the question, "Shall a constitutional convention be held?" If a majority answer "yes," then convention delegates would be elected at the next general election. Finally, any revisions or new document recommended by a convention would have to be approved by the voters in a following general election.

DIRECT VERSUS REPRESENTATIVE DEMOCRACY

The initiative and referendum provide for *direct democracy*—the people themselves initiating and deciding issues by popular vote. In contrast, *representative democracy*, or "republicanism" as it was termed by the writers of the U.S. Constitution, envisions decision-making by representatives of the people (elected legislators) rather than by the people themselves. The nation's founders were profoundly skeptical of "the follies" of direct democracy; hence there is no provision in the U.S. Constitution for national initiative or referenda. This form of direct democracy is found today only at the state and local government levels.

Pros and Cons of Initiatives

There are good arguments both for and against the use of the initiative to make constitutional and policy changes.

Opponents of the use of the initiative argue that:

- It encourages majorities to sacrifice the rights of individuals and minorities.
- It facilitates the adoption of unwise and unsound policies.
- It requires voters to decide on issues on which they are not sufficiently informed to cast intelligent ballots.
- It does not allow consideration of compromise or modifications of proposals.
- It enables special interests to mount expensive statewide campaigns on their behalf.

Supporters of the initiative process argue that:

- It enhances government responsiveness and accountability to the people.
- It allows the people to restrict self-interested public officials to limit their terms or compensation or their ability to raise taxes.
- It enables citizens to bypass the legislature when it becomes unresponsive to the majority on specific policy issues.
- It stimulates popular debate about policy issues and can increase turnout.
- It increases popular trust in government and reduces alienation—the feeling that citizens can do little to influence public affairs.

Restricting Elected Officials

Florida's citizens have made numerous constitutional changes by popular initiative and referendum that placed restrictions on government or lawmakers that elected legislators were unwilling to put on themselves. Florida's "sunshine" amendment, adopted by popular initiative and referendum in 1976, was supported by Governor Askew but opposed by many in the legislature. It requires public officials to make "full and public disclosure of their financial interests" and their campaign finances. Enforcement is the responsibility of a constitutional Commission on Ethics. Term limits for state legislators (eight years) were adopted by an overwhelming 77 percent of the vote in 1992 following a successful citizen group effort called "Eight Is Enough." And, in 2010, voters approved a pair of "Fair Districts" initiatives that create standards for redistricting state legislative and congressional seats. The standards forbid partisan and incumbent gerrymandering by the legislators who are responsible for drawing their own district maps.

Finally, Florida's citizens, not surprisingly, have shown a strong propensity to limit the ability of their government to raise taxes.[16] In 1992, they supported the Save Our Homes constitutional initiative to limit the annual growth of property tax assessments on homes by three percent or the inflation rate. In 2008, they approved a legislative proposal to make those property assessment savings portable. In 1994, Floridians voted for an initiative that allows all future initiatives to cover more than one subject if they involve limiting government revenue. In 1996, voters overwhelmingly passed an initiative to require a two-thirds majority of voters to approve any new constitutionally-imposed taxes. Florida voters have approved numerous other constitutional amendment proposals to limit taxes put before them by the legislature or the commissions. (See Chapter 9.)

Bypassing the Legislature to Make Policy

A variety of public policies have been instituted by Floridians through the initiative process. In many instances the legislature or governor opposed the changes and would not pass them legislatively. The Florida lottery was adopted in 1986 by petition and referendum over the opposition of Governor Bob Graham. In 1988, voters overwhelmingly (84 percent of the vote) approved an initiative declaring English as the official language of Florida. In 2002, voters adopted an anti-smoking amendment, followed in 2006 by an amendment requiring more money won in a lawsuit against cigarette companies to be spent on anti-smoking advertisements targeting kids. The legislature was reluctant to act because of the power of the tobacco lobby and the desire to spend tobacco settlement money on other areas. In 2002, voters supported initiatives to reduce class sizes in public schools out of frustration with high student-teacher ratios throughout much of the state. Governor Bush and much of the Republican legislature opposed the proposal because of the cost. Also in 2002, voters approved an amendment giving rights to pregnant pigs that the conservative pro-agriculture legislature would not pass. In 2004, Floridians passed an amendment increasing the minimum wage which labor leaders had sought unsuccessfully for years in the business dominated legislature.

In 2008, an initiative recognizing marriage in Florida as between just one man and one woman became part of the Florida Bill of Rights. In this case the legislature had passed a similar Defense of Marriage Act, but proponents argued a constitutional amendment was needed to stop a future legislature or the Florida Supreme Court from overturning the law. (It was eventually overturned by the *federal* courts. Same-sex marriage became legal in Florida in 2015.) Interestingly, Floridians voted for an initiative petition in 2000 requiring the state to build and operate a high speed rail system between five metropolitan areas in Florida but then voted in favor of another initiative petition in 2004 that repealed the requirement for high speed rail. The governor and the legislature had opposed the high speed rail amendment because of its enormous cost. It was unclear whether voters who changed their minds did so because of cost arguments made by the legislature or whether they did not pay attention to changes in the wording. (A "yes" vote in 2000 was a vote to support high speed rail while a "yes" vote in 2004 was a vote to repeal.)

In 2010, a coalition of Democratic, liberal, and good government groups successfully sponsored the Fair Districts Amendments, changing the redistricting standards.

Initiative Campaigns

Initiative campaigns in Florida have become more sophisticated and costly over time. Most successful initiative campaigns must raise millions of dollars. Supporters of an initiative often use paid workers and volunteers to obtain the necessary number of signatures on petitions.[17] Then they must obtain legal counsel to help convince the Florida Supreme Court that the initiative covers only a single topic and that the title of the initiative properly describes its content. Once on the ballot, an initiative campaign can become very expensive, with television "infomercials," celebrity endorsements, and election-day get-out-the-vote efforts.

Special Interests Often Sponsor Initiatives

Initiative campaigns are often sponsored by special interests such as: specific businesses or industries; labor unions, including government employee unions; religious organizations; environmental groups; and public interest groups. The gambling industry, for example, backed three unsuccessful "citizens' initiatives" to legalize gambling in 1978, 1986 and 1994 and one successful, but limited, one in 2004. The Save Our Sea Life Committee, a coalition of environmental groups and the sports fishing industry, backed a successful

1994 amendment to limit commercial fishing with large nets. In 2002, the Florida Education Association strongly supported initiatives to reduce class sizes and to provide universal voluntary pre-school. In 2004, Florida trial lawyers got two initiatives approved attacking doctors, and Florida doctors got one approved attacking lawyers. Animal rights groups backed the "pregnant pig" amendment in 2002 and anti-smoking groups successfully pushed smoke-free workplaces in 2002 and an increase in government funded anti-smoking advertisements in 2006. Employee unions sponsored the 2004 amendment to create a Florida minimum wage and index it to inflation. Religious conservatives sponsored the marriage amendment in 2008. A coalition of Democratic, liberal and good government groups were behind the fair districting amendments in 2010. In 2014, environmental groups successfully convinced voters to support an amendment requiring legislators to spend no less than 33 percent of the revenue generated by a specific tax on land and water conservation after the legislature and governor had deeply cut funding for such programs for several years.

Opposition to Initiatives

Opposition to initiatives is often well funded by organized interests.[18] For each proposal by a union or environmental group there is likely business opposition, socially conservative proposals engender opposition from social liberals, and proposals to raise taxes are resisted vigorously by taxpayers. However, statistics indicate that the opposition in any initiative campaign has its work cut out for it once an initiative petition proposal makes the ballot; only 7 of 33 have been voted down. The more effective strategy statistically is to file briefs and give testimony to try to influence the Florida Supreme Court in the ballot review process. (Recall that 22 out of 55 proposals that gathered enough signatures to trigger ballot review were removed by the Court.) Of course now that proposals require 60 percent to pass, the opposition may have an easier time defeating proposals that are placed on the ballot.

Lobbying groups that are well entrenched in state capitals are often skeptical of citizens' initiatives. The influence that different interest groups have on the Florida Legislature has changed somewhat over time as Democratic dominance has given way to Republican dominance in Tallahassee. Traditional Democratic allies like labor, environmental and public health groups who were once more likely to oppose initiatives have become more apt to sponsor them since the 1990s. Political officeholders are also generally cautious about citizen initiatives, even though they may occasionally endorse particularly popular ones. After all, the initiative process is designed to bypass the state capital and its power holders.

At times the legislature may be goaded into enacting legislation by the threat of a popular initiative. Recognizing that a popular initiative may gain a position on the ballot and win voter approval, legislators may prefer to head off a citizen-initiative-drafted amendment by passing a law or by putting their own constitutional amendment on the ballot for voter approval. For example, under pressure to get tough on crime, the legislature passed a law requiring prisoners to serve at least 85 percent of their sentences causing the group STOP (Stop Turning Out Prisoners) to abandon its own initiative drive to place the same language in the Constitution.

Wording and Timing of Proposals

The wording of the text can be absolutely vital to the success or failure of constitutional referenda, especially on tax-related proposals. In 1996, environmentalists succeeded in get¬ting the word "fee" (favorable) used in a proposed amendment which would have allowed the South Florida Water Management District to impose a one-cent per pound fee on sugar grown in the Everglades Agricultural Area to be earmarked for the protection and clean-up of the Everglades. In turn, the Florida sugar industry spent millions in a campaign to convince voters the "fee" was really a "tax" (unfavorable) and the proposed amendment was defeated.

Political timing can also be a crucial factor in determining whether a proposal is approved by voters. In June 2003, a political committee called Hometown Democracy organized and registered with the state. They started an initiative petition to require a local referendum anytime the local government sought to change its comprehensive growth plan. Hometown Democracy believed that rampant development was hurting the state's quality of life and that local officials were too quick to grant changes and variances to the growth plan and that local residents should have the final say on such questions.

When originally conceived by environmentalists and growth management advocates, Florida was in the midst of an economic boom with the lowest unemployment rate in the nation and gaining 1,000 new residents a day. Further, polls showed that many residents were concerned about quality of life issues (traffic, overcrowded schools, and pollution). However, because the initiative process is long and drawn out, it took Hometown Democracy until 2010 to get Amendment 4 on the ballot. By then the economy in Florida had deteriorated with housing prices down, the unemployment rate among the highest in the nation, and population growth at a standstill. An assortment of business groups spent millions of dollars opposing Amendment 4 making the case that it would hurt Florida's already ailing economy. In the end despite raising and spending $2.4 million in support of Amendment 4, Hometown Democracy was defeated 67 percent to 33 percent.

In 2010, realtors and homebuilders spent a lot of money to convince voters to defeat the proposed "Hometown Democracy" constitutional amendment.

Reforming the Initiative Process

Reformers have argued that initiative voting is becoming too common. Multiple initiatives on the ballot overload and confuse voters because they are often poorly drafted. Voters are often poorly informed about the real purposes and intent of an initiative. Reformers recommend that neutral voter guides summarizing arguments for and against initiative questions be printed by the state, and that the names and affiliations of major contributors to initiative campaigns be published.[19]

Voters See Problems with the Process

A statewide survey of Floridians confirms many of the reformers' claims. (See Figure 2-1.) Only one-quarter of voters think they have enough information about the pros and cons of proposed amendments. Eighteen percent think they only receive one side of the information. A majority, 55 percent, do not feel they have enough information—an increase of almost 10 percentage points over a decade. A voter's educational level matters when it comes to feeling well-versed about proposed amendments. Less-educated voters are the least likely to say they are sufficiently informed.[20] Three-quarters of all Floridians believe that proposed amendments are usually put on the ballot by special interests (a level of skepticism that has not changed much over the decade). Just 17 percent think they are usually sponsored by average citizens.

Figure 2-1. Voters' Opinions on Florida's Constitutional Amendment Process

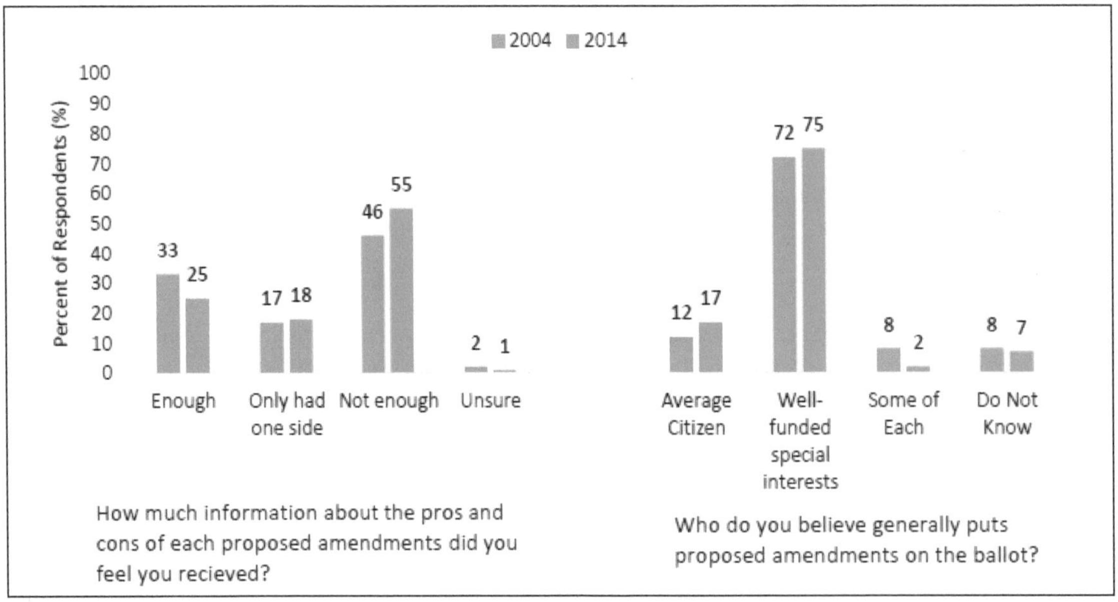

Source: Collins Center for Public Policy and the James Madison Institute, December 7-24, 2004, and University of South Florida-Nielsen Sunshine State Survey (2014).

Public Officials Worry about the Cost

Florida officials have also become increasingly worried about the costs of initiatives and now require a financial impact statement to accompany all initiatives that gain ballot access. In their opinion voters have approved measures that sound good without thinking about how to pay for them. This concern arose with the passage of two initiatives in 2000 and 2002. In 2000, voters passed an initiative requiring the state to start building a high speed ground transportation system connecting the five largest urban areas by a November 1, 2003 deadline. The state had already examined this idea in the 1990s and rejected it as too expensive—an estimated cost of $20 billion. Floridians frustrated with transportation problems narrowly voted for the amendment. The legislature delayed the start date and in 2004, nearly two-thirds (64 percent) of the voters approved an initiative to repeal the high speed rail amendment after being exposed to a lot of publicity about its costs and limited routes.

Cost concerns also drove the governor and state legislature to oppose the 2002 initiative that mandates reducing the size of K-12 classrooms over time: no more than 18 in grades K-3; no more than 22 in grades 4-8; and 25 in grades 9-12. Further, studies available at the time showed that reducing class size has little impact on learning gains except in the early grades. However, parents frustrated by the large class sizes in their own children's schools voted for the amendment which passed with just 52 percent of the vote. By 2010, the state had spent an estimated $18 million to comply with the class size amendment. Frustrated legislators put a proposal on the ballot to ease the strict class size limits. Over half (54.5 percent) of the voters supported the amendment—a higher percentage than when the initial size-limiting proposal was passed but not high enough to hit the required 60 percent threshold. Facing a disastrous budget situation in 2011, legislators cut K-12 spending by about $500 per pupil and passed a law narrowly defining the core classes that must meet the class size limits to try and reduce costs and assist districts in meeting the requirements.

Requiring a Supermajority Vote

Prior to 2006, constitutional amendments in Florida required a 50 percent vote for passage regardless of how they were proposed. Reformers suggested requiring a supermajority vote for initiative proposals to change the Florida Constitution. Proponents argued that changes to the fundamental governing document should require more than a simple majority, just as amending the U.S. Constitution requires approval by three-fourths of the states. Opponents believed a supermajority requirement worked against grassroots democracy and was an effort by legislators to protect their lawmaking power at the expense of the public. Lawmakers liked the idea of requiring a supermajority to ratify suggested constitutional amendments, although the idea was not as popular with Democrats in the minority who viewed the initiative as a way to achieve some of their goals by bypassing the Republican-dominated legislature. Nonetheless, in 2006 the Florida Legislature put a proposed amendment on the ballot calling for a 60 percent "yes" vote to ratify all future proposed amendments to the Florida Constitution regardless of how they were proposed. The voters approved it. The irony was that it passed by only a 58 percent "yes" vote!

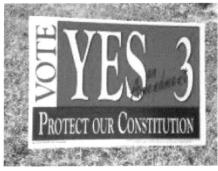

In 2006, Florida voters approved an amendment requiring broader public support for constitutional amendments or revisions." Passage now requires 60 percent of the voters to approve amendments or revisions as opposed to a simple majority. The group in favor of passing the amendment used "Protect Our Constitution" as its slogan. The group opposed to the amendment chose "Trust the Voters" as its theme.

What about the Statutory Initiative as an Alternative?

Florida is one of 18 states that allow *constitutional* initiatives. Florida does not allow *statutory* initiatives. Citizens can use the initiative (petition process) to amend the state's Constitution, but not to change ordinary laws. This anomaly in the Florida Constitution forces citizens and groups to amend the Constitution when they petition for change, rather than to simply change statutory law.

Some reformers have suggested that Florida amend its Constitution to allow statutory initiatives, and make them easier to pass than constitutional initiatives. For example, signature requirements might be made more difficult for constitutional initiatives than for statutory initiatives. In addition while a supermajority (60 percent) is required to ratify a constitutional initiative, a statutory initiative might require only a simple majority (50 percent plus one). If both these changes were adopted citizens might be more inclined to change state statutes instead of *constitutionalizing* their policy preferences. The idea of allowing citizens to propose and vote on legislation directly has not gotten very far with the Florida Legislature. However, support for citizen-driven statutory initiatives has re-surfaced on the heels of the legislature's failure to implement the land and water conservation amendment overwhelmingly passed by voters in 2014 in a way that satisfied the amendment's supporters.

Reforming the Petition Signature Process

Some good government groups have recommended cracking down on abuses by those who gather petition signatures. The vast majority of Floridians agree: 87 percent favor stiffer penalties for petition signature collectors who fraudulently sign someone else's name to the petition and 83 percent favor clearer rules against signature collectors badgering, harassing, or intimidating persons to sign a petition.[21] In 2004, Floridians passed a constitutional amendment placed on the ballot by the Florida Legislature that requires groups to gather their signatures by an earlier date (February 1st of the election year) to give Florida voters more time to learn about the proposed changes and more time to county supervisors of elections to verify petition signatures.

WHAT HAPPENS AFTER AN AMENDMENT PASSES?[22]

Proposed amendments receive the most media attention before they are voted on, but the real consequences surface soon after their passage. A "yes" vote on a constitutional amendment is just the first step down the long road to full implementation. Amendments may cause unintended consequences once the state legislature sits down and writes the implementing statutes.

State legislatures often have the last word, even on citizen-initiated constitutional changes that were designed to bypass state representatives. But legislatively-initiated amendments can share the same fate—difficulties and delays in "putting meat on the skeletons" of broadly-worded proposals. Legislators must fill in the how-to-do and how-to-pay-for details.

The Florida Legislature's implementation plans often involve other state and local entities. State agencies are frequently instructed to adopt rules. Counties, municipalities, and school districts may be required to pass legislation putting various components of the amendments into place. Implementation deadlines established by the amendment may extend several years into the future, allowing new circumstances to alter original plans. And in other instances, litigation may halt or delay full implementation. Delay, delegation of authority, and other difficulties are typical. At

College campuses are a favorite place to collect signatures to put various constitutional amendment proposals on the ballot. Signature collectors appeal to the students' propensity to "let the voters decide" by informing them that their signature merely puts the issue before the voters and does not necessarily reflect the petition signee's support for the amendment.

any rate, voter-approved constitutional changes always face hurdles before they are fully implemented. (See Table 2-1.)

Table 2-1. Implementing Constitutional Amendments after Passage

Problem	Consequences
A larger "yes" vote on an amendment does not necessarily mean government officials will more quickly implement it.	Many amendments passed overwhelmingly by voters are not implemented fully two or three years later, leaving the voters cynical about the process.
In a diverse state like Florida, implementation will not be uniform, even when universally mandated.	Florida's counties each have very different economic realities when it comes to the funding of mandates. The fierce fight in the legislature over the funding formula often results in small rural counties losing out.
Amendments with the most "actors" involved in their ultimate implementation will generate the most controversy as the legislature establishes rules, regulations, and funding. The more persons or agencies involved, the greater the likelihood of fierce disagreements and lawsuits.	Implementation becomes a battle of experts. Each actor enters the fray armed with mountains of reports, statistics, and dollar estimates. The courts often have the last say. The result is often the threat of a reversal or a re-vote on the amendment.
Broadly or vaguely written amendments often slow down the implementation process. They quickly become politicized once the debate over specifics begins. Initial support wanes as the real impact becomes more apparent.	The lack of detail gives legislators bold license to interpret what the voters meant. Political and legal battles over the breadth of authority granted under each vaguely worded amendment slows down implementation.
The greater the complexity of an amendment the more difficult it may be to anticipate all the possible results, and the more likely unintended consequences will become apparent.	Confusion over defining the terms of a complex amendment often leads to litigation, slowing implementation.
Amendments that deal with issues perceived by some as unconstitutional are the most likely to generate lawsuits, slowing down implementation. Issues seen as trampling on individual freedoms protected by the Bill of Rights or those with a religious or moral dimension are the most likely to ignite court challenges.	Due to the controversial nature of such issues, litigation is common. This results in delayed implementation.

Source: Susan A. MacManus, "Implementing Florida's Constitutional Amendments: Truth and Consequences," *The Journal of the James Madison Institute* 31 (Spring 2005).

ONLINE SOURCES FOR DATA AND INFORMATION UPDATES

Florida Senate: Constitution

The Florida Senate provides an e-version of the Florida Constitution for searching and browsing.
http://www.flsenate.gov/Laws/Constitution

Florida Memory: Past Constitutions

Florida Memory is dedicated to Florida history and provides histories, texts, pictures, statistics, and audio/video recordings. The Constitutions page provides the text of past Florida Constitutions.
https://www.floridamemory.com/collections/constitution/

Florida Division of Elections

The Florida Division of Elections is an arm of the Florida Department of State and is responsible for assisting the state to ensure fair and accurate elections. They have information on how to participate in elections, ballots initiatives, voter statistics, and the legal rules of elections.
http://dos.myflorida.com/elections/

Florida Division of Elections: Constitutional Amendment Process

"Constitutional Amendment Process" explains the constitutional amendment process and outlines how to start an initiative.
http://dos.myflorida.com/media/695015/initiative-petition-handbook.pdf

Florida Division of Elections: Legal References

"Legal References" presents information on and links to the constitutional and statutory authority for the amendment process and rules governing the process.
http://dos.myflorida.com/media/695015/initiative-petition-handbook.pdf

Florida Division of Elections: Voters and Signatures

"Voters and Signatures" has a table of the up-to-date signature requirements needed to place an initiative on the ballot per congressional district.
http://dos.myflorida.com/media/695015/initiative-petition-handbook.pdf

Florida Division of Elections: Forms

This is a source of the forms necessary to place an initiative on the ballot that also details the signature verification procedure for groups unable to pay the costs (undue hardship).
http://dos.myflorida.com/elections/forms-publications/forms/

Florida Division of Elections: Initiative Index

This is a searchable index of all proposed constitutional amendments since 1978, including currently active citizen petition drives underway throughout the state.
http://dos.elections.myflorida.com/initiatives/

Sunshine State Survey: Results

The Sunshine State Survey polls Florida residents for their opinions on national and local issues, and includes statistics on the respondent's age, race, gender, party affiliation, employment, etc. The survey has data available from 2006 to 2014 (excluding 2013). Specific data can be found on trust in government leaders, the most important issue facing Florida, opinions on taxing and spending (tax revenue, least fair revenue source, and budget), issue stances, biggest divide for public officials, and the most important leadership quality.
http://sunshinestatesurvey.org/results/

Chapter 3. Public Opinion in Florida

Politicians read opinion polls. And, even though most elected officials claim to exercise their independent judgment in decision making, we can be reasonably sure that their judgment is influenced in part by what they think the voters want. People read polls, too. In fact, polls are one of the most effective attention-grabbing news items. Everyone likes to know what everyone else is thinking about key issues of the day and about various candidates seeking office.

Florida is a pollster's paradise because of the state's diverse population as measured by age, race/ethnicity, and political party affiliation. But it is also a pollster's nightmare due to its ever-changing population makeup that poses a special challenge when it comes to drawing an accurate sample.

Major shifts in public opinion in Florida and the nation are generally reflected in policy change over time. While public officials enjoy considerable leeway in fashioning the details of broad public policy (e.g., education), they often respond to sharp upswings in public opinion, calling for government action on a hot button issue of the day (e.g., oil drilling off Florida's coast).

While polls are common tools used by elected officials to gauge the public's policy preferences, they must be analyzed with caution. Not all polls are equal in their accuracy or objectivity. And a bad poll may be worse than no poll at all. (See Table 3-1 for instructions on "How to Read Political Polls Like a Pro.") The polling industry is undergoing a lot of changes in the methodologies it uses to tap the opinions of voters. (See Table 3-2, "Common Types of Polling Methodologies.") Modern technology (namely the cell phone) and a growing concern among respondents that their responses will not remain private are making traditional methods of telephone polling more difficult. Telephone surveys that target a combination of land-line and cell phones have proven to be the most accurate. A big challenge for telephone-based pollsters is the percentage of their calls to make on cell phones as more Floridians give up their land-line phones. Self-administered surveys, in response to an automated phone call, an online poll, or a highly targeted request via mail (address-based sampling) have become a much larger part of survey research.[1]

Florida's constantly changing demographics due, at least in part, to constant in- and out-migration and generational replacement often explain shifts in public opinion and policy priorities. Political consultants are fond of reminding their Sunshine State clients that "An elected official who relies on yesterday's demographics might very well lose today's election!"

THE CHALLENGES OF ASSESSING PUBLIC OPINION IN FLORIDA

Public opinion in Florida is often described as somewhat conservative, distrustful of government, opposed to higher taxes, yet unrealistic in its demand for more and better government services. As we shall see, this generalization is not far from the mark, especially during economic downturns. Another common description of Floridians is that they tend to be "fiscal conservatives and social moderates." Indeed, more recent polls show that Floridians have become more moderate on social issues like same-sex marriage and the legalization of marijuana.

However, Floridians do not always have well-formed opinions on specific public issues. In the words of one analyst, "Modern polling can give us back only what citizens know the moment the phone rings"[2] or the moment they interact with an online or mail survey request.

The "softness" or shallowness of many voters' opinions on various issues makes them more persuadable by political leaders, candidates for office, the mass media, and well-publicized events. The strong opinions they do have are often about hot button moral issues like the death penalty that are often intertwined with their religious beliefs. Few Floridians see politics through the same lenses as the academics and researchers who design polls. Persons from varying racial/ethnic, cultural, age, and gender groups may interpret a poll question differently than the pollsters envisioned. These realities of voter behavior and Florida's population diversity make polling in our state quite challenging.

Table 3-1. "How to Read Political Polls Like a Pro"

Things to Look For	Reason
Be careful of polls taken more than six weeks before an election.	Most voters make up their minds about who they will vote for shortly before Election Day. Polls taken too early detect off- the-cuff responses that are often not accurate. [In Florida, there are multiple "Election Days" due to Early Voting.]
Expand margin of error by half or more	Polls are purported to be a snapshot in time. But polls are based on many assumptions that make the analogy of a snapshot faulty. Polls are estimates.
Look at the source	Do the people paying for the poll have an interest in a certain result? A candidate's internal poll can be particularly dangerous. Use reputable polls for reputable data.
Be careful of polls that do not use a random sample	Internet polls are a common unscientific poll. Unless a poll is scientific and each person has an equal chance of being selected, it does not necessarily give a true glimpse of public opinion.
Look at question wording	Even subtle differences in the wording of a question can change the outcome of the poll. Make sure that there is no use of loaded words.
Be careful of comparison among subgroups	A poll's margin of error is for the entire sample. Any subgroup comparison is less accurate. The smaller the size of the sample, the less accurate the information will be.
Look for the missing facts	There are 12 pieces of information you should be able to find: • Whether the poll was scientific (respondents chosen randomly). • Margins of sampling error for each group [even small groups] whose opinion is estimated. • The number polled; if less than 600, it probably isn't worth reading and will be unreliable because of a large margin of error. • Who was polled (e.g., adults, registered voters, likely voters). • How those people were identified (from voter registration lists, taking their word). • The actual wording of key questions. • The dates of the poll. • Who conducted the poll. • Who paid for the poll. • How the poll was conducted (telephone, Internet, in person, mail). • The response rate; if it dips much below 50%, it isn't a scientific poll and margins of error are meaningless. • The language used in the interview (if in any area with a lot of non-English speakers).

Source: Abstracted from John McManus, "How to Read Political Polls Like a Pro." http://gradethenews.org, accessed May 25, 2006. McManus directs Grade the News, a media research project in the San Francisco Bay Area.

Table 3-2. Common Types of Polling Methodologies

Live Interviewer Polls: In what were once called traditional telephone polls, a random sample of telephone numbers is dialed and a human interviewer reads the questions to the respondent and records the answers. It can be land-line, cell phone, or combination (most accurate). A random sample is taken of telephone numbers. Samples can also be drawn from registered voter databases or telephone numbers matched to those databases (called registration based sampling or RBS).

Interactive Voice Response (IVR) Polls: In a pure IVR poll, a random sample of telephone numbers is dialed by computer and a recorded voice asks questions. Respondents enter their answers using the numeric key pad on their telephone.

In a mixed mode IVR survey, human interviewers conduct either some portion of the interview or some percentage of the total interviews, with the IVR process completing the remainder of the interview process or the other portion of the interviews.

Internet (Online) Polls: One type (panel) recruits people via e-mail to participate in the survey. The panel member logs onto the survey website and completes the survey online. The recruitment of panel members and the selection of the survey participants (panel members) may or may not be random.

Another type simply posts a survey online and asks people visiting that website to respond. Such a poll can be useful in generating instant opinions about breaking news, issues, candidate debates, even online ads posted by parties, candidates, or advocacy groups. It is difficult to construct a random sample using this type of poll. But as the reach of the Internet gets broader, that will be less of a problem.

Address-Based Sampling (Mail) Polls: ABS polls are examples of micro targeting. A mail survey is sent to a carefully selected group of people. The address list is constructed by merging postal service addresses with household data from business and consumer database companies, and voter registration and voter history files available from county supervisors of elections (Florida). Research has found that the response rates and the quality of data are comparable to those obtained by telephone surveys.

Exit Polls: Polls taken of a small sample of voters selected from key precincts as they leave the polling place. These polls enable researchers and campaigns to answer the questions of who voted, how, and why. With a higher proportion of early voters (either in person or via an absentee ballot), today's exit polls are a mixture of in-person polling (Election Day) and a telephone survey of early voters. Exit polls are extremely expensive and are usually paid for by a conglomerate of major news media.

Sources: National Council on Public Polls, "NCPP Analysis of Final Statewide Pre-Election Polls 2010." Available at http://ncpp.org/files/NCPP%20Election%20Poll%20Analysis%202010%20-%20Final-%200202.pdf. Scott Keeter, "Ask the Expert," Pew Research Center Publications, December 9, 2010.
Available at http://pewresearch.org/pubs/1770/ask-the-expert-pew-research-center AA POR Report on Online Panels, March 2010. Available at
http://www.aapor.org/AM/Template.cfm?Section=AAPOR_Committee_and_Task_Force_Reports&Template=/CM/ContentDisplay.cfm&ContentID=2223.

Absence of Opinion and Lack of Knowledge

Most Floridians do not follow politics closely enough to have well-formed opinions on many issues. Low levels of political knowledge are common. For example, most Floridians know little about the duties of the state's three Cabinet officers (Attorney General, Chief Financial Officer, and Agriculture Commissioner) even though they are called upon to vote for candidates for these offices every four years. Likewise, most Floridians do not know the names of their elected state and local representatives nor do they know exactly which level of government is responsible for specific services and activities.

Halo Effect and Question Wording

Often, people respond to opinion polls by giving "good citizen" or socially desirable answers, whether truthful or not, even during anonymous interviews. This is known as the "halo effect." Nowhere is the tendency to give "good citizen" answers more evident than in questions asking respondents how frequently they vote. Even in presidential elections, the turnout rate is in the low-to-mid 50 percent range, yet more than 60 percent say they always vote. "Good citizen" answers are especially problematic when surveyors want to get accurate information on citizen opinions about sensitive issues like race, religion, or substance abuse.

The 2014 gubernatorial election between Rick Scott (R) and Charlie Crist (D) was extremely close. The polling firms that were the most accurate will certainly advertise that accomplishment.

The "halo effect" can be exaggerated by the wording of questions. People respond positively toward positive phrases (for example, "helping the poor," "improving education," "cleaning up the environment") and negatively to negative phrases (for example, "raising taxes," "expanding government," "increasing power," "restricting choice").

Shaping Opinion and Push Polls

Interest groups will often conduct polls that are designed to shape voter responses. The groups then report that public opinion is "on their side." Clearly, such polls do not accurately reflect true public opinion. In addition, campaigns will often use polls either to seek information through clever question wording or to measure change in a voter's opinions in response to learning information, often derogatory, about a candidate. These types of polls are often erroneously described as "push polls." A *true* push poll would offer up a statement about a person that is knowingly *false* such as "How likely are you to vote for [candidate's name] if you knew he/she was a child molester?" Push polls are usually very short and typically used on a very large group of voters with the intent of smearing the opponent. True push polls have been condemned by the American Association of Political Consultants and are illegal in some places. And, as one polling expert pointed out, "A true push poll is not a poll at all. It is a telemarketing smear masquerading as a poll."[3] However, many voters wrongly describe any poll that posits something negative about someone as a push poll, particularly if they favor the candidate.

Change over Time

Advanced opinion research tries to avoid misconceptions stemming from question wording by asking the *same* questions over time and focusing analysis on the *change* in responses. This type of survey research allows us to observe trend lines—directions of movement over time in response to particular words and phrases. When analyzing longitudinal (over time) data, it is a good idea to make sure the wording of the question is exactly the same in order to avoid misinterpretation.

Language, Age, and Cultural Issues

Florida's diverse population requires interviewer skill sets that are not needed in more homogeneous states. A reputable polling firm that surveys in Florida must have interviewers who can communicate in Spanish and even Creole, are familiar with the special challenges of interviewing seniors, and are sensitive to cultural differences regarding attitudes toward surveys (e.g., privacy concerns).

Divergence in Number of Issues Followed

Scholars have found that there are groups within the electorate who are concerned with one or two public issues but indifferent toward others. Top issues of interest may shift over time as an individual's life circumstances change. The point is that *while survey respondents may give an answer when asked about a specific policy, the policy may not be one that they use as a voting cue.*

MAJOR STATEWIDE ISSUE-BASED POLLING IN FLORIDA

In the past, it has often been said that Florida is over-surveyed when it comes to preferences for political candidates but under-surveyed on key issues facing the nation's third largest state. As Florida has become a more preeminent player in presidential politics, the number of polling firms doing business in the state has escalated. Some conduct polls for candidates, political parties, super PACs, or issue advocacy and adversarial groups, and others for news outlets. Many of these firms do not ask the same questions over time, making it difficult to examine trends in Floridians' opinions.

The Florida Annual Policy Survey (FAPS): 1979-2004

Statewide issue- and performance-oriented longitudinal polling began in 1979. The Florida Annual Policy Survey (FAPS), conducted by the Survey Research Laboratory at Florida State University,[4] provided such data to public policy makers, academics, and the public until 2004, when it was discontinued. (Much of the public opinion data included in the first two editions of this book came from the FAPS survey.)

The Sunshine State Survey: 2006-Present

For several years after FAPS was discontinued, no such trend-line data were available. In 2006, Leadership Florida stepped into the void and began its annual Leadership Florida Sunshine State Survey, in partnership with Kaplan, then The Nielsen Company (2010). In 2014, the University of South Florida's School of Public Affairs in partnership with The Nielsen Company took charge of the annual survey. (For annual updates, see sunshinestatesurvey.org.) The Sunshine State Survey is a series of questions asked annually, which provides leaders and academics in the public and private sectors with much-needed trend-line data, while questions on newly emerging issues give leaders an invaluable up-to-date look at where a wide cross-section of our state's residents stand on them. The survey focuses on policy and civic engagement issues rather than on which candidate is ahead in a political race.

While some Sunshine State Survey questions differ from year-to-year, reflecting newly emerging issues and problems, many key questions are asked annually, including questions about:

- The "most important issue" confronting the state.
- Evaluations of the overall performance of governments (federal, state, county, city, school board, and the state's courts).
- Evaluations of a number of specific state services.
- The most important qualities desired of the state's leaders.
- Trust and confidence in the state's leaders—business, government (federal, state, local), and social service/nonprofit.
- Fairness of Florida government revenue sources (gas tax, lottery, property tax, sales tax, and others).
- Education (K-12, higher education); the economy; the environment; transportation; crime; health; election administration; growth management.

In summary, the annual USF-Nielsen Sunshine State Survey provides benchmark data on citizen opinions about issues and institutions—public, private, and nonprofit—and leadership.

Other Florida-Based Surveys

The state's two major nonpartisan think tanks—the more liberal leaning Collins Center For Public Policy, Inc. and the more conservative leaning James Madison Institute—occasionally conduct issue-specific polls, sometimes jointly, on critical public policy questions. So, too, do various interest groups like the Florida Education Association and the Florida Chamber of Commerce.

Other state universities conduct polls but they are not as issue inclusive as the Sunshine State Survey and do not extend for as long a period. The University of North Florida Public Opinion Research Laboratory conducts specific issue and political horserace polls. The questions asked are often not repeated over time. Polls conducted by Florida International University's Cuban Research Institute largely focus on the South Florida Cuban population's views on specific issues and political races. The University of Florida's monthly Florida Consumer Attitude Survey asking about Floridians' confidence in the state's economy is conducted by the University of Florida's Survey Research Center in the University's Bureau of Economic and Business Research.

Variations among and within Groups

Public opinion not only changes over time but also varies across social and political groups. Depending on the issue, opinions may differ from North, to Central, to South Florida. Opinions often differ among Florida's major racial and ethnic groups and among age and income groups. A gender gap sometimes emerges as well. Differences are also observable *within* these groups. We should be careful when generalizing, for example, about "white," "black," "Asian," or "Hispanic" opinions, because individuals within these groups may hold very divergent viewpoints. In addition, the sample size for these minority subgroups may be far too small to get meaningful results.

DECLINING TRUST IN GOVERNMENT

Floridians have little trust in government—either the government in Washington or the government in Tallahassee. That is not terribly surprising. Trust in government among the American public, as revealed in public opinion surveys over time, plunged during the Vietnam War, the Watergate scandal, and the forced resignation of President Richard Nixon. Trust was partially restored during President Ronald Reagan's first term in the early 1980s, but, except for a momentary rebound after the terrorist attack on 9/11, the trend has generally been downhill. In fact, it tracked sharply downward during the Great Recession. It began improving after the Great Recession ended, although the pace has been slow, partially because the economy's recovery has been slow. (See Chapter 1.)

"Re-elect No One" or voting for "None of the Above" sentiments are highest when trust in government is the lowest.

Floridians' trust of their government has eroded over time. Officials in Tallahassee can take small comfort in knowing that Floridians trust them "to do what is right" only slightly more than they trust officials in Washington. Not surprisingly, trust in government closer to home (local governments) is higher—a pattern evident across the United States for many years. (See Figure 3-1.) But the highest marks go to non-governmental entities—social service/nonprofit agencies and businesses. (See Figure 3-2.)

Figure 3-1. Floridians' Trust in Their Government Leaders: National, State, Local

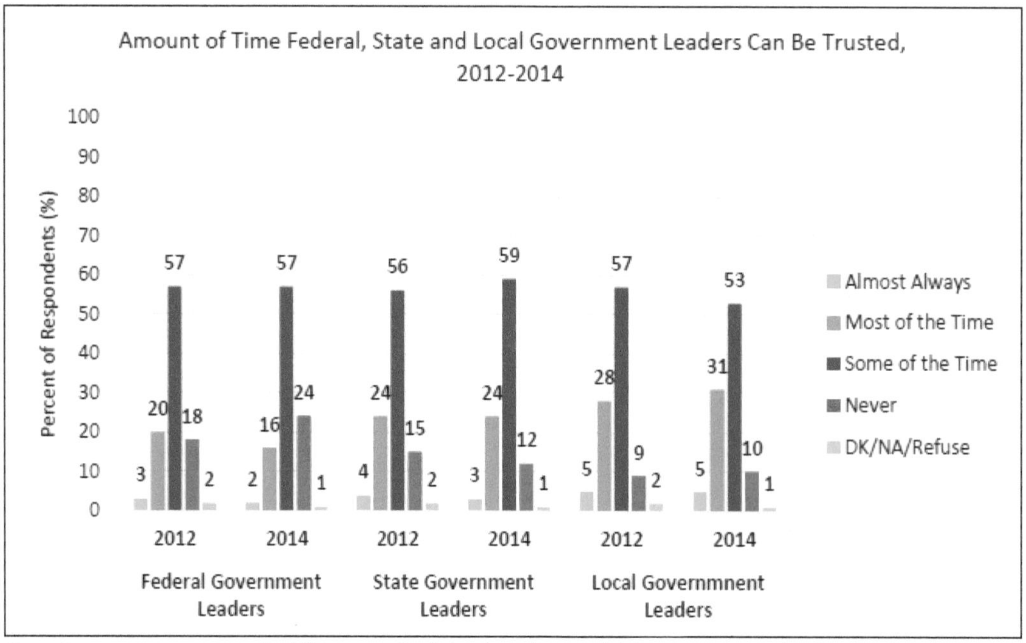

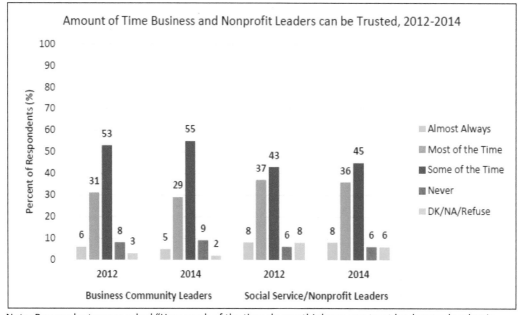

Note: Respondents were asked "How much of the time do you think you can trust leaders to do what is right for Floridians?" Responses may not add to 100% due to rounding.

Source: Leadership Florida-Nielsen Company Sunshine State Survey (2010-2012), and University of South Florida-Nielsen Sunshine State Survey (2014).

Figure 3-2. Floridians' Trust in Their Business and Social Service/Nonprofit Leaders

Note: Respondents were asked "How much of the time do you think you can trust leaders to do what is right for Floridians?" Responses may not add to 100% due to rounding.

Source: Leadership Florida-Nielsen Company Sunshine State Survey (2010-2012), and University of South Florida-Nielsen Sunshine State Survey (2014).

EXPLAINING THE DECLINE IN TRUST

Why has trust in government among Floridians declined so much in recent years? Political scientists have investigated the decline in trust nationally and offered various explanations.

Response to Events

An events explanation for the decline in trust cites scandals, incompetence, and ineffectiveness of government in dealing with major crises. The strongest evidence for this explanation is the drop in trust in Washington that accompanied the Vietnam War, and later the Watergate scandal and the Iranian hostage crisis. National opinion polls reported that 75 percent of adult Americans said they trusted the government in Washington "always" or "most of the time" in 1964, but only 24 percent did so by 1980.[5] Floridians and Americans generally registered a brief upward spike in trust during the Persian Gulf War and in the aftermath of the terrorist attacks on 9/11. But they plummeted again as the Great Recession worsened and unemployment rates and home foreclosures continued to rise. More recently, trust levels at the national level have been low, driven by continued conflict in the Middle East, rising national debt levels, national security breaches, and concerns about invasion of privacy and the erosion of individual rights. At the state and local levels, trust levels have taken a beating due to the seeming inability of officials to resolve partisan bickering, budgetary disputes, infrastructure needs, and privacy concerns, to name a few. The implication of these trends is that government failure and success greatly influence people's trust.

The Leadership Factor

A leadership explanation focuses on the public's evaluation of particular executive leaders over time— presidents at the national level and governors at the state level. The reasoning is that these most visible officeholders symbolize government, and, therefore, their popularity largely determines trust in government generally. A series of unpopular presidents—Richard Nixon (R), Gerald Ford (R), and Jimmy Carter (D)—led to a decline in trust in Washington, while public trust in government rose during the popular presidency of Ronald Reagan (R). Trust resumed its downward spiral under George Herbert Walker Bush (R), except during the Persian Gulf War, and Bill Clinton (D), although trust numbers began to rise slightly during the late Clinton years due in part to the strong economy. It can be argued that, without the personal scandals that plagued Clinton's final two years in office, trust would have gone up even more, due to his job performance ratings, which were higher than his personal approval ratings. George W. Bush (R) helped restore trust in the federal government with his initial response to 9/11 terrorist attacks, but trust in government quickly declined after the inept response to Hurricane Katrina and the wars in Iraq and Afghanistan dragged on and casualties rose. Trust in government rose in the early days of the Barack Obama (D) administration but fell off as a result of a worsening economy, problems with the Affordable Health Care program, and his inability to work with a divided Congress. The implication is that a leader who inspires respect and optimism can help restore trust in government generally, while leaders who are perceived as weak, dishonest, or misguided lead to more distrust of government—at every level (national, state, and local).

Voters angry with government often cite the Preamble to the Constitution to remind officials that the real power in a democracy lies with "We the People."

Floridians' trust in state government varies with the popularity of their governors. Bob Graham (D) was an especially popular governor of Florida (See Chapter 7.), and trust in Florida government was high during his years in Tallahassee. In contrast, Governor Bob Martinez (R) was not especially popular with Floridians; trust in the state government declined during his tenure. Governor Lawton Chiles (D) started out as governor with a great deal of public support but gradually saw it drop. His successor, Governor Jeb Bush (R), started off with strong job ratings from two-thirds of Floridians, came under criticism as he attempted to reform the state's educational system, but left office with high approval ratings stemming from his leadership through two severe hurricane seasons. Governor Charlie Crist (R, then independent, then Democrat) had high approval ratings for much of his tenure but lost favor with the public near the end of his term when he appeared to be changing his mind on key issues and abandoned his party to run for the U.S. Senate as an independent. By that time, the economy had declined significantly. Governor Rick Scott (R) took office at a time when trust in government was at nearly an all-time low. The inability to quickly lead Florida out of a deep economic downturn, followed by difficulties in addressing the state's health care, correctional (prisons), and environmental issues reinforced Floridians' views that politicians cannot be trusted to do what they promise on the campaign trail. The bottom line is that the public expects its governors to lead the state's recovery, whether from hurricanes or fiscal crises, and trust in government falters when they fail to do so.

Negative Politics

Pundits frequently refer to a negative politics explanation for declining trust, suggesting that public cynicism and distrust are nourished by special interest influence, unsavory campaign finance practices, negative campaign advertising, and the like. Reformers argue that public confidence in government could be restored by tightening lobbying regulations, eliminating political action committees (PACs), banning "soft-money" contributions to parties (contributions to party building and voter registration activities that traditionally have not been limited), regulating campaign practices, and strengthening government ethics laws. But "dirty politics" is hardly new to the American scene. In 1800, Federalists argued that if Thomas Jefferson was elected, "We will see our wives and daughters the victims of legal prostitution." And lobbying, both in Washington and Tallahassee, was probably more corrupt in the 19th century than it is today. Even before Will Rogers, most Americans regarded the term "honest politician" as an oxymoron. But perhaps recent decades of declining trust can be attributed to the greater exposure of Americans to the negative aspects of political life through the media, especially television, but more recently online via viral videos and blogs. And, of course, television advertising is largely responsible for pushing up the costs of political campaigning, thus forcing both incumbents and challengers into desperate scrambles to raise more funds, thereby strengthening the influence of individuals and organizations that make big campaign contributions.

Cultural Erosion

A cultural explanation for declining trust cites the long-term erosion of cultural values in America. It is argued that mass distrust and cynicism are engendered by the bad-news bias of television reporting and our fascination with scandals, rip-offs, and violence; by the anti institutional bias of the entertainment industry, portraying government as corrupt, corporations as greedy, the military as warmongers, and so forth; and by revisionist historians and teachers who describe America and its government as racist, sexist, oppressive, or worse. Support for the cultural explanation is found in declining levels of trust expressed toward virtually all societal institutions including corporations, unions, banks, schools, medicine, and even religion. Additional support for the cultural explanation is found in a rise in public cynicism, especially toward government. An overwhelming majority of Americans and Floridians believe government is run for special interests rather than for the benefit of all. (See annual Gallup Polls measuring confidence in various American institutions.) Declining trust and rising cynicism have occurred in tandem, as if responding to a broader cultural malaise.

IDEOLOGY IN FLORIDA: CONSERVATIVE OR MODERATE?

A look at shifts in the ideological breakdown of voters over the past 10 years, as gleaned from exit polls, shows that Floridians are more conservative than liberal in their politics, but a plurality of voters identifies themselves as moderates. (See Figure 3-3.) The greatest fluctuations have been in the percentages who label themselves as a conservative or moderate.

Figure 3-3. Ideological Identification in Florida

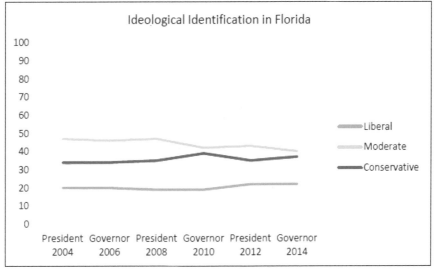

Source: Presidential and gubernatorial exit polls for Florida.

It is easy to see why some analysts divide the state into three ideologically diverse regions—the conservative North, the moderate Middle, and the liberal South. Conservatives are more concentrated in the Panhandle and rural areas, while moderates dominate the central part of the state (the I-4 Corridor in particular). Liberals tend to be concentrated in the state's large urban areas, university towns and Southeast Florida. Self-described liberals include Florida's African-American and Jewish communities, feminist and gay rights organizations, environmentalists, public employees, and college and university faculty and students.

Floridians, like most other Americans, do not always approach public issues in ideological terms. They are not necessarily consistent in the application of their self-described "liberal," "conservative," or "moderate" beliefs to specific issues. We usually think of the liberal-conservative dimension as referring to the role of government in society, with liberals favoring a strong, active government, conservatives favoring a smaller, limited government, and moderates falling in between. But Floridians often favor the expansion of some government services (liberal), while at the same time opposing big government and higher taxes (conservative). This can also be seen in the constitutional amendments for which Floridians have voted. They have voted a number of times to restrict taxes (See Chapter 9.) but have also voted for increasing the minimum wage, banning smoking in public places, and for voluntary universal pre-K education. (See Chapter 2.)

FLORIDA'S MOST IMPORTANT PROBLEMS

In a representative government, we expect voters' perceptions of important social problems to set the policy-making agenda. Over the years, in response to the question, "What is the most important issue facing the State of Florida today?"[6] the people of Florida frequently cited four topics of concern: crime, the economy, education, and community development (managing growth and the environment). Other problems were consistently mentioned, although not by as many voters: health care, taxes, government, transportation, immigration, racial conflict, and rising insurance rates. However, since the beginning of the Great Recession in 2007, the economy/jobs has been the dominant issue on Floridians' minds. (See Figure 3-4.)

Figure 3-4. *The* Most Important Issue Facing Florida

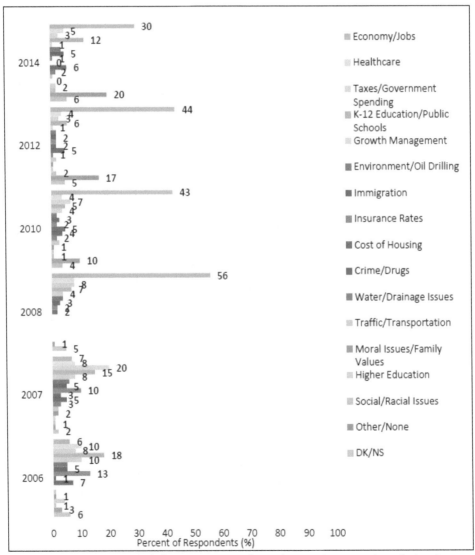

Note: Respondents were asked, "In your opinion, what is the most important issue facing the State of Florida today?

Source: "Leadership Florida Sunshine State Survey (2006-2008), Leadership Florida-Nielsen Company Sunshine State Survey (2010-2012), and University of South Florida-Nielsen Sunshine State Survey (2014).

Variations in problem identification from year to year reflect events affecting the state at the time. Crime was the number one problem for six years in a row, from 1994 through 2000, when Florida's crime rate was the highest in the nation. Whether due to public concern, tougher crime laws, better enforcement, or simple demographic changes, the crime rate dropped every year during that span in Florida (and has continued to decline—See Chapter 8.). By 2001, crime was no longer the number one problem issue.

When the economy takes a downturn and unemployment rises, the economy becomes Floridians' biggest problem. That was true in the late 1970s, early 1980s, early 1990s, and the Great Recession (2007-2009). Events like increasing unemployment rates, rising gas prices, escalating health care costs, and jumps in property insurance premiums can quickly turn the economy into the number one issue.

When the economy improves, the percentage of Floridians identifying education as the number one problem increases, as does the proportion that sees no problem at all. (Education was the number one issue from 2001-2006—before the recession hit.) When the population is growing rapidly, growth itself and the problems it creates for communities (congestion, over-crowded schools, pollution) become the most pressing problems in the eyes of the voters. This was true in the mid-1980s when growth was chosen as the most important problem and the landmark 1985 Growth Management Act was passed. (See Chapter 12.)

Attitudes toward Spending

During Florida's high growth years, public support for spending more on education and crime control was strong. Support for increasing state spending on health care, elderly assistance, help for low-income families, and colleges and universities was also high. Budget allocations for those programs increased.

During tough times, when revenues drop, deciding which programs, activities, or infrastructure to cut back or eliminate entirely becomes the challenge for state and local governments. *Decisions about what to cut back first are excruciatingly painful for elected officials, primarily because there is little consensus among Floridians.* Such decisions serve to remind politicos that spending money is far more pleasurable than taking it away!

During recessions, it is not uncommon to see more *"self-regardingness"* in attitudes toward government spending.[7] For example, people seem more willing to cut prisons, public employee benefits, public assistance, and transportation primarily because these functions of government directly affect only highly exclusive groups of people (convicted criminals, government employees, the impoverished, and those who use public transportation, respectively). On the other hand, more people seem unwilling to cut things

While Floridians generally put schools at the top of their funding priority lists, "education" may mean K-12 for some, but college for others.

like education, health care, law enforcement, and economic development (job creation) primarily because these services are perceived to benefit a larger share of the population.

Personal circumstances can affect one's outlook on government spending priorities, as reflected in some differences by age[8] and race/ethnicity. For example, young Floridians are far more willing to cut back spending on prisons/correction facilities and law enforcement than older Floridians. Why? Because younger persons are generally less concerned about crime and more supportive of rehabilitation than are their elders. African Americans are also considerably more in favor of the state reducing prisons/correction facility spending but for a different reason—a belief that there is racial bias in the prison system, as evidenced in their disproportionate representation among the imprisoned population. White and Asian Floridians are more supportive of reducing public employee benefits and pensions than blacks or Hispanics. This is not surprising in light of the income and educational differences across these racial/ethnic groups.

The bottom line is that it is difficult to get consensus among the population on spending priorities when the public is split over which approach the legislature should use when drawing up the annual budget. (See Figure 3-5.) Spending decisions are contingent on the amount of revenue available. (See Chapter 9.)

Attitudes toward Taxes

It comes as no surprise to learn that Floridians are less enthusiastic about taxing than spending. Part of the explanation for this lies in the fact that a sizable portion of the electorate feels that the state does not spend tax dollars efficiently. (See Figure 3-6.)

The sales tax is the principal source of revenue for Florida's state government, and property taxes are the principal source of revenue for city and county governments in the state. The property tax is the least popular major tax in Florida, unless gas prices go up, and then the gas tax replaces the property tax as the most unpopular. (See Figure 3-7.) Animosity toward user fees and "sin" taxes (liquor, cigarettes) also increases when there are sharp increases in those rates. Not surprisingly, the most complaints come from the "users." (See Chapter 9 for more discussion of the state's revenue system.)

Local elected officials frequently hear citizen complaints about their property taxes rising due to high growth. But when a large influx of young families with school-age children occurs, local governments often ask citizens to approve higher property taxes or local sales taxes to pay for new school buildings to replace portables.

DISASTER PREPAREDNESS AS AN IMPORTANT ISSUE

Florida is geographically, economically, and demographically more vulnerable to both human-made (terrorism; environmental) and natural disasters than are many other states.[9] The Florida Hazard and Risk Assessment, contained in the State's Comprehensive Emergency Management Plan, warns that "The potential for terrorism remains high in the State of Florida."[10] The assessment rates the impact of a terrorist attack on the state's population, property, and environment as "High." The same plan rates the impact of a large-scale natural disaster as "Catastrophic."

Terrorism (homeland security and, more recently, cyber security) was—and is—a bigger issue in Florida than elsewhere for many reasons: our larger-than-average number of military installations, deep-water ports, commercial and private airports; the state's extensive coast line—the longest of any continental state; and Florida-based terrorism incidents and impacts—the anthrax death in South Florida, the flight school training of the terrorists who flew into the World Trade Center, and the devastating economic impact of 9/11 on the state's tourism-based economy.[11]

Figure 3-5. Floridians Divided Over Which Combination of Taxing and Spending State Should Use

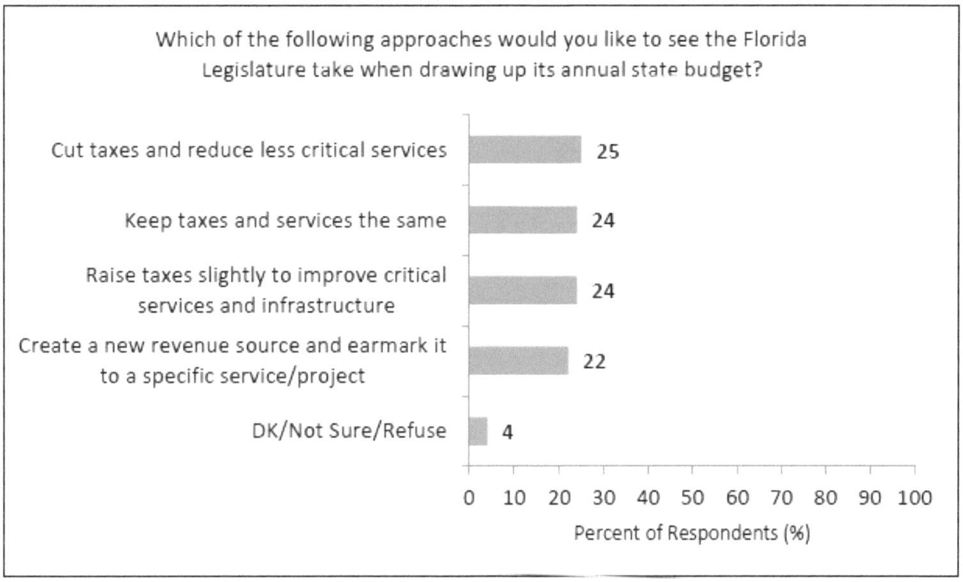

Which of the following approaches would you like to see the Florida Legislature take when drawing up its annual state budget?
Cut taxes and reduce less critical services
25
Keep taxes and services the same
24
Raise taxes slightly to improve critical services and infrastructure
24
Create a new revenue source and earmark it to a specific service/project
22
DK/Not Sure/Refuse
4
0 10 20 30 40 50 60 70 80 90 100
Percent of Respondents (%)

Source: University of South Florida-Nielsen Sunshine State Survey (2014).

Figure 3-6. Attitudes on How Tax Revenue Is Spent by the State Government

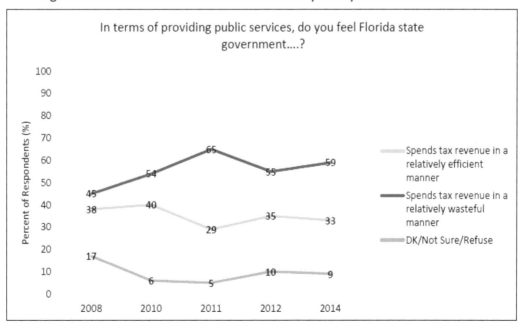

In terms of providing public services, do you feel Florida state government....?
Percent of Respondents (%)
100
90
80
70
60
50
40
30
20
10
0
2008
2010
2011
2012
2014
45
54
65
55
59
38
40
29
35
33
17
6
5
10
9
Spends tax revenue in a relatively efficient manner
Spends tax revenue in a relatively wasteful manner
DK/Not Sure/Refuse

Source: "Leadership Florida Sunshine State Survey (2006-2008), Leadership Florida-Nielsen Company Sunshine State Survey (2010-2012), and University of South Florida-Nielsen Sunshine State Survey (2014)."

Figure 3-7. Citizens' Evaluations of the Least Fair of Florida's Revenue Sources

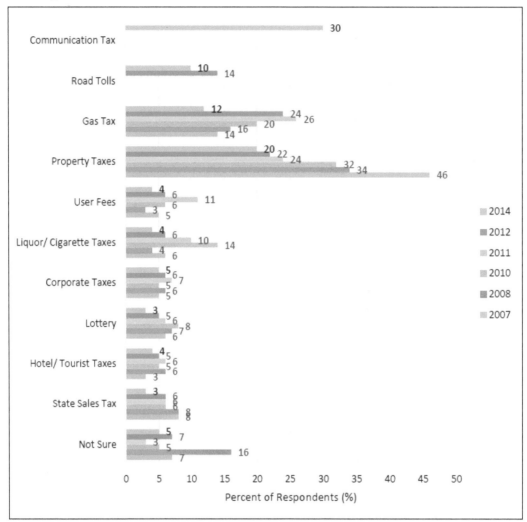

Note: Respondents were asked, "Which one of the following Florida government revenue sources do you feel is the least fair?" Responses may not add to 100% due to rounding.

Source: "Leadership Florida Sunshine State Survey (2006-2008), Leadership Florida-Nielsen Company Sunshine State Survey (2010-2012), and University of South Florida-Nielsen Sunshine State Survey (2014)."

The state's vulnerability to natural disasters was made crystal clear when eight major hurricanes hit the state in two successive years (2004 and 2005). Ever since, rising homeowner and property insurance rates and property taxes have been key concerns of voters. Both have strained the personal finances of many Floridians. Other surveys and reports show that emergency management-related concerns still linger among Floridians, especially worries about evacuation plans for the elderly and infirm.

Florida's 8,426-mile-long tidal shoreline makes it vulnerable to environmental accidents like the massive BP oil spill in the Gulf of Mexico that began on April 20, 2010, with an explosion aboard the Deepwater Horizon oil rig. The spill nearly devastated the economies of many communities in the Panhandle, whose livelihoods heavily depend on tourism and Gulf-related industries, namely seafood and petroleum. Even though the physical damage was not as catastrophic as initially envisioned, the economic and political fallout was substantial. The Obama administration's slow handling of financial assistance for Panhandle businesses and people harmed by the spill had major consequences for the 2010 gubernatorial election. High turnout Panhandle voters heavily supported Republican candidate Rick Scott, who went on to a narrow victory against Democrat Alex Sink. She attributed a major portion of her loss to the Obama-appointed administrator's slow pace of responding to oil-spill victims' reimbursement requests.

Offshore oil drilling has long been a controversial issue (see Chapter 12 Up-Close: Oil Drilling off the Florida Coast). Floridians' opinions about it rise and fall with gas prices... or in response to a major environmental accident like the BP oil spill. (See Figure 3-8.) Opinions also differ considerably by the degree to which a person owes his/her economic livelihood to the industry. Just one month after the BP spill, a Mason-Dixon poll showed that a plurality (47 percent) of Panhandle residents still supported offshore oil drilling, whereas large majorities were against it in other regions of the state. At the same time, there was broad support in both the Panhandle and the state at large for targeting spill-related fines paid by BP to Gulf Coast area restoration.

Another oil drilling practice—hydraulic fracking—has become a controversial issue in Florida. Initial debates over the practice in the Florida Legislature found legislators most strongly against the practice were from non-oil producing districts—a pattern similar to opinions on permitting offshore oil drilling.[12]

Figure 3-8. Floridians' Support of Offshore Oil Drilling

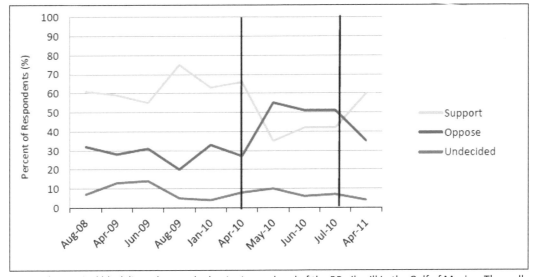

Notes: The vertical black lines denote the beginning and end of the BP oil spill in the Gulf of Mexico. The well was capped on July 15, 2010 but was officially sealed and closed on September 19, 2010. Gas prices spiked in early summer 2008 and spring 2011.

Sources: This chart was derived from several different polls of Floridians' support for offshore oil drilling: Mason-Dixon (August 2008, April 2009, June 2009, and May 2010); Associated Industries of Florida poll by McLaughlin & Associates (August 2009); Quinnipiac University (January 2010, April 2010, June 2010, July 2010, April 2011). The Question wording differed slightly among the polls but all had the same response categories: Mason Dixon – Do you generally support or oppose drilling for oil in the waters off of the coast of Florida; AIF – When it comes to the issue of drilling for oil and natural gas off the coast of Florida, which of the following comes closest to your own personal opinion? 1. Drilling should be allowed anywhere off the coast of Florida. 2. Drilling should not be allowed at all off the coast of Florida; Quinnipiac – In general, do you support or oppose the United States increasing the amount of drilling for oil and natural gas in offshore waters?

Most Divisive Issues

Floridians may not be all that interested in most policy debates, but they certainly have strong opinions about issues that have moral, religious, racial, and equity (fairness) dimensions. The five issues that have been the most divisive in recent years have been: (1) offshore drilling for oil and gas, (2) the Stand Your Ground law, (3) same-sex marriage, (4) Common Core standards in public schools, and (5) casino gambling. (See Figure 3-9.) Of course, other issues like reproductive rights, the death penalty, gun laws, school vouchers, affirmative action, and immigration have been controversial for some time. Predictably, opinions on all these hot button issues tend to vary by gender, race, ethnicity, party, or region of the state.

Here we take a closer look at opinion differences concerning the five most divisive issues identified in the Sunshine State Survey. Those queried were presented with a long list of issues and asked, "If the State of Florida were to [do this_____], would you say that was going in the right direction or the wrong direction, or do you have no opinion about it?" What is particularly interesting is the high percentage of Floridians who do not have opinions on these volatile issues. This confirms research showing that a growing number of voters do not *closely follow* the news and are ill-informed about specific public policies. It also confirms that not all voters are equally informed about, or interested in, every issue.

Offshore Drilling for Gas and Oil

Offshore drilling for oil and gas is the most closely divided issue, with 44 percent saying it is the right direction, 39 percent saying it is the wrong direction, and the remaining 17 percent undecided. Support for drilling in Florida has fluctuated considerably based on gas prices and disasters. Those in favor of drilling tend to be older with some college education. Opponents are more likely to be Millennials—a generation that is more environmentally conscious than their elders. (For more on the environment, See Chapter 12.)

Stand Your Ground Law

Florida was the first state in the nation to adopt a Stand Your Ground law (2005).[13] It "allows people to defend themselves with deadly force as long as they reasonably believe it is necessary to protect themselves."[14] Former Governor Jeb Bush signed the legislation into law because "when faced with a serious threat to one's life, to have to retreat and put yourself in a very precarious position defies common sense."[15] A simplistic summary of the pros and cons of the law boils down to this:[16]

> Pros: "Bad people are armed and good people need to be able to use deadly force if necessary to defend themselves."
> Cons: The law "gives too much freedom to use such force, making the law a license to kill rather than a protective measure."

The law came under intense scrutiny in 2012 with the high profile killing of Trayvon Martin—a black teenager—by George Zimmerman (a Hispanic male). Zimmerman was acting as a neighborhood crime watch volunteer in his Sanford neighborhood and claimed he was acting in self-defense when he shot Martin, who was unarmed. Ultimately, Zimmerman was acquitted because it was not clear whether Martin had attacked Zimmerman using his fists as a weapon. A public outcry ensured and protest rallies were held across the country. Martin became a national symbol of the racial injustice in the legal system to minorities. However, subsequent demands for reform of the state's Stand Your Ground law were, and are still, opposed by strong proponents of the Second Amendment and persons fearful of not being able to defend themselves. Floridians remain divided.

Repealing the Stand Your Ground law is seen by 41 percent of Floridians surveyed as the wrong direction but by 33 percent as going in the right direction, with 26 percent undecided. The strongest proponents of the repeal are African Americans and persons living in the Miami/Palm Beach media markets. Those more in favor of keeping the law are Caucasians, males, and residents of North Florida—the most conservative part of the state. (For more on legal issues, see Chapter 8—courts, crime, and corrections.)

Figure 3-9. Issue Stances

Source: University of South Florida-Nielsen Sunshine State Survey (2014).

Same-Sex Marriage

Legalizing same-sex marriage is viewed by 40 percent as the right policy direction, and by 31 percent as the wrong direction, with 29 percent undecided. Floridians' views on same-sex marriage have changed considerably over the past decade. A 2004 poll by *The Miami Herald* and *St. Petersburg Times* (now *Tampa Bay Times*) found just 27 percent of Floridians in favor of same-sex marriage.[17] Seven years later, it was just 28 percent (survey by Public Policy Polling[18]). But by 2014, a plurality of Floridians (40 percent) supported it. A federal court ruling in January 2015 made the issue moot by legalizing same-sex marriage in Florida.

Much of the change in Floridians' attitudes can be attributed to generational replacement and education, although there is still some resistance to it from older voters and religious conservatives. The strongest support for same-sex marriage comes from young Floridians and college graduates. From a partisan perspective, Democrats and independents are more in favor of it than Republicans, although younger Republicans also favor it. Age is the biggest differentiator in opinions—and Millennials are a large age cohort.

Common Core Standards in Public Schools

Common Core standards lay out what students in grades K-12 should learn in certain areas (math and language arts), then monitor whether they have learned the material using standardized tests. More than 40 states and the District of Columbia have adopted them, including Florida. The goal is to better prepare students for college or a career.[19] Former Republican Governor Jeb Bush was, and is, a strong proponent of national Common Core standards on the grounds that they are necessary to make Americans more competitive in the global economy.

Polls have shown that semantics (wording) matters. When surveys avoid using the label "Common Core," respondents are in favor of the policy. For example, when voters were asked whether they approved of adopting standards in math and reading that were shared among several states, two-thirds of the respondents said "yes." But when the Common Core label was used, just over one-third approved. For that reason, Florida changed the name to the Next Generation Sunshine State Standards and finally to just Florida Standards.[20]

Implementing the Common Core standards in public schools is seen as the right direction for 42 percent of Floridians and the wrong direction for 28 percent. The remaining 31 percent—a high proportion—are undecided. Initially, support for the standards was strong, but it has gradually weakened. Opponents of Common Core standards argue "they require too much of [students], lead to too much high-stakes testing, and limit local control of schools."[21] Opposition from others, especially conservatives, is based on what some experts say are "widespread misperceptions" that the standards "extend to topics such as sex education, evolution, global warming, and the American Revolution."[22] In Florida, a slight majority of African Americans, parents with a child in school, and divorced/separated individuals view the standards positively. Opposition is higher in the more Republican areas of the state, and is growing among liberals and teachers who strongly oppose the *frequency* of standardized testing more than testing itself. In response to pressure from both conservatives and liberals, in 2015, Governor Scott signed a bill reducing the number of tests public school students take each year. (For more on education issues, see Chapter 11.)

Expansion of Casino Gambling

The gambling industry in Florida is a multi-billion dollar business, with many components—including casinos on Indian reservations, pari-mutuel gambling (betting on dog and horse races), and more.[23] In recent years, there has been a push to permit Las Vegas-style casinos to operate in the Sunshine State—a highly controversial proposal. Proponents see it as a form of "destination tourism"—a type of tourism that is growing in popularity—and as a big revenue producer for the state and its localities. Opponents see expanded casino gambling as threatening Florida's family-friendly tourism image. They point to the fact that casinos did not bring the expected revenue into Atlantic City, where many casinos have closed and local businesses have gone bankrupt. Opponents also fear rising social costs and crime.[24] Many casino gambling expansion bills have been introduced in the legislature in recent years but thus far without much success.

A plurality (43 percent) of Floridians see allowing more casino gambling as pushing the state in the wrong direction, while 29 percent believe just the opposite; 28 percent have no opinion. The strongest opposition comes from the state's seniors, African Americans, and women. Proponents are more likely to be males, Generation Xers, and non-college educated persons. (For a discussion of another popular type of gambling—the lottery—see Chapter 9.)

Moral, racial, religious, or equity-related issues often drive citizens to speak their minds about them at public forums.

RATING GOVERNMENT PERFORMANCE

Governments are increasingly turning to citizen surveys to grade their overall performance. These surveys are, in effect, a government's report card—an evaluation by the citizenry of how well government is performing a whole host of activities. The Sunshine State Surveys show that Floridians give the highest marks to state and local governments for promoting political participation—making it convenient to vote, providing election equipment that is highly dependable, and informing citizens about election laws and procedures. The lowest marks are given to governments' efforts to create jobs, manage their finances, provide for adequate transportation, and meet the needs of Florida's "dependent" children, elderly, disabled, and minority populations. (These ratings are discussed in the appropriate chapters.)

WHAT DIVIDES FLORIDIANS THE MOST POLITICALLY?

Floridians see political differences as the deepest divide among the populace—the one that makes finding solutions to problems the most difficult for public officials. (See Figure 3-10.) Nearly half (45 percent) identify either partisan differences (Democrats vs. Republicans) or differences between elected officials vs. average citizens as the sharpest dividing line. The income gap (rich vs. poor) ranks third, followed by the racial/ethnic divide. Citizens *generally* see far fewer differences along gender, age, religious, sexual orientation, and citizenship status lines than are portrayed in the media. However, it is also true that the divides may differ depending on the issue at hand.

Figure 3-10. Biggest Divide Between Floridians

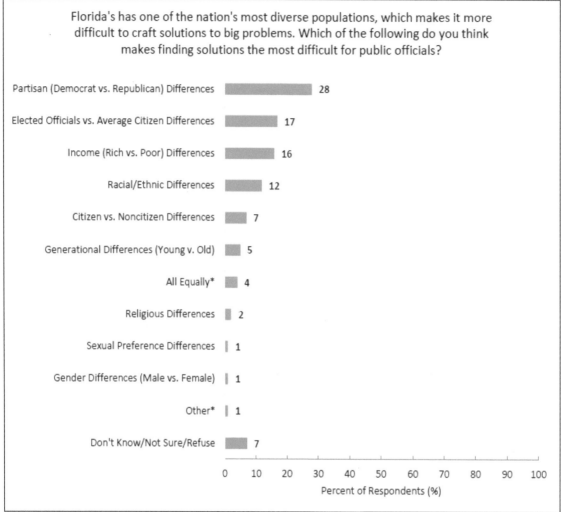

Florida's has one of the nation's most diverse populations, which makes it more difficult to craft solutions to big problems. Which of the following do you think makes finding solutions the most difficult for public officials?

	Percent of Respondents (%)
Partisan (Democrat vs. Republican) Differences	28
Elected Officials vs. Average Citizen Differences	17
Income (Rich vs. Poor) Differences	16
Racial/Ethnic Differences	12
Citizen vs. Noncitizen Differences	7
Generational Differences (Young v. Old)	5
All Equally*	4
Religious Differences	2
Sexual Preference Differences	1
Gender Differences (Male vs. Female)	1
Other*	1
Don't Know/Not Sure/Refuse	7

Source: University of South Florida-Nielsen Sunshine State Survey (2014).

FOLLOWING OR LEADING PUBLIC OPINION?

The influence of public opinion over government policy has been the subject of great philosophical controversy in the classic literature on democracy. The English statesman and political philosopher, Edmund Burke, argued in 1790 that democratic representatives should serve the interest of the people but not necessarily conform to their will in deciding questions of public policy. In contrast, some democratic theorists have measured the success of democratic institutions by the degree to which there is a close congruence between public opinion and public policy. Elected officials in diverse Florida struggle with which of these two representational paths to follow, knowing full well

Floridians look for integrity in their leaders and hold them accountable for doing what they promise when in the spotlight.

that politicians that regularly go outside the bounds of public opinion or consistently ignore it do so at their own peril.

Leadership Qualities

What qualities do Floridians want most in their leaders? Results of the annual Florida Sunshine State Surveys clearly show the vast majority prefers someone of honesty and integrity, whether that person is a leader in the public, private, or nonprofit sector. (See Figure 3-11.) Floridians also expect their leaders to be knowledgeable, competent, decisive, open-minded, enthusiastic, confident, and good listeners, communicators, and motivators. Florida's most successful politicians embody most, if not all, of these characteristics, whether in Washington, Tallahassee, or in local governments throughout the state. They do not just follow public opinion; they help to shape it for the good of the state and for future generations.

Figure 3-11. Most Important Leadership Quality for Good Leaders to Have

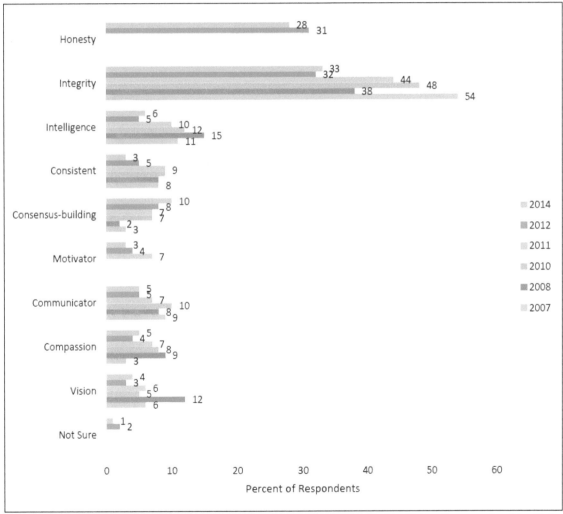

Source: "Leadership Florida Sunshine State Survey (2006-2008), Leadership Florida-Nielsen Company Sunshine State Survey (2010-2012), and University of South Florida-Nielsen Sunshine State Survey (2014)."

Note: Respondents were asked, "Which one of the following qualities do you feel is most important for a good leader to have?" Motivator is a new trait added in 2011. Responses may not add to 100% due to rounding. The "All Other Responses" category is not included in the graphic.

Source: Sunshine State Surveys.

Ultimately, it is the responsibility of political leaders to find policy solutions that satisfy the often seemingly inconsistent views of the electorate. And if public opinion ever presents an obstacle to sound policy, it is the responsibility of leadership to educate the public. Indeed, the very definition of leadership is the ability to articulate the public interest and bring people together in support of it. Because of Florida's "rootless" political culture, diverse population and simultaneous preference for low taxes and more spending, strong political leadership is in great demand in the Sunshine State.

According to public opinion surveys, services for Florida's youngest, oldest, and disabled residents (its "dependent" populations) are high priorities.

ONLINE SOURCES FOR DATA AND INFORMATION UPDATES

Sunshine State Survey: Results

The Sunshine State Survey polls Florida residents for their opinions on national and local issues, and includes statistics on the respondent's age, race, gender, party affiliation, employment, etc. The survey has data available from 2006 to 2014 (excluding 2013). Specific data can be found on trust in government leaders, the most important issue facing Florida, opinions on taxing and spending (tax revenue, least fair revenue source, and budget), issue stances, biggest divide for public officials, and the most important leadership quality.
http://sunshinestatesurvey.org/results/

Florida Annual Policy Survey

The Florida Annual Policy Survey focuses on the policy interests and attitudes of Floridians on decisions and issues facing local and state governments and has annual public opinion data from 1979 to 2003-04.
http://coss.fsu.edu/d6/srl/content/reports

National Council on Public Polls

The NCPP is an organization dedicated to setting the highest standards in polling, as well as informing citizens, media, and politicians alike of how to organize, conduct, and understand polls and their results.
http://www.ncpp.org/?q=home

Sayfie Review

Sayfie Review, "what Florida's most influential people read daily," is a news aggregator with local and national pieces about Florida politics.
http://www.sayfiereview.com

Real Clear Politics

Real Clear Politics compiles pre-election polls from all over the country for presidential, gubernatorial, and select congressional races, including many Florida-specific polls.
http://www.realclearpolitics.com

Chapter 4. Parties and Elections in Florida

For years, the primary symbols representing the two major political parties have been a donkey (Democrats) and an elephant (Republicans). Now the parties are also portrayed in colors. States that are dominated by one party are described as either "red" (Republican) or "blue" (Democrat). A handful of states—the nation's premier battleground states—are "purple" (a combination of both colors). Florida is a purple state. In fact, "Florida's hue is *bright* purple."[1] But it hasn't always been so.

Transition from a One-Party State

A half-century ago, when political parties played a more central role in the political life of the nation, the distinguished political scientist V.O. Key, Jr., observed that, in contrast, politics in Florida was "every man for himself." In the traditional one-party Democratic system of Florida, party held little meaning. Everyone was a Democrat. Electoral politics centered on Democratic primary elections. The winner of the Democratic primary was seldom, if ever, challenged by a Republican in the general election. Even within the Democratic Party, there were no clear liberal or conservative factions as in some other Southern states.

But Florida politics has changed remarkably in recent decades as the state has grown. The influx of Republican-leaning retirees from the Midwest and immigrants from Cuba and the Caribbean, along with conservatives from other Southern states, increased the number of Republicans and brought two-party competition to Florida. The parties are most competitive in *statewide races* for president, governor, the Cabinet, and the U.S. Senate, depending on the candidates. There is less partisan competition in contests for state legislative and congressional seats. In recent years, the GOP (the Grand Old Party) has held the edge there, primarily due to controlling the redistricting process in 2002 and 2012, but also due to unequal geographical concentrations of Democrats and Republicans across the state. (See Chapter 6 for a review of the redistricting process that takes place every 10 years after a new U.S. Census.)

As Florida's political landscape has changed, so, too, has campaigning. Targeting specific slices of the electorate and more intense get-out-the-vote (GOTV) turnout efforts have become the critical campaign tools used by political parties and candidates. (See Chapter 1.) Technology—better data bases and specially designed campaign management software, vastly improved interactive communication mechanisms (social media, smartphones, tablets), more rapid video production capabilities, "YouTube," online polls, and apps—all have made contacting and GOTV efforts easier and more precise. Obviously, there is still nothing like meeting a candidate in person. If a voter meets a candidate, chances are higher that he/she will turn out to vote *and* vote for that candidate. However, in a large state like Florida, candidates cannot meet every voter. The challenge then becomes how to reach voters in ways that make them feel personally connected to the candidate. What is effective in creating that sense for one group of voters may not be so for another.

In any campaign, the biggest challenge is still turnout. One turnout tool regularly used by both political parties has been the constitutional amendment. Whether placed on the ballot by the Florida Legislature or voter petitions (constitutional initiative), amendments are viewed as a way to get people to vote. (See Chapter 2.) Economic and moral issue-related amendment proposals stir voter emotions the most. A classic example of the "amendment turnout technique" was evident in 2004. On the ballot were several constitutional amendment proposals (minimum wage, parental notification of a minor's termination of pregnancy plans) placed there precisely for the purpose of turning out infrequent voters. The minimum wage amendment was seen by Democrats as a great GOTV tool; for Republicans, it was parental notification. Another example was the medicinal marijuana amendment placed on the ballot in 2014 by voter petition. The collection of petition signatures was funded largely by a wealthy Democratic supporter. The proposed amendment was seen by many as a way to increase young Democrats' turnout in a midterm election. (Young voter turnout typically plummets in non-presidential election years.) The proposal was narrowly defeated by the voters; young voter turnout did not spike, as projected.

THE FUNCTIONS OF PARTIES

The development of political parties in virtually all the world's democracies testifies to the importance of parties to democratic governments. The principal function of parties is to organize elections. Parties narrow the field of aspiring office seekers in party primary elections and offer voters a choice of a Democratic, Republican, or third party candidate in the general election. Very few independent candidates are elected to high office in the United States without first securing a Democratic or Republican Party nomination. Few legislators and no governor, cabinet official, or U.S. senator have ever been elected as an independent in Florida. But a few legislators have been elected from other political parties, often referred to as minor parties. (For a list of Florida's minor parties, see Table 4-2 later in the chapter.)

Lawton Chiles leads a get-out-the-vote rally at the State Capitol.

A second function of parties is to organize leadership within the government, notably in the legislature where leadership posts are chosen by the members of the majority party in each house. Party identification and party loyalty are stronger among elected officeholders than among voters. Thus, after legislators select their leaders in a party caucus, they unite behind their party's choice when the formal vote is taken on the floor of the House or Senate. Seldom do members cross party lines in leadership votes, even when they may be unhappy with their own party's nominee. This means that the party that wins a majority of house or senate seats in the November election will see its choices for leadership posts and committee chairs take charge in the following spring legislative session. (See Chapter 6.)

Parties also function to help direct the course of public policy. This is perhaps their weakest function. In a strong responsible party system, each party would develop clear policy options to present as platforms to the voters; they would recruit candidates for public office who supported the platform; they would educate the voters about the issues during the political campaign; and then later they would hold the party's elected officials responsible for enacting the party's platform pledges into law.

But the Democratic and Republican parties in Florida, as in other states and in Washington as well, are not really disciplined, responsible, issue-oriented parties. Although Democratic Party candidates and officeholders are generally more liberal than Republicans, and Republican candidates and officeholders are typically more conservative than Democrats, these ideological lines are frequently blurred during general election campaigns. Candidates in each party usually try to "center" their image with the voter.

They try to appear moderate in their views and avoid being labeled as "extremists," especially in light of the growing number of independents.

Moreover, party officials cannot deny their party's nomination to the winner of their party's primary. Anyone, regardless of ideological positions or views on major issues, may register as either a Democrat or a Republican and enter his or her name as a candidate in that party's primary. Party officials may endorse a candidate (officially declare a candidate in the party primary as the party's preferred candidate), but voters in primary elections often ignore (or have no knowledge of) these endorsements. Whoever wins a party's primary election becomes the party's nominee, whatever their policy views. Despite these weaknesses, both the Republican Party of Florida and the Florida Democratic Party play a vital role in Florida politics.

PARTY ORGANIZATIONS

Florida's Democratic and Republican state party organizations resemble those of other states—a state committee and state chair, offices in the state capital with full-time staff, and party committees in each county. Typically, state party chairs ascend to the position in one of two ways—by elective office or up through the ranks of local, state, and national party or fundraising committees. Twice in recent history both the Democratic and Republican state party chairs have been women—Democrat Karen Thurman and Republican Carole Jean Jordan (2004-2006); Democrat Allison Tant and Republican Leslie Dougher (2014).

Florida's political party organizations have become much more important in recent years as grassroots-level voter-contacting efforts have become more critical to winning and Florida's political clout has increased. Local party organizations, especially in heavily populated metropolitan areas, hold candidate forums, host presidential candidates and national party leaders, and annually sponsor major fundraising events (Democrats—Kennedy-King dinners and Blue galas; Republicans—Lincoln and Reagan Day dinners).

County Committees

The county committees are the building blocks of the state party organization. Members are elected in each party's primary elections. However, in many counties it is difficult for a party, especially the minority party, to fill all of its committee seats. Committee members are usually recruited as friends and neighbors of current party activists; intraparty competition for committee seats is rare.

Some Democratic and Republican county committees are active and well organized. They regularly engage in candidate recruitment, fundraising, campaign and media activities, and occasionally even door-to-door canvassing of voters. They maintain voter registration lists that can help their party's candidates. They may undertake to recruit candidates for local government offices and occasionally for state legislative seats. But this candidate recruitment task is especially difficult in counties where a party suffers minority status.

A sizeable number of Florida legislators run unopposed in general elections. Vacant party nominations at any level of public office reflect weak party organizations. Strong parties try to put forward a full slate of nominees in every general election. Even against strong incumbents, active party committees seek out "sacrificial lambs" to carry the party banner. And active committees routinely promote candidates on their websites, in social media and in print, distribute flyers and brochures, put up signs, and sponsor rallies and candidate forums.

State Committees

Florida's state Democratic and Republican committees have become professionalized in recent years. Both committees maintain well-staffed offices in Tallahassee, and have computerized lists of likely financial contributors, mass printing and mailing operations, regular party newsletters, training workshops for new candidates, and close contacts with professional advertising and polling organizations. State party committees also have the honor of appointing their party's presidential electors, who are required by Florida law to sign a pledge to support the winner of the presidential primary vote in Florida.

Members of the state Democratic and Republican committees are elected by each party's county committees, not by the party's voters. State chairs are officially elected by the state committees. Intraparty competition for this post is often vigorous, with aspirants vying for the recommendation of the governor or other leading public figures in the state. This high level of competition is not surprising. It is merely a mirror of Florida politics in general.

THE RISE OF PARTY COMPETITION IN FLORIDA

Historically, competition within Florida's one-party system centered on local and regional loyalties, friends and neighbors, and personal followings, rather than along party lines or even along clear factions within the ruling Democratic Party. The prevailing political culture was conservative, fundamentalist in religion, segregationist, and solidly Democratic.[2]

Traditional Democratic Control of the Capitol

For many years, with few exceptions (Republicans Claude Kirk in 1966 and Bob Martinez in 1986), Democrats dominated the governorship and maintained control of both houses of the state legislature. Democratic Governor LeRoy Collins[3] led the state peacefully through early desegregation efforts in the late 1950s. Succeeding Democratic Governors Farris Bryant and Haydon Burns were somewhat less successful in uniting the state, but in the 1970s a group of younger, progressive Democratic leaders emerged: Reubin Askew, who served two full terms as governor after his election in 1970[4]; Bob Graham, who followed in 1978, serving two full terms; and Lawton Chiles, who was first elected to the U.S. Senate in 1970, served three terms in Washington before retiring in 1988, and then ran successfully for governor in 1990 and 1994. It is likely that these popular political figures kept the Florida statehouse Democratic longer than it would have without their skillful political leadership.

Democrats dominated state-level politics for many decades and in two different Capitol buildings (the old on the right, the new on the left).

Early Republican Inroads

Republican voting in Florida is considered a "top down" phenomenon. It started first at the presidential level and only over time did it move down the ticket to other races. Republican President Dwight D. Eisenhower first cracked the solid Democratic South and set a pattern for Florida voting in presidential contests that lasted nearly 30 years. (See Table 4-1.) After 1952, Florida voted Republican in most presidential elections but remained heavily Democratic in state elections. Florida voted for Eisenhower in 1952 and 1956, for Richard Nixon in 1960, 1968, and 1972; for Ronald Reagan in 1980 and 1984; and for George H.W. Bush in 1988 and 1992 (see Table 4-1). Many Florida Democrats, especially old-line conservatives, saw Democratic presidential nominees as too liberal for the state, except when Southern Democrats ran (Lyndon Johnson from Texas, Jimmy Carter from Georgia, and Bill Clinton from Arkansas). Democrat Al Gore from Tennessee came within 537 votes of winning Florida in 2000. But John Kerry from Massachusetts was seen as too liberal for many conservative Florida Democrats in 2004. Kerry lost to George W. Bush by a margin of five percent.

Table 4-1. Florida's Votes in Presidential Elections

Year	Republican		Democrat		Third Party	
	Candidate	% of Vote	Candidate	% of Vote	Candidate	% of Vote
1952	Eisenhower	55.0	Stevenson	45.0		
1956	Eisenhower	57.3	Stevenson	42.7		
1960	Nixon	51.5	Kennedy	48.5		
1964	Goldwater	48.9	Johnson	51.1		
1968	Nixon	40.5	Humphrey	30.9	Wallace	28.5
1972	Nixon	71.9	McGovern	27.8		
1976	Ford	46.6	Carter	51.9		
1980	Reagan	55.5	Carter	38.5	Anderson	5.1
1984	Reagan	65.3	Mondale	34.4		
1988	Bush	60.1	Dukakis	38.0		
1992	Bush	40.9	Clinton	39.0	Perot	19.8
1996	Dole	42.3	Clinton	48.0	Perot	9.1
2000	Bush	48.8	Gore	48.8	Nader	1.6
2004	Bush	52.1	Kerry	47.1		
2008	McCain	48.2	Obama	51.0		
2012	Romney	49.1	Obama	50.0		

Source: Florida Division of Elections.

This presidential voting pattern was broken in 2008 when Florida voters rejected Republican John McCain, and instead selected Illinois Democrat Barack Obama—the first Northern Democratic presidential candidate to win the Sunshine State in over fifty years. In 2012, Democrat Barack Obama narrowly beat Republican Mitt Romney in the second closest presidential election in Florida (the 2000 election was the closest). In both 2008 and 2012, Republican turnout was lower than expected for a variety of reason. (See discussions of each race later in the chapter.)

At the same time Republican strength waned somewhat in presidential elections, it increased in both the 2010 and 2014 *midterm* (non-presidential) election years. In both elections, GOP candidates swept all the statewide offices (governor, Cabinet offices, U.S. Senate—2010 only).

The Rising Republican Tide

Early growth in Republican identification and voting in Florida has been linked to the popularity of Ronald Reagan, heavy migration to Florida, the increasing liberalism of the Democratic Party, and superior Republican organizational strength. Republicans Ronald Reagan and George H. W. Bush (at the beginning of his term) were extremely popular in the state. During their presidencies, an increasing number of Floridians began identifying themselves as Republicans in opinion polls. Indeed, it was during the Reagan years that Republican identification in Florida leaped from 20 to 40 percent of the electorate, and for the first time in the state's history surpassed Democratic Party identification. Party identification is measured in opinion polls by responses to the question: "Generally speaking, do you think of yourself as a Republican, a Democrat, an independent, or what?"

The growth of Republican Party identification in the Florida electorate has also been attributed to the state's explosive population growth.[5] New residents migrating from other states and countries bring their traditional party identification with them. Republicans from Midwestern states flowed down I-75 to Central and Southwest Florida, while Democrats from Northeastern states streamed into the state via I-95 to Miami-Dade, Broward (Fort Lauderdale), and Palm Beach counties. The tide of middle class, suburban retirees brought a mix of Democrats and Republicans that better reflected national party affiliations. New Republican arrivals began swelling the ranks of the GOP. Democrats moving into Florida from liberal Northeastern states pulled the Florida Democratic Party in a more liberal direction.

Increased Democratic liberalism is a third factor contributing to the growth of Republicanism in Florida and throughout the South.[6] Traditionally the Democratic Party in Florida and the South was very conservative. However, white Southern Democrats began to permanently defect over the race issue when Democrat Lyndon Johnson began to strongly support civil rights in 1964, while GOP presidential candidate Barry Goldwater opposed violating "states' rights." Over time, the national Democratic Party was perceived as becoming too liberal on a host of social, economic, and moral issues. As traditional conservative Florida Democrats saw their party becoming more liberal, they began switching their party affiliation and voting Republican in state and local elections.

Finally, the Republican Party's well-organized candidate recruitment, registration, and GOTV efforts prompted more Floridians to identify with and vote for Republicans.[7] Democrats were so dominant for so long that they saw little need for formal organizational structures at the state or grassroots levels. Meanwhile, Republicans began investing money in a formal party organization to recruit candidates, assist with campaigns, and mobilize voters.

Initially, many new residents who came to Florida and voted Republican in presidential elections registered as Democrats. Moreover, many native Floridians who were conservative Democrats retained their Democratic registration despite casting presidential votes for Republicans. Both groups knew that, historically, the only real contests for state and local office were Democratic primary races, and they wanted to be able to participate in these races. Florida law traditionally held that only registered members of a party could vote in the party's primary (a *closed* primary). Consequently, Republican registration in the state lagged well behind opinion poll data showing higher levels of self-identification with the GOP.

As the GOP began winning races, it began attracting even more party identifiers once there was a viable option to the Democratic Party. Republican successes forced Florida Democrats to re-organize their party organization structure to remain competitive. They had to step up their fundraising efforts both inside and outside Florida to improve the party's outreach to newly arrived residents, plus improve their candidate recruitment efforts.

Major Parties Come Closer to Parity, but Share of Registrants Shrinking

As late as 1980, Democratic registrations outnumbered Republican registrations by more than 2 to 1. During the Reagan Bush years, Republican registration leaped upward, while Democratic registration stagnated, allowing the gap between Democrats and Republicans to narrow. But since the early 1990s, the sharp increase has been in independents—voters registering as having no party affiliation (see Figure 4-1). Each major party's share of registered voters has declined.

Both parties have had to bolster their efforts to improve their targeting of new immigrant groups, especially Hispanics, and the large, diverse, and more independent Millennial generation.

Figure 4-1. Florida Voter Party Registration Percentages: 1972-2015

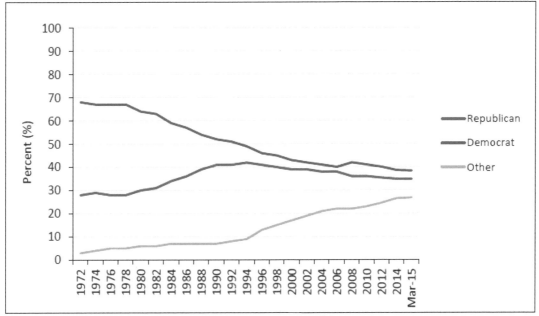

Source: Calculated from data available from the Florida Division of Elections.

No Party Preference and Third (Minor) Parties

The biggest gains in registration after the passage of the federal Motor-Voter Act (1993) have come among voters with no party preference and those who choose a third party (labeled a "minor party" under Florida law). These two groups rose from eight percent of all voters in 1995 to more than one-fourth of all voters by the early 2010s.

People with strong party attachments were motivated to register before the Motor-Voter Act made it possible to register at driver's license and social service agencies starting in 1995. Once registration became easier, people with less interest in, or a great dislike for, the two major parties became registered voters. Some chose not to register with any party. Others formed new political parties—a process that for many years was easier in Florida than in many other states. A casual observer once described it: "In Florida, if someone names a chairman and treasurer, and files quarterly financial reports with the Secretary of State's office, they're official; there are no fees, and there seems to be no standing regulation on party names or purpose, much less on good taste."[8]

The 2006 gubernatorial debate sponsored by the Florida NBC stations featured (left to right) Republican candidate Charlie Crist, Democratic candidate Jim Davis, and Reform Party candidate Max Linn. A last-minute court order allowed Linn to participate in the debate.

Now the process is more rigorous. Legally, a minor political party is "a group which on January 1 preceding a primary election does not have registered members consisting of five percent of the registered voters of the state" (Section 97.021(18), *Florida Statutes*). To become a minor party, a group of citizens must submit a certificate showing the name of the organization and the names and addresses of its current officers, including the members of its executive committee. The application must also include a voter registration application for each of its officers and executive committee members listing the proposed minor political party as their official party affiliation. A copy of the group's constitution, bylaws, and rules and regulations must also be submitted to the Florida Division of Elections. The division reviews the application to determine whether it meets all the requirements, then notifies the group whether its status as a minor political party has been approved. However, Florida's recognition of a group as a minor political party does not mean the group is recognized as a party in other states or at the federal level.

The three largest minor parties are the Independent Party of Florida, the Independence Party, and the Libertarian Party. The first two should be called "accidental parties" because the vast majority of people who are registered with this party have done so without realizing it. They think they are registering as true "independents," meaning they do not belong to any political party. Those with such a preference should actually register as having "No Party Affiliation (NPA)."

There are 13 minor parties in Florida, many with fewer than 1,000 registrants. Rarely do candidates from these small, minor parties run for office, so it grabs people's attention when they do.

Prior to Motor-Voter, most new registration was done directly with an employee or volunteer of a Supervisor of Elections office who would clarify the intent of the new registrant. Since Motor-Voter became law, many citizens no longer have direct contact with the elections supervisor office when they register, so no such clarification is offered. Thus when Floridians say "independent" to an employee at the driver's license office, or write "independent" on a registration form and send it by mail, they often are registered as a member of the Independent or Independence Party instead of "No Party Affiliation" (NPA).

Table 4-2. Florida Political Parties: Major and Minor

Major Political Parties	
Florida Democratic Party (DEM)	Republican Party of Florida (REP)
Minor Political Parties	
America's Party of Florida (AIP)	Constitution Party of Florida (CPF)
Ecology Party of Florida (ECO)	Florida Socialist Workers Party (FSW)
Green Party of Florida (GRE)	Independence Party of Florida (IDP)
Independent Party of Florida (INT)	Justice Party of Florida (JPF)
Libertarian Party of Florida (LPF)	Party for Socialism and Liberation-Florida (PSL)
Peace & Freedom Party of Florida (PFP)	Reform Party (REF)
Tea Party of Florida (TPF)	

Source: Florida Division of Elections, October 15, 2014.

The Libertarian Party is the largest *active* minor party. Its members support reduced government regulation in both social and economic affairs. The Libertarian Party actually fielded more candidates for the 2002 statehouse races (72) than the Democrats (69). A Libertarian candidate, Adrian Wyllie, ran for governor in 2014 and got a considerable amount of media coverage—more than any prior Libertarian had garnered.

The Green Party is more familiar to many Floridians than many other minor parties. Its platform focuses largely on seeking more protection for the environment and more stringent regulation of business. Another third party that was once quite active in the state is the Reform Party, which was started nationally by Ross Perot in 1992 to challenge the major parties on budget and trade issues. By 2002, the Reform Party was wracked with internal strife after the controversial selection of Pat Buchanan as the presidential nominee split the party. But the party experienced a rebirth in Florida in 2006. Max Linn, the party's nominee for governor, got lots of publicity, participated in the statewide televised debate sponsored by Florida's NBC stations, and ultimately received two percent of the vote. Since then, the party has not had a high profile candidate for any state-level office.

The Tea Party: Political Party or Political Movement?

The answer is "both."[9] The Florida Tea Party, an official political party, was founded in August 2009.[10] It was the first such party in the nation. There was always some controversy about who founded the official Tea Party and for what purposes, although most agree its formation tracked with the national movement's focus on taxation. In Florida, both major parties were skeptical of the motivations of those behind this new party. Republicans claimed it was created by liberals to split the Republican vote (conservatives and moderates) and help elect Democrats.[11] Conversely, Democrats saw it as a Republican tool to increase the turnout of conservatives in a midterm election.

Initially, the tea party movement was considerably larger than the official Tea Party. At the time of its formation, the nearly 250 groups scattered across the state were mostly grassroots groups joined together by their concerns about the direction of the country, the expansion of government, out-of-control spending, and rising national debt, not by any formal party organization. When Republican Marco Rubio began his improbable race for the U.S. Senate against fellow Republican, later independent (NPA) Charlie Crist, he gained a lot of support from those who identified with the movement. (He later sought distance between himself and the group.)

By the time the 2010 election took place, many of those in the movement looked with disdain upon the official Tea Party, even going so far as to label it the "fake tea party." One activist took the media to task for treating the two as one and the same. As it turned out, the voters were able to make the distinction:

> "The tea party, the movement, had a great week. The Tea Party, the party, not as much. Members of the loosely organized and hard-to-define tea party movement were generally jubilant with Tuesday's election with conservatives backed by the anti-spending, small government crowd having success around the country [and in Florida]. But for the Florida Tea Party, an official political party that tried to capitalize on the national tea party tide, Tuesday was rough—none of its [20] candidates in the state were elected."[12]

The national media never really picked up on this difference. Many outside (and inside) Florida, still erroneously view "tea-partiers" as monolithic in their politics.

The Impact of Minor (Third) Parties

While third party candidates in Florida have almost never won election, they have impacted politics. In 1998, voters approved the Constitutional Revision Commission's proposal to make ballot access laws for the third parties the same as that for Republicans and Democrats (Article VI Section 1). Prior to 1998, it was more difficult for third parties to get on the ballot. Indirectly, this constitutional change caused Al Gore to lose Florida, and thus the presidency, and altered the course of U.S. and, perhaps, world history. As a result of the change, the Florida 2000 ballot had presidential candidates from 10 different political parties, up from just four in 1996. Ralph Nader, the Green Party candidate, pulled almost 100,000 votes.

Conventional wisdom and exit polling suggest that the majority of liberal and progressive "green" voters would have voted for Al Gore rather than George Bush if the Green Party had not been on the ballot, more than enough to overcome the eventual 537-vote Bush win. Of course, the Green Party may have made it on the ballot even under the more restrictive rules.

In addition, putting all 10 candidates on a single ballot was a challenge for county elections supervisors in 2000. Much of the brouhaha and chaos of that election stemmed from supervisors creatively placing the candidates' names on the ballot. Most notable was Palm Beach County's infamous "butterfly" ballot that caused some voters to punch the wrong hole and mistakenly vote for third party candidate Pat Buchanan. In Duval County, the 10 presidential candidates were on two consecutive pages because of a lack of space. About 9,000 voters in predominantly black precincts voted for Al Gore on the first page and then turned the page and voted for Harry Browne (the Libertarian Party candidate), thus spoiling their ballot with an over-vote. Much of their confusion may have stemmed from campaign ads for Corrine Brown, a popular African-American Congresswoman running for re-election. Her ads urged black voters to "vote for Gore and vote for Brown."[13] In summary, the constitutional change making it easier for third parties to get on the ballot in Florida has, on occasion, had unintentional and dramatic consequences. The law of unintended consequences often yields unpredictable outcomes when it comes to election reforms.

Partisan Alignments and Geographical Concentrations

Voter registration figures, election outcomes, exit polls, and the annual Sunshine State Surveys have shown fairly consistent patterns of group attachment with the two major political parties. Historically, the strength of the Republican Party in Florida has been among white voters, Cuban Hispanics, men, and more affluent, Protestant, college-educated, and conservative voters. Democrats have drawn greater support from blacks, some non-Cuban Hispanic groups, women, Jewish and non-religious persons, lower-income, less-educated, and liberal voters. (See Table 4-3.) As previously noted, recent influxes of immigrants and generational replacement have begun to alter some of the traditional party-identification patterns. Naturally, Democrat and Republican Party support levels from these different demographic groups may differ, depending on who is running.

Symbols of each major political party (elephant—Republicans, donkey—Democrats) are prominently displayed in a tamper-free case in the Florida Capitol.

For decades North Florida remained Democratic by registration, but voters in the region would cast their ballots for Republicans in statewide elections when a Democratic candidate was perceived as too liberal. Now, more voters register as Republicans and the region consistently votes Republican as well. The Southeast part of Florida, particularly Broward and Palm Beach counties, is strongly Democratic. The Southwest region is the most heavily Republican area. Central Florida is the most competitive part of the state and home to a large number of independent or swing voters who have less loyalty to either major party. The I-4 Corridor is considered to be a microcosm of Florida at large in both its registration and voting patterns. (See Figures 4-2 and 4-3.)

Table 4-3. Vote Patterns of Floridians: 2000-2012 Presidential Elections

Category	2000		2004		2008		2012	
	Bush (R)	Gore (D)	Bush (R)	Kerry (D)	McCain (R)	Obama (D)	Romney (R)	Obama (D)
Gender								
Male	54	42	53	46	47	51	52	46
Female	45	53	50	49	47	52	46	53
Race								
White	57	40	57	42	56	42	61	37
African American	7	93	13	86	4	96	4	95
Latino	49	48	56	44	42	57	39	60
Other	*	*	66	34	*	*	39	59
Age								
18-29	40	55	41	58	37	61	29	68
30-44	50	47	53	46	49	49	46	52
45-59	49	49	57	42	*	*	*	*
60 and older	51	47	52	47	*	*	*	*
45-64	*	*	*	*	47	52	52	48
65 and Older	*	*	*	*	53	45	58	41
Income								
Less than $15,000	37	62	40	59	33	66	40	59
15,000-30,000	36	60	39	59	37	62	55	43
30,000-50,000	47	48	48	51	39	59	*	*
50,000-75,000	53	45	54	45	52	47	*	*
75,000-100,000	59	40	62	37	58	39	*	*
Over $100,000	66	33	*	*	55	44	43	57
100,000-150,000	*	*	56	44	58	40	*	*
150,000-200,000	*	*	60	38	54	45	*	*
$200,000 or More	*	*	59	41	48	51	*	*
Education								
No High School	47	50	45	53	29	70	32	66
High School Graduate	42	56	48	51	41	58	47	52
Some College	49	48	51	48	49	49	50	49
College Graduate	57	39	56	44	53	45	52	46
Postgraduate Study	52	45	53	45	41	58	46	53
Vote by Party Identification								
Democrat	13	86	14	85	12	87	9	90
Republican	91	8	93	7	87	12	92	8
Independent	46	47	41	57	45	52	47	50
Ideology								
Liberal	17	79	18	81	8	91	13	86
Moderate	46	51	43	56	41	57	46	53
Conservative	77	21	86	13	77	21	78	20
Have You Ever Voted Before?								
No	*	*	43	56	40	59	*	*
Yes	*	*	53	46	48	50	*	*
Religion								
Protestant	66	32	59	40	55	43	58	42
Catholic	54	42	57	42	49	50	52	47
Jewish	*	*	20	80	*	*	30	66
Other	*	*	29	69	18	80	28	68
None	*	*	31	66	26	71	26	72

Note: * Indicates that the category was not used in that year's exit poll or that the sample size was too small to be representative of the category.

Source: Florida presidential exit polls. (The 2000 Exit Poll results were contested.)

Figure 4-2. Party Registration Patterns of I-4 Corridor Voters Mirror State

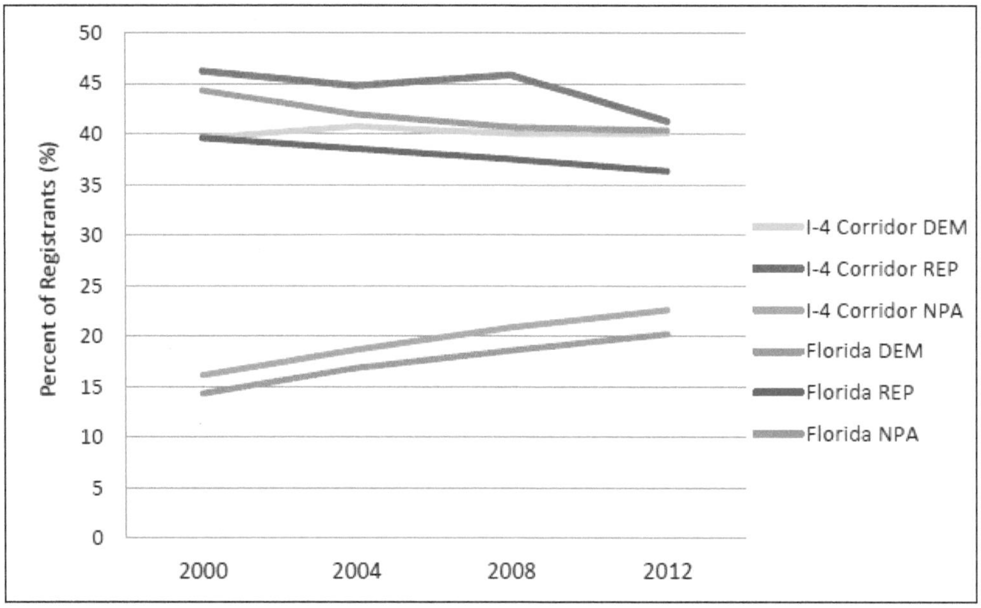

Note: The counties in these calculations are those included in the F-DOT definition of the I-4 Corridor:
• Sarasota-Bradenton MSA (Sarasota and Manatee counties).
• Tampa-St. Petersburg-Clearwater MSA (Hernando, Pasco, Pinellas, and Hillsborough counties).
• Lakeland-Winter Haven MSA (Polk County).
• Orlando MSA (Lake, Orange, Osceola and Seminole counties).
• Daytona Beach MSA (Flagler and Volusia counties.
• Melbourne-Titusville-Palm Bay MSA (Brevard County).

Source: Calculated from data available from the Florida Division of Elections.

Figure 4-3. Presidential Election Results of I-4 Corridor Voters Mirror Statewide Results

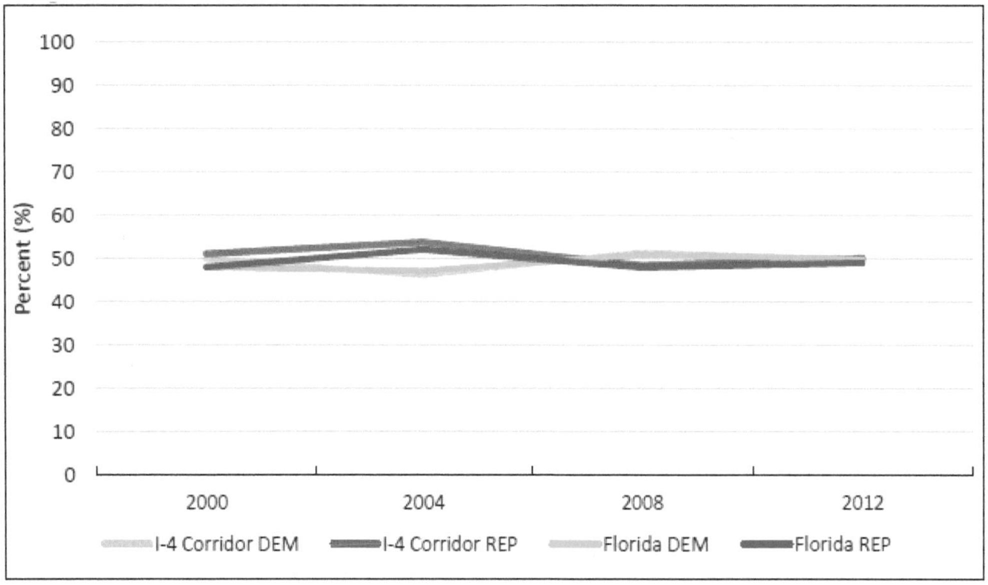

Source: Calculated from data available from the Florida Division of Elections.

FLORIDA ELECTIONS: COMPLEX, VOLATILE, AND UNPREDICTABLE

A great deal of the instability of Florida politics is attributable to the state's demographic shifts due to population in-migration. New arrivals have little knowledge of Florida's political traditions and no strong local political allegiances. They are moving targets for expensive media campaigns. Media ads focus on candidates, enhancing their images, and in the case of negative attack videos, besmirching the images of their opponents. Party affiliations and specific issue stances are seldom mentioned—intentionally. With few ties to political organizations and little knowledge of the records of incumbents, Florida's newcomers are especially dependent on the media for political information—and not just about candidates but also about the voting process.

Florida's election system is often confusing, especially to voters who have moved to Florida from a state with different registration laws, election types and timing, and party structures. Florida's election system is more decentralized as well (See Table 4-4.), although the Florida Legislature has given more power to the secretary of state (the state's chief election official) in recent years.

Table 4-4. The Complexity of Florida's State and Local Election Administrative Structure

Secretary of State
1. Chief election officer – Appointed by the governor beginning January 2003
2. Provides guidance to 67 supervisors of elections, but does not supervise them
3. Provides technical assistance to elections supervisors
4. Prescribes voter registration forms and procedures
5. Prescribes rules concerning voting systems
6. Qualifies federal, state, and multi-county candidates
Election Canvassing Commission
1. Three members of the Florida Cabinet
2. Canvasses all county returns and prepares election abstract
County Supervisors of Elections
1. Local chief election official; elected*; a four-year term—no term limits.**
2. Appoints other local election officials; qualifies county and local candidates; mails and receives financial disclosure statements
3. Administers voter registration; prepares ballots
4. Administers absentee voting
5. Conducts poll worker training
6. Prepares and distributes election materials to each precinct
County Canvassing Board
1. Supervisor of Elections, County Court Judge, chair of the Board of County Commissioners
2. Tabulates county vote and prepares abstracts for transmittal to secretary of state
Election Day Officers
1. Election Board: inspectors and clerks (appointed by county elections supervisor)
2. Administers elections at precincts

Note: *The Miami-Dade County Supervisor of Elections is appointed. **There are term limits in Duval and Orange counties.

Sources: Federal Elections Commission and Federal Statutes; 2002 Governor's Select Task Force on Election Procedures, Standards, and Technology. Tallahassee: Office of the Governor, December 30, 2002, p. 26; Florida Secretary of State update, July 22, 2011.

Primary Elections: Closed and Universal (Open)

Florida has traditionally been a *closed primary* state. That means that in order to vote in a party primary, a voter has to be registered with that party at least 29 days before the election. It also means that voters registered with No Party Affiliation cannot vote in either the Democratic or Republican Party primary. However, there is one exception.

When only one party has candidates running in a primary and the winner will face no opposition in the general election, *all* voters, even independents, may vote in that party's primary election since winning the race effectively elects a candidate for that position.[14] Such an election is called a *universal primary*. Voters approved this change in 1998. (It was a constitutional amendment sponsored by the Constitutional Revision Commission.)

Supporters of the universal (open) primary law argued it would increase participation, ensure that elected officials reflect majority views, and stop a small minority from selecting a winner.[15] Opponents vehemently objected, charging that it would weaken a political party's right to control its own candidate nomination process.

There is a major loophole in Florida's universal (open) primary law that political parties quickly figured out. If a write-in candidate files to run for an office, he/she would run in the general election. It would effectively close what would have been a universal primary open to *all* voters. The Florida State Association of Supervisors of Elections, as well as the editorial boards of many state newspapers, have repeatedly urged the state legislature to ban the use of write-ins in a general election to block a universal primary. (One newspaper has referred to the tactic as "write-in trickery,"[16] another as an example of "Republicans and Democrats... corrupting the system by unleashing bogus write-in candidates that shut out voters."[17])

Runoff (Second) Primaries—Gone!

Until 2005, Florida, like several other Southern states, required a runoff election (a second primary) if no candidate received a majority in the first primary.[18] The runoff primary was held between the two top vote getters. The runoff primary was a holdover from the days of one-party Democratic domination when there were almost no Republicans running. A second primary was held between the top two finishers to ensure that the winner could claim at least 50 percent of the vote. In those days, Florida's Democratic primary voters often defeated the top vote getter in the first primary. In fact, some of the state's leading political figures—Democrats Reubin Askew (1970), Lawton Chiles (1970), and Bob Graham (1978)—came from behind to win a runoff primary, then went on to victory in the general election, which is why some citizens did not want to see it eliminated.

Opposition to the second primary came from some minorities who saw it as potentially disadvantageous to a minority candidate who might end up in a runoff against a white candidate. Others who wanted to get rid of it, like some elections supervisors, pointed to cost savings. Other supervisors asked for its removal, pointing out that it was difficult to prepare ballots and hold three elections (first primary, second primary, general election) in just 60 days. With the elimination of the runoff, the top vote getter in a primary election wins the party's nomination even if the candidate receives less than 50 percent of the vote.

Nonpartisan Primaries Held Simultaneously with *Party* Primaries—Confusing

In Florida, candidates for county and circuit court judgeships and for school boards run in *nonpartisan elections* (with no political party label after their name). These elections are held the same day as the *party* primaries. Many minor party and independent voters do not realize they can go to the polls on a primary election day to vote in these judicial and school board races. This helps explain why turnout in primary elections is typically low in Florida. Many voters simply are unaware that these nonpartisan races are on the ballot and that *all* registered voters may vote in these contests on primary Election Day.

If none of the candidates for a specific nonpartisan position gets a majority of the vote, the top two vote getters then run against each other in the general election. This is, in effect, a runoff election, although it is not held on a separate day as was once the case with runoff elections for partisan races.

Presidential Preference Primary

The presidential preference primary is an election in which the registered voters affiliated with each political party choose whom they prefer to be their party's presidential candidate.[19] In a way, the primary is a "beauty contest" featuring candidates who have been identified as presidential hopefuls. Votes cast for a presidential contender are actually votes cast for the delegates pledged to that candidate at the national party conventions where the official nomination occurs. Unless a political party has several candidates seeking the presidential nomination, the voters affiliated with that party have nothing on which to vote.

For many years, Florida's presidential preference primary was held on the second Tuesday in March of presidential election years. Beginning with the 2008 presidential election cycle, a number of states began moving up the date of their primaries (front-loading)—even defying national party calendar rules—to have more influence over the selection of the nominee. Florida was one. In 2008, the legislature moved the primary to the last Tuesday in January of a presidential election year. At the time, it created a lot of controversy. Democratic candidates Barack Obama and Hillary Clinton refused to campaign in the state. Both national parties threatened not to seat Florida delegates at their national conventions. But of course, as soon as it was clear who the parties' nominees would be, all was forgiven. Florida delegates even got premier seating locations on the convention floor—indicative of the crucial role the state plays in national elections.

The battle to go early (ahead of Iowa, New Hampshire, South Carolina, and Nevada) began anew in 2011. The Florida Legislature passed a law requiring a date selection committee to set the date of the 2012 presidential preference primary election no earlier than the first Tuesday in January and no later than the first Tuesday in March. It chose the January date—which was ahead of the date set by national party rules. Again, by going earlier than national party rules dictated, Florida's Republicans lost half their delegates to the national convention which, ironically, was held in Tampa!

In 2013, legislators from both parties agreed to end the eight-year battle with the national parties over the timing of the presidential primary. A bill was passed setting the 2016 presidential preference primary date to conform with national party rules. (The date set was March 15, 2016.) At the time, some speculated that the potential candidacy of several prominent Florida Republicans pushed the Republican-controlled legislature in that direction, while others pointed to a stiffer penalty from the national Republican Party that would have cost Florida Republicans all but a handful of delegates to the national convention (in Cleveland, Ohio).[20]

Resign-to-Run

The resign-to-run law prohibits an elected official holding one office from "qualifying as a candidate for *another* state, district, county or municipal public office if the terms or any part of the terms overlap with each other if the person did not resign from the office the person presently holds."[21] It creates an interesting dilemma for many officeholders considering a run for higher office. It requires all elected officials to announce a resignation date for their current post before filing to run for another office. It also prevents candidates from running for, or holding, more than one office at a time.[22]

Under the law, "a resignation must be submitted in writing at least 10 days prior to the first day of qualifying for the office the person intends to seek."[23] The actual resignation must occur either by the date the official would take office if elected or by the date the official's successor is required to take office—whichever date is earlier. Once an official submits a resignation, it cannot be revoked. Candidates whose campaigns appear to be going badly cannot change their minds and resume their previous posts. Confusing? You bet. Nearly every election cycle, some officeholder runs afoul of Florida's resign-to-run law. The law does not apply to state officials seeking federal office—thus, if a Florida governor was selected to be a vice presidential candidate, the governor would not have to resign his seat to be on the presidential ticket.

Voter Registration

Florida requires its eligible citizens to register at least 29 days prior to Election Day. Registration has always been available at the Supervisor of Elections offices in each county and at registration drives sponsored by these officials. The federal National Voter Registration Act (Motor-Voter Act) in 1993 mandated that registration must also be made available at driver's license offices, public assistance offices, veterans' offices, and libraries and by mail. Once registered, voters' names remain on election rolls; they cannot be purged from the rolls for failing to vote.

Every state but North Dakota requires voter registration. The registration process is designed to prevent voter fraud, including multiple voting, voting in other people's names, and phantom or "graveyard" voting. There have been several high profile cases of vote fraud in Florida including a Miami mayoral election in the 1990s that resulted in a court order overturning the election results due to rampant absentee ballot fraud. Another was in a South Florida congressional race (2012) in which a candidate's chief of staff went to jail for directing staffers to make almost 500 fraudulent online ballot requests. (Florida elections law prohibits anyone other than a voter or an immediate family member from submitting online ballot requests.[24])

Of course, registration imposes additional burdens on citizens in the exercise of their vote. They must figure out where and how to register, take the time to do so, and change registration each time they take up a new residency. All of these burdens come into play in Florida because many new people move to the state and many residents move within the state each year. But it is also the responsibility of the state's election officials to keep citizens informed about changes in voting-related procedures.

The most common reasons given by Floridians for not registering to vote are ineligibility (non-citizens, felons whose rights have not been restored), failure to move one's registration to current residence, lack of time, a belief that their votes will not matter, a feeling that there is no difference between the candidates running, a language barrier, lack of knowledge about the candidates or issues, or a dislike of politics.[25] (See Figure 4-4.) A few do not register because they believe it will cause them to be called for jury duty, although Florida has not used voter registration rolls to select its juror pools for many years. (It uses driver's license lists instead.) Sunshine State Survey data show that the percent citing "ineligibility" as a reason for not voting has declined the most, while the greatest increase has been in the percent pointing to their "failure to transfer their registration from another location."

Voter IDs

Voters in both primary and general elections must present valid identification (photograph and signature) at the polling precinct in which they are registered in order to cast a ballot, although voters who have lost their identification may sign an affidavit at the polling place and still vote.[26] A valid ID is one that is current, with a picture and a signature. Approved forms of *picture identification* include a Florida driver's license; Florida identification card issued by the Department of Highway Safety and Motor Vehicles; United States passport; debit or credit card; military identification; student identification; retirement center identification; neighborhood association identification; or public assistance identification.[27] If the picture ID does not contain the signature of the voter, some other form of identification that has the voter's signature on it must be provided. In many states, requirements to present voter identification cards at the polling location have been extremely controversial.[28] It is far less so in Florida because the state has long accepted a wide variety of forms of identification. It is important for voters to update their signatures on their voter registration because signatures change as one ages. And to be valid, a person's signature must match the signature on their voter registration record on file with the county elections supervisor.

Figure 4-4. Reasons Floridians Give for Not Registering to Vote

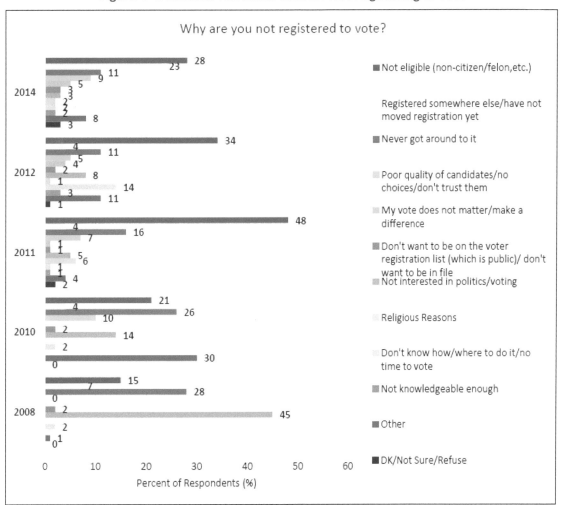

Source: "Leadership Florida Sunshine State Survey (2006-2008), Leadership Florida-Nielsen Company Sunshine State Survey (2010-2012), and University of South Florida-Nielsen Sunshine State Survey (2014)."

Voter Turnout

Voter turnout in Florida fluctuates considerably from one election to another, depending on the competitiveness of top-of-the-ticket contests (president; governor) and whether it is a presidential election year. (See Figure 4-5.) Turnout is higher in presidential election years than in non-presidential election years.

Figure 4-5. Turnout Rates in Florida Elections: 1954-2014

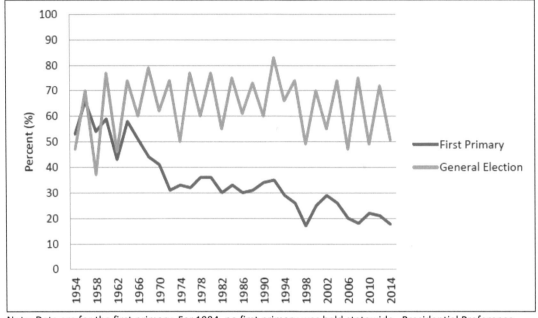

Note: Data are for the first primary. For 1984, no first primary was held statewide. Presidential Preference primary data was used instead.

Source: Florida Division of Elections turnout Data. Available at http://election.dos.state.fl.us/online/voterpercent.shtml.

There are two ways of measuring turnout rates. One calculates the number of persons who cast ballots as a percent of the voting age (18 and older) population (VAP). The other method computes the percentage of registered voters who actually voted. The second method yields a higher turnout rate and is used by the Florida Division of Elections. For example, in the 2012 presidential election only 56 percent of Florida's voting age population turned out but 72 percent of its *registered* voters cast a ballot.[29]

Why do so many Floridians who are registered fail to vote? For a lot of reasons, including cynicism, alienation, lack of interest, disgust with the candidate choices, or time pressures. For others, illness, an unexpected job conflict or trip out of town on Election Day, or the lack of transportation keep them from voting. The truth is that most non-voters cite their indifference to politics or their dislike of the candidates as their principal reason for staying home, not voting laws. Nonetheless, reformers are always in search of ways to improve turnout rates. Early voting (in-person) and "no fault" absentee voting are recommendations that the legislature has adopted. Today, more than half of all Floridians who vote do so *before* Election Day—either by casting absentee ballots or in-person early voting. (See Figure 4-6.) The reality is that Florida no longer has a single Election Day. Rather it has *multiple* Election Days.

Figure 4-6. Timing of Vote—Before or On Election Day

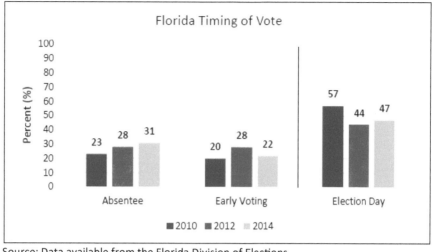

Source: Data available from the Florida Division of Elections.

Early Voting: In-Person or Absentee

Early voting, or "convenience" voting, was adopted by the legislature in the aftermath of the 2000 presidential election as a way to improve voter turnout. (Thirty-three states now have early voting laws.)[30] Polls show that Florida voters like the opportunity to vote early, particularly seniors, students, and persons who travel out of town frequently in their jobs.

The change in *when* Floridians vote has altered how candidates and parties plan their campaigns. Campaigns are now two-stage efforts. In the first stage, attention is focused on early voters. But once the early voting period ends (usually the weekend before the election), they aim their GOTV efforts at potential Election Day voters—the second stage. The pitches used are quite different. Early campaign ads are structured to appeal more to senior voters. Later ads are more likely to be pitched to women and younger voters who traditionally make up their minds last about whether to vote, and if so, for whom.

The result of more Floridians choosing to vote before Election Day has been to cost campaigns "millions of additional dollars as political parties are forced to start their mobilization efforts and buy ads earlier to get their supporters to the polls."[31] Some say it has also made campaigns more negative. Ironically, it has not been shown to increase turnout.

Each party makes special efforts to encourage pre-election participation by calling voters, sending reminder mailers, or helping with transportation (in the case of early voting). Of those who vote before Election Day, a higher percentage of Democrats tend to vote early in person, while a higher proportion of Republicans vote absentee. Although Democrats began intensifying their efforts to encourage more registered Democrats to vote absentee in the mid-2010s, the pattern has prevailed. Independents are the least likely to vote early perhaps because they do not receive as many of these prompts or reminders.

Both the Democrat and Republican parties have encouraged their supporters to vote early. It is a form of "convenience" voting.

FLORIDA'S ELECTION SYSTEM: REFORMS ARE THE NORM

No state's election system has been in the national spotlight more than Florida's—beginning with the 2000 presidential election. In fact, Florida (or "Florid-duh") is still remembered for its election system meltdown in 2000, even after a decade of election reforms.

For days on end after the 2000 presidential election, Florida's voters, poll workers, and election officials were skewered by the national and international media and caricatured as "buffoons."[32] News of confusing ballot formats designed by local elections supervisors, inept and inappropriate actions by poll workers, and voters "spoiling" their ballots, thereby rendering them uncountable, caused a national uproar and got nearly as much attention as the partisan activities of key state officials.[33]

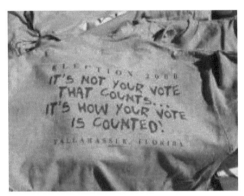

Controversies over how to recount ballots cast in the 2000 election prompted Florida to revise its election laws after a loud outcry for reform from the citizens.

Inside the state, loud, angry voices demanded a major overhaul of the election system. In addition to demands for new voting equipment, uniformity in ballot design, standardization of recount rules, and a rule prohibiting Cabinet officials from campaigning for others, there was considerable pressure for more voter education and better training for election officials and poll workers.[34] State officials responded by enacting reforms in the 2001 and 2002 legislative sessions—prior to passage of the federal Help America Vote Act (HAVA). In virtually every legislative session since, there have been changes in some dimension of Florida's election system. (For a summary of major changes enacted between 2000 and 2010, see Table 4-5.) *Florida has clearly shown the nation that election reform is an ongoing task—and seldom without controversy.*

The Most Commonly Debated Election Practices

Florida's election officials have come to expect challenges every election cycle. They are routinely cross-pressured to provide greater voter access while protecting the integrity of the voting process by preventing fraud. It is a difficult balancing act. At the same time, they may face budget challenges that can impede their ability to purchase new technologies, especially during economic downturns. The chair of the national Elections Assistance Commission (EAC) puts it this way: Neither other elected officials nor voters "think much about the resources necessary to running elections, unless something goes wrong. [Yet] there is zero tolerance for error in elections, so elections officials are constantly challenged with maintaining perfection on tighter and shrinking budgets."[35] (In Florida, each county elections supervisor's budget must be approved by the Board of County Commissioners.)

Florida no longer has punch card ballots.

Election officials and voting rights advocates tend to agree that certain election system practices are the most subject to change in response to either citizen demands or the availability of new technology. Consequently, they are also the most likely to generate controversy. Among these are the following:

- **Registration.** Debates are ongoing over how and when to register, when and where a person can change his/her party affiliation, and who can engage in registering voters. The fight is between those who want to make voting as open and easy as possible and those who want to maintain the integrity of the voting process (prevent fraud). Currently Floridians can register in person at a number of different types of locations or they can go online and print out an application—but it must be mailed in or hand delivered to a county Supervisor of Elections office. In 2017, voters will be able to submit a voter registration application online.

- **Online Registration.** After a long battle, in 2015, online registration was approved by the legislature and signed by the governor—but it will not be available until October 2017. There was considerable debate on whether to allow online registration, although over two dozen states already permit it. Those opposed to it were concerned about potential cyber-attacks in an era of increased identification theft. Proponents favored it for two major reasons—to boost voter registration and save money because election office employees would not have to enter the information into a data base by hand. The details of how to design the system have yet to be finalized and are sure to generate debate.

- **The Voter Registration Roll.** Keeping the state voter registration roll (Florida Voter Registration System-FVRS) current and free of ineligible or deceased voters is extremely difficult. Yet the integrity of the voting process is at stake. In the past, the state aggressively sought to remove non-citizens from voter rolls—a process known as purging—by using driver's license data. But there was a backlash against the process by elections supervisors who asserted that the lists of non-citizens provided to them by the state were inaccurate and unreliable. Voting rights groups also harshly criticized the purge, saying it disproportionately targeted minority voters. The state backed off the practice in 2014.[36] But criticism of the accuracy of the voter registration is ongoing. In every election cycle, ineligible voters are detected, including persons registered in two states.

- **Absentee Ballots.** Florida is a state in which any registered voter can request an absentee ballot without having to give a reason. Historically, election officials and citizens alike have identified <u>absentee balloting</u> as the most vulnerable to fraud both in requesting and completing ballots. Because nearly every election cycle brings arrests for such illegalities, legislation designed to deter fraud is often proposed. Such was the case in 2013 when a law was passed that requires a voter who requests that an absentee ballot be mailed to an address other than the address for that person on file in the county elections office where one is registered, has to make the request in writing. (In the past, a request could be made online or by phone.) The new law continues to generate opposition because of its perceived disproportionately negative impact on college students. (Active duty military personnel were exempted.) Other debates are over: (1) how best to reduce the number of absentee ballots not counted because of a missing signature, (2) how to improve the return rate, and (3) the handling of "in-person absentee" ballots (a person can request an absentee ballot, then fill it out at a Supervisor of Elections office) —a practice that contributed to excessively long lines in the 2012 presidential election.[37]

  Other controversies regarding absentee balloting are more likely to stem from voter protection activists' belief that voters who cast absentee ballots do not have the same opportunity to correct an error as those voting in person. They suspect some sort of bias in the disqualification of voters by county canvassing boards making judgments on voter intent.

- **Early In-Person Voting.** Controversies surrounding early in-person voting center on the number and location of polling places, as well as the days and hours of operation. This battle is often viewed through partisan lenses—each party accusing the other of trying to get an advantage. Democrats accuse Republicans of trying to suppress minority votes. Republicans charge Democrats with labeling every change in election law as racial discrimination. For example, a 2011 law that cut early voting days back from 14 to 8 (but allowed the polls to stay open longer each day) generated considerable high profile criticism from voting rights groups for being discriminatory and for causing exceedingly long lines.

In 2013, the legislature responded by expanding early voting to a minimum of 64 hours over eight days and a maximum of 68 hours over 14 days. It also allows each county elections supervisor to determine whether to conduct early voting the Sunday before Election Day (known as "souls to the polls" day within the black church community). Supervisors are also given more options on where early voting may take place—elections offices, city halls, and libraries plus fairgrounds, civic centers, courthouses, county commission buildings, stadiums, convention centers, government owned senior centers and community centers.

The lack of uniformity of days and voting hours across all 67 counties remains a point of debate. Some see that policy as in violation of state law mandating uniformity in the state's election system. But for others, a one-size-fits-all approach does not work in a state with some sparsely populated rural counties with limited budgets.

- **Average wait time in line to vote.** Long lines to vote—either early or on Election Day—can signal greater-than-expected turnout. But they can also signal poor decisions about the location and staffing (poll workers) of polling places, inefficient check-in procedures, long ballots, or outdated and malfunctioning voting equipment, including scanners. Long wait times can also be cast as discriminatory if they occur more often in minority neighborhoods. Florida garnered unwanted attention in 2012 when it had *the* longest wait (45 minutes) of any state and the largest increase in wait time (up 16.1 minutes from 2008).[38] The most egregiously long times were in precincts with more black and Latino voters (Miami-Dade, Orange, Hillsborough, Broward counties) where there were fewer poll workers and machines per registered voter.[39] Once again, Florida was at the epicenter of negative national news coverage of its elections, and again, the legislature responded with extensive election reforms in its 2013 session. Wait times were considerably shorter in 2014. But debates over poll worker assignment and training, proposed changes in polling locations, certification of new voting equipment and software, and responsibility for funding new technology (state vs. local), among others, will continue to take place.

- **Disabled Voters and Touch Screen Voting Machines.** In 2013, the legislature passed a law extending the deadline from 2016[40] to 2020 that mandates that voters with disabilities have the option to vote on an accessible device that marks a paper (optical scan) ballot rather than on an electronic touch screen voting machine. (Touch screens for non-disabled voters were outlawed in 2008.) Some counties already have the mark-sense equipment, while others do not due to fiscal constraints. The delay and the lack of uniformity across all 67 counties have angered some disabled voter advocacy groups, such as the Florida Rehabilitation Council for the Blind.

- **Felons Waiting to Have Their Voting Rights Restored.** Florida is one of four states that does not automatically restore felon voting rights once they have met the terms of their sentences. Here, felons who have paid restitution and who have not been convicted of a certain class of offenses may have their civil rights restored by petitioning the state's Board of Executive Clemency (made up of the governor and cabinet). Once the board has restored a person's rights, the individual can register to vote. The Florida Parole Commission's website enables felons to determine whether or not their rights have been restored. For years, the clemency board had a huge backlog of requests for reinstatement of rights. Lawsuits and threats from groups like the ACLU asserted that the law disproportionately impacts African Americans because a higher percentage have been convicted of felonies.

In 2007, in response to complaints from civil rights groups, the Office of Executive Clemency (at the urging of Governor Crist) voted to amend the state's voting rights restoration procedure to automatically approve the reinstatement of rights for many persons who were convicted of nonviolent offenses. This decision was reversed by Governor Scott and the new Republican Cabinet in 2011. Persons seeking rights restoration must now wait at least five years after completion of sentence.[41] Felons' rights advocacy groups, including the NAACP, ACLU, and Florida League of Women Voters, vehemently objected. In 2014, these groups and Floridians for a Fair Democracy began collecting petition signatures to place a proposed constitutional amendment on the ballot in 2016 calling for the automatic restoration of a felon's civil rights upon completion of their sentencing. Such a proposal, if approved by 60 percent of the voters, would make it easier for ex-felons to get back their right to vote.

- **Provisional Ballot Invalidation.** Provisional ballots are given to voters who come to the polls without proper identification or whose eligibility is in question because their name does not appear on the voter registration roll for that precinct. Many people are under the false impression that provisional ballots (like absentee ballots) are counted only where there is a close race. (Both are myths.[42]) But a provisional ballot is always counted when the voter is shown to be registered and eligible. The ballot does, however, have to be cast at the precinct in which the voter is registered; otherwise it will not be counted. One study of provisional ballots in Palm Beach County found that the most common reason for rejecting a provisional ballot was that the voter was simply not registered.[43] Casting a provisional ballot at the incorrect precinct was the second most common reason. This practice, again designed to prevent fraud—persons casting ballots at multiple polling places—is highly debated on who is responsible. Is it the voter for not properly changing his/her address or paying attention to precinct location information sent by the county elections supervisor? Or is it the county elections office for changing precinct numbers or location? Regardless of which, provisional ballot policies and procedures evoke lots of discussion every election cycle.

Table 4-5. A Decade of Changes to Florida's Election System: 2000-2010

More Uniformity	Ensure uniformity across all counties with regard to recount procedures, determination of voter intent, ballot design (type size, placement, etc.), poll worker training, logic and accuracy testing of equipment, post-election audits, and the distribution and counting of absentee ballots for overseas and military voters.
New Voting Equipment	The state now uses optical scan systems, which replaced touch screens, and before that, punch cards. Paper-based optical scan systems with precinct tabulation permit more accurate recounts and determination of intent should such a question arise. If used at a polling site, optical scan systems can inform a voter if he/she has under-voted and will not count an over-voted race. Replacements are made available should either situation arise.
Ballot-Testing	There is also now a ballot-testing law requiring supervisors to fill in the ovals to test ballots that will be used by voters to ensure that the ballots can be read by the voting equipment.
Early (Convenience) Voting	Early voting can be done either through absentee ballot or in person at selected locations. This system is widely popular among voters and county election supervisors. Changes in absentee voting rules mean that (1) voters no longer have to give a reason for voting absentee, (2) they may ask to be put on a list of voters to whom absentee ballots are automatically mailed every election, (3) they no longer must have a witness sign their return envelope; (4) they are offered clear instructions reminding them to sign the outside of the return envelope containing their absentee ballot. Early voting gives the voter more choice about the day and time he/she votes and reduces long lines on Election Day that might deter a voter from casting a ballot. And if there are problems at the polling place, the voter still has other times he/she can vote.
More Efficient Voter Education	County elections supervisors are now required to prepare and use a voter guide and make it available on his or her website and at a variety of locations and events. Each website must include detailed voter and voting information such as a sample ballot and notice of any change in polling place location. Supervisors are required to conduct voter registration, education, and training programs, such as voter registration/education programs in each public high school and college campus in the county
Centralized Voter Registration System	(Florida Voter Registration System-FVRS) The federal Help America Vote Act required all states to create an official, uniform, and nondiscriminatory statewide computerized voter registration list by January 2006. The FVRS allows local election officials to enter information and have access to the list, but the program is under the authority and responsibility of the Secretary of State. This centralized list has helped to eliminate duplicate registrations.
Better Protection Against Disenfranchisement at the Polls	The Voter's Bill of Rights and Responsibilities must be posted at each polling place and at the county supervisor's office during the early voting period and on Election Day. Voters who cast provisional ballots at a polling place must receive a written notice of their rights that includes information about how to certify their eligibility and informing them of their right to find out if their ballot was counted and, if not, the reason why. To make sure that poll workers properly implement election procedures and laws, a Polling Place Procedures Manual must be made available.
Protecting the Voting Rights of Military and Overseas Civilians	Passage of the federal Military and Overseas Voter Empowerment (MOVE) Act in 2010 requires that absentee ballots for all elections be sent at least 45 days before an election to all military and overseas voters through an e-mail transmission, which can be returned by the voter by mail or by fax, not via e-mail. County election supervisors can communicate directly with these voters via e-mail, which is faster and more efficient than regular mail. The Act also requires that these voters be able to track the status of their ballot, from request, to receipt, to return.
Checking Voter Ineligibility	In 2005, Florida Department of State established a new Bureau of Voter Registration Services that is charged with conducting research to determine a person's potential ineligibility on the basis of a court order of mental incapacity or a felony conviction. In 2009, the Bureau began checking the legal status of thousands of alleged felons to determine their removal from the voter registration rolls. Procedures are in place to notify felons, give them a hearing if requested, and inform them of how to request restoration of their voting rights.

Source: Susan A. MacManus, Florida 10 Years After the 2000 Election. Available at http://www.sayfiereview.com/featured_column?column_id=34.

Voters Grade the Election Process

Beginning with the first Sunshine State Survey, respondents have been asked to judge how good a job the state is doing in three election-related areas. The state consistently gets its highest marks for "making it convenient to vote" (Figure 4-7), with more than two-thirds giving the state a positive rating ("excellent" or "good").

Figure 4-7. Voters Rate State on How Good a Job it Does Making It Convenient to Vote

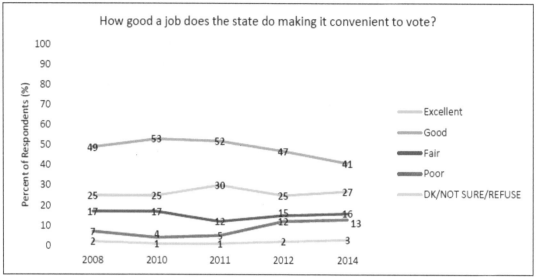

Source: "Leadership Florida Sunshine State Survey (2006-2008), Leadership Florida-Nielsen Company Sunshine State Survey (2010-2012), and University of South Florida-Nielsen Sunshine State Survey (2014)."

Voters are more mixed in their opinions about the state's performance in "providing election equipment that is highly dependable." (See Figure 4-8.) The lower rating for election equipment dependability is partially a product of lingering memories of problems caused by punch card ballots and electronic voting machines in the early 2000s. But it may also be a product of "obligatory" Election Day TV news coverage of equipment breakdowns (and there are always a few)—jammed scanners, malfunctioning electronic poll books, or laptop memory card failures.

The weakest ratings are for the job the state does in informing citizens about election laws and procedures (Figure 4-9). This is not surprising in light of the constant stream of election reforms, the frequent relocations of precinct locations, and the wide variation in voter outreach techniques used by the state's 67 county election supervisors—which can range from simple voter forums, informational brochures, and websites to more sophisticated online interactive educational programs, how-to YouTube videos, and popular forms of social media. Younger voters are the most likely to say they do not get enough information about election laws and voting processes.

Figure 4-8. Voters Rate the Job the State Does Providing Highly Dependable
Election Equipment

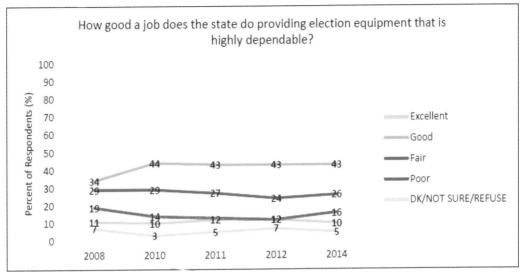

Source: "Leadership Florida Sunshine State Survey (2006-2008), Leadership Florida-Nielsen Company Sunshine State
Survey (2010-2012), and University of South Florida-Nielsen Sunshine State Survey (2014)."

Figure 4-9. Voters Rate State on How Good a Job it Does Informing Citizens About
Election Laws and Procedures

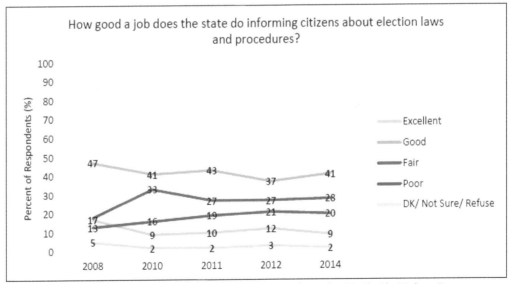

Source: "Leadership Florida Sunshine State Survey (2006-2008), Leadership Florida-Nielsen Company Sunshine State Survey (2010-2012), and University of South Florida-Nielsen Sunshine State Survey (2014)."

A Big Wish for Future Elections

At the end of the day, election officials and voters alike want no repeat of the 2000 election… ever! In the words of one election supervisor who lived through those stressful days: *"Please, no recount… They always get ugly."* The most worrisome races are always the highly visible contests appearing at the top of the ballot.

PRESIDENTIAL ELECTIONS IN FLORIDA

Presidential elections in Florida in 2000, 2004, and 2008 were among the most competitive in the nation. The 2012 presidential race was *the* closest of any state—just 0.9 percent separated Barack Obama (D) and Mitt Romney (R).   In each election, the Sunshine State was labeled a "key battleground state" by national-level analysts. All four were classic nail-biters—close right down to the wire. Nowhere was the vote more split than in the central part of the state—the Orlando and Tampa media markets located on the bellwether I-4 Corridor. (See Table 4-6.) Each election had frequent visits by the candidates, millions of dollars spent on television ads, and plenty of controversy.

Table 4-6. Presidential Elections in Florida: Close!

Presidential Election Results by Florida Media Market, 2000-2012								
Media Market	2000		2004		2008		2012	
	DEM	REP	DEM	REP	DEM	REP	DEM	REP
Florida	49	49	47	52	51	48	50	49
North								
Pensacola	30	68	27	72	33	66	31	69
Panama City	35	63	30	69	29	70	28	72
Tallahassee	55	43	56	43	55	44	55	45
Jacksonville	38	60	37	63	42	58	40	60
Gainesville	52	43	51	48	54	45	53	47
Central (I-4 Corridor)								
Orlando/Daytona Beach	47	51	45	54	51	49	50	50
Tampa/St. Petersburg	47	50	45	54	50	49	49	51
South								
Naples/Fort Meyers	39	59	38	61	43	56	40	60
Palm Beach/Fort Pierce	57	40	56	44	57	42	54	46
Miami/Fort Lauderdale	59	39	58	41	62	38	64	36

Source: Compiled by the authors from data from the Florida Division of Elections.

The 2000 Presidential Election in Florida

The 2000 presidential race was one of the closest in American history. The outcome hinged on who would win Florida's 25 electoral votes (to be 27 in 2002). In the end, Bush won the state and the presidency, but not before a heated legal battle that lasted more than a month and not before the whole nation called into question Florida's ability to competently conduct an election.[44] Media mistakes contributed greatly to the confusion: The major networks declared Gore the winner early in the evening, rescinded the call, declared George W. Bush the winner, and then finally declared the election "too close to call" when Bush's lead shrank to 1,784 votes out of 6 million cast.[45]

It quickly became clear that many ballots cast in Florida were not properly marked. There were *over-votes* (people voting for more than one presidential candidate) and *under-votes* (people did not vote in the presidential race at all). Odd ballot designs and the unreliable punch card system contributed to the balloting problems that caused some votes to be invalidated. Both Gore (D) and Bush (R) sent teams of lawyers and political operatives to Florida. The Gore strategy focused on getting ballots recounted as fast as possible in four heavily Democratic counties by enlisting support from local Democratic officials in the legal process (and in the media), and getting the Democratic-leaning Florida Supreme Court to make a ruling mandating the recount. The Bush team's strategy revolved around slowing down the process, stopping the recount, enlisting support from Republican state officials, and getting the case to the Republican-leaning U.S. Supreme Court. Meanwhile, both teams were well aware of the federal law that set December 12 as the deadline for selecting presidential electors from each state (including Florida).

The Recount and Legal Battle

A mandatory mechanical recount and a partial hand recount in the four counties focused on by the Gore campaign (only one county finished by the state deadline) completed one week after the election cut Bush's lead to just 327 votes. A few days later, the tabulation of absentee ballots from military and overseas voters pushed the lead up to 930 votes. Democrats sued to get more time to complete the manual recounts, and the Florida Supreme Court unanimously agreed to extend the deadline and ruled that Secretary of State Katherine Harris had to accept revised manually recounted vote tallies until then.[46] Canvassing boards in each of the three counties used different standards in recounting the punch card ballots, and Palm Beach failed to finish its recount by the deadline. On November 27, Katherine Harris officially certified the vote, without including the partial recount results from Palm Beach, and declared George W. Bush the winner by 537 votes. However, on December 8th the Florida Supreme Court reinstated all votes turned down by Katherine Harris, bringing Bush's lead down to a mere 154 votes, and ordered a manual recount of under-votes in all Florida counties with voter intent to be decided at the local level. But the next day the U.S. Supreme Court halted the recount while it heard the case[47] and finally on December 11th officially ended the recount, clearing the way for Bush to win Florida's 25 electoral votes and the presidency.[48] By a 7-2 vote, the U.S. Supreme Court found the Florida Supreme Court's decision ordering recounts unconstitutional because it did not establish a statewide (uniform) standard by which to recount votes and thus violated the Fourteenth Amendment to the U.S. Constitution, which guarantees to citizens equal protection under the law. By a 5-4 vote, the Supreme Court ruled that state legislatures, not the courts, should decide the process for selecting presidential electors.

Who Really Won?

Two different groups of media consortiums conducted extensive analyses of some 175,000 ballots in Florida that did not have a *legal* vote cast for president. They asked the question: "Who really won Florida?"[49] The overall conclusion of both groups was that the standard employed for determining voter intent on under-votes directly impacted who won. Ironically, one group found that if the under-votes had been tallied using the looser standards suggested by Al Gore, then Bush would have tripled his winning vote margin to 1,665 votes. If the votes were counted using the stricter standard advocated by Bush, then Gore would have won Florida by exactly three votes out of more than 6 million cast! The other group found that Bush would have won in four scenarios and Gore in five. Both groups agreed that if voter intent could be pulled from ballots containing more than one vote for president—*over-votes*—then Gore would have won the race because far more over-voted ballots included a vote for Gore. However, over-votes were always clearly invalid under any interpretation of the law. The bottom line was that officially George W. Bush defeated Al Gore by a mere 537 votes in Florida, and Floridians became the object of many jokes about their counting skills.

The 2004 Presidential Election: Security

All eyes were on Florida in 2004, especially after the 537-vote 2000 election.[50] Democrats hoped to capitalize on lingering and festering anger stemming from Al Gore's narrow loss in 2000 to turn out their supporters. Republicans expected Governor Jeb Bush's popularity and his knowledge of how to win Florida (he won re-election in 2002 by a 13 percent margin) to be real assets in mobilizing voters sympathetic to his brother's presidential re-election campaign. Both Senator John Kerry (D) and President George W. Bush (R) visited Florida multiple times over the course of the campaign, as did their vice presidential running mates and their spouses.[51] Each presidential campaign spent more than $40 million on television commercials alone between March and November. When the polls closed at 7 P.M. on November 2, nearly everyone expected a repeat of 2000—an election so close a recount would be needed. It did not happen. Bush easily won the state by a five percent margin over Kerry (52 percent to 47 percent). The intense GOTV efforts of both parties pushed the turnout rate up—from 70 percent in 2000 to 74 percent in 2004.

The president carried 56 of 67 counties and increased his share of the vote over the 2000 results by at least five percent in 51 counties. In contrast, in only six counties did Kerry's share exceed Gore's in 2000 by at least five percent. In a repeat of the 2002 gubernatorial election, Republicans bested Democrats at the turnout game. The GOP's 72-hour plan of action primarily staffed by volunteers was more effective at turning out Republicans than the Democratic Victory 2004 coordinated campaign that relied more heavily on paid activists to get Democrats to the polls.

Nationally, "moral values" was the most important reason affecting voters' choice for president. But in Florida, it was terrorism, 24 percent compared to 20 percent for moral issues. From the start, the Kerry campaign (and the Betty Castor U.S. Senate campaign) understood that, to carry Florida, Democrats would have to change the subject from terrorism and homeland security to domestic issues. It was just beginning to work when the national news coverage reverted to terrorism-related stories because of the release of an Osama Bin Laden tape.

The state did have its share of lawsuits related to the election system. Lawsuits were filed challenging everything from the lack of paper trails for touch screen voting machines to the constitutionality of state laws requiring provisional ballots to be cast in the precinct in which a voter is registered for it to be counted. Fortunately for Florida, most of the major lawsuits were resolved in the state's favor prior to the election. The early resolution of legal challenges and the state's two-week period for early voting greatly minimized the projected Election Day chaos. The lack of election night drama sent scores of national and international reporters scurrying from Florida to Ohio.

In the closing days of presidential campaigns, it is common for the candidates to hold rallies in cities along the I-4 Corridor, long considered Florida's major political battleground. On the weekend prior to the 2004 presidential election, both Republican George W. Bush and Democrat John F. Kerry held rallies on the same day in Tampa.

The 2008 Presidential Election: An Amazing Race; Florida Turns Blue[52]

The incredibly exciting, highly engaging, suspenseful 2008 presidential election had all the elements—and more—of a top-rated reality show. It was the year when conventional wisdom often got turned on its head. There was no better place to watch the drama unfold than in the Sunshine State. When the race was over, Democrat Barack Obama had narrowly won Florida (51 percent vs. 48 percent for McCain). The state turned blue, and the nation had its first African-American president. The state's longstanding bellwether status remained intact: "As Florida goes, so goes the nation."

The race began in 2007 with a larger-than-usual field of candidates (8 Democrats, 11 Republicans) expressing interest in being president. No incumbent was in the race (although McCain was cast in that light by the Democratic contenders), nor was any vice president throwing a hat into the ring. Early polls showed Democrat Hillary Clinton and Republican Rudolph (Rudi) Giuliani as the likely winners in their respective presidential preference primaries in Florida. Only half of that prediction turned out to be true. Hillary won big, but a last-minute endorsement of John McCain by Governor Charlie Crist produced an upset and virtually ended Giuliani's campaign.

It was the *timing* of Florida's primary that created an uproar. Florida (and Michigan) dared to buck party rules and scheduled their presidential primary elections in advance of Super Tuesday (February 5th). Both states argued they were more diverse and representative of the nation's electorate than Iowa or New Hampshire. This raw and unscripted drama yielded months on end of highly contentious debates, particularly among Democrats, about whether Florida and Michigan delegates would be seated at the national conventions and the consequences if not. The national Democratic Party had to convene an unprecedented two-day nationally televised hearing by its Rules and Bylaws Committee in late May to attempt to untangle what had become a giant mess. The issue of the seating of the Florida delegates was at the center of the controversy.[53] When the state had held its primary earlier than national party rules had called for, the national party had suggested Florida Democrats conduct caucuses (in effect, a re-vote) so that their delegates could be seated at the national convention. They refused. The chair of the Florida Democratic Party cited the unfairness of caucuses, which disproportionately tamp down the participation rates of elderly, disabled, shift workers, and active-duty military stationed outside their communities. Actually, the delegate seating issue was not fully resolved until the day before the convention in Denver, when it was announced that all Florida delegates would be seated and have full voting rights.

Many have speculated that Florida's defiant stance against party rules regarding the timing of the primary may ultimately have cost Hillary Clinton the Democratic nomination.[54] She easily won the Florida primary over Obama (Clinton 49.7 percent, Obama 33.0 percent).[55] Had the Florida Legislature voted to hold the state's primary on February 5th instead of January 29[56], the results would likely have been the same. Hillary would have won the support of Florida's delegates to the national party convention. She would have exited from Super Tuesday (February 5th) with her front-runner status secure, having carried three of the nation's four largest states (California, New York, Florida) and a passel of others. It would have made it considerably more difficult for Obama to win in states holding their primaries or caucuses after Super Tuesday. But, of course, that did not happen because Florida did hold its primary in January.

The race between Obama and McCain remained close in the Sunshine State, with the lead in the polls changing periodically, particularly when the dominant issue changed. Initially, the central issue was the *War in Iraq*. Nearly everyone assumed that it would dominate all the way to Election Day. That prognostication, like so many others, turned out to be way off the mark. When *gas prices* hit $4.00+ a gallon, the war took a backseat to energy costs. McCain and Sarah Palin, his running mate from oil-rich Alaska, were much better positioned on that issue than the war. Their "Drill Here, Drill Now" message resonated with an irate public whose attitudes on offshore oil drilling had changed virtually overnight. The race narrowed. McCain even took a brief lead. Then *the economy* took a nosedive and suddenly there was no other issue: "[The] meltdown on Wall Street brought the economy roaring back... and the question for the final seven weeks of the general-election campaign [was] whether Barack Obama or John McCain [could] convince voters that he is capable of leading the country out of the morass."[57] It was a ready-made issue for Democrat Obama and a nightmare for Republican McCain who had to live with an ill-timed comment made at a Jacksonville, Florida, rally right after the meltdown. After acknowledging that the economy was a serious problem, he said he still thought "the fundamentals of our economy are strong." The Obama campaign made hay of the issue, even running powerful ads using McCain's own words against him. McCain rebounded by strengthening his strong anti-tax message using "Joe the Plumber" to put a real face on the issue. Many pundits said the election was really lost when the economy became the issue rather than energy costs, national security, or terrorism.

As the campaign unfolded, competition intensified, and candidate visits escalated, the crowds at rallies, town hall meetings, and debates swelled. Who would have thought that so many Americans would have stood in lines for hours to see a candidate in person? Record-level crowds were the norm, rather than the exception. Most recognized they were watching history in the making, especially in the case of Obama, Clinton, and Palin, and they wanted to say, "I was there." For others, it was an opportunity to take a firsthand look at the candidate, rather than rely on secondhand accounts from media that some found biased. And many created their own "media" coverage, by posting personal photographs and accounts of the events on social networking sites and/or blogs.[58] For others not lucky enough to be there in person, they could still see these momentous events firsthand via online streaming or YouTube.

In the end, Obama was able to tremendously outspend McCain and, with a barrage of ads, introduce himself to Florida voters, reassure them that he was not a traditional liberal but, rather, a centrist with common sense solutions to the economy and health care, and make the case that a vote for McCain was a vote to continue the failed policies of unpopular President George W. Bush. In addition, his huge money advantage allowed him to out-organize McCain in the state, mobilize huge numbers of younger voters and minorities and get them to the polls, and have direct voter contact with large numbers of independent voters who swung heavily for Obama. The 2008 presidential campaign underscored the importance of candidate visits to Florida. Winning campaigns start and end in the "purple" state.

Presidential Election 2008 saw Florida in the national spotlight again. It is one of the nation's key battleground states. As Florida goes, so goes the nation.

The 2012 Presidential Election: Florida's Race Closest in the Nation

Heading into the 2012 election, everyone knew Florida would be close... and it was. For months on end, most horse race polls (partisan and nonpartisan) pitting Barack Obama against Mitt Romney were within the margin of error—virtually tied. And that is the way the race ended—with Obama winning Florida by less than one percent (50 percent vs. 49.1 percent for Romney). Just 74,309 votes out of the more than 8 million cast separated the two front-runners.

From beginning to end, Florida was seen as one of the nation's premier battleground states—a bigger prize than any other swing state with its 29 Electoral College votes (two more than in 2008). The state's sheer size, demographic diversity, and partisan competitiveness ensured that the state would yet again be in the national spotlight. With early prognostications of another nail-biter election, each major political party began positioning itself for contesting or defending the election results should a repeat recount be in the cards. Thankfully, that did not happen—although it took four days before the vote count was completed. The razor-thin margin "narrowly avoided an automatic recount that would have brought back memories of 2000."[59] (An automatic computer recount is triggered if the vote margin is a 0.5 percent or less.)

The campaign was intense. Prior to Election Day, Florida was home to four televised GOP primary debates, one nationally televised presidential debate (the last of three), and 40 visits from presidential and vice presidential candidates. More money was spent on TV ads in Florida's 10 media markets than in any other state, and both parties engaged in highly targeted GOTV mobilization efforts. At the outset, analysts agreed that without a win in Florida, Romney had little chance of capturing the presidency, while a victory by President Obama would virtually guarantee his re-election.

There was never any doubt that the economy would be the top concern of Florida voters, regardless of party affiliation. After all, the state's unemployment and home foreclosure rates were higher than the national average and the median family income of Floridians had dropped at a sharper rate than in many other states. Republicans assumed that "economic voters" would be highly critical of President Obama's handling of the economy and lean heavily toward Romney, while Democrats bet that lower- and middle-class voters would be drawn back to Obama by his proposals to tax the wealthy at higher rates. Exit polls showed that among those saying the economy was their chief concern (62 percent), Romney won (53 percent to 46 percent), but he gained only a majority of those identifying taxes as their premier economic concern. Obama won among voters pointing to the housing market, unemployment, and rising prices as their chief concern—a real shocker to the Romney campaign.

Nowhere was the highly sophisticated micro-targeting of key constituencies more evident than in the Sunshine State with its racial/ethnic, age, gender, and geographical diversity. The targeting of Hispanic voters was a central part of both parties' outreach. Each focused considerable attention on the burgeoning Puerto Rican community in the Orange and Osceola county areas. In fact, President Obama's first post-Democratic National Convention stop in Florida was a rally at the Kissimmee Civic Center in Osceola County. Democrats counted on the anti-immigration stances of Republicans to help them win the Puerto Rican vote. Republicans were hopeful that they could make inroads by emphasizing higher-than-average unemployment rates among minorities because polls showed that Hispanics, like other Floridians, consistently ranked the economy as their top issue of concern.

Turnout rates and cohesion among Hispanic voters were higher than anticipated. Hispanics increased their share of the electorate from 14 percent in 2008 to 17 percent in 2012; 60 percent voted for Obama—up 3 percent from 2008. The unexpectedly large vote for Obama was driven by a higher-than-expected vote for him among Cubans. Generational replacement has made the Cuban vote less solidly Republican. Younger Cubans born in the United States are more interested in domestic than foreign policy and lean more Democratic than their parents or grandparents. Spanish language media (Univision, Telemundo) also played a big part in promoting cohesiveness among Hispanics in order to increase the political clout of Hispanics overall. Spanish language TV and radio stations constantly pushed Hispanics to register and vote and downplayed country-of-origin differences.

Initially, the major worry within the Obama campaign regarding black voters was a lower level of enthusiasm for the president than in 2008 when he made history by breaking the racial barrier. Specifically, there was some concern that enthusiasm for the president had fallen among African Americans because of the president's stance on gay marriage. But when voter suppression claims surrounding changes in the election laws that limited early voting became a rallying cry, blacks responded. Exit polls showed that blacks as a share of all Florida voters were at the same level as in 2008 (13 percent) and solidly behind Obama (95 percent), with just a one percent slippage from 2008.

Both parties engaged in sophisticated age-based targeting of younger voters. While many outside Florida still assumed that the state's senior voters were the dominant cohort, a pre-election analysis of registered voters showed that 52 percent of Florida's voters were 50 years of age or older, but 48 percent were under that age, with the largest cohort being 30- to 49-year-olds. Republicans believed they could erode Obama's 2008 margin of victory among young voters by focusing on high unemployment rates and the rapidly growing national debt and arguing that each had disproportionately landed on their shoulders. Democrats knew full well that the younger cohort (18 to 29) was the most solidly Democratic (and liberal) in its vote patterns and more pro-government than their elders. They fully understood that Obama's biggest challenge was getting younger voters to turn out, particularly young women and persons of color. Post-election results showed Democrats had a much better plan for targeting young voters, often described as "low propensity" voters.

The Obama campaign was effective in GOTV efforts aimed at traditional late deciders—mostly young and female voters—primarily by relying on embedded staff and a superior data base that constantly informed the campaign about who had not yet voted but had pledged to do so. (In Florida, exit polls showed that three percent of the voters made up their minds about voting on Election Day; another five percent did so just a few days ahead.) President Clinton's visits to college campuses, along with those by Obama in South Florida, and First Lady Michelle Obama in Tallahassee, Orlando, Jacksonville, Gainesville, and Davie also helped mobilize younger voters in the closing days of the election. They stressed Obama's college loan policies and his health care plan that allowed younger voters to remain on their parents' health insurance policies. Younger women were also pushed to vote by contraception and reproductive rights issues. Many post-election analyses labeled the turnout and cohesion of younger voters as the election's biggest surprise. No one had projected that the youth vote as a proportion of the electorate would increase in 2012, but it did (from 15 percent in 2008 to 16 percent in 2012).The youth vote was solidly for Obama; two-thirds of those younger than 30 cast their ballots for him. The 2012 election left many concluding that the 18- to 29-year-old cohort had become the state's most consistently solid Democratic voting bloc (by age), whereas in the past it had been the senior vote.

More fluctuation occurred in gender support patterns throughout the campaign in Florida than nationally. Several times in the course of the campaign, the divide among women voters was considerably narrower here, giving hope to the Romney campaign. (It is often said that if the women's vote in Florida is split, Republicans will win the state.) Some analysts attributed the fluctuation to suburban women—who voted for Obama in 2008 but for Republicans in 2010, largely over economic issues. Democrats were optimistic that these women could be drawn back to Obama by reproductive rights issues and health care for themselves and their children. Democrats worried about turnout among younger minority women—a larger portion of Democratic-voting women, while Republicans were confident in their ability to turn out older and married women with historically higher turnout rates.

The women's vote expanded (from 53 percent in 2008 to 55 percent in 2012) and ended up more solidly behind Obama (53 percent) than polls taken earlier in the campaign had suggested. Post-election studies point to a surge in the younger women's vote near the end of the campaign, moved by powerful Amendment 6 ads on TV (reproductive rights; abortion) and by active women's groups on campus. Social issues like gay marriage and abortion ended up being more important than economic issues to younger, single women voters. In fact, the gender gap between unmarried women and men was wider (six percent) than between married women and men (four percent). A majority of unmarrieds supported Obama, while marrieds preferred Romney. And some suburban Republican women also moved back to Obama at the campaign's end, pushed by concerns about pay equity and health care availability.

In geography, the I-4 Corridor was once again the state's premier battleground. More than 40 percent of all Florida registered voters lived in either the Tampa or Orlando media market, and I-4 Corridor voters were nearly evenly divided from a partisan perspective. Both campaigns located their state headquarters in the I-4 Corridor, specifically in Tampa—the state's largest media market, housing one-fourth of all Florida's registered voters. Candidate visits and TV ads flooded the Tampa and Orlando media markets, offering further proof that both parties saw the I-4 Corridor as critical to winning the state.

The suburban areas surrounding key urban centers were seen as the key to a Romney victory. Republicans calculated that suburban turnout and vote patterns in 2012 would lean their way due to slower-than-average economic recovery rates in many of these areas. But turnout of middle-class suburbanites was lower than expected in several vital suburban counties along the I-4 Corridor. Some have speculated that turnout among middle-class white suburbanites (swing voters) in these highly TV-ad saturated areas fell because neither candidate convinced these voters that they had a clear plan on how to fix the economy and fix it fast. Overall, Obama did better among voters with incomes under $50,000—a group that grew from 39 percent of the electorate in 2008 to 45 percent in 2012. A majority of those voters cast their ballots for Obama, while voters with incomes of $50,000 and up supported Romney.

As the campaign progressed, the Obama team increasingly realized that South Florida would be the key to eking out a victory. A high Democratic turnout in Broward, Palm Beach, and Miami-Dade counties could offset Republican votes in other counties. As it turned out, the biggest gains for Obama were in Democratic vote-rich South Florida, with Miami-Dade County giving President Obama a much larger margin of victory than in 2008 (204,000 vs. 140,000).The late visits to the area by President Obama, President Bill Clinton, First Lady Michelle Obama, and Vice President Joe Biden were effective. The Obama turnout machine was in full force here, yielding much-needed support from African Americans, older Jewish voters, and young voters (minorities, including Cubans, and single females).

In spite of the intense competition, there was no record turnout in Florida; the voter turnout rate actually fell by four percent. The over-saturation of ads, and the sharp increase in early voters, meant that last-minute GOTV tactics— phone calls (in person or robo), TV ads, and mailers—that used to work to mobilize late deciders did not. Neither did the GOP's GOTV plan that heavily relied on a dysfunctional data base. The superiority of the Democrats' "Big Data"-driven micro-targeting efforts by a large team of embedded organizers across the state was quite evident. And it was the Democrats' edge in GOTV that narrowly pulled Obama across the finish line in Florida—once again turning the Sunshine State blue.

The 2016 Presidential Election: Florida Again a Key Battleground State

The 2016 race to the White House began early—with more than a dozen wannabes finding their way to Florida to gin up support… and money. Why? As one longtime reporter has observed, "There's an underlying truth that crosses both party lines and lures anyone on the presidential campaign trail [to Florida]. It's very tough to become president of the United States without Florida. So no matter what, you've got to start building your networks [early].'"[60] By the time Election Day—November 8, 2016—rolls around, millions of dollars will have been spent convincing Floridians to vote for a particular candidate. The candidates will travel all across Florida, but much of their time in Florida will be spent trying to energize voters in the I-4 Corridor and South Florida. Local party activists and campaign volunteers will expend thousands of hours contacting fellow Floridians on behalf of their chosen favorite. Media coverage (local, state, national, even international) will be nonstop, based on the belief that in Florida, one should always expect the unexpected when it comes to high profile elections.

GUBERNATORIAL RACES

Political competition for the Florida governorship has intensified over the years as the Republican Party rose to challenge the traditional Democratic monopoly. Under one-party rule, competition for the office was limited to the Democratic gubernatorial primary. And prior to 1968, the Florida Constitution limited the governor to a single term. In that year, Florida adopted a new constitution that allowed the governor to run for a second four-year term. Two years earlier, the state had elected its first Republican governor since Reconstruction, the flamboyant Claude Kirk. For a summary of Florida's governor, U.S. Senate, and U.S. House of Representatives races, see Table 4-7.

Kirk and Askew

A former Democrat, Kirk had led "Floridians for Nixon" in 1960, winning the state's electoral votes for the Republican presidential candidate. As a successful insurance company founder and investor, Kirk mobilized the nascent Republican Party in the state. He was unsuccessful in his first statewide race, trying to oust four term incumbent U.S. Senator Spessard Holland. But in 1966, Kirk broke the Democratic monopoly on the governor's office, defeating Miami Mayor Robert King High, who had ousted incumbent Governor Haydon Burns in a bitter Democratic primary battle. Kirk benefited from the growing Republican leanings of the electorate, but his victory was largely due to the large number of crossover votes he received. Many Central and North Florida Democrats thought High was too liberal on civil rights, and that split the Democratic Party.

Kirk's administration was both colorful and controversial, marked by confrontations with the Democratic

Governor Claude Kirk (left) welcomes newly elected Governor Reubin Askew and his wife to the Governor's Mansion.

legislature, an unprecedented statewide teachers' strike, and crises over forced school busing. His personal flamboyant leadership style came under attack from media around the state and turned off many former supporters. He was defeated in his bid for re-election in 1970 by a young Pensacola Democratic state senator, Reubin Askew. Askew successfully pushed comprehensive tax reform through the state legislature during his first term. He easily won re-election in 1974 to become the first Florida governor to serve two four-year terms. As a progressive Democrat from North Florida, Askew was able to reunite the Democratic base. His re-election was aided by the fallout from the Watergate scandal that hurt Republicans across the country at every level of office.

Graham and Martinez

Media campaigning came to dominate governors' elections in the 1970s. Media campaigns thrive on gimmicks that attract cameras and audiences. A Harvard-educated millionaire lawyer and real estate developer from Miami, Bob Graham, a former legislator, turned to professional media consultants in 1978 to develop an image with which working people could identify. They selected a campaign theme for his gubernatorial race, "Bob Graham—Working for Governor," which featured well publicized working days for the candidate. Graham's television ads showed him collecting garbage, picking oranges, herding cattle, and so forth. Critics complained that the wealthy Graham's televised working days may have been the only days of his life that he ever worked, but the approach was so successful that Graham continued his work days even after he won the governorship. As we shall see in Chapter 7, Graham won highly favorable ratings in opinion polls during his governorship. After two terms in the state capital, Graham easily won a seat in the U.S. Senate. Although from South Florida, Graham was a moderate Democrat who captured much of the same constituency that had voted for Askew. His re-election was aided by an economic recovery that was beginning in 1982 and the perception that he was an effective leader who worked well with the Democratically controlled legislature.

Table 4-7. Election Outcomes in Florida Races for Governor, U.S. Senate, and U.S. House

	Governor	U.S. Senate	U.S. Senate	U.S. House of Representatives
2014	(R) Rick Scott 48.1% over (D) Charlie Crist	–	–	Democrats 10 Republicans 117
2012	–	–	(D) Bill Nelson 55.2% over (R) Connie Mack IV	Democrats 10 Republicans 17
2010	(R) Rick Scott 49% over (D) Alex Sink	(R) Marco Rubio 49% over (D) Kendrick Meek and (NPA) Charlie Crist	–	Democrats 6 Republicans 19
2008	–	–	–	Democrats 10 Republicans 15
2006	(R) Charlie Crist 52% over (D) Jim Davis	–	(D) Bill Nelson 60% over (R) Katherine Harris	Democrats 9 Republicans 16
2004	–	(R) Mel Martinez 49% Over (D) Betty Castor	–	Democrats 7 Republicans 18
2002	(R) Jeb Bush 56% over (D) Bill McBride	–	–	Democrats 7 Republicans 18
2000	–	–	(D) Bill Nelson 52% over (R) Bill McCollum	Democrats 8 Republicans 15
1998	(R) Jeb Bush 55% over (D) Buddy MacKay	(D) Bob Graham 63% over (R) Charlie Crist	–	Democrats 8 Republicans 15
1996	–	–	–	Democrats 8 Republicans 15
1994	(D) Lawton Chiles 51% over (R) Jeb Bush	–	(R) Connie Mack III 70% over (D) Hugh Rodham	Democrats 8 Republicans 15
1992	–	(D) Bob Graham 65% over (R) Bill Grant	–	Democrats 10 Republicans 13
1990	(D) Lawton Chiles 56% over (R) Bob Martinez	–	–	Democrats 9 Republicans 10
1988	–	–	(R) Connie Mack III 50% over (D) Buddy MacKay	Democrats 10 Republicans 9
1986	(R) Bob Martinez 55% over (D) Steve Pajcic	(D) Bob Graham 55% over (R) Paula Hawkins	–	Democrats 12 Republicans 7
1984	–	–	–	Democrats 12 Republicans 7
1982	(D) Bob Graham 65% over (R) Skip Bafalis	–	(D) Lawton Chiles 62% over (R) Van Poole	Democrats 13 Republicans 6
1980	–	(R) Paula Hawkins 52% over (D) Bill Gunter	–	Democrats 11 Republicans 4
1978	(D) Bob Graham 56% over (R) Jack Eckerd	–	–	Democrats 12 Republicans 3
1976	–	–	(D) Lawton Chiles 63% over (R) John Grady	Democrats 10 Republicans 5
1974	(D) Reubin Askew 61% over (R) Jerry Thomas	(D) Richard Stone 43% over (R) Jack Eckerd	–	Democrats 12 Republicans 3
1972	–	–	–	Democrats 9 Republicans 3
1970	(D) Reubin Askew 57% over (R) Claude Kirk	–	(D) Lawton Chiles 54% over (R) Bill Cramer	Democrats 9 Republicans 3
1968	–	(R) Edward Gurney 56% over (D) LeRoy Collins	–	Democrats 9 Republicans 3
1966	(R) Claude Kirk 55% Over (D) Robert King High	–	–	Democrats 9 Republicans 3

Note: U.S. Senators are elected for six-year terms. The terms are staggered so that both of a state's U.S. Senate seats do not go up for election in the same year.

Source: Florida Division of Elections.

Newly elected Bob Martinez leaves a meeting with Governor Bob Graham.

Republican Bob Martinez, former Democratic mayor of Tampa, took advantage of the state's conservative leanings in 1986 and used extensive television advertising to successfully label his Democratic opponent, Steve Pajcic, as an unrepentant liberal—a charge that had first been leveled against him by his Democratic opponent Jim Smith in the primary election. Although Pajcic was from Jacksonville, North Florida Democrats defected to Martinez believing Pajcic was too liberal, while the turnout rate among South Florida Democrats was lower than usual. Martinez became the state's first Hispanic governor, winning a solid 55 percent of the vote. He did well among all Republican constituencies and especially Hispanic voters. He ran on a platform of low taxes and social conservatism. But as governor, Martinez lost favor by first supporting—and later disavowing and repealing—a sales tax on services that would have enlarged the state's tax base. He also called an unsuccessful special session on abortion and generally had a difficult time with the Democratically controlled legislature. By 1990, Republicans felt they could not trust Martinez on taxes, and moderate Democrats felt he was much too conservative on social issues. He lost to Democratic U.S. Senator Lawton Chiles.

Lawton Chiles

Perhaps no Republican would have been able to defeat the popular Democrat Lawton Chiles. Chiles retired from his safe U.S. Senate seat in 1988 after three terms, citing burnout, depression, and an inability to get Congress to deal honestly with federal budget deficits in his role as chair of the Senate Budget Committee. A reenergized Chiles decided to enter the Florida governor's race in 1990 and handily beat Bill Nelson in the Democratic primary. He reassumed his populist political style, announcing that he would not accept campaign contributions over $100, and blasting incumbent Martinez's $1,500-per-plate fundraising dinners. Chiles easily defeated Martinez, winning almost 57 percent of the vote. He stressed right-sizing government, as opposed to raising taxes, and successfully unified the Democratic base across the state.

Folksy Governor Chiles enjoys a moment with his dog Tess.

Under the Constitution of 1968, gubernatorial candidates in Florida run together with their handpicked nominees for lieutenant governor in both primary and general elections. These running mates are usually selected to balance the ticket geographically, ideologically, or both. Lawton Chiles, widely perceived as a moderate-to-conservative North Florida Democrat (although he was originally from Polk County), chose the more liberal Buddy MacKay (who had earlier been defeated in a hotly contested Senate race in 1988 by Republican Connie Mack using the attack line "Hey, Buddy, You're a Liberal!").

Chiles was not as popular a governor as his many supporters had expected. Governor Chiles faced tough budget times due to the national recession in the first two years of his term. In his second year, he supported an extension of the sales tax to services, the same rock on which Governor Martinez had stubbed his political toe. When Republicans won a 20 to 20 tie in the state Senate in 1992, Chiles's legislative proposals were effectively curtailed. His public approval ratings sagged (See Chapter 7.), inspiring Republicans to believe he could be defeated.

Chiles (The "He-Coon") vs. Jeb Bush

Indeed, Chiles's perceived vulnerability brought a crush of Republican gubernatorial primary candidates in 1994, including Secretary of State Jim Smith who had switched from the Democratic Party, Insurance Commissioner Tom Gallagher, Senate President Ander Crenshaw, and Jeb Bush, the youngest son of former President George H.W. Bush. Jeb Bush had served as chair of the Florida Republican Party in 1992 and helped carry the state for his father. He enjoyed high name recognition and the ability, with the help of his mother and father, to raise huge amounts of campaign funds. He garnered 45 percent of the vote in the Republican primary against seven candidates, causing distant runner-up Jim Smith to abandon the runoff and accept the GOP agriculture commissioner nomination (only to lose in the general election). Bush concentrated his fire on Chiles, with tough television ads attacking the governor as a liberal "taxer and spender" who was "soft on crime."

Governor Lawton Chiles (right) meets with newly elected Governor Jeb Bush. In the previous election in 1994, Chiles had narrowly defeated Bush.

Chiles responded with the most conservative and hard-hitting campaign of his career. Behind in early polls, he counterattacked, citing Bush's lack of experience, past business dealings, and dependence on his father's name to get ahead. Chiles boasted of his prison-building program, his willingness to carry out the death penalty, and his battles with the Clinton administration over Haitian and Cuban refugees. Chiles benefited from the perception that Bush was too conservative for moderate voters and also from voter backlash created by a Bush ad that used the mother of a murder victim to suggest that Chiles did not support the death penalty. His stellar performance in the final debate included a reference to the "He-Coon" (male raccoon) rising at dawn. This stumped Bush and new arrivals to the state, but the symbolic reference to leadership, experience, and a last-minute comeback resonated with North Florida Democrats who stuck with their party for Chiles's last political race. Chiles wore a coonskin cap as a campaign gimmick over the final weeks and was affectionately labeled the old "He-Coon" by supporters. In the end, Chiles squeaked out the closest win (51 percent) of his long political career in what was at the time the closest governor's race in modern Florida history.[61] Chiles's victory was even more impressive because it came during a nationwide Republican sweep in 1994, when many popular Southern Democrats were defeated.

A New Jeb Bush vs. Buddy MacKay

Jeb Bush came back to win the governorship in 1998. Bush's victory can be attributed to several factors. First, Bush kept his campaign team together after his 1994 loss and stayed involved with policy by starting a nonprofit think tank called Foundation for Florida's Future. Second, he repositioned himself as a "compassionate conservative" who reached out to minorities and sought to help the poor through innovative programs, while still keeping taxes low. Third, Bush balanced his ticket by selecting a more moderate lieutenant governor running mate (popular Education Commissioner Frank Brogan) than his 1994 selection, Tom Feeney, who was widely criticized in the media for being too conservative. Fourth, Bush managed his campaign ads and campaign funding better than in 1994. However, Bush's biggest break in 1998 was a weaker opponent. Buddy MacKay was considerably more liberal than Lawton Chiles and a less effective campaigner. Jeb Bush won going away by 55 percent to MacKay's 45 percent. Bush's 2.1 million votes were only slightly up from 1994 (2 million), but MacKay at 1.7 million received about 400,000 fewer votes than Chiles had four years earlier, indicating that the deciding factor was a lower Democratic voter turnout rate.

Incumbent Bush vs. Novice Bill McBride

Florida's Election 2002 was three elections rolled into one: presidential election 2000, the governor's race, and presidential election 2004. From the beginning, it was cast as a highly competitive race because of the incredibly close 2000 presidential election, decided in Florida for George W. Bush by just 537 votes. Even the White House's own political advisor worried that Florida's governorship was a "Possible D Pickup." Winning the Florida governor's race became the primary goal for both Democrats and Republicans once Democratic National Committee Chairman Terry McAuliffe identified "defeating Jeb Bush as the Party's No. 1 priority." Some saw the governor's race as a surrogate grudge rematch between George W. Bush and Al Gore—a chance to prove once and for all who really won Florida in 2000. Both the current president and former vice president visited the state a number of times. Inside Florida, most saw the election as a fight over the direction the state would take in the next four years. Republican Governor Bush and Democratic nominee McBride, offered Floridians clear choices on everything from education to taxes to adoptions by gay couples.[62]

Ultimately, Bill McBride, a lawyer with Holland and Knight, who had never run for public office before, proved to be an inexperienced candidate with poor public speaking skills who was painfully naïve about modern campaigning (even though he did defeat former U.S. Attorney General Janet Reno and State Senator Daryl Jones, both from the Miami area, for the Democratic nomination). McBride centered his entire campaign on one issue—education— and was heavily backed by the Florida teachers union. At one point, McBride pulled to within five points of Jeb Bush, according to polls taken about three weeks before the election. But his support faded by Election Day after a lackluster performance in the final debate. When he was unable to answer moderator Tim Russert's question on how to pay for a proposed constitutional amendment to reduce classroom size, his poll numbers plummeted. Worse than that, McBride opened himself up to GOP charges that he would raise taxes.

And, of course, Jeb Bush ran a strong campaign. First, he raised a lot of money for the campaign and, more importantly, for the state Republican Party. The state GOP out-raised and out-spent the Democrats by more than 2 to 1. Second, Bush and the Republican Party used the money to effectively attack McBride on taxes—even going so far as to suggest that McBride might consider an income tax! Third, Bush effectively stressed the most positive parts of his record: a $3 billion increase in education spending, a declining crime rate, lower taxes, and job creation. Fourth, he aggressively courted Hispanic voters, and even won about two-thirds of the growing non-Cuban Hispanic vote. Fifth, he came off well in the debates, looking smooth and sounding informed, with many facts and details to support his positions. Sixth, he successfully finessed the education issue. He came out against the constitutional amendment to reduce class size because of the cost, but argued for smaller classes for younger grades and provided a detailed plan to finance it that included no tax increases.

The biggest factor outside Governor Bush's control, which ended up helping him inside Florida, was the terrorist attack of 9/11 and the subsequent popularity of his brother, President George W. Bush. Republican candidates across the country benefited from the record-high midterm approval ratings of the president that inspired extremely high turnout among Republican and independent voters.

Governor Bush won re-election in a landslide by carrying 55 of 67 counties and receiving 656,619 votes more than McBride. He became the first Republican Florida governor to be reelected. How badly did Democrat Bill McBride do? One reporter said McBride's defeat was "the worst showing of a Democrat running for governor since 1868."

The governor's, and arguably President Bush's, coattails were long. For the first time in Florida's history, Republicans controlled the governorship, all three Cabinet posts, 18 of 25 Congressional seats, 26 of 40 state Senate seats, and 81 of 120 state House seats.

Crist vs. Davis: The Race to Replace Term-Limited Jeb

No doubt about it—both parties wanted to win the 2006 governor's race. With no Jeb Bush on the ballot, Florida Democrats were hopeful they could recapture the Governor's Mansion. For the Republican Party of Florida, holding on to the governor's chair was its top priority. The race was a classic pocketbook election, in which rising homeowners' insurance rates and escalating property taxes dominated even education and the FCAT.

For the first time in years, both major parties had a highly contested gubernatorial primary.[63] Initially, most analysts projected the Republican primary between two experienced Cabinet officials—Attorney General Crist and Chief Financial Officer Gallagher—would be the "bloodiest" and most damaging to the eventual nominee. But as it turned out, the Democratic primary between U.S. Congress member Jim Davis, Tampa, and State Senator Rod Smith, Alachua (near Gainesville), was the most competitive... and damaging to the party's nominee. Smith leveled charges of racial insensitivity against Davis. While a legislator, Davis had voted against compensating two African Americans wrongly convicted of murder—Freddie Pitts and Wilbur Lee. Big Sugar, a powerful lobby, spent millions spreading this message, along with one that pointed out Davis' poor attendance record during his last year in Congress. Ultimately, Davis apologized to Pitts and Lee, who then endorsed him, and selected an African-American running mate, former State Senator Daryl L. Jones from South Florida. Davis won the primary over Smith by 47 to 41 percent, but the intra-party battle for the nomination left Davis wounded and short of funds.

The Republican primary, which pitted Crist against the religious right candidate, Tom Gallagher, was less contentious than expected, making it easier for the party—and critical campaign contributors—to coalesce behind Crist's candidacy once he won the nomination. Governor Jeb Bush's refusal to take sides during the primary made it easy for him to become a Crist cheerleader the day after. The Crist campaign correctly predicted that fiscal issues and anti-crime messages would easily trump moral issues like embryonic stem cell research, abortion, and same-sex civil unions. In fact, the percentage of the GOP vote that Gallagher received—just 33.5 percent—was viewed as evidence that the social and religious conservatives sometimes referred to as the "born-again" vote, make up a far smaller portion of the Florida GOP than some analysts commonly assume.

Governor Charlie Crist receives congratulatory hug from departing Governor Jeb Bush on Crist's inauguration day.

The Crist-Davis match-up was never viewed as overly competitive by national handicappers. Perhaps it was due to Governor Jeb Bush's high approval ratings, his brother George's unexpected five percent margin of victory in the 2004 presidential contest, or the magnitude of the Crist fundraising machine early in the campaign. But certainly part of it was the recognition that the national Democratic Party and Democratic congressional campaign committees in each house had as their top priority winning back Congress, leaving much of the responsibility for capturing governors' races to state parties. And Florida's Democratic Party was at best in a rebuilding mode heading into the 2006 election cycle.

Davis' biggest problem was money. His campaign lagged behind Crist's in fundraising, as did that of the Florida Democratic Party. Without enough money for statewide television ads, Davis could not muster enough name recognition even among Democratic registrants to compete with the better known Crist. It was when Davis got money for television ads linking Crist to the insurance industry and performed well in statewide televised debates that he gained some ground on Crist—but not enough. Low voter turnout, particularly among blacks in South Florida, was "a key factor in the loss of Democratic gubernatorial candidate Jim Davis… A *South Florida Sun-Sentinel* precinct analysis showed that only one in three black voters in Broward and Miami-Dade went to the polls. The turnout was lower than in the 2002 governor's race, a fact some attribute to a lack of spending and outreach in the black community…"[64] and to the Pitts-Lee issue raised by Rod Smith in the primary. Davis was also hampered by party organizational problems that had still not been fully tackled by the party's new leadership in Tallahassee after Kerry's defeat in the 2004 presidential race. Specifically, Democrats lagged in their registration efforts after the 2004 election and allowed Republicans to close the registration gap a bit. In 2004, there were three percent more Democrats registered than Republicans. By the general election in 2006, the gap had closed to just two percent.

Money was a definite factor in Crist's success. He raised nearly $20 million on his own[65] (compared to Davis's $6.7 million), and the Republican Party of Florida contributed generously—$42 million in the last two months alone.[66] Equally important were his upbeat "I love Florida" temperament and his message of fiscal conservatism, especially doubling the homestead exemption for property owners, and moderation on social issues. He indicated tolerance on some social issues (abortion, civil unions, stem cell research) but steadfastness against others (gay marriage, gay adoption).[67] Crist successfully posited himself as independent of the Bush brothers, especially the president, opting not to appear side-by-side with him at a rally in Pensacola in the waning days of the campaign. At the time he was heavily criticized for the decision, but the criticism ended when he held on to the Florida governor's chair for the GOP by a seven percent margin (52 to 45 percent). By the time of the next gubernatorial election, Crist had announced he would not run for re-election, but rather for the open U.S. Senate seat created when Senator Mel Martinez decided not to seek another term.

Rick Scott vs. Alex Sink: Battle of the CEOs

Florida's 2010 gubernatorial race was all about Florida's sagging economy. Florida's unemployment and foreclosure rates were among the highest in the country. The BP oil spill in the Gulf (April) wreaked havoc on coastal counties' economies, particularly those in the Panhandle. It was the perfect time for two business executives to run. It was a battle over who could best restore Florida's economy. Would it be the former president of a large banking chain and the state's chief financial officer at the time

Gubernatorial candidates Democrat Alex Sink and Republican Rick Scott shake hands before a debate. The two CEOs ran hard-hitting ads against each other. After all the votes were in, Scott won but in the closest race in Florida gubernatorial history up to that time.

(Democrat Alex Sink)? Or would it be the wealthy CEO of a large hospital corporation—a political newcomer who had never run for office before (Republican Rick Scott)? The race gave Floridians a firsthand look at the difficulties corporate business leaders encounter when they seek top-level posts in the public sector. Few realized when the race began just how much each candidate would be *open game for any and all corporate-related actions that occurred under their watch*.

Nationally, it was a closely watched race because of the key role Florida's governor plays in the congressional redistricting process that would soon begin.[68] (The governor has a veto power over congressional redistricting plans submitted to him by the state legislature.) Redistricting took on added importance once it was announced that the state would gain two new congressional seats and thereby increase the state's presence on the national political stage. At one point, President Obama even remarked that winning the governor's race in Florida was more important to the administration than capturing the U.S. Senate seat.

Democrat Alex Sink had no opposition in the Democratic primary. Republican Rick Scott spent millions to win his party's primary against Attorney General Bill McCollum. He then spent millions more to win the general election against Sink, ultimately setting a record for campaign spending for state office in Florida—most of it from his own fortune. All the while, he had to spend a lot of time trying to repair the schism within the party created by his decision to run against the party establishment's favored candidate (McCollum).

As the race tightened, the negative ads escalated. The ad war disintegrated into résumé-bashing, an exercise made easier by each candidate's having served as a corporate CEO. Sink took every opportunity to label Scott a crook. She questioned Scott's integrity and raised the issues of the record-level Medicare fraud fine paid by his former company, his invoking of the Fifth Amendment 75 times during a deposition, and his unwillingness to make public the content of that deposition. Her campaign theme of honesty and accountability was well grounded in polling data. The 2010 Sunshine State Survey (conducted by Leadership Florida & The Nielsen Company in February), had shown that the quality Floridians want most in their leaders is *integrity*.

Scott went after Sink's business practices as well. He accused her of failing to rein in Nations Bank's (later Bank of America) scams against the elderly and of poor oversight of the state's pension fund as chief financial officer. His attacks on her banking career were grounded in polls showing growing fears of bank closings; anger at banks for their unwillingness to restructure mortgages, renegotiate loans, or even make small loans to struggling Floridians; and disdain for huge CEO bonuses. Scott was, in effect, betting that voters would be more critical of a banker than of a hospital CEO and of a "Tallahassee insider" (her) than a new face (his). Scott also ran numerous ads connecting Sink to President Obama, whose popularity had sunk since winning the state two years earlier.

The candidates participated in three televised debates hosted by Univision, Florida PBS stations/Leadership Florida, and CNN/the *St. Petersburg Times*/University of South Florida. For the most part, their answers to moderators' questions mirrored the content of their television ads. It was in the third and final debate just a week away from the election that both candidates stumbled. In a highly embarrassing moment, neither candidate (both wealthy CEOs) could accurately identify the current minimum wage ($7.25 per hour), yet both were running on a job creation platform. But it was Sink's simple glance at a text message on an aide's cell phone during a break, in violation of debate rules, that created a post-debate storm broadcast across the nation. It was a devastating moment for a candidate running on an integrity platform. Even so, Sink and Scott stayed neck-and-neck to the end.

The 2010 gubernatorial election turned out to be the closest one in the state's modern history. Scott won by only 1.2 percent. The contest was decided largely by voters who were angry at Washington and took it out on Democrats running for office at all levels—federal, state, and local. For these voters, Scott, the outsider, had more appeal with his "Let's Get to Work" anti-Washington message than Sink, the insider, with her honesty, integrity, and accountability message. In the words of one Florida journalist: "In a normal election year, Scott's baggage might have been too much to overcome, even with his record-shattering personal spending... But this is a year when Republicans and independents alike are so angry and fed up that such issues [had] little traction."[69]

Incumbent Rick Scott vs. Charlie Crist: Governor vs. Former Governor

The 2014 governor's race was one of the most expensive in Florida history, and the campaign was one of the longest and most negative. It was also one of the most unusual, featuring an incumbent Republican governor (Rick Scott) running against a former Republican governor, turned independent, turned Democrat (Charlie Crist).

It was a first—a sitting governor (Republican Rick Scott-left) running against a former governor, Democrat Charlie Crist (right). In another first, both chose Hispanic running mates from South Florida: Scott—Cuban Carlos Lopez-Cantera; Charlie Crist—Colombian Annette Taddeo. It was the closest governor's race in Florida history.

The negative tone of the multi-million dollar TV ad campaign can be summarized by the taglines to the most frequently aired commercials.

"Charlie Crist, Slick Politician, Lousy Governor"
"If you liked the last six years of Obama, you'd love the next four years of Charlie Crist"
"Charlie Crist, Typical Flippin' Politician"

"Rick Scott, "Too Shady for the Sunshine State""
"Rick Scott, for the Powerful Few, Not You"

By the time the campaign was winding down, many Floridians did not like either candidate. That scenario set the stage for a strong finish by third party candidate—Libertarian Adrian Wyllie—but that did not

happen either. Wyllie was excluded from the three statewide televised debates by debate sponsors that dashed any hopes he had of being a spoiler. With little funding or name recognition, his campaign got little traction outside the Tampa media market—his home base where he ran his only TV ad. Wyllie ended up with just 3.75 percent of the vote, although that was a record high for a Libertarian candidate.

Adrian Wyllie was the Libertarian Party's candidate for governor. He was excluded from the debates but showed up at all of them and generated lots of publicity for his party and his candidacy. But he had little money to run TV ads in all 10 media markets.

While Democrats had the upper hand in registration, Republicans turned out at a higher rate and ended up narrowly holding on to the Governor's Mansion. Typical of most midterm elections, turnout among three key portions of the Democratic base was markedly lower than in the 2012 presidential election—young voters, minorities (especially Hispanics), and unmarried females. Even a proposed constitutional amendment to legalize medicinal marijuana failed to bring young Democratic voters to the polls. So did the micro-targeting of young women using the reproductive rights appeal that had worked in the 2012 election. Crist's selection of a Colombian female (Annette Taddeo) from Democratic vote-rich South Florida as his lieutenant governor running mate also failed to mobilize Hispanics, especially non-Cubans, to the degree expected.

Well in advance of the campaign, analysts raised several key questions—the answers to which help explain the ultimate outcome:

To what degree would the 2014 election be nationalized—intertwined with Washington politics? Polls were showing a huge disconnect between voters and Washington. High proportions of voters believed the country was headed in the wrong direction and President Obama's favorability ratings were slipping. It turns out opinions about Obama did matter. Exit polls showed among Scott voters, 74 percent disapproved of the way President Obama was handling his job, while among Crist voters, 88 percent judged his job performance positively. But there ended up being more Scott than Crist voters.

Would either party have a truly competitive gubernatorial primary? Party activists who preferred candidates other than Charlie Crist or Rick Scott doubted it, believing that big money behind the two governors would chase away primary challengers who, ironically, might have been stronger candidates for their respective parties in the general election. In the end, only the Democrats had a contested primary. Former Senator Nan Rich (Broward County) ran against Crist but got little support from the party establishment. Crist refused to debate her—which some say may have cost him the election. A sizeable number of Democrats and independents, especially females, simply did not vote in the governor's race in protest of what they perceived to be sexist behavior—uncalled for in a party that touts its inclusiveness.

If the nominees were Crist and Scott, to what degree would political ad-makers take their records and paint them as flip-floppers? Both Crist and Scott had dramatically changed their positions on key issues. Party activists rightly anticipated that campaign ads would paint the candidates as flip-floppers. The label stuck more to Crist than Scott for several reasons. First, the Scott campaign and its supporters ran TV ads far in advance of the Crist campaign, branding Crist as a flip-flopper and job-hopper. Second, Crist *had* changed his position on some high profile issues (same-sex marriage), changed his party affiliation, and run for multiple offices. Crist countered this line of attack by stating that voters cared less about changes in issue positions that genuinely occurred due to a change of heart than about Governor Scott's failure to resolve some of the state's pressing problems—like education. Actually, Governor Scott had changed *his* position on education funding, but the number one issue for voters was the economy. Exit polls showed that 73 percent of those who voted were very or somewhat worried about the direction of the nation's economy in the next year. Scott's campaign never wavered from its theme—"Let's Keep Working"—and focused on Jobs! Jobs! Jobs. And it paid off.

Would either or both parties have racial/ethnic or gender diversity on their governor/lieutenant governor ticket? It turned out that the answer was "Yes" for racial/ethnic diversity. Scott's running mate was Carlos Lopez-Cantera, a Cuban American and former state legislator from Miami. Crist chose Taddeo—a female Colombian also from Miami—giving both racial/ethnic and gender diversity to the Democratic ticket. Florida's increasing diversity has made racial/ethnic diversity on the ticket a must. Each party is well aware of the importance of image and of the role path-breaking candidates can play in mobilizing turnout, although the consensus of analysts was that Lopez-Cantera was the more effective campaigner of the two.

Would President Obama and/or the First Lady campaign for the Democratic nominee? Once Crist became the party's nominee, the real question became whether Crist would *want* President Obama to campaign for him in light of the president's plummeting approval ratings. Crist was also wary of re-igniting the images of the famous "hug" he had given to Obama after accepting federal stimulus package funding for the state while governor. The ultimate decision to opt for the First Lady's presence more than the president's was a controversial one that split the Democrats. After Crist narrowly lost, those who had argued for bringing

President Obama to South Florida near the end of the campaign to increase minority turnout said, "I told you so."

How much influence would the gubernatorial debates have? How many and where will they be and who will sponsor them? In the past, Floridians had acknowledged debates to be a critical source of information affecting their eventual vote choice. But the proliferation of debates in 2012, candidate and audience dissatisfaction with various formats and moderators, and claims of media bias depending on the ideological bent of the cable/network carrying them made the 2014 gubernatorial candidates less eager to engage in more than three debates—all in October. Two were held in South Florida—one sponsored by Telemundo, a second by Leadership Florida and the Florida Press Association carried by public television stations, and a third in Jacksonville hosted by CNN. The most bizarre of the three was the Leadership Florida/Florida Press Association debate that was labeled "FanGate." One "pop" media outlet described the event to its readers like this: "The nation was introduced to Charlie Crist's fan fetish, when Crist broke the rules at [the] debate and snuck a fan into the hall. Current Fla. Gov. Scott hung out backstage in protest, causing Crist to get seven solo minutes on stage, bewildering the moderator who called it 'the most unique beginning to any debate not only in Florida, but anywhere in the country.'"[70] As it turned out, even FanGate did not have much impact, although at the time, some thought it had ended Scott's re-election bid. Many Floridians, however, just saw it as an extension of the months-long pattern of back-and-forth negatives—and two negatives did not make the campaign or the debate positive in their minds.

As we look back, it is clear that in the 2014 election, the Republican Scott's goals were to split the women's vote, get 40 percent of the Hispanic vote, split the independent vote, and win the turnout battle. Tracking back to the 1990s, Republican victories in statewide races had occurred when these goals were achieved. The Scott campaign also focused on winning the I-4 Corridor (Tampa and Orlando media markets), recapturing some of the suburban vote it lost in 2012, and ramping up vote totals and margins of victory in rural areas. According to exit polls, he came closer to achieving his goals than Crist—nearly splitting the women's vote (Crist 49 percent, Scott 47 percent), getting 38 percent of the Hispanic vote, narrowly winning both I-4 Corridor media markets, winning a majority (52 percent) of the suburban vote that Obama carried in 2012, and handily winning the rural vote (57 percent). Scott spent a lot more time than Crist in what some call the I-10 Corridor—Jacksonville west to Pensacola.[71]

The Crist campaign had counted on the 2012 Obama machine and "big data" to yield presidential-election-year turnout rates among youth, minorities, and unmarried females—three key constituencies with histories of low midterm-election turnout. Geographically, the focus was on pushing up turnout in areas with the heaviest concentrations of low-turnout Democratic registrants. Specifically, Crist spent more time in South Florida to energize black and Hispanic voters, in the Orlando area to reach Puerto Ricans, and in college towns to garner the important youth vote.

When Scott narrowly won (one percent), it was evident that Crist's efforts to produce presidential-election-year turnout among young, minority, and female voters fell short. Democratic turnout in vote-rich South Florida lagged again, as it had in the 2010 governor's race. And Republicans held on to the Governor's Mansion by a sliver. Scott's victory meant that Republicans had won five gubernatorial elections in a row, beginning with Jeb Bush's victory in 1998. Scott became just the second Republican governor in state history to win re-election.

U.S. SENATE RACES

U.S. Senate races in Florida, like presidential and gubernatorial contests, have become more competitive in recent years. Some of these races have been heavily influenced by national-level politics (the elections were *"nationalized"*), while others have turned on mostly Florida issues. Two of the three most recent contests have been highly competitive races featuring strong candidates vying for open seats created when an incumbent U.S. senator decided to retire.

First Republican Victory

Prior to 1968, no Republican had been elected to the U.S. Senate from Florida since Reconstruction. In that year of racial and antiwar turmoil, Richard Nixon won Florida's presidential election with 40 percent of the state's popular vote. Segregationist and former Democrat George Wallace (29 percent), running as a third party candidate, split the remainder of the state almost evenly with Democrat Hubert Humphrey (31 percent). Florida's former, and very popular, Democratic Governor LeRoy Collins had been an early supporter of civil rights and had later served under President Lyndon Johnson as director of the Equal Employment Opportunity Commission. In the 1968 U.S. Senate race pitting Collins against Republican Representative Edward J. Gurney, Collins fell victim to the "Liberal LeRoy" label and the voters' general unhappiness with the national Democratic Party. Indeed, the back-to-back statewide victories by Republican Claude Kirk in 1966 and Edward Gurney in 1968 shook the state's traditional Democratic establishment.

Popular Democrat Lawton Chiles Wins

In 1970, the task to rescue the Florida Democratic Party fell to two young, charismatic, and responsible reformist candidates—Reubin Askew, who thwarted Republican Governor Claude Kirk's bid for re-election, and Lawton Chiles, who kept Florida's other U.S. Senate seat in Democratic hands. Chiles had the more difficult obstacle to overcome—he faced former Democratic Governor Farris Bryant, who won the first primary, but was forced to confront Chiles in the runoff. In an original and colorful campaign, "Walkin' Lawton" garnered local news coverage by walking the length of the state (actually riding between towns). His upset of Bryant and subsequent victory in the 1970 general election was the beginning of his long career in Washing¬ton (he was reelected in 1976 and 1982). Republican Senate incumbent Gurney did not run for re-election in 1974, and Democrat Dick Stone won a tight open seat race over drug store magnate Jack Eckerd. Stone was vulnerable in the Democratic primary in 1980 and lost to Bill Gunther. However, Gunther could not hold the seat for the Democrats, losing to Paula Hawkins in the general election.

Republican Paula Hawkins was the first woman to win a U.S. Senate seat from Florida.

Paula Hawkins: Florida's First Female U.S. Senator... Then Comes Bob Graham

Paula Hawkins was the first woman, and second Republican, to win a U.S. Senate seat from Florida. (The first Florida female representative was Democrat Ruth Bryan Owen of Miami, elected in 1928 and reelected in 1930.) Hawkins had a successful run as a "housewife" for the state Public Service Commission in 1972 and won re-election in 1976. She lost her bid to be lieutenant governor in 1978 but gained name recognition. In 1980, running with future President Ronald Reagan at the head of the Republican ticket, she squeezed by her Democratic opponent for the U.S. Senate with 52 percent of the vote. But she fell victim to Governor Bob Graham's

Governor Bob Graham, famous for his work days and his Florida ties, easily won election to the U.S. Senate in 1986 (over Hawkins), 1992, and 1998 after being term-limited as governor.

popularity with Florida's voters when Graham chose to run for the Senate in 1986, after term limits forced him out of the governor's office. Graham was reelected easily in 1992 and 1998 with more than 63 percent of the vote both times.

The *Close* Mack v. MacKay Race

Republican Connie Mack III (popularly known as Connie Mack) holds the distinction of winning his U.S. Senate seat by the narrowest margin (0.8 percent in 1988) recorded in the history of Florida U.S. Senate races. Three-term incumbent U.S. Senator Lawton Chiles stunned Democrats in 1988 with his announcement of retirement from the Senate (he later ran for governor and won). A second blow to the Democrats came when the popular Reubin Askew, leading in the Senate preference polls, dropped out of the Senate race. The task fell to Congressional Representative Buddy MacKay from Ocala to keep Chiles's seat for the Democrats. But MacKay was vulnerable to attack as a liberal in a state that was increasingly conservative and Republican. His Republican opponent, Congressional Representative Connie Mack, enjoyed some name recognition: his grandfather had been the legendary owner of the Philadelphia Phillies and a pioneer in major league baseball. Mack blanketed the state with attack ads that had the same tagline: "Hey Buddy, You're a Liberal!" The vote was so close that some media outlets actually declared MacKay the winner late in the evening. However, Mack squeaked by the next morning after the absentee ballot count. Mack became increasingly popular during his first term. Ironically, after winning the seat in such a close fashion, Mack went on to win re-election in 1994 over Hugh Rodham (Hillary Clinton's brother) with 70 percent of the vote—the widest margin of victory in a Florida U.S. Senate race in the competitive two-party era dating back to the 1960s.

Republican U.S. Senate candidate Connie Mack III is surrounded by Democrat Buddy MacKay's supporters. Mack won in one of the closest U.S. Senate races in Florida history.

An Open Seat: Nelson vs. McCollum

Mack's retirement for health and family reasons cost the Republicans the U.S. Senate seat in 2000. Democrat Bill Nelson ran against Republican Bill McCollum. Nelson had excellent name recognition as a former Space Coast Congressman who flew on the space shuttle and as a two-time winner of the office of state treasurer and insurance commissioner. He had gained favorable press coverage over the preceding six years for dealing with the insurance crisis in Florida and for fighting to keep rate increases to a minimum. McCollum, on the other hand, had served 20 years in the U.S. House from Central Florida and had gained national notoriety as one of the House managers of President Bill Clinton's impeachment. But Nelson, running as a conservative Democrat, was able to keep most Democratic voters and polled well among swing voters who found McCollum too conservative and who did not like his role in the impeachment process. Nelson's solid victory (51 percent vs. 46 percent) showed that Democrats could still win statewide office in Florida, despite Republican gains over the past two decades.

A Historic First: Martinez vs. Castor

Republican Mel Martinez's victory over Betty Castor made history. Martinez is the first Cuban-born American to be elected to the U.S. Senate.

The 2004 Florida U.S. Senate race was a fiercely fought contest from start to finish. (U.S. Senator Bob Graham, a Florida political icon, retired after a heart problem derailed his plans to make a serious run for president that year.) The race, for one of the nation's eight open Senate seats, generated a crowded field of candidates in both the Democratic and Republican party primaries. Moreover, it was filled with political "firsts": It was the first time 527 groups surfaced and played such a critical role in fundraising, television and direct mail advertising, and voter mobilization (Get-Out-the-Vote) efforts. It was also the first time Hispanics outnumbered African Americans at the polls.[72] Perhaps more important, the Florida race was one of only two U.S. Senate contests in the nation not featuring a white male.[73] Either of the two ultimate opponents stood to make history: Republican Mel Martinez could become the nation's first Cuban-American U.S. senator,[74] or Democrat Betty Castor could become the state's first female Democratic U.S. senator.

As it happened, the Senate race turned out to be even more competitive than the much-anticipated presidential contest in Florida. Democrats were determined not to lose the seat held by Graham for 18 years, and Republicans saw the 2004 election as an opportunity to reclaim one of the state's Senate seats for the GOP.[75] Ultimately, the race ranked eighth among the costliest Senate contests in the nation. As the race progressed, the advertising and personal attacks became more venomous. The terrorism issue dominated both the primary and general election campaigns. It was cited by voters as the most important issue in their vote decision, according to exit polls.[76]

The general election focused mainly on the issue of alleged terrorist and former University of South Florida professor Sami Al-Arian.[77] One of Castor's primary opponents had attacked her for not doing enough to fire Al-Arian from USF after he was accused by the federal government of terrorist activities. In a proactive attempt to get ahead of the issue, the Castor campaign ran ads early in the general election saying Betty Castor was the only candidate in the race with real experience in fighting terrorism. That ad gave the Martinez camp an opening to begin a barrage of attack ads questioning Castor's decisions in the case and suggesting she had gone too easy on a suspected terrorist. Castor's camp responded with ads showing Martinez at the Florida Strawberry Festival with Al-Arian standing next to him, implying that Martinez was either soft on terrorism himself or that Al-Arian was clearly not a threat.

Martinez relied heavily on his ties to President Bush and the Republican Party during the campaign to highlight his White House connections. In contrast, Castor rarely campaigned with Democratic presidential nominee John Kerry, who was perceived as too liberal by many conservative Florida Democrats in North Florida. In the end, Castor failed to get enough support from those North Florida Democrats, and Martinez got enormous support from Florida Hispanic voters (Democrats and Republicans alike). Martinez squeaked out a 49 percent to 48 percent victory, once again proving that Florida is a highly competitive state.

An Easy Win for the Incumbent: Nelson vs. Harris

A year before U.S. Senator Bill Nelson (D) began his 2006 re-election quest, many Republicans thought he might be vulnerable because his public approval numbers hovered near the 50 percent mark. However, controversial GOP nominee Katherine Harris proved to be no match for Nelson due to her political baggage, the national anti-Republican mood, allegations of scandal, lack of support from the Republican Party, an erratic campaign, and a series of personal challenges.[78] Harris's role as Florida's Secretary of State in the controversial 2000 presidential election left her with high name recognition but also with an unfavorable rating almost three times greater than her favorability rating. In addition, Harris was linked with taking campaign donations and an expensive dinner from a defense contractor found guilty of bribery in Washington. Fearing Harris would be a drag on the GOP ticket in Florida, the national and state Republican Party leadership, including President Bush, Governor Jeb Bush, and the State Party Chair Carole Jean Jordan, all undercut Harris by trying to recruit other candidates, publicly stating that she could not win, and providing no campaign help or resources. The Harris campaign contributed to its own problems by failing to develop a clear message, making extremely controversial remarks or statements that were not credible, and suffering from wave after wave of staff turnover. Finally, Harris herself suffered through the unexpected death of her father and an ovarian mass that required surgery.

The 2006 U.S. Senate race featured Republican Congresswoman Katherine Harris against incumbent Democratic U.S. Senator Bill Nelson.

In contrast, Nelson ran a disciplined textbook race by raising millions of dollars, running a positive campaign that largely ignored his floundering opponent, and playing up his "everyman" moderate centrist image with saturation advertising in Florida's 10 media markets. Nelson was easily reelected with 60 percent of the vote, getting virtually every Democratic vote in the state and most of the independents' votes as well.

A Three-Way Race that Intrigued the Nation: Rubio vs. Meek vs. Crist[79]

Florida's 2010 U.S. Senate race was fascinating for a number of reasons. First, it was the only race in the country featuring a prominent African American (Meek), a Cuban American (Rubio), and the grandson of a Greek immigrant (Crist). Florida's racial/ethnic mix has long mirrored the nation's more than any other large battleground state—a well-known fact among the national and international media. Second, the race raised the question of whether a popular statewide elected official (Crist) could abandon a major party and successfully win an important statewide office as an independent. Had Crist's independent run been successful in the nation's fourth largest state at the same time more voters were labeling themselves independents, it would likely have prompted independent candidacies to spring up in other states.

The three candidates for the U.S. Senate relax in a Tampa television station before they debate each other. It was one of the most closely watched U.S. Senate races in the nation. L to R: Charlie Crist- NPA, Kendrick Meek-D, Marco Rubio-R.

The drama began on December 2, 2008 when Republican U.S. Senator Mel Martinez shocked Floridians by announcing he would not run for re-election in 2010. Rumors immediately began circulating that popular Republican Governor Charlie Crist would make a run for the U.S. Senate in spite of being seen as a shoo-in for re-election as governor. On May 5, 2009, Republican Marco Rubio, former Florida House Speaker, beat Crist to the punch by announcing his candidacy, forcing Crist to decide more quickly than he might have wanted. On May 12, 2009, Crist finally confirmed his candidacy. He was immediately considered the front-runner.

It was not until late January 2010 that a poll showed Rubio had inched ahead of Crist among likely Republican voters. So what contributed to Rubio's gains? For months, Rubio had crisscrossed the state, visiting local party organizations and speaking to any group he could. His candidacy caught the attention of high profile conservative groups, columnists, Fox News broadcasters, and tea partiers. Campaign contributions started rolling in, and his lead over Governor Crist in the polls widened as the Republican base became convinced that Crist was too moderate and that Rubio was a rising conservative star. On April 29, 2010, Crist made national headlines by announcing he was leaving the Republican Party to run as an independent (no party affiliation). Attention quickly shifted to the Democratic Party primary race.

That primary race already had a contender. On January 13, 2009, Democratic Congressman Kendrick Meek[80] from Miami had announced his candidacy for the U.S. Senate. An African American, Meek was convinced he could replicate Obama's victory in Florida through a coalition of moderate and liberal Democrats and independents with higher-than-average turnout by young and minority voters. The lack of enthusiasm for Meek's candidacy among some Democrats undoubtedly played a role in billionaire real estate developer Jeff Greene's decision to enter the primary on April 30, 2010. Like many self-financed candidates, Greene immediately cast himself as the outsider and labeled Meek, Rubio, and Crist as insiders. While Greene's questionable past made it easy for Meek to attack him, the billionaire's money advantage put Meek at a disadvantage. Only when Presidents Barack Obama and Bill Clinton came to Democratic vote-rich South Florida to campaign for him did Meek surge ahead in the polls. He ultimately beat Greene for the

Democratic nomination despite being outspent by Greene by 5 to 1.[81] Meek quickly turned his attention to Crist and Rubio.

A record six debates gave Floridians many opportunities to see the three candidates side-by-side. With each debate, Crist increasingly became subjected to double-barreled claims by both opponents of flip-flopping on key issues and being an opportunist. The debates allowed each candidate to clearly lay out his action plan. Rubio claimed to be the outsider who would oppose the Obama agenda, Meek pledged to support Obama and Democratic policies aimed at helping the middle class, and Crist pledged to turn his back on partisan politics and "fight for the people of Florida." Rubio's strong anti-Washington, fiscally conservative message won out.

Rubio won with 49 percent of the vote. In addition to solid Republican support, he captured a majority of the state's sizeable independent vote. (Exit polls showed that independents made up 29 percent of those voting.) Crist and Meek divided up the liberal and moderate Democratic and independent vote that did not go to Rubio. Like Rick Scott, Rubio won big in the rural and suburban areas of the state.

Perhaps the most surprising aspect of the high profile campaign was the tepid response Democrats gave to Meek's candidacy. A hefty portion of Florida Democrats abandoned the party's first African-American nominee for the U.S. Senate to support a former conservative Republican governor they had found repulsive just four years earlier. Endorsements of Crist by some Democratic elected officials, contributions to him by big Democratic donors, and President Clinton talking to Meek about dropping out of the race made big headlines and further angered Meek supporters and Democratic Party loyalists. The intraparty spats undoubtedly tamped down critical Democratic turnout in South Florida and cost Meek the election (and Alex Sink her bid for governor as well).

Cuban-American Marco Rubio's victory in the 2010 Florida U.S. Senate race had some Republicans already mentioning him as a possible vice presidential candidate in 2012. In 2015, he announced his candidacy for president of the United States in the 2016 election.

The election dashed the hopes of the eternally optimistic Crist, who wanted to make history as an independent, and the dreams of Meek, who would have been Florida's first African-American U.S. senator. It was Rubio who drew a record number of media from around the world to his victory party in Miami, with speculations that he might one day be president. In the end, "With uncompromising conservatism, Rubio proved to be the perfect candidate at the perfect time," wrote Adam Smith, the St. Petersburg Times' political editor.[82]

An Open U.S. Senate Seat in 2016

Senator Marco Rubio's six-year term ends in 2016. But in 2015, he announced he would not run for re-election but rather seek the Republican Party nomination for president. That left a wide open race in the nation's most competitive state. Early estimates were that it would be costly, probably in the neighborhood of $40 million to $50 million. When Rubio won the race in 2010, he spent $21.6 million, Crist spent $13.6 million, and Meek, slightly less than $9 million.[83] And that race wasn't as close as the 2016 race will likely be. The 2016 race will be hard fought as each party sees the seat as critical to its control of the U.S. Senate.

Cabinet Races

Until 2002, the Florida Cabinet was made up of six statewide elected officials (attorney general, comptroller, secretary of state, education commissioner, agriculture commissioner, treasurer and insurance commissioner). But in 1998, Florida voters approved a constitutional amendment (effective in 2002) that reduced the size of the Cabinet to three statewide elective offices (attorney general, chief financial officer, agriculture commissioner).

Florida's Cabinet is historically unique among the 50 states. Its members are independent of the governor. Each Cabinet member serves a four-year term with a two-term limit. Each Cabinet member is wholly responsible for the administration of at least one state department, while the governor is responsible for the administration of most other state departments. Cabinet members, like the governor, are elected statewide.[84] There are conditions under which the governor and Cabinet meet collectively to make executive decisions but technically the governor is not a member of the Florida Cabinet. (More will be said about that in Chapter 7.)

Until the 1980s, all of Florida's Cabinet members were well-entrenched Democrats who were consistently reelected. (Nathan Mayo served as agriculture commissioner from 1923 to 1960.) But Republicans have slowly gained control of the Cabinet just as they have the state legislature. The first Republican Cabinet member to be elected in the modern era was Jim Smith, who was appointed by Governor Martinez to fill a vacancy as secretary of state in 1987, then won the office as the incumbent in 1988.

By 1994 Florida's six member Cabinet was equally divided—three Democrats and three Republicans. (At the time, Democrat Lawton Chiles was governor, giving Democrats the voting edge in collective body decisions.) The Cabinet was also equally divided in 1998, when Republican Jeb Bush was elected governor. In 2002, Republicans won all three races for the smaller three-person Cabinet and the governor's race. While a Democrat was competitive in the attorney general's race, the Florida Democratic Party did not field a candidate for chief financial officer and put up only token opposition for the agriculture commissioner post. The result was that in 2002, Republicans achieved total control of the executive branch for the first time since Reconstruction. The GOP's exclusive control of the Cabinet was short-lived, however. In 2006, Democrat Alex Sink was elected chief financial officer (CFO). Her victory in this statewide race was celebrated by Democrats who saw her win as good news for the future of the party and immediately began talk of her potential as a gubernatorial candidate.

Democrat Nathan Mayo served as Florida's agriculture commissioner from 1923 to 1960, before there were term limits on Cabinet officials. A state building in Tallahassee bears his name.

Sink's decision to run for governor in 2010 rather than for re-election as CFO created a unique situation. For the first time in Florida's history, the governorship and all three Cabinet posts had no incumbents running (Crist ran for the U.S. Senate, CFO Sink and Attorney General McCollum ran for governor, and Agriculture Commissioner Charles Bronson was term limited). The Republican candidates won all three Cabinet offices. Republican Pam Bondi became Florida's first female attorney general, former Congressman Adam Putnam was elected agriculture commissioner, and State Senator Jeff Atwater became CFO. In hindsight, it is easy to see that the poor state of Florida's economy was a powerful mobilizing force that made "anti" messages (anti-tax, anti-spending, anti-national debt, anti-establishment, anti-incumbent) an easy sell in 2010. The 2014 Cabinet races were a repeat of the 2010 races, with Republicans Bondi, Putnam, and Atwater all easily winning re-election. (See Table 4-8.)

Table 4-8. Statewide Cabinet Elections: 1998 to 2014
(Winner's Percent of Vote)

Election	Attorney General	Secretary of State	Comptroller	Treasurer	Education Commissioner	Agriculture Commissioner
1998 (3D's, 3R's)	Bob Butterworth (D) 59.6%	Katherine Harris* (R) 53.7%	Bob Milligan* (R) 60.6%	Bill Nelson* (D) 56.5%	Tom Gallagher* (R) 56.5%	Bob Crawford (D) 61.8%
(Cabinet Size Reduced)	Attorney General	X	Chief Financial Officer		X	Agriculture Commissioner
2002 (3R's)	Charlie Crist (R) 53.4%		Tom Gallagher (R) No Opposition			Charles Bronson (R) 57.4%
2006 (1D, 2R's)	Bill McCollum (R) 52.7%		Alex Sink (D) 53.5%			Charles Bronson (R) 57.0%
2010 (3R's)	Pam Bondi (R) 54.8%		Jeff Atwater (R) 57.3%			Adam Putnam (R) 55.9%
2014 (3R's)	Pam Bondi (R) 55.1%		Jeff Atwater (R) 58.9%			Adam Putnam (R) 58.7%

Note: *1998 was the last year these positions were elected. In 1998, Floridians amended the Constitution to reduce size of the Cabinet from six to three. The chief financial officer position was created by merging the comptroller and treasurer positions.

Source: Florida Division of Elections.

U.S. CONGRESSIONAL RACES

Congressional races, like state legislative races, are district-based. The districts are drawn by the state legislature often to protect incumbents or to expand the power of the party in control. That is why Florida looks like a *very Republican* state when judged by the number of Republicans in its congressional delegation and in the state legislature but looks *very competitive* in statewide elections (presidential, U.S. Senate, gubernatorial, Florida Cabinet).

Florida's electoral shift to the GOP is evident in the changing partisan composition of its congressional delegation. In 1955, voters from the St. Petersburg area elected Bill Cramer to Congress, making him the first Republican congressman elected from Florida since the post-Civil War era. He was joined in the 1960s by two other Republicans—Lou Frey from Orlando and Edward Gurney. Other early Republican stalwarts in Congress—Clay Shaw, Bill Young, Bill McCollum, and Michael Bilirakis—were joined by several newcomers, including Connie Mack III, after the reapportionment in the early 1980s that expanded Florida's congressional delegation from 15 to 19.[85]

Republicans picked up additional congressional seats in 1984 and 1988 and finally won a slim 10 to 9 majority in the 1990 midterm congressional election. Key to the switch was the victory of Cuban born Republican Ileana Ros-Lehtinen, who won the Miami seat long held by Democrat Claude Pepper. He had served Florida first as a U.S. senator, then later as a U.S. House member from Miami-Dade County. Pepper was perhaps best known for his advocacy work on behalf of senior citizens and for bringing new federal jobs, contracts, and military bases to Florida during the Depression and World War II.[86]

Florida's huge population growth during the 1980s gave the state four more congressional seats after the 1990 Census. Republicans picked up three of these new seats for a total of 13 out of 23 seats in the delegation. Florida was a major component of the earth-shattering Republican victory in the 1994 congressional elections that, for the first time in 40 years, gave Republicans control of the U.S. House of Representatives. The GOP won 15 seats in Florida in 1994; it held on to these seats despite Clinton's victory in the state in 1996.

The partisan makeup of the state's congressional delegation did not change in 2000; it stayed at 15 Republicans and 8 Democrats. However, it did change after the 2002 redistricting. Again, Florida's population growth during the 1990s gave Florida two more congressional seats, bringing the delegation total to 25. With Republicans in control of the Florida Legislature—and the redistricting process—Republicans were able to shore up several weak GOP districts, create new Republican districts in Central and South Florida, and considerably weaken the Democratic District Five in West Central Florida.

In the 2002 elections, under the new redistricting plan, Republicans picked up three seats in the congressional delegation (won by Tom Feeney, Mario Diaz-Balart, and Ginny Brown-Waite) giving the GOP 18 of the 25 seats, leaving the Democrats with just seven seats. (See Figure 4-10.) Republican gains in Florida accounted for the majority of new seats won by Republicans in the U.S. Congress as they beat historical odds to increase seats when their party controlled the White House.

The 2004 election did not change the partisan makeup of Florida's congressional delegation, although one new Republican was elected (Connie Mack IV, son of the former senator) replacing one who was retiring. However, 2006 proved to be a good year for Democrats who took advantage of the national anti-Republican mood brought on by the war in Iraq and scandals in Washington. The Democrats recruited and supported a number of quality candidates to challenge GOP incumbents in vulnerable districts and in open seats. Ultimately Democrats regained control of Congress and picked up two seats in the Florida delegation, reducing the Republican advantage in the congressional delegation to 16-9.[87] Democratic State Senator Ron Klein was able to unseat long-term GOP incumbent Clay Shaw by nationalizing the race in a district that had trended Democratic (it went for John Kerry in 2004 by two percent). Democrat Tim Mahoney was able to win a squeaker in Mark Foley's formerly safe Republican seat after Foley resigned in the wake of press reports of sending salacious e-mails to teenage congressional pages. Because the resignation occurred after the primary, Foley's name remained on the ballot although all votes cast for him were assigned to GOP replacement candidate Joe Negron.

Figure 4-10. The Partisan Makeup of Florida's U.S. House Delegation: 2002-2014

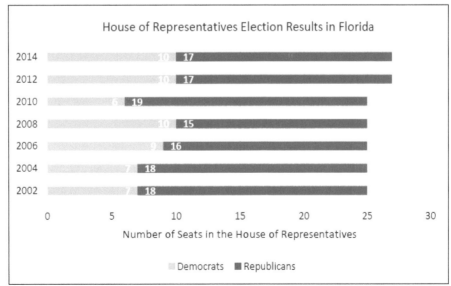

Note: In the 2012 reapportionment, Florida gained two seats in the U.S. House of Representatives
Source: Federal Election Commission.

The other seven Florida Democrats who won congressional seats in 2006 were mostly from heavily Democratic districts in highly urbanized areas: South Florida (Kendrick Meek, Robert Wexler, Debbie Wasserman-Schultz, and Alcee Hastings), Tampa (Kathy Castor), and Jacksonville (Corrine Brown). The one exception was conservative Allen Boyd from the Panhandle area west of Tallahassee, a member of the Democratic Blue Dog coalition (mostly Southern fiscal conservatives). Three of the nine Democrats in Florida's congressional delegation were active members of the Congressional Black Caucus (Meek, Hastings, and Brown).

The 2008 U.S. Congressional races in Florida were mostly business-as-usual, with the exception of two Central Florida races that, at least at the time, appeared to be positive indicators for future Democratic candidates in Florida. In District 24, Democrat Suzanne Kosmas unseated Republican Tom Feeney, whose campaign was overshadowed by an ethical misjudgment. Democrat Alan Grayson, a wealthy, flamboyant, and liberal business executive, defeated Republican incumbent Ric Keller, despite winning only one of four counties in District 8. Grayson was able to win the district by achieving a sizeable margin in Orange County, which is by far the district's largest county. Grayson and other Democrats throughout the state enjoyed high turnout among the loyal Democratic base that resulted from Obama's groundbreaking candidacy. These Democratic victories would be short-lived, however, as both Kosmas and Grayson would lose their seats in the next election cycle (2010). Neither Democrats nor Republicans could have fully anticipated the economic downturn that would follow, and, as a result, what was largely a product of special circumstances was mistaken for a more predictable Democratic resurgence in the state.

Although the 2008 election suggested more competitive congressional elections to come, a deepening recession all but ensured that Republicans would win big in 2010. And, they did, dominating races across the state, due in part to unusually low black turnout. The turnout problem proved insurmountable for Democrats.

In 2010, Kosmas shifted to a more moderate platform in an effort to stay afloat in a largely conservative district; this strategy backfired, as her indecision on health care reform (first voting against it, then voting for it) managed to upset both the Democratic base and members of the tea party movement. Former State Representative Sandy Adams (R) ran against Kosmas in a district that mostly overlapped her former state legislative district, and Adams coasted to victory. In District 8, Republican Daniel Webster ran a frugal, yet successful campaign against both Alan Grayson and Florida Tea Party candidate Peg Dunmire.

A three-way race for Congressional District 12, an open seat vacated by Republican Adam Putnam, who successfully ran for state agriculture commissioner,[88] saw Republican Dennis Ross (a former state legislator) defeat Tea Party candidate Randy Wilkinson and Democrat Lori Edwards.

Elsewhere in the state, Republican Allen West, a retired Army lieutenant colonel who had served in Iraq, upset Jewish Democrat Ron Klein, whom many expected to win in a South Florida district with strong Jewish communities. West, a favorite of the tea party movement, drew support from the movement's energized conservative following in the state and the nation and went on to become Florida's first Republican African-American Congressman since Reconstruction, whereas other 2010 candidates who ran with the Florida Tea Party failed to capture the support of a movement more interested in its ideology than in fielding candidates.

The strength of the Republican wave in 2010 could also be seen as Democrat Allen Boyd, whose seat was long considered safe, especially after winning handily in 2008, was upset by a political novice, Republican Steve Southerland, of Southerland Family Funeral Homes. Boyd, like Kosmas in District 24, decided to support Obama's health care reform after originally opposing it, a grave misstep that weakened his traditionally popular image as a Blue Dog, conservative-leaning Democrat. A handful of Democrats survived the Republican tidal wave, including Frederica Wilson, who filled Kendrick Meek's newly vacant seat, winning handily in South Florida's heavily Democratic multicultural District 17. In general, Republicans successfully rode the anti-incumbent wave across the state, propelled by low turnout among the Democratic base, particularly in critical South Florida. This confirmed that, while Democrats successfully catered to the desire for change in health care and other key policy areas in 2008, *nothing* breeds more urgent public demand for a changing of the guard like a tough economy.

The congressional delegation grew in 2012, with the addition of two new seats after the 2010 Census. District lines were altered to comply with the equal population requirement. In some cases district numbers were even changed. As noted in Chapter 1, court cases ensued, led by plaintiffs charging that the state had violated the Fair Districts amendment that prohibited any partisan favoritism. But the map that was used in the 2012 election was not declared unconstitutional until 2014, and a new one would not be put in place until 2016. The 27-member map used in 2014 was configured so that there were nine districts favoring Democrats, 16 favoring Republicans, and two that could swing either way.[89] As with any round of redistricting, some incumbents decided not to run for re-election (Connie Mack IV who ran unsuccessfully for the U.S. Senate). Others chose to run in a different district and lost (Allen West-R). (Congress members do not have to live in the district they represent.) Still others got thrust into a district with another incumbent from the same party and ended up losing to a colleague (Sandy Adams-R lost to John Mica-R). Republicans ended up winning 17 seats, and Democrats 10—but that was a pickup of four House seats for Democrats and a loss of two seats for Republicans.

Several key congressional races in the 2010 election cycle were heavily influenced by activists in the Tea Party movement.

The 2014 congressional election cycle saw two newcomers beat two incumbents in that year's two most competitive districts—one in the Panhandle (District 2), the other in South Florida (District 26). In the Panhandle, newcomer Gwen Graham-D (daughter of former Governor and U.S. Senator Bob Graham) beat Republican Steve Southerland. In South Florida, Carlos Curbelo-R defeated Democrat Joe Garcia. Both Graham and Curbelo campaigned against Washington, reflective of voter disillusionment with the lack of leadership there. The Florida delegation remained heavily Republican (17 Republicans and 10 Democrats).

The 2016 congressional races are likely to see a lot of candidates running for the House for three reasons—court-ordered, newly drawn congressional districts, record low ratings of Congress, and decisions by some incumbents not to seek re-election. For example, Democratic Congressman Patrick Murphy's decision to run for the open U.S. Senate seat creates an open seat in District 18, and open seats draw a lot of candidates.

STATE LEGISLATIVE RACES: FLORIDA SENATE AND FLORIDA HOUSE

For many years, the Florida Legislature was dominated by Democrats. But, as mentioned earlier, that began to change in the 1960s as Florida's political landscape became more competitive and Republicans steadily gained seats in each house. (See Figures 4-11.) One hundred twenty years after Reconstruction ended in Florida, the state's voters finally elected Republican majorities to both houses of the state legislature in 1996.

Figure 4-11. Party Seats Won in Florida State House & Senate Elections

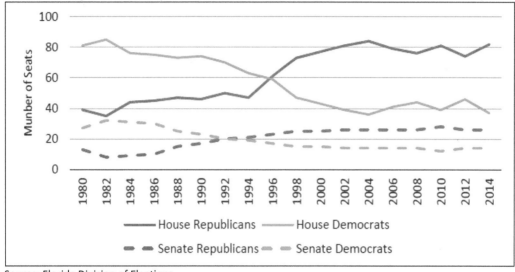

Source: Florida Division of Elections.

The Republican victory in 1996 was by no means unexpected. The steady gains by the GOP in state House and Senate races made such a forecast fairly easy, although there were a few stumbles and scares along the way. In 1976, Republican gains during the 1960s were erased by voter outrage over Watergate. That year Florida Republicans won only 28 of 120 House seats (23 percent). But then they continued their gains. By 1994, Republicans had gained control of the Florida Senate after an awkward two years in which each party held exactly half (20) of the chamber's seats. And in 1996, they won the Florida House by a slim 61 to 59 margin.

Between 1996 and 2004, Republicans increased their margin of control in both houses of the state legislature. Their gains came about as a result of redistricting in 2002 (more Republican districts), the party's recruiting of more and better candidates, and its success in generating campaign contributions (the power of incumbency). Republicans have also been aided by several conservative Democratic legislators switching parties. By early 2006, Republicans expanded their control of legislative seats 85-35 in the House and 26-14 in the Senate. However, Democrats rebounded in the fall of 2006 using the national tide to help win back seven House seats (although one conservative Democrat switched to the GOP right after the election) bringing the GOP edge to 79-41. The Senate remained at 26-14 in favor of the Republicans.

Democrats made smaller gains in the 2008 election cycle, picking up only three seats in the House and no seats in the Senate. It was a disappointing result in what should have been a good year to be running as a Democrat, with Barack Obama heading the national ticket. Still, Democrats throughout the state took the Obama victory as a sign the party was on the rebound. They anxiously awaited 2010. But on November 3, 2010, Floridians woke up to the news that Republicans had won both the U.S. Senate and gubernatorial races, four congressional seats held by Democratic incumbents, all three statewide Cabinet post contests, and a large number of seats in both the Florida House (81-39) and Senate (28-12).

In 2012, Democrats counted on regaining some of the state legislative seats they lost in 2010. After all, it was a presidential election year when Democratic turnout rates are typically higher. Plus, every legislator would have to run for newly configured districts as a consequence of redistricting—a process they assumed would yield more Democratic-leaning districts to conform to the Fair Districts amendment outlawing partisan gerrymandering. Democrats picked up two seats in the Florida Senate (from 12 to 14) and eight seats in the House (38 to 46)—enough seats to block any legislative efforts to overturn a governor's veto. However, Republicans remained in control of both chambers (Senate 26 to 14; House 74 to 46). The gains were enough to make Democrats believe it was the start of a rebirth of Democratic strength. It was not.

In 2014, Republicans did well in the state legislative races—a pattern reflecting the wave of Republican victories across the United States. (It meant that Republicans hold more state legislative seats in the 50 states than at any time since 1928.)[90] The result was that the GOP gained seven seats in the Florida House (up from 74 in 2010 to 81). The Democratic loss in the House was so severe that the party lost its ability to hold up legislation procedurally. The good news for Democrats was that they lost no seats in the Senate. The bad news was that they still had just 14 seats to the Republicans' 26. A court challenge to the 2012 Senate redistricting map claiming it was partisan gerrymandering had not progressed in time for the map to be altered. The challenge will be resolved before the 2016 Senate elections.

The pressure is on Florida Democrats to do a lot better in legislative races over the next few years. One post-2014 election analysis in a major newspaper pointed to the party's "decade-long tradition of losing in a state where they outnumber Republicans" and "ignor[ing] races they could win [because] they have no bench."[91] Some party activists are "worried that Democrats are going to have a hard time winning state legislative control... before the next round of redistricting in 2020."[92] Republicans, on the other hand, have to be concerned about the state's changing demographics—increases in the number of more Democratic-voting racial/ethnic minorities and Millennials, although Millennials are a little more up for grabs. How Millennials vote will make a big difference in future elections because they are now larger in numbers than Baby Boomers. One prominent demographer has observed that "the data says that if Republicans focus on economic issues and stay away from social ones like gay marriage, they can make serious inroads with Millennials."[93] Democrats doubt it.

Florida's Bellwether Status in National Politics

Tracing the evolution of Florida into one of the nation's most competitive battleground states shows just how much the state's political parties and elections have mirrored what was happening nationally. From the 1990s forward, the state has been the nation's largest swing state, sharply divided and capable of shifting between political parties."[94] Florida's role as a barometer is likely to continue so long as the state's population continues to look more like America at large than most other states.

ONLINE SOURCES FOR DATA AND INFORMATION UPDATES

Florida Division of Elections: Statistics

This page features statistics on voter registration, voter turnout (absentee, early voting, election day), election results, political parties (major and minor), and general facts about elections, (general, primary, and special) in Florida, and its counties or districts. Data is also broken down by age, race, income, and political party.
http://dos.myflorida.com/elections/data-statistics/

Florida Division of Elections: Candidates

This is searchable index of all candidates in current and past elections.
http://dos.elections.myflorida.com/candidates/index.asp

Federal Election Commission: Federal Statutes

The FEC is responsible for regulating the financing of all elections. "Federal Statutes" contains copies of election rules regarding contributions and disclosures.
http://www.fec.gov/law/law.shtml

Federal Election Commission: Data Summaries

This is a source of summaries of all election data in both national races and state races, specifically regarding the financial records of each race.
http://www.fec.gov/finance/disclosure/ftpsum.shtml

Sunshine State Survey: Results

The Sunshine State Survey polls Florida residents for their opinions on national and local issues, and includes statistics on the respondent's age, race, gender, party affiliation, employment, etc. The survey has data available from 2006 to 2014 (excluding 2013). Specific data can be found on trust in government leaders, the most important issue facing Florida, opinions on taxing and spending (tax revenue, least fair revenue source, and budget), issue stances, biggest divide for public officials, and the most important leadership quality.
http://sunshinestatesurvey.org/results/

Republican Party of Florida

The official home of the Republican Party of Florida has information about the party, fundraising, candidates, and leadership.
http://www.florida.gop/

Democratic Party of Florida

The official home of the Democratic Party of Florida provides information about the party, fundraising, candidates, and leadership.
http://www.floridadems.org/

Chapter 5. Power, Money, and Influence in Florida

Florida's growth and diversification over the years brought about a gradual fragmentation of the state's traditional power structure. It is no longer possible for a few powerful individuals—like the late Ed Ball, who headed the extensive DuPont land and railroad holdings in the state, the late Chester Ferguson of Lykes Meat Company, the late Ben Hill Griffin of agribusiness, or the late attorney Chesterfield Smith of Holland and Knight, who wrote the Florida Constitution—to dictate policy in the state capital. Traditionally strong interests in Florida—citrus, cattle, horse racing, phosphate, electric power, and liquor industries—now share power with tourism and the service sector, builders and contractors, banking and insurance, health care providers, labor unions, teachers, public employees, environmentalists, gun owners, feminist and civil rights organizations, trial lawyers, and Tribes. And, of course, in Florida the influence of senior citizens, including AARP (formerly known as the American Association of Retired Persons), is especially important. The increase in the number of interest groups active in Florida over time mirrors a trend found in most states.[2]

Some interests are more powerful than others. That is, some interests are more likely to see their concerns placed high on the agenda of the state's decision makers, more successful in developing a consensus on behalf of their preferences, more active in electoral campaigns and in contributing money to candidates, more skillful in guiding their initiatives through the legislative process, and generally more successful in enacting their preferences into public policy. In Florida, business interests, especially the Associated Industries of Florida and the Florida Chamber of Commerce, tend to be most influential. Indeed, in Florida, as elsewhere, the public perception is that government is "pretty much run by a few big interests." One survey found that three out of four Floridians believe that "the country is pretty much run by a few big interests looking out for themselves."[3] Fewer than one in five expresses the more benign view that the country "is run for the benefit of all people."

The public's suspicion of lobbyists and powerful special interest groups has been around since the days of the constitutional convention in Philadelphia. However, when it is an issue a group of citizens becomes keenly concerned about, a "special interest group" suddenly becomes an "advocacy group," which conjures up a more positive image. Collective action on the part of the citizenry has always been an important source of influence. The old saying "There's strength in numbers" often turns out to be true in a representative democracy. On contentious issues, the "law of lobbyist physics" often prevails: "For every powerful interest group pushing one side of an issue, there is an equally powerful interest group advocating the other side." In a diverse state like Florida, powerful interest groups represent virtually every sector of the economy.

THE ECONOMIC INTERESTS

Economic interests dominate politics in Tallahassee and nearly everywhere else, as well. More than two hundred years ago James Madison observed that "the most common and durable source of factions, has been the various and unequal distribution of property... A landed interest, a manufacturing interest, a mercantile interest, a moneyed interest, with many lesser interests, grow up of necessity in civilized nations."[4] And modern studies of power in Washington and state capitals conclude that economic interests are more numerous, better organized, better financed, and more influential in policy making than other groups and organizations.[5]

The Florida economy is heavily dependent on services including tourism, banking, insurance, real estate, and construction. Agribusiness, particularly citrus, sugar, fresh vegetables and greenhouses, is still important, and the health care industry is growing rapidly due to the large number of seniors. Electric utilities have expanded to serve the state's rapidly growing population. While manufacturing has never been a very large part of the Florida economy, despite the presence of Lockheed Martin on the Space Coast, there has been an upswing in the production of communications equipment, defense electronics, and photonics. During the 1990s, Florida became a leader in high-tech industrial employment, especially in the areas of communications and engineering services, computer-related services, and information services. Local governments, the state, and its universities have sought to attract more high-tech industry by establishing research parks and providing incentives to firms that move to or expand in Florida. International trade and travel has become a bigger part of Florida's economy as well. The state's top five exports are motor vehicles, aircraft engines and parts, telecommunications equipment, computers and components, and gold.[6] In fact, it is the desire of state politicians to keep Florida's economy growing that gives economic interests such clout. Because businesses provide jobs and generate sales taxes, and because states compete with each other for new business, economic interests carry great sway in the state capital.[7]

Corporations

The largest public and private corporations based in Florida as ranked by annual revenue are summarized in Table 5-1. The largest public corporations include World Fuel Services, Tech Data (a computer distributor), Auto Nation, NextERA Energy, Office Depot, Carnival, Jabil Circuit, WellCare, CSX and Hertz. Large private companies include Publix, Sun Capital Partners, H.I.G. Capital Management, JM Family Enterprises, Southern Wine and Spirits, Southeastern Grocers, Brightstar, Adventist Health, Oasis Outsourcing, and Fanjul Florida Crystals. Public corporations are owned by shareholders who purchase the stock on the open market while private corporations are owned by private investors. These large public and private

Publix, a majority employee-owned company, has repeatedly been named as one of Fortune Magazine's "100 Best Companies to Work For."

corporations are usually among the biggest donors to candidates, committees, and political parties in the state.

Banks and Insurance Companies

Table 5-2 displays the largest banks and insurance companies operating in Florida. Because of mergers and buy-outs, most of the large banks and insurance companies operating in Florida have their corporate headquarters out of state, with just a regional office in Florida or somewhere in the southeast (except for residential property insurers who are largely Florida-based). However, health care access, costs and regulations are enormous issues in the state because of Florida's large elderly population and the sizable number of its residents without health insurance. Containing health insurance costs, while trying to expand health insurance coverage, have been important but conflicting priorities in the Florida Legislature over the last decade. (See Chapter 11.)

The Great Recession spelled bad times for homeowners and the state's large banks and insurance companies as Florida led the nation in home foreclosures. Fortunately, the economy is on the rebound.

Table 5-1. Florida's Largest Corporations

Rank	Institution	Corporate Headquarters
Corporations—Public		
1	World Fuel Services	Miami
2	Tech Data	Clearwater
3	AutoNation	Fort Lauderdale
4	NextEra Energy	Juno Beach
5	Office Depot	Boca Raton
6	Carnival	Miami
7	Jabil Circuit	St. Petersburg
8	WellCare Health Plans	Tampa
9	CSX Corp.	Jacksonville
10	Hertz Global Holdings	Estero
Corporations--Private		
1	Publix Supermarkets	Lakeland
2	Sun Capital Partners	Boca Raton
3	H.I.G. Capital Management	Miami
4	JM Family Enterprises	Deerfield Beach
5	Southern Wine & Spirits of America	Miami
6	Southeastern Grocers	Jacksonville
7	Brightstar	Miami
8	Adventist Health Systems	Altamonte Springs
9	Oasis Outsourcing	West Palm Beach
10	Fanjul/Florida Crystals	West Palm Beach

Source: Top Rank Florida, ©*Florida Trend*, July 2015 issue, used with permission. Further reproduction prohibited.

Property and Casualty Insurance

The homeowners insurance market has been problematic in Florida since Hurricane Andrew in 1992. The record-setting four major hurricanes in 2004 followed by another heavy hurricane season in 2005 caused many of the largest insurance companies to stop writing policies in Florida and in some cases to even shed policies to limit their risk. In addition, the companies sought big rate increases in an effort to recoup their losses and regain profitability. The state insurance commission reduced some of the requests, but that had the effect of causing the companies to write even fewer policies in Florida, making it very difficult for homeowners near the coast to get coverage.

After Hurricane Andrew, the Florida Legislature created Citizens Property Insurance Corporation to insure properties that private insurers will not cover—primarily homes near Florida's beaches. But the rates charged by Citizens were not nearly enough to cover the losses incurred in 2004 and 2005. Homeowners across the state have been forced to pay extra charges on top of their own premiums to help keep Citizens solvent. The situation has turned angry homeowners into political activists. Lawmakers acted quickly to use more general revenue money to cover the shortfall and reduce the extra charge on insurance policies. The quick reaction of the legislature to rapidly escalating citizen complaints demonstrates that it is not always just the big corporations that win at the lobbying game. Each year that passes without a major hurricane allows the insurance market to stabilize, Citizens insurance to shed policies, and the extra charges that have incensed property owners to be phased out. But the issue remains unsettled with private insurance companies arguing for more freedom to raise rates, coastal homeowners demanding affordable coverage, inland residents insisting that they stop being asked to subsidize Floridians who live near the beach, and all taxpayers at risk should damages caused by a major hurricane be greater than the funds available to Citizens Insurance to pay all the insurance claims.

Table 5-2. Florida's Largest Banks and Insurance Companies

Rank	Institution	Location
Banks (By Florida Deposits)		
1	Bank of America	Charlotte, NC
2	Wells Fargo	Sioux Falls, SD
3	SunTrust Bank	Atlanta, GA
4	JPMorgan Chase Bank	Columbus, OH
5	Regions Bank	Birmingham, AL
Health Insurance (By Number of Customers)		
1	UnitedHealth	Minnetonka, MN
2	Blue Cross Blue Shield of FL	Jacksonville, FL
3	Humana	Louisville, KY
4	Aetna	Hartford, CT
5	WellCare	Tampa, FL
Residential Property Insurance (By Total Premiums)		
1	Citizens Property	Jacksonville, FL
2	University Property & Casualty	Fort Lauderdale, FL
3	Tower Hill Insurance Group	Gainesville, FL
4	State Farm	Winter Haven, FL
5	ARX Holding Corp (Progressive)	St. Petersburg, FL
Automobile Insurance (By Number of Customers)		
1	Berkshire Hathaway (GEICO)	Washington, D.C.
2	State Farm	Bloomington, IL
3	Progressive American	Cleveland, OH
4	Allstate Insurance	Northbrook, IL
5	USAA	San Antonio, TX

Source: Bank Holding Companies, ©*Florida Trend*, October 2014 (as updated by the authors from the FDIC Deposit Market Share Report as of June 2015). *Fast Facts* Florida Office of Insurance Regulation, October 2014.

Construction and Real Estate

Florida's rapid growth over the last decades has been a boon to construction companies and commercial real estate firms. (Frankly, so, too were the hurricanes). (See Table 5-3.) Land development, construction and real estate industries have been particularly important engines for economic growth and tax generation. Growth management is always a major issue of interest to the construction and real estate industry. As a rule, they view restrictions on growth as bad for their business. (See Chapter 12.)

Utilities

New homes and businesses require increasing amounts of electricity, and have made generating and distributing power an extremely profitable and fast growing business in Florida. The issues of energy deregulation, competition, disaster recovery, nuclear power, energy prices, and rate increases have dominated the agenda of electric utilities over the years. And, of course, as a heavily regulated industry, utilities constantly lobby the legislature and the Florida Public Service Commission that has oversight responsibility for the industry. Some electric utilities are privately owned, while others are run by municipalities.

Table 5-3. Florida's Largest Construction, Real Estate Firms, and Utilities

Rank	Institution	Location
Construction		
1	Lennar	Miami
2	Coastal Construction Group	Miami
3	GL Homes	Sunrise
4	Haskell	Jacksonville
5	Stellar	Jacksonville
Real Estate Development		
1	Related Group	Miami
2	Villages of Lake Sumter	The Villages
3	St. Joe	WaterSound
4	Rayonier	Jacksonville
5	Stock Development	Naples
Utilities		
1	Florida Power & Light (FPL) / NextEra Energy	Juno Beach
2	Duke Energy (formerly Progress Energy)	Raleigh, NC
3	Tampa Electric / TECO Energy Inc.	Tampa
4	Gulf Power Company / Southern Company	Pensacola
5	Jacksonville Electric Authority (JEA)	Jacksonville

Source: Annual Top Rank Florida, ©Florida Trend, July 2015, used with permission. Further reproduction prohibited. Utilities, ©Florida Trend, July 2015, used with permission. Further reproduction prohibited. As updated by the authors from Facts and Figures of the Florida Utility Industry March 2015, Florida Public Service Commission, Available at http://www.floridapsc.com/publications/pdf/general/factsandfigures2015.pdf

Tourism and Agribusiness

Table 5-4 lists the largest companies with headquarters in the state from the top two sectors of Florida's economy: tourism and agriculture. Tourism is the number one industry in Florida and one of the state's top employers with nearly 1 million people directly employed by the industry (many in low-wage service jobs). Tourism leaders include cruise and entertainment giants Carnival and Royal Caribbean, low cost Spirit Airlines, and Sea World (which also owns Busch Gardens). The out-of-state parent companies of Walt Disney World and Universal Studios and Islands of Adventure are tremendously influential as well. Florida's taxpayers depend on tourists to pay a healthy percentage of total sales taxes. In 2014, an estimated 97 million tourists visited Florida. They spent $82 billion and paid almost $5 billion in sales taxes. Demonstrative of Disney's clout is the fact that when they came to Florida in the 1960s, the state legislature actually allowed them to form and control three local governments: Reedy Creek Improvement District, Bay Lake, and Lake Buena Vista.[9] (See Chapter 10.)

Agriculture is the second largest portion of the Florida economy and citrus is still the signature Florida product. In addition, Florida ranks first or second among all states in greenhouse and nursery products, peppers, tomatoes, strawberries, snap beans, squash, sweet corn, cucumbers, and watermelons.[10] The citrus industry faces major challenges from damaging winter frost, pressure to sell land to developers, competition from Brazil, and diseases such as citrus canker and the even more deadly citrus greening. The tomato and vegetable industry has faced significant challenges from Mexico under NAFTA (the North American Free Trade Agreement) and has brought formal complaints alleging "dumping" of tomatoes in the U.S. market below actual costs in order to drive the U.S. producers out of business. The sugar industry in South Florida depends on federal tariffs on imported sugar to stay profitable and is impacted by environmental regulations and cleanup efforts in the Everglades and thus lobbies heavily in Washington, as well as in Tallahassee.

Tourism is the number one industry in Florida.

Agribusiness is big business in Florida.

Table 5-4. Florida's Largest Tourism Firms and Agribusinesses

Rank	Institution	Location
Tourism		
1	Carnival Corp.	Miami
2	Royal Caribbean Cruises	Miami
3	Spirit Airlines	Miramar
4	Sea World Entertainment	Orlando
5	Westgate Resorts	Orlando
Agribusiness		
1	Fanjul Corp. / Florida Crystals	West Palm Beach
2	Fresh Del Monte Produce	Coral Gables
3	Florida's Natural Growers	Lake Wales
4	A. Duda & Sons	Oviedo
5	Peace River Citrus Products	Vero Beach

Source: Annual Top Rank Florida, ©*Florida Trend*, July 2015, used with permission. Further reproduction prohibited.

THE LAW FIRMS

As early as 1832, Alexis de Tocqueville observed that the legal profession in the new American republic was becoming the "new aristocracy."[11] The historic prevalence of lawyers among political leaders in Florida, and the nation, is well documented. Lawyers are still quite prevalent among Florida's legislators. (See Chapter 6.) But the real power of the legal profession is found in the state's large, prestigious, and influential law firms. The senior partners of these firms are "the professional go betweens," bringing together the economic and political worlds "to unify the power elite."[12]

Identification of the top law firms in Florida is necessarily subjective. Prestigious firms do not provide full lists of clients, claiming that to do so would violate "lawyer-client confidentiality." But Table 5-5 provides the names of firms believed to be the most influential in the state ranked by the number of lawyers employed in Florida. All the firms listed employ over two hundred lawyers and have considerable clout in Tallahassee. Many law firms lobby on behalf of their clients on a wide variety of issues. Law firms also lobby directly on behalf of their own interests such as fighting tort reform efforts that seek to make it more difficult to sue corporations or doctors. Business groups argue that tort reform is needed to encourage economic growth. Lobbyists for doctors argue that reform is needed to keep their insurance costs down and encourage doctors to continue practicing in high risk specialty areas like obstetrics. Law firms argue that tort reform makes it difficult for consumers or patients to receive compensation for serious injuries.

Table 5-5. Florida's Largest Law Firms

Rank	Name	Main Office
1	Ackerman LLP	Miami
2	Holland and Knight	Miami
3	Greenberg Traurig	Miami
4	Carlton Fields Jorden Burt	Tampa
5	Gray Robinson, P.A.	Orlando

Source: Biggest Florida Law Firms, ©*Florida Trend*, January 2015, used with permission. Further reproduction prohibited.

THE MEDIA

Media power in Florida is somewhat diffused, owing to the large number of media markets in the state. Whereas some states only have one television market, Florida has 10. The state's largest is the Tampa Bay media market, which reaches one-fourth of all the state's voters.[13] The same pattern of diversity holds true for newspapers—dailies and weeklies, English and non-English language—and radio stations.14 Florida has a lot of each. By one count, Florida has almost 100 television stations, representing all networks, and almost 500 radio stations, public and private.[15] It has about 50 daily newspapers and over 250 weeklies.[16] Florida also has one of the largest Capitol Press Corps, full-time newspaper, radio, television, wire service, and online news publication reporters assigned to Tallahassee.

Editorial decisions about state news—what will be selected as news, how it will be presented, how much time or space it will occupy, what editorial slant it will be given—rest largely with newspapers and independent stations throughout the state. The state's 12 largest circulation newspapers are listed in Table 5-6. The largest newspaper by daily circulation is the *Tampa Bay Times* (formerly the *St. Petersburg Times*). A number of Florida papers are owned by national chains such as Gannett. Although Florida's population has been growing rapidly, the state's major newspapers have struggled to sustain their paid circulation and advertising revenue. All papers have launched online editions to target younger Americans who are turning to local and cable television and the Internet for their news rather than traditional printed newspapers. Yet, newspapers continue to hold influence. They impact the policy agendas of state and local officials by bringing problems to light, getting them on the agenda in Tallahassee, and drumming up public support for passage through editorials and news coverage.

Media Segmentation

Increasingly, Floridians, like Americans in general, select the news sources that are most in sync with their own ideology. The proliferation of newspapers, radio stations, and cable stations has created a very segmented media, which makes it easier for citizens to select their "news of choice." Most of the major media markets in Florida have at least four broadcast network affiliate television news stations (ABC, NBC, CBS and FOX) and a local PBS affiliate as well. Several also have Spanish-speaking television—Univision and Telemundo—and radio stations. Almost every market has one or two dominant "news, weather, sports" radio stations that provide state and local news to commuters and workers. Typically, on the AM dial, the station that carries the Rush Limbaugh or Sean

Florida's multi-lingual population has given rise to Spanish-language media and brought politics to life for the state's growing Hispanic population.

Hannity show will be a ratings powerhouse among political conservatives and also carry one or more talk shows catering to state and local events. Public radio stations, especially those that are part of National Public Radio (NPR), attract listeners with more moderate-to-liberal views. Newspapers provide the most thorough coverage of state and local politics although on average they have reduced the number of reporters covering the state capitol.[17] There is considerable variation in the ideological slant of the state's newspaper editorial boards. For instance, *The Florida Times-Union* is considered quite conservative, while the *Palm Beach Post*, more liberal. With most papers having on-line versions, it is easy for politically-attentive Floridians to read whichever of the state's papers they would like and for advocacy groups to circulate "friendly" editorials or candidate endorsements to their members

Television coverage of Florida politics focuses more on campaigns than on the day-to-day operations of state and local governments.

Media Coverage

In general, local television news programs do not cover state and local politics very extensively, except in the heat of an exciting campaign season. One study has found that almost 55 percent of local news stories focus on crime; another 30 percent on soft or "fluff" news.[18] In Florida, the best media coverage of the state legislature while it is in session can be seen on "Capitol Update" which is broadcast on local PBS affiliates or heard on "Capitol Report," aired by Florida's public radio stations. The real power of state and local media stems from the fact that the public trusts them to deliver the news in a more objective manner than the national media.

Table 5-6. Florida's Largest Circulation Daily Newspapers

Rank	Name	Location
1	Tampa Bay Times	Tampa/St. Petersburg
2	Orlando Sentinel	Orlando
3	Miami Herald	Miami
4	South Florida Sun Sentinel	Ft. Lauderdale
5	Tampa Tribune	Tampa
6	Palm Beach Post	West Palm Beach
7	Florida Times-Union	Jacksonville
8	Vero Beach Press Journal	Vero Beach
9	Daytona Beach News Journal	Daytona Beach
10	Sarasota Herald Tribune	Sarasota
11	Florida Today	Melbourne
12	El Nuevo Herald	Miami

Source: Alliance for Audited Media, 2015, http://auditedmedia.com/ cross-referenced with Mondotimes, Highest Circulation Florida Newspapers, http://www.mondotimes. com/newspapers/usa/florida-newspaper-circulation.html.

Media as an Interest Group

While the media often lobbies for what they perceive to be the public good, they occasionally use their influence to secure special breaks for themselves. The best example is the sales tax exemption that media advertising receives. The Florida media, with few exceptions, fought successfully to reinstate the exemption after sales taxes were imposed on it, and many other services, when Bob Martinez was governor. They continue to vigorously, and successfully, resist all subsequent attempts to take the exemption away. (See Chapter 9 for more on the sales tax.)

Media as Watchdog

Most news operations are profit-seeking businesses. There is a strong incentive to cover stories that will increase the number of people watching, listening, or reading so that higher advertising rates can be charged. "Bad news" sells more than "good news" even though the public says otherwise (parallel to their proclaimed dislike of negative political ads, while admittedly being heavily influenced by them). Polls show the public strongly supports the media's watchdog role. Stories focusing on scandal, government waste, bad news, or sensationalism draw viewers and readers far more than those focusing on competent governance or on politicians who work hard to represent the views of their constituents. Politicians are aware of the critical role press coverage can have on their popularity and hence their re-election chances and try to follow the old adage "don't do anything you would not want to see on the front page of your local paper."[19] They do their best to attract positive coverage and escape negative scrutiny. Former Florida Congressman Lou Frey has two rules for politicians dealing with the press.[20] The first is "Don't get in a fight with someone who buys their ink by the carload [i.e., the print press]." And the second is "If you have to explain, you're in trouble."

THE ASSOCIATIONS

The number and variety of organized associations operating in state capitals has mushroomed over the past two decades. It is difficult to name a business, trade, or profession that has *not* organized an association to protect its members' interests—from police, firefighters, nurses, and teachers, to horse breeders, dog racers, used car salesmen, and doctors. Even paid lobbyists have their own association: the Florida Association of Professional Lobbyists! Most associations have offices and full-time representatives or lobbyists in Tallahassee.

Business, Trade and Professional Associations

Business, trade, and professional associations outnumber other types of organizations in Florida as in most other states. The largest business and professional associations as measured by the size of their membership include the Florida Education Association, the Florida Association of Realtors, the Florida Bar Association, the Florida Chamber of Commerce, Associated Industries of Florida, the Florida Institute of CPAs, the Florida Home Builders, the National Federation of Independent Business, and the Florida Medical Association. Sometimes, these professional associations are at loggerheads with each other, as when Florida's doctors and lawyers oppose each other on the volatile topic of tort reform. While the number of members an association has can be one indicator of its clout in the Capitol, membership numbers alone do not always translate into political influence.

Public-Interest Groups

Public interest groups (PIGs) have multiplied very rapidly in recent years, representing a vast array of social, ideological, consumer, and environmental interests. Many of these associations have lofty-sounding names, like Common Cause, Mothers Against Drunk Driving, Save the Manatee Club, Florida Public Interest Research Group (F-PIRG), and Florida Defenders of the Environment. They claim to represent the "public interest" against the "special interests," presumably the business, trade, and professional associations. Among the most influential of these groups is the Florida League of Women Voters which pushed successfully for both the Fair District Amendments and the Water and Land Conservation Amendment. (See Chapter 2.) F-PIRG operates on several college campuses and lobbies on behalf of a number of environmental, consumer, and civil rights causes in the Sunshine State. One of the most powerful groups in Tallahassee is Florida TaxWatch, an extremely influential statewide organization devoted entirely to taxing and spending issues facing the state. Florida TaxWatch officials conduct a lot of in-depth studies designed to monitor whether the state's taxes are equitable and not excessive. Other TaxWatch studies regularly focus on generating recommendations as to how government agencies can be more responsive and productive in the use of hard-earned tax dollars.

Governments

It is very common for governments to lobby other governments. Local governments lobby state government (the executive and the legislative branches); state agencies lobby the state legislature; all frequently lobby Congress. Associations of local governments and local officials proliferate in Tallahassee. The Florida League of Cities and the Florida Association of Counties are the largest of these organizations. Individual cities and counties, such as Fort Lauderdale, Miami Beach, Tampa, Metropolitan Dade County, and Hillsborough County, also employ registered lobbyists to monitor what's going on in Tallahassee. The state legislature passes local bills that affect these counties and cities, adopts funding formulas for distributing state shared tax dollars to the local level, and funds locally-administered grant programs. Thus, local governments as a group, and individually, lobby for more favorable laws and more money. An equally large number of government lobbyists come from state government itself. Major state agencies, ranging from the state university system and state employee organizations to the Florida Association of State Troopers, maintain registered lobbyists in Tallahassee, although there are restrictions on this type of activity.[21] Since the Florida Legislature controls the state budget and sets out state policy, state agencies lobby vigorously in hopes of getting more money for raises and agency programs in order to shape the direction and scope of their mission.

Unions

The most influential unions in Florida are the Florida Education Association (FEA), representing the state's teachers, and the American Federation of State, County and Municipal Employees (AFSCME), representing public employees. The FEA is the largest union and association in the state based on membership (over 140,000). It was created from a merger of two different teacher groups who fought for control throughout the 1990s. Both the FEA and AFSCME lost political clout when Republicans took control of state government but are still extremely influential within the Democratic Party. While education unions in over forty states are ranked as very effective lobbyists, often ranking second to business interests,[22] they lack this kind of political clout in Florida. Conservative legislators have passed laws removing tenure protection, tying salary increases to student learning gains, and requiring state employees to begin putting three percent of their salary into their retirement accounts. However, voters did approve two constitutional amendments heavily pushed by the state's education groups—the class size amendment and pre-kindergarten for four-year olds—and defeated an amendment that sought to water down the class size amendment. (See Appendix A.)

Unions representing employees in the private sector are less influential in Florida than in many other states as well. The Florida AFL-CIO has offices in Tallahassee, but only about 6 percent of the state's work force is unionized—placing Florida in the bottom 10 among the 50 states. (By comparison, the top-ranked states are California at 16 percent and New York with 25 percent.[23]) The right-to-work provision in the Florida Constitution prevents mandatory union membership as a condition of employment. Even when Democrats were in charge of state government, private unions usually lost battles against Florida business to control labor policy. For example, workers' compensation reform in Florida has usually been dominated by business interests who seek to reduce premiums by making it tougher for workers to get workers' compensation and by reducing the benefits paid out when a claim is successful.[24] Unions scored a rare victory when they bypassed the legislature and convinced voters to support a constitutional initiative to increase Florida's minimum wage and index it to inflation. Their timing was right. Surveys showed a lot of Floridians were still struggling financially.

Interest Group Strategy

Interest groups seek to achieve their goals in different ways. Interest groups in Florida pursue rational strategies to obtain their goals by emphasizing their strengths and downplaying their weaknesses.[25] For example, a group with broad public support but little money may seek publicity to bring pressure on the legislature to pass or defeat a bill. A well-funded group with reasonable popularity may rely on campaign donations and a team of full-time lobbyists to get bills introduced and passed through the normal legislative process. Conversely, an established group with a questionable policy aim may seek to work quietly behind the scenes to change a simple phrase or word in a bill to make it less objectionable or more favorable. As a general strategy, all interest groups acknowledge that it is easier to play defense (kill or change a bill) than it is to play offense (pass a bill). The simple fact is there are many ways to kill a bill and it is very difficult to pass one. Of course if a group has a fair amount of public support, it may opt to bypass the legislature entirely and conduct a petition drive to get a constitutional amendment placed on the ballot for direct voter approval. (See Chapter 2.)

Most Powerful Interest Groups

One study conducted over a decade ago asked Florida's legislators' and lobbyists' to identify the most influential interest groups in Florida.[26] Many of the same groups identified then would most likely be among the same ones identified today if a similar study were conducted—Associated Industries of Florida, the Florida Association of Realtors, the Florida Home Builders Association, the Florida Chamber of Commerce, and the Florida Bankers Association. All five of these groups have an interest in promoting growth in Florida because the influx of new residents results in new customers, business and home construction, land deals and home sales, and loans. These groups were strong in the days when Democrats controlled the capitol but they have become even more influential now that control lies with the Republicans. In contrast, no union group, including FEA, the largest association by membership, makes the top ten list of influential Florida interest groups.

The Voices of Florida Business

While groups promoting development and growth are generally the most powerful in the state, Associated Industries of Florida, the self styled "voice of Florida Business," is regularly designated by legislators, lobbyists, and reporters in Tallahassee as the state's single most powerful interest group. Its members include the state's corporate giants as well as thousands of small businesses attracted by the organization's array of business services including insurance. AIF's computerized Florida Business Network provides subscribers with current reports on state legislative committee hearings and actions, members' voting records, campaign fund accounts, bill tracking, issue analysis, and tips on contacting senators and representatives. This communication network can generate a barrage of phone calls, emails, texts, or tweets to legislators' offices in a matter of hours. Its campaign division endorses, as well as targets, legislative candidates. It helps its friends in the legislature with polling, video production, advertising, and, of course, with campaign contributions. AIF publishes a voting scorecard at the end of each legislative session ranking all representatives and senators according to their support of AIF positions and releases the rankings to its membership. While AIF did quite well when Democrats controlled Tallahassee, they have done even better since Republicans became the majority party.

The Florida Chamber of Commerce is the one other interest group in Florida that can rival the influence of AIF. Established in 1916 as Florida's first statewide business advocacy organization, the Florida Chamber claims to be the state's most powerful federation of employers, chambers of commerce, and associations, representing more than 139,000 grassroots members with more than 3 million employees.[27] The Florida Chamber unites Florida's business community through use of its extensive legislative, grassroots, and political tools. The Florida Chamber's Political Institute recruits and vets pro-business candidates, gathers information on upcoming political races, and provides Florida's employers with essential statistics and analyses to help support pro-job initiatives in the legislature. The Florida Chamber takes a stance on a wide range of issues after thoroughly researching each topic and consulting with its members throughout the state. The Chamber's annual Legislative Scorecard grades and ranks the members of the legislature on their pro-business voting record. Like AIF, the Florida Chamber has become even more successful since the Republican majority took control of the legislature.

LOBBYING IN TALLAHASSEE

"Lobbying" is generally defined as any communication directed at a government decision maker with the hope of influencing policy. The *Florida Statutes* define *a lobbyist* as "a person who is employed and receives payment, or who contracts for economic consideration, for the purpose of lobbying, or a person who is principally employed for governmental affairs by another person or governmental entity to lobby on behalf of that other person or governmental entity."[28] Under Florida law, the act of *lobbying* is defined as "influencing or attempting to influence legislative action or nonaction through oral or written communication or an attempt to obtain the goodwill of a member or employee of the legislature."[29]

During a legislative session, lobbyists huddle around TV monitors, tracking legislation of interest to them and waiting to "button-hole" a legislator leaving the House or Senate Chamber.

In Session

When the legislature is in session, the Capitol gets crowded.
Lobbyists congregate in the offices, hallways, and central rotunda. They are officially banned from the floor of both houses. But they can sit in on committee and subcommittee hearings. If a chamber is in session, they huddle around television monitors posted strategically around the rotunda to watch the proceedings, exchange insights with each other ("gossip"), and wait to corner a key legislator when he or she leaves the House or Senate floor. Lobbyists can also be observed waiting in the outer offices of the governor, lieutenant governor, and the elected Cabinet members. Skilled lobbyists make it their business to know and visit key staff aides in both legislative and executive offices. Finally, lobbyists regularly assemble in Tallahassee's Adams Street bars and restaurants, although the passage of a stringent limit on free food and drink has tamped that activity down a bit from days gone by.

Lobbying Staff

One form of lobbying that is becoming more critical is communicating with legislative staff personnel. The number of professional lobbyists has mushroomed, primarily because of an increase in the number of full time staff for standing committees, house and senate leaders, and majority and minority party caucuses. Lobbyists have come to recognize that these "staffers" can have as much or more to do with the specific content of bills as the legislators themselves. Even with trying to influence professional staff members, personal interaction is a far more effective method of lobbying than simply giving them long letters or reports, although those are often necessary as well.

Providing Information

Persuasion is usually more than just a matter of argument or emotional appeal. It involves the communication of useful technical and political information. Legislators are required to vote on, or decide about, hundreds of questions each year. It is impossible for them to be fully informed about the wide variety of bills and issues they face. Consequently, many legislators depend upon skilled lobbyists to provide technical information about matters requiring action as well as to inform them of the political preferences of important segments of the population. Lobbyists have become more critical players in the legislative process since term limits have reduced the level of experience among legislators.

Lobbying Reform in the Florida Legislature

Lobbying is an important and constitutionally protected activity. Legislators want and need to hear from their constituents. Indeed, excessive restrictions on the U.S. Constitution's First Amendment right "to petition the government for a redress of grievances" are likely to be declared unconstitutional by the federal courts. However, individual legislators worry about the public's perception that lobbyists have

too much influence over them and that public policy too often represents the interests of a small number of people or groups rather than the broader public interest.

In 2005, the Florida Legislature passed stricter reporting and disclosure requirements for lobbyists. Senate President Tom Lee and Speaker of the House Allen Bense pushed the reforms through, arguing that greater transparency of the lobbying process was needed to restore the public's faith in the legislative process. Since then, both the House and Senate have continued with these reforms by adopting Joint Rule One Lobbyist Registration and Compensation Reporting at the beginning of each legislative session.

The first day of any legislative session, state legislators receive flowers, cards, and well wishes from their supporters, including many interest groups and their lobbyists.

Lobbyist Registration

There are about 2,000 registered lobbyists in Tallahassee (over 12 for each of the state's 160 legislators) representing around 3,600 principals. Many are registered to lobby both the legislature and the executive branch.[30] They must register separately to do so. Florida law requires all lobbyists to register with the Lobbyist Registration Office and to identify the clients, or principals, they represent. A *principal* is defined as "the person, firm, corporation, or other entity that has employed or retained a lobbyist." They must also pay an annual registration fee to the Lobbyist Registration Office. The amount is set annually by the President of the Senate and the Speaker of the House of Representatives. Currently, to lobby the legislature, the fee is $50 for their first registration (one principal), plus an additional $20 for each additional principal client a lobbyist registers to represent. A lobbyist may register and lobby just one chamber for half the cost—$25 and $10.[31]

Compensation Disclosure Requirement

In a move fought by many lobbyists but pushed for and applauded by citizens, good government groups, and the press, the legislature imposed a strict *compensation disclosure requirement* on lobbyists. Each lobbying firm must now file quarterly reports that detail the total compensation *received by the firm* from all its principals (clients) within set ranges: $0; $1 to $49,999; $50,000 to $99,999; $100,000 to $249,999; $250,000 to $499,999; $500,000 to $999,999; $1 million or more. Each firm's report must also list *for each of its principals* their name and contact information and total compensation provided or owed to the firm within set ranges: $0, $1 to $9,999; $10,000 to $19,999; $20,000 to $29,999; $30,000-$39,999; $40,000-$49,999; or $50,000 or more. Over the past few years, principals paid registered lobbyists a total of $110-130 million dollars a year.[32] These figures reinforce citizens' views that money and power dominate Tallahassee politics. But, while some Florida lobbying firms do make millions of dollars a year, most do not.

Gift Limits

When the legislature rewrote the laws on making the lobbying process more transparent, it also cracked down on gifts from lobbyists. As of 2006, Florida law prohibits lobbyists from making direct or indirect "expenditures" to members and employees of the Florida Senate or House and prohibits members and employees from directly or indirectly taking any "expenditure" from a lobbyist. Much to the dismay of restaurant owners in Tallahassee, lobbyists can no longer buy legislators lunches, dinners, or even a cup of coffee. And if legislators attend a reception put on by an interest group, including one in their home town, they must reimburse the group for the cost of their meals and drinks. When the bill was passed in 2005, one newspaper described this "catastrophic" event as follows: "Florida lawmakers, some of them reluctantly, approved Thursday a ban on gifts from lobbyists, agreeing to end the flow of food and drink that has lubricated deal making in Tallahassee for decades."[33] Some remain skeptical of the long-term impact of the ban, expecting lobbyists (and legislators) to find ways around it through soft-money fundraising committees or through the state's political parties.[34] (See end of chapter.)

Lobbyists' Background

Many successful lobbyists are former legislators or legislative leaders, executive officials, party leaders, or top gubernatorial or legislative aides who have turned their previous state government experience into a new career. They offer their services—access to legislative and executive officials, knowledge of the lawmaking process, an ability to present information and testimony to key policy makers at the right time, political skills and knowledge, personal friendships, and "connections"—to their clients at rates that usually depend upon their reputation for influence. Some professional lobbyists are attached to law firms or public relations firms and occasionally do other work. Others are full time lobbyists with multiple clients.

Lobbying Tactics

Most professional lobbyists publicly attribute their success to hard work, persistence, information, and an ability to get along with others: "Being prepared, personal credibility"; "Legislators know I'm going to present the facts whether they're favorable to my client or not"; "I'm a forceful advocate—determined"; "Doing my homework on the issues"; "Knowledge of the issues I'm dealing with and knowledge of the system"; "I try to understand the political pressures on elected officials." Yet in more candid moments, professional lobbyists will acknowledge that their success is largely attributable to personal friendships, political experience, and financial contributions: "I raise a lot of money for people."[35] It is unwise for lobbyists to threaten legislators—for example, by vowing to defeat them in the next election. This is the tactic of an amateur lobbyist, not a professional. It usually produces a defensive response by the legislator and ruins the lobbyist's effectiveness. As one lobbyist put it: "Once you have closed the door, you have no further access to the individual. Once you've threatened an individual, there is no possibility of winning in the future."[36]

LOBBYIST—LEGISLATOR INTERACTION

Legislators depend on lobbyists for much of their information on public issues. Although legislators are aware of the potential for bias in information given them by lobbyists, the constant proximity of lobbyists to legislators facilitates information exchange. Testimony at legislative committee hearings links lobbyists and legislators. Often this testimony is a legislator's primary source of information about a subject addressed in a proposed bill. Meetings in legislators' offices are also frequent and effective. Before the gift ban, social gatherings where the food and liquor were furnished by the lobbyist afforded them a way to establish connections with and gain the trust of key legislators. However, even before the gift ban, some legislators viewed the wining and dining scene as more of a chore than a pleasure. There were simply too many lobbyists vying for their attention and expecting them to show up at their hosted events. Under the new rules the number of parties and receptions has dropped off sharply since legislators must pay for any food or drink they consume. They can still go free if they do not eat or drink anything, but since attendance has plummeted, so, too has the number of parties.

Most Successful Lobby Firms

Who are the most successful lobbyists in Tallahassee? It is difficult to judge which lobbyists are most successful since so much lobbying activity focuses on relatively narrow issues like the wording of regulatory authority, obscure exemptions in tax laws, or specific monetary amounts in appropriations bills. Some lobbyists might boast a 100 percent batting average on a very limited number and range of legislative actions. Others might experience some defeats but succeed on a larger, more sweeping scope of proposals. Some lobbyists are self-employed small business people with expertise in a limited number of policy areas who represent only a handful of clients. Other lobbyists work for very big firms that take on a large number of clients with wide-ranging issue concerns. One way to judge success is to compare how much each lobby firm earns. This is not a perfect measure but it does give some indication of which firms are perceived to be successful by interest groups and individuals who are willing to pay for their services. Table 5-7 lists the top five lobby firms in Florida based on their median three-month total compensation and a sample of their clients.[37] The top two firms, and many of the others, were founded by, or employ, notable Republicans seeking to influence the Republican-dominated legislative and executive branches.

Table 5-7. Florida's Five Largest Lobby Firms Represent Diverse Clients

Rank	Name	Estimated Revenue	Notable Clients
1.	Southern Strategy Group	$2.2 million	3-M, Apple, BP, CVS, FL Chamber, FL Girl Scouts, Jacksonville Jaguars, Mosaic Fertilizer, Nemours Foundation, TECO Energy, Walt Disney World
2.	Ballard Partners	$2 million	Amazon.com, FPL, Geico, Harris Corp., Herbalife, Honda, New York Yankees, Tampa General Hospital, U.S. Sugar, Verizon, Walmart, Xerox
3.	Ronald L. Book	$1.9 million	AT&T, AutoNation, FL Apartment Asstn, FL HS Athletic Asstn, FPL, Republic Services, Sun Life Stadium, Title Clerk Consulting, U of Miami
4.	Capital City Consulting	$1.3 million	Aetna, American Traffic Solutions, AT&T, Cigna, Citibank, Delta, Dosal Tobacco, Everglades Fndtn, Office Depot, U. S Chamber Institute, Visa
5.	Gray Robinson	$825,000	Canaveral Port Authority, Darden Restaurants, FL Asstn of Broadcasters, JP Morgan Chase, Lockheed Martin, Orlando Magic, Target, UCF Fndtn

Source: Florida Lobbyist Compensation Report, Legislature, 1st Quarter 2015. Compensation is reported in ranges by the firms. Estimates are the sum of the median range of each reported payment.

Individuals Can Make a Difference

Not every decision made in Tallahassee is directly influenced by paid lobbyists. Occasionally "little people" capture the hearts of citizens and legislators alike when a tragic circumstance makes news and reveals shortcomings in the law. Mark Lunsford, whose daughter Jessica was murdered by a registered sex offender living in his neighborhood, tearfully and successfully pleaded for the legislature to shore up laws dealing with child molesters. The legislature passed, and the governor signed, one of the toughest child-sex laws ("Jessica's Law") in the U.S.[38] Other states soon adopted their own Jessica's laws. When Martin Lee Anderson, a young African American boy, died after injuries sustained in a Florida boot camp for juveniles, his mother would not give up her fight to abolish boot camps until the legislature passed and the governor signed the "Martin Lee Anderson Act." The law changed how the state provides intensive services to at-risk youth. These examples go to show that it is not *always* about power and money in Tallahassee, although admittedly the two go hand-in-hand in many situations.

MONEY IN FLORIDA POLITICS

Money drives the political system in Florida, as it does in other states and in Washington, D.C. Campaign contributions are the key links between the state's major power centers—corporations, banks, utilities, insurance companies, health care providers, real estate developers, professional associations, agribusiness, public employee and teacher unions—and elected officials. Driven by television advertising, the costs of campaigning have skyrocketed everywhere, but especially in large states like Florida with its multiple television markets. Campaign fundraising has become the central activity in the political process. Indeed, most political candidates now report that they devote more time to fundraising than to all other campaign activities. Large sums of money are also spent independent of candidates in order to influence elections or public opinion on issues.

New records in campaign spending are set in nearly every election cycle—not surprising in light of increases in the cost of living and advertising rates. In 2002, over $150 million was spent on state elections in Florida. In 2014, candidates and committees raised over $289 million to influence election outcomes—$34 million for the governor's race, $14 million for Cabinet races, $30 million for 120 House seats, $9 million for 20 senate seats, $13 million for ballot initiatives, and $139 million to political party committees.[39] Anyone considering a serious campaign for a state legislative seat must begin by thinking about how to raise $200,000 or more in campaign funds. In recent elections, the average amount raised by the winners in Florida house races was about $180,000 and in state senate races about $400,000. Simply put, it costs a lot of money to get your name and message out in a state as large and diverse as Florida, with so many newcomers that a campaign needs to reach. In addition, a tricky, and often confusing, part of running for office is that the campaign laws are constantly changing. Contribution laws for candidates seeking federal offices (Congress, president) are different than those covering candidates running for state-level offices (governor, Cabinet, state legislators, judges, and other judicial officials).

Individuals and organizations can make unlimited contributions to Florida's Democratic and Republican parties. "Soft money," as this type of contribution is called, is to be used for general party-building activities.

Florida's Campaign Finance Act

Both Florida and the U.S. government regulate campaign finance. They set the rules for how much money may be donated to candidates, political parties and political action committees (PACs). Florida rules apply to state races and federal rules apply to national races (presidential, congressional). Donations that are limited are called *hard money* and donations that are not limited are called *soft money*.

The Florida Election Commission enforces state law by requiring candidates to file campaign finance statements and identify contributors. It can levy civil fines against candidates for violations of the law. The Federal Election Commission performs the same functions at the national level. Table 5-8 lists the different limits put on different types of donations by the state of Florida and by the federal government. It is easy to see how difficult it is to understand the intricacies of campaign finance.

Florida's Campaign Finance Act limits individual and organization contributions to $1,000 per election for most state and local offices. A primary election and a general election are treated as two *separate* elections meaning a person could contribute $2,000 to a candidate (primary + general = $2,000). Candidates for statewide office (governor, Cabinet and Supreme Court justice) may collect up to $3,000 per election for a maximum of $6,000 per individual donor. Before these limits were raised from $500 in 2013, Florida had the lowest limit in the country for statewide races and was lower than 47 other states for state legislative races.

The Federal Election Campaign Act (FECA) sets separate limits on individual contributions to congressional and presidential candidates: individual contributions to $2,700 (indexed to inflation meaning they go up over time) and PAC contributions to $5,000. Before 2002, the federal limit for individuals was just $1,000. (PAC donation limits were not changed.)

Florida and the national government also treat donations to political parties quite differently. Federal rules limit individual donations to national political parties to $33,400 (indexed to inflation) and limit most PAC donations to national parties to just $15,000. Donations to state and local political parties are also limited by federal law if the money is to be used for campaigns for federal office. Prior to 2002 and passage of the Bipartisan Campaign Reform Act (BCRA—also known as the McCain-Feingold Act after the sponsors), contributions to national political parties were unlimited. This was called the *soft money loophole* since a wealthy person could donate only a small amount directly to a federal candidate but a very large sum to a national political party that could, in turn, use it indirectly to help those same federal candidates.

Unlike the federal government and most other states, Florida still allows individuals and organizations to make unlimited contributions to the Democratic, Republican, and third (minor) parties in the state. The Sunshine State is just one of 13 states that places no limits on donations to state political parties.[40] In Florida, as in the other 12 states, the state parties have become more important vehicles for raising money, especially for Get-Out-The-Vote activities, than they used to be when the national parties could also raise soft money. "Soft money" contributions are supposed to be used primarily for general party building activities (like voter registration drives), but often this money seeps into specific candidates' campaigns. In addition, Florida's state political parties can legally contribute up to $50,000 directly to a state candidate's campaign or $250,000 to a candidate for statewide office (like governor or Cabinet)—50 to 80 times more than the limit for individual or PAC donations.

Table 5-8. Campaign Contribution Limits: State v. National Offices

Donation Limits on:	Florida Regulations	National Regulations (2015-2016 Cycle)
Individual to Campaign (per election cycle)*	$1,000 to candidates for state/local offices EXCEPT $3000 to candidates for statewide office (Governor, Cabinet, SC Justice)	$2,700** to candidates for federal office
PAC to Campaign (per election cycle)*	$1,000 to candidates for state/local offices EXCEPT $3000 to candidates for statewide office (Governor, Cabinet, SC Justice)	$5,000 from multi-candidate PAC*** to candidate for federal office $2,700** from other PAC to candidate for federal office
Party to Campaign (per election cycle)*	$50,000 to candidate for state office**** $250,000 to candidate for statewide office (Governor or Cabinet)****	$5,000 from national party to U.S. House candidate $46,800** from national party to U.S. Senate candidate $5,000 from state and local party combined to House or Senate candidate for federal office
Individual to Party (per year)	Unlimited to state party	$33,400** to national party
PAC to Party (per year)	Unlimited to state party	$15,000 from multi-candidate PAC*** to national party $33,400** from other PAC to national party

Notes: * In both state and national elections, contributors can give the maximum amount in both the primary election and in the general election. For example, a person could contribute $1,000 to a state House candidate's primary campaign and another $1,000 to that candidate's general election campaign. Or in a federal election, a person could donate $2,700 to a congressional candidate's primary campaign and another $2,700 to that candidate's general election campaign.
** Amounts indexed to inflation.
*** Multi-candidate PACs must have been registered for at least 6 months, received contributions from more than 50 contributors, and made contributions to at least 5 federal candidates.
**** Political parties may provide polling services, research services, and the cost for campaign staff, professional consulting services, and telephone calls. The contributions are not counted toward the contribution limits, but must still be reported by the candidate.
Sources: Florida Division of Elections and the Federal Election Commission.

Campaign Finance and the Constitution

The U.S. Supreme Court upheld campaign donation limits established by FECA in *Buckley* v. *Valeo* in 1976, but also ruled that individuals have a constitutional free speech right to spend as much of their own money as they wish on their own campaigns, and that individuals and groups also have a constitutional right to spend as much of their own money independently to publish or broadcast their own views on issues or elections.[41] The Court reasoned that restrictions on political speech were only permissible to further a compelling government interest such as reducing corruption. The rationale was that unlimited donations to a candidate might lead to corruption while candidates spending large sums of their own money might actually reduce the likelihood of corruption. While this court decision established that there could be limits on donations to campaigns, it also declared that there could be no mandatory limits on campaign spending. Thus, candidates can spend however much they can legally raise or donate to their own campaign.

Campaigns cost millions in Florida with its 10 media markets. Party activists know campaign contributions are vital, while citizens are greatly offended by the amount of money it takes to win.

The personal wealth of candidates has become an even more important qualification for successful campaigning. Through BCRA, Congress attempted to even the playing field by increasing the legal contribution limit for a candidate who faced a wealthy self-funded opponent spending large sums of their own money. However, in *Davis* v. *FEC* the U.S. Supreme Court struck down the *"millionaire's amendment"* relying in part on the precedent it established in *Buckley* v. *Valeo*, namely that an even playing field was not a compelling government interest.[42] In *Citizens United* v. *FEC*, the Court struck down another part of BCRA when it found that the government could not ban independent political advertisements paid for directly by corporations and unions since this was protected political speech under the First Amendment.[43] And in *McCutcheon* v. *FEC*, the Court ruled that aggregate donation limits were also unconstitutional.[44] In essence, the Court ruled that money is speech.

Individual Contributor Reports

Almost everyone agrees that the public should know who is contributing to a candidate's campaign and how the candidate is spending the money. Florida's Campaign Finance Act requires candidates to report the names and occupations of individuals who give to their campaign, along with the amount. The contributions picture has become considerably more transparent now than it used to be because all contributions are posted quarterly on the Division of Elections website. However, Florida's contributor disclosure law gives us only a glimpse of the real sources of funding for two major reasons. First, it is not always clear from these reports exactly who the contributing lawyers, lobbyists, and consultants (perennial big donors) represent. Second, some individual contributors seek additional influence through a process called *bundling*. Bundling occurs when one individual solicits campaign donations from many other individuals and then delivers all of them at one time to the candidate.

Influencing Florida Elections

Florida law establishes five types of groups that can be formed to raise and spend money to influence state elections. These include Political Committees—commonly called Political Action Committees (PACs), Electioneering Communication Organizations (ECOs), Independent Expenditure Organizations (IXOs), Political Party Committees, and Affiliated Party Committees.[45] Each of these groups must register with the Florida Division of Elections and report their contributions and expenditures. But they differ in a number of other ways—their purpose, how they can raise money, and how they can spend money. There are legal restrictions on which groups can donate directly to candidates, make independent expenditures, and engage in electioneering communication.

Under Florida law an *independent expenditure* is money spent to expressly advocate the election or defeat of a candidate or issue that is made without consulting or coordinating with any candidate or committee. An *electioneering communication* is any communication publicly distributed through radio, television, telephone, magazine, newspaper, or direct mail that refers to or depicts a clearly-identified candidate for office but does not expressly advocate the election or defeat of the candidate, yet leaves no doubt that it is an appeal to vote for or against that candidate. Table 5-9 compares Political Action Committees and Electioneering Communication Organizations in Florida.

Political Action Committees have the broadest purpose and thus may support or oppose any candidate, issue, PAC, ECO, or political party and may engage in independent expenditures and electioneering communication. Contributions to PACs are unlimited. Contribution reports are required frequently (at first weekly, and then daily within 10 days of the election). PACs may contribute up to $1,000 to candidates ($3,000 to statewide candidates) and unlimited amounts to political parties, ECOs, or other PACs. PACs are extremely common in Florida. There are some 870 currently registered with the state. The number has grown ever since the legislature changed the law in 2013 to allow them to take in unlimited donations. (Prior to 2013, PACs were limited to $500 contributions.)[46]

PACs are a major source of funding for candidates and for independent expenditures. Many candidates actually open up their own PACs in addition to their regular campaign account (although legally they must make sure that the PAC expenditures are not coordinated with the official campaign). In the 2014

election cycle, Florida PACs raised $219 million dollars. Some of the biggest PACS were: Governor Rick Scott's "Let's Get to Work" PAC which raised $46 million for the Governor's re-election; the "Charlie Crist for Florida" PAC ($30 million) promoting his candidacy for governor; the "People United for Medical Marijuana" PAC supporting passage of Amendment 2 ($8 million); the "Drug Free Florida Committee" PAC opposing Amendment 2 ($6 million); and the "Florida's Water and Land Legacy Inc. PAC" promoting Amendment 1 ($6 million).

Electioneering Communication Organizations may only make electioneering communications as defined by Florida law. The most important part of the definition is that the advertisement cannot say "vote for" or "vote against" a candidate. There are no limits on either contributions to ECOs or on how much they can spend. While they cannot make contributions to campaigns or PACs, they can shift money to other ECOs. An ECO must disclose its contributions frequently (weekly, then daily starting 10 days before the election). Just as with PACS, many candidates for state office have established their own ECOs. It is another way to take in more money to help a candidate appeal to voters and at the same time evade the hard limit on direct contributions to their campaigns. However, now that Florida PACs can also

Election laws governing candidate and interest group communication with the public via the airwaves are quite confusing and often challenged in court.

accept unlimited donations, there are fewer ECOs than there once were. Today there are some 130 ECOs registered in Florida, down from more than 200 at their peak.

Table 5-9. Influencing Florida Elections: PACs and ECOs

Attributes	PAC (Political Action Committee)	ECO (Electioneering Communication Organization)
Primary Purpose	To support or oppose any candidate, issue, PAC, ECO, or political party.	To make electioneering communications
Limits on Donations To the Group	No monetary limit	No monetary limit
Limits on Spending By the Group	Contributions to a candidate - $1000 per election, except limit to candidates for statewide office or Supreme Court Justice - $3000 (donations to candidates cannot be made within 5 days of the election) PAC to a political party, ECO or another PAC – no limit.	ECO on electioneering communications - no limits ECO to another ECO – no limits May not make contributions to a candidate, political party or a PAC
Additional Clarifications	May expressly advocate the election or defeat of a candidate May make independent expenditures but cannot coordinate with candidate when doing so May make electioneering communications which are not considered candidate contributions	May not "expressly advocate" the election or defeat of a candidate May not make independent expenditures May coordinate with candidates May make electioneering communications which are not considered candidate contributions

Source: Created by the authors from data found at the Florida Division of Elections.

In 2014, ECOs raised almost $68 million dollars to influence Florida elections. Among the largest ECOs were: Governor Scott's "Let's Get to Work" ($27 million); the "NextGen Climate Action Committee – Florida" seeking to defeat Scott ($21 million); the Florida Realtor's Association "Citizens for a Better Florida" ($1.4 million); the one established by the "Florida Federation for Children" to promote school choice and vouchers ($1.3 million); and the "SEIU Florida Community Alliance" supporting union issues ($1.2 million).

Independent Expenditure Organizations can also raise unlimited sums of money, but unlike ECOs, IXOs may expressly advocate the election or defeat of a candidate or issue as long as they do not consult or coordinate with any candidate or committee. To date, very few IXOs have organized in Florida.

Federal Campaign Law: Super PACS and Non-Profit Tax Exempt Groups

Changes in federal campaign finance law and Supreme Court decisions have resulted in an explosion of independent advocacy groups that can raise unlimited amounts of money and influence elections in Florida. For example, federal Political Action Committees that only engage in independent expenditures and do not make contributions to candidates may now receive unlimited donations despite the $5,000 limit established by the BCRA for normal PACs that donate to candidates. These rapidly proliferating groups are commonly known as *Super PACs* because of the huge sums of money they can raise and spend. Florida-based PACs are actually more versatile than federal Super PACs since they can raise unlimited sums of money *and* can also contribute directly to individual campaigns at the state level.

A variety of non-profit groups can be set up under different sections of the IRS tax code and can then work to influence elections:

- *501(c) organizations* are nonprofit tax exempt groups that are not supposed to engage in direct political activity as a primary purpose, but may provide "educational" material on public policy with a political or ideological point of view; *501(c)3 groups* must report their donors, while *501(c)4 groups* are not required to do so.

- *527 groups* are also tax exempt. They can raise unlimited amounts of money specifically for political activities like voter mobilization and issue advocacy but they must report their donors.

- *Non-federal groups* can organize to raise unlimited amounts of soft money to influence state or local politics through voter mobilization or issue ads that criticize or promote a candidate's record.

Neither 501(c) nor 527 groups may expressly advocate the election or defeat of a federal candidate. These groups file disclosure reports with the IRS rather than the Federal Elections Commission. Both 501(c) and 527 groups may raise non-federal funds.

It is clear that big donors will give more if the group they donate to does not have to report them by name. The 501(c)4 groups have become more popular in recent elections as donors realized they could give big money to influence elections yet still remain anonymous. In addition, 501(c) and 527 groups can work together to "launder" political donations. 501(c)4 groups can donate unlimited sums to 527 groups thus allowing more direct political spending but still shielding their donors from publicity. While the 527 groups do have to list their donors, on the form they simply list the name of the 501(c)4 thus shielding the original source of the money.

Lots of national Super PACs, 501s, and 527s spend money in Florida to influence elections—particularly federal races—presidential, U.S. senatorial, and congressional. It is also common for Florida political party officials, interest groups, and candidates to create their own non-profit 501(C) or 527 groups under the federal IRS tax code, then promptly register them as ECOs in Florida. (When Rick Scott first ran for governor, he funded a "Let's Get to Work" 527 that helped him win his race.) Unlike the official campaign accounts, these nonprofit groups can accept donations no matter how large. It can also mean that they raise large sums of money from just a few or even a single donor that can be used for ads spelling out candidate and party stances on issues important to the group. Of course the ads must stop short of explicitly saying "Vote For (or Against) Candidate X" or "Issue Y" but they can certainly help boost a candidate's name recognition and create a positive image for him or her. More commonly, ECO funds are used to attack and "sling mud" which allows the formal campaigns to deny that they are responsible for negative advertising.

Money Flows to Incumbents and Leaders

PACs are politically sophisticated contributors. They do not like to back losers. Since incumbent members of state legislatures running for re-election seldom lose (See Chapter 6.), PAC contributions are heavily weighted in favor of incumbents seeking re-election over their challengers. Of course there are times when PAC money does go to challengers—usually when an incumbent is perceived as likely to lose for whatever reason or has greatly offended PAC contributors. Challengers rely more on contributions from interest groups in sync with their views, individual supporters, and other members of their political party. PAC contributions also flow heavily to leaders in the house and senate. Presiding officers in each chamber, committee chairs, and majority and minority leaders have more influence over the legislative process and over certain policies than other members.

Leadership Funds and Political Parties

In addition to collecting money for their campaigns, legislative leaders can collect money for their own *Affiliated Party Committees*. These so-called "leadership funds" allow each political party conference (Democratic and Republican) of the state House of Representatives and Senate to establish a separate, affiliated party committee to support the election of candidates of the leader's political party. Leader is defined as President of the Senate, Speaker of the House of Representatives, or the minority leader of either house of the legislature. A total of four affiliated party committees can be created (Republican House and Senate and Democratic House and Senate). These funds are separate from those donated to the state political parties and the contributions and expenditures are tracked and reported. Like donations to the state parties, there is no limit on contributions to the affiliated party committees, and, like spending by the state party, contributions made by these leadership funds are limited to $50,000 to an individual party candidate and $250,000 to candidates for statewide office (like governor or Cabinet officer).[47]

Affiliated Party Committees have always been quite controversial. They were, and are, viewed by many as simply slush funds for legislative leaders. At one time, the legislature had gotten rid of them, only to revive them in 2010. Since then, only one leadership fund has been created (the Florida House Democratic Caucus Affiliated Party Committee in 2013) and it was quickly shut down after attracting too much hostile attention. All of the Committee's money was transferred to the Florida Democratic Party.

As discussed in Chapter 4, state political parties have many functions, but their primary goal is to help their candidates win office. Florida laws allow unlimited contributions to political parties and permit the parties to spend that money on anything except a direct campaign ad for an individual candidate (soft money as described above). State law actually allows political parties to skirt this restriction by running so-called *"three pack"* ads—political ads that must mention at least three party candidates in order to support party building efforts. In 1998, this amounted to running a regular TV campaign ad for a candidate, then rapidly mentioning two additional candidates in the last three seconds. By 2002, it meant running a regular campaign ad for one candidate (most often the governor) and just listing the two additional candidates in the small print at the bottom of the television screen rather than mentioning them verbally. This practice has continued to date.

The two major state political parties are enormously important vehicles for collecting and spending money to help candidates get elected. In 2014, the Republican Party of Florida raised $115 million and the Florida Democratic Party over $52 million. This was a record amount for both parties but the differential between the two reflected the realities of Republican domination in the state capitol. Overall, interest groups gave disproportionately to the Republicans to help ensure continued access in Tallahassee. However, some industries gave much more to one party than the other (trial lawyers, unions and liberal policy organizations to the Democratic Party and business associations and conservative policy organizations to the Republican Party). Other groups (like utilities, gambling interests, and health care) tilted Republican but gave large sums to both parties. Of course Florida's political parties also received financial help from various national party groups such as the Republican or Democratic Governors Association or the Republican or Democratic National Committee.

The Largest Contributors

It is no easy task to determine exactly what interests the state's largest political contributors represent. Contributions from individuals may not precisely spell out their corporate, professional, trade, or union affiliations in official reports. PACs and ECOs often mask their real sponsor with lofty-sounding names—Citizens for a Better Florida (realtors), Committee for Effective Representation (Associated Industries of Florida), or Florida for All (a coalition of union groups). It is not clear from the name, for example, whether the officially registered PAC-Y-DERM PAC represents elephants, Republicans, or dermatologists. (It is the dermatologists.)

Some individuals make campaign contributions to state legislators to develop a more personal connection that makes it easier to directly communicate with the lawmaker.

While lawyers (or lobbyists) may accurately list their occupation as required by law when they make a campaign contribution, there is often little indication of why they are donating to a candidate. (Trial lawyers might be hoping to influence tort reform, while corporate lawyers may want to push for revisions in the tax code.) That said, it is possible to see what industries are giving the most money to influence Florida elections. Table 5-10 shows the top industries by average amount donated in the past two election cycles. This includes all money donated to campaigns, political committees, political organizations, and political parties. By industry, the heaviest political hitters are lawyers and lobbyists, and those from the real estate and insurance worlds.

Table 5-10. Largest Contributors in Florida Elections*

Top Industries	Avg. in Millions	Top Industries	Avg. in Millions
Lawyers & Lobbyists	$19.7	Business Associations	$4.0
Real Estate	$12.2	Hospitals & Nursing Homes	$3.7
Insurance	$9.75	Health Services	$3.2
Public Sector Unions	$7.4	General Contractors	$3.15
Liberal Policy Org.	$6.9	Telecom Services	$2.5
Health Professionals	$6.75	TV & Movie Production	$2.2
Conservative Policy Org.	$6.2	Retail Sales	$2.1
Crop Production	$6.05	Energy	$2.1
Securities & Investment	$4.8	Automotive	$2.0
Gambling & Casinos	$4.7	Lodging & Tourism	$1.8

*Excludes candidate self-funding, candidate committees, party funding, and public subsidy.

Source: Compiled by the authors from followthemoney.org, "Florida Elections, General Industry Contributions."

What Contributors "Buy"

Campaign contributions in state races are made for a variety of reasons. Some individuals may contribute $50 or $100 to an acquaintance, co worker, fellow club member, or church parishioner simply as a friendly gesture. Others make contributions based on their perception of the issue or ideological position of the candidate, expecting nothing personal in return other than the satisfaction of knowing that they are financially backing a cherished cause. Still others simply want to have a "photo-op" with the candidate. However, organized groups and lobbyists give money with the hope of gaining access to elected officials, assistance with state agencies and contracts, and influence over voting behavior. While research clearly shows that money buys access, the link between campaign donations, assistance, and influence is much harder to prove.[48]

Access

Large organizational contributors expect that their money will at the very least buy access to elected officials. They expect to be able to call or visit and present their views directly to legislators, Cabinet officials, and the governor's key staff members, if not directly to the governor. Legislators often boast of responding to letters, emails, calls, and visits from their constituents back home whether they were campaign contributors or not. However, *contributors* (individual and groups) expect more immediate and direct responses to their requests for a face-to-face meeting with elected officials or an appearance before a scheduled legislative hearing to present their views.

Assistance

Many large contributors do business with state government agencies or are directly regulated by them. They expect legislators or Cabinet members they have supported to help them deal with these bureaucracies, sometimes acting to cut red tape, ensure fairness, and expedite their cases, and other times pressuring the agencies for a favorable decision. Few questions are raised when the intervention merely expedites consideration of a contributor's case, but pressure to bend rules or regulations to get favorable decisions creates ethical problems for officeholders. The State Ethics Commission is responsible for investigating such situations but a complaint must first be brought to the Commission before it can take action. Of course, if a criminal allegation is involved, the appropriate state law enforcement officials take over.

Actually, the evidence is mixed as to whether contributors really get greater assistance from legislators and their staff than non-contributors. For the most part, state legislators make responding to, and helping, constituents a high priority simply because it is excellent way to boost positive name recognition. "Service beyond the call" for a constituent may prompt that person to tell friends and neighbors, which is, in effect, invaluable word-of-mouth advertising that can help an official get re-elected. Even constituents who may have backed an opponent can expect diligent casework on their behalf. Incumbents know that by assisting them with their dealings with state agencies, they may be converted into supporters by the time of the legislator's next re-election campaign.

Influence

Contributors hope to influence policy making. However, *quid pro quo* deals, giving votes in direct exchange for money, are illegal. Scandals involving the direct purchase of special favors, privileges, exemptions, and treatments do not happen very often in Florida politics, although the media justifiably highlight them when they do happen.[49] In reality, campaign contributions are rarely made in the form of a direct trade off for a favorable vote. Such an arrangement risks exposure as bribery and may be prosecuted under the law. Campaign contributions are more likely to be made with a general understanding that the contributor has confidence in the candidate's good judgment on issues important to the donor. In fact, most politicians say that when they accept campaign donations, it is with the understanding that the individuals or groups giving money *share* the candidate's issue stance, not because the donors are trying to change it. For example, when labor gives money to Democratic candidates and those candidates vote a pro labor position, the candidates will argue that they would have voted for a labor-friendly bill regardless of donations because they believed in it themselves. The same can be said about Republicans and business donations. That is why it is very difficult to show that donations cause a change in voting behavior. In most circumstances, it is more likely that the previous voting record "caused" the donation.

PUBLIC CAMPAIGN FUNDING

Florida is one of only a few states that provide public funds for its gubernatorial and Cabinet races. Candidates in competitive races for governor who raise at least $150,000 (Cabinet offices $100,000), limit donations from their own personal funds and from political parties, and agree to limit their overall spending to no more than $2 per registered Florida voter ($1 for Cabinet races) are eligible for the matching funds. For example, in 2010 and 2014, candidates for governor who agreed to voluntarily limit their campaign expenditures to $25 million could have received public funding if they chose to take it. The limit for Cabinet candidates was $12.5 million. The limit was raised significantly by the legislature after the 2004 election. The public money is distributed to the candidates as matching contributions to campaign donations raised from Florida residents. The maximum matching amount from the state is $250—thus a $500 donation from a contributor is only matched with $250 from the state.[50]

Originally, if a candidate for office did *not* participate in the state matching program and exceeded the limit, then the opponent who was participating was allowed to exceed the limit and received additional public funds equal to the amount by which the nonparticipating candidate exceeded the limit. In 1994, Republican Jeb Bush did not take public money and exceeded the limit (at that time only about $6 million), allowing Democrat Lawton Chiles to receive an additional one million dollars in public money and win re-election. However, in 2010, Rick Scott decided not to abide by the limits in the Republican gubernatorial primary, calculating that he would need to spend far more of his own money to have a chance to beat well-known Attorney General Bill McCollum. Scott successfully sued to invalidate the provision that would have given McCollum additional matching funds arguing that the provision was no different than the national BCRA millionaire's amendment that had been recently struck down by the U.S. Supreme Court. Without the extra state money, McCollum was badly outspent in the waning days of the campaign and lost a close Republican primary election to Scott. Democrat Alex Sink, who ran against Scott in the general election, also decided to forego public money in an effort to try and keep up with Scott campaign's war chest, but she was badly outspent anyway and lost to Scott in a tight race.

While Governor Scott again did not take public money in his successful 2014 re-election campaign, most other statewide candidates did. Charlie Crist took $2.6 million in his losing battle against Scott. Jeff Atwater received over $740,000 in 2010 and $418,000 in 2014 for his two successful CFO races. Likewise, Pam Bondi got $430,000 (2010) and $328,000 (2014) in public funds for her winning attorney general campaigns. Adam Putnam benefitted from almost $590,000 (2010) and $460,000 (2014) in public funds on his way to twice winning the Agricultural Commissioner post.[51]

Support

The main argument for public (taxpayer) funding of political campaigns is that it reduces the influence of the "fat cats"—heavy political contributors, including individuals, corporations, and PACs. Presumably officeholders who are less reliant on campaign contributions from special interests will be freer to pursue their own interpretation of the public interest in their official duties. It reduces the public perception that special interests are buying favors and helps restore public trust in representative government. Public campaign financing may also open the electoral process to people of more modest personal wealth. Finally, many officeholders support public campaign funding because it helps relieve them of the time consuming task of fundraising and allows them to spend more time governing. Some states, like Vermont, Maine, Massachusetts, and Arizona, have approved a public financing system even more expansive than the one in Florida.[52]

Members of the Capitol Press Corps lean over the railing and strain hard to hear what is being said on the floor below.

Opposition

There are a fair number of citizens who strongly oppose giving taxpayer-generated dollars to office-seekers for campaign purposes—often derisively dubbed as "welfare for politicians." Because public funds used for campaigning take money away from other public purposes, the idea of using tax money in this way is not very popular with citizens who would rather see those funds be spent on schools, roads or police. Because so many campaign ads are negative, some taxpayers also resent subsidizing mud-slinging attack ads, particularly for candidates they disagree with. It is also argued that public funding and limits on campaign spending favor incumbents by denying challengers the additional funds needed to overcome the advantages of incumbency. Opinion polls in Florida and the nation rarely show majority support for the idea of public funding. In fact, 52.5 percent of Floridians voted to *eliminate* public campaign financing in the 2010 election after the legislature had placed the proposal to repeal it on the ballot. But since constitutional proposals need 60 percent of the vote to pass, the measure fell short and public campaign financing for statewide offices remains the law in Florida.

Impact of Campaign Finance Regulations

Florida's campaign finance laws restrict what candidates for statewide office can spend overall if they want taxpayer money and restrict individual and PAC donations to state campaigns. However the U.S. Constitution protects political speech and state law allows Florida political parties, ECOs and PACs to raise money in unrestricted amounts. In summary, public financing, restrictions on campaign donations, and other attempts to reduce the influence of money on Florida politics have failed. Money is more important than ever, but now flows in a torrent to the state parties, PACs and ECOs because of limits placed on donations to an individual candidate's campaign.

The Changing Florida Interest Group System

How has Florida's interest group system changed since Republicans took unified control of state government in 1998 after many decades of Democratic dominance? One study summarized the most important findings:[53]

- Generally the most influential interest group sectors have remained the same although some of the important issues they face and largest specific corporations within industry categories have changed.

- Florida business continues to be influential in the new Republican era, while unions and newspapers have lost influence.

- Republicans have passed laws banning lobbyist gift giving, restricting lobbying by former colleagues, and requiring more financial disclosure by lobbyists.

- In 1998 the largest and most successful lobbyists in the state generally had connections to the Democratic Party, but the most influential lobbyists today tend to have Republican ties.

- Florida Republicans have modified rules regulating groups that can be formed to influence elections, increased the amount of money that can be donated to campaigns, permitted PACs to take unlimited donations, and continued to allow political parties to receive unlimited donations.
- There has been an increase in campaign spending (generally favoring Republicans) and an increase in the use of independent spending groups like ECOs to influence election outcomes (typically dominated by Republican conservative pro-business groups).
- Overall, many of the top donor industries and some of the specific donor groups are the same although Republicans now typically receive more money than Democrats.
- The two major political parties continue to draw disproportionate support from different groups: lawyers, unions and liberal policy groups give more to the Democratic Party, while business associations, individual business interests, and conservative policy groups give more to the Republican Party.

ONLINE SOURCES FOR DATA AND INFORMATION UPDATES

Florida TaxWatch

Florida TaxWatch provides data analysis of economic and fiscal policies and how they affect the people of Florida. TaxWatch also compares taxes between Florida and the rest of the nation.
http://www.floridataxwatch.org/home.aspx

Florida Division of Elections: Campaign Finance

The Florida Division of Elections is responsible for ensuring fair and accurate elections in the state. The "Campaign Finance" page includes information about the rules and regulations governing campaign finance in Florida, and also provides and index of contributors.
http://election.dos.state.fl.us/campaign-finance/cam-finance-index.shtml

Federal Election Commission: Campaign Finance

The FEC is responsible for regulating campaign finance for each election. This site includes information about the rules and regulations governing campaign finance, and also provides compiled data on who is giving and receiving money.
http://www.fec.gov/disclosure.shtml

Follow the Money

The National Institute on Money in State Politics tracks campaign donations in all 50 states.
www.followthemoney.org

Florida Legislature: Lobbyists

The Florida Legislature's lobbyist registry provides information about all the lobbyists registered with the state of Florida, as well as a searchable index.
http://www.leg.state.fl.us/lobbyist/index.cfm.

Florida Lobbyist: Registration and Compensation

The Florida Lobbyist registry provides lobbying requirements, public records about all the lobbyists registered with the state of Florida, as well as a searchable index.
https://www.floridalobbyist.gov

Associated Industries of Florida: Legislature

The AIF is an association of Florida's main industries and provides a forum for their goals. Specifically, the "Legislature" page provides a list of key legislative priorities and voting scorecards for the legislators.
http://aif.com/menu_priorities.html

Florida Chamber of Commerce

The Florida Chamber of Commerce is a business advisory service, and they offer a list of issues, a list of key priorities, and legislative scorecards or voting records on the Chamber's goals.
http://www.flchamber.com/issues-legislation/overview/

Florida Trend

This magazine's website focuses on Florida's economy and its politics; it regularly ranks Florida's key economic sectors and covers critical issues facing the state. Their data includes information on Florida's largest corporations, construction, real estate firms, utilities, tourism firms, agribusinesses, and lobbying firms.
www.floridatrend.com

Chapter 6. Legislative Politics in Tallahassee

Architecturally, the Florida Capitol Complex reflects both the state's modern growth and its historical tradition—a twentieth-century high-rise tower overlooking a preserved nineteenth-century Capitol. (For a pictorial overview of the evolution of the Capitol buildings, See Figure 6-1.) The plaza level of the modern Capitol building houses the Office of the Governor, as well as Lieutenant Governor and the three Cabinet officials: Attorney General, Chief Financial Officer, and the Commissioner of Agriculture. The 22-story tower houses many departments, agencies and divisions.

On an average working day, the building hosts about 3,000 people, but every spring when the legislature is in session that number swells to 4,500 or more. The 120 member House of Representatives and 40 member Senate meet in their respective chambers under twin domes at each side of the skyscraper office building, and separate House and Senate office buildings adjoin the main complex on either side. The legislative chambers are separated by a majestic high-rising lobby, where visitors, lobbyists, staff, the media, and legislators constantly mill about. Observation windows at the top of the Capitol building provide an almost limitless view of the rolling North Florida hills surrounding Tallahassee.

Tallahassee becomes the focus of citizens, interest groups, and the media when the state legislature is in session.

FUNCTIONS OF THE FLORIDA LEGISLATURE

The primary function of the state legislature is to "pass laws"—that is, to enact statutory law. State senators and representatives also adopt resolutions congratulating or recognizing special people or events, propose amendments to the Florida Constitution, and occasionally, but infrequently, they vote on proposed amendments to the U.S. Constitution. Legislators must pass a budget every year so state government can function. Legislators hold oversight hearings to ensure that the appropriated money is spent, and that programs created by law are being run, as the legislature intended. Finally, legislators and their staff also spend a great deal of time responding to constituent complaints and requests. Some of these activities take place during their annual 60-day session. Others they engage in year-round.

Enacting Laws

Since 1997, Florida legislators have introduced about 2,200 bills every session or almost 14 bills per member. (See Table 6-1.) On average, nearly 380 of these proposed bills become law each year. Although the number fluctuates from session-to-session, the average number of bills introduced and laws passed over the past several years has declined to about 1,770 and 266 respectively. Many proposed bills are never *expected* to pass. Some are introduced merely as a favor to a constituent or an interest group or to get a headline in a newspaper back home. Others simply fail to generate enough support and die in committee or while waiting for floor action. Some pass one chamber but not the other. Still other bills actually pass both the House and Senate but are then vetoed by the governor.

Figure 6-1. The Capitol of Florida

Above Top Left: In 1824 the Florida Legislative Council met in its first permanent capitol in Tallahassee – a log cabin. **Above Top Right:** In 1825 construction began on a larger two-story capitol building, although only this one wing was completed as the Legislative Council ran out of money to complete the project. **Above Lower Right:** The U.S. Congress appropriated money for Florida to build its third capitol and construction was completed shortly before the Territory of Florida became a state on March 3, 1845. **Above Lower Left:** The current Capitol Complex, finished in 1977 at a cost of $43 million, consists of: 1. A 22-story executive office tower with Senate Chambers and Governor's offices on the left and House Chambers and Cabinet offices on the right; 2. The restored Old Capitol, now the Museum of Florida History (the dome was added in 1902); 3. The Senate Office Building; and 4. The House Office Building.

Above Left: The Senate Chamber includes a rostrum at the front for the Senate President and staff, desks for the 40 Senators, and a visitor's gallery. **Above Right:** The House Chambers includes a rostrum at the front for the House Speaker and staff, desks for the 120 Representatives, and a visitor's gallery.

Source: The Florida Legislature http://www.leg.state.fl.us/kids/tour/index.html and the Florida Department of State http://dhr.dos.state.fl.us/kids/capitol.cfm.

Table 6-1. The Florida Legislative Scorecard

Year	Bills Introduced	Acts Passed	Acts Vetoed	Laws Enacted
1997	2,540	464	19*	445
1998	2,131	549	17	532
1999	2,377	498	10	488
2000	2,502	497	7	490
2001	2,316	395	15	380
2002	2,323	420	16	404
2003	2,505	448	22	426
2004	2,435	506	22	484
2005	2,253	399	37	362
2006	2,227	379	14	365
2007	2,380	357	22	335
2008	2,245	308	10	298
2009	2,196	280	9	271
2010	2,247	292	18**	274
2011	1953	277	10	267
2012	1851	280	12	268
2013	1657	283	11	272
2014	1620	256	1	255
2015***	1574	227		
Average	**2,175**	**377**	**15**	**368**

Source: Florida Legislature Bill Citator (Regular and Special Sessions, General and Local Bills).
* Two of these vetoes were overridden by the legislature in 1998.
** Nine of these vetoes (and one line item veto) were overridden by the legislature in fall 2010 and spring 2011.
*** Through June 5th 2015. Data does not include 2015 Special Session. Vetoes and Laws Enacted data not available as 125 bills from the regular session were still pending for action by the governor.

The laws that do pass each year become part of the *Florida Statutes*. The Statutes are organized into 48 Titles or broad subject areas covering over 1,000 Chapters or specific topics and represent the wide range of issues the legislature may address every year. (See Table 6-2.) For example, Title XLVI (46) consists of over 100 chapters detailing Florida laws concerning crime—homicide, prostitution, burglary, computer crime, child abuse, animal cruelty, obscenity, drunkenness, terrorism, drug abuse, and many other offenses.

Hot Topics and Pressing Issues

Let's face it. There are plenty of pressing issues facing a large, diverse state like Florida. Recent legislative sessions have tackled a many tough topics:

- Attracting more businesses and rebuilding Florida's economy.
- Providing affordable property insurance to homeowners, reducing the number of Floridians who received coverage from the state-backed insurance company, and mitigating the housing crisis.
- Privatizing prisons to save money on the exploding costs of corrections, requiring inmates on death row to receive the death penalty more quickly, and establishing new drug protocols to execute prisoners.
- Revising health care programs to try and control costs while extending coverage to poor people and children who lack insurance while fighting Obamacare.
- Reforming education by adopting Common Core standards, ending tenure for new K-12 teachers, replacing FCAT with the Florida Standards Assessment, and expanding school choice options.
- Reforming welfare by requiring recipients to train or work and setting time limits on benefits.

- Establishing new rules for planning and growth management that reduce state oversight.
- Seeking protection for environmental resources like the Everglades, the aquifer, and endangered species like the panther and manatee.
- Cutting taxes while balancing the state budget.
- Passing conservative, and often controversial, social legislation on issues like abortion and gun rights.

Table 6-2. Florida Statutes: Titles and Chapters

TITLE I	CONSTRUCTION OF STATUTES	Ch.1-2
TITLE II	STATE ORGANIZATION	Ch.6-8
TITLE III	LEGISLATIVE BRANCH; COMMISSIONS	Ch.10-11
TITLE IV	EXECUTIVE BRANCH	Ch.14-24
TITLE V	JUDICIAL BRANCH	Ch.25-44
TITLE VI	CIVIL PRACTICE AND PROCEDURE	Ch.45-88
TITLE VII	EVIDENCE	Ch.90-92
TITLE VIII	LIMITATIONS	Ch.95
TITLE IX	ELECTORS AND ELECTIONS	Ch.97-107
TITLE X	PUBLIC OFFICERS, EMPLOYEES, AND RECORDS	Ch.110-122
TITLE XI	COUNTY ORGANIZATION & INTERGOVERNMENTAL RELATIONS	Ch.124-164
TITLE XII	MUNICIPALITIES	Ch.165-185
TITLE XIII	PLANNING AND DEVELOPMENT	Ch.186-191
TITLE XIV	TAXATION AND FINANCE	Ch.192-221
TITLE XV	HOMESTEAD AND EXEMPTIONS	Ch.222
TITLE XVI	TEACHERS' RETIREMENT; HIGHER ED. FACILITIES BONDS	Ch.238-243
TITLE XVII	MILITARY AFFAIRS AND RELATED MATTERS	Ch.250-252
TITLE XVIII	PUBLIC LANDS AND PROPERTY	Ch.253-274
TITLE XIX	PUBLIC BUSINESS	Ch.279-290
TITLE XX	VETERANS	Ch.292-296
TITLE XXI	DRAINAGE	Ch.298
TITLE XXII	PORTS AND HARBORS	Ch.308-315
TITLE XXIII	MOTOR VEHICLES	Ch.316-324
TITLE XXIV	VESSELS	Ch.326-328
TITLE XXV	AVIATION	Ch.329-333
TITLE XXVI	PUBLIC TRANSPORTATION	Ch.334-349
TITLE XXVII	RAILROADS AND OTHER REGULATED UTILITIES	Ch.350-368
TITLE XXVIII	NATURAL RESOURCES; CONSERVATION, RECLAMATION, & USE	Ch.369-380
TITLE XXIX	PUBLIC HEALTH	Ch.381-408
TITLE XXX	SOCIAL WELFARE	Ch.409-430
TITLE XXXI	LABOR	Ch.435-452
TITLE XXXII	REGULATION OF PROFESSIONS AND OCCUPATIONS	Ch.454-493
TITLE XXXIII	RGLTN. OF TRADE, COMMERCE, INVESTMENTS, & SOLICITATION	Ch.494-560
TITLE XXXIV	ALCOHOLIC BEVERAGES AND TOBACCO	Ch.561-569
TITLE XXXV	AGRICULTURE, HORTICULTURE, AND ANIMAL INDUSTRY	Ch.570-604
TITLE XXXVI	BUSINESS ORGANIZATIONS	Ch.606-623
TITLE XXXVII	INSURANCE	Ch.624-651
TITLE XXXVIII	BANKS AND BANKING	Ch.655-667
TITLE XXXIX	COMMERCIAL RELATIONS	Ch.668-688
TITLE XL	REAL AND PERSONAL PROPERTY	Ch.689-723
TITLE XLI	FRAUDS, FRAUDULENT TRANSFERS, & GENERAL ASSIGNMENTS	Ch.725-727
TITLE XLII	ESTATES AND TRUSTS	Ch.731-739
TITLE XLIII	DOMESTIC RELATIONS	Ch.741-753
TITLE XLIV	CIVIL RIGHTS	Ch.760-765
TITLE XLV	TORTS	Ch.766-774
TITLE XLVI	CRIMES	Ch.775-896
TITLE XLVII	CRIMINAL PROCEDURE AND CORRECTIONS	Ch.900-985
TITLE XLVIII	K-20 EDUCATION CODE	Ch.1000-1013

Source: *Statutes of Florida*, Online Sunshine, http://www.leg.state.fl.us/statutes/, 2014.

Florida's diverse population ensures that there will be differences of opinion about what types of subjects the state legislature should address in its annual sessions.

Adopting Resolutions and Memorials

A bill that is not subject to action by the governor is called a resolution. There are three types of resolutions: a Senate or House Resolution, a Joint Resolution, and a Concurrent Resolution. A *Senate or House Resolution* is a one-house document for matters not involving the other chamber. Resolutions are often ceremonial in nature and frequently used to express recognition, congratulations, or condolences. (Examples are resolutions declaring Florida National Guard Day, congratulating the Florida State Seminole football team for winning a national championship, or honoring the memory of former Florida Governor Reubin Askew.) This type of resolution does not have the effect of law and almost always passes. In one recent session, 64 out of 64 in the House passed and 53 out of 59 in the Senate.

A *Joint Resolution* is the method by which the legislature can propose amendments to the Florida Constitution. It requires a three-fifths vote in each house before it can be placed on the ballot for a decision by Florida voters. A joint resolution is more difficult to pass. Recently there were 23 Joint Resolutions filed, but only one proposed constitutional amendment passed both chambers: a measure that would have allowed the governor to make prospective appointments of departing judges under some circumstances. (It was defeated by voters.) Joint Resolutions are also the form of legislation used to redistrict state legislative seats.

A *Concurrent Resolution* must be adopted by both houses and is limited to procedural and organizational legislative matters and ratification or rejection of proposed U.S. constitutional amendments or requesting action on U.S. constitutional amendments. In one recent session there were seven proposed Concurrent Resolutions, but only two passed both houses of the legislature. One was to clarify factors used to establish that legislative members are legal residents of their districts. The other called for the Senate and the House of Representatives to convene in joint session for the purpose of receiving a message from the governor.

Voting on proposed U.S. constitutional amendments is a rare event since few are proposed by Congress. In the 1970s and 1980s, the Florida Legislature chose not to ratify either the Equal Rights Amendment or the Washington D.C. Voting Rights Amendment. Neither of these proposed amendments ever obtained the required vote of three-fourths of the nation's state legislatures. Florida is also one of only eight states that never ratified the successful 26th Amendment that gave 18 year-olds the right to vote in 1971. In 1990, the

Florida Legislature did vote for the 27th Amendment that mandates congressional pay increases cannot take effect until after a congressional election has occurred, which became part of the U.S. Constitution.

A *Memorial* is a special form of Concurrent Resolution addressed to an executive agency or another legislative body, usually Congress, that expresses the sentiment of the Florida Legislature on a matter outside its legislative jurisdiction. In one recent session, 40 Memorials were filed but only six passed both chambers. One of these urged Congress to repeal all taxes on income and enact a national retail sales tax (the "Fair Tax").

Approving Budgets

Passing the annual appropriation bill (the budget) is perhaps the single most important function of the legislature. Adopting the budget is the only task that the Florida Constitution requires the legislature to accomplish each year. No state monies may be spent without a legislative appropriation, and it is difficult to think of any governmental action that does not involve some financial expenditure. Potentially, the legislature can control any activity of the state government through its power over appropriations—the "power of the purse." Each year Florida lawmakers consider the authorization of *billions* of dollars of state spending. (A more detailed description of the budget process appears in Chapter 7 and of the budget itself in Chapter 9.) Budgetary fights among legislators are commonplace due to differences in their taxing and spending priorites—and those of the citizens they represent.

Appropriations Committee members listen intently to a presentation on the proposed education budget.

Overseeing State Agencies

Legislative oversight of state agencies and programs is another important function. After the legislature creates and funds a program, they have a responsibility to ensure that the executive branch carries out the policy and spends the money as the legislature intended. Legislators frequently challenge state administrators to explain why they are doing what they do. Committee hearings, and budget hearings in particular, provide opportunities for legislators to put administrators "through the wringer" about programs and expenditures. Often embarrassed administrators feel harassed at these meetings, but the true purpose is to remind state administrators that elected representatives of the people are the final legal authority. For instance, when problems arose in Florida's prisons with unexplained inmate deaths the head of the Department of Corrections was grilled by legislators. Florida has many "sunset" laws that call for the legislature to reenact programs every few years or see them go out of existence. Few programs or agencies are ever "sunsetted," but such laws force periodic legislative reexamination and evaluation of the performance of state bureaucracies. One program that may actually see the "sunset" is Enterprise Zones scheduled to expire at the end of 2015 and not reauthorized during the regular session. Enterprise Zones give incentives to attract companies to locate in economically-depressed areas but have shown little return on investment.

Serving Constituents

Legislators and their staff spend a great deal of time answering requests from constituents, known as "servicing the district." Many e-mails, letters, and phone calls come from interest groups in their districts—business, labor, agriculture, teachers, municipal employees, and so on. These communications may deal with specific bills or with items in the state budget. Other communications may come from citizens who want specific assistance or favors such as help getting a state job, help with permits or licenses, voicing an opinion about proposed increases in state university tuition, and so forth. Most legislators willingly invest time in constituent service as they believe that it helps solidify their chance for re-election and because they find helping constituents to be a rewarding and fulfilling part of their job.[1]

LEGISLATIVE QUALIFICATIONS, ELECTIONS, & SESSIONS

All legislators are elected by the voters. There are 160 Florida legislators: 40 state senators and 120 state representatives. They are directly elected by voters in their districts. Senate districts are larger than House districts because there are considerably fewer Senate districts.

Qualifications

The only constitutional qualifications for House or Senate membership are that a candidate be 21 years of age or older, a resident of Florida for two years prior to election, and a resident of the district from which elected.

Filling Vacancies

When a legislative seat becomes vacant due to a death or resignation, the vacancy is filled in a special election, not by gubernatorial appointment.

Elections

Legislative elections are held in even numbered years for all House members (two-year terms) and one-half of Senate members (four-year terms). Florida's legislators are subject to term limits (eight years), which generally means two consecutive four-year terms for senators and four consecutive two-year terms for House members. It is possible to run again after sitting out a term.

Legislative Sessions

Florida's Constitution requires the regular legislative session to start in March in odd-numbered years but leaves it up to legislators to fix the date in even-numbered years. Legislators every 10 years meet in January when they are drawing new Congressional and legislative districts. During the 2014 session, they decided to meet in January 2016 ahead of the presidential preference primary scheduled for March. Most years, the legislature officially convenes for its annual *regular session* in March for a constitutionally-limited sixty days. Given the inefficiency of the legislative process, *special sessions* are very common. *Special sessions* may be called by either the governor or jointly by the President of the Senate and Speaker of the House. Special sessions are generally called when the state faces some financial or legal emergency or when an important issue that needs to be resolved was not adequately addressed during the regular session. Such was the case with the state budget in 2015. A special *organizational session* is convened following the November general election (even-numbered years) to swear in newly-elected members, select a new House Speaker and Senate President, and appoint committees before the next regular session begins.

REAPPORTIONMENT & REDISTRICTING

Every 10 years, there is a new U.S. Census of Population. After each Census, the number of seats each state has in Congress may increase, decrease, or stay the same, depending on a state's population growth rate over the past decade. This recalculation of how many seats in the U.S. House of Representatives a state will have is the responsibility of the U.S. Congress. Florida has gained congressional seats every decade since 1950 because of the state's rapid population growth.

When the new Census numbers are available, it is up to the state legislature to determine precisely how many people need to be placed in each congressional and state legislative district to meet the "one person, one vote" standard. The process of making such calculations is known as *reapportionment*. The actual drawing of the lines is known as *redistricting*. After each Census, the Florida Legislature has to redraw each congressional district, all 40 state Senate districts, and all 120 House districts. Each chamber draws their own new districts. However, the Florida House of Representatives and the Florida Senate must adopt a joint resolution apportioning the legislative districts in accordance with federal and state constitutional requirements. Both must also pass legislation creating the new congressional seats. The governor can veto the proposed congressional districts but has no say in the new legislative districts.

Redistricting is a highly contentious process. Legislators are often fighting to keep their own seat or to help their party gain seats. They may even be interested in designing a seat they might run for in the future (e.g., a house member looking ahead to running for a senate seat). When legislators draw districts for political advantage, it is called *gerrymandering*. Two constitutional amendments passed by Florida voters in 2010 prohibit partisan and incumbent gerrymandering during the redistricting process but require the legislature to take into account racial and ethnic minority access. They also require that lines be drawn to follow local governmental and natural geographic boundaries as much as possible.

Florida's Early Reapportionments

Prior to 1962, the Florida Legislature was malapportioned—that is, there were unequal numbers of people in each district. Each county got at least one seat in the Florida House regardless of its population size. That practice allowed just 18 percent of Florida's population to elect a majority to the state legislature.[2] It gave the rural Democratic panhandle legislators (nicknamed "pork-choppers" because they fought for pork rather than principle) enormous power to bring money and programs into rural communities at the expense of the growing urban and suburban areas.[3] Many attempts were made in the 1950s and early 1960s to reapportion Florida's electoral districts fairly, but the pork choppers in the legislature were able to defeat every meaningful reform.

Two former state legislators who lived through the early days of redistricting have written fascinating memoirs that recount those hectic times (top, Frederick B. Karl; bottom, Buddy MacKay). Both went on to higher office after leaving the legislature. Karl became a Florida Supreme Court Justice; MacKay became Governor.

The U.S. Supreme Court's *Baker* v. *Carr* ruling in 1962, and the subsequent decisions mandating one-person, one-vote in legislative districting,[4] had a profound effect on the Florida Legislature.[5] Reapportionment broke the grip of the rural North Florida "pork choppers" and distributed legislative power to urban counties like Dade (Miami), Duval (Jacksonville), Hillsborough (Tampa), Orange (Orlando), Pinellas (St. Petersburg), and Broward (Fort Lauderdale).[6] It allowed African Americans to win state legislative office for the first time since Reconstruction. It brought a new generation of urban legislators to Tallahassee like Reubin Askew and Bob Graham who became governors.

Reapportionment also dramatically increased Republican representation in the Florida House. Following a special election in 1967, Republicans went from having less than 10 members to 39 members. The 1967 special election was conducted under the direction of a federal court. The long term impact of the ruling was to help translate growing Republican strength in Florida's urban and suburban areas into more Republican legislative seats.[7]

The switch from multi-member state legislative districts (which allow two or more legislators to be elected from the same district) to single-member districts in 1982 created an even more representative legislative body whose membership more closely mirrored the demographics of the state. Single-member districts allowed the creation of districts with larger and more concentrated populations of minority groups. Blacks and Hispanics both gained a number of seats in 1982. While Republicans actually lost seats in the 1982 election, they began gaining ground in subsequent elections.

Race and Redistricting

The Florida Constitution places the responsibility for apportionment and redistricting on the legislature itself. If the legislature fails to do it, the Florida Supreme Court is authorized to perform the task. But the federal courts often become involved because of Acts passed by Congress or U.S. Supreme Court rulings on the use of race in the redistricting process.

The federal Voting Rights Act (VRA) lays out quite explicit rules that state and local governments must adhere to when engaging in redistricting to protect the voting power of minorities. For example, Section 2 of the VRA protects minority voters from practices and procedures that deprive them of an effective vote because of their race, color or membership in a particular language minority group. The VRA also prohibits *minority vote dilution* (depriving minority voters of an equal opportunity to elect a candidate of their choice) and *retrogression* (a voting or redistricting change that puts minorities in a worse position under the new scheme than under the existing law or districts). Until 2013, under the VRA, some states with a history of discrimination, including Florida, were required to have their proposed redistricting plans pre-cleared by the U.S. Department of Justice before they could go into effect. Now, pre-clearance is no longer required of any state as a result of the U.S. Supreme Court's ruling in *Shelby County* v *Holder*[8] unless Congress changes the law. The purpose of pre-clearance was to make sure the proposed changes did not violate the VRA. Florida's growing and diverse minority populations (racial, language) make it more difficult to draw districts that satisfy federal law than is the case in states and localities with less diverse populations.

Civil rights groups are always on the lookout for districts that *effectively* limit, or dilute, their opportunity to elect representatives. *Splintering* (or *cracking*) is the term used for spreading the minority population across several districts. *Packing* refers to excessively concentrating the minority population into fewer districts. Over the years, intense debates have ensued over what should be the minority population makeup of a district. Even within the minority community, there is often disagreement as to whether majority-minority districts would expand minority representation more than would minority influence, coalition, or crossover coalition districts.

Federal court rulings, like *Thornburg* v. *Gingles* in 1986, *Shaw* v. *Reno* in 1993, and *Miller* v. *Johnson* in 1995[9] have spelled out how states are to take race into consideration when redrawing districts. The *Thornburg* v. *Gingles* ruling required state legislatures to create "majority-minority" districts where possible to enhance the chances that minorities could elect a representative of their own choice.[10] This ruling guided the actions of the Florida Legislature in its 1992 redistricting efforts. Later, however, the U.S. Supreme Court backed off its earlier "majority-minority" district dictate and ruled that drawing congressional districts based *solely* on racial composition violated the 14th and 15th amendments to the U.S. Constitution which prohibit election practices based on race.[11]

With the constant changes in judicial rulings and Florida's increasingly racially and ethnically diverse population, it is not surprising that a number of the legislature's redistricting plans have ended in the federal courts.

Redistricting in 1992

The 1992 redistricting centered on arguments over how many minority leaning districts should be drawn. Republican, Hispanic, and black legislators sought to maximize the number of minority seats while white Democrats sought somewhat fewer fearing that increased racial gerrymandering would help Republicans win more seats. The state Senate plan and the House plan created by the legislature ended up in federal district court before a three-judge panel as a consequence of lawsuits brought by Hispanic and African-American plaintiffs (the DeGrandy case). The federal judges approved the plan drawn for the Senate but redrew the House boundaries in 31 districts and created five more favorable Hispanic (and thus Republican) districts in South Florida. But the state appealed that decision and ultimately the U.S. Supreme Court overturned the lower court and reinstated the House plan approved by the state legislature and the Senate plan drawn by the Florida Supreme Court.[12] In the end, the House plan included 13 districts with majority black populations and 9 with majority Hispanic populations and the Senate plan included three districts with majority black populations and three with majority Hispanic population.[13] The creation of these minority access districts brought a record number of minorities into the legislature and helped Republicans take control of the Florida Senate in 1994 and the Florida House in 1996.

Florida gained four additional congressional seats in 1992 for a total of 23. The political infighting in the legislature over congressional redistricting created gridlock. The federal district court was obliged to draw the state's congressional district map after the legislature failed to approve a map. The court did so by creating three heavily African-American districts, subsequently won by African-American Democrats who became the first black members in the Florida congressional delegation since before the Civil War and two heavily Hispanic districts won by two Cuban-American Republicans—one new and one an incumbent who had won a special election a few years earlier. Adjustments to the black majority district running from Jacksonville to Orlando (and several surrounding districts) were ordered by the federal courts later in the decade.

Redistricting in 2002

The 2002 legislative redistricting process brought fewer charges of *racial gerrymandering* and more accusations of *partisan gerrymandering*. This was hardly surprising in light of the fact that Republicans were in total control of redistricting for the first time. The GOP legislators followed three guidelines: the constitutional obligation to create districts of relatively equal size based on Florida's 2000 population of 16 million; the civil rights law prohibiting dilution of black and Hispanic voting strength; and the desire to create as many Republican leaning districts as possible by packing Democrats together in relatively fewer districts. With the aid of sophisticated software, Republicans were able to take partisan gerrymandering to new heights (or lows depending on one's point of view). Minority districts were created for black Democrats, and white Democrats were packed into relatively few districts to leave surrounding districts leaning Republican. In South Florida, minority districts were also created for Cuban Republicans. The end result was that although Democrats had a slight lead in statewide voter registration, Republicans took an 81-39 seat lead in the Florida House, a 26-14 lead in the Florida Senate, and an 18-7 lead in the congressional delegation. (Florida gained two more congressional seats after the 2000 Census.) While the Department of Justice reviewed all of the 2002 redistricting plans, and several interested parties filed lawsuits, only a small change boosting the number of Hispanics in a Senate district in South Florida was required. Florida courts and federal courts had long held that partisan gerrymandering may be unfair, but it was not unconstitutional.

Redistricting in 2012: The Fair Districts Amendments

The redistricting process in 2012 was considerably different than in 2002 for a number of reasons—voters' approval of two constitutional amendments (Fair Districts) changing the standards for drawing districts, the release of 2010 Census figures awarding Florida two new seats in the U.S. House of Representatives, growth in the state's "racial and language minorities," significant within-state population shifts, major U.S. Supreme Court rulings on how to draw minority districts, better software by which to draw districts, and more aggressive citizen watchdog groups.

Upset about the partisan gerrymandering that took place in 2002, reform groups like the Committee for Fair Elections tried to take redistricting out of the hands of the Florida Legislature altogether, judging the process to be unfair and a threat to good government. The Fair Districts group circulated a petition calling for an amendment to the Florida Constitution that would have turned the responsibility over to an independent redistricting commission, similar to the process in place in some other states. The proposal almost made the 2006 ballot but was rejected by the Florida Supreme Court for two reasons—it did not comply with the constitutional requirement of a single-subject and the ballot summary was misleading.[14] Somewhat reluctantly, the group abandoned the idea of the independent commission, went back to the drawing board, and crafted two new amendments focused more on setting clear standards than on who would do the drawing. These were referred to as the "Fair Districts" amendments, both of which were handily approved. Each got 63 percent "Yes" votes in November 2010.

One amendment sets the standards for drawing the *congressional* districts, the other for creating the state *legislative* districts (Senate and House) although the standards for both are identical. Two separate amendments were needed to comply with Florida's single subject rule for initiatives proposing changes to the Florida Constitution. The specific Florida constitutional standards for drawing congressional redistricting boundaries are:

(a) No apportionment plan or individual district shall be drawn with the intent to favor or disfavor a political party or an incumbent; and districts shall not be drawn with the intent or result of denying or abridging the equal opportunity of racial or language minorities to participate in the political process or to diminish their ability to elect representatives of their choice; and districts shall consist of contiguous territory.

(b) Unless compliance with the standards in this subsection conflicts with the standards in subsection (a) or with federal law, districts shall be as nearly equal in population as is practicable; districts shall be compact; and districts shall, where feasible, utilize existing political and geographical boundaries.

(c) The order in which the standards within subsections (a) and (b) of this section are set forth shall not be read to establish any priority of one standard over the other within that subsection.

Redistricting in 2012: Strategy and Process

Publicly, the Republican legislators sought to follow the letter of the law of the new Fair Districts and the VRA. But as with most redistricting, they hoped to end up with districts favorable to the GOP. Their major strategy to accomplish these goals was to maximize opportunities for minorities and create a number of districts favorable to black candidates that were heavily Democratic thus leaving surrounding districts "bleached"—more white and favorable to Republican candidates.

Before the redistricting session began, legislators held a number of meetings around the state where large numbers of citizens and groups gave input and also submitted a variety of proposed maps online.[15] Once the legislature met, drew, and passed the three redistricting plans, the Florida Supreme Court automatically reviewed the two new legislative maps. The Court declared the Senate map unconstitutional because of intentional partisan and incumbent gerrymandering while ruling the House maps to be in compliance. (Congressional districts do not undergo automatic review by the Florida Supreme Court.) After the Florida Senate redrew their maps the Florida Supreme Court eventually ruled them in compliance as well.

A coalition of Democrats and "good government" groups filed a lawsuit asking a Florida District Court to summarily declare the new congressional districts unconstitutional.[16] After a facial review, the judge refused to issue a summary judgement, clearing the way for the congressional districts to be used, but also allowing the trial to move forward. All three plans were submitted to the U.S. Justice Department who pre-cleared them for use. Elections were held using the new maps in 2012 and 2014, but after a lengthy trial the District Court eventually ruled that the congressional maps were unconstitutional because of partisan gerrymandering. In the course of the trial, emails were discovered showing that several GOP consultants conspired to secretly draw districts favoring Republicans. The court ordered changes to several Central Florida districts. The legislature promptly redrew the congressional map and the judge found the new districts in compliance. The coalition then appealed the decision asking the Florida Supreme Court to order further changes to the congressional map. A similar court challenge was made to the state Senate map. In each instance, those challenging the maps hoped for court-ordered new maps with more competitive districts and fewer safe (heavily one-party) districts.

Redistricting in 2012: Evaluating Outcomes

How well did the new process work? One study that evaluated redistricting outcomes under Fair District standards concluded the following:[17]

- Despite some problems, the new redistricting process worked fairly well compared to redistricting efforts in previous decades.
- On average, the new process produced legislative and congressional districts that were more compact and split far fewer cities and counties than the districts created in 2002.
- The new process protected minority voting rights and resulted in a greater number of black and Hispanic leaning districts and record numbers of minority members in the legislature.
- The House and congressional districts did not favor or disfavor incumbents (many Republican incumbents were put in less favorable districts or with other GOP incumbents) although very few incumbent senators were put at risk.
- The new process fell short on producing districts that were neutral towards political parties. On the one hand, Democrats were able to make some gains at all three levels, on the other hand, Republican maintained solid majorities despite the statewide Democratic advantage in voter registration.

Obviously, Fair Districts supporters are particularly concerned with the last point (partisan gerrymandering) and have continued their fights in court.

A PROFILE OF FLORIDA'S LEGISLATORS

Why do people run for the state legislature? A combination of motives draws people into politics. For many it is their interest in public affairs. They see themselves as "doing good," serving the public, and performing a civic duty. They may believe that they know better than others what is truly in the public interest. For others, it is an overriding commitment to a particular policy that has prompted their candidacy, such as tax limits, better educational funding, environmental protection, "save the beaches," school choice, or police protection. For some candidates, politics is a fun hobby; they enjoy meeting people, attending gatherings, giving speeches. The prestige and attention received from holding a high office in state government are very appealing. For still others, legislative office enhances their business and professional contacts. "For nearly all, in some way or another, politics is an 'ego trip,' a means of receiving approval, support, and attention."[18]

How representative is the Florida Legislature? To what degree do the characteristics of elected legislators match the characteristics of Florida's population? The answer is on race and ethnicity, "somewhat" representative, but on party, being native to the state, education, religion, political experience and gender, "not very" representative. On average, Florida legislators are more likely to be white, Republican, Florida natives, well-educated, religious, politically experienced, male, wealthy, and lawyers. (See Figure 6-2.)

The proportion of African-American state legislators nearly equals the percentage of blacks in Florida's population while the proportion of Hispanic state legislators is less than the percentage Hispanic in the population at-large. The number of Hispanics serving in the legislature has grown over two decades, but has not kept up with exploding Hispanic population growth. Part of the reason is that some of the new arrivals are not citizens and are therefore ineligible to vote.

In terms of political party representativeness, all legislators are either Republicans or Democrats, even though 26 percent of Floridians are not registered with a major party.[19] And although there are more Democrats in the state than Republicans by about four percentage points, the 2015 legislature had 107 GOP members but only 53 Democrats—a 2:1 Republican advantage.

Background and Experience

Legislators generally have deep roots in their communities, even in Florida where non-natives constitute about 67 percent of the population. (See Chapter 1.) State senators and especially state representatives are more likely to have been born in the state than the general population. Legislators are more likely to have business or professional ties in their community, to belong to churches and service clubs, to be property owners and investors in their community, and to have attended colleges and universities in the state. Most members express a religious preference. In the legislature overall, about 71 percent are Christian Protestant, 21 percent Catholic, and 7 percent Jewish. The average age of Florida house members is 49 and Florida senators 54 whereas the average age of Floridians overall is 39.

A little less than a third (29 percent) of Florida's house members had experience in previous elected office prior to running for the legislature, mostly as city or county commissioners or school board members. However, for many, their House race was their first try at elected office. Increasingly, state house seats are seen as excellent entry points into politics—a sharp change from the past when local offices were regarded as the launching pad for a political career. In reality, many of these first-time candidates have had some previous experience in politics, frequently as legislative staff members or aides to individual legislators. Such staff positions allowed them to use their experience, knowledge, and contacts to launch their own campaigns for the legislature when a seat was vacated.

Senators are more likely than house members to have had experience in elective office before winning a seat in the Senate. In fact, only two members of the 2015 Florida Senate did not have previous political experience. Over 90 percent served in the House before they "moved up" to the Senate. While the two chambers are technically co-equal branches, as a more exclusive body with only 40 members, the Senate promises more power and perks than a seat in the 120-member House. Because of their smaller numbers, senators serve on more committees and are more likely to become a committee chair if their party wins a majority of seats in the chamber.

Minority Path-Breakers

The first African American to serve in the Florida House since the Reconstruction era was Joe Lang Kershaw, a junior high school civics teacher from Coral Gables who first won office in 1968.[20] In the following 1970 election, Miami attorney Gwen Cherry, a graduate of Florida A&M University, won election to the House and became the first black woman to serve in the legislature. Mrs. Cherry died in an automobile accident in 1979 and was succeeded by another Florida A&M University graduate, Carrie Meek, who in 1982 became the first African-American woman elected to the Florida Senate. She later served in the U.S. House of Representatives, and upon her retirement, was replaced in Congress by her son Kendrick Meek. Arnett Girardeau, a dentist from Jacksonville, was also elected to the Senate in 1982 and thus became the first black man elected to that body since Reconstruction. Les Miller became the first black Minority Leader for the Democrats in 1998. The 2004-2006 legislature saw blacks serving as Minority Leader in both the House (Chris Smith) and Senate (Les Miller) for the first time in Florida history.[21] As this rise to leadership indicates, black members are extremely influential within the legislature's Democratic Caucus. Nearly half of the House Democrats (21 of 39) and Senate Democrats (6 of 14) are African-American or Afro-Caribbean.

After the Civil War, most blacks who served in the legislature were Republicans, but in the modern era, almost all black legislators have been Democrats. In 1980, John Plummer of Miami became the first black Republican elected to the legislature since Reconstruction but he served just one term. His election came about in large part due to voter confusion. Plummer shared the same last name as another Democratic member of the House and engaged in a "stealth" campaign that avoided photographers and public appearances. Jennifer Carroll from Jacksonville became the first black Republican woman elected to the House in April 2003 and was elected Lt. Governor in 2010. All but one of the current black members of the legislature are Democrats. Almost all black members are elected from majority or near-majority black districts. Florida's black

When state legislators take the oath of office, they are ever mindful of the make-up and priorities of the people back home they represent.

legislators also come from diverse backgrounds: in 2015, one member was Haitian and one was Jamaican. Black members have formed the Florida Conference of Black State Legislators and the Florida Legislative Black Caucus to advocate for policies to help the black community.[22] On average black legislators in most states[23] and in Florida specifically[24] compile more liberal voting records than other Democrats (or Republicans).

The first Hispanic elected to the Florida legislature after statehood was Fernando Figueredo in 1885 from Monroe County. Democrat Maurice Ferré, a native of Puerto Rico, was elected to the House in 1966—the first Puerto Rican to serve in the modern era since 1925. In 1982, Republican Ileana Ros, a Cuban, became the first Hispanic woman elected to the House. She later married Representative Dexter Lehtinen, the first marriage of two Florida legislators. Ileana Ros-Lehtinen now serves in the U.S. House of Representatives.

She was not only the first Hispanic elected to serve in Congress from Florida when she won a special election in 1989, but was also the first Cuban elected to the U.S. House of Representatives.

Figure 6-2. Characteristics of Florida Legislators Compared to Floridians At-Large

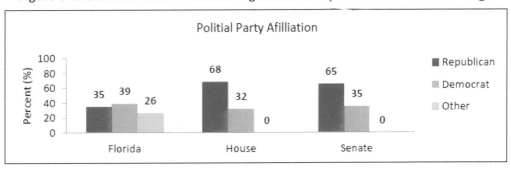

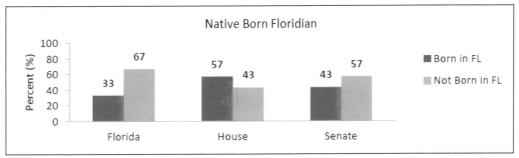

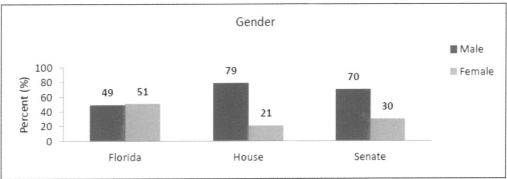

Sources: Data for Florida comes from the U.S. Census and Florida Division of Elections. Legislative data are from the Florida House and Senate member directories for the 2015-16 legislative sessions.

The Cuban-American Caucus was formed in 1988 and evolved into the Hispanic Caucus in 2004 to reflect the growing numbers of non-Cuban Hispanics in the state and in the legislature. The Hispanic Caucus has come out strongly against what they viewed as punitive legislation targeting illegal immigrants. Cuban legislators are usually Republican and generally conservative, although Cuban House members did support Democratic leadership from 1988 to 1992 to gain influence for South Florida until redistricting disputes split the alliance.[25] Only four of the 22 Hispanic members of the Florida Legislature in 2015 are Democrats (only one is Cuban). Most Hispanic legislators are Cuban although five members are Puerto Rican, one traces his roots to Spain, and another member has Cuban and Puerto Rican ancestry. All of the non-Cuban legislators are from Central Florida.

Women in the Legislature

Nationwide 24 percent of all state legislators are women—up from only about 5 percent in 1970.[26] Women constitute 21 percent of the Florida House and 30 percent of the Florida Senate—up dramatically from 1970, but relatively stable in recent years. (See Figures 6-3.) In 1928, Edna Giles Fuller from Orange County was the first female elected to the Florida Legislature (the House). Beth Johnson (D-Orlando) was the first woman elected to the Florida Senate (1962). While women candidates in Florida and elsewhere are just as successful as men in primary and general elections, fewer women than men choose to run for legislative seats. Scholars frequently cite women's traditional family roles of wife and mother as obstacles to a political career. Female legislative candidates with young children are very rare; newly elected female legislators are four years older on average than newly elected male legislators—a fact generally attributed to women waiting until their children are older to run.[27] One study found that more women serve in the legislatures of states whose capitals are located close to the major population centers than in states where the capital is more remotely located and requires a long commute from home.[28]

Some gender differences in politics have been declining over time. In Florida, gender differences in family commitments, early political experiences, and political ambitions are diminishing, especially among younger women. A study that interviewed Florida legislators found that:

- Women do not enter elective office later in life than men. The average age of entry is virtually identical.
- An equally high percentage of both men and women legislators in Florida bypassed local elective offices, choosing instead to enter elective politics at the state legislative level.
- The fact that the average age at which women are running for office is *declining* reflects the fact that women no longer have to wait until the children are grown to run for office—no doubt an outgrowth of higher incidences of working women of all ages and greater reliance upon child care by all households with children of school age or younger.
- Female and male legislators have remarkably similar histories of being elected to legislative bodies, beginning for many as far back as their high school student council days and continuing through college student government and adulthood.
- Nearly equal proportions, of men and women legislators held elective posts as adults in nonpolitical organizations (civic, business, professional, cultural, church, service) and in political party organizations prior to running for office.[29]

Figure 6-3. Political Party Make-Up of Women in the Florida House and Senate

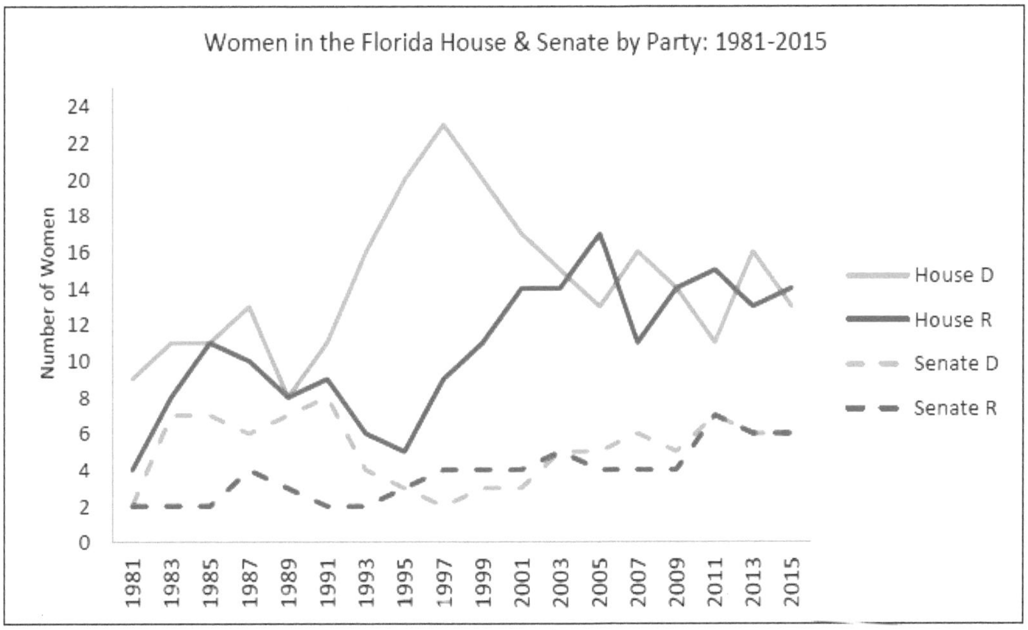

Women in the Florida House & Senate by Party: 1981-2015

Source: Center for American Women and Politics. Available at
http://www.cawp.rutgers.edu/fast_facts/resources/state_fact_sheets/FL.php.

While there is plenty of evidence that both the Florida Democratic Party and the Republican Party of Florida put a premium on women winning state legislative offices,[30] the proportion of women in the Florida Legislature has not risen dramatically in recent years. One of the reasons is that many local government elective posts are becoming more attractive than state legislative posts. Higher salaries, no term limits, smaller constituency bases (and thus lower campaign costs), along with more favorable ratings from the public than those garnered by the state legislature are all reasons why more women are opting to run for local offices rather than for the state legislature.[31]

Personal Wealth

Legislators frequently claim that public service is a financial burden. Many legislators put in full time hours but receive only around $30,000 year. While this may be true, legislators are generally recruited from among the more affluent members of society, and they become even more affluent during their tenure. Indeed, there is evidence that the average net worth of new legislators is increasing over time, and the average legislator increases his or her net worth while serving in the legislature. (Net worth is the total value of all assets—houses, autos, stocks, bonds, property, etc.—after subtracting the total value of all outstanding debts, mortgages, loans, etc.) Asked to explain these increases in personal wealth, one legislator said, "Maybe they do well because they're achievers. That's why they win when they run for office and that's why they make money."[32] But it is also likely that legislative service—and the name recognition and personal contacts that go with it—enhances a legislator's legal practice, real estate or insurance business, and investment opportunities. The Director of Integrity Florida, a nonpartisan good government group, says many lawmakers get significant income from another source as well—special interests who lobby the legislature.[33] Citizens now have access to the legislators' financial disclosure reports which are posted on the Ethics Commission's website, thanks to legislation passed in 2013.

Occupation

Since Florida is considered a part-time legislature, it is not surprising that most members have full time jobs in addition to serving. In fact, less than 10 percent of state legislators (two senators and nine house members) have no other occupation. Most of these are retired. Since the Republican takeover of the Florida Legislature, there has been an increase in the number of business people elected. Some 49 percent of the House and 42.5 percent of the Senate are businesspeople from various sectors including banking, insurance, accounting, real estate, public relations and advertising, and management. About 6 percent of the members of both houses are educators, 6 percent are in the medical field, and another 2.5 percent are in agriculture.[34] A handful of legislators work in the non-profit sector, for local governments, or for unions.

Lawyers are the largest and most over-represented single occupational category in the Florida Legislature (26 percent of the House members and 27.5 percent of the state senators). In comparison, less than one percent of all Floridians are lawyers. The traditional explanation for the dominance of lawyers is that they are trained to represent clients and to deal with state laws. They are therefore well prepared to represent the district's constituents and write and rewrite state laws. But a more practical explanation is that service in the legislature enhances one's legal practice through increased name recognition and contacts with potential clients. Many young people who aspire to careers in politics apply to law school, well aware of the American tradition of the lawyer-politician.

What is the effect of having so many lawyers in the legislature? Lawyers represent a full range of Democratic, Republican, liberal, conservative, and interest-group views. They seldom vote as a bloc in the legislature. However, the one important issue that unites most lawyer-legislators is tort reform. (See Chapter 8.) Lawyers are almost uniformly opposed to reforms that limit jury awards, restrict their fees, limit medical malpractice or product liability cases, prevent attorneys from suing deep-pocketed third parties, or otherwise adversely affect the financial interests of trial lawyers.

INCUMBENT ADVANTAGE, TURNOVER, AND TERM LIMITS

Over the years the *incumbent re-election rate* has averaged over 90 percent. That is, over 90 percent of incumbent state legislators running for re-election are successful. The power of incumbency is so great that well over half of Florida House and Senate incumbents regularly run unopposed in the November general election.

Incumbent Advantage

Why do incumbents win so often, especially when most Floridians give poor ratings to the Florida Legislature itself? The answer lies in the many advantages enjoyed by incumbents over challengers in wooing voters. As senators and representatives, incumbents are frequently invited to speak to civic groups, service clubs, neighborhood associations, colleges and universities, and other public forums in their districts. In effect, they are campaigning during their entire term and gaining valued name recognition. Challengers do not usually fire up their campaigns until a few months before the election. Incumbents have full-time legislative staff working for them in offices in Tallahassee and in their home districts. Careful attention to calls and requests from voters (casework) wins loyalty. But perhaps most important, incumbents enjoy a huge advantage in campaign contributions, enabling them to outspend their challengers, often by 2, 3, or 4 to 1. Lobbyists and political action committees contribute much more to incumbents than to challengers because officeholders are already in a position to respond to requests and are more likely to win re-election. Challengers have no immediate favors to offer, and many political contributors do not want to offend incumbents by being publicly listed as financial supporters of their opponents. (See Chapter 5.)

Turnover

Turnover is higher than the incumbency return rate because not every incumbent seeks re-election. Before term limits took effect in 2000, turnover in the Florida Legislature averaged about 25 percent. This meant that in any two-year session approximately one-quarter of the House and Senate members were "freshmen." Turnover occurs when legislators vacate their seats to run for another office at the national, state, or local level. Turnover also occurs when legislators decide that they have made enough trips to Tallahassee, that their business or professional interests are sufficiently advanced that further service in the legislature is not worth the effort, that they have grown tired of legislative business, or that they have accomplished most of what they came to Tallahassee to do. Redistricting after each ten-year Census can create turnover whenever legislators are deprived of their customary constituents or they end up in a newly-configured district where another incumbent legislator also lives. Occasionally, however, turnover results from the rare defeat of an incumbent. Three or four two-year terms as a House member and two four-year terms in the Senate was close to the average service, even before term limits were mandated by the Florida Constitution.

Term Limits

The citizens' initiative "Eight Is Enough" won an overwhelming 77 percent voter support in a statewide referendum in 1992. It mandated eight-year term limits on Florida House members (four two-year terms), Senate members (two four-year terms), and all Cabinet officials (two four-year terms). Similar eight-year term limits had been set for the governor and lieutenant governor in the 1968 Constitution. The ban is for consecutive years and is actually a ban on a candidate's name appearing on the ballot if they will have been in office for eight years at the end of their current term. Because of this wording, some senators actually get to serve 10 years total if their first term in office comes during a redistricting year and they are assigned a two year term initially. Proponents of term limits argue that they inspire greater competition for legislative seats and encourage more qualified people to run for office. Proponents also believe that term limits reduce the influence of well-entrenched interest groups and make legislators more responsive to public opinion. Opponents of term limits counter that they weaken the power of the legislature in relation to the governor, executive branch, bureaucracies, and interest groups. They insist that term limits lead to less experienced legislative leadership and membership, a loss of institutional memory and policy expertise, and less professional legislators.

State legislators are ever-mindful of term limits. State Representative Arthenia Joyner, D-Tampa, was scheduled to be term-limited out of the House in 2008 but decided to run for the Florida Senate in 2006 when the District 18 seat opened up as a consequence of former Senator Les Miller's decision to seek a congressional seat. She was reelected and served as the first black female Minority Leader in the Senate before being termed out in 2016.

Term limits took effect in Florida for the first time in 2000 and researchers are now able to assess their impact.[35] Initally, term limits increased turnover in a highly cyclical manner, particularly in the House. In the 2000 election, 55 of 120 House members were forced out due to term limits followed by 14 more in 2002, 7 more in 2004 and 19 in 2006. In 2008, 47 members were forced to leave who had originally entered office because of term limits! However the dramatic eight-year turnover swings (2000 and 2008) have faded over time: only 16 members of the

House have to leave office in 2016. The turnover in the Senate caused by term limits has been less cyclical and more spread out since Senate terms are staggered. In the Senate, 11 of 20 Senators whose terms were up in 2000 left office, followed by 12 of 20 in 2002. No senators were forced out in 2004, but five were forced out in 2006 and in 2008 and seven more were termed out in 2010. Seven more members of the Senate have to leave office in 2016.

The most thorough study of term limits in Florida[36] found that:

- Competition for most seats has decreased. Forced turnover has increased competition for open seat races, but once a legislator wins a seat, competition declines dramatically until the incumbent retires since prospective challengers know the incumbent will be forced out in the near future and their chance of winning increases in an open seat race.

- Term limits have had little impact on the number of women and minorities in the legislature. Open seats create new opportunities for women and minority candidates but also force many existing female, black and Hispanic legislators out of office. Term limits have increased the number of younger and older members namely those seeking to begin a career in politics or seeking to serve after retirement.

- Term limits have not created citizen legislators. Many politicians elected under term limits have significant electoral experience before joining the Florida House or Senate. Once in office many do not serve a full eight years, instead quitting early to run for a different office. And many term limited legislators do not return to their private lives; instead many decide to run for local office.

- Forced turnover has dramatically accelerated the race for leadership positions as newly elected legislators begin to seek and often lock up pledges to become House Speaker or Senate President before finishing their first year in office.

- Term limits have caused a loss of institutional memory. There are fewer members who actually know what has been tried and done in the legislature before or have an in-depth knowledge of procedural rules. These problems are more acute in the House than in the the Senate because most senators have served in the House. This has enhanced the power of legislative leaders and the majority party (Republicans to date).

- The legislative branch overall has been weakened by term limits. The governor to some degree, and particularly executive branch staff and lobbyists have increased in power relative to the legislature since they ofter serve in their positions far longer than the legislators. In addition, more legislators become lobbyists after leaving office due to term limits.

PUBLIC IMAGE OF THE FLORIDA LEGISLATURE

Popular approval of the Florida Legislature declined between 1980 and 1992, rebounded quite strongly until 2000, then began declining again, leveling off in the last few years in the low to mid 30 percent range. (See Figure 6-4.) Perhaps this decline merely reflects the public's declining confidence and greater distrust of all government institutions (see Chapter 3). But it may also reflect a growing awareness of partisan bickering in the legislature. While political scientists may praise a competitive two-party system with clear ideological divisions between the parties, many voters want to see more cooperation between Democratic and Republican legislators, an end to party strife and bickering, and a common devotion to serving the public interest.

The combination of a recession in 1991-1992 and the highly publicized battle over redistricting in 1992 contributed to the rock bottom 18 percent legislative approval rating in 1992. In 1995, the House commissioned a study *Making Florida Democracy Work*, "to change the way the legislature responds and makes itself acceptable to the people it represents" and "to repair the ties between the people and the government."[37] The legislature's approval rating began to climb and accelerated after the Republican takeover of the Senate in 1994 and the House in 1996. The improvement was short-lived. Voter assessments of legislative performance fell after the 2000 presidential election chaos, rebounded in 2006 when Republican Charlie Crist was elected Governor, then plummeted on the heels of the Great Recession. The "ups-and-downs" since then have largely reflected brief blips in the state's slowly-recovering economy, the sometimes strained relationship between the governor and legislature and between the House and Senate.

Figure 6-4. Citizen Evaluation of the Florida Legislature

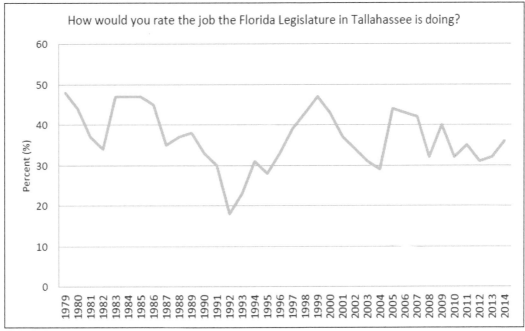

Note: Through 2004 percent responding "excellent" or "good"; from 2005 percent approving.
Source: Florida Annual Policy Survey, 1979 through 2003-2004, Florida State University. Quinnipiac from 2005.

Even as Floridians are highly critical of "the legislature in Tallahassee," they are paradoxically highly supportive of "their own representative." As noted earlier, over 90 percent of incumbent state legislators who seek re-election win, and for the most part they win easily. This same apparent paradox—poor popular ratings for the legislature as an institution, yet approval of the voters' own representative—has been reported for the U.S. Congress and various explanations have been offered. Perhaps voters have different expectations of the legislature as a whole than they have for their own representative.

Voters expect the legislature to deal effectively with state problems, to reduce crime, keep taxes low, and provide good services. These high expectations are seldom met. But voters expect their own representative to deal with local concerns, perhaps even personal problems they may have with state or local government agencies. They cast their vote for their own representative based on his or her name recognition or because of some personal service rendered (from major favors to small courtesies), common membership in church, service club, neighborhood association, or other civic organization, or because of a legislator's support for local projects—"bringing home the bacon" from Tallahassee.

Popular distrust and lack of confidence in the legislature has some important consequences. Perhaps most obvious is the willingness of citizens to bypass the legislature by signing petitions and putting policy proposals on the ballot in the form of constitutional amendments. (See Chapter 2.)

THE LEGISLATIVE PROCESS

On average, some 2,200 bills are introduced in the Florida Legislature each session. Proposed bills are then filtered through a daunting legislative process. (See Figure 6-5.) Less than 20 percent of them will become law. Only a member of the House or Senate or a committee can introduce a bill. But most bills are actually written by the governor's staff, attorney general's office, state agencies, city or county attorneys, or lawyers for interest groups. Legislators themselves can call on bill drafting offices in the House and Senate to assist them in putting their ideas into statutory language. In fact, there are about 2,000 legislative employees to help process legislation in Tallahassee. They provide professional assistance to the members, committees, and leadership. Many bills are "prefiled"—written and filed with the Clerk of the House or the Secretary of the Senate in advance of the legislative session. Each bill begins with the phrase "Be it Enacted by the Legislature of the State of Florida..." Without this phrase a bill cannot become a law. Opponents occasionally kill a bill by offering an "amendment" to "strike the enacting clause."

Figure 6-5. How an Idea Becomes a Law in Florida

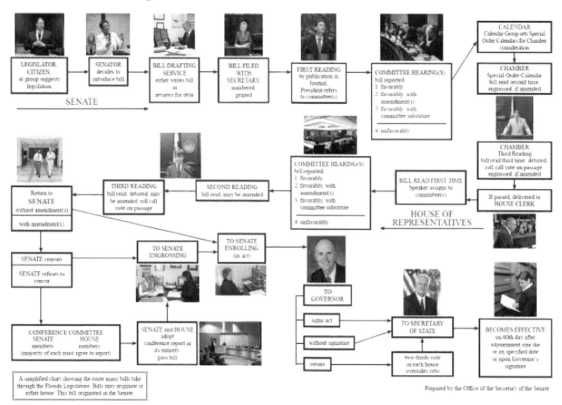

Source: Office of the Secretary of the Senate.

Legislative Leadership

Florida's legislative leaders—the Speaker of the House of Representatives and the President of the Senate—are more powerful in several areas (appointments, committee control, managing legislative procedures) than their counterparts in most other states.[38] They are elected in brief organizational sessions of the legislature held after each November election. By tradition they are elected on straight party-line votes. And by tradition they serve only one term as the head of their chamber. Maneuvering among contenders for these posts begins almost as soon as they are elected, with their solicitation of pledges from other legislators. Term limits have accelerated the time line for seeking a leadership position and brought more instability to the process as well.

Over the past decade, most House Speakers and Senate Presidents have locked up enough pledges to secure the position after just their first year in office and thus a line of leadership succession is set up many years in advance. In the House for instance, Speaker Designates include GOP Representatives: Corcoran (2016-2018), Oliva (2018-2020), and Eisnaugle (2022-2024). Of course this presupposes that the Republican Party will maintain its majority, that the designated leaders will continue to win office, and that members will not change their pledges. This does not always happen. House Speaker Steve Crisafulli (2014-2016) got the position only after Speaker Designate Chris Dorworth became embroiled in scandal and was defeated for re-election in 2012. It is doubtful that this process yields the best leaders as it does not give members time to actually assess the longer term performance of leadership candidates. Critics see this method of picking a "speaker-D" as a "precarious way to run a democracy... There's no audition for the job. You don't get a chance to see how the prospective leader performs under stress, how he/she resolves conflicts, or even how she/he feels about many issues. But you do know her/her political pedigree and which lobbyists and fundraisers back them."[39]

All House Speakers and Senate Presidents prior to 1992 were Democrats elected by party-line voting. In 1992, Senate elections produced an evenly divided chamber—20 Democrats and 20 Republicans. This situation created a real dilemma. Who would become the Senate president? (In Florida, the lieutenant governor does not preside over the Senate as he or she does in some other states.) The parties were deadlocked. After intense efforts by each party to lure defectors from the other party failed, a compromise was reached: the Republicans elected a President for the first year of the session (Ander Crenshaw), and the Democrats elected the President for the second year (Pat Thomas). In 1994, Republicans won their first Senate majority and installed the first full-term Republican Senate President, Jim Scott. In fall 1996, Republicans took control of the House for the first time with a 61-59 margin and Dan Webster became the first Republican House Speaker since Reconstruction. Republicans have maintained control of both chambers since that time.

Legislative leaders are sworn into their offices during the organizational session that is held after every general election. Leaders for the 2015-16 sessions are House Speaker Steve Crisafulli, R-Brevard (left), and Senate President Andy Gardiner, R-Orlando.

The House Speaker's and Senate President's power derives from control over their chamber's floor proceedings as well as their control over committee and leadership posts. Both leaders appoint the members of all committees and choose the chairs of all committees. Unlike the U.S. Congress, seniority in the Florida Legislature does not entitle members to leadership posts. The leaders also decide what legislation reaches the floor. This power is particularly important in the traditional end-of-session "logjam," when many bills are overlooked in the press of time. As one representative explained, "Enormous power resides in the Speaker's office—always has and always will. The Speaker controls everything-from where members park, to where they sit on the floor, to when their bills are heard, and where those bills are referred, and whether those bills ever get to the House floor."[40]

In Committee

Bills are filed with numbers to enable legislators, interest groups, and citizens to follow them through the legislative process. Computer systems now enable skilled observers to "track" a bill through the legislature. The "reading" of a bill is a misleading term. The first "reading" is simply the bill's introduction; it is not read but simply published in the *Journal*. Usually only the title is read on second and third "readings," and sometimes only the number.

Committees are where most of the in-depth discussion of bills that have been filed takes place. The Speaker of the House and the President of the Senate assign all bills to standing committees based on their policy focus.

The Speaker of the House and the President of the Senate assign all bills to standing committees based on their policy focus. (See Table 6-6.) This power of assignment is formidable. It allows the leadership to send bills to committees that are likely to look favorably (or unfavorably) upon them. Most bills die in committee, usually because the chair does not place them on the committee agenda or hold hearings on them. Occasionally a bill will be amended or rewritten as the *"committee substitute bill"* before being voted on by the full committee. Committees must vote approval of a bill to move it to the floor. In both the House and the Senate, bills approved by a standing committee go to the Rules and Calendar Committees for placement on the calendar or second reading. A negative vote by a committee almost always kills a bill. A two-thirds floor vote is required to review a bill rejected by a committee.

Traditionally, both House and Senate members prefer appointment to committees dealing directly with each year's appropriations bill (the state budget). In both the House and Senate, the budget is dealt with by the Appropriations Committee. (Until recently, the Senate called it the Budget Committee.) Both these committees have large numbers of subcommittees and many members. Members of these committees have more opportunities to slip in appropriations that directly benefit their constituents and supporters. Members also tend to seek committees that are directly related to their own expertise or to the interests of people in their district.

In addition to standing committees which continue to exist between sessions, each body will usually create some temporary *select* committees during a session to look at particular pressing issues—for instance in one session the House created a select committee on government reorganization and another on water policy. The House and Senate also usually decide to form some *joint* committees each session to allow members from both bodies to work together directly. Some examples are the Joint Administrative Procedures, Joint Legislative Auditing, Joint Public Counsel Oversight, and Joint Budget. Occasionally there are even *joint select* committees like a recent one on Collective Bargaining.

On the Floor

The Speaker of the House and the President of the Senate control floor proceedings in each chamber. Members usually begin debate or questions by addressing "Mister Speaker" or "Mister President" or "Madame President" as Toni Jennings was addressed when she was President (for two terms). These presiding officers decide which bills will come to the floor, allocate precious time to members for debate, and allow or disallow votes on amendments. It is true that the Constitution and the formal rules of each chamber provide for bill reading on separate days, for notification of members when bills will be considered, and other reasonable yet time-consuming procedures. But most floor business is conducted under a waiver of the rules. The Speaker and President frequently ask for, and almost always receive, "unanimous consent to suspend the rules" in order to proceed to pass favored bills and amendments.

Both House and Senate members are allocated specific amounts of time to debate bills and amendments. As Table 6-4 demonstrates, member comments during debate can be quite comical. A bill can be defeated by adopting a "killer" amendment—a motion to strike the clause "Be it enacted..." Debate can be cut off if the Speaker or President recognizes a "motion for the previous question" and it passes (by a majority in the House and two-thirds majority in the Senate). But the Speaker and President are often reluctant to cease debate or halt amendments because they do not want to irritate members who wish to speak.

A *yea* floor vote on the second reading of a bill is often swiftly followed by a third reading and final passage. Any member who voted with the majority may move for *reconsideration*. A vote to reconsider a previously passed bill usually kills the bill by sending it back to committee. Often an opponent of a bill will swing over to its majority supporters on final passage just to give him or her the right to move for reconsideration, presumably after having changed some minds. Often proponents of a bill move immediately for reconsideration just to forestall any second guessing. No bill may be reconsidered twice.

Legislators can get quite animated when trying to persuade fellow legislators about how to vote on a bill that is being debated on the floor.

In Conference

Legislation must pass both houses in identical form in order to go to the governor for signature into law. Most key bills have identical "companions" in each chamber. Even if one chamber amends the bill, the other may adopt this bill as its own *"substitute" bill*. Occasionally *conference committees*, with members from both houses, are required to find compromises between different versions of bills passed by the House and Senate. Conference committee members are appointed by Senate President and House Speaker. Most conference committees have three to five members from each chamber. But the powerful conference committee for the General Appropriations Bill (the state's annual budget) may have up to 30 or more "conferees."

Bills fashioned by conference committees must go back to the floor of both houses for approval. Conference committee-approved bills *("reports")* may not be amended. Each chamber must vote the report up or down. If either house rejects it, the bill is sent back to the conference committee, which may or may not try to reach a more acceptable compromise.

Table 6-3. Florida Legislative Committees, 2015-2016

Senate	House of Representatives
Standing Committees & Subcommittees	**Standing Committees & Subcommittees**
Agriculture	Appropriations
Appropriations	Agriculture and Natural Resources
Criminal and Civil Justice	Education
Education	Government Operations
General Government	Health Care
Health & Human Services	Justice
Transportation, Tourism & Econ. Development	Transportation & Econ. Development
Banking & Insurance	Economic Affairs
Children, Families and Elder Affairs	Econ. Development & Tourism
Commerce and Tourism	Highway & Water Safety
Communications, Energy, & Public Utilities	Transportation & Ports
Community Affairs	Education
Criminal Justice	Choice & Innovation
Education Pre-K-12	Higher Ed. & Workforce
Environmental Preservation & Conservation	K-12
Ethics & Elections	Finance and Tax
Finance & Tax	Health and Health Services
Fiscal Policy	Children Families & Seniors
Governmental Oversight & Accountability	Health Innovation
Health Policy	Health Quality
Higher Education	Judiciary
Judiciary	Civil Justice
Military, Veterans, Space & Domestic Security	Criminal Justice
Regulated Industries	Local Affairs
Rules	Local Government
Transportation	Veterans & Military
	Regulatory Affairs
	Business & Professions
	Energy & Utilities
	Insurance & Banking
	Rules, Calendar & Ethics
	Rulemaking Oversight & Repeal
	State Affairs
	Agriculture & Natural Resources
	Government Operations
Joint Committees	
Administrative Procedures	
Public Counsel Oversight	
Legislative Auditing	
Legislative Budget (Commission)	
Collective Bargaining (Select)	

Source: Florida House, http://www.myfloridahouse.gov/Sections/Committees/committees.aspx;
Florida Senate. Available at https://www.flsenate.gov/Committees/#com-list.

Table 6-4. Classic Quotes from Debates in the Florida House of Representatives

"Anyone can get a good bill passed. It takes real skill to get a bad one through."
"These are not my figures I'm quoting. They're the figures of someone who knows what they're talking about."
"I believe in capital punishment as long as it's not too severe."
"This body is entirely too laxative about some matters."
"I don't think people appreciate how difficult it is to be a pawn of an interest group."
"We're caught between the dog and the fire hydrant on this vote."
"Mr. Speaker, what bill did we just pass?"

Source: Collected by Thomas R. Dye.

To the Governor

Legislative power is shared by the governor who can sign bills before they become law, allow them to become law without his signature, or veto bills. Florida's governor, like most governors, also has *line-item veto* power over the General Appropriations Bill—that is, the ability to veto particular sections of it without vetoing the entire bill. Thus, the governor may veto particular *"turkeys"* in the appropriations bill if he chooses to risk offending the legislator in whose district the "turkey" is to "roost." It requires a two-thirds vote of both chambers to override the governor's veto of a bill and thus veto overrides are typically quite rare. Until 2010, there had only been three overrides since 1986. However, in 2010, the legislature overrode nine vetoes and one line item veto of Governor Charlie Crist (see Chapter 7).

The Logjam

The Florida Legislature officially meets for sixty days, but typically most legislation is passed in the last forty-eight hours of the session. This end-of-session *"logjam"* is the most disorderly phase of lawmaking. Both chambers become scenes of noisy confusion, with legislators voting blindly on bills often described only by numbers. The logjam is caused somewhat by procrastination, but more by the desire to trade support for bills and the need to rally support for some controversial legislation. The logjam further strengthens the power of the House Speaker and Senate President. They select from among scores of bills approved by committees which bills will come to the floor. They decide what are "must-pass" bills and what bills will get on the *"train."* One legislator has described a train this way:

> We regularly have what's called "trains." Trains are what happens to your amendment in the last days of the session if it hasn't made it through the process and been passed by the House and Senate. You find what's called a "must-pass" bill, one that the House Speaker, the Senate President, and the governor all must have. You tag your little amendment or proposal onto the must-pass bill as an amendment. (We call this a "train" because there might be fifty to sixty amendments that may or may not be germane to the underlying bill.) This is a very bad way to make policy. It's a mistake to do most of your serious work on the last two days of session.[41]

In an effort to reform the end-of-session confusion, especially to end the practice of slipping in wasteful expenditures or unseen "turkeys" into the General Appropriations Bill, the Constitution was amended to require that "all general appropriation bills shall be furnished to each member of the legislature, each member of the Cabinet, the governor and the chief justice of the Supreme Court *at least seventy-two hours* before final passage thereof by either house of legislature."

With so many places for a bill to get hung up, it is no surprise that a relatively small proportion of all the bills introduced ever make it into law. Some citizens like it that way. They feel that the less government does, the better. Others are exasperated by the process, impatient with its slow, deliberative nature.

PARTY AND IDEOLOGY

Traditionally, political parties in southern state legislatures were not differentiated along ideological lines. Both majority Democratic and minority Republican legislators reflected generally conservative views. Factionalism within the dominant Democratic Party developed around colorful personalities with constituencies made up of "friends and neighbors" and, except for the race issue, largely lacked policy coherence from one election to the next. But with the rise of party competition over the years, legislative politics changed remarkably.

Beginnning in the 1990s, party politics dominated the legislature, and Democratic and Republican Party members were highly polarized on the issues. In fact, party was the principal voting cleavage within both the House and Senate. Party cleavages appeared more often than splits based on race, or gender, or region. Party was, and still is to a certain extent, the strongest single determinant of voting behavior in the Florida Legislature on many issues. Democratic legislators, with a few exceptions, reflect liberal views in their voting, and Republican legislators, almost always, reflect conservative views.[42]

But as Republicans have come to really dominate the legislature, the intensity of fighting *between* the parties has actually lessened. In the House, Democrats make liberal arguments but basically conservative Republicans can, and usually do, ignore them since they outnumber the minority party by about two to one. In the Senate, typically an atmosphere of moderation is encouraged and the minority party usually has more say.

Predictably, as the Republicans' margin of control of the legislature grew larger, *intra-party* squabbles among various factions (usually between the House and Senate over leadership posts or "turkey projects" for their districts) surfaced and at times have become more intense than their fights with Democrats. A recent example of intra-party conflict was more philosophical in nature yielding a deeper party divide. It was the intense and fractious fight between Republicans in the House and those in the Senate over accepting more federal Medicaid money to help expand health care to some 800,000 uninsured low income Floridians. Republicans in the Senate favored accepting the funds whereas a majority of those in the House did not. The high profile conflict led one newspaper to begin a story detailing the conflict with this line: "Republicans in the Florida Legislature have met the enemy, and it is them."[43] The bottom line is that when one party so heavily controls both houses of the legislature, fights within the dominant party move to the front burner. These differences may fall along ideological (conservative, moderate, liberal) or geographical (urban, suburban, rural) lines or be between the two chambers.

Ideological Differences

The ideological polarization of the legislature can be observed in liberal/conservative voting divisions over the years. If we define modern *liberalism* as support for an activist government role in redistributing and regulating goods, services, and civil rights, and modern *conservatism* as a preference for limited government activity and markets free from extensive regulations, and support for traditional social values, then it is possible to identify key votes reflecting these divergent views. A study that identified key liberal and conservative votes of House members over two decades found that Democratic House members have voted increasingly liberal over the years, while Republican members have voted more solidly conservative.[44] While the study may be imperfect (votes in different years are necessarily based on different pieces of legislation), the trend toward greater polarization of the parties is clear. Increasingly, so too is the growing polarization between conservative and moderate Republicans.

Responsible Parties

The clear liberal/conservative cleavage between the Democratic and Republican Parties in the legislature provides a basis for developing a *"responsible-party" model* in Florida politics. Florida voters may come to know that electing Democrats or Republicans to the legislature has policy consequences. Voters can influence policy in a liberal or conservative direction by casting their votes along party lines. If each party's candidates are differentiated ideologically, voters can make a rational choice based on party labels, without necessarily investigating the specific policy positions of individual candidates for the state legislature. In recent years, the clearest party differences have been on tax and moral issues. When legislators look to party leadership for cues on how to vote on controversial issues they are acting in the role of a *partisan*. For instance several Republican representatives said they would support Medicaid expansion while campaigning. However, once in office, they voted against expansion after a closed-door meeting of the House GOP Caucus made it clear that all Republican House members were expected to vote the way party leaders wanted.[45]

Day-at-the-Capitol events are very popular. Here a group from Miami-Dade County serves up big helpings of paella.

CONSTITUENCY AND LEGISLATIVE VOTING

Most legislators see themselves as *trustees*—performing their duties and casting their votes according to their own best judgment about what is best for their constituents. More than two hundred years ago, the English political philosopher Edmund Burke urged members of Parliament to vote according to their own conscience about what is good for the country. The classic alternative role for legislators is that of *delegate*— performing duties and casting votes in response to the wishes of constituents, even when they conflict with the legislator's own judgment.

When Florida legislators were asked to identify themselves along a ranking of 1 (pure delegate) to 10 (pure trustee), the majority placed themselves much nearer to the pure trustee role. Florida legislators justify their trustee role on the basis of the importance of their own beliefs, their confidence that they know more about the issues than their constituents, and their certainty that if their constituents were well-informed, they would agree with the legislator's judgment.

Nothing is more welcome after a particularly contentious session than its end. A crowd watches House Sergeant-at-Arms Earnest Sumner, left, and Senate Sergeant-at-Arms Donald Severance, right, drop the traditional handkerchiefs in the Capitol rotunda signaling adjournment of the Legislature "sine die."

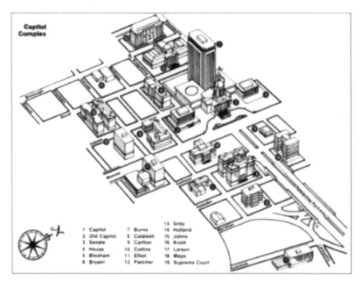

But legislators' self-identification as trustees may be in part self-laudatory. The trustee role appears more courageous and less political than that of delegate. Yet in truth, all legislators function as delegates from time to time, especially when performing personal services, favors, and conflict resolution for constituents and bringing state projects and money to their home districts, often in the form of "pork," "turkeys," and local-aid formulas. And legislators are much more likely to function as delegates at the request of constituents who contribute money to their campaigns.

The truth is that most legislators vote as trustees on low profile issues but as delegates on "hot button" high profile issues. (Some call this the *"politico"* model of legislative behavior.) Legalized gambling, the death penalty, and racial issues, for example, may produce clear constituency pressures. Only the most confident legislators from very "safe" districts would likely ignore constituency views on such issues.

On the great majority of votes that are cast in committee or on the floor, legislators receive little input from constituents.[46] Voters have no opinion on many issues, and on many other issues voter opinion is divided. Polls are not completely reliable because they depend heavily on the wording of questions (see Chapter 3). Calls, letters, faxes, emails, and tweets are more likely to be generated by interest groups than by constituents acting on their own. Legislators know that "grass-roots campaigns" generated by special interests do not necessarily represent the views of their district. (The tricky part of being a legislator is knowing when they do.)

Actually, there may be little difference between legislators' views on issues and those of their constituents. After all, legislators are products of their constituencies. They have roots in their district's churches, clubs, neighborhood associations, local governments, and racial and ethnic affiliations. If they did not think like their constituents, they would not have been elected in the first place. Political scientist Alan Rosenthal writes:

> The representative's action inevitably involves discretion and judgment, and the potential for conflict between the representative and the represented about what is to be done always exists. But such conflict must be the exception and not the rule, for a representative cannot be persistently at odds with the wishes of the represented. In view of the desires of representatives to be in step with their constituents, the frequency of elections, and the potential (if not the guarantee) of opposition, it is extremely unlikely that representatives will deviate too far from constituency mandates, if and when such mandates exist.[47]

The Florida Legislature is arguably the most important branch of government. Legislators pass laws, propose constitutional amendments, draw district lines, and adopt an annual budget. It will be a continuing challenge for the legislature to adequately represent the people of this state as it becomes increasingly large and diverse in the decades ahead.

ONLINE SOURCES FOR DATA AND INFORMATION UPDATES

Florida Legislature: Bill Citator

The "Bill Citator" has statistics, histories, and reports of all bills in session from 1998 to 2015.
http://billinfo.leg.state.fl.us/

Florida Legislature: Statutes

This is an online copy of all Florida statutes up to 2014.
http://www.leg.state.fl.us/STATUTES/

Florida House: Directory

This is a directory of all current members of the Florida House of Representatives.
http://www.myfloridahouse.gov/FileStores/Web/HouseContent/Approved/ClerksOffice/HouseDirectory.pdf

Florida Senate: Directory

This directory lists all current members of the Florida Senate.
http://www.flsenate.gov/PublishedContent/ADMINISTRATIVEPUBLICATIONS/sdir.pdf

Florida House: Committees

This list of committees and subcommittees for any legislative session in the House through 2014-2016 also includes all proposed committee bills.
http://www.myfloridahouse.gov/Sections/Committees/committees.aspx

Florida Senate: Committees

This list of all committees and subcommittees for any legislative session in the Senate through 2014-2016 also includes all proposed committee bills.
http://www.flsenate.gov/Committees/

U.S. Census

The U.S. Census publishes information on population and demographics of U.S. regions.
www.census.gov

Florida Division of Elections

The Florida Division of Elections provides data on past and current Florida elections- including presidential, congressional, and state legislature races. The data also includes voter turnout, results, candidates, and information on political parties.
http://election.dos.state.fl.us/

Center for American Women and Politics

The CAWP offers helpful information on women in elected offices nationwide and locally and statistics on women in elections, women voting, minority women, and the current number of women in political positions.
http://www.cawp.rutgers.edu/

Chapter 7. Florida's Governor and Cabinet

The governor is the central figure in Florida politics. (See Table 7-1 for a list of all Florida governors.) While many Floridians do not follow state government very closely, most know who the governor is. Florida's governors are always in the news, whether they are signing an important bill into law, attending the annual "Possum" Festival & Funday in West Florida (seriously, a must-attend event for candidates for statewide office),1 or testifying before a congressional committee as to how federal emergency management policies need to be structured.

What few Floridians realize is that Florida's governors have traditionally been, in *constitutional* terms, less powerful than governors in many other states. At one time, Florida's governor was ranked 46th out of 50 in the formal powers of the office.[50] The state's gubernatorial power ranking has improved somewhat over time with Florida now tied for 32nd place and just slightly below average compared to other state governors.[3] Still, our governors must share some of their executive authority with three Cabinet officials (attorney general, chief financial officer, commissioner of agriculture) and with a number of independent boards and commissions. Cabinet members are elected statewide at the same time the governor runs. Both the governor and Cabinet members have four-year terms and are limited to two consecutive terms.

Former Governor Bob Graham knows that if you want to win the Panhandle vote, you go to the Wausau Possum Festival, hold one of the little critters, and make a contribution to the local volunteer fire department.

Governors can overcome some of their formal power limitations with their own personal powers of persuasion and political skills, strong media presence, and national visibility. Florida's governors always get national attention, especially during presidential election years, due to the crucial role that Florida plays in determining the outcomes of presidential elections. Florida's size and population diversity also thrust its governors onto the national political stage. A number of Florida's modern era governors have gone on to hold top positions in various presidential administrations; several have run for president. The state has had its share of governors with unique personalities—the "he-coon" "Walkin' Lawton" Chiles, "teetotaler Reubin Askew," "work days" Bob Graham, "Jeb!" Bush, the "People's Governor" Charlie Crist, and "Let's Get to Work" Rick Scott.

Regardless of whether their power stems from the Constitution or their own personality and leadership style, Floridians expect the governor to: take the lead in helping solve pressing state problems; initiate programs and push them through the state legislature; oversee the state bureaucracy, prevent corruption, and deal with administrative foul-ups; negotiate with federal agencies on behalf of the state; represent the state and its people in public ceremonies; grow the Florida economy so that there are more and better paying jobs; and manage crises in the state—from hurricanes, serious droughts, or recessions to immigration tides and urban unrest.

FLORIDA'S UNIQUE—AND CONFUSING—EXECUTIVE BRANCH

While many states elect statewide officials in addition to the governor, no other state has an executive structure like Florida. The state's Constitution establishes a plural executive—a unique Cabinet system in which the governor shares control over the executive branch with other statewide elected officials.[4] Until 2002, the Florida Constitution divided executive power between the governor and six separately-elected statewide officers (Cabinet members): secretary of state, attorney general, comptroller, treasurer, commissioner of education, and commissioner of agriculture. These Cabinet officers headed their own departments of state government: State, Legal Affairs, Banking and Finance, Insurance and Treasurer, Education, and Agriculture and Consumer Services. As the Cabinet, they joined the governor to collectively make policy for a number of other boards, commissions, departments, and divisions. The governor alone was responsible for a number of other agencies, boards, commissions, and departments. That system has changed somewhat. Now, Florida's Cabinet has only three members: attorney general, chief financial officer, and commissioner of agriculture. Governors now appoint the Secretary of State and members of the State Board of Education which, in turn, selects the Commissioner of Education. These changes and others, which we will examine, were all made in an effort to give Florida's governor more power commensurate with the public's expectations. After all, almost every Florida governor runs on an education platform, yet prior to 2002, the winning candidate had very little power to actually do what was promised unless the independently-elected Commissioner of Education agreed.

Table 7-1. Florida Governors by Date of Service and Political Party

Andrew Jackson* Mar. 10, 1821 - Nov. 12, 1821	George Franklin Drew (D) Jan. 2, 1877 - Jan. 4, 1881	Fuller Warren (D) Jan. 4, 1949 - Jan. 6, 1953
William Pope DuVal * Apr. 17, 1822 - Apr. 24, 1834	William D. Bloxham (D) Jan. 4, 1881 - Jan. 7, 1885	Daniel T. McCarty (D) Jan. 6, 1953 - Sept. 28, 1953
John H. Eaton* Apr. 24, 1834 - Mar. 16, 1836	Edward Aylsworth Perry (D) Jan. 7, 1885 - Jan. 8, 1889	Charley E. Johns (D) Sept. 28, 1953 - Jan. 4, 1955
Richard Keith Call* Mar. 16, 1836 - Dec. 2, 1839	Francis P. Fleming (D) Jan. 8, 1889 - Jan. 3, 1893	(Thomas) LeRoy Collins (D) Jan. 4, 1955 - Jan. 3, 1961
Robert R. Reid* Dec. 2, 1839 - Mar. 19, 1841	Henry Laurens Mitchell (D) Jan. 3, 1893 - Jan. 5, 1897	(Cecil) Farris Bryant (D) Jan. 3, 1961 - Jan. 5, 1965
Richard Keith Call* Mar. 19, 1841 - Aug. 11, 1844	William D. Bloxham (D) Jan. 5, 1897 - Jan. 8, 1901	(William) Haydon Burns (D) Jan. 5, 1965 - Jan. 3, 1967
John Branch* Aug. 11, 1844 - June 25, 1845	William S. Jennings (D) Jan. 8, 1901 - Jan. 3, 1905	Claude R. Kirk (R) Jan. 3, 1967 - Jan. 5, 1971
William Dunn Moseley (D) June 25, 1845 - Oct. 1, 1849	Napoleon Bonaparte Broward (D) Jan. 3, 1905 - Jan. 5, 1909	Reubin O'D. Askew (D) Jan. 5, 1971 - Jan. 2, 1979
Thomas Brown (Whig) Oct. 1, 1849 - Oct. 3, 1853	Albert W. Gilchrist (D) Jan. 5, 1909 - Jan. 7, 1913	Daniel R. "Bob" Graham (D) Jan. 2, 1979 - Jan. 3, 1987
James E. Broome (D) Oct. 3, 1853 - Oct. 5, 1857	Park Trammell (D) Jan. 7, 1913 - Jan. 2, 1917	(John) Wayne Mixson Jan. 3, 1987 - Jan. 6, 1987
Madison Starke Perry (D) Oct. 5, 1857 - Oct. 7, 1861	Sidney J. Catts (Prohibition) Jan. 2, 1917 - Jan. 4, 1921	Robert "Bob" Martinez (R) Jan. 6, 1987 - Jan. 8, 1991
John Milton (D) Oct. 7, 1861 - Apr. 1, 1865	Cary A. Hardee (D) Jan. 4, 1921 - Jan. 6, 1925	Lawton M. Chiles (D) Jan. 8, 1991 - Dec. 12, 1998
Abraham Kurkindolle Allison (D) Apr. 1, 1865 - May 19, 1865	John W. Martin (D) Jan. 6, 1925 - Jan. 8, 1929	Kenneth H. "Buddy" MacKay (D) Dec. 12, 1998 - Jan. 5, 1999
William Marvin (None) July 13, 1865 - Dec. 20, 1865	Doyle E. Carlton (D) Jan. 8, 1929 - Jan. 3, 1933	John E. "Jeb" Bush (R) Jan. 5, 1999 - Jan. 2, 2007
David S. Walker (Conservative) Dec. 20, 1865 - July 4, 1868	Dave Sholtz (D) Jan. 4, 1933 - Jan. 5, 1937	Charles J. "Charlie" Crist (R; NPA) Jan. 2, 2007 - Jan. 4, 2011
Harrison Reed (R) July 4, 1868 - Jan. 7, 1873	Frederick P. Cone (D) Jan. 5, 1937 - Jan. 7, 1941	Richard L. "Rick" Scott (R) Jan. 4, 2011 -
Ossian B. Hart (R) Jan. 7, 1873 - Mar. 18, 1874	Spessard L. Holland (D) Jan. 7, 1941 - Jan. 2, 1945	
Marcellus Lovejoy Stearns (R) Mar. 18, 1875 - Jan. 2, 1877	Millard F. Caldwell (D) Jan. 2, 1945 - Jan. 4, 1949	

* Appointed as Territorial Governors

Source: Florida Memory Project, http://www.floridamemory.com/Collections/governors/.

The Old System

The weak formal powers of the governor and the diffusion of political accountability, due to the seven separately-elected executive officials (governor + six Cabinet members), troubled reformers in Florida for many years. In 1968, they approved a new Florida Constitution that strengthened the independence of Cabinet members by deleting the phrase "the Governor shall be assisted by" the Cabinet to make it clear that Cabinet members were equal members with the governor. However, until 1998, Florida voters had rejected any constitutional changes. A Constitutional Review Commission placed amendments on the 1978 ballot that would have reduced the number of separately-elected executive officials from seven to three (governor, secretary of state, and attorney general) and would have established the governor as the head of most state departments. Those proposals were strongly opposed by entrenched interest groups from agriculture and citrus, to banking, insurance, teachers, and others who favored retaining the independence of their "own" executive agencies. These amendments were trounced at the ballot box by an average 75 percent "No" vote.

Until 2002, the Florida Constitution divided executive power between the governor and six separately-elected statewide officers (the Cabinet).

Voters Change the System

In 1998, 20 years later, the Constitutional Revision Commission again proposed strengthening the power of the governor by reducing the size of the Cabinet to just three members. The smaller Cabinet would include an attorney general, agriculture commissioner, and chief financial officer (an office combining the old treasurer and comptroller positions), while the education commissioner and secretary of state would come under the governor's control. On the campaign trail, Jeb Bush, a candidate for governor in 1998, spoke out in favor of the proposed changes: "Most people in this state believe the governor is accountable for all this anyway, and he might as well get the power to be able to carry out what people expect him do to."[5] Florida voters liked what they heard. They elected Jeb Bush as governor and approved the constitutional amendment reducing the size of the Cabinet effective January 7, 2003. That meant that in 2003, when Governor Bush officially began his second term, he assumed office with more power than he had in his first four years and relatively greater formal powers than any Florida governor elected before him.[6]

A Closer Look at the New System

With the shrinking of the Cabinet, Florida's governor gained power in three ways. First, the governor is now more directly responsible for education policy in Florida, although the making and implementing of education policy is still widely dispersed. (See Chapter 11.) Under the old system a separately-elected Commissioner of Education reported directly to the voters, meaning the governor did not have direct authority over the Commissioner or the Department of Education. Now the governor appoints members to the State Board of Education, who in turn appoint the commissioner giving the governor more, if still indirect, influence.

Second, under the old system the secretary of state reported directly to the voters. Under the new system, the secretary of state is now directly appointed by the governor. This gives a governor full responsibility for the Department of State and the Florida Division of Elections, which is housed within that department. Florida's Secretary of State and the Department of State have many duties, including overseeing elections, promoting the state's history, culture, and arts, providing library and archival services, registering all corporations doing business in Florida, issuing corporate charters, and recording financial information. But it is the Division of Elections that continues to receive most of the public's scrutiny as a consequence of the 2000 election. Democrats complained bitterly about some of the decisions made by the last elected Secretary of State, Katherine Harris, during the 2000 *Bush* v. *Gore* presidential campaign. Much of the criticism stemmed from the fact that she was a Republican and an honorary co-chair of the Bush campaign. In fairness, at the same time, Democrat Bob Butterworth, the Attorney General, was co-chair of the Gore campaign. While many voted to create an *appointed* Secretary, some see little difference in the appearance of conflict of interest, when it comes to overseeing elections. Election and appointment both yield a partisan, rather than a nonpartisan, Secretary.

Third, when making decisions in conjunction with the Cabinet (e.g., collectively sitting as the state's Board of Administration), the governor now shares power with just three other members as opposed to six. Florida's Constitution says that in the case of a tie vote on such collective bodies, the side on which the governor votes prevails. The awkwardness here stems from the fact that technically the governor is not a member of the Cabinet.[7] Now the governor only needs one Cabinet official to agree with his position in order to set policy. Obviously, this greatly increases the governor's power. Under the old system, the larger number of Cabinet officials meant they could prevail over the governor if they chose. The only exception to this rule is the Board of Clemency which requires at least three of the four votes to take action.

THE ORGANIZATION OF FLORIDA'S EXECUTIVE BRANCH

Under the Florida Constitution, the state's executive branch powers are assigned to: (1) the governor who exercises independent power over certain departments, boards and commissions, (2) three other statewide officials (Cabinet members) who exercise independent power in their respective areas, and (3) the governor and various combinations of the three Cabinet officials who share decision making power over several state departments, boards, and commissions. This means that even under the reformed system, Florida's governors must share their executive power to a greater degree than some governors in other states.

A reading of Article IV, Section 6 of the Florida Constitution makes it clear that the governor controls some of the state's "no more than 25" executive departments, has no control over others, and shares the control of several more with various Cabinet members:

It is not uncommon for newly-elected governors to reorganize existing state agencies and departments to better reflect their priorities. In his first election bid, Governor Rick Scott and his Lt. Governor Jennifer Carroll ran on a platform of job creation. The Governor successfully urged the Florida Legislature to create a new Department of Economic Opportunity and eliminate the old Department of Community Affairs

The administration of each department, unless otherwise provided in this constitution, shall be placed by law under the direct supervision of the governor, the lieutenant governor, the governor and Cabinet, a Cabinet member, or an officer of board appointed by and serving at the pleasure of the governor (with a few exceptions[8]).

This shared executive authority, like we have in Florida, is often referred to as a *"plural," "split"* or *"splintered"* executive system.

The Governor

The governor oversees more than 20 agencies, boards, commissions and departments within the executive branch. (See Figure 7-1.) The number of agencies and their missions is set by the state legislature. New agencies are sometimes created and old agencies are sometimes eliminated or split up. For instance, in 2011, the state legislature decided to abolish the Department of Community Affairs and create a new Department of Economic Opportunity in its place to emphasize economic growth rather than growth management (See Chapter 12.) and in 2014 the legislature established a new Agency for State Technology to oversee information technology projects and create Florida's first Chief Information Officer (CIO). In most cases, the governor selects the heads of agencies and departments and members of commissions with the approval of the Florida Senate. The governor has enormous influence over public policy based on who he selects to serve in these positions.

Departments and Agencies under the governor's control include:

- Agency for Health Care Administration – administers the Florida Medicaid program.
- Agency for Persons with Disabilities – serves the needs of disabled Floridians.
- Department of Business and Professional Regulation – regulates one million professionals and businesses across 200 licensee categories in Florida.
- Department of Children and Families – protects vulnerable Floridians and promotes strong families.
- Department of Citrus and the Florida Citrus Commission – department, under the direction of the commission, markets, researches, and regulates Florida citrus.
- Department of Corrections – operates the state prison and community correction system.
- Department of Economic Opportunity – coordinates economic and workforce development, community planning, and affordable housing.[9]
- Department of Education, State Board of Education, and Statewide Board of Governors – department, under direction of the state board, coordinates Florida K-20 education policy; Board of Governors is specifically responsible for state universities.
- Department of Elder Affairs – administers human service programs for Florida's elderly.
- Department of Environmental Protection – protects Florida's air, water, and land resources.
- Department of Health – promotes and protects public health of Floridians and coordinates efforts of 6 7 local county health departments.
- Department of Juvenile Justice – seeks reduction of juvenile crime and rehabilitation of young offenders.
- Department of Lottery—operates the Florida lottery and provides money for the state budget.
- Department of Management Services and Agency for State Technology – the department seeks to efficiently manage costs associated with running Florida government; the agency oversees information technology standards and projects for the state.
- Department of Military Affairs – protects Florida and the U.S. as the home of the Florida National Guard.
- Department of State – coordinates elections, keeps corporate records, promotes culture and history, and records official acts of legislative and executive branches in Florida.
- Department of Transportation – seeks to provide a safe transportation network that efficiently moves Floridians and fosters economic growth.
- Fish and Wildlife Conservation Commission – manages fish and wildlife resources in Florida.

Qualifications: Governor and Cabinet

Florida's governor, lieutenant governor, and Cabinet members must each be a registered voter, at least 30 years old, and a resident of the state for the preceding seven years. In addition, the attorney general must have been a member of the Florida Bar for the preceding five years. Governors are elected in non-presidential years. The term of office for each post is four years, with a limit of two consecutive terms.

The maximum number of years a governor can serve consecutively is ten years—two full four-year terms plus two years—but no more—of serving out the term of a governor who resigned or died in office. The governor and Cabinet members earn about $130,000 a year.

Figure 7-1. Agencies, Boards, Commissions, and Departments Under the Governor's Control

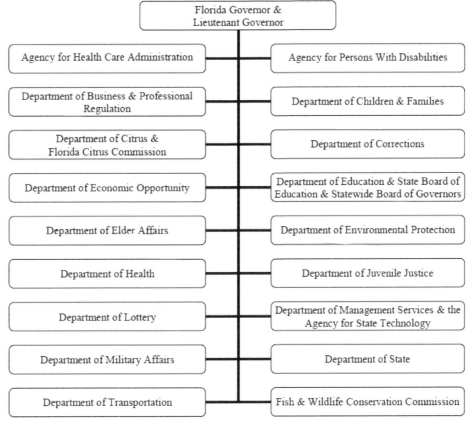

Note: Several boxes include more than one entity controlled by the governor.
Source: Created by the authors from the Florida Government Organizational Chart, Office of the Governor.

Cabinet Officers

The Florida Constitution creates the offices of attorney general, chief financial officer, and commissioner of agriculture and gives them each specific responsibilities:

> Article IV, Section 4:
> (b) The attorney general shall be the chief state legal officer.
> (c) The chief financial officer shall serve as the chief fiscal officer of the state, and shall settle and approve accounts against the state, and shall keep all state funds and securities.
> (d) The commissioner of agriculture shall have supervision of matters pertaining to agriculture except as otherwise provided by law.

The duties and responsibilities of these officials have been further detailed in laws passed by the Florida Legislature.

The *attorney general* is the chief legal officer of the state and is the head of the Department of Legal Affairs. The attorney general represents Florida in legal proceedings as prosecutor or defense attorney depending on the situation, serves as legal advisor to the governor, other executive officers, the legislature, and other state and local public officials, and indexes legislative statutes and resolutions and makes suggestions for revising and improving them.

The *chief financial officer* (CFO) heads the Department of Financial Services. The CFO collects certain taxes, deposits state funds, pays the state's bills including salaries and claims, supervises banks, credit unions, and insurance companies, administers Florida's workers compensation program, and oversees the state fire marshal.

The *commissioner of agriculture* heads the Department of Agriculture and Consumer Services. The "Ag" commissioner ensures the safety and wholesomeness of food and consumer products, protects consumers from unfair and deceptive business practices, assists Florida's farmers with production and promotion of agricultural products, and helps conserve and protect Florida's natural resources.

The Florida Cabinet and Governor, 2011-2019, from left to right: Attorney General Pam Bondi (R), Agriculture Commissioner Adam Putnam (R), Governor Rick Scott (R), Chief Financial Officer Jeff Atwater (R). When they first took office in 2011, it was the first time in modern Florida history that the Governor and Cabinet were all new.

Cabinet Responsibilities

The governor, together with the Cabinet or some of its members sit as the governing boards of about a dozen boards, commissions, departments, and divisions. (See Figure 7-2.) For the four departments they head, the governor and Cabinet appoint an administrator to handle the day-to-day operations. These bodies can be abolished and new ones can be created. For example, the legislature established the Agency for Enterprise Information Technology in 2007 but then disbanded it in 2011. Many of its function were eventually taken over by the Agency for State Technology in 2014, but placed under control of the governor rather than the Cabinet.

The Cabinet offices and their primary functions include:

- Administration Commission (Governor and Cabinet sit as)—responsible for more than 25 functions per statute including resolving disputes in seven situations (i.e., budget appeals by sheriffs or property appraisers), adopting rules for state employees, establishing guidelines for growth management and encouraging efficiency in state government.
- Board of Trustees of the Internal Improvement Trust Fund (Governor and Cabinet sit as)—acquires, manages, conserves, and disposes of state land.
- Department of Highway Safety and Motor Vehicles (Governor and Cabinet head but choose administrator)—licenses automobile dealers, tests and licenses drivers, and enforces traffic and safety laws through the Florida Highway Patrol.
- Department of Law Enforcement (Governor and Cabinet head but choose administrator)—investigates multi-jurisdictional crime and coordinates investigation and enforcement between different law enforcement agencies.
- Department of Revenue (Governor and Cabinet head but choose administrator)—collects taxes according to *Florida Statutes*.

- Department of Veterans' Affairs (Governor and Cabinet head but choose administrator)—assists former, current, and future members of the Armed Forces including dependents.
- Electrical Power Plant and Transmission Line Sitting Board (Governor and Cabinet sit as)—reviews applications for power plant and transmission line certification.
- Financial Services Commission (Governor and Cabinet sit as)—serves as the agency head for the Offices of Financial Regulation and Insurance Regulation which regulate and enforce regulation of those industries in Florida.
- Land and Water Adjudicatory Commission (Governor and Cabinet sit as)—hears appeals of local government land use decisions and water management district decisions.
- State Board of Administration (Governor, attorney general, CFO sit as)—–the board invests and manages the assets of the state pension fund and various trust accounts; the Division of Bond Finance (Governor and Cabinet sit as) issues bonds for all state agencies for construction of infrastructure projects and purchase of land.
- State Board of Executive Clemency (Governor and Cabinet sit as)—authorized to commute sentences, suspend fines, grant pardons and restore civil rights.

It is doubtful that many Florida voters realize the collegial nature of executive decision-making in the state—that, for example, the person they elect as chief financial officer will be voting on everything from electric power plant certification to pardons.

Figure 7-2. Boards, Commissions, Departments, and Divisions Under the Control of the Governor and Cabinet

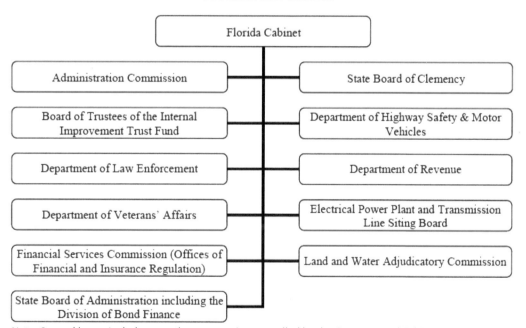

Note: Several boxes include more than one entity controlled by the Governor and Cabinet.
Source: Created by the authors from data found at http://www.myflorida.com/myflorida/cabinet/.

Cabinet Decision Making

Cabinet meetings ("Cabinet days") are usually convened every other week on a Tuesday in a spacious auditorium in the new Capitol. The decision making process occurs in several steps that begin well before the actual Cabinet meeting. First, the board, commission, or department submits an agenda and back-up material. Next, Cabinet aides review these items and hold a meeting to discuss proposed items. (Citizen input is solicited at that meeting and at the actual Cabinet meeting.) Cabinet aides prepare notes and each briefs their respective Cabinet member. The beginning of most Cabinet meetings is devoted to ceremonial activities, like officially recognizing the state's Teacher of the Year or commending winning state football teams. In an interesting but somewhat confusing process, the Cabinet then reconvenes itself into the different boards and commissions to address the issues on the agenda of relevance. Citizens appear before the board or commission that is handling the issue of concern to them. Action is then taken on each agenda item in the form of a voice vote: approval, denial, deferral, or withdrawal.[10]

Diffused Responsibility

It is easy to see how Florida's plural executive structure forces the governor to share control over the executive branch, even after the restructuring of the Cabinet. Sometimes the "sharing" goes more smoothly than at other times. Some governors have had the luxury of working with Cabinets whose members are all from the same political party as the governor. Others have not. Democratic Governor Lawton Chiles faced three Republicans and three Democrats at Cabinet meetings during his second term. Republican Jeb Bush faced three Democrats and three Republicans in his first term but all Republicans in his second. Republican Charlie Crist worked with a Cabinet made up of two Republicans and one Democrat. Governor Scott (R) took office with an all Republican Cabinet. But even having Cabinet members from your own party is no guarantee they will always go along with the governor since Cabinet members may have their own agendas, constituencies, and political ambitions.

The Lieutenant Governor

The Constitution adopted in 1968 provides for a lieutenant governor. (The previous Constitution of 1885 did not.) Compared to the formal powers granted lieutenant governors in many states, Florida's lieutenant governor is extremely weak.[11] Here is how Article IV, Section 2 defines the position:

> There shall be a lieutenant governor. He shall perform such duties pertaining to the office of governor as shall be assigned to him by the governor, except when otherwise provided by law, and such other duties as may be prescribed by law.

Candidates running for governor select a running mate for lieutenant governor and they run on a ticket together, although a gubernatorial candidate does not have to select his or her running mate until after the primary election is over. Article IV, Section 5 describes the way Florida voters are to select the governor and lieutenant governor:

> In the general election, all candidates for the offices of governor and lieutenant governor shall form joint candidacies in a manner prescribed by law so that each voter shall cast a single vote for a candidate for governor and a candidate for lieutenant governor running together.

In some states, lieutenant governors preside over the state senate. So did Florida's lieutenant governor under the Constitutions of 1865 and 1868. The 1885 Constitution eliminated the position altogether. While the 1968 Constitution restored the office, it did not designate the lieutenant governor as the Senate presiding officer.

Lieutenant governors in some states may also be given the formal responsibility for acting as governor in the governor's absence from the state. Not so in Florida. Here, lieutenant governors mostly do what their governors ask them to do—usually based on their interests, backgrounds, and skills. For example, Governor Jeb Bush asked Lt. Governor Toni Jennings to assist with workforce development and welfare reform because she had been a construction company president and had worked on these issues extensively as Senate President. Governor Lawton Chiles asked Lt. Governor Buddy MacKay to assist with his efforts to reform state government and make it more efficient. Other governors have asked their second-in-commands to head up departments. For example, Governors Reubin Askew, Bob Graham, and Bob Martinez each had their lieutenant governor serve as Secretary of Commerce. Being the governor's liaison with the legislature is another common role for lieutenant governors. Governor Charlie Crist selected a former legislator, Jeff Kottkamp, as his. Governor Rick Scott chose former legislators as well—first Jennifer Carroll, then Carlos Lopez-Cantera following Carroll's resignation. Each of these selections also provided balance to the electoral ticket—Kottkamp to shore up Crist's conservative base, Carroll to bring gender and racial diversity to the team, and Lopez-Cantera for ethnic and regional diversity.

Toni Jennings, left, was Florida's first female Lieutenant Governor. She was appointed by Governor Jeb Bush when former Lt. Gov. Frank Brogan resigned to become president of Florida Atlantic University. Jennings also has the distinction of being the only person in Florida history to have served two consecutive terms as President of the Senate. Jennifer Carroll, center, became Florida's first black lieutenant governor when she was selected as Governor Rick Scott's first running mate. Carroll, born in Trinidad, is a retired Navy Lieutenant Commander and former legislator and Director of the Florida Department of Veterans' Affairs. After Carroll resigned in March 2013, Scott eventually appointed Carlos Lopez-Cantera in February 2014 and they won re-election as a team that fall. Lopez-Cantera is Florida's first Hispanic lieutenant governor. He served eight years in the legislature (the last two as House Majority Leader) and then was elected Property Appraiser of Miami Dade County before joining Scott in the executive branch.

Becoming Governor

The most important constitutional function of Florida's lieutenant governor is to succeed the governor should he or she die, leave office, or be otherwise incapacitated. Article IV, Section 3(a) spells out that "upon vacancy in the office of governor, the lieutenant governor shall become governor." Throughout Florida's history, there have been vacancies due to deaths and resignations. Most recently, Lt. Gov. Wayne Mixson became governor for three days in 1986 when Governor Bob Graham resigned from office 72 hours early in order to be sworn in as a U.S. Senator. Lt. Gov. Buddy MacKay became governor for a little over three weeks in 1998 when Governor Lawton Chiles suddenly died in office just 24 days before the end of his term. Ironically, MacKay became governor before Jeb Bush, albeit for just a brief period, although Bush had beaten MacKay in the November gubernatorial election. If a governor leaves office without a lieutenant governor in place (Governor Scott went 11 months without one after the resignation of Jennifer Carroll), then Florida law states that the Attorney General would become governor.

GUBERNATORIAL LEADERSHIP

The constitutional weakness of Florida's governors makes their interpersonal and political skills critical to their success in office. These informal, or personal, powers might include the governor's margin of electoral victory (winning big gives a governor more clout), political ambition and connections (like being the son of one president and brother to another), time left in office (Florida governors are perceived as weaker in their second term because they cannot run again), and public approval ratings (higher ratings translate into more influence).[12] Political skills and informal power are especially important when governors face opposition party control of one or both houses of the legislature. Republican Governors Claude Kirk and Bob Martinez both faced a legislature under complete Democratic control. Governor Lawton Chiles faced a Republican Senate and then a Republican House and Senate during his last four years in office.

Even unified party control of state government is no guarantee of gubernatorial success. While Governor Jeb Bush dealt with a Republican-controlled legislature throughout both his terms, disagreements between the more conservative House and the more moderate Senate on occasion made it more difficult for the Governor to pass his conservative legislative agenda than one might have expected. After Governor Charlie Crist left the Republican Party in the last year of his term, the relationship between the legislature and Governor deteriorated significantly. And Governor Rick Scott's self-proclaimed outsider status, low approval ratings, and budget challenges have made for several rancorous sessions even though both the House and Senate were heavily Republican. In the end, to effectively lead Florida, governors must use all the sources of power at their disposal (formal and informal) and play many different roles—from state cheerleader to crisis manager.

Executive Orders

Governors make policy through the use of executive orders. Governors Scott, Crist and Bush averaged over 250 executive orders a year during their terms.[13] Many executive orders made by governors are ceremonial proclamations. Others routinely instruct one official to take over the duties of another in a specific case involving a conflict of interest, or suspend local officials for misconduct, or call for a special election when a vacancy occurs in an elected office. Occasionally, governors issue executive orders that mandate significant policy changes for their executive agencies. Some executive orders also create significant controversy.

For instance, Governor Bush established the One Florida program prohibiting the use of race in decisions for college admission and as a criterion for granting state contracts. Many Democrats in the state legislature vehemently opposed Bush's One Florida policy, particularly his use of an executive order to create it. While executive orders do not require legislative approval or action, the legislature can pass a law countermanding an executive order or codifying or modifying one if they choose. That did not happen with the Republican-controlled legislature. Bush also issued an executive order to mandating that comatose patient Terri Schiavo be provided food and water through a feeding tube. This created a legal and political firestorm in the right to die case and the courts quickly ruled that the governor had exceeded his authority.

Governor Charlie Crist issued a number of highly visible executive orders including: extending early voting in the 2008 elections; extending the eligibility period for unemployment benefits; setting energy efficiency, carbon emission and climate change goals for state government; and assisting coastal homeowners affected by the BP oil spill in the Gulf of Mexico. Governor Rick Scott issued four executive orders on his first day in office shortly after being sworn in. Scott's first-day executive orders put a freeze on new government regulations, required state agencies to verify legal immigration status, established a new ethics policy and the office of open government, and affirmed his commitment to diversity in employment.[14] One of Governor Scott's more controversial executive orders mandated pre-employment and random drug testing for state employees. The American Civil Liberties Union (ACLU) sued and the courts eventually declared the action an unconstitutional violation of privacy for most state workers but did allow some employees with jobs related to public safety to be randomly tested.

Appointment Powers

The Florida Constitution proclaims that "supreme executive power shall be vested in the governor"— an overly inflated proclamation since the same Constitution then proceeds to weaken and divide executive powers. While Florida's governor does have the power to appoint many state officials to head agencies and serve on commissions, many appointments require senate confirmation. The governor also has the power to appoint county and state government officials when vacancies occur either through death, resignation, or retirement. The governor makes about 1,200 of these appointments each year. They can include U.S. Senators, Cabinet officers, state appellate court judges and Supreme Court justices (merit-retention, see Chapter 8), sheriffs, county commissioners, and other county officials. For example, Governor Crist appointed his former Chief of Staff George LeMieux to be the interim U.S. Senator from Florida when Senator Mel Martinez resigned from office. Interim appointments last until the next general election. However, the persons appointed by the governor usually have a head start against their challengers should they decide to run for a full term. Florida's governors are constitutionally prohibited from filling vacant seats in the state legislature or in Congress. These seats may only be filled by an election.

Removal Powers

The governor's power of removal is far-reaching. The governor can suspend any state or county official in Florida for malfeasance, neglect of duty, incompetence, or inability to perform official duties. "If the Governor believes an official is guilty of one or more of the grounds specified in the Florida Constitution, he may file an Executive Order of Suspension with the Secretary of State, and the named official is automatically but temporarily stripped of all rights, power, emoluments, and accoutrements of the office."[15] As one expert describes the power: "It provides the Governor with the ability to effectively watch over all the public offices in the state... It actually helps to make all of Florida's 67 counties perform as a cohesive state."[16] Suspensions of state and county officials are subject to review and possible reinstatement by the Senate. The governor may also suspend municipal officials indicted for crime or misconduct; they can be reinstated only if subsequently found not guilty in a court.

Each term on average, governors suspend several mayors, sheriffs and other county constitutional officers, and city and county commissioners; a few are usually reinstated. For example, in 2002 Governor Bush suspended four members of the five-member Escambia County Commission when they were indicted (and later convicted) of bribery, extortion, and theft.[17] In 2013, Governor Scott suspended Miami Lakes Mayor Michael Pizzi who was then replaced in a special election as called for by the town charter. However, after Pizzi was found not guilty of federal bribery charges he sued and eventually was reinstated as mayor in 2015.[18] Governor Claude Kirk still holds the record for the most suspensions in a single term.[19]

The governor *cannot* suspend state officials subject to impeachment. Governors themselves are subject to impeachment, although no modern Florida governor has been impeached. In Article III, Section 17, the Constitution spells out officials who can only be removed by impeachment, for misdemeanors: "The governor, lieutenant governor, members of the Cabinet, justices of the Supreme Court, judges of district courts of appeal, judges of circuit courts, and judges of county courts shall be liable to impeachment for misdemeanor in office." Under the Constitution, the Speaker of the House can at any time appoint a committee to investigate charges against any official subject to impeachment. It takes a two-thirds vote of the Florida House to impeach (formally accuse). The actual trial takes place in the Florida Senate, to be presided over by the Chief Justice of the Florida Supreme Court (or a designate) or by the governor if it is the chief justice being tried. A two-thirds vote of the senators present is necessary to convict at which point the official is removed from office and may be prohibited from running for any other office.

Media Access and Opinion Leadership

As the state's chief executive and its most visible political figure, a governor has greater access to the media than any other state official. The governor's comments and appearances make news. The governor is heavily sought after for television, radio, and public appearances. The media gives governors a platform from which they can influence public opinion and educate the public about their high priority issues. A prudent governor will select a limited number of priorities—perhaps in education, or crime control or health care—and mobilize public opinion and political pressure behind these priorities. A reputation for success becomes a source of power and can lead to still more success. Governors want to keep public approval ratings high, knowing how important they are as a source of informal power. Highly popular governors have more leverage over the legislature and are treated more favorably by the state's press corps, who regularly report poll results and tally up policy scorecards showing how many of a governor's campaign promises have come to fruition. Governor Crist was generally considered to be quite adept at getting positive media coverage throughout most of his time in office. Governor Scott got off to a rocky start with the Tallahassee press corps because they felt the Governor limited media access to him and his events. Governor Scott eventually began to cultivate the traditional media as part of his re-election strategy but still had a strained relationship with many reporters.

Agenda Setting

The governor is expected to provide leadership in legislative affairs, to provide a clear and forceful answer to the question frequently asked in legislative debate, "What does the governor want?" The governor largely sets the legislative agenda. At the opening session of the Florida Legislature each March, the governor reports on "the State of the State." Newly-elected governors lay out their vision for the next four years. After that, each year's address evaluates how Florida has fared over the previous year under the governor's leadership and spells out the governor's policy priorities for that legislative session. Governor Bush identified the top three priorities for his new administration in his first State of the State speech: reforming education through his A+ Plan, helping the most vulnerable Floridians (children on welfare and in foster care, seniors and the disabled), and making "historic" tax cuts. These three themes figured prominently in each of his next seven addresses including his final "State of the State" address.

Charlie Crist stressed a number of recurring themes in his first State of the State address, including: mitigating the housing and property insurance crisis; improving education by spending more money on teacher pay and the class size amendment; and protecting Florida's environment. He also struck a more bipartisan tone than Jeb Bush and continued his campaign promise to be the "People's Governor."

Rick Scott emphasized his conservative-outsider image and focused on job creation in his first State of the State speech. While his primary focus was on creating jobs, he also stressed the importance of making Florida more competitive in attracting new businesses by cutting regulations and corporate income taxes, reducing government spending, reducing the size of government, consolidating economic development into a single new agency run by the governor, and reforming education. He promised to improve education by implementing innovative teaching, encouraging competition, and measuring performance. He closed with his tag line "Let's get to work!" His first address to the legislature after re-election noted the economic progress that Florida made over his first four years in office, then laid out a five point agenda for the next four years—cutting taxes, keeping college tuition affordable, and investing in workforce development, K-12 education, and the environment.

Perhaps more important than the State of the State speeches, governors also establish their priorities by presenting an annual recommended budget. Each department and agency submits its budget request, and these requests, together with the governor's recommendation, go to the legislature for consideration for enactment as appropriations laws. (See the end of this chapter.)

Special Sessions

The governor can call a special session of the legislature "by proclamation stating the purpose" of it. Most Florida governors have used this power to push their policy agenda forward when the state legislature was dragging its feet or was heading in a different direction. Governor Bob Martinez called a special session to seek (unsuccessfully) more restrictions on abortion, Lawton Chiles to increase education funding, Jeb Bush to reform Medicaid, and Charlie Crist (unsuccessfully) to propose a constitutional amendment to ban oil drilling off of Florida's coast. No other business can be taken up at a special session, except by a two-thirds vote of each house. Governor Scott called a special session in 2012 so the legislature could redraw Senate districts after the Florida Supreme Court declared the original plan unconstitutional.

Lobbying

Governors must do more than simply propose legislation. They must also be the lobbyist-in-chief on behalf of their own proposals. A governor's *"outside" lobbying strategy* may include public appearances throughout the state to rally popular opinion and create pressure on the legislature. It may include mobilizing interest groups to help force the legislature's hand. The *"inside" lobbying strategy* usually involves direct appeals to legislative leaders as well as rank-and-file legislators. Such appeals are often made at breakfasts, luncheons, or even late-night sessions with legislators. Tactics include "pork barrelling," "log-rolling," and arm-twisting, and occasionally even appealing to legislators' public spirit. Governors are not above rallying the support of legislators' friends and relatives, including their spouses and children!

The Veto Power

The veto power lies at the heart of the governor's legislative powers. The governor has seven days to veto a bill while the legislature is in session, and fifteen days to do so if the legislature has adjourned. Most legislation is passed at the end of a session, so the governor's veto cannot be overridden until the next legislative session. Since 1968, Florida governors have averaged about 17 vetoes a year. (See Table 7-2.) Republican Claude Kirk in his contentious four years with a Democratic legislature averaged a high of 27 vetoes a year, while Republican Rick Scott averaged just 8.5 a year with a Republican legislature— including just one veto in 2014. By contrast, Democrat Reubin Askew averaged over 19 per year with a Democratic legislature and Republican Jeb Bush averaged almost 18 per year with a Republican-controlled legislature.

Table 7-2. Florida Governor Vetoes, 1968-2010

Governor	Vetoes	Years in Office	Veto Average per Year
Claude Kirk	108	4	27.0
Reubin Askew	157	8	19.6
Bob Graham	105	8	13.1
Bob Martinez	72	4	18.0
Lawton Chiles	126	8	15.8
Jeb Bush	140	8	17.5
Charlie Crist	55	4	13.8
Rick Scott	34	4	8.5
Total (1967-2014)	**797**	**48**	**16.6**

Note: *Does not include line item vetoes.

Source: Information from *The Florida Handbook 2005-2006*, as updated by the authors.

The Line-Item Veto

On appropriations bills, the governor enjoys the *line-item veto* power—also rarely overridden. Each year's General Appropriations Bill contains hundreds of separate money lines, any of which the governor can strike out while still approving those that remain. Each year the governor can go on a "turkey hunt," identifying particularly fat pieces of legislative "pork" and striking them from the General Appropriations Bill. Of course, he risks alienating a legislator each time he "kills a turkey." An independent watchdog organization, Florida TaxWatch, puts out a list of "turkeys" each year, keeps track of how many of them a governor kills, and how much money was saved.

Through his eight years in office, Governor Bush vetoed well over 1,000 individual projects (430 in his last year alone) worth over $2 billion dollars, including many desperately wanted by *Republican* legislators. That earned him the nickname "Veto Corleone" from Florida lobbyists and lawmakers.[20] Populist Charlie Crist surprised most legislators when he outdid Jeb in his first year in office by vetoing a then record $459 million. Cumulatively, Crist cut almost $1.1 billion over four years. But in an interesting twist, Crist actually line item vetoed about $121 million in proposed spending *cuts* in 2009, thereby increasing rather than decreasing spending.[21] Governor Rick Scott, following up on his pledge to reduce government spending, set a new one year veto record by cutting $615 million during his first year in office, followed by cuts of $142, $368 and $69 million for a first term total of about $1.2 billion.

All governors have their own informal rules for which lines they choose to veto. But under Governor Bush, the rules were spelled out and made quite transparent—if an item did not go through the proper appropriations "vetting" process, it would be axed. In the Governor's words: "Call me whacky, but it is important for the governor to be immersed in the details of the budget because money should follow policy, not the other way around."[22] One scholarly study of Bush's line item vetoes concluded that they were really "part of a larger goal to redefine the role of the governor in state budgeting in Florida... by attempting to shift [budgeting] powers held for a long time by the state legislature back to the executive branch."[23] Charlie Crist was less systematic in his use of the veto and prone to let public opinion polls influence his decisions. Rick Scott's criteria for line item vetoes involves looking for proposed spending that avoids the regular legislative process or that falls outside the traditional limited functions of state government.

Veto Override

The governor's veto can only be overridden by a two-thirds vote of both houses. Most governors have enough support in the legislature to sustain a veto, so overrides have usually been very rare, with only 13 occurring since 1986. (See Table 7-3.) During the 24-year period from 1986 to 2009, there were only three veto overrides involving two governors. In 1986, the Democratic legislature overrode Democratic Governor Bob Graham's veto of a health care bill that required chiropractic treatment to be included in health insurance policies. Twelve years later a Republican legislature overrode two vetoes made by Governor Lawton Chiles. One changed the rules of evidence by allowing the use of previous testimony in retrials of civil cases—Governor Chiles actually withdrew his objection to the measure and did not oppose the override. The other was much more volatile because it banned the procedure known as "partial birth abortion" and many Democrats joined Republicans to override Chiles' veto."[24]

Table 7-3. Veto Overrides in Florida, 1986 to 2011

Governor/ Party*	Legislative Majority	Year	Issue
Graham (D)	D	1986	Health insurance mandate for chiropractic care
Chiles (D)	R	1998	Allow previous testimony in retrial of civil cases
Chiles (D)	R	1998	Ban "partial birth" abortion procedure
Crist (NPA)	R	2010	Limit state agency rule making authority
Crist (NPA)	R	2010	Restore $9.7 million line item for Shands Hospital
Crist (NPA)	R	2010	No duty to tell windstorm rating when selling home
Crist (NPA)	R	2010	Require DOT public hearing for new road medians
Crist (NPA)	R	2010	Allow Class 1 landfills to accept yard waste
Crist (NPA)	R	2010	Tax break on sold farm land if still used for farming
Crist (NPA)	R	2010	Allow landowners to avoid underground tank cleanup
Crist (NPA)	R	2010	Provide rebates for high efficiency AC unit purchase
Crist (NPA)	R	2011	Block locally imposed fees on farmland
Crist (NPA)	R	2011	Allow leadership committees that raise campaign $

*Governor party affiliation at the time of veto override.
Source: Compiled by the authors.

In 2010 and 2011, the Republican legislature overrode an unprecedented 10 vetoes made by Governor Charlie Crist. The governor upset Republicans when he left the Republican Party during his bid for the U.S. Senate when it became clear he would lose to Marco Rubio in the GOP primary. Crist officially ran with no party label and campaigned heavily to get independent and Democratic votes. Republicans gained so many legislative seats in 2010 that they had over a 2/3 majority in both the House and Senate and could easily override vetoes without any support from Democratic legislators. So GOP leaders called a special session in late fall 2010 and overrode eight of Crist's vetoes (seven regular and one line item), then overrode two more in the opening days of the 2011 regular session.

One common factor shared by the veto overrides of Graham, Chiles, and Crist was timing: they each came in the final year of a lame duck governor who was leaving or had just left office. Only one override occurred when the governor and legislative majority were of the same political party at the time of the override—Bob Graham. The other 12 involved the majority party in the legislature leading the override effort against a governor who was not a member of their party. Finally 12 out of 13 overrides were for regular legislation. Only one was for a line item of spending—restoring $9.7 million to pay for hospital care for indigent patients.

Chief Economic Manager and Trade Ambassador

Floridians expect their governor to help grow the state's economy and create new jobs. Over the decades, Florida has often been a leader in population and job growth, although the housing crisis and recession that began in 2007 hit Florida hard. The traditional formula for attracting new residents and jobs has been to keep taxes low and regulations at a minimum, invest in infrastructure like roads and ports, and promote Florida as a great place to visit, move to, and buy from. (See Chapter 12 for more details on economic development strategies.) Florida's governor plays a key role in promoting the state's economic assets to other states and to foreign countries. In fact, international trade has become one of the fastest growing portions of the state's economy. In one year alone, Florida's international merchandise trade (imports and exports) exceeded $131 billion with over $59 billion in exports and $72 billion in imports.[25]

Governors, working with Enterprise Florida,[26] often travel to other countries to promote Florida's products, location, and business climate, as well as its vacation and cultural amenities. The Governor's Office of Tourism, Trade, and Economic Development plays a major role in coordinating special social, cultural, and educational activities between foreign governments and Florida. There are over 100 consular missions and official trade/tourism offices representing 78 countries in the state.[27] Governors in their role of chief trade ambassador often interface with dignitaries in these offices. For instance, Jeb Bush made 24 trips during his eight years in office focusing especially on Latin America (15 countries) and Europe (4 countries) and Canada and Israel.[28] Charlie Crist made fewer trips but focused on similar regions. He went on at least three high profile missions to Israel, Brazil, and Europe. Governors do need to be careful that their trade missions are not perceived as wasteful taxpayer-funded vacations. Crist's trip to Europe was heavily criticized for visits to London, Paris, St. Petersburg, and Madrid and for including more than two dozen state employees, first class flights, and high-priced hotels at a total cost to the taxpayers of over $430,000.[29] During the first week in office, Rick Scott, seeking to fulfill his pledge to be the Chief Economic Development Officer for Florida and create 700,000 new jobs in seven years, met with the foreign minister of Japan and announced plans to visit Japan to increase exports from Florida.[30] Governor Scott undertook 10 trade missions during his first three years in office (to Panama, Canada, Brazil, Israel, Spain, the United Kingdom, Colombia, Chile, France and Japan) but took none during 2014 while running for re-election.

On Governor Scott's first trade mission to Canada, First Lady Ann Scott (3rd from right) meets with members of the Ontario Literacy Coalition.

Party Leadership

The Florida Democratic Party and the Republican Party of Florida each have executive directors to oversee their party's day-to-day operations. Each party also has a Chair, elected by the state party's executive committee. However, the governor is usually regarded as head of the political party he/she represents, both in the public's eye and in the eyes of state and local elected officials from that party. These officials know that the fortunes of their party and their own political futures are tied to the success of the governor. This is particularly true when it comes to dealing with the legislature. Governors who are fortunate enough to deal with a legislative majority from their own party are usually more successful (Reubin Askew, Bob Graham, and Jeb Bush). Governors who must deal with a majority from the opposite party usually have more mixed results (Claude Kirk, Bob Martinez, and Lawton Chiles). Charlie Crist was considered a savior for the Republican Party when he won election in 2006 (a very good year for Democrats nationwide) but later was viewed as a political "traitor" when he left the party his last year in office. Governor Rick Scott had an awkward adjustment period in assuming the unofficial role of party leader. Scott ran as an outsider against Republican establishment favorite Bill McCollum in the primary election, and most party leaders had publicly supported McCollum. Although the factions came together for the general election, some intraparty tensions continued throughout his first term and into his second. After his reelection, party members voted to replace Governor Scott's hand-picked choice to chair the Republican Party of Florida. This was believed to be the first time a governor's preference for party chair has been defeated.[31]

The first Governor's Mansion in Tallahassee was built in 1907 and occupied for nearly 50 years by a succession of 11 governors. The new Mansion was completed in 1957 on the same site.

Crisis Management

The governor is expected to deal with crises occurring within the state. These include natural disasters like hurricanes, tornados, freezes, floods, droughts, and fires. It also includes other people-made challenges like urban riots, public employee strikes, environmental disasters, economic strife, and waves of immigration. The state Constitution declares the governor "commander in chief" of the military forces of the state, that is, the Florida National Guard. The governor may call out the National Guard to deal with emergencies or, in the words of the Constitution, "to preserve the public peace, execute the laws of the state, suppress insurrection, or repel invasion." More commonly, the governor acts in crises to mobilize state agencies to provide assistance, to call upon the federal government for aid and, perhaps most importantly, simply to reassure people that *something* is being done.

Nearly every governor has had to deal with some type of crisis during his administration. Claude Kirk dealt with a teacher strike, Bob Graham with the Mariel boatlift from Cuba to South Florida, Lawton Chiles with Hurricane Andrew and widespread wildfires in Central Florida during a drought, Jeb Bush with four Category 3 or higher hurricanes in six weeks, and Charlie Crist with the BP Gulf Oil Spill. Coming into office, Rick Scott had to deal with a budget crisis (a shortfall of almost $4 billion), a jobs crisis (one of the highest state unemployment rates in the country), and an ongoing housing crisis (with one of the highest home foreclosure rates in the country).

There is plenty of evidence that "performance under fire" (in a crisis) has political consequences. For example, polls taken after the hurricanes in 2004 showed each Bush brother's favorable ratings rising among Floridians. The 2004 presidential election exit poll showed that of the 87 percent of the voters who approved of the government's response to the hurricanes, 57 percent voted for George Bush.[32] Throughout the BP oil spill in the Gulf of Mexico and cleanup, Charlie Crist remained a visible figure in all coastal counties organizing the state response, coordinating assistance with President Obama and the federal government and putting pressure on BP to provide more financial help to Florida families and businesses hurt by the spill. The extensive media coverage of Crist's efforts, and the perception that he was on top of the crisis response, kept his pubic approval numbers high for many months. As the crisis was mostly resolved and his free media exposure was winding down, his poll numbers dropped and he began to lag behind Marco Rubio in the race for the U.S. Senate.[33] In 2014, Rick Scott was able to win reelection (against Crist) in part because of the impression that he handled the state's economic crisis adequately.

RATING THE PERFORMANCE OF GOVERNORS

Evaluating political leadership is a complex task. Some strong and effective leaders may take the state or nation in directions we consider wrong. Others may not achieve a great deal, yet we appreciate their goals, sincerity, and hard work. Some may govern in a time of crisis that brings out their better qualities; others may never really be tested. But leadership evaluation is not wholly subjective. We can examine the success of modern era governors in getting their policies and programs established, their popularity with the general public, and their reputation among historians and political scientists. Naturally, nearly every governor had his "ups" and "downs"—with the legislature and with the public at-large—not much different from what the average person goes through, just a lot more visible. Governors live in "fish bowls." What is interesting about Florida's governors is how many go on to hold an executive position at the national level and how many later run for other offices, often losing.

Florida governors' leadership skills are tested when a major hurricane hits. Governor Jeb Bush's job approval ratings went up when he skillfully led the state's recovery after two back-to-back years of multiple hurricanes.

UP-CLOSE: THE WIT AND WISDOM OF FLORIDA'S GOVERNORS

In spring 2006, Jeb Bush and five of the six living former governors participated in a one-day symposium organized by the Lou Frey Institute of Politics and Government at the University of Central Florida.* Listed below are some of their recollections about serving as Florida's governor. Comments are also included for Governor Crist and Scott who took office after 2006.

Shown left to right: Buddy MacKay (D), Claude Kirk (R), Reubin Askew (D), Bob Graham (D), Bob Martinez (R), and Jeb Bush (R).

Claude Kirk 36th governor (1967-1971): First Republican governor since Reconstruction.

I was the most productive governor in history. I had two children on state time on state property.

On the day I took office it was stormy, cold and rainy at 11 a.m. By noon the sun was shining down when I took the oath of office. We cleansed the temple and drove out the money changers.

(Speaking of the three other Democratic governors on stage with him) Had I not been governor, these good guys would not be here today—they are the fruit of my loins! (Governor Askew laughed and responded) Governor Kirk did unite the Democratic Party like it had never been united before!

Reubin Askew 37th governor (1971-1979): First governor to be reelected with a four year term.

We had six Cabinet members, three of whom were under investigation and three members of the Supreme Court under investigation. The legislature refused to pass (reform) laws. So I went to the people, and the people passed (the Sunshine Amendment) overwhelmingly.

LeRoy Collins, Bob Graham, and Lawton Chiles would not have been governors without run-off elections. I would not have been state senator. I would like to see run-offs reinstated.

Bob Graham 38th governor, (1979-1987): Most popular governor in modern Florida history.

When my father was defeated, they said it would be a cold day in hell before a candidate from Miami would become governor. On the day I took the oath of office, it snowed in Tallahassee.

My daughter went to my wife and said 'Mommy I don't want Daddy to run.' And Adele said 'Don't worry. There is no chance he will win!' After the election, Sissy told her mother 'you lied,' and then she threw up. On my first day in office, Sissy came to me and said 'Daddy, I'm glad you won.'

Bob Martinez 40th governor, (1987-1991): First Hispanic governor.

There's a huge change in demographics in this state. We need to find a way for them to be a part of Florida.

Every governor does what he can do to move the state forward and then the next governor picks it up.

Buddy MacKay lieutenant governor and then 42nd governor after the death of Lawton Chiles (1991-1999).

> *There are two Floridas and at least two cultures. In the rural counties there are no jobs and no growth. The growth policy for young people in these areas is 'Move Out!'*

> *I supported term limits strongly. I think now that it was a mistake. Term limits assure that about the time (legislators) figure out how things work, they move on.*

Jeb Bush 43rd governor, (1999 - 2007): First Republican governor to be reelected.

> *Big things require doing the little things over and over again. . . . Success is never final; the job is never finished. . . . Some people think I'm stubborn. I think its determination.*

> *I've had a chance to work with the most dedicated individuals I've ever seen – the first responders.*

> *This has been the greatest job in the world!*

Charlie Crist** 44th governor, (2007 – 2011): Populist governor who left the Republican party when he ran for U.S. Senate.

Charlie Crist (R)

> *I'm pro-life, pro-family, pro-business, pro-Republican (running in the GOP gubernatorial primary in 2006).*

> *You know there is a new show on TV called "Entourage." Well, I don't have one (in response to criticism of the cost of, and number of people who went on, a trade mission to Europe).*

> *I haven't supported an idea because it's a Republican idea or Democratic idea. I support ideas because they are good ideas for the people (announcing his bid to run for the U.S. Senate as an independent).*

Rick Scott** 45th governor, (2011 -): Outsider who spent a record amount of his own money to win the closest governor's race in Florida history.

Rick Scott (R)

> *Let's get to work! (Campaign theme, closing line from his first State of the State speech, and the name of his political committee).*

> *Doing what must be done will not make me "Most Popular," but I'm determined to make Florida "Most Likely to Succeed." (First State of the State speech).*

> *So now it's time for another state of the state speech, or as I like to call it — a chance for me to show off my world renowned oratorical skills. It's ok, you can laugh, it was meant to be a joke. (Second State of the State speech).*

Note: * See www.loufrey.org for more information on the governor's conference and for upcoming events.
** The symposium occurred before Crist and Scott became governor. Their quotes were collected by the authors.
Sources: Quotes selected by the authors from the DVDs of the program and from the Daytona Beach News-Journal, Sunday April 2, 2006 "Ideas" Section (1B and 3B).

LeRoy Collins and the Civil Rights Revolution

Among modern Florida governors, historians generally agree that LeRoy Collins (1955-61) brought the state through a period of great change with minimum disruption.[34] A graduate of Tallahassee's Leon High School, Collins received a law degree from tiny Cumberland College and was promptly elected to the state legislature from Leon County in 1934, serving in both the House and Senate. He married the wealthy great-granddaughter of Richard Keith Call, an early governor of the state, and moved into the Call family home, "The Grove," across the street from the Governor's Mansion.[35] In 1954, Collins was elected governor to complete the term of Governor Dan McCarty, who died in office.

Thomas LeRoy Collins, Florida's 33rd governor, served from 1955-1961. Historians regard Collins as one of Florida's (and the South's) most outstanding governors for his progressive stance on civil rights.

Although a North Florida legislator himself, Collins led the fight to reapportion the state legislature to give equal representation to urban South Florida voters. This was at a time when 14 percent of the state's population could elect half of the Senate and 18 percent could elect half of the House. Rural North Florida legislators, dubbed the "pork chop gang" by the *Tampa Tribune*, dominated the Capitol. Collins was unsuccessful in getting the legislature to reapportion itself. Reapportionment would not come until ordered by the U.S. Supreme Court in *Baker* v. *Carr* (1962) and later in *Reynolds* v. *Sims* (1964) in which the Court ordained that both houses of state legislatures must reflect the principle "one person, one vote."[36] But in 1956, with the strong support of urban South Florida voters, Collins made political history by winning the first Democratic primary over five opponents, thus making a gubernatorial runoff primary unnecessary.

Florida politics during and after the Collins governorship was dominated by the issue of race—notably the implementation of the U.S. Supreme Court decision in *Brown* v. *Board of Education of Topeka* in 1954 that segregation in public schools violated the Equal Protection Clause of the Fourteenth Amendment.[37] Politically, Collins was obliged to announce his opposition to the decision, but he sought to keep Florida's public schools open, counseled conformity to the Constitution, and worked to avoid the violence and disorder that characterized desegregation in other southern states. He fought successfully against various proposals by militant segregationists to close the public schools and openly defy the federal law. Rather than exploit the race issue, he focused on economic development and strengthened Florida's educational system from grade school to the university level.

Collins' relatively progressive and moderate stance won him the chairmanship of the National Governors' Conference. In 1960, he was selected as the chair of the Democratic National Convention. Later President Lyndon Johnson asked him to serve as the president's principal civil rights adviser. But when Collins returned to Florida and ran for the U.S. Senate in 1968, he lost to a relatively unknown Republican, Edward J. Gurney. Collins' association with Lyndon Johnson and the National Democratic Party in a year of racial and anti-Vietnam War discord ended Collins' political career. Gurney would later be indicted on bribery and conspiracy charges.

Farris Bryant and Haydon Burns: One-Termers

After LeRoy Collins came two competent, but lower-profile, one-term governors. These two gentlemen fit a pattern observed at the presidential level, namely that, often, after a period of turmoil or intensity with a high profile leader in charge, the public turns to more calming figures. Farris Bryant, a Harvard Law School graduate from Marion County, and an accountant, served from 1961 to 1965. He had been in the legislature for ten years, including one term (1953) as the Speaker of the House. As governor, Bryant fought to improve higher education, including raising the salaries of professors and pushing through a constitutional amendment allowing the state to issue bonds for the construction of higher education facilities. During his administration, more than one billion dollars was raised to construct new buildings on the state's college campuses. Bryant also pushed hard for water control projects and got the state to purchase land for conservation and recreation purposes. Perhaps his biggest legacy was repeatedly calling the legislature into special session until it finally produced a reapportionment plan somewhat in line with the "one person, one vote" standard ordered by the U.S. Supreme Court in its landmark 1962 *Baker v. Carr* ruling. While the 1963 plan was struck down by the courts for not exactly meeting the "one person, one vote" rule, it was the state's first step toward giving urban areas more representation—a move that would ultimately change the whole face of Florida politics. Down went the "pork choppers" and in marched the urban Democratic progressives. Bryant did not seek re-election as governor but he did accept an appointment by President Lyndon Johnson to the National Security Council and the Office of Emergency Planning. He later (1970) ran for the U.S. Senate but was defeated by Lawton Chiles in the runoff primary.

Florida's 34th and 35th governors: Cecil Farris Bryant (top) served from 1961-1965. William Haydon Burns (bottom) served from 1965 to 1967. Both were low profile one-term (half-term for Burns) governors.

Haydon Burns, Florida's 35th governor, followed Bryant for one two-year term after serving 14 years as the Mayor of Jacksonville. Burns had unsuccessfully run against Bryant and many other Democrats for the party's gubernatorial nomination in 1960. Burns' term was a short one – only two years long. Voters had approved a constitutional amendment changing the timing of Florida's gubernatorial election so that it would no longer be concurrent with the presidential election cycle. During his short tenure in office, he "oversaw progress on constitutional revision, outdoor recreation, industrial development, and tax reform."[38] Burns is remembered more for losing the Democratic runoff primary in 1966 to the liberal Robert King High of Miami than he is for any particular policy initiative. High supported the Civil Rights Act and Voting Rights Act of 1965, while Burns opposed the measures. The primary was bitter and resulted in a split of the Democratic Party in the general election because of Burns' refusal to endorse High. The split enabled the election of Florida's first Republican governor since Reconstruction, Claude Kirk. Burns later ran again for Mayor of Jacksonville in 1971 but was defeated.

Claude R. Kirk, Jr., the state's 35th governor and first Republican to win the governorship since 1872, often clashed with the legislature's Democratic majority.

Claude Kirk: First Republican since 1872, Flamboyant

In 1966, many conservative Democrats from the Panhandle, including former Democratic Governor Haydon Burns, abandoned their party's nominee and joined the growing number of GOP voters in Central and Southwest Florida to elect Kirk, the first Republican governor of Florida since Reconstruction. Kirk, too, had been a Democrat but switched parties in 1960 and led the "Floridians for Nixon" campaign. He ran unsuccessfully for the U.S. Senate as a Republican in 1964, before running for governor in 1966.

Kirk's personal life made the news a lot and was of great interest to Floridians. He married and had two children while in office. The governor's administration was both colorful and controversial, marked by confrontations with the Democratic legislature and Republican colleagues, an unprecedented statewide teachers' strike, and crises over forced school busing.[39] However, one of Governor Kirk's lasting achievements was helping to shape the 1968 Florida Constitution which, when adopted, allowed Florida governors to seek a second four year term and re-established the lieutenant governor position. But Kirk was defeated in his bid for reelection in 1970 by a young Pensacola state senator, Democrat Reubin Askew who was able to pull the Democratic Party back together. Kirk would later run (unsuccessfully) for statewide office three more times: for governor (in 1978 as a Democrat), for the U.S. Senate (in 1988 as a Democrat), and for Commissioner of Education (in 1990 as a Republican).

Reubin Askew, Reformer Extraordinaire

Askew seemed destined for high political office from his days as student body president at Florida State University (FSU) and class president at the University of Florida Law School. He began his career as Assistant County Solicitor for Escambia County in 1956. He was elected to the state House in 1958 and to the Senate in 1962. Young, personable, and hardworking, Askew stood out in a legislature with many progressive urban legislators recently elected following reapportionment.[40] He was elected president pro tempore of the Florida Senate by his colleagues in 1969, setting the stage for his race for the governorship in 1970. By then Claude Kirk's many controversies and elaborate lifestyle in the Governor's Mansion had worn thin with voters. Askew defeated the incumbent Republican governor with 57 percent of the vote. Life in the Governor's Mansion changed dramatically. Askew was a non-drinking, non-smoking Presbyterian elder who served orange juice at cocktail parties. (Great for Florida's citrus industry and a boon to local bars. Guests would leave early and drink elsewhere!)

Reubin O'Donovan Askew, the state's 36th governor, successfully pushed for major tax reform and "Government in the Sunshine" requiring financial disclosure by elected officials.

A committed reformer, Governor Askew sought to enact a corporate income tax, first winning legislative approval to place the measure on a state referendum, then campaigning successfully for its approval. Askew's corporate tax referendum won with over 70 percent of the vote. When the legislature failed to pass his "government in the sunshine" amendment, he lent his support to a citizen's initiative that won nearly 80 percent of vote. Askew was easily re-elected in 1974 by a landslide 61 percent. Askew named the first African American to the Florida Supreme Court and appointed the first woman to head a state agency.

Like Governor Collins, Askew served as chair of the National Governors' Conference. He failed in subsequent efforts to reform the Cabinet system and strengthen the governorship, suffering voter rejection in 1978 of constitutional revisions that he supported, but left office with high public approval ratings. His subsequent attempts to enter Democratic presidential politics failed, apparently dashed by the perceived failure of fellow southern governor Jimmy Carter, for whom Askew served as Special Trade Representative. Askew finished last in the New Hampshire presidential primary in 1984. He briefly considered running for the U.S. Senate in 1988 but decided to continue in law and university teaching. He has the distinction of having taught at each state university before choosing FSU as his permanent academic home. Both of his alma maters carry his name on important programs. Florida State University currently houses the Reubin O'D. Askew School of Public Administration and Policy, where Askew was a professor, and the University of Florida hosts the Askew Institute.

Bob Graham and His Popular Work Days

The Florida Annual Policy Survey (FAPS) polls show that Bob Graham has been the most popular governor since regular reliable polling began in 1979 (see Figure 7-3). Graham's father was a multimillionaire land developer in [Miami-] Dade County and a state senator who unsuccessfully ran for governor. Graham himself was Phi Beta Kappa at the University of Florida and a 1962 graduate of Harvard Law School. His uncle, Philip Graham, was publisher of the *Washington Post* and *Newsweek* magazine and was succeeded after his death by Washington's most powerful woman publisher, Katherine Graham. Bob Graham started at the top, as principal developer of the Miami Lakes residential community. He was elected to the Florida House in 1966 and the Senate in 1970. He was defeated in the first Democratic primary in the 1978 governors' race but came back to win the runoff with an expensive professional media campaign (see Chapter 4). In the general election that year, two multimillionaires faced off in the most costly governors' race to that time. Bob Graham defeated Republican drug store magnate Jack Eckerd with 56 percent of the vote.

Daniel Robert "Bob" Graham, the 38th governor of Florida, coped with a Cuban and Haitian refugee crisis, pushed through the Growth Management Act of 1985 and increased support for higher education.

Graham continued his popular media style of governing in office. He put in "working days" throughout the state, as everything from police officer, teacher, and social worker to construction worker, fisherman, and restaurant busboy. He performed the role of crisis manager extraordinarily well during hurricanes, strikes, and civil disturbances. He maintained a moderate-to-conservative image—tough on crime and willing to sign death warrants to implement capital punishment. Graham was also a forceful advocate for public education, particularly higher education. He was easily re-elected in 1982, with a landslide 65 percent of the vote. In his second term, he pushed the state's most comprehensive environmental protection program through the legislature, including the far-reaching 1985 Florida Growth Management Act. (See Chapter 12.) Among the more controversial provisions of this act was a "concurrency requirement" that barred private development, unless supporting public facilities (roads, schools, sewers, etc.) were either already in place or were built concurrently with new development. (The Growth Management Act was significantly changed in 2011. See Chapter 12.) Graham ran for the U.S. Senate in 1986, while still governor, and won, easily defeating Republican incumbent Senator Paula Hawkins. He had to resign 72 hours before his gubernatorial term ended to take his seat in the U.S. Senate, which allowed his Lt. Governor, Wayne Mixson, to fill out his term. Graham continued his "working days" as a U.S. Senator and routinely won high approval ratings from Florida voters. A heart problem stalled his presidential bid in 2004 and Graham retired from the U.S. Senate.[41]

Figure 7-3. Florida Governors' Performance Ratings

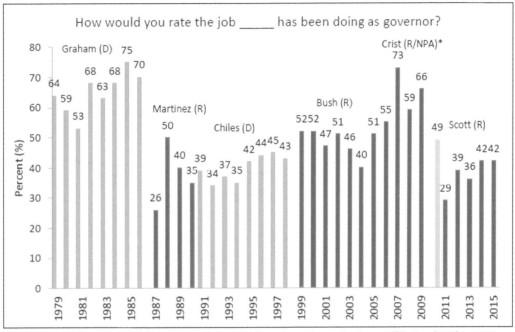

*Charlie Crist left the Republican Party and changed his registration to No Party Affiliation (NPA) in 2010.
Source: 1979-2004, Florida Annual Policy Survey, Florida State University; 2005-2015, Quinnipiac University Polling.

Bob Martinez: Taxes, No; Environment, Yes

The Florida sales tax exempts more items than it taxes.[42] Most of these exemptions involve services—from accounting, insurance, travel, media advertising, and real estate services to the politically most sacred exemption of all, lawyers' fees. Also exempted are groceries, rent, and medicine—exemptions most people support as equity measures. The untaxed service sector of the Florida economy is growing more rapidly than retail product sales subject to taxation. Thus, over time, the base of the sales tax has diminished as a portion of the state's economy. For years, tax reform proponents have pushed for a change in the tax laws to deal with this problem. But Florida's governors, Democrats and Republicans alike—have proven unequal to the task of expanding the sales tax base by eliminating the services exemptions. Nearly every governor that has tried to eliminate these "sacred cows" has failed. Some, like Republican Governor Bob Martinez, ended up losing their re-election bid because of trying.

The Florida public gave Republican Governor Bob Martinez very low ratings during his tenure and denied him re-election. Yet Martinez, the first governor of Hispanic heritage and a graduate of the University of Tampa, had earlier proven successful as mayor of Tampa. It is not surprising that he frequently fought with the Democratic legislature over budgetary items (he was clearly a fiscal conservative opposed to waste in government). But his low ratings more likely resulted from his stand on taxing services. When he ran for office against the liberal Democrat Steve Pajcic, Martinez promised to cut or at least keep taxes at their current level. However, in his first year, he urged Republican and Democratic legislators to join together to eliminate sales tax exemptions on many services, including newspaper and television advertising. When the predictable firestorm of media criticism reached the Governor's Mansion, he quickly reversed his position and urged the legislature to repeal the reforms he had so recently touted. It was too little, too late. The damage had been done. The result was that he alienated citizens on each side of the issue and never fully recovered politically. The whole episode demonstrates the power of taxes as a perennially simmering issue in Florida politics that can boil over at any time.

The tax issue shadowed some of Martinez's most significant accomplishments as governor. He initiated and expanded a number of environmental initiatives that were very popular with the public. He "won bipartisan legislative support for SWIM [Surface Water Management and Improvement Act], creating for the first time uniform policies for the management and protection of Florida's surface waters."[43] Martinez played a major role in pushing Florida's Republican Party toward a more pro-environment position. The shift has been critical to the party's long-term success in a state filled with people who move here for the state's beautiful beaches and pristine lakes. Martinez was also a staunch supporter of a get tough on drugs policy. After he left office, President George H. W. Bush appointed him Director of the National Campaign Against Use of Drugs. Martinez became the nation's "drug czar."

In the end, Martinez lost his re-election bid to Democrat Lawton Chiles. Ultimately conservatives did not think they could trust Martinez on taxes and moderates were alienated by his conservative stance on social issues (anti-abortion), although many analysts simply hand his defeat to the fact that he had to run against 'Walkin' Lawton.

Robert "Bob" Martinez, the state's 37th governor, was a strong conservationist who initiated Preservation 2000, a large environmental land acquisition program.

"Walkin" Lawton Chiles

Governor Lawton Chiles frequently urged tax reform for Florida, including the elimination of many exemptions to the sales tax. But, as popular as he was, he did not have any better luck than Martinez. Chiles graduated from the University of Florida and the University of Florida Law School. Three years after finishing law school, he won election in 1958 to the Florida House of Representatives, moved to the Senate in 1966, and then upset former Governor Farris Bryant in the U.S. Senate Democratic runoff primary that featured Chiles' famous walk over the length of the state (1,033 miles from Pensacola to Miami-Dade County), earning him the nickname "Walkin" Lawton.[44] While in the U.S. Senate, Chiles' chairmanship of the Senate Budget Committee added to his expertise in budget and tax matters and gave him a lot of visibility. Chiles stepped down from the U.S. Senate in 1988 after 18 years, admitting that he suffered from depression and needed a break. But, after two years, he jumped into the governor's race and beat Martinez handily (57 percent to 43 percent).

Chiles appeared well aware of the need to keep the state's revenue base abreast of its population growth and the equally compelling need to achieve greater fairness in the distribution of the tax burden. While carefully avoiding the politically dangerous call for a tax "increase," Chiles continually attacked the maze of exemptions to the state's sales tax. He wisely began his efforts to reform the tax structure by announcing his intentions to "right size" state government, to adopt the citizen-as-consumer recommendations of the "reinventing government" movement, and to reduce bureaucratic waste and inefficiency The idea was to first convince Floridians that he was doing everything possible to save taxpayers' money before asking for an expansion of the sales tax. But the following year his proposals to tax services were met by a powerful array of interest group opponents. The insurance and real estate industries, newspaper and television owners, bankers, accountants, and lawyers easily derailed the governor's plans. His proposals to expand state-supported health care met a similar fate. When the Republicans won a 20 to 20 tie in the state Senate in the 1992 midterm elections, Chiles saw his approval ratings sink dangerously low. (See Figure 7-3.) He appeared vulnerable to defeat in his 1994 bid for reelection.

Chiles came back to win a razor-thin victory over Jeb Bush in November, after trailing in opinion polls for most of the summer and early fall. He did so in part by shelving his more progressive plans for tax reform and expanded health care and touting his more conservative policy positions—prison building, the death penalty, and opposition to unchecked immigration. Chiles joined with some other border state governors in suing the U.S. government to recover the costs of providing services to illegal immigrants due to the federal government's failure to control the borders. They lost the suit, but the governor's position resonated with Floridians.

In his second term, Chiles struggled to avoid the "lame-duck" syndrome. According to the Florida Constitution, he could not run again for the state's top post. Politically, he faced a legislature controlled by the opposition party, Florida's first Democratic governor ever to be in such a situation. Yet clearly Chiles wanted to lead the state. He was not content to simply occupy the Governor's Mansion for his final term. He correctly judged that moderate and conservative initiatives—such as deregulation, no-new-taxes budgets, and anti-crime measures—were more likely to succeed than proposals calling for additional taxing, spending, or regulation.

Lawton Mainor Chiles, Jr. was Florida's 41st governor. A populist from Polk County, he was nicknamed the "he-coon" after an old country saying he evoked in his debate with Jeb Bush during the 1994 governor's race. (You can see the old coon through the window in the governor's official portrait. First Lady Rhea's reflection can be seen in the mirror over the Governor's left shoulder.)

Chiles' renewed conservative rhetoric helped to raise his approval ratings in his second term. His Second Inaugural Address indicated that he understood the frustration of Floridians with their government:

I have 200 acres of woods north of Tallahassee where I have an old log cabin. I wanted to build a cook shack out back-wood poles, tin roof, screened sides, old stove. I've been trying to get a permit for over a year. "You must have plans," they say. But, a cook shack is unusual; there are no regulations for one. So they ask: "Does it have a stove?" YES. "Does it have a toilet?" YES. "Well, the closest thing we have is a single-family residence; so it needs steel tie-downs; it must withstand Andrew-type winds, etc." That could cost from $15,000 to $65,000. I've concluded the Lord gave me this problem so I could understand why people hate government so much.[45]

Chiles wisely chose to publicize a battle with the tobacco industry, positioning himself as the white-hatted defender of children's health against the greedy black-hatted tobacco companies. He inspired a lawsuit against the tobacco industry claiming compensation and punitive damages for the ill-effects of cigarette smoking on state-supported Medicaid patients. Eventually the tobacco companies settled and Florida was projected to receive $11.3 billion over 25 years to compensate the state for Medicaid costs incurred by treating smoking-related illnesses. The tobacco companies agreed to limit advertising in the state and to stop vending machine sales. With money from the tobacco settlement, Chiles was able to expand health care opportunities for Florida children who lacked health care. The only new taxes he proposed were an additional ten cent per pack cigarette tax and a tax on "lap dancing" at nude adult entertainment establishments. In 1997 he called a special session of the legislature to deal with school overcrowding, hoping, perhaps, to force the Republican leadership to approve some form of revenue increase. (See Chapter 9.) But the issue was dealt with by reallocating funds rather than increasing taxes. Tragically, Chiles died of a heart attack in the gym of the Governor's Mansion with just 24 days remaining in his term. His Lt. Governor Buddy MacKay filled out the last days of his term.[46] When the new governor, Jeb Bush, took office, one of his first acts was to name the tobacco settlement fund the Lawton Chiles Tobacco Endowment for Children and Elders.

Lt. Governor Buddy MacKay (D) takes the oath of office as Governor, following the sudden death of Governor Lawton Chiles.

Jeb Bush Makes History

Jeb Bush, a Miami businessman in real estate, had never held public office before he ran for governor. The closest he had come to public service was serving as Governor Martinez's Secretary of Commerce. To say that Jeb Bush made history is somewhat of an understatement. He has the distinction of losing what was at the time the closest governor's race in modern history to Lawton Chiles in 1994, then winning two of the state's biggest landslide elections when he handily beat Buddy MacKay in 1998 by a 55 percent to 44 percent margin and Bill McBride in 2002 by 56 percent to 43 percent. With his victory over political novice McBride, Bush became the first Republican governor to ever win re-election. Bush's finest moments, according to polls, were in crisis situations—first, the economic crisis that struck Florida's tourism industry after 9/11 when his creative fiscal policies helped jumpstart the industry. Second, when powerful hurricanes ripped apart the lives of many Floridians, Bush's management expertise, attention to detail, calm demeanor, and empathy helped them recover from one hurricane, while preparing for the next.

John Ellis "Jeb" Bush, the state's 43rd governor, was given high marks by the public for creative fiscal policies after 9/11 that helped Florida's vital tourism industry recover from the devastating event that had made Americans afraid to travel.

While Jeb remained fairly popular throughout his two terms in office, he had his share of "negative moments," one being the large protest march on Tallahassee by minority groups opposed to his "One Florida" program. While the majority of Floridians supported doing away with racial preferences in college admissions and government contracting, minorities, especially African Americans, were concerned about access to higher education and to government jobs and contracts. The biggest controversy of the Bush governorship was surely the 2000 presidential election (Review Chapter 4.) which put the Sunshine State under the microscopic eye of the world's media. Although Bush removed himself from the canvassing board that certifies election results, it was not enough for ardent Gore supporters—half of Florida. However, the imbroglio did push Florida to the forefront of the election reform movement. Another misstep in the minds of many Floridians was Jeb's intervention in the Terri Schiavo right-to-die case.

Many close observers labeled Governor Bush "a policy wonk"—someone who is very focused on changing the course of public policy. He made his mark in several key policy areas—education, fiscal policy, and law enforcement. He was also credited with bringing the "high tech" revolution to state government operations. Bush's signature education program is the *"A+ Plan."* All public schools receive letter grades based on their students' scores on standardized tests. Proponents cite rising test scores as evidence the program is increasing student performance and shrinking the achievement gap between minority and white students. Opponents say that an overemphasis on testing is actually hurting education, as teachers "teach to the test" at the expense of critical thinking. In the area of taxation, Bush was a tax cutter, not a tax reformer. His focus was on improving Florida's business climate, diversifying the state's economy, and getting Florida's credit rating raised to AAA (the highest level). Under his administration, all three goals were met. But that did not quell the debate over his tax cuts (projected to have been over $15 billion during his eight year term). Supporters pointed to the consistent economic growth in Florida and high rate of job creation, while critics pointed to the unmet needs of the state including education, welfare, and the environment. To help curtail rapidly rising Medicaid costs, the governor sought and was granted waivers from the federal government to experiment with HMOs. In the area of law enforcement, Bush pushed through the 10-20-Life program for criminals convicted of using a gun when committing a felony. (See Chapter 8.) Finally, nothing better demonstrates the "high tech" revolution than the governor's e-budget (making the state's finances more transparent and readily accessible online in an easy-to-comprehend format). In general, Florida's web-based communication system continues to be a leader among the states.[47]

When Governor Bush left office, he indicated that he was not interested in running for public office again and returned to Miami. He continued to be heavily involved in promoting education reform around the country. Few political analysts really believed it was the end of his political career. In fact, many believed it was not a matter of *if* he would one day run for president, but *when*. He left the governor's office a young man of 53, having been proclaimed the "best governor in America" by one national conservative magazine.[48] In 2015, Governor Bush announced he would run for president in 2016.

Charles "Charlie" Joseph Crist, Jr. "The People's Governor"

For the first time since the 1870s, one Republican succeeded another as governor when Charles "Charlie" Joseph Crist, Jr. became Florida's 44th governor. Crist ran as a populist, promising to be "the people's governor" and to govern by adhering to the core principles of less taxes, less government, and more freedom. Crist is proud of his Greek heritage and of the fact that his grandfather emigrated from Cyprus "seeking the promise of a better life that only America could provide."[49]

Crist's political experience before becoming governor was somewhat unique in that it cut across all three branches of state government. He served as a state senator from 1992-1998. His executive branch experiences included being Deputy Secretary of the Florida Department of Business and Professional Regulation (1999-2000), Florida Education Commissioner (2000-2002), and Florida Attorney General

(2002-2006). As attorney general, he frequently interacted with the state's judicial branch as the state's chief lawyer.

Crist took office already perceived as more socially moderate and centrist than his predecessor Jeb Bush, having expressed his support of civil unions and embryonic stem cell research during his campaign. His sunny, easy-going inclusive personality and his centrist campaign platform led many to predict he would be more willing to reach out to Democrats in the Cabinet and state legislature and this turned out to be the case. As he took office, his biggest challenge was projected to be dealing with the sizable number of Republican legislators and voters who were more conservative than he—the reverse of the situation faced by Governor Bush. This also turned out to be true. However, Crist's victory in 2006, a year when Republican candidates for governor across the U.S. did not fare very well, gained him respect both in Florida and nationally. In fact, a year after taking office, he was given serious consideration as a potential GOP vice-presidential candidate by Republican nominee John McCain. Two short years later, during his last year in office, Crist actually left the Republican Party to run with no party affiliation in a failed attempt to become a U.S. Senator.

Charles J. "Charlie" Crist, Florida's 44th governor, a populist who billed himself as "the people's governor," chose to run for the U.S. Senate rather than for a second term as governor.

Crist accomplished a number of changes that were generally popular with Democrats and independents, but tended to alienate the GOP conservative base. One of his early successes was getting the Florida Cabinet (acting as the State Board of Clemency) to automatically restore the voting rights of nonviolent felons who had served their time and paid restitution. Many of those affected were minorities and poor people who generally vote Democratic. Crist also lobbied successfully for the legislature to provide a paper trail for the voting system as one of the continuing reforms in the aftermath of the 2000 presidential election. Democrats, especially African Americans, were thrilled with this move. On the environment, the governor announced his intention to make Florida a leader in the fight against global warming and hosted a major conference on the issue, much to the chagrin of many conservatives who doubt that global warming is a major problem caused by human activity.

During the 2008 election, Crist issued an executive order to keep early voting sites open longer, knowing that this would likely help Democratic candidates, since many standing in line were voters who were very enthusiastic about voting for Barack Obama. Crist's outreach to the minority community extended into his court appointments. He appointed an African-American judge from Orlando to serve on the Florida Supreme Court—again, an action applauded by black voters and Democrats but denounced by Republicans and conservatives. He vetoed a Republican-passed law that would have tied teacher pay raises to student performance as measured by test scores—a move that upset conservatives but delighted the Democratic-aligned teacher's union. And, finally, Crist unapologetically took federal stimulus dollars to stave off deep cuts to the state budget. He even appeared on stage with President Obama in Florida and gave him a hug to thank him for his largess. This enraged the Republican base and the growing Tea Party movement, which had cast the midterm elections as a referendum on Obama and his policies.

Despite, or perhaps because of, many of these policies, Crist's popularity ratings were quite strong during his first three years in office which was impressive considering the economy in Florida was in terrible shape. Although his overall poll numbers were higher than Jeb Bush's had been, Crist was never as popular with Republicans as Bush. Crist's high poll numbers were more the result of being well-liked by Democrats and independents. Still, when Crist announced he was going to run for the open U.S. Senate seat that was being temporarily filled by his former Chief of Staff (George LeMieux, whom Crist had appointed when Senator Mel Martinez resigned), most polls showed him comfortably ahead of primary opponent Marco Rubio and also leading any Democratic candidate by a large margin in the general election. When the BP oil spill and clean up dragged on for months, it gave Crist an opportunity to lead in a crisis, gave him lots of free publicity, and kept his poll numbers up. Eventually, however, Rubio became a Tea Party and conservative favorite and opened up a sizable advantage over the Governor. At that point, facing the reality that he could not win the primary, Crist decided to leave the Republican Party to run as an independent. But he lost a three-way race to Rubio as Democratic and independent voters largely split their votes between Crist and the Democratic nominee Kendrick Meek. Fittingly, after leaving office, the self-proclaimed "people's governor" went to work with a large, high profile, Orlando-based law firm whose long time slogan is "Morgan and Morgan: For the People!" Eventually Crist registered as a Democrat, won the Democratic nomination for governor, but lost his bid to unseat Rick Scott.

Rick Scott: Let's Gets to Work – Jobs! Jobs! Jobs!

When Governor Rick Scott first decided to run for governor, almost no Florida voters had heard of him. By the time he finished spending a Florida record $85 million on his campaign (including $73 million of his own money), voters knew his name, his face (he joked about his bald head), his campaign slogan ("Let's get to work"), his likes (less government and lower taxes), his dislikes (anything related to President Obama), his successes (building a large profitable hospital chain), his failures (forced out of his company, HCA, which paid a record $1.7 billion in fines for Medicare fraud), his mother ("Rick's a good boy"), and his background (a poor family that worked its way out of public housing). Scott first came out of nowhere to beat well known party establishment favorite Attorney General Bill McCollum in a primary memorable for the quantity and variety of nasty attack ads. Next, GOP leaders who had desperately fought to beat Scott quickly jumped in to support him. Scott then heavily outspent Democratic candidate Alex Sink (who had herself set a Florida Democratic spending record of $17.5 million). She was still outspent by almost 5:1 in another attack-filled campaign that left some voters wondering if Scott was running against Sink or President Obama because of the number of times he mentioned the president in his

Richard "Rick" Scott, the state's 45th governor, entered office in the midst of a recession and promised to run Florida like a business, reflecting his CEO background.

advertisements. In the end, Scott relied heavily on an energized conservative Republican base, the fast emerging Tea Party movement, and a lower turnout among dispirited Democrats to win the governor's office with less than 50 percent of the vote and by the closest margin in Florida history (1.2 percent).

Upon election, Governor Scott's overriding goal was to create 700,000 new jobs over seven years using seven steps. The 7-7-7 plan proposed to: implement accountability budgeting, reduce government spending, reduce regulations, recruit new business and retain existing ones, invest in universities to make them world class, reduce property taxes, and eliminate the corporate income tax. Scott's outsider status and lack of political experience, combined with the sagging Florida economy and nearly $4 billion budget shortfall, made implementing this plan difficult and got him off to a rocky start in his first few months in office.

One of Governor Scott's first big decisions made national headlines when he turned down $2.4 billion in federal grant money to build a $2.7 billion high-speed rail line from Orlando to Tampa that President Obama and many Floridians wanted. (See Chapter 9.) Scott and his supporters thought the project was wasteful, inefficient, and would be underutilized, thus putting the State of Florida on the hook for major building and operating expenses in the future. Critics pointed out that the federal money would just go to other states and would not save taxpayers a dime, and that private business would take the risk of the additional building and operating expenses. Critics also pointed out that the State of Florida typically pays much more in taxes than it receives in grant money from the federal government, and that the high speed rail line would have created thousands of construction and service jobs to build and operate the system. Some legislators were so angry that they filed a lawsuit to try to force the governor to change his mind. It did not work.

Scott and the Republican-dominated legislature had a somewhat strained relationship even though both were from the same party. In the end, Scott presided over one of the most ideologically conservative sessions in Florida history. The GOP legislative leadership was sympathetic to many of Scott's economic goals, but also aware of what was possible in a tight budget year from a political perspective. In the end, they passed a budget that was about $4 billion dollars less than the previous year's and did not raise taxes. However, they were able to cut taxes marginally with a small reduction in the number of businesses that would have to pay the corporate income tax. They approved a sales tax holiday for school shoppers and a rollback of property taxes collected by the Water Management Districts. They cut K-12 education spending by about $500 per pupil, funds for Medicaid to provide health care for poor families and children and numerous other programs. They tied teacher pay to student test scores, required welfare recipients to submit to random drug tests (Scott, on his own, ordered state employees to do the same), mandated that women seeking abortions pay for and view an ultrasound of the fetus before termination of pregnancy, threatened to fine doctors who asked their patients about gun ownership, changed election laws that some said would lower voter registration and turnout among young and minority voters, and abolished most state oversight of local government land use and development decisions. In turn, a number of citizens and groups filed lawsuits against many of these new laws in the hopes that a court would strike them down as unconstitutional.

Whether because of the budget cuts, conservative social policy, or the bad economy, Florida citizens gave Governor Scott the lowest approval rating, 29 percent, of any governor in the country just four months after he was sworn in. (His approval rating was just three points higher than the lowest rating of any Florida governor in the past 30 years—Bob Martinez, who hit 26 percent in his first year.) Scott's initial response was that he was not seeking to be the most popular, but rather to do what he said he would do— make hard choices that can no longer be avoided. However, while he remained focused on job creation throughout his first term, Governor Scott did undergo a style and policy "makeover" as he moved into his third and fourth years and sought re-election.

Governor Scott began to speak to a wider variety of groups and cultivate the traditional media. Where Governor Scott once opposed Obamacare, he said he would support Medicaid expansion to bring coverage to low income Floridians (although he switched back to opposing expansion after getting re-elected). After arguing loudly for a harsher policy against illegal immigrants during his first campaign, he ignored the illegal immigration issue for the remainder of his term. After cutting K-12 education funding in his first session, he touted the record overall amount that was being spent in his fourth session and promised if re-elected he would increase education spending to record per-pupil levels. After pushing job creation at the expense of growth management, he began to advance a variety of environmental initiatives. And where once he bragged about budget austerity after his first year in office, he began bragging about passing the largest budget in Florida history during his fourth year in office. These changes and the improving economy pulled Governor Scott's approval ratings up to the low 40s by his fourth year.

Ultimately, Governor Scott was able to squeak by former Governor Charlie Crist by about 1 percent and win a second term despite never getting over 50 percent in approval ratings. In fact, his four year average approval rating is the lowest of any Florida governor since tracking began. Governor Scott's victory can be attributed to several factors. First, the national electoral cycle worked in his favor as President Obama approval ratings were low. Historically the president's party does poorly in the sixth year of a president's term. And it was true that Democratic turnout sagged in 2014 compared to 2008 and 2012. Second, Governor Scott had a huge monetary advantage over Crist. While the actual donations to the official campaigns were fairly close, the Republican Party of Florida and outside groups (including Scott's own Let's Get to Work) enabled the Scott "team" to outspend Crist by about a 2:1 margin. Scott's funds included a $12 million infusion from his own personal account the last week of the campaign that proved to be critical. Third, the Florida economy had improved over the four years of Scott's term with more jobs created, a rising economic growth rate, and more revenue raised for the state. Finally, while Crist was arguably the best candidate Democrats could field, he was hampered with high negative public approval ratings (about the same level as Governor Scott) and saddled with the image that he was a flip flopper who switched political parties out of personal ambition rather than a desire to help Floridians.

Although Gov. Scott is term limited, he may have other political ambitions. He continues to raise and spend large amounts of money through his political committee and seems to be veering to the right politically now that he has been safely re-elected. He continues to focus on attracting jobs to Florida and stimulating economic growth by cutting taxes and reducing regulations. As governor of the nation's largest swing state, Scott's profile is also rising because the early 2016 presidential race features four Florida Republican candidates—Jeb Bush, Marco Rubio, Mike Huckabee, and Dr. Ben Carson. Early on in the race, Gov. Scott attracted a lot of national media when he played host to an Economic Summit featuring seven GOP presidential candidates. While the governor said his primary goal was to elect a Republican president, others were already speculating it was about a future run for office.

THE GOVERNOR'S BUDGET

The budget is the most important single policy statement of any government. It sets forth what the government proposes to do in the coming year and how much it will cost. The Florida Constitution (Article IV) provides that the "Governor shall be the chief administrative officer of the state responsible for planning and budgeting for the state." It requires the governor to submit an annual balanced budget to the legislature after receiving agency budget requests and holding at least one public hearing on the budget. However, Article VII gives the legislature the final responsibility to enact appropriations: "No money shall be drawn from the treasury except in pursuance of an appropriation made by law." Nonetheless, the General Appropriations Act passed each year by the legislature usually reflects the Governor's Budget Recommendations fairly closely. Indeed, the governor is constitutionally entitled to line-item veto specific expenditures that he opposes. A two-thirds vote in both the House and Senate is required to overturn a veto, a very rare occurrence under normal circumstances.

The Budget Process

The state budget process is outlined in Figure 7-4. Each state agency starts with a base budget of current positions and dollars authorized in the previous General Appropriations Act (GAA). Agencies are obliged to prepare their Legislative Budget Requests (LBRs) almost a year in advance of the beginning of the state's fiscal year, which begins July 1 and ends June 30. This requirement allows time for the Governor's Office of Policy and Budget (OPB) to review, and in most cases reduce, the agencies' requests. The governor then formally recommends a budget to the legislature.

Figure 7-4. Florida's State Budget Process: Major Actors & Time Table

Governor/ Office of Policy and Budget and the Legislature	State Agencies	Governor/ Office of Policy and Budget	Legislature	Governor/ Office of Policy and Budget
• Provide Instructions to Departments for: ○ Long-Range Program Plan ○ Legislative Budget Request ○ Capital Improvements Program Plan ○ Information Technology Plan	• Prepare Long-Range Program Plan • Prepare Legislative Budget Request • Prepare Capital Improvements Program Plan • Prepare Information Technology Plan • Prepare Internal Operating Budget	• Review/Analyze: ○ Long-Range Program Plans ○ Legislative Budget Requests ○ Capital Improvements Program Plans ○ Information Technology Plans • Hold Public Hearing • Develop Recommendations Based on Governor's Priorities and Available Revenues	• Prepare Appropriations Act • Review Governor's Recommendations • Review/Analyze/ Revise Budget • Appropriations Act Passed by Both Houses	• Governor may Line Item Veto Specific Appropriations • Governor Signs Budget into Law • Create Agency Operating Budgets from General Appropriations Act
May - July	**May - October**	**September - January**	**December - May**	**May - July**

Source: Governor's Budget from http://letsgettowork.state.fl.us/overview.aspx.

The Appropriations Process

The final Governor's Budget Recommendations must be sent to the legislature 45 days before the regular session begins in March. The budget is initially considered by the House and Senate Appropriations Committees, both of which hold extensive hearings with input from interest groups, lobbyists, the governor's staff, agency representatives, and occasionally individual citizens. Committee staff play an important role in writing the General Appropriations Act (GAA). The Constitution requires that the GAA be presented to each house of the legislature 72 hours before a vote on passage, presumably to limit a once-common practice of slipping in appropriations items that legislative leaders hoped would pass unnoticed. Like all legislation, if the House and Senate pass different versions of the GAA, the differences must be resolved by a conference committee and the final version voted up or down by each chamber. The Constitution also specifies that appropriations in excess of $1 million must be itemized so that the governor can veto any single item without affecting other items in the budget. The governor has 15 days following enactment of the GAA to exercise his vetoes. As noted earlier, he is often urged by tax savings groups such as Florida TaxWatch to veto "turkeys" in the budget, but just as often, he is urged not to by legislators and benefactors back home, each wanting to preserve their cherished items which they view as "essential" to their community.

Even with all the headaches that come with the job, lots of Floridians would love to become governor. It is a title one carries for a lifetime. As most former governors say, "It is the best job in politics."

Florida's governors have a very nice office suite in the state Capitol.
Left: The entrance to the office of the Governor and Lt. Governor.
Right: The spacious waiting room inside the office suite.

ONLINE SOURCES FOR DATA AND INFORMATION UPDATES

Florida's Governor

The online home of the state's chief executive has "News, initiatives, executive orders, appointments and office links."
http://www.flgov.com/

Florida's Attorney General

The State of Florida features reports from the office of the Attorney General on crime/justice.
http://www.myfloridalegal.com/

Florida's Chief Financial Officer

The Florida Department of Financial Services provides finance-related news and resources, as well as information about the organization of the department.
http://www.myfloridacfo.com/

Florida's Secretary of Agriculture and Consumer Services

The Florida Department of Agriculture and Consumer Services offers information about its divisions and offices, a variety of publications, and forms for individuals and organizations.
http://www.freshfromflorida.com/

The Florida Cabinet

This is the official site of the state's executive branch, with historical records of Cabinet meetings, an overview of the Cabinet, and descriptions of the primary boards and commissions.
http://www.myflorida.com/myflorida/cabinet/

Florida Board of Executive Clemency

The Office of Executive Clemency page contains explanation of clemency and its types, historical data on sentences commuted since 1980, and answers to frequently asked questions.
https://www.fcor.state.fl.us/clemency.shtml/

Florida TaxWatch: Budget Turkeys

Florida TaxWatch identifies "budget turkeys" and keeps a scorecard for how many TaxWatch "turkeys" the governor vetoed.
http://www.floridataxwatch.org/researchareas/TURKEYS.aspx

Florida Department of State: Florida Governors

The Florida Department of State's portraits and brief biographies of all Florida governors.
http://dos.myflorida.com/florida-facts/florida-history/florida-governors/

Chapter 8. Courts, Crime, and Corrections

State courts are powerful "political" institutions because they seek to resolve many of the most important conflicts in society. This is especially true in Florida, where the Florida Court System exercises some powers even beyond those exercised by federal courts in the U.S. court system. For example, the Florida Supreme Court can deny a place on the ballot to a citizen initiative if the Court determines that it covers multiple topics or that it fails to provide an accurate descriptive title (see Chapter 2). And the Florida Supreme Court, unlike federal courts, can render advisory opinions to the governor and legislature. Occasionally, the state and federal court systems clash as they did on the 2000 presidential election and the Terri Schiavo cases.

The Florida Supreme Court building is stately in its appearance.

The Florida Constitution vests the "judicial power" in the Supreme Court and the Florida Court System (Article V). According to former Florida Supreme Court Chief Justice B.K. Roberts:

> The judicial power is, essentially, the authority of a judge to decide, according to the law, controversies of which the law takes notice, and to secure the enforcement of the decision rendered. We commonly say that the judicial power is the power to administer justice; and that "equal justice under the law "is the supreme object of all courts which perform their proper function.[1]

More specifically, judicial power in Florida includes the power to interpret the Constitution and laws of the State of Florida. All state courts, including Florida's, are obliged by the Supremacy Clause in the U.S. Constitution (Article VI) to be bound by the Constitution and laws and treaties of the United States. The judicial power exercised by the Florida Court System includes the power of *judicial review* of the laws of Florida to determine if they conform to both the Florida Constitution and the U.S. Constitution. The Florida Supreme Court has the final authority to determine the meaning of the Florida Constitution and to decide whether laws passed by the state legislature, as well as county and municipal ordinances, are in conformity with it. State laws that the Florida courts rule to be in conflict with the Florida Consti¬tution are "null and void."

While the Florida Supreme Court can also interpret the meaning of the U.S. Constitution and can strike down Florida laws that violate it, most "federal questions" are decided in federal courts. In the rare instances that the Florida Supreme Court decides a "federal question," the decision may be appealed to the Supreme Court of the United States. Most of the cases that move from the state court system to the federal court system involve the 14th amendment to the U.S. Constitution (equal protection under the law; due process).

The interiors of Florida's old (left) and new (right) Supreme Court facilities are both very elegant.

What's Different about the Judicial Branch?

The judicial branch, like the legislative and executive branches, ends up "making" public policy by their rulings. But what is different about *judicial decision-making* is that it is:[2]

- Passive (courts rarely initiate policy decisions).
- Governed by special rules of access (through cases filed by an accusing party—the plaintiff).
- Bound by different types of procedures (writs, motions, written briefs, oral arguments).
- Limited in scope (the decision is for the specific case at hand).
- Expected to be objective (judges must not appear to base their decision on partisan considerations, to bargain, or to compromise in decision making).

Florida's Court System

Article V of the Florida Constitution establishes a four-tiered court system. (See Figure 8-1.) The top two tiers are the *appellate courts* (Florida Supreme Court, District Courts of Appeal). The lower two tiers are the *trial courts* (Circuit Courts, County Courts). Decisions at the appellate level are made by judges; decisions at the trial court level, by juries unless otherwise requested by the defendant. In recent years, Floridians have been mostly satisfied with the performance of Florida's court system, although few rate the performance as excellent. (See Figure 8-2.)

Appellate court-level justices and judges are selected/elected via a merit-retention process (discussed later in the chapter). Trial court level judges are elected via nonpartisan elections. They do not run with a political party label after their name. There are no term limits on judges. Judges at all levels are subject to mandatory retirement at age 70, although some judges may serve a little longer depending on when their birthday falls during their final term.[3] The legislature sets judicial salaries. Supreme Court justices make about $162,200 a year, district judges $154,140, and trial court judges $146,080. While judges sometimes complain about their salaries, Florida's salaries for its judges and justices (all four levels) are competitive with other states. Of the 50 states, Florida's Supreme Court, district courts, and trial courts rank about 26th, 21st, and 24th, respectively.[4]

To be eligible for judgeships, one must have been a member of the Florida Bar Association for a certain period of time. For appellate-level judges, it is 10 years. For circuit court judges and county court judges in counties with populations larger than 40,000, it is at least 5 years. However, in counties smaller than 40,000, a county judge must simply be a member of the Bar. There are also residency requirements. Judges must be residents of the county, circuit or district in which they preside. At least one Supreme Court Justice must come from each of the five appellate court districts.

Figure 8-1. The Florida Court System

Appellate Courts	Trial Courts
Supreme Court	**20 Circuit Courts**
7 Justices	599 Judges
	(Number of judges per circuit based on caseload)
Sit in Tallahassee (5 Justices constitute a quorum;	Preside individually
4 Justices necessary to render a decision)	
6 year terms	6 year terms
Selected by merit plan	Selected by nonpartisan election
	(Interim appointment by governor for vacancies)
5 District Courts of Appeal	**67 County Courts**
64 Judges	322 Judges
	(At least one judge in each of the 67 counties)
Cases reviewed by three-judge panels	Preside individually
6 year terms	6 year terms
Selected by merit plan	Selected by nonpartisan election
	(Interim appointment by governor for vacancies)

Source: Florida Supreme Court, 2014. The number of judges for district, circuit, and county courts reflect that authorized by the Florida Legislature as of 2014.

Figure 8-2. Rating the Performance of Florida's Court System

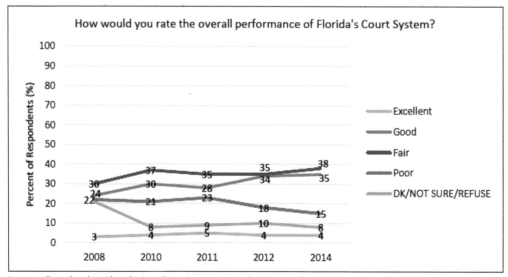

Source: "Leadership Florida Sunshine State Survey (2006-2008), Leadership Florida-Nielsen Company Sunshine State Survey (2010-2012), and University of South Florida-Nielsen Sunshine State Survey (2014)."

The Florida Supreme Court

The Florida Supreme Court, also known as the court of last resort, has both *appellate jurisdiction* (reviewing decisions of lower courts) and *original jurisdiction* (hearing a case first). It has constitutionally mandated jurisdiction to hear appeals from any lower court that declares a state law unconstitutional and to hear appeals of the death penalty. It also has <u>mandatory</u> appellate jurisdiction under state statute on questions concerning bond validation and public utility cases (see Figure 8-3). It has <u>discretionary</u> appellate jurisdiction to review any other decisions by the state's District Courts of Appeal and even intervene in lower courts to expedite decisions "of great public importance." It sets the rules of conduct for judges and attorneys which the legislature can only repeal by a two-thirds vote of its membership. It also oversees the disciplining of judges and attorneys by the Judicial Qualifications Commission.

The Florida Supreme Court also has *original jurisdiction* when the issue at hand involves some rather unique situations. The Court has the authority to issue four types of writs:[5] w*rit of prohibition*—to prevent an action; *writ of mandamus*—to compel performance of a public duty that the petitioner has a right to have performed; *writ of quo warranto*—to determine by what authority one holds office or presumes to act; and the *writ of habeas corpus*—to obtain the release of any person allegedly wrongfully deprived of liberty.

Unlike the U.S. Supreme Court or the federal judiciary, the Florida Supreme Court may be required to render an *advisory opinion* if asked to do so by the governor or the attorney general. The Florida Constitution specifically authorizes the governor to request advisory opinions regarding the interpretation of the Constitution relevant to gubernatorial powers and duties. Also unlike the U.S. Supreme Court, by tradition, the Chief Justice of the Florida Supreme Court serves for two years and the position then rotates to the member serving the longest who has not been Chief Justice.

Figure 8-3. Jurisdiction of Florida Courts

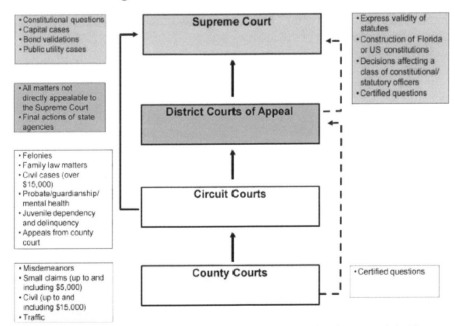

Note: A visual representation of the jurisdiction boundaries within the State of Florida Court System.

Source: Florida Supreme Court, 2015. Available at: http://www.floridasupremecourt.org/pub_info/system2.shtml.

District Courts of Appeal

Florida's five District Courts of Appeal (Tallahassee, Lakeland, Miami-Dade County, Palm Beach County, and Daytona Beach) have appellate jurisdiction over all trial courts. In most instances, cases arise from the Circuit level, but *certified questions* can come directly from the County Courts. A *certified question* is a formal request by one court to one of its sister courts for an opinion on a question of law. DCAs have jurisdiction on all matters not directly appealable to the Supreme Court and on final actions of state agencies. Appeals are usually heard by rotating *three-judge panels*, although occasionally decisions of great magnitude may be heard *en banc* with all of a specific District Court's eligible judges participating. In most cases, the decision of a District Court of Appeal is final because most requests for further review by the Florida Supreme Court are denied. District appeals courts can also issue the same four types of writs as the Florida Supreme Court (appellate jurisdiction). The Florida Legislature sets the number of judges per appellate district. The term of office is six years. There are no term limits.

Circuit Courts

Florida's 20 circuit courts have original jurisdiction in felony[6] criminal cases and civil cases in which the amount in dispute exceeds $15,000. These courts conduct trials and carry the principal burden of administering justice in the most serious cases in the state. In addition to civil and criminal divisions, there are also divisions for family law, probate, and juveniles. A *civil case* is one "brought by a private individual to enforce a private right." In a civil case, the prosecutor and the defendant are both private individuals. A *criminal case* involves an "offense punishable by a governmental body."[7] In criminal cases, the government is the prosecutor and the individual charged is the defendant.

While most cases heard by circuit courts are heard first at that level (original jurisdiction), circuit courts do have appellate jurisdiction in that they may hear appeals from the county courts. They, too, can issue any one of the four types of writs. The number of judges per circuit court is set by the Florida Legislature. Circuit courts serving larger populations are assigned more judges. Circuit court judges have six-year terms. Each circuit court has a Clerk of the Circuit Court—an elective post. The county sheriff serves as the executive officer of the circuit court of the county.

County Courts

Under the Florida Constitution, each of the state's 67 counties has a county court. These courts hear criminal misdemeanor[8] cases, simple divorce cases, and civil cases involving not more than $15,000. In addition to civil and criminal divisions, county courts also have a traffic division for adjudicating accidents and citations and a small claims division for litigants who want to represent themselves in civil disputes over small amounts of money. County courts hear the most cases of any type of Florida court and have the most interaction with average Floridians. County judges are elected for six-year terms. There are no term limits.

Court Reforms

The current Florida Court System was established by constitutional amendment in 1972, largely through the efforts of former Florida Supreme Court Justice B.K. Roberts. The amendment completely revamped the former court system, which was a confusing, complex, and cluttered system. In fact, under the old court system, "Florida had a greater variety of trial courts than any state except New York."[9] A variety of city courts, justices of the peace, and county courts operated throughout the state, often levying traffic fines against tourists in order to help fill local treasuries. Now all fines are forwarded to the state, reducing the local incentive to create "speed traps." (As of 2015, it is illegal for localities to have ticket quotas for their law enforcement officers.) After voters accepted Constitutional "Revision 7" in 1998, the state became responsible for funding almost the entire court system, although counties still provide courtroom space.

It is not uncommon for proposed court reforms to come from the legislature. In 2011, several Republican lawmakers filed a bill to split the Florida Supreme Court into separate criminal and civil divisions. The proposal stemmed from the Court's removal of several legislatively proposed constitutional amendments from the ballot in 2010. (See Chapter 2.) Supporters of the proposed reform argued it would be more efficient, while critics complained that it is just an effort to "pack the court" with new conservative Republican-appointed justices. While the bill did not pass, debate over the idea itself has continued.

Many courts in Florida have heavy caseloads, often involving persons for whom English is a second language. In Orange County, Court Administration Interpreter Services are provided to the Criminal Divisions in the Circuit, County, Juvenile, and Traffic Courts as well as to Child Support Hearings and Mental Health Hearings.

Workload

Floridians are involved in over 2.7 million civil filings a year in circuit and county courts. (See Figure 8-4.) A number of these are civil traffic infractions involving a judge or hearing officer. Two million more traffic infractions are processed by the county court system each year that do not involve an actual hearing. Many civil filings are lawsuits filed against other Floridians, businesses, or corporations, with the active encouragement of the state's 80,000-plus eligible lawyers.[10] The judicial system also handles about 850,000 criminal cases ranging from simple misdemeanors at the county level to serious felonies at the district level. Cases may be initially filed in either county courts or circuit courts depending on the severity in criminal cases and the amount at stake in civil cases. These are the state's "trial courts," which initially hear all cases in the state system. In trial courts, judges and/or juries weigh the facts of the case, as presented in an adversarial process, and determine guilt or innocence in a criminal trial or negligence in a civil trial. The circuit court also reviews about 280,000 family filings (divorces, custody, adoption, etc.) and over 110,000 probate filings to settle the affairs of the deceased.

The Florida Supreme Court and the state's District Courts of Appeal, with few exceptions, hear only appeals from the decision of the trial courts. As appeals courts, they read briefs filed by opposing council, hear oral arguments, and are primarily concerned with questions of law and how the law has been applied to the actual facts of the case. The District Court of Appeals handles thousands of filings for appeal, while the Florida Supreme Court reviews about 2,500 filings, of which about 100 are mandatory reviews.

JURIES

The Florida Constitution guarantees a trial by jury. There are two types of juries: trial (petit), and grand. *Petit juries*, seated to hear cases in trial courts, determine the guilt or innocence of the accused. *Grand juries* (larger) have two primary functions—investigation and indictment.

Trial (Petit) Juries

Under Florida law, the number of jurors on a trial jury varies by type of case. Civil cases require a six-person jury. The exception is an eminent domain case (involving the taking of a person's land) in which case there must be a 12-person jury. A criminal case punishable by death requires a 12-person jury, while any other criminal case requires a six-person jury. The verdict in a criminal case must be unanimous.

Grand Juries

A grand jury is made up of 15 to 21 persons. It "investigates crimes, hears testimony, and receives evidence in secret before determining whether to issue an indictment."[11] Twelve grand jurors must concur in order to issue an indictment.

Juror Qualifications and Selection

In Florida, jurors must be at least 18 years old, a legal resident of the state, and have an address in the county in which they are called to jury duty. Contrary to popular opinion, jurors' names are selected from Florida driver's license lists, not from voter registration lists (as they once were).

Juror Disqualifications and Exemptions

Not everyone is eligible to serve on a jury in Florida. Those who may not serve include a person who: has been convicted of a felony, unless their civil rights have been restored; is currently being prosecuted for any crime—felony or misdemeanor; is the governor, lieutenant governor, a Cabinet officer, a clerk of the court or a judge; or has an interest in the case (a conflict). Some citizens may be excused from jury duty if they request it: law enforcement officers and investigators; expectant mothers and parents not employed full time who have children younger than six; full-time students; persons 70 or older; those responsible for the care of an incapacitated person; and persons for whom service would be a hardship.[12]

While many Floridians try to avoid jury duty, studies show that those who serve end up feeling more positive about the court system than their fellow citizens who do not serve.[13]

Some Floridians still believe that jurors are selected from voter registration lists and subsequently do not register to vote to avoid jury duty. In fact, jurors are pulled from driver's license lists.

Figure 8-4. The Workloads of Florida's Courts

APPELLATE COURTS		TRIAL COURTS	
Supreme Court		**20 Circuit Courts**	
Total Filings	2,521	Total Filings	770,840
Mandatory Review Filings	112	Criminal Filings	176,768
Discretionary Review	1,013	Family Filings	281,168
Original Proceedings	1,396	Other Civil Filings	198,858
		Probate Filings	114,046
5 District Courts Of Appeal		**67 County Courts**	
Total Filings	24,861	Total Filings	2,831,304
Criminal Appeals	14,647	Criminal Filings	669,554
Civil Appeals	6,102	Civil Filings	2,161,750
Workers' Compensation	231		
Other Appeals and Petitions	3,881		

Sources: Circuit and County Court statistics from Florida Office of the State Courts Administrator, FY 2013-14 Statistical Reference Guide, available at http://www.flcourts.org/core/fileparse.php/541/urlt/reference-guide-1314-chp2.pdf; Supreme Court statistics from Florida Supreme Court (data for 2014). Available at http://www.floridasupremecourt.org/pub_info/documents/caseload/2014_Florida_Supreme_Court_Caseload.pdf; District Court of Appeals statistics from The Office of the State Courts Administrator, 2013-2014 Annual Report. Available at http://www.flcourts.org/core/fileparse.php/248/urlt/annual_report1314.pdf.

OTHER IMPORTANT JUDICIAL ACTORS

In addition to the justices, judges, and jurors, there are a number of other players that are crucial to the judicial system's smooth operation. There are judicial nominating commissions to screen applicants for judgeships and make recommendations to the governor. A judicial qualification commission performs an oversight role on judges once they are in office. The Office of the State Courts Administrator helps keep records for, and provides information on, the court system as a whole. Each county has a clerk of court to handle administrative duties for the court system within the county. Each circuit has an elected state attorney to prosecute criminal acts and a public defender to provide legal representation to poor criminal defendants. Last but not least, there is the Florida Bar Association, which governs all the practicing Florida lawyers who must belong.

Judicial Nominating Commissions

According to the Florida Constitution, a separate judicial nominating commission (JNC) is required for the Supreme Court, each district court of appeal, and each judicial circuit, for a total of 26 JNCs. Each judicial nominating commission looks over applications for judicial vacancies that arise for their level of the court system. (The circuit-level JNCs also review applications for county court judge vacancies.) Each JNC then submits a list of three to six names of qualified nominees to the governor within 30 days of the announcment of the vacancy. The governor then has 60 days to make the appointment. Governor Charlie Crist rejected a list of nominees from the 5th District Court of Appeals JNC asking that they submit another list with more minorities on it. When the JNC re-submitted the same list, the governor did not make an appointment. Ultimately, the Florida Supreme Court ruled that the Florida Constitution mandates that the governor must make the appointment within 60 days and has no authority to reject the list or extend the time period.[14]

The Florida Constitution also requires that a uniform set of procedures be established for the JNCs at each level and leaves the composition of the judicial nominating commission up to the legislature. Originally, the judicial nominating commissions were made up of three members selected by the Florida Bar Association's Board of Governors, three appointed by the governor, and three lay persons chosen by the other members. However, in 2001, following the controversial 2000 presidential election in Florida, with the rulings by the Florida Supreme Court favoring Democrat Al Gore, the legislature changed the process. Now the selection of each nine-member judicial nominating commission is more directly under the control of the governor. This move came about in reaction to what the Republican majority saw as an activist judiciary controlled by liberal Democratic-appointed judges who sought to thwart the conservative agenda promoted by the GOP-controlled legislature and governor.

Judicial Qualification Commission

Florida's judges have very limited accountability to the electorate. For that reason, the state's 15-member Judicial Qualifications Commission (JQC) plays a very important role in overseeing the judiciary. Constitutionally, the JQC is comprised of six judges (two each from the district courts of appeals, the circuit courts, and the county courts), four members of the Florida Bar, and five lay persons. The commission is constitutionally charged with the responsibility to "investigate and recommend to the Supreme Court the removal from office of any justice or judge whose conduct... demonstrates a present unfitness to hold office," as well as to recommend reprimands and other disciplinary actions. The JQC is structured between an investigative panel that acts as a prosecutor and a hearing panel that acts like a panel of judges reviewing a case. Commission proceedings are confidential prior to bringing formal charges so that unfounded complaints will not besmirch a judge's reputation. After the Florida Supreme Court receives the JQC's recommendations it may accept, modify, or reject them. Over the years, the JQC, through the

Supreme Court, has reprimanded, fined, suspended or removed numerous judges. (See Up-Close: When Good Judges Go Bad.)[15]

County Clerk of Court

Each county elects a Clerk of the Circuit Court for a four-year term. The office of the clerk performs a wide range of record keeping, information management, and financial management functions in the judicial system and county government. One Florida study found that clerks were charged with some 1,000 different tasks.[16] In most Florida counties, the Clerk is not only Clerk of the Circuit Court, but also the County Treasurer, Recorder, Auditor, Finance Officer, and Ex-Officio Clerk of the County Commission.

Office of the State Courts Administrator

The Office of the State Courts Administrator was created in 1972 to develop a uniform case reporting system. The system is designed to collect and analyze information on activity in the judiciary to be used in preparing the court's operating budget and to estimate the need for more judges and specialized court divisions. The State Courts Administrator serves under the direction of the Florida Supreme Court Justices and is responsible for overseeing the operation of numerous court programs, initiatives, and administrative functions. The State Courts Administrator also serves as the liaison between the court system and the legislative branch, the executive branch, the auxiliary agencies of the court, and national court research and planning agencies.

State Attorneys and Public Defenders

State attorneys, as well as public defenders, serve in each of the state's 20 circuit courts. They are elected for four-year terms. The *state attorney* is responsible for conducting grand jury investigations and prosecuting criminal cases. The *public defender* is responsible for defending accused persons who are unable to afford an attorney. Most actual trial work is done by assistant state attorneys, many of them fresh out of law school, seeking courtroom experience and personal contacts. Historically, state attorney posts have been stepping-stones to higher political office in the state. Public defender offices are considered to be at a disadvantage relative to state attorney offices. Public defender offices usually have fewer resources and greater difficulty in recruiting top notch lawyers to do public defense work. It does not help that the public has a tendency to hold public defenders in low esteem since they represent accused criminals who are often found guilty of high profile crimes that citizens find reprehensible (e.g., sexual molestation of children).

Florida Bar Association

Only members of the Florida Bar Association may practice law in Florida courts. However, nonmembers may practice in federal courts in Florida. Admission to the Florida Bar is based upon background investigations and written examinations given to graduates of law schools anywhere in the nation. Out-of-state law school graduates generally take special prep courses to prepare for the Florida Bar exam. The Florida Bar Association is empowered to reprimand, suspend, and in extreme cases "disbar" lawyers for unethical practices. Over 80,000 lawyers are eligible members of the Florida Bar – about 63 percent are male and 37 percent are female.[17]

UP-CLOSE: WHEN GOOD JUDGES GO BAD

Judges are supposed to conduct themselves in a way that inspires the public to have confidence in the judges, the court system, the trials, and the decisions. This applies to their conduct inside and outside the courtroom. Specifically, Florida judges are supposed to follow seven judicial Canons:[a]

1. A Judge Shall Uphold the Integrity and Independence of the Judiciary.
2. A Judge Shall Avoid Impropriety and the Appearance of Impropriety in all of the Judge's Activities.
3. A Judge Shall Perform the Duties of Judicial Office Impartially and Diligently.
4. A Judge Is Encouraged to Engage in Activities to Improve the Law, the Legal System, and the Administration of Justice.
5. A Judge Shall Regulate Extrajudicial Activities to Minimize the Risk of Conflict With Judicial Duties.
6. Fiscal Matters of a Judge Shall be Conducted in a Manner That Does Not Give the Appearance of Influence or Impropriety; etc.
7. A Judge or Candidate for Judicial Office Shall Refrain From Inappropriate Political Activity.

Almost all judges have a track record of exhibiting good behavior—they would not have won election or been appointed if they had not. But when people believe that judges are acting badly and not following the canons, they can file a complaint with the Judicial Qualifications Commission (JQC). The JQC investigative panel confidentially looks into the accusations. The panel brings formal charges if they believe the evidence supports the accusations. The charges lay out the specific complaints and the specific canons that have been violated. If the JQC hearing panel finds the judge in violation, then it recommends a sentence to the Supreme Court which has the final say. Penalties include admonishment, public reprimand in front of the Supreme Court, imposition of a fine and/or court costs, suspension from the bench, removal from office, or dismissal of the charges. Multiple penalties may be, and often are, applied to the same case.

Since 2001, the JQC has closed disciplinary cases against 57 judges. Only one judge received a dismissal without qualification—the equivalent of a "not guilty" verdict (but the case lasted 18 months and involved over 50 filings before the JQC was satisfied that no violation had occurred). Two others received dismissals with strings attached: one issued a written apology and the other agreed to take anger management classes. Only one judge received the lightest slap on the wrist—a written admonishment by the Supreme Court to be more careful about *ex parte* communication (discussing a case outside of the courtroom). The most common penalty (34 judges) was a public reprimand requiring the judge to go in person to Tallahassee, appear before the Supreme Court, and actually receive a verbal tongue lashing from the justices in open court. Nine judges were ordered to pay fines (the largest was $40,000) or court costs (more than $8,500 in one case) or both. Four judges received suspension from duty ranging from two weeks to four months. Three judges were given involuntary retirement due to serious medical issues that made it impossible for them to continue to serve. Finally, 16 judges lost their jobs because of their conduct: 6 were directly removed from office and 10 others either resigned or were defeated for re-election while their case was still in progress. Their resignation or defeat prompted the charges against them to be dismissed.

What did these judges do to earn these charges and punishments? Eighteen engaged in bad behavior outside of the courtroom (intervening to have a friend released from jail, entering the locked office of another judge, demeaning other judicial officers in public, extravagantly spending money on a new courthouse and furnishings). Twelve judges engaged in improper campaign activity (failing to report $200,000 in campaign contributions, misrepresenting an opponent or themselves in campaign literature, taking large illegal campaign donations). Fifteen exhibited bad behavior that impacted activities in the courtroom (habitually late to trials and hearings, *ex parte* communication, imprisoning 11 traffic defendants for failure to appear even after being told that the defendants had been directed to the wrong courtroom by court personnel, having a close personal relationship with the prosecuting attorney during a death penalty case). Eleven judges repeatedly used abusive or inappropriate speech (demeaning comments to witnesses, intemperate behavior towards counsel, threatening messages to the Bar Association). Four judges were guilty of sexual harassment (unwanted sexual advances to a student, habitual viewing of pornography on the courthouse computer). Four others became involved in improper relationships of a personal or financial nature, including one with a stripper, another with a drug abusing felon, one a romantic interlude with a lawyer appearing before the court, and one with a bailiff. Finally, five judges had drug or alcohol related problems (public intoxication that led to a whole host of infractions—inappropriate conduct of an intimate nature, prowling and attempted forcible entry, and making a material false statement to the police; several with driving under the influence with one also in possession of cannabis and drug paraphernalia; and another who took the bench while impaired).

Most judges follow the canons of judicial ethics. But when judges go bad, the JQC is there to mandate corrective actions, dish out punishment, or remove the judge from the bench altogether. The Florida Supreme Court has the final say.

Notes:
ªThe canons are available at http://www.floridasupremecourt.org/decisions/ethics/index.shtml.
ᵇData on charges and penalties from 2001-2011 collected by Hannah Jewett, Historian of the Paul J. Hagerty High School 2010-11 Law Society, Seminole County Florida; subsequent data collected by the authors. All data from the Judicial Qualifications Commissions archives: http://www.floridasupremecourt.org/pub_info/jqcarchives.shtml.

Trial Lawyers

The Florida Association of Trial Lawyers is a very powerful group that often flexes its political muscle in state politics. The group can easily raise millions in campaign contributions for candidates who support the Association's positions on various legal issues. In recent years, no issue has mobilized the trial lawyers more than tort reform. A tort "involves an injury to a person or to property caused intentionally or through someone's negligence." Usually, the plaintiff (the person who filed the lawsuit) is suing for money damages to compensate the plaintiff for a loss.[18] Doctors, corporations, and state and local governments have pressed state lawmakers hard for tort reform, hoping to reduce the number of frivolous lawsuits they assert are causing undue and unfair financial and professional burdens. Specifically, these groups have pushed for changes in liability laws, such as capping the award for "pain and suffering," eliminating punitive damage awards, restricting lawyer fees, adopting "loser pays" laws, and ending the rule of "joint and several liability." Not surprisingly, the trial lawyers have vigorously fought these reform efforts. They argue that every person is entitled to his or her "day in court"—the right to seek justice, including compensation for damages incurred by the wrongful acts of others. And they argue that tort liability—responsibility for "pain and suffering" incurred by a civil wrongdoing—protects everyone from harmful activities and products, thereby making society safer. The clash between the trial lawyers association and the Florida Medical Association came to a head in 2004 when each group placed constitutional amendments on the ballot articulating their position. (Voters passed them all!)

The tort reform battle is far from over in spite of the fact that the Florida Legislature eliminated the doctrine of "joint and several liability" in its 2006 session. "Joint and several" liability allows a plaintiff to collect the entire court award from any party that contributes to their loss regardless of that party's degree of fault. Opponents of it argue that it is grossly unfair to make a party with a limited degree of fault bear the entire cost of a judgment simply because of its "deep pockets." Proponents defend it, believing that it allows injured parties to be fairly compensated without burdening the taxpayers who otherwise might have to pick up the tab for health care, rehabilitiation, or long term care. In 2011, business groups applauded the passage of two more tort reform bills.[19] Florida now allows the introduction of evidence relating to the driver's condition at the time of an automobile crash when that driver is suing an auto manufacturer over the "crashworthiness" of the vehicle. Before the change, Florida was the only state in the nation that prohibited the introduction of such evidence. The other reform bill grants immunity to businesses and individuals who voluntarily provide housing and shelter to first responders during natural disasters.

In 2014, the Florida Supreme Court ruled the $500,000 to $1,000,000 caps on pain and suffering for medical malpractice cases passed by the legislature in 2003 were unconstitutional. The ruling was a blow to those calling for more tort reforms.

JUDICIAL SELECTION IN FLORIDA

Florida uses two different methods to select judges and justices. Trial court judges are selected by nonpartisan election; appeals court judges and justices are selected through the Merit Retention System (also known as the Missouri Plan after the first state to adopt it). Merit retention for appellate level judges and justices was adopted by Florida voters in 1976 following a series of judicial scandals that brought into question the competency and legitimacy of the judiciary in a very public way.[20] Two Supreme Court Justices were accused of criminal misconduct, resigned, and were disbarred; another was publicly identified as suffering from alcoholism by the Judicial Qualifications Commission; and still another was required by the commission to undergo psychiatric treatment.[21] Prior to 1976, Florida's judicial elections were partisan and competitive.

Merit System: Appointment and Retention Election

Supreme Court Justices and District Court of Appeals Judges in Florida are selected by the merit system—a hybrid system that combines appointment and election. Here is how it works: when a vacancy on the Florida Supreme Court (or District Court of Appeals) occurs, Floridians interested in serving apply to a Judicial Nominating Commission. The JNC reviews the applications, narrows the list down to between three and six names, then submits those names to the governor.

The governor then selects the new justice from that list. In the next general election (but at least more than one year following the appointment), the new justice's name goes on the ballot so that the voters can decide whether the new appointee should be given a full six-year term. The ballot only poses this question to voters: "Shall Justice _____ be retained in office?" The choices are "Yes" or "No." No opponent is listed on the *judicial retention ballot*, nor is the justice's party affiliation listed. In the unlikely event that a majority of voters say no, the nominating process starts over again. However, this has never happened in Florida. So for most justices, their name is again submitted to the voters for a merit retention vote every six-years. Supreme Court Justices and District Appeals Court judges can continue to serve as long as they are retained until they face mandatory retirement at age 70. (If a justice turns 70 after the first three years of a six-year term, they may serve until the end of the term.) Table 8-1 lists the current Florida Supreme Court Justices, their first year of appointment, and their next scheduled retention election and mandatory retirement date.

Table 8-1. Justices of the Florida Supreme Court

Justice	Appointed	Governor Appointing	Law School	Date of Birth	Term Expires	Mandatory Retirement*
Barbara Pariente	1997	Chiles	GW	1948	2019	2019
R. Fred Lewis	1998	Chiles	Miami	1947	2019	2019
Peggy Quince	1998	Chiles & Bush	Catholic	1948	2019	2019
Charles Canady	2008	Crist	Yale	1954	2017	2024
Ricky Polston	2008	Crist	FSU	1956	2017	2029
Jorge Labarga	2008	Crist	UF	1952	2017	2023
James Perry	2009	Crist	Columbia	1944	2017	2017

Note: * Mandatory retirement date for judges who are eligible for retention assumes the justice is retained in future elections.

Source: Compiled by the authors from Florida Supreme Court website.

Four justices face mandatory retirement on or before January of 2019. If Governor Scott were to make all the replacements, he would be able to shift the balance of the court in a conservative direction and thus impact Florida politics long after he leaves office. Currently the court has a majority of moderate to liberal justices that have acted as a check to a number of conservative policies and actions taken by the Republican legislature and governor. However, at present it is unclear whether Gov. Scott or his successor will appoint the new justices who will replace the three that are slated to retire in 2019. Technically, their terms will expire at the exact moment as Governor Scott ends his term of office, unless they choose to step down earlier. The last time this scenario occurred outgoing Governor Chiles (D) and incoming Governor Bush (R) made a joint appointment—of Justice Peggy Quince. Anticipating that the same situation could occur in 2019, the Republican legislature proposed a constitutional amendment making it clear that the *outgoing* governor should make the appointments. Florida voters disagreed. The amendment failed (2014). Opponents of the proposed amendment had argued that the *incoming* governor should make the choices. That way, voters would be able to hold the newly-elected governor responsible for his or her appointments if that governor ran for re-election.

Florida voters have never ousted a Supreme Court Justice or a District Court of Appeals judge on a merit retention vote. Although Supreme Court Justices on occasion have been targeted because of particular decisions they made, all have been retained. For example, Justices Rosemary Barkett and Leander Shaw, came under attack from the National Rifle Association and several pro-life groups for being soft on criminal defendants and liberal on abortion issues.[22] More recently, three justices up for retention (Peggy Quince, Barbara Pariente, and Fred Lewis) were targeted by some conservative groups for being too liberal and legislating from the bench. The conservatives were upset that a few years earlier the Court had kept a proposed anti-"Obamacare" amendment off the ballot for its lack of clarity. (Florida is the only state that gives its highest court the right to remove a proposed constitutional amendment from the ballot if it is not clearly worded or addresses multiple subjects.) But that effort failed as all three justices were retained by the voters. Although Florida voters have yet to reject a justice or judge, it is important to note that giving citizens the right to vote on retention helps keep judges within the mainstream of Floridians' political attitudes.

Nonpartisan Judicial Elections: Low Information Contests

Circuit court and county court judges are elected to six-year terms (county court judges used to be elected to four-year terms). Both circuit and county judges run in nonpartisan elections, meaning that no party label appears after their name on the ballot. Candidates running for these judicial posts are not supposed to engage in *partisan* political campaigns or advertising. They do campaign and promote their candidacies via advertisements, although the content of the ads is restricted. Prohibited are statements about how they would rule in certain situations. While voters expect their judges to be apolitical and objective, the limited information they get about judicial candidates is frustrating. Some voters in this situation simply skip over the judicial contests.

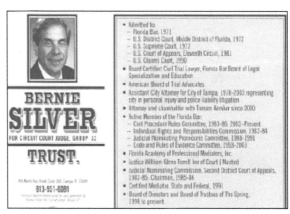

Florida law greatly restricts the content of political advertising by nonpartisan candidates for county and circuit judgeships. Most judicial candidates stress their legal credentials, training, experience, law firm, community involvement, professional memberships, and integrity. Voters feel such information is not very helpful to them in deciding which judicial candidate to vote for since most of the ads seem to be highly similar.

Interim Appointments

When vacancies occur in between elections, the governor makes an interim appointment from a list of three or more names supplied by a Judicial Nominating Commission. As a practical matter, most sitting judges actually got their position initially through an interim appointment by the governor. And, of course, governors are inclined to appoint judges of similar political party or political philosophy. After the interim appointment term expires, the sitting judge has the advantage of being the incumbent in the subsequent election. Being an incumbent increases the appointee's probability of winning the election since judicial elections are such low visibility affairs and incumbents have higher name recognition than challengers. Being an incumbent also deters opposition. Potential opponents are hesitant to run. They know that if they lose, they may have to face the judge in court when representing a client.

Governors, Judicial Appointments, and Diversity

Gubernatorial appointments have a higher profile in Florida than in many other places, primarily due to the state's diverse population, its political competitiveness, and the priority governors have placed on diversity. In 2001, the Florida Legislature strengthened the hand of governors by giving them the power to appoint *all* members of the state's Judicial Nominating Commissions. These commissions submit nominee lists to the governor who, in turn, appoints one from the list to the bench.

An analysis of gubernatorial appointments of circuit court judges from 2005 through 2008 (the last two years of the Jeb Bush administration and the first two years of the Charlie Crist administration) found that a majority of female gubernatorial appointments came when new judgeships were created by the legislature to meet growing caseloads. The same study found that governors are more likely to appoint racial/ethnic minority females to a vacancy, thereby achieving greater gender and minority diversity with the same appointment. For example, in one year, 35 percent of Governor Bush's 17 female appointees were racial/ethnic minorities (4 Hispanics and 2 African Americans). In contrast, just 11 percent of his 45 male appointees were minorities (4 Hispanics and 1 African American).[23]

A more recent study of judges in Florida showed that Governor Scott in his first term appointed a lower percentage of blacks but a higher percentage of women than either Bush or Crist (and a higher percentage of Hispanics than Crist but lower than Bush). Under Scott, the Judicial Nominating Commissions that review and forward a short list of judicial nominess to the governor have become less diverse. Overall, about 84 percent of all Florida judges are white, 9 percent are Hispanic, and 7 percent are black.[24]

Florida's current Supreme Court justices are quite diverse.
Back row (L-R): Ricky Polston, Peggy Quince, Charles Canady, James E.C. Perry.
Front row (L-R): Barbara Pariente, Chief Justice Jorge Labarga, R. Fred Lewis.

The Pros and Cons of Electing Judges

Three arguments are often given *for* electing judges. First, one can argue that electing judges is more democratic than appointment; a process that is good enough to elect governors and legislators is good enough to elect judges. Second, having to run for office keeps judges more accountable to state residents and ensures that judicial decisions are in line with the prevailing value system of the citizens served by the court. Third, and perhaps most importantly, Floridians like to elect their county and circuit judges. A constitutional initiative placed on the ballot in 2000 to select trial judges through the merit plan was defeated in every single county and judicial circuit in Florida.

There are an equal number of plausible reasons why judges should *not* be elected. One is that judges should base their decisions on the law and the facts of the case in an unbiased fashion, without being influenced by campaign contributions or public opinion. Further, electing judges makes it difficult for minorites to become judges in a diverse state like Florida. Finally, it could be argued that without more information about a judicial candidate's background or an incumbent judge's record of decisions, voters are asked to make uninformed decisions.

In 1975, Joseph Hatchett became the state's first African American to serve on the Florida Supreme Court. Hatchett was appointed by Governor Reubin Askew.

Fundraising Limits on Judicial Candidates

The Florida Supreme Court's Canon 7C (1) of its Code of Judicial Conduct, provides that judicial candidates "shall not personally solicit campaign funds . . . but may establish committees of responsible persons to raise money for election campaigns." This rule was challenged by a judicial candidate from Tampa who mailed and posted online a letter soliciting financial contributions to her campaign for judicial office. The Florida Bar disciplined her for violating a Florida Bar Rule requiring candidates to comply with Canon 7C (1). She contended that the First Amendment protects a judicial candidate's right to personally solicit campaign funds in an election (the money is speech argument). The case was ultimately decided in 2015 by the U.S. Supreme Court (*Williams-Yulee* v. *Florida Bar*). In the majority opinion, Chief Justice Roberts wrote: "Judges, charged with exercising strict neutrality and independence, cannot supplicate campaign donors without diminishing public confidence in judicial integrity. Simply put, the public may lack confidence in a judge's ability to administer justice without fear or favor if he comes to office by asking for favors."[25]

Who Serves on the Bench?

Historically, Florida's judges were predominantly white, wealthy, middle-aged, male Democrats. Few women or minorities went to law school. Both of these situations have changed. Consequently, the courts are becoming more diverse in terms of gender, ethnicity, and party leanings (although judicial posts are nonpartisan).[26] In 1985, Governor Bob Graham appointed Rosemary Barkett to the Florida Supreme Court, making her the state's first female Supreme Court Justice. In 1975, Governor Reubin Askew appointed Joseph Hatchett as the first African-American justice to the Florida Supreme Court. In 1976, Hatchett became the first minority to win a statewide election in Florida when he ran successfully for a full term. In late 1998, Governor Lawton Chiles and Governor-elect Jeb Bush together appointed Peggy Quince as the first black woman Supreme Court Justice. When Quince joined Barbara Pariente and African American Leander Shaw on the court, it marked the first time there were two women and two blacks on the Florida Supreme Court. When Jeb Bush appointed Raoul Cantero to the bench in 2002, the Florida Supreme Court had its first Hispanic justice.

It is not just the highest court whose judges have become more diverse. Overall, about 33.5 percent of Florida judges are women which is the second highest rate in the country behind only Massachusetts (the national average is 29.2 percent).[27] Over 15 percent of state judges in Florida are minorities, placing it near the top 10 stes in terms of judicial diversity.[28] Currently, the Florida Supreme Court has four white justices, two black justices, and one Hispanic justice. Five are men and two are women. The picture on the previous page shows the diversity of Florida's Supreme Court in 2015.

Across the U.S., interest in becoming a judge has escalated, perhaps because of the emphasis law schools place on the judiciary, the esteem accorded judges and justices, and the experience students get while serving as law clerks. Recruitment efforts and election-related seminars sponsored by women and minority lawyer associations have also contributed to higher candidacy rates and electoral successes, particularly at the trial court level.

The gap between women and men serving on the bench is narrowing. The gains by women have occurred for a number of reasons: (1) a growing pool of female law school grads and practicing attorneys; (2) greater interest among women in serving on the bench; (3) higher female candidacy rates and electoral successes at the trial court level; (4) more strategic decisions by women on when and where to run and who to run against; and (5) their improved odds of being tapped by a governor for a prized appointment when a vacancy occurs.[29]

Can a Non-Citizen Be Admitted to the Bar?

In 2014, the Florida Board of Bar Examiners requested an advisory opinion on whether Jose Manuel Godinez-Samperio, the son of undocumented immigrants, could be admitted to the Florida Bar because he was not a citizen. The young man had come to the United States from Mexico at age 9 with his parents on a tourist visa, stayed after they left to continue his schooling, graduated with honors from the FSU law school, and passed the Florida Bar exam. The Supreme Court ruled him ineligible but noted that the state could allow eligibility to the young man if the state legislature enacted a law to that effect which it did. On November 2014, Cuban-born Chief Justice Jorge Labarga, who fought hard to have the law passed, officiated at the ceremonial swearing in of Godinez-Samperio to the Florida Bar.

CRIME IN FLORIDA

Crime is an issue that always seems to be on the minds of Floridians. It is not at all surprising in light of the state's age profile (older voters are the most fearful for their own personal safety), its large transient population, and loads of politicians who stand ready to use the issue in their campaigns. From the late 1980s through much of the 1990s, Floridians identified crime as "the most important problem" facing the State of Florida. (See Chapter 3.) While the issue's ranking has slipped as the crime rate has declined, the Federal Bureau of Investigation's *Uniform Crime Report* shows that Florida had one of the nation's highest overall crime rates over most of the last two decades. The *overall crime rate* is the number of serious crimes, violent and property, divided by the resident population. The *violent crime rate* is the number of serious violent crimes divided by the state's total resident population.

Reported Crime

FBI crime reports are based on figures supplied by state and local police agencies. The FBI has established a uniform classification for serious crimes: *violent crimes* (crimes against persons) include murder and non-negligent manslaughter, forcible rape, robbery, and aggravated assault; and *property crimes* (crimes committed against property only) include burglary, larceny, arson, and theft, including auto theft. But one should be cautious in interpreting official crime statistics. They are really a function of several factors: (1) the willingness of people to report crimes to the police; (2) the adequacy of the reporting system that tabulates crime; and (3) the amount of crime itself. The only two crimes that appear at the same rate as the officially reported figures are murder and car theft. All other types of crime are typically underreported.

Around one million persons are arrested in Florida each year and about 8 percent of these arrested persons are juveniles. Of the crimes reported in 2014, 86.5 percent were non-violent crimes, and 13.5 percent violent crimes.[30] Some $1.2 billion in property was reported stolen with less than $300 million recovered. Fewer than 1,000 murders occurred in the state that year, although that is still a disconcerting figure. Domestic violence crimes are tracked separately. The bulk of those crimes generally are for simple and aggravated assault.

Non-Serious Crimes

The FBI's *Uniform Crime Reports* actually understate the true crime rate in another way as well because there are five times as many arrests for non-serious as for serious crimes. Yet, the FBI does not include the so-called "non-serious crimes" in its crime rate index. Ironically, the non-serious crimes like drug violations, prostitution, sex crimes, gambling, fraud, forgery, driving while intoxicated, and liquor law violations are seen as "very serious" by the victims, even devastating. They are also what make some citizens identify crime as one of the state's most serious problems.

Explaining Florida's High Crime Rate

There are numerous explanations for Florida's high crime rankings over the last two decades. These include:

- *Climate*. In northern states, crime rates typically decline in the winter and rise in the summer. However, since Florida is relatively warm year-round, crime flourishes year round.

- *Demographics*. Florida leads the nation in the percent of its population that are senior citizens, and older people are more likely to be victims of crime because they are considered easy targets as age and ill health makes them easier to rob and less likely to fight back. Florida also has a large and growing population of young people in the crime-prone 15-24 age group.

- *Growth*. Florida is a constantly growing state with a population that is always churning. Growth leads to neighborhoods which might more accurately be called "strangerhoods." In such settings people do not know each other and often fail to look out for each other. This type of environment does not do much to prevent criminal behavior.

- *Urbanization*. Florida is a highly urbanized state (ranked seventh). Urban areas are much more likely to have higher incidences of crime than rural areas. In rural areas, residents often know and watch out for each other. In urban areas, residents usually mind their own business. Further, packing people together into densely-populated geographies encourages and creates more opportunities for criminal behavior.

- *Drugs*. Florida is a major drug conduit for the rest of the country with its long coastline, many ports, and proximity to Latin America's drug-producing cartels and gangs. Much crime in Florida is drug-related and involves the transporting, controlling, and/or selling of drugs inside and outside the state.

- *Tourism*. Florida is the top tourism destination in the country. Tourists are prime targets for thieves, as they often carry cash and are easy prey in hotels and at rest stops as they are often unfamiliar with their surroundings.

- *Statistics*. Florida's high crime rate ranking is at least partially a product of how the statistic is calculated. The rate is expressed as crimes per 100,000 population. The key word to focus on is population. Because Florida has millions more visitors on any given day than most states, the actual number of people in Florida is much higher than the official Census population figure shows. Thus, Florida's crime rate would drop if the number of crimes would stay the same but be divided by a larger number of people in the state at any one time.

Trends in Florida's Crime Rate

Crime rates in Florida have fluctuated considerably over the years. (See Figure 8-5.) Florida's overall crime rate peaked at 8,938 (crimes per 100,000 population) in 1988 and its violent crime rate in 1992 at 1,200 (crimes per 100,000 population). Both the overall and violent crime rates have declined by about 60 percent from their peaks. By 2014, the state's violent crime rate stood at 467 and its overall crime rate at 3,451—the lowest rates in 40 years. Coinciding with the reduction in crime, the public's perception of the job that the state does in prosecuting criminals has improved gradually, with the percent of Floridians giving "poor" ratings falling from 25 percent in 2008 to 18 percent in 2014. (See Figure 8-6.)

Figure 8-5. Crime in Florida: Trends

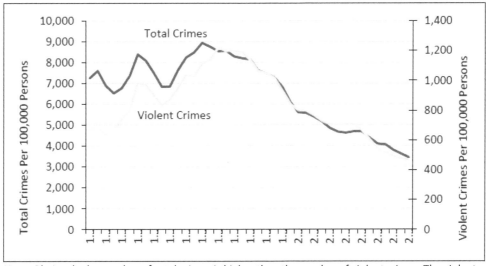

Note: Obviously the number of total crimes is higher than the number of violent crimes. The violent crime and total crime measures are drawn to different scales. The purpose is to show how the trends in these two statistics track with each other.

Source: Florida Department of Law Enforcement website, *Florida Crime Trends*.

Figure 8-6. Floridians' Perception of State's Prosecution of Criminals

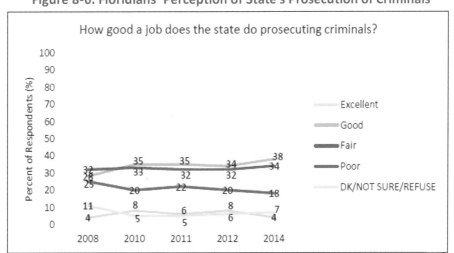

Source: "Leadership Florida Sunshine State Survey (2006-2008), Leadership Florida-Nielsen Company Sunshine State Survey (2010-2012), and University of South Florida-Nielsen Sunshine State Survey (2014)."

Criminologists and other social scientists have offered different explanations for the rise and fall in crime rates. One explanation is generational. The rapid rise in the 1970s was widely attributed to the "Baby Boomers" who, at the time, were in the most crime-prone age group (15-24). Crime rates appeared to level off somewhat in the early 1980s, when this age group was older. But then, in the late 1980s, crime rates unexpectedly soared upward again. The new factor in the equation appeared to be the widespread popularity of crack cocaine and the drug violence that accompanied it. According to some researchers, as the crack epidemic subsided and the population aged, crime rates went down. Other researchers have suggested that the economy impacts crime rates with a strong economy reducing crime and a bad economy "forcing" people into crime because they cannot find a legitimate job. This explanation has little support as the crime rate has continued to drop, even during the tough economic times that began in 2007.

What else accounts for the progress in the fight against crime in Florida and the nation since 1990? Law enforcement officials attribute decreases in crime rate to police "crackdowns," more aggressive "community policing," longer (and more prevalent) mandatory minimum sentences for certain crimes (gun-related) or types of criminals (repeat felons), and requirements for those convicted to serve a higher percentage of their sentence. In support of this claim, law enforcement officials note that the greatest reductions in crime have occurred in the nation's largest cities, especially those like New York City that have adopted tougher law enforcement practices. However, by the mid-2010s high profile incidences of police corruption and brutality pushed some to question the "toughness" approach. The pendulum began slowly swinging away from rigid punishment philosophies back toward rehabilitation. Before this redirection effort, the state had passed many stringent anti-crime laws.

Juvenile Crime

Like adult crime rates, juvenile crime rates have also declined at a steady pace in Florida since the early 1990s. (See Figure 8-7.)[31] Since 1995 (the high point), the rate of referrals per 1,000 population age 10-17 has dropped 65 percent. Juvenile offenders are primarily male (75 percent) and disproportionately minorities (50 percent African American and 14 percent Hispanic). Referral rates are higher among older children, especially those in their mid-teens. For example, in fiscal year 2014, only 623 five to ten-year-olds were referred compared to 9,445 eleven to thirteen-year-olds and 45,316 fourteen to seventeen-year-olds. In that year, 44 percent were referred for misdemeanors (theft and assault, marijuana, disorderly conduct, tresspassing), 33 percent for felonies (burglary, aggravated assault, grand larceny, non-marijuana drug crimes, auto thefts and the more serious crimes of armed robbery, sexual battery, attemped murder, and murder), and 23 percent for "other" violations (probation violation, previously deferred prosecution, contempt). Those who committed the most serious offenses were transferred to adult court (1,832 in fiscal year 2014). Because a juvenile arrest record, even for nonviolent offenses, can haunt an individual in adulthood, there has been a push for less permanent alternatives, like civil citation programs or participation in similar diversion programs, as a consequence for childhood mistakes.[32] The governor signed such a bill in 2015. It authorizes a law enforcement officer to issue a warning to a juvenile who admits having committed a misdemeanor or to inform the child's parent or guardian of the child's infraction. It also permits a law enforcement officer who does not exercise one of these options to issue a civil citation or require participation in a similar diversion program.[33]

Guns and Crime in the "Gunshine" State

Article I, Section 8 of the Florida Constitution gives people the right to "keep and bear arms in defense of themselves." The Florida Constitution clearly establishes that the right to keep and bear arms is an *individual* right. It is much more precisely written than the Second Amendment to the U.S. Constitution. As written, the U.S. Constitution's second amendment has sparked heated debates over whether the national right to bear arms is a collective right tied specifically to "a well-regulated militia" or an individual right.

The U.S. Supreme Court settled the argument more recently with a pair of decisions that reaffirmed that the Second Amendment is an individual right.[34]

Gun politics is always evident in Tallahassee since the National Rifle Association is a strong lobbying group in Florida and there are millions of gun owners in the state. Florida's Constitution gives the legislature the power to regulate the "manner of bearing arms" and specifically requires a three-day waiting period for the purchase of a handgun. In 1987, the legislature passed a law ("right to carry") making it easier to get a concealed weapon permit. Over 1.3 million Floridians now have one.[35] A debate has ensued over whether the large number of concealed guns has contributed to the state's high violent crime rate overall or to the downward trend in crime rates that began a few years after passage of the "right to carry" law.[36] The debate did not stop Governor Scott from signing a bill that allows Floridians who do not have concealed weapon permits to carry concealed firearms when evacuating due to a disaster.[36] Not everyone was in favor of the bill. Floridians remain somewhat divided on gun laws. While 43 percent of Floridians think the level of restrictiveness of Florida's gun laws is about right, 46 percent think the laws are not restrictive enough. (See Figure 8-8.)

Figure 8-7. Delinquency Referrals in Florida per 1000 population (Population Age 10 to 17)

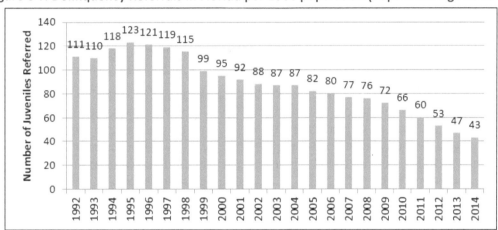

Source: Florida Department of Juvenile Justice Delinquency Profile.

Figure 8-8. Few Floridians Perceive State's Gun Laws as Too Restrictive

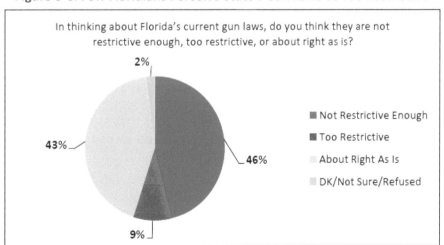

Source: Leadership Florida Sunshine State Survey (2006-2008), Leadership Florida-Nielsen Company Sunshine State Survey (2010-2012), and University of South Florida-Nielsen Sunshine State Survey (2014).

Two other widely debated gun laws passed the Florida Legislature in 2005—the "Castle Doctrine" and the "Stand Your Ground" law. The Castle Doctrine defines a person's home as their "castle," and permits them to use deadly force against an intruder to defend it. The law was later expanded to include a person's vehicle. One of the first persons to take advantage of the law was an elderly woman who shot and killed a man who forcefully entered her home.

Florida became the first state to adopt a Stand Your Ground law. A majority of other states have done so since. The Stand Your Ground law allows Floridians to use deadly force if they reasonably believe they are facing a deadly threat (or great bodily harm or a forcible felony). It removes a traditional duty to retreat first before using deadly force. If a defendant invokes the Stand Your Ground defense, a judge holds an evidentiary hearing (before the actual trial) to see if the law applies. If the judge decides that it does, then the accused receives immunity from criminal and civil prosecution. The debate over Stand Your Ground laws hit a fever pitch in the aftermath of George Zimmerman's acquittal for the shooting death of Trayvon Martin. (Zimmerman's attorney did not actually invoke the Stand Your Ground defense, but it sparked a national debate and protests in Florida nonetheless.) Critics of the law argue that it will lead to people taking the law into their own hands, increased gun violence, and racial bias. One study of Florida Stand Your Ground cases found disparities based on the race of the victim. Killers of blacks went free 73 percent of the time while those who killed whites went free only 59 percent of the time. The study noted that most of the racial differential could be explained by higher incidences of gun possession and in-progress criminal activity among black victims. The study also found that white defendants were just as likely to be charged and convicted as black defendants.[37]

Florida's lack of gun control laws have earned it a top 10 ranking as a "Best State for Gun Owners" for a number of years and the "Gunshine" State nickname.[38] In addition to the laws discussed above, the NRA has pushed for "open carry" laws that would make it legal in most circumstances to carry a weapon out in the open. A watered down version prohibiting prosecution for accidental disclosure of a weapon did pass. The NRA also backed a controversial law that forbids doctors from routinely asking their patients about gun ownership and safe gun storage (Docs versus Glocks)—typically asked by pediatricians concerned about children. A group of doctors sued the state to declare the law an unconstitutional violation of the doctors' free speech rights and won at the Circuit Court level but then lost at the Circuit Court of Appeals.[39] Florida forbids local government from adopting more stringent gun control laws than the state, prohibits firearm registration, makes it quite easy to open up a backyard gun range even in urban and suburban areas, and does not require a permit to own a gun.

Keeping Floridians Safe and Protecting Their Privacy

A key function of government is to keep citizens (and their privacy) safe from criminals. Most Floridians feel that the state does at least a fair job ensuring public safety. Fewer Floridians believe the state does a good job protecting individual rights and privacy. (See Figures 8-9 and 8-10.) This discrepancy comes as rapid advances in technology expose people to new forms of exploitation. Some of these incidents, including using airborne drones to photograph people on private property without their consent, could be classified as only potentially harmful. A bill signed by Governor Scott in 2015 made such unauthorized photography illegal, even if done by government (utilities and property appraisers are exempt).[40]

Other modern forms of invasion of privacy are inherently malicious. In 2015, the Florida Legislature took steps to address the growing problem of individuals sharing sexually explicit content without consent, including "revenge porn,"[41] to intentionally cause emotional distress.[42] More alarmingly, Florida has ranked as high as third in the nation in recent years in human trafficking reports. Human trafficking does not necessarily involve movement of people, but refers to modern-day slavery in which U.S. citizens and immigrants, alike, are forced to work in sex, tourism, personal services, and other industries. State law enforcement officials believe that "human trafficking is thriving here because the state is a destination for tourists, transients, runaways, migrant workers, and organized crime."[43]

Personal safety and privacy issues have become a subject of great debate in law enforcement, a field marked by recent high-profile cases of alleged police brutality and even unjustified shootings. Critics of Florida law enforcement agencies' tactics cite that "the number of fatal police shootings has tripled in the past 15 years, even as crime has plummeted."[44] They argue that the police can do no wrong in the eyes of the courts, and suspicion of cover-ups abounds as law enforcement agencies conduct internal investigations. As tension between police and the communities they serve mounts, both reformers and law enforcement officers want more transparency which is why the idea of body cameras worn by the police has been so appealing. Body cameras are used in an effort to bring hard evidence to cases involving allegations of improper force, although the implementation has created other privacy concerns.[45]

Another issue contributing to the seemingly growing distrust of law enforcement is the unpopular use of red light cameras. Recipients of citations from red light camera programs have fought, winning big in some cases, to have their citations dismissed. In a 2015 Broward County ruling, judges determined that use of red light cameras violates state law by delegating too much authority to vendors, and 24,000 pending citations totaling over $6.3 million were dismissed.[46] Following this and other similar rulings, governments continuing to use the cameras have acted to move the operations in-house. Red light camera critics claim that the programs have been pursued with the intention of generating revenue, rather than promoting safety. That assertion may be supported by the fact that, as citations and, consequently, revenues have fallen in some jurisdictions, governments have acted to end their contracts and discontinue the programs. The vendors explain that their goal is to reduce violations, which naturally leads to reduced revenues.[47]

Even if red light camera programs prove to be unsustainable, safety and privacy concerns stemming from cultural events and enhanced by technological advancements are now a permanent fixture of the law enforcement landscape. If agencies wish to repair damaged relationships with communities and maintain their public images, they will need to carefully address technological opportunities and challenges with programs that are legally sound and consistently enforced.

The damaged citizen-police relationship problem is not one-sided. Law enforcement officers say a growing anti-cop sentiment is making their jobs more dangerous on the streets. They and their families worry about the increase in attacks on them, the repercussions of defending themselves, public humiliation, and the lack of support from elected officials in the event of a protest-gone-violent and viral in the media. They even worry about the availability of "apps" that allow criminals to see exactly where they are hiding. In some high crime areas, there have already been slowdowns in arrests, officer resignations, and recruitment difficulties. Morale has worsened, which saddens many law-abiding officers. "Most get into this line of work for their love of their community. Nobody goes into law enforcement wanting to be hated," says the CEO of the Law Enforcement Research Group.[48] The situation poses big challenges to government officials who are responsible for protecting the public. They do not want to see any increase in constituents' feelings of being unsafe in public places or worries about the invasion of their individual rights or privacy. (See Figures 8-9 and 8-10.)

Figure 8-9. Floridians Mostly Satisfied with Safety in Public Places

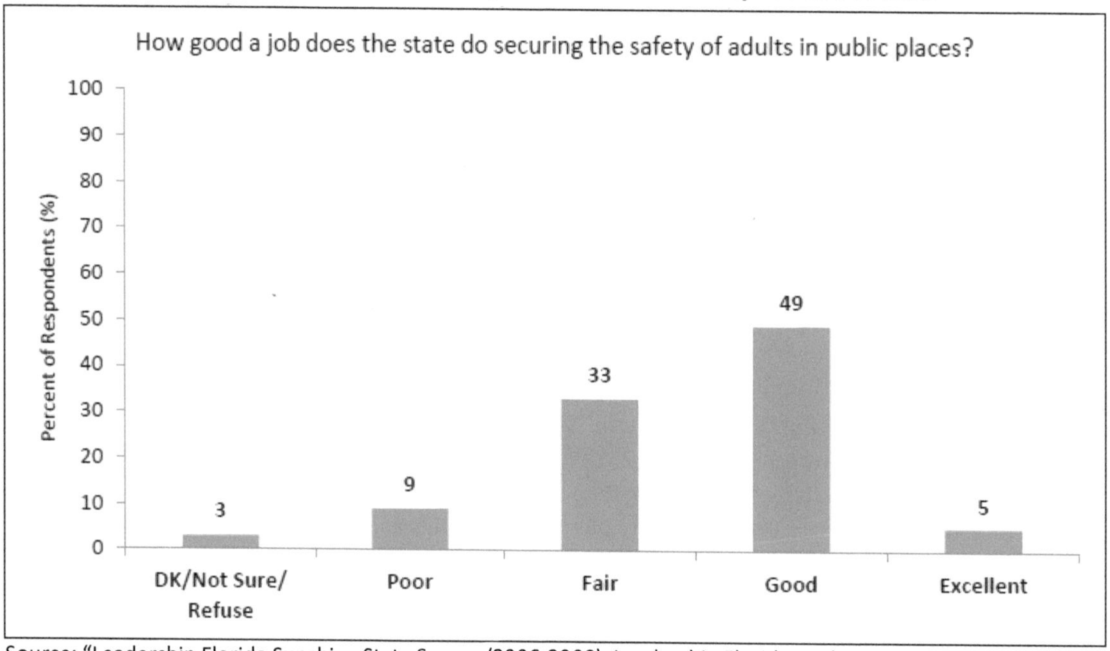

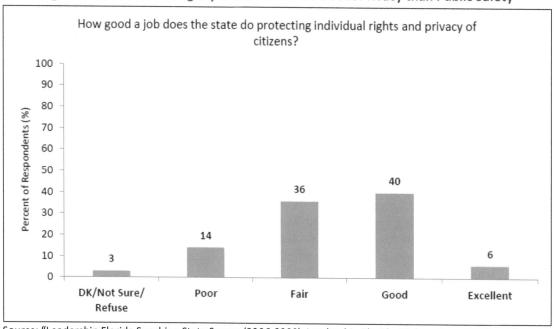

How good a job does the state do securing the safety of adults in public places?

Source: "Leadership Florida Sunshine State Survey (2006-2008), Leadership Florida-Nielsen Company Sunshine State Survey (2010-2012), and University of South Florida-Nielsen Sunshine State Survey (2014)."

Figure 8-10. Floridians Slightly More Concerned about Privacy than Public Safety

How good a job does the state do protecting individual rights and privacy of citizens?

Source: "Leadership Florida Sunshine State Survey (2006-2008), Leadership Florida-Nielsen Company Sunshine State Survey (2010-2012), and University of South Florida-Nielsen Sunshine State Survey (2014)."

CORRECTIONS

Florida's prison population grew very rapidly in the 1990s and 2000s (See Figure 8-11.), growing by 20 percent just between 2005 and 2010. However, that growth has slowed in recent years. In 2014, Florida housed about 100,873 inmates in 71 corectional institutions and prison annexes, 64 work camps and release centers, and 7 road and other prisons.[49] An additional 146,000 offenders were under community supervision including regular probation, drug offender probation, community control, and pretrial intervention. *Probation* is a court-ordered term of community supervision under specified conditions for a specific period of time that cannot exceed the maximum sentence for the offense.

The huge influx of prisoners in recent years has strained the Florida Department of Corrections budget, making it hard to hire and retain prison guards. A high profile investigation of what goes on behind the state's prison walls by an award winning investigative reporter revealed "well-documented and flagrant brutality that has been allowed to fester."[50] Outrage intensified as testimonies before state legislative committees revealed widespread corruption and atrocities—beatings, rapes, gassings, retaliations against whistleblowers, and corruption. Legislative inaction during a regular session (2015) pushed Gov. Scott to issue an executive order designed to clean up Florida's broken prison system. It requires a major overhaul of prison-related regulations, processes, and management: *"The steps outlined in today's executive order present a clear path forward for the Florida Department of Corrections. The Department's number one focus is the safety of Florida's correctional officers, communities and the inmates in state custody and supervision."*[51] No longer is prison reform just about saving money. It is also about saving lives and that means sharpening the focus on rehabilitation.

Figure 8-11. Crime Rate and Prison Population Trends in Florida

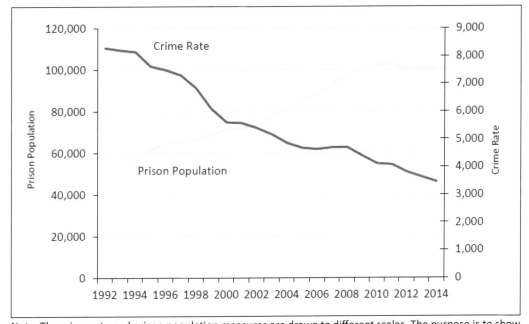

Note: The crime rate and prison population measures are drawn to different scales. The purpose is to show how the trends in these two statistics track with each other.
Source: Florida Department of Corrections, 2013-2014, Agency Statistics from the Florida Department of Corrections website.

Florida's Prison Population

Similar to the juvenile offenders, young black males make up a disproporionately large percentage of Florida's prison population compared to the African-American population overall (48 percent v. 17 percent). Approximately 46 percent of the state's inmates are 34 years of age or younger. However, the average age of inmates in Florida is increasing as inmates serve longer sentences. The growing number of aging prisoners is causing prison health care costs to rise at a sharp rate.[52] Only about 7 percent of Florida's prisoners are women.

Nearly half (46 percent) of all inmates are *recidivists*, that is, they served a prior sentence in the Florida prison system before their current admission. The recidivism rate has actually dropped slightly with more inmates serving longer sentences. But the recidivism rate is still unacceptably high for many Floridians. More of them think the state does a "poor" job rehabilitating ciminal offenders than think the job done is "fair", "good", or "excellent" combined. (See Figure 8-12.)

Figure 8-12. Floridians Are Critical of How Well State Has Rehabilitated Criminal Offenders

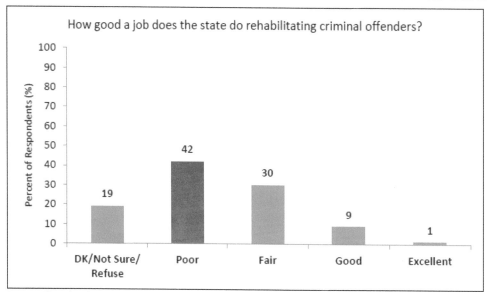

Source: "Leadership Florida Sunshine State Survey (2006-2008), Leadership Florida-Nielsen Company Sunshine State Survey (2010-2012), and University of South Florida-Nielsen Sunshine State Survey (2014)."

Incarceration Rate

Florida's incarceration rate was 524 prisoners per 100,000 population in 2013 which placed it in the top 10 among all states—a ranking it has held for many years.[53] Some of the increase in the prison population in the 2000s was due to the state's rapid growth rate over that decade; more people usually means more crime. But more of the increase in inmates over those years was due to Florida laws that stiffened punishment and did not allow parole for offeners who committed crimes after October 1983.[54] Over the past few years, Florida's prison population has leveled off somewhat. It is too early to tell if this trend will continue, but part of the explanation has been the steady drop in crime rates.[55]

Prison overcrowding can create serious legal and financial problems for states when lawsuits are brought against the prison system. Federal courts have determined that prison overcrowding may be a violation of the U.S. Constitution's Eighth Amendment prohibition of "cruel and unusual punishment."[56] When faced with the possibility of such a ruling, states have little choice other than to build more prisons or to give prisoners an *"early release."* During the 1980s and 1990s, many states opted to grant prisoners early release based on the amount of their sentence they had served, simply to make room for more prisoners.

Early releases, together with time off for good behavior, meant that most prisoners served as little as one-third of their mandated sentences in most states. When crime rates started rising, states then turned to building prisons. But when states began experiencing major budget shortfalls in the late 2000s, many, including Florida, began reconsidering their "lock'em up and throw away the key" policies.

Stop Turning Out Prisoners

Florida's prison-building program doubled statewide capacity over the past two decades. Under legislation known as STOP—Stop Turning Out Prisoners—the governor and the legislature mandated that all prisoners serve at least 85 percent of their sentenced time. Persons convicted after 1995 are now required by state law to serve 85 percent of their sentences. The rule does not apply to inmates convicted before that date. (The courts ruled such a retroactive action would be illegal because it would be an *ex post facto law*—changing the law and then applying it retroactively.) The effect of the law has been to substantially increase the length of sentences actually served in Florida. In 1991, the average offender served only one-third of his or her sentence—considerably less than the 85 percent required today. Department of Corrections' statistics show that prisoners, on average, are actually serving slightly more than 85 percent of their sentences.[57] However, inmates who are not serving life sentences are still awarded "gain time" based on good behavior, meritorious deeds, and educational achievement in prison. Gain time can be forfeited for violation of prison rules. Correction officials generally consider gain time a useful tool in prison management.

Mandatory Minimum Sentences

In Florida, the legislature passed two laws in 1999 at the urging of Governor Jeb Bush that require felons to serve longer prison sentences: the *10-20-Life law* and the *3 Strikes law*. Under 10-20-Life, a felon who uses a gun to commit a crime like armed robbery faces at least 10 years in state prison. If he or she shoots the gun, 10-20-Life increases the mandatory prison penalty to 20 years. If the armed robber shoots someone, the 10-20-Life law increases the mandatory prison sentence to 25 years-to-life. In addition, the Governor's office ran a high profile public service announcement campaign warning would-be criminals of the severe penalties for using a gun in Florida: "Use a gun, and you're done."

The 3 Strikes law mandates longer prison sentences for repeat felons. Under the 3 strikes provision, judges must give convicts the maximum sentence for a third felony. For example, the most severe penalty for armed robbery is life in prison, so a felony offender with three strikes would have to get a life sentence. The Florida Supreme Court ruled the law constitutional in 2004.[58]

There are contradictory claims as to whether the 10-20-Life and 3 Strikes laws have actually reduced Florida's crime rate. A report by the Department of Corrections concluded that the results of "10-20-Life" were impressive. Over a six-year span (1998-2004), 10-20-Life helped drive down violent gun crime rates by 30 percent statewide. Armed criminals robbed over 10,000 fewer people and killed 380 fewer Floridians than they would have had the crime rate remained the same as in 1998. The report noted that these crime rate reductions occurred even though the state's population had increased 17 percent over that period.[59] Another study came to the opposite conclusion—that laws like 10-20-Life and 3 Strikes had little effect on reducing the crime rate. That study found that there had been a greater drop in crime *before* the laws went into effect. Between 1994 and 1998, the years before the 10-20-Life and 3 Strikes laws were passed, crime had fallen by 16 percent, compared with a 13 percent decline between 2000 and 2004, the period immediately after the laws went into effect.[60] Whether the laws have had a direct effect on crime rates is still up for debate, but there is little doubt the laws have increased the state's prison population.

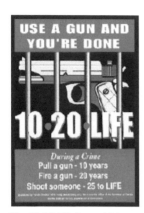 

The 10-20-Life law, which provides mandatory penalties for using a gun while committing a crime in Florida, has been widely publicized since its passage in 1999. At left is a poster that was put up all over the state and at right a billboard on the side of a well-trafficked street.

Parole and Life Sentences

Parole is a program that allows inmates to leave prison before the completion of their sentence under the supervision of the Department of Corrections. The number is relatively low. In 2014, only about 2,000 inmates were on parole in Florida; three-fourths were actually on parole from other states.[61] The legislature has eliminated parole for those committing non-capital felonies on or after July 1, 1984 and for capital felonies committed after October 1, 1995. Of the 100,884 inmates in Florida prisons in 2013, just 5 percent remained parole eligible. Only 22 (less than 0.1 percent) of the 33,137 inmates released from Florida prisons in FY 2012/13 were actually paroled.[62] The bottom line is that a prisoner sentenced to life in prison in Florida actually serves life in prison. In January 2014, there were some 12,501 of these "lifers" in Florida prisons (8,407 life without parole and 4,094 life with parole).[63]

More Prisoners, Less Crime

One explanation for the decline in national and state crime rates, is the increase in the prison population. The effect of longer sentences and larger prison populations is to incapacitate likely wrongdoers. There appears to be a close relationship between increases in the state's prison population and decreases in its overall crime rate (see Figure 8-5). Florida began a prison-building program in the 1990s that has doubled the number of prison beds.

The evidence is rapidly accumulating that the cost of housing criminals is far less than the cost of allowing them to roam the streets. In other words, prisons pay.[64] Taxpayers are understandably upset with the prospect of spending $50,000 to $75,000 for each new prison cell and $15,000 to $25,000 per year to keep a single prisoner behind bars. It costs $17,338 a year or $47.50 a day to feed, clothe, house, educate and provide medical services for an inmate at any state facility.[65] Those figures are destined to escalate as the health costs for aging prisoners rise. But if the costs of incarceration are weighed against its benefits to society, taxpayers may feel better about prison construction and maintenance. One study estimates the dollar value of crimes committed by the typical convict in a year prior to incarceration runs from $200,000 to $400,000, that is, 10 to 20 times the cost of a year's incarceration.[66] Such cost-benefit analyses often do not tell the full story—that of human costs.

While Florida's crime rate is falling, it remains 15 percent higher than the national average. According to a major analysis of Florida's crime rates and its correction system by the Florida TaxWatch Center for Smart Justice, "tough-on-crime policies are doing the state more harm than good."[67] More than 40 percent of those released from prison are re-arrested for another offense within three years of release.[68] Any calculation of the high human costs of the failure of prisons to rehabilitate inmates must include costs to the inmates, correction officials, individual citizens, and society at-large.

Prison Privatization

As of 2015, seven prisons were being privately operated in Florida by three different companies. During several recent legislative sessions, some lawmakers sought unsuccessfully to turn over the operations of 27 state prisons and work camps in an 18 county area in South Florida over to private companies. The primary reason given for privatization was to save money. Companies bidding on the contracts were required to show that their operation could yield at least a seven percent saving over what it would cost state workers to do the job. Opponents of privatization argued that even if a company promised such savings, there is no guarantee that it can actually do so without paying workers substantially less and greatly reducing their benefits, thereby hurting working families. Opponents also argued that private companies are not very accountable to the public and are more likely to cut corners on safety and services. There was plenty of politics involved in the privatization decision. The private prison industry donated about $1 million dollars to Florida politicians (mostly Republicans) in the year before the privatization vote, while the state's Democratic-leaning public (and private) employee unions lent their support to candidates opposed to privatization.

There have been conflicting evaluations of prison privatization. State accountants and legislative committee analysts have produced several reports concluding that private prisons cut corners on staffing, offer fewer education programs, return inmates to the state system if they have major medical needs, cherry pick the least troublesome offenders and shift administrative costs to the state.[69] But another study of the state's currently-privatized prisons found that the companies had met the seven percent savings standard. The Department of Management Services (which oversees the private prison vendors) rated the prisons "acceptable" and attributed the savings to lower retirement contributions, lower administrative costs, lower rehabilitative program costs, and the fact that no women's prisons were included (women's prisons are more costly to run).[70] The legislature has discussed the creation of a joint legislative board to provide oversight to the Department of Corrections after a number of complaints including: suspicious inmate deaths, substandard medical care, nursing shortages, excessive force, and numerous lawsuits alleging inadequate care.[71]

 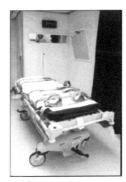

The electric chair (left) was used for executions in Florida from 1923 to 1999. The original "Old Sparky" was built by inmates. When constitutional concerns over cruel and unusual punishment arose, the legislature changed the law. Starting in 2000, lethal injection with a prisoner strapped to a gurney (right) became the default method. Previous to 1923 executions were mostly done at the county level by hanging.

The Death Penalty

Florida is one of 31 states that can impose the death penalty.[72] In 1976, the U.S. Supreme Court specifically upheld Florida's rewritten death penalty law.[73] It provides for two trials by the same jury in capital cases: one to determine guilt or innocence, and a second to determine the penalty. At second trial, evidence of "aggravating" and "mitigating" factors are presented to the jury. Some examples of possible *"aggravating" factors* are a crime that was: "heinous, atrocious, or cruel," or "committed in a cold and calculated and premeditated manner, and without any pretense of moral or legal justification." Some examples of possible *mitigating factors* include "no significant history of prior criminal activity," "extreme mental or emotional disturbance," and "the age of the defendant at the time of the crime." The jury's recommendation is almost always imposed by the judge. The death penalty is automatically appealed to the Florida Supreme Court. Some Supreme Court justices, usually the more liberal ones, are more willing than others to overturn a death penalty. One study found that among Florida's Supreme Court justices, the overturn rate ranged from 55.7 percent to just 7.5 percent.[74]

The governor, together with at least two of the three Cabinet officers, may *commute* a death penalty sentence (reduce the punishment to a life sentence) when sitting as the State Board of Executive Clemency. The federal courts may also intervene when a defendant's lawyers (usually provided by the public defender's office) raise a U.S. Constitution-based question. Florida has Capital Collateral Regional Counsels (attorneys) who represent indigent individuals convicted of a capital crime and automatically appeal the individual's death sentence verdict.[75] Capital collateral representatives were initially created to prevent death penalty convictions from being overturned because of inadequate or incompetent legal representation.

Over the past several decades, judges and juries in Florida have given the death penalty to hundreds of convicted murderers, although fewer defendants have been given the death sentence in recent years. Just 90 executions have occurred since Florida reinstated the death penalty in 1976. Frustrated by the slow pace of executions, in 2013 the legislature passed the Timely Justice Act to speed up the process and Governor Scott has been more aggressive in signing death warrants than any other modern Florida governor. Consequently, the "death row" population of the Florida State Prison at Starke grew steadily until leveling off over the past few years. (See Table 8-2.) *Death row* is the term given to prisoners condemned to death who are awaiting final disposition of their cases. Florida ranks second among all states in the number of inmates on death row but also leads the country in the number of inmates released from prison who were once there.[76] In Florida, the average time on death row before execution is about 14 years. More than 100 death row inmates have been there for over 10 years.[77]

Opponents of the death penalty protest against it at every execution.

Polls show that the average Floridian supports capital punishment. However, there are a number of controversies regarding the state's death penalty that extend beyond the traditional debates about the morality of the action or its impact as a deterrent to murder. At the heart of these debates are these questions:

- Is there a racial and economic bias in the application of the death penalty?
- Is Florida's method of execution, lethal injection, "cruel and unusual punishment?"
- Should limits be put on the appeals process?
- How should laws be written to prevent innocent people from being executed?
- Should a unanimous jury verdict be required to impose the death penalty?
- Do defendants in death penalty cases receive adequate legal representation?

The lethal injection controversy stems from a botched execution in Florida a few years ago.[78] Similar problems with the three-drug protocol ("cocktail") have occurred in several other states. Lawsuits filed by prisoners and groups opposing the death penalty allege that one of the three drugs has not been proven to be effective in rendering and keeping inmates unconscious and thus its use violates the Constitution's prohibition of cruel and unusual punishment.[79] The controversy ended up in the U.S. Supreme Court in April 2015. Even if the Court upholds the drug, one of the key companies that makes the drug (a sedative) is strongly opposed to the use of its products in capital punishment and has announced that neither the company nor its distributors will sell the drug directly to prisons.[80]

Table 8-2. Florida's Death Row Population

Year	Murders	Rate per 100,000	Executions	Death Row Population
1983	1,203	11.4	1	193
1984	1,264	11.6	8	215
1985	1,297	11.5	3	227
1986	1,371	11.8	3	254
1987	1,368	11.4	1	283
1988	1,008	8.1	2	287
1989	1,405	11.0	2	285
1990	1,387	10.7	4	291
1991	1,276	9.7	2	310
1992	1,191	8.9	2	312
1993	1,187	8.7	3	324
1994	1,152	8.3	1	342
1995	1,030	7.3	3	365
1996	1,077	7.6	3	367
1997	1,014	6.9	4	381
1998	966	6.4	0	367
1999	856	5.6	5	377
2000	890	5.6	3	368
2001	867	5.3	1	371
2002	906	5.5	3	372
2003	924	5.4	3	367
2004	946	5.4	2	366
2005	881	4.9	1	369
2006	1,129	6.2	4	377
2007	1,202	6.4	0	380
2008	1,168	6.2	2	391
2009	1,017	5.4	2	391
2010	987	5.3	1	394
2011	985	5.2	2	399
2012	1,009	5.3	3	402
2013	970	5.0	7	405
2014	981	5.0	8	403

Source: Florida Department of Corrections, and Florida Department of Law Enforcement.

FRAGMENTED LAW ENFORCEMENT

Law enforcement in Florida is highly fragmented. At the state level, law enforcement responsibilities are divided among several departments: the Department of Legal Affairs, headed by the attorney general; the Office of Statewide Prosecutor, appointed by the attorney general; the Florida Department of Law Enforcement (FDLE), headed by the governor and Cabinet; the Department of Juvenile Justice, whose secretary is appointed by the governor; the Office of Executive Clemency composed of the state's cabinet and the governor; the Department of Corrections, whose secretary is appointed by the governor; the Department of Highway Safety and Motor Vehicles, which includes the Florida Highway Patrol (FHP); the

Game and Fresh Water Commission; and a host of special commissions on such topics as corrections, criminal justice standards, training, parole, and sentencing. Moreover, Florida's twenty state attorneys (each elected by voters within a circuit) have considerable discretion over criminal prosecutions. At the local level, Florida counties elect their own sheriffs, who oversee a force of deputies, and cities maintain their own police departments, whose chiefs are accountable to the mayor and council.

The Coordination Challenge

Coordinating the activities of these many separate law enforcement agencies with each other and with federal law enforcement offices is a major challenge. Over the years, more and more crimes have become *"federalized"*—that is, declared by Congress to be federal crimes, as well as state crimes. Examples of federalized crimes are drug trafficking, bank robbery, kidnapping, hostage taking, interstate criminal activity, assault on a federal official, and obstruction of civil rights. These laws are enforced throughout the nation by the Federal Bureau of Investigation (FBI), the Drug Enforcement Administration (DEA), the Bureau of Alcohol, Tobacco and Firearms (ATF), the Internal Revenue Service (IRS), as well as the U.S. Coast Guard, Customs Bureau, and Immigration and Customs Enforcement. It is not uncommon at a major crime scene to see FBI, DEA, and ATF agents mingling with FDLE agents, FHP officers, county sheriff's deputies, and local police. Since many crimes violate both state and federal laws, federal and state attorneys must decide who will undertake prosecution. And it is possible to be prosecuted in both federal and state courts for the same crime, despite the U.S. Constitution's Fifth Amendment prohibition against double jeopardy.

Attorney General

Florida's elected attorney general heads the Department of Legal Affairs and is a member of the Cabinet. The attorney general performs a wide variety of functions—overseeing the provision of legal services to all state agencies, defending the state in legal proceedings, opposing appeals from criminal convictions, advising the governor and Cabinet in legal affairs, and providing advice and interpretation of state laws to city, county, and state agencies upon request. The attorney general also appoints the *statewide prosecutor*, whose responsibilities include the investigation and prosecution of organized crime in the state—crime that crosses the boundaries of Florida's 20 judicial circuits and the jurisdictions of state prosecutors in each circuit.

Florida Department of Law Enforcement (FDLE)

The FDLE is headed by an executive director appointed by the governor and Cabinet. It is authorized to investigate crime, especially organized, complex, and multi-jurisdictional crime in the state. It is also supposed to support local law enforcement agencies with information, intelligence, laboratory, forensic, training, and staff assistance.

Florida Highway Patrol (FHP)

The FHP is a division of the state's Department of Highway Safety and Motor Vehicles, whose secretary is appointed by the governor. Its primary responsibility is the enforcement of traffic and safety laws, although it does investigate crimes that take place on the state's highways.

Police and Sheriff's Deputies

Most law enforcement activity in Florida and other states is undertaken by city and county officers. In addition to fighting crime, these officers perform a host of other duties—taking accident reports, directing traffic, escorting crowds, and so on. Florida has approximately 68,000

State troopers, gathered in front of the Capitol, await the beginning of an inaugural parade.

full-time law enforcement employees.[81] The state ranks eighth among the 50 states in full-time law enforcement employees per 10,000 population, down from fourth in 2004. The slippage in the ranking is attributable to declining crime rates and budget shortfalls.

Department of Juvenile Justice

The Department of Juvenile Justice was established in 1994. It is headed by a secretary who is appointed by the governor. It assumed the responsibilities of the former juvenile program office in the old Department of Health and Rehabilitative Services. As juvenile crime became a more serious issue in the early 1990s, state officials thought that creating a separate department would create an organizational structure that would be more effective in addressing the problem. The Department operates the state's juvenile detention centers and residential and nonresidential commitment, probation, and prevention programs. It also cooperates with local communities and school districts in juvenile crime prevention.

Florida's judicial branch plays a major role in helping resolve conflicts in society. The state's large and increasingly diverse population creates special challenges to those responsible for keeping Floridians safe and protecting their individual rights. Over the years, Florida's crime rate has fluctuated dramatically. When crime rates rise and citizen fears increase, policymakers impose "get tough" policies, with an emphasis on punishment and deterrence. When crime rates fall and the per capita costs of keeping offenders in prison rise, there is a renewed call for more rehabilitation-centered policies and programs.

ONLINE SOURCES FOR DATA AND INFORMATION UPDATES

Florida Supreme Court

The Florida Supreme Court provides information on justices, court opinions, oral arguments, and dockets. Oral arguments are also provided to the public as a webcast.
http://www.floridasupremecourt.org/

Office of the State Courts Administrator: Publications and Statistics

The Florida Courts site offers annual reports, publications, and statistics on trial courts, judgeships, and other data. Statistics are from the Supreme Court, circuit courts, and county courts.
http://www.flcourts.org/publications-reports-stats/

Florida Department of Juvenile Justice: Research Reports

The Department of Juvenile Justice deals exclusively with juvenile offenders and offers research reports, including the annual Delinquency Profile, which features intake, disposition, court-diversion programs, juvenile probation, and transfers. The research also includes more in-depth research into delinquency in schools, disproportionate minority contact reports, a DJJ monthly scorecard, and current performance measurements.
http://www.djj.state.fl.us/research/reports/research-reports

Florida Department of Corrections: Agency statistics

The Florida Department of Corrections is responsible for public safety, safety of corrections officers, and providing the proper care and supervision of offenders. Annual reports from 1995-2014 contain statistics on budgets, facilities, sentencing, current and former inmates, and community supervision.
http://www.dc.state.fl.us/pub/index.html

Florida Department of Law Enforcement

The FDLE works in partnership with local, state, and federal law enforcement to ensure public safety and domestic security. This site offers quick-facts, budget information, and annual performance reports.
http://www.fdle.state.fl.us/Content/getdoc/036671bc-4148-4749-a891-7e3932e0a483/Publications.aspx

Chapter 9. Financing State Government: Taxing, Spending, and Borrowing

The Florida of today faces many challenges: a slower pace of population growth, an increasingly diverse population (as measured by race/ethnicity and generational makeup), a changing economic base, above-average vulnerabilities to natural disasters, especially hurricanes, homeland security breaches, increased use of constitutional amendments as a way to dictate budget priorities, and a politically-divided electorate.

Each of these trends affects the budgets of Florida's many governments but not always in the same way. The economies, population makeup, and politics of various regions of the state vary considerably, as they do among different types of governmental units (state, county, municipal, school district, special district). The fiscal pressures facing these governments differ by their location—rural, suburban, or metropolitan. There is no "one size fits all" approach to raising money or paying for state or local governments in the Sunshine State. It is the state's finances that are the primary focus of this chapter. Local governments' finances are discussed in more detail in Chapter 10.

Florida law requires that financial operations of the state be maintained through the General Revenue Fund, various trust funds, and the Budget Stabilization Fund (the "rainy day fund") administered by the Chief Financial Officer (CFO)—a statewide elected post. The General Revenue Fund, funded largely by taxes, "can be spent pretty much on anything because it is the money the state most directly controls. Trust funds are monies that are collected for a specific purpose such as tolls paid on Florida roads that are then earmarked specifically for road projects or money that comes from the federal government that has a specific purpose like funding a portion of the state's Medicaid program."[1] The Revenue Stabilization Fund, required by law, is funded by state funds set aside for emergencies.

The governor and CFO are responsible for ensuring that sufficient revenues are collected to meet appropriations and that no deficits occur in state funds. Decisions regarding the state's finances involve elected officials, economists, policy analysts, and the public.

The State's Roller Coaster Economy

"Getting a balanced budget in hard economic times is not easy and sure as sunrise, some people are not going to be happy as tough decisions are made."[2] Reaching a consensus on how to pay for government, what the top spending priorities should be, and whether to borrow to balance the budget is *always* difficult no matter whether the economy is booming or in decline.

Florida's economy has been on a roller coaster ride in recent years, outpacing the nation in economic growth (gross domestic product) in the early 2000s, plummeting far below the national average during the Great Recession, and catching up to the growth of the national economy in recent years. (See Figure 9-1.) During the boom times, Florida's governors and legislators have struggled to meet sharply rising demands for services associated with rapid population growth in a fiscally conservative state. (Florida has long been labeled a "low tax" state.) In the midst of the Great Recession, officials agonized over whether to increase taxes and fees, significantly reduce spending on some popular programs, or borrow more money, possibly lowering Florida's credit rating. As the economy began its recovery in the 2010s, new pressures have faced budget makers—what to spend money on first to meet demands that went unmet during the Recession, whether to take federal money for health care programs, and whether to increase certain fees or taxes to cover rising costs. It is crystal clear that the volatility of Florida's economy, its sharp "ups-and-downs," makes it more difficult to accurately forecast revenue and expenditure demands and craft the state's budget.

Figure 9-1. Florida's "Roller Coaster" Economy Fluctuates More than the U.S. Economy

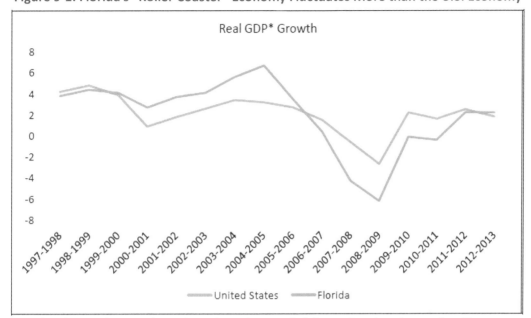

Note: *Real GDP is the gross domestic product—the sum of all the goods and services produced in a year—adjusted for price changes (inflation or deflation).

Source: Bureau of Economic Analysis, *Economy at a Glance,* Bureau of Labor Statistics. Available at http://www.bls.gov/eag/eag.fl.htm.

The Public's Preferred Method of Balancing the Budget

It is not surprising, that during the recent economic downturn, over 10 times more Floridians favored reducing spending over increasing taxes to bridge the state's huge budget shortfalls.[3] However, a majority preferred a dual approach to budget-balancing—increasing taxes and fees while cutting back spending. As the economy began to rebound, Floridians were evenly split between those who favor raising taxes or expanding services and those who do not—46 percent and 49 percent, respectively. (See Figure 3-5.)

There is *little consensus about what is the fairest way to raise more revenue or on which programs to reduce spending first.* One person's "high priority" program is seen by another as "wasteful and expendable." These different perspectives among Floridians explain why fiscal decisions are among the most painful for elected officials to make. Equally challenging is the fact that lawmakers have little control over the economic conditions during the time they must govern. Legally, however, they have no choice but to approve a budget. It is the *one* task the Florida Constitution requires. That is why in 2015, the legislature's delay in doing so before the regular session ended was so heavily criticized. The legislature had to come back into special session to pass a budget. Special sessions cost $75,000 a day which is seen by many taxpayers as wasteful and inexcusable.[4]

Florida's legislators must also pass a balanced budget which the federal government does not—a difference that annoys a great many Floridians. In 2010, 72 percent of the state's voters voted for a non-binding referendum calling for a balanced federal budget amendment to the U.S. Constitution. Balancing the state's budget is made more difficult by fluctuations in federal budget decisions and concerns about placing too heavy a tax burden on Florida residents.

TAX FLUCTUATIONS AND TAX BURDENS IN FLORIDA

A state's tax burden can be computed in several ways, but the Tax Foundation method is to calculate the total amount paid by the residents in taxes, and then divide those taxes by the state's total income. Florida's state and local tax burden has remained consistently lower than the U.S. average, but the gap is closing as the state makes the tough decisions necessary to balance the budget. (See Figure 9-2.)

Despite Floridians' seemingly increasing anti-tax sentiment, general revenue collections as a percentage of income decreased sharply during the late 2000s. (This is another way to measure tax burden.) (See Figure 9-3.) Many cheer Florida's traditionally low tax burden as a primary reason for the state's past economic growth (Florida's state and local tax burden compared to the other 50 states has typically been in the bottom half, which gives the state a competitive advantage in attracting new business). Others see it in a less positive light, believing that, in the long run, higher taxes could help produce a better-educated workforce and improved infrastructure. Critics also point to the fact that the state's tax burden is heaviest on the poorest Floridians.[5]

Public finance reformers continue to press for a revenue system for the state that is fairer, more diversified, and more broad-based. They favor more wealth-based taxes, more graduated (needs-based) rate structures on existing fees and taxes, and the elimination of various loopholes.

FLORIDA'S REVENUE STRUCTURE

Florida relies heavily on sales taxes, which are the state's largest single source of tax receipts.[6] During the 2000s, the recession had a particularly stinging impact on several revenue sources, including the documentary stamp tax, which is directly tied to real estate transaction volume, and interest earnings, which only flourish when the state has excess funds to invest. Its general sales tax rate (six percent) is similar to that of many of the other states. Usually, people regard a consumption tax like a sales tax as fairer than income-based taxes.

Florida Revenue Sources (State Receipts)

All the monies the State of Florida receives are from general revenue sources (mostly taxes collected by the state), the federal government (federal aid), trust funds (earmarked for a specific purpose), and taxes which are shared with local governments. In recent years, the two largest sources have been federal aid and general revenue, followed by trust funds and, lastly, transfers to local governments.[7]

Changes in Florida's Tax Structure

Over the years, the state's tax structure has been altered as its economy and population make-up have changed. In examining the state's tax history, the authors of *Florida's Tax Structure* conclude that: "Florida's tax structure has changed significantly since 1949 when Florida received 41.4 percent of state revenues from gasoline and motor vehicle taxes and 30.3 percent from so-called "sin [alcoholic beverage, cigarette and tobacco, pari-mutuel] taxes." In 1949, a three percent sales and use tax was enacted. Today, sales taxes make up a far larger portion of the state's revenue pie than either "sin taxes" or gas taxes.

Changes in Florida's tax structure in the 1990s and 2000s were largely "incremental." Small rate increases for existing taxes and the closing of some loopholes (exemptions) were more common than the adoption of *new* tax sources. State lawmakers are quite aware of the population's animosity toward taxes.

With the exception of the lottery, which the citizens approved in 1986, Florida's voters have rejected most *new* revenue proposals put before them and approved a host of revenue-restricting amendments. (See Appendix A.) Both Democratic and Republican officials have run on "no new taxes" platforms in recent election cycles and promised to keep Florida's tax burden from getting too much heavier.

Figure 9-2. Florida's Total State-Local Tax Burden below U.S. Average

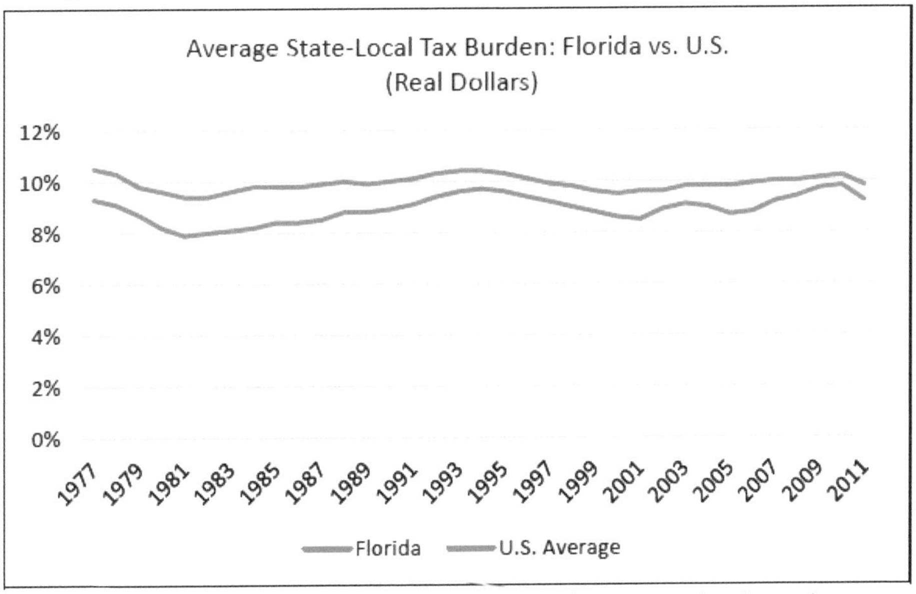

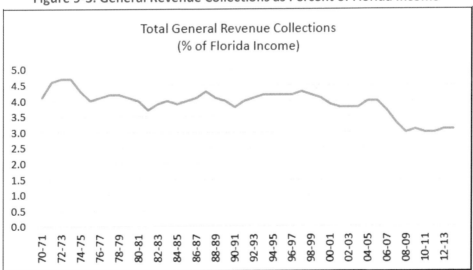

Note: Per the Tax Foundation, "A state's state-local tax burden, In general, is the total amount residents of that state pay in state and local taxes (even if some of those payments go to out-of-state jurisdictions). Our measure expresses this tax burden as a proportion of total state income. This means that two broad statistics are needed to make the calculation for each state: total state and local taxes paid by state residents (what we call the tax burden) and total state income."

Source: Chart created from data from the Tax Foundation calculations. For full methodology see Tax Foundation Working Paper 10. Inflation adjustment done using Bureau of Labor Statistics. Available at http://taxfoundation.org/article/state-and-local-tax-burdens-all-years-one-state-1977-2011.

Figure 9-3. General Revenue Collections as Percent of Florida Income

Source: Florida Revenue Estimating Conference, "Long-Term Revenue Analysis," fall 2014. Available at http://edr.state.fl.us/Content/conferences/longtermrevenue/2014longtermrevenueanalysis.pdf.

STATE SALES TAXES: GENERAL AND SELECTIVE

The *general sales tax* is the most important source of revenue for the state. Florida's general sales tax is a six percent levy on "retail sales of most tangible personal property items, admissions to amusements, transient lodgings, commercial rentals, motor vehicles, and ships and commercial fishing equipment."[8]

The state's general sales tax raises about three-quarters of the monies going into the state's General Fund—the major source of most of the state's current operations. (See Figure 9-4.) Despite low population growth, per capita state sales tax collections fell dramatically from 2006 to 2012, down $257, before increasing by $63 in 2013.[9]

Local governments have the option of adding discretionary sales surtaxes; counties have several options at their disposal, depending on the circumstances, including a Charter County and Regional Transportation System Surtax and an Emergency Fire and Rescue Services and Facilities Surtax (each up to one percent), and school districts can levy a School Capital Outlay Surtax of up to 0.5 percent.

The general sales tax is a big revenue producer for the State of Florida and its local governments, especially in affluent areas.

Figure 9-2. State Revenues Making Up the $26 Billion General Fund

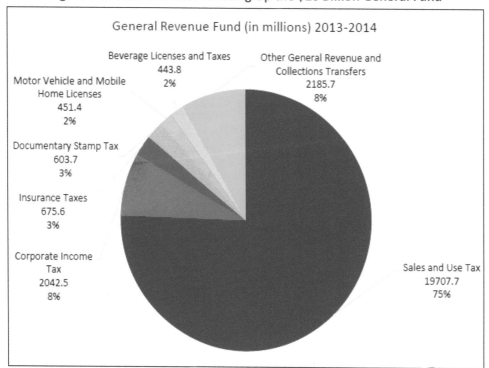

General Revenue Fund (in millions) 2013-2014

- Beverage Licenses and Taxes 443.8 2%
- Other General Revenue and Collections Transfers 2185.7 8%
- Motor Vehicle and Mobile Home Licenses 451.4 2%
- Documentary Stamp Tax 603.7 3%
- Insurance Taxes 675.6 3%
- Corporate Income Tax 2042.5 8%
- Sales and Use Tax 19707.7 75%

Source: Florida Revenue Estimating Conference, Long-Term Revenue Analysis. Available at http://edr.state.fl.us/Content/conferences/longtermrevenue/2014longtermrevenueanalysis.pdf.

Tax Exemptions

Florida exempts a number of necessities from its general sales tax (groceries, prescription drugs, etc.). Once instituted, these tax exemptions (formally labeled "tax expenditures") are very rarely repealed, if they are even reviewed at all for fear of a backlash from the public. This lack of scrutiny is in sharp contrast to the relatively high frequency and intensity with which appropriations are reviewed and revised. Often, appropriations are seen as more tangible expenses, whereas tax expenditures, despite having the same budgetary effect, are perceived as merely lost income. This lost income may seem more harmless than the more visible appropriations, but its economic opportunity cost is just as real as the costs of appropriations.

Sales tax exemptions are not the only type of exemption that results in lost revenue to the state. One estimate of the lost revenue from all current tax exemptions, deductions, allowances, exclusions, credits, preferential rates, and deferrals contained in Florida's tax laws put the figure at nearly $50 billion. Reformers' attempts to close many of these loopholes have largely been unsuccessful. Such proposals usually evoke fierce political battles in Tallahassee and/or in the courts because many of the loopholes are designed to spur the growth of certain sectors of the economy or areas of the state or to give taxpayers some relief. For example, back-to-school sales tax holidays have become extremely popular with taxpayers and merchants. And even though the holidays have been estimated to cost the state millions in lost sales tax revenue, eliminating them has proved to be quite difficult politically.

Selective Sales Tax

Florida also levies *selective sales taxes* on the sale of beer, wine, and spirits and on cigarettes ($1.339 dollars per pack).[10] Selective sales taxes are also imposed on documentary stamps (real estate transactions, bonds, notes, etc.); on insurance premiums; on the severance of solid minerals, including phosphate; on gross receipts of electric, gas, and telecommunication services, including municipal corporations; on gasoline;[11] and on various other products and activities. The documentary stamp tax, which is directly tied to real estate transaction volume, soared with the housing boom and plummeted when it burst, further emphasizing the volatility of the state's tax system. In summary, Florida relies considerably more on transaction taxes (General Sales + Selective Sales) than the U.S. at large: 83 percent v. 49 percent.[12]

Selective sales taxes have, on occasion, been heavily criticized by taxpayers. During the Great Recession, it was the gas tax. More recently it has been the telecommunications tax (Florida's cell phone taxes are among the nation's highest).[13] Anytime there has been a proposal to tax the Internet or online purchases made in a different state it has been met with strong opposition from the public.[14]

Politics of Sales Taxes

No one likes to pay taxes, but Floridians report that the sales tax is the least objectionable major tax source. Consumers are a weak pressure group. It is difficult for them to count pennies dribbled away six at a time. Few people have any idea how much they pay each year in Florida sales taxes. They do not involve obvious payroll deductions, or lump-sum bills as in the case of property taxes. However, Floridians who itemize their deductions can now deduct their sales taxes when computing their federal tax returns. This change in federal law was spearheaded by the Florida congressional delegation.

Are Florida Sales Taxes Regressive?

Sales taxes are often criticized as *regressive*; that is, these taxes take a larger proportion of the incomes of the poor than they do the incomes of the wealthy. This belief is based on the knowledge that low-income groups must use most, if not all, of their income for purchases, while high-income groups devote larger shares of their income to savings, and, of course, income saved is not subject to the sales tax. However,

Florida excludes some of the basic necessities of life, including packaged food bought at the grocery store, rent, prescription drugs, and medical expenses. These exclusions remove some of the regressivity from the Florida sales tax. Nonetheless, Florida's poor still pay a higher share of their income in sales taxes than Florida's wealthy.[15]

Arguments for the Sales Tax

Besides being less objectionable to the public, there are several other arguments supporting Florida's heavy reliance on sales taxation. First of all, it is the only major source of revenue left mostly to the states. Local governments rely primarily on property taxes, and the federal government relies primarily on income taxes. An additional state bite on paychecks or year-end property tax bills would be very painful, more so than sales taxes paid pennies at a time. Second, sales taxation reaches tourists who make purchases within the state. Florida would be particularly disadvantaged if it placed the full burden of its taxes on the state's almost 19 million residents, while allowing its over 93 million annual visitors[16] to avoid support of highways, parks, recreation, police and fire protection, and other public services from which they benefit.

Sales Taxes on Services?

The service sector, much of which is not included in the sales tax base, comprises a major and growing part of the state's economy. This means that sales tax collections do not keep pace with economic growth over time since the service sector is becoming an increasingly larger share of the gross domestic product. But powerful political interests oppose the extension of the sales tax to their services, notably newspapers, radio and television stations, lawyers and accountants, and real estate dealers. (Of course, they usually phrase their argument as protection for barbers, beauticians, and other small service providers.) Taxes on services were briefly enacted in 1987 under Republican Governor Bob Martinez, but he quickly reversed himself under interest group pressure, and the legislature repealed these taxes—although the legislature then raised the sales tax rate from five to six percent. (See Chapter 7.) His successor, Democratic Governor Lawton Chiles, frequently urged tax reform, suggesting that various service exemptions should be reconsidered—but to no avail. Republican Governor Jeb Bush, Chiles' successor, was a "no new taxes" governor who had no interest in reviving the sales tax on services. Neither did Governor Charlie Crist or current Governor Rick Scott.

INCOME TAXES: PERSONAL AND CORPORATE

Florida is one of seven states without a *personal* income tax. (The others are Alaska, Nevada, South Dakota, Texas, Washington, and Wyoming; New Hampshire and Tennessee tax interest, dividends, and capital gains but not wage income.) Florida's prohibition against income taxation is lodged in the state's Constitution (Article VII, Section 5). Thus only a constitutional amendment, approved by the voters in a statewide referendum, could impose an income tax. Voters' approval of such an amendment is very unlikely. In surveys taken over the years, a state income tax has never won the support of more than 15 to 20 percent of the Florida public. Opposition is especially strong among Florida's large elderly population.

Progressive Income Taxes

It is frequently argued that Florida's tax structure is antiquated, designed for a small rural state that produced citrus and sugar and entertained tourists in the winter months. Reformers have long recommended that the state adopt a progressive personal income tax. The first state to adopt income taxation was Wisconsin in 1911. The federal government adopted the principle of progressive income taxation with the passage of the Sixteenth Amendment in 1913. Progressive income taxation, with rates rising with increases in income, is usually defended on the principle of "ability to pay." The theory is that high income groups can afford to pay a larger percentage of their income in taxes than poorer people. The theory may be sound, but the practical realities of Florida politics will likely continue to keep the state from adopting a personal income tax. As a result, Florida's overall tax system has been ranked as the second most regressive in the country by one tax and policy institute.[17]

State Corporate Income Taxes

Florida's *corporate* income tax provides only 8 percent of General Fund revenue. The corporate tax rate of 5.5 percent of net profits is roughly comparable to other state corporate income taxes. Four states (South Dakota, Wyoming, Nevada, and Washington) have no such tax, while some other states, including Iowa, tax corporate income at up to 12 percent. In 2011, Governor Rick Scott, in keeping with his campaign pledge, "Let's get to work!" fought to scale-back the state's corporate income tax, arguing that, as a progressive income tax levied against businesses, it hinders economic development. Scott argued that the tax discourages businesses from relocating to Florida and existing Florida businesses from creating new jobs.[18] Opponents to Scott's plan argued that repealing the tax would leave less funding for key government services that also attract relocating businesses. Scott did not quite get his wish of a reduction in the corporate income tax rate, but he did get his foot in the door with an annual tax break of $1,100 to small businesses.

OTHER STATE TAXES

Florida, like other states, imposes other types of taxes in addition to sales and corporate income taxes. For example, real-estate related collections contribute significantly to state revenues. However, the housing market crash had a strong negative impact on these collections, which fell from $276 per capita (2006) to $76 (2012). Foreclosures flooded the market and home values plummeted in a vicious cycle. Lower sale prices and a general downturn in the housing market caused decreased documentary stamp and real estate transfer tax collections. As the real estate market has rebounded, so have housing related collections, marked by an increase to $100 per capita in 2013.[19]

The Intangible Personal Property Tax: Going, Going, Gone!

For years, Florida imposed an "intangible" personal property tax—an annual tax placed on the value of stocks, bonds, mutual funds, accounts receivable, and other personal assets owned by Floridians. It excluded real estate, leaving this form of "tangible" property taxation to local governments. It also excluded bank deposits. In 1997, the Florida Legislature passed a law to phase out the intangibles tax over several years. It was seen by Republican state legislators as a deterrent to businesses (and jobs) relocating to Florida and as a tax that is discriminatory toward the state's elderly—a tax on "seniors and savers" since a greater proportion of the incomes of elderly residents are in the form of stocks and bonds.[20] Democrats complained that this was a tax break for the wealthy. The tax was completely abolished during the 2006 legislative session. There has been little discussion of reinstating it.

Licenses, Fines, and Fees

As the economy declined, licenses, fines, and fees became the fastest growing type of revenue in Florida with the legislature approving almost a billion dollar increase in them. The reason for this growth is three-fold: (1) each individual license tax, fine, or fee is relatively low; (2) Floridians generally find them more fair than an across-the-board tax increase, rationalizing that they are mostly paid by people who benefit from the service being paid for (or in the case of fines, who deserve the punishment); and (3) conservative politicians who vote to increase licenses, fines, and fees can still claim that they did not vote to increase taxes (making a distinction between general taxes and licenses, fines, and fees). Local governments have been raising them as well. Thus, Florida has seen increases in occupational licenses, marriage licenses, pet licenses, hunting licenses, fishing licenses, driver's licenses, automobile registration fees, environmental disposal fees, divorce fees, local and state park fees, and fines for traffic infractions and other violations. While growing rapidly, they still do not account for a very large share of Florida state and local revenue.

There is a point when the public starts to see fees as taxes. In fact, the term "fee tax" has become a fairly common one. Some politicians even run on an anti-"fee tax" platform. As an example, in 2014 (a gubernatorial election year), Governor Rick Scott proposed, and the legislature approved, a reduction in vehicle registration fees.[21]

HOW FLORIDA SHARES ITS TAX REVENUE WITH LOCAL GOVERNMENTS

The State of Florida shares some of its tax revenues with its county governments, including shares of beverage license taxes, various gas, fuel, and road taxes, cigarette taxes, insurance license taxes, general sales taxes and user fees, intangible property taxes, mobile home license taxes, oil, gas and sulfur production taxes, and the phosphate rock severance tax.

The state's municipalities are also recipients of shares of some state taxes, including beverage licenses, insurance premiums, gas, fuel, and road usage, and general sales. As with counties, use of many of these revenues is generally unrestricted (with the exception of gas, fuel, and road usage taxes which are earmarked to roads and transportation and the documentary stamp tax which is earmarked for affordable housing). The state's school districts receive portions of the state revenues, including lottery proceeds.

Local Sales Tax Options Granted by State

For years, local governments in Florida were considerably more restricted in their ability to impose local sales taxes (on top of the state sales tax) than their counterparts in many other states. But between 1976 and 1996, the Florida Legislature authorized 15 new local sales tax options. While an important step in the right direction, these options are still *much* more restrictive than local officials believe they should be in terms of which local governments can use them, how the funds must be spent, and how they are adopted. Larger jurisdictions are generally given more authority to levy these local option taxes than smaller jurisdictions.

Limits and Conditions

Most local option general sales taxes permitted by the Florida Legislature have been earmarked for limited purposes (e.g., transit systems, indigent care, public hospitals, infrastructure, school construction). They can be adopted only by voter approval or, in some cases, by an extraordinary majority vote of the local legislative body. Generally, counties have broader authority to use these taxes than cities or special districts.

Occasionally, the legislature has granted local governments the right to impose sales taxes of a selective nature (e.g., on fuel, hotel and motel rooms, restaurant food and beverages). But these, too, must be approved by voters or extraordinary votes of the county commission or city council and be used for specific purposes. Many are restricted to jurisdictions meeting certain size thresholds. It was not until 1995 that the state legislature first granted school boards the right to impose any kind of local option sales tax. Now, districts can propose a half-cent general sales tax, but it cannot be levied without voter approval and it must be used for school construction. The electoral successes of these sales tax votes, where put to a vote, have been mixed.[22] Some counties have taken greater advantage of local option sales taxes than others. (See Table 9-1.)

Table 9-1. Local Option Sales Tax Rates in Florida Counties

Rate	Counties
1.50%	Calhoun, DeSoto, Escambia, Gadsden, Jackson, Leon, Liberty, Madison, Monroe, Walton
1.00	Baker, Bradford, Charlotte, Clay, Columbia, Dixie, Duval, Flagler, Franklin, Gilchrist, Glades, Gulf, Hamilton, Hardee, Hendry, Highlands, Hillsborough, Holmes, Indian River, Jefferson, Lafayette, Lake, Levy, Miami-Dade, Nassau, Okeechobee, Osceola, Pasco, Pinellas, Polk, Putnam, Sarasota, Seminole, Sumter, Suwannee, Taylor, Union, Wakulla, Washington
0.50	Bay, Brevard, Manatee, Orange, St. Lucie, Santa Rosa, Volusia
No Tax	Alachua, Broward, Citrus, Collier, Hernando, Lee, Marion, Martin, Okaloosa, Palm Beach, St. Johns

Source: Table created from Discretionary Sales Surtax Information For Calendar Year 2015, Florida Department of Revenue. Available at http://dor.myflorida.com/Forms_library/current/dr15dss.pdf.

FEDERAL FUNDS IN FLORIDA

Florida's state and local government officials are well aware of how important federal funds are to their economies, especially when disasters hit, such as a major hurricane or oil spill in the Gulf like the Deepwater Horizon ("BP") catastrophe. Florida officials frequently lobby Congress, the president, and Cabinet-level administrators to make sure Floridians get back a fair share of the federal tax dollars they send to Washington. This has rarely happened, much to the dismay of Florida officials. Among the states, Florida ranks 48th in the per capita federal aid the state and its local governments receive. (See Figure 9-5.) That was why when Governor Scott turned down billions in federal funds for high speed rail in 2011, many state and local officials, particularly those in the areas it would have gone, were stunned. (See Chapter 7.) What was not surprising were the reasons he gave for rejecting the monies. (More will be said about this later.)

Multiple Sources of Federal Monies[23]

Billions of dollars of federal funds flow into Florida annually from a variety of sources. Twenty-seven percent is via direct expenditures to individuals, governments, businesses, and not-for-profits. Seventy-three percent is in the form of other financial assistance (insurance coverage, guaranteed loans, and direct loans). Reported dollar amounts for these other assistance programs represent the face value of insurance coverage or the dollar volume of loans made rather than actual expenditures.

Florida has long complained that the federal grant-in-aid formula for highway funding *shortchanges the state.*

Figure 9-3. Federal Aid to State and Local Governments, Per Capita Ranges: Florida Ranks 48th

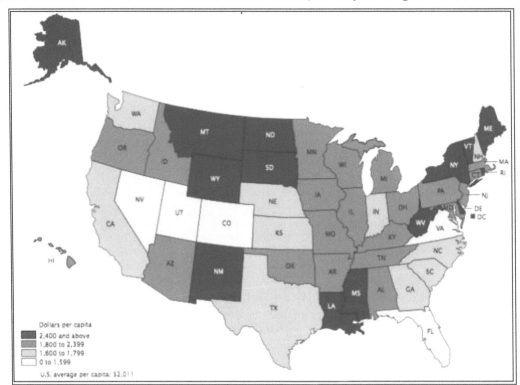

Source: U.S. Census Bureau, Federal Aid to the States for Fiscal Year 2010, September 2011. Available at https://www.census.gov/prod/2011pubs/fas-10.pdf.

Direct Federal Spending in Florida (27 Percent)

- Direct federal payments to individuals for Retirement and Disability (35 percent). This category includes four types of payments: 1) Social Security payments, 2) federal retirement and disability payments, 3) veterans benefits, and 4) other payments. *Social Security* payments account for 80 percent. Florida gets more direct payments to individuals than most other states because of its larger elderly population.

- Direct payments for Individuals Other Than for Retirement and Disability (34 percent). Included here are nine types of payments (Medicare benefits, unemployment compensation, excess earned income tax credits, supplemental nutrition assistance program, housing assistance, agricultural assistance, federal employees life and health insurance, student financial assistance, and other). *Medicare* benefits alone account for 74 percent of all these payments.

- Grants to state and local governments and non-governmental entities (15 percent). Grants received help support a wide range of activities such as child nutrition programs, special milk programs, state and private forestry, disaster relief, construction of wastewater treatment facilities, low income home energy assistance, *Medicaid*, public housing, highways, and airports, to name a few. A number of state agencies administer the grants: Children and Families, Health, Agency for Health Care Administration, the Agency for Persons with Disabilities, Community Affairs (disaster related grants),[24] and Health and Human Services. Grants to Health and Human Services make up the majority of grant funding.

- Procurement contracts (10 percent). This category includes contract awards by the Department of Defense and non-defense agencies. In Florida, contracts awarded by the Department of Defense account for 71 percent of total federal procurement contracts awarded in 2010.

- Salaries and wages paid to federal employees working in Florida (7 percent). Salary and wage payments are divided into two categories: those paid to Department of Defense employees and those to federal employees working in non-defense agencies.

Other Federal Financial Assistance (73 Percent)

- Insurance coverage (95 percent). Florida ranks first among the states in the face value of federal insurance coverage. Most (99 percent) is for *flood* insurance; the rest is for crop insurance, foreign investment insurance, life insurance for veterans, and various other types.
- Guaranteed loans (4 percent). *Mortgage insurance for homes* accounts for 59 percent of the total dollar volume of federal guaranteed loans. The remainder is for the federal family education loan program, veterans housing loans, mortgage insurance for condominiums, and Department of Agriculture guaranteed loans.
- Direct loans (1 percent). Federal direct *student loans* are the largest category (89 percent). Commodity loans (price supports) and other Department of Agriculture loans make up 7 percent.

How Does Florida Compare?

Watchdog groups, like Florida TaxWatch, routinely track how well the state does. Historically, Florida's state and local governments have received less back in federal grants than most other states. When measured as federal aid per capita, Florida generally ranks near the bottom of the 50 states and has been slipping. In 2003, Florida ranked 46th, but, by 2009, it had dropped to 48th.[25]

Pros and Cons of Federal Aid

Some analysts attribute this federal aid "inequity" to uncoordinated efforts by various state agencies, decisions by Congress to use "old" Census figures (which greatly disadvantages high growth states like Florida), and the general redistributive nature of many federal grants programs designed to aid poorer entities and individuals. Those who believe Florida is still being short-changed, especially on transportation funds, advocate pushing harder for more federal funds on the premise that Florida deserves a more equitable share of federal aid.

State and local governments often worry about how they would fund certain programs and construction projects without federal aid. That's why governments themselves may hire lobbyists to keep an eye on what Congress is doing and then to pressure them if it looks like funds will be reduced or cut altogether.

Others warn that too much reliance on federal funds can backfire. They argue that Congress has a habit of reducing or redirecting aid, particularly during economic slumps. Critics also warn that becoming too dependent on federal funds, especially for essential programs, can put state and local governments in a fiscal squeeze if the federal monies are cut. There is also a certain wariness about the accuracy of cost estimates and revenue projections, which, if grossly underestimated, could create major fiscal problems for the recipient governments which might entail raising taxes, borrowing, or cutting other programs.

The latter argument was how Governor Scott defended rejecting the federal government's offer of $2.4 billion to build a high speed rail line in Florida. The three reasons he gave were: (1) construction cost overruns would likely put Florida taxpayers on the hook for $3 billion; (2) low ridership would require state subsidies; and (3) if the project were shut down, the state would have to return the $2.4 billion to Washington. "The truth is that this project would be far too costly to taxpayers and I believe the risk far outweighs the benefits," Scott said.[26] But for many other state and local officials (Republicans and Democrats alike) who had experienced the difficulties of securing money to pay for major infrastructure projects, it was still hard to accept. For them, even though the odds of securing a major federal grant are steep, applying for a grant is nearly always worth the gamble and getting it is worth the strings and guidelines attached.

The fierce battle over whether the state of Florida should accept federal funds to expand its Medicaid program reflected the same basic arguments. Proponents saw it as a return of federal income taxes paid by Floridians and as money that would permit the state to spend more in other pressing areas. In contrast, opponents worried that the federal government's funding promises might be broken, leaving Florida to pick up 100 percent of the cost and thereby requiring the state to reduce its funding for other important programs, like education. (See more about Medicaid later in the chapter and in Chapter 11.)

LOTTERY, GAMING, AND OTHER REVENUE

The Florida lottery was approved by the voters in 1986 after an extended debate over whether the state ought to encourage and profit from gambling. While Governor Bob Graham opposed the lottery, voters approved it by a lopsided 64 to 36 margin. (See Appendix A.) The Department of the Lottery was created during the 1987 Regular Session and the state lottery officially began selling tickets on January 12, 1988. The lottery's stated mission is "to maximize revenues for educational enhancement in Florida."[27]

Lottery funding has contributed to K-12 programs in Florida's 67 school districts, community colleges and state universities, the Bright Futures Scholarship Program, other state student financial aid, and the construction and maintenance of public schools through the Classrooms First and Classrooms for Kids programs. To date, more than 700,000 Bright Futures scholarships have been awarded statewide, making it possible for many of Florida's future leaders to enroll in state universities, community colleges, and workforce education programs of their choice.[28]

State Senator Betty Castor (D, Tampa) pushed hard for the lottery to help fund education. Some years later, she was elected the state's Education Commissioner.

Initially, lottery proceeds were distributed roughly as follows: 50 percent for prizes, at least 39 percent to the state's Educational Enhancement Trust Fund, and the remainder to the Department of the Lottery for advertising and administrative expenses (including a 5 percent retail dealer allowance).[29] More recently, approximately 64 percent was spent on prizes, 8 percent on administration (retailer compensation, vendor fees, and operational costs), and 28 percent was transferred to the Educational Enhancement Trust Fund. Lottery games are popular. One survey found that 66 percent of adult Floridians acknowledged they had played at least one Florida Lottery game over the past year; 54 percent had played over the past month.[30]

The Lottery Shell Game

Of all the state's revenue sources, the most misunderstood and controversial is the lottery. Soon after its approval by Florida's voters following an expensive high-profile marketing campaign, many citizens became somewhat disillusioned with the lottery. They discovered that lottery funds were being substituted for tax dollars that had previously been earmarked for education. In other words, rather than *enhancing* the overall proportion of the state's budget going to education, lottery funds were merely being *substituted* for other state funds which were transferred elsewhere. There was no net gain in the percentage of the state's budget going to education.

Funding Bright Futures

In 1997, Florida's lawmakers enacted the Bright Futures Scholarship Program which is funded by the lottery proceeds, to attempt to restore the public's faith in the lottery. The program rewards graduating high school students for their academic achievements by providing lottery funding to pursue postsecondary educational and career goals in Florida. Over the years, the legislature has passed laws giving more authority to local school districts, community colleges, and universities to decide how they will spend the funds, rather than leaving the decision to the State Department of Education in Tallahassee.

The cost of the program ballooned from $70 million when it began to $437 million in 2011. By then, lottery funds were not sufficient to fund the total cost of the program. Lottery proceeds dipped during the recession. At the same time, the state lost millions of dollars in federal aid for education due to cutbacks at the federal level, while the number of Bright Futures-eligible students continued to rise. (Some 88 percent of in-state freshmen qualified for the scholarship.)[31] The state legislature reacted by restructuring the Bright Futures Scholarship program in 2011. It tightened eligibility and reduced the amount of the grant. To receive Bright Futures scholarships, school students graduating in the 2013-14 academic year were required to score higher on the SAT and engage in more community service hours, and they received a lower stipend. Legislators said the changes were necessary just to keep the program afloat.

Economic Stimulus

Occasionally, Florida's lottery has been used to help boost the state's economy, especially its tourism industry, following disasters.[32] In the days following 9/11, Florida faced a projected $7 billion loss in tourism spending, with an expected accompanying loss of $434 million in state sales tax revenue. Both the private and public sectors were suffering. Thus, it was fitting that help came via several coordinated public-private partnerships—one, a rather unusual one involving Florida's lottery. It was one of the nation's first uses of a state lottery as an economic stimulus tool. When state leaders sat down to devise a road map to recovery, one path they took was to develop a highly publicized state lottery scratch-off game designed to encourage Floridians to play the game *and* vacation in their home state (the "Stay Here, Play Here" theme). The press release announcing the game made it clear that the game was intended to boost revenues in both the private and public sectors:

Florida's lottery has occasionally been used as an economic stimulus tool to boost the state's tourism-based economy following disasters like 9/11 and hurricanes. Games are promoted with that goal in mind. The Play FLA USA campaign after 9/11 had as its theme "Stay Here, Play Here."

> "Featuring more than $10 million in cash prizes and 90 vacation packages, the Florida Lottery's new Scratch-Off game, PLAY FLA USA, leverages the Lottery's strength in the retail marketplace in an effort to boost the Sunshine State's vital tourism industry."

While no one would argue that the "Play FLA USA" game was in and of itself the *sole* factor jump-starting the tourism sector, sales and tax receipts clearly show it had some impact in combination with the large-scale VISIT FLORIDA advertising campaign. Similar uses of the lottery as an economic stimulus tool were made following disastrous hurricane seasons that also threatened to harm Florida's important tourism industry and in the midst of both the oil spill in the Gulf and the Great Recession.

The Lottery: More Misunderstandings

Several other areas of misunderstanding about the lottery still persist. First, many voters believe that the state reaps a large share of the state's revenue from lottery proceeds. Wrong. In actuality, the lottery generates only a very small percentage of total state revenues. Second, many citizens believe that the amount generated by lottery ticket sales is sufficient to fund the entire cost of education in all the state's school districts, community colleges, and universities. Wrong. The lottery funds only about seven percent of the state's annual educational appropriation.[33]

Floridians initially approved the Lottery after promises from the state that the proceeds would go to fund education.

The Lottery's Impact on Public Opinion

To many, the lottery remains a symbol of government's failure to spend Florida taxpayers' dollars as "promised." It has made it very difficult for other local governments to use earmarking strategies to get voters to approve new local revenue sources. Surveys asking voters why they would (or did) vote against a half penny sales tax earmarked for local school construction or some other local project often find disillusionment with the lottery to be a major reason for voting "No."

Pari-Mutuel Revenue

Florida allows three types of pari-mutuels—horse racing, jai alai, and greyhound racing—and derives less than one percent of state revenue from taxes and licenses on these activities. Once the state lottery was established, pari-mutuel betting in the state and the taxes derived from it began to stagnate. Lobbyists representing these types of gaming pushed hard to allow citizens to vote on a proposed constitutional amendment allowing slot machines at these facilities. In 2004, voters narrowly approved (51 percent) a constitutional amendment allowing such a local vote to be conducted in two South Florida counties (Miami-Dade and Broward) and for the State of Florida to tax the slots and earmark the revenue for education. Subsequently, Broward County approved slots at its pari-mutuel facilities; Miami-Dade did not in a first vote but then did in a second. Pari-mutuels are constantly fighting for survival against any form of competition in the gaming industry, especially new, more lucrative forms of gambling.

Florida's pari-mutuel industries—horse racing, jai alai, and greyhound racing—are constantly fighting for survival against other forms of legalized gambling.

UP-CLOSE: NATIVE TRIBES AND CASINO POLITICS IN FLORIDA

In 2010, the state of Florida and the Seminole Tribe of Florida signed a compact allowing expansion of gambling at the tribe's casinos and guaranteeing the state at least $1 billion from the Tribe over the next five years. The agreement ended a political and legal battle that stretched back thirty years and involved the Seminole Tribe, governors, legislatures, state courts, presidents, Congress, the U.S. Supreme Court, multiple proposed constitutional amendments, the public, and numerous interest groups from the casino industry, theme parks, the pari-mutuel industry (horse and dog tracks and jai alai frontons), business associations, education interests, law enforcement, and religious and social conservatives.

Gambling and the Seminole Tribe

The biggest source of revenue, and political conflict, for the Seminole Tribe is gambling money generated by reservation casinos.[34] The Seminole Tribe was the first native tribe in the country to offer high stakes gambling when they opened up a bingo hall in Hollywood in 1979. After surviving legal challenges, the practice spread and today about 200 tribes in 28 states have gambling operations bringing in over $27 billion a year.[35] The Seminole Tribe operates seven casinos in the state including five Seminole Casinos (Brighton, Big Cypress, Coconut Creek, Hollywood, and Immokalee) and two Seminole Hard Rock Hotel and Casinos (Hollywood and Tampa). The Hard Rock facilities are the most recent additions. Hoping to compete with Las Vegas, the Seminoles signed a joint venture with Hard Rock Café International to replace the older gambling halls in Tampa and Hollywood with brand new luxury casino resorts and in 2006 agreed to buy Hard Rock Café company for about $965 million. The casinos have been quite popular and Tribe members have benefited greatly. After opening the Hard Rock casinos, gambling surged from $200 million a year to $500 million a year in tax-free profits to the Tribe. In 1979, the entire tribal budget was only $400 per person with most of the money coming from federal aid. Twenty years later, the per-Tribe-member dividend had climbed to $18,000 per person. Today, payments have soared to over $7,000 a month for each man, woman, and child in the 3,300 member Tribe.[36] With the signing of the new compact, revenues to the Tribe will likely increase even more.

The Seminole Hard Rock Hotel and Casino in Tampa

Indian Gaming Regulatory Act

The 1988 Indian Gaming Regulatory Act passed by Congress gives tribes the right to regulate gaming on Indian land as long as it is not prohibited by federal or state law. Traditional Indian games, Class 1 gambling, are left unregulated. But the law places Class 2 gaming (gamblers play each other and not against the house) under federal supervision by the National Indian Gaming Commission and allows Class 3 gambling only where states permit such gambling and only when a compact is reached between the tribe and the state. The law allowed tribes to sue states in federal court if the states did not negotiate a gambling compact in good faith. And since Florida refused to sign a compact allowing expanded gambling, the Tribe sued. However, in that case, the U.S. Supreme Court ruled the section of the law allowing a lawsuit unconstitutional, holding that it violated the Eleventh Amendment giving states immunity from lawsuits in federal court.[37] Thus, since Florida did not allow Class 3 gambling, and since the Tribe had no agreement with the state, the Seminole Tribe was limited to certain "low stakes" games by their federal Class 2 gambling license, although the term "low stakes" is somewhat of a misnomer. Seminole bingo games had jackpots as high as $130,000 and video slot machines had jackpots as high as $10,000. The video slot machines operate like lottery scratch off cards revealing combinations of numbers and issuing paper receipts to winners that can be exchanged for cash. All the while, the Seminole Tribe actively sought to upgrade to a Class 3 license to allow full-fledged casino gambling: regular slot machines and games like roulette, blackjack, and high-stakes poker. Florida officials continued to refuse and also believed the video slot machines were illegal but were unsuccessful in federal court in their attempts to remove them.

The Battle over Expansion

Native tribes in Florida sought to convince lawmakers to sign a voluntary compact with the tribe and allow expanded casino gambling by promising Florida a portion of the projected enormous profits. Casino interests, the native tribes, and the pari-mutuel industry regularly lobby in Tallahassee and are heavy campaign contributors to state elections. Casino backers placed three proposed constitutional amendments in three different decades to expand gambling in the state, but each was defeated by the voters. The public, most politicians, and a number of interest groups in Florida fought this expansion even though it meant passing up extra revenue from a voluntary source of taxation. A number of socially conservative individuals and groups believe that gambling is morally wrong and exploits poor people and that the government should not encourage it. In addition, other legislators and more established tourism interests fight expansion of casino gambling because they worry it will change Florida's family friendly image and hurt existing theme parks and tourist attractions. Finally some "law and order" opponents worry about the potential increase in criminal activity that often accompanies casino gambling: from theft and prostitution to organized crime.

The Stalemate Ends

The stalemate over expanded casino gambling in Florida ended for two reasons: a constitutional amendment and a bad economy. In 2004, Floridians voted to allow slot machines at race tracks in Broward and Miami-Dade counties if the residents of those counties approved a referendum to do so. Broward residents approved it quickly and Miami-Dade residents approved it after first rejecting it. Since federal law allows native tribes to have any form of gambling allowed elsewhere in the state, the Seminoles argued that they had the right to slots and to all other forms of Class 3 gambling and began expanding operations. At the same time the economy in Florida began to stagnate with unemployment rising and the state budget facing multi-billion dollar shortfalls. Facing the prospect of the Seminoles expanding gambling with the state receiving nothing from them, Governor Crist, on his own, negotiated a compact with the Seminoles, but the legislature sued and the Florida Supreme Court invalidated the agreement saying it required legislative approval. Governor Crist negotiated a second deal getting some legislative input but the legislature voted it down fearing it expanded gambling too much without providing enough for Florida. Finally the legislature itself entered the negotiations and an agreement was reached and passed into law in April of 2010.[38]

The Las Vegas of the South?

The compact guaranteed the state at least $1 billion payable over five years with the possibility of up to $500 million more depending on how much the Tribe made on card games. In return, the Seminoles got exclusive rights to run banked card games (like blackjack, baccarat and chemin de fer) at its Tampa and Hollywood Hard Rock resorts and at its Hollywood, Coconut Creek and Immokalee casinos and official permission to run slot machines at all seven casinos. As a sideline of the deal, the pari-mutuels in Broward and Miami-Dade also got a reduced tax rate from 50 to 35 percent and expanded gambling hours and higher betting limits—but were prohibited from the banked card games. After five years the deal could be renegotiated with more expansion of gambling (like roulette or craps) a possibility. When asked if the compact was poised to make Florida the "Las Vegas of the South," the House chief gambling negotiator Representative Bill Galvano said: "That's a very real probability. Yes."[39] In 2015, the Seminole Tribe's monopoly on gaming was threatened when a coalition of in-state and out-of-state gambling interests fought against the renewal of the compact hoping to expand the lucrative gaming industry in South Florida. While the legislature and governor did not vote to expand gambling, they also have yet to extend the agreement with the Tribe (the Seminole Tribe would like to renew the agreement).

LINKING TAXES AND SPENDING: HOW THE PUBLIC JUDGES SPENDING DECISIONS

Nothing better reflects the priorities of a government than its budget. In people's personal lives, it is common to require someone to "put your money where your mouth is" as proof of a true commitment to a promise. It is no different in the public sector. However, from a constituent's perspective, it is important to feel that public officials' promises about spending tax dollars in the most efficient and effective way are not just hollow campaign rhetoric. In the wake of the Great Recession, a majority of Floridians do not feel that either the State of Florida or their local government (county) spends its tax revenues efficiently, although local government is generally seen as somewhat more responsible. (See Figure 9-4.)

REVOLTING AGAINST TAXES

The anti-tax sentiments of Floridians are not limited to opinion polls. Floridians have directly expressed their opposition to taxes on a number of referenda votes over the years.

Voting to Limit Taxes

Constitutional amendments to limit taxes have fared very well with Florida voters. (See Appendix A.) In 1980, over 80 percent of Florida voters approved a property tax homestead exemption of $25,000. In 1986, they approved a state-operated lottery in the hopes of keeping taxes low. In 1990, they approved a constitutional prohibition on unfunded mandates on local governments. In 1992 a "Save Our Homes" constitutional amendment, limiting annual property tax assessment to the lower of three percent or the inflation rate, was approved by the voters, despite vigorous opposition by many city and county officials, school board members, and educational groups. Following Florida Supreme Court decisions to keep tax-limiting constitutional amendments off the ballot because they violated the single topic rule, anti-tax forces succeeded in a 1994 initiative effort to eliminate the single topic constitutional provision for tax limiting amendments. And even though Floridians are very supportive of education, in 2008 voters rejected an amendment to allow higher taxes to fund local community colleges.

Figure 9-4. Public Sees Tax Dollars for Services Being Spent Wastefully: State v. Local

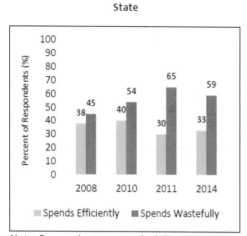

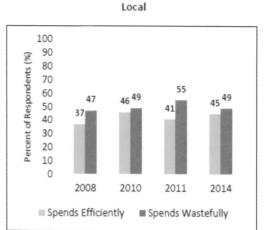

Note: Respondents were asked, "In terms of providing public services, do you feel Florida state government... spends tax revenue in a relatively efficient manner or spends tax revenue in a relatively wasteful manner?" Responses may not add to 100% due to rounding.
Source: "Leadership Florida Sunshine State Survey (2006-2008), Leadership Florida-Nielsen Company Sunshine State Survey (2010-2012), and University of South Florida-Nielsen Sunshine State Survey (2014)."

Note: Respondents were asked, "In terms of providing public services, do you feel your local county government... spends tax revenue in a relatively efficient manner or spends tax revenue in a relatively wasteful manner?" Responses may not add to 100% due to rounding.
Source: "Leadership Florida Sunshine State Survey (2006-2008), Leadership Florida-Nielsen Company Sunshine State Survey (2010-2012), and University of South Florida-Nielsen Sunshine State Survey (2014)."

Granting Exemptions

Floridians have been more than willing to grant tax exemptions or tax relief to certain types of individuals and properties. In 2006, Floridians gave disabled veterans property tax relief and counties the option of increasing the homestead exemption for poor senior citizens over age 65. (See Chapter 2.) In 2008, a number of property tax-related exemptions were approved for homeowners, as well as land used for conservation purposes. In 2010, voters overwhelming voted to grant property tax credits to deployed military personnel.

A Supermajority to Raise Taxes

Perhaps the most sweeping tax limiting initiative approved by Florida's voters was the 1996 constitutional amendment requiring a two-thirds statewide referendum vote on any new constitutional state tax or fee. Presumably, an income tax proposal would need to win a two-thirds majority of the voters to be approved. Since polls show that an income tax is not likely to be approved by even a majority, this provision may have little meaning. But it raises questions about the possible adoption of other constitutional taxes—that is, revenues

The sentiments of these protesters add to the image of Florida as an "anti-tax" state.

that can be raised only by constitutional amendment. Perhaps a 60 percent majority vote to rescind the two-thirds requirement must precede any vote to add a new tax or fee.

The Sugar Fee

The large and powerful sugar industry aroused anti-tax sentiments to defeat a proposed one cent per pound "fee" on sugar that was to be earmarked for Everglades cleanup. Environmentalists succeeded in getting the initiative on the state ballot with the word "fee" in the title. Generally the word "fee" generates less opposition than the word "tax," and early opinion polls showed widespread support for a fee on sugar to clean up the Everglades. But the sugar industry responded with a well-funded media campaign to equate fee with tax. Indeed, "Fee = Tax" was the centerpiece of its ads. By Election Day, the voters were convinced that the "fee" really was a "tax," and they rejected it.

Repeal of the High Speed Rail System

Occasionally voters change their minds after learning of the costs of approving an expenditure called for in an amendment (or the possibility of higher taxes to pay for it). Such was the case in 2004 when Florida's citizens overwhelmingly (64 percent) voted to repeal the high speed rail system they had approved in 2000.

Strong Popular Support for Tax Holidays

Republican Governor Jeb Bush, with help from the Florida Legislature, pushed through popular sales tax holidays on low cost clothing items in five different years of his administration. Three of the holidays also included school supplies selling for less than $10 and two of the holidays included books selling for less than $50. Over the years, these holidays have become very popular both among residents and merchants. But tax holidays are not always just about giving taxpayers relief for school clothes, books, shoes, and supplies. The list has been expanded to include clothes, books, shoes, and supplies. Some have been offered to prompt voters to make certain types of purchases. In 2005, a new sales tax holiday for the purchase of hurricane preparedness supplies was approved. (It ended in 2007.) In 2006, there was relief for purchase of new energy efficient appliances less than $1,500. In 2015, one legislator even proposed creating an Independence Day tax holiday to encourage Floridians to buy hunting, camping, and fishing gear, linking these activities to the Founding Fathers![40] In fact, only twice (2008 and 2009) since the sales tax holidays were first implemented has the legislature not offered any type of tax holiday, and that was due to major budgetary constraints.

A CLOSER LOOK AT STATE SPENDING (APPROPRIATIONS)[41]

The monies the state receives from its many revenue sources are spent on (or appropriated to) many different programs, services, and facilities throughout the state. While funds from some of the state's revenue sources are earmarked and not at the discretion of the state, funding from other sources can be spent by the legislature for whatever purposes it sees fit (discretionary funds). What is confusing is how different revenues are placed in different funds to be in line with government accounting standards. Because of this, there is often confusion about how much of the state's budget is spent on specific functions. Perhaps most importantly, by law, the state must run a balanced operating budget (money appropriated annually to run the day-to-day operations of the state) and cannot borrow money to make up shortfalls in the annual appropriations bill. Thus, during recessions, when revenues decline, state legislators must either cut spending or raise taxes. They cannot put off hard choices like the federal government.

Two Ways to Look at Spending Priorities

The state really has several different budgets, including the "All Funds" budget and the "General Fund" budget. Both are considered operating budgets. They present a slightly different picture of the state's spending priorities. The ˆ Budget (the '"big picture" budget) includes federal aid money, state trust funds, and taxes collected by the state (like sales taxes). Federal aid includes money for health care (including Medicaid), children and family welfare, and unemployment compensation. State trust funds include gasoline taxes earmarked for highways and taxes collected that under law must be shared with cities and counties. The revenues in the All Funds budget that are dedicated to specific spending categories are often referred to as *"nondiscretionary"* funds. These funds are excluded from the *General Fund* budget.

The *General Fund* budget is more "discretionary" in nature and is primarily funded by sales tax revenues the state has collected. It is the General Fund budget that the Florida Legislature has more control over, and it is the General Fund spending plan that gets the most news media attention and, thus, is what most citizens believe is "the state's budget." As shown in Figure 9-7, the proportion of the total budget pie that is spent on specific programs differs depending on what revenues go into the pie—although Education and Human Services (health and welfare) are the largest two categories in both budgets.

While political commentators often focus on the state's General Fund budget, the All Funds budget gives a more comprehensive look at where the state's money is spent. For example, a casual review of the General Fund budget indicates that 52 percent is spent on education. However, this is only the proportion of the General Fund budget, not the much larger All Funds budget, which actually appropriates more to human services than it does to education.

Figure 9-5. "ALL FUNDS" and "GENERAL FUND" Budgets: $77 Billion vs. $28 Billion

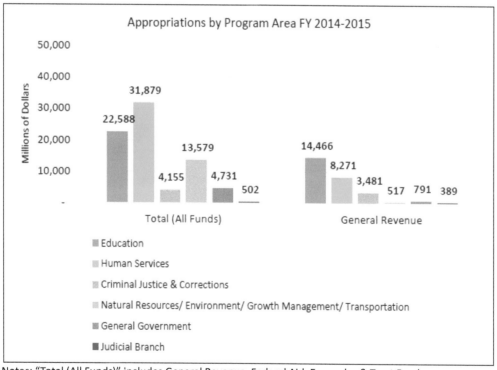

Notes: "Total (All Funds)" includes General Revenue, Federal Aid, Earmarks, & Trust Funds.
Source: Florida Revenue Estimating Conference, 2015 Florida Tax Handbook. Available at
http://edr.state.fl.us/content/revenues/reports/tax-handbook/taxhandbook2015.pdf.

Billions of Dollars Spent

Total state government spending in Florida amounted to around $77 billion in FY 2015—that is, about $3,903 per person in the state (with an estimated population of almost 19 million). (See Figure 9-8.) This does not include the billions spent by Florida's local governments.

The General Appropriations Act is difficult to prepare because it has a lot of moving parts. The funding sources are restricted by different rules, and some offer more flexibility than others. As shown in Figure 9-9, the sources for each broad program area differ. While some program areas are funded primarily by state trust funds (Health and Human Services; Transportation, Tourism, and Economic Development; and General Government), others are funded mostly by general revenue (Education and Criminal and Civil Justice). Education also receives substantial funding from local governments.

Figure 9-6. Total Per Capita State Appropriation

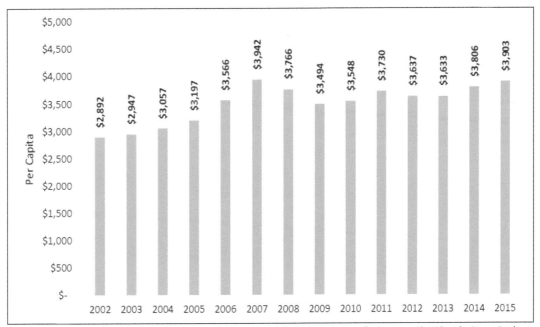

Source (2002 through 2011): Florida Center for Fiscal and Economic Policy, "Primer on the Florida State Budget and Tax System," June 2010. Available at http://www.fcfep.org/attachments/20100630--Primer.pdf.

Source (2012 through 2015): Per capita appropriation calculated using appropriations from *Florida Tax Handbook* (available at http://edr.state.fl.us/content/revenues/reports/tax-handbook/) and population estimates from Office of Economic and Demographic Research (available at http://edr.state.fl.us/Content/population-demographics/data/).

Figure 9-7. Source of Funds for Different Program Areas (General Fund Appropriations)

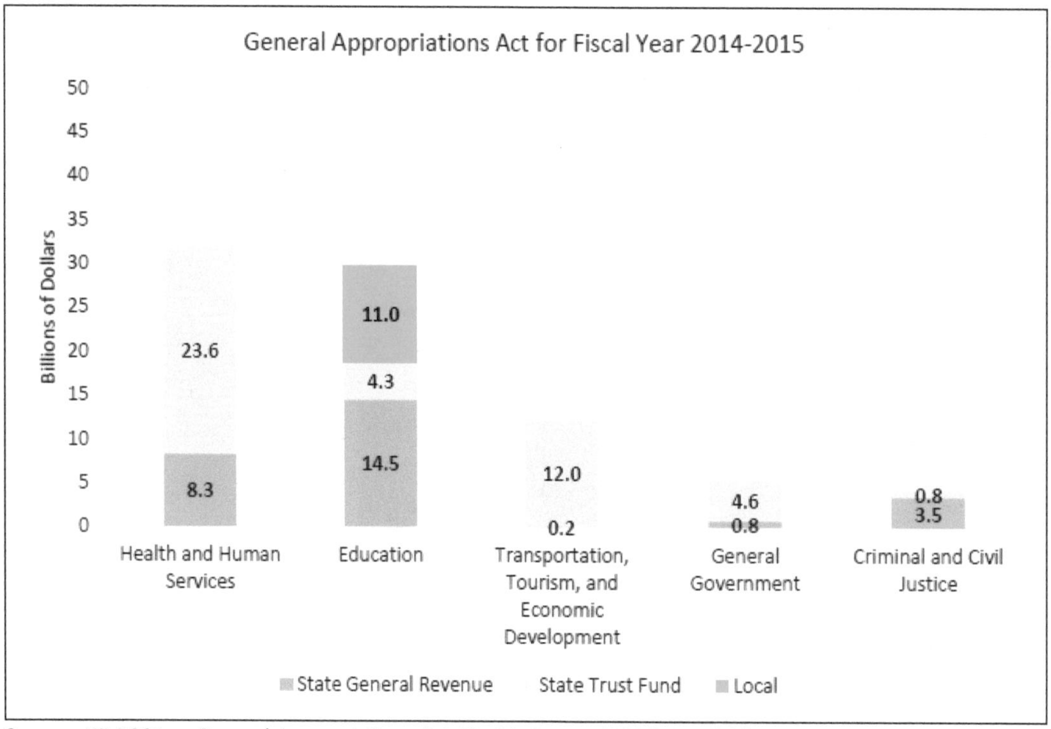

General Appropriations Act for Fiscal Year 2014-2015

Source: *HB 5001 — General Appropriations Act*, Florida Senate (2014). Available at http://www.flsenate.gov/PublishedContent/Session/2014/BillSummary/Appropriations_AP5001ap_5001.

Earmarking of Tax Revenues for Specific Policy Areas

Not only are federal funds and trust funds earmarked to specific types of spending, so, too, are certain tax revenues. For example, Lottery monies are earmarked for education, and the tobacco tax is earmarked exclusively to human services.

In 2014, a coalition of conservation and civic groups worked hard to get Florida voters to approve Amendment 1 (The Water and Land Conservation Amendment) mandating that one-third of the funds raised by the real estate transactions tax (documentary stamp tax) be spent on water and land conservation.[42] Specifically, they wanted to make sure that monies raised by the tax and dedicated (earmarked) to conservation projects would actually be spent on it rather than diverted to more general use via the state's general revenue fund. In selling the idea to the voters, the group emphasized that no *new* tax was needed. The voters overwhelming approved it; 75 percent voted "Yes."

Once a revenue source becomes linked to a specific function (or functions), it is quite difficult politically to reverse this linkage. The more earmarks are in place constitutionally or statutorily, the more difficult it becomes to adopt significant shifts in budgetary priorities.

Human Services

The human services appropriation, which comprises a major portion of the state's All Funds budget, has been placing great strain on the state's finances. Arguably one of the most pressing financial challenges facing the state, Medicaid costs have skyrocketed at the worst possible time. Caseloads expand as more citizens lose their jobs and can no longer afford rising health care costs. These indigent citizens who qualify for Medicaid are entitled to receive care, meaning, by law, they cannot be denied. (See Figure 9-10 for trends in Medicaid costs and caseloads.)

Figure 9-8. Explosion in Medicaid Caseloads and Spending

Medicaid Caseload and Expenditures in Florida

(Bar chart showing Average Monthly Caseload in Millions and line chart showing Service Expenditures in Billions, by fiscal year)

Fiscal Year	Average Monthly Caseload (Millions)	Service Expenditures (Billions)
2006-07	2.1	$14.4
2007-08	2.2	$14.8
2008-09	2.4	$16.0
2009-10	2.7	$17.9
2010-11	2.9	$19.3
2011-12	3.1	$19.6
2012-13	3.3	$20.4
2013-14*	3.5	$22.2
2014-15*	3.7	$23.3
2015-16*	3.8	$21.7
2016-17*	3.9	$22.9
2017-18*	4.0	$24.1

Average Monthly Caseload (Millions)   Service Expenditures (Billions)

Note: *Estimates based on June 2014 Social Services Estimating Conference
Source: Office of Economic & Demographic Research, *State of Florida Long-Range Financial Outlook, Fiscal Year 2015-16 through 2017-18*, 2014. Available at http://www.edr.state.fl.us/Content/long-range-finacial-outlook/3-Year-Plan_Fall-2014_1516-1718.pdf.

The fact that the state receives federal assistance to help fund Medicaid means that the state must comply with the demands of the federal government. In 2015, this proviso took center stage, as Republican Governor Rick Scott and the Florida House, along with Texas and Kansas, led the fight (against President Obama and the Florida Senate) to reject Medicaid expansion. Expansion opponents claimed that Obama tried to coerce states into Medicaid expansion by tying it to federal funding for hospitals.[43] It was interesting that the same legislators opposed to taking federal money for Medicaid expansion were in favor of continuing to accept federal funds for Florida's Low Income Pool (LIP)—the program aiding hospitals that serve the poor. The bottom line is that there have always been tensions between the national and state governments over federal funds whether it be the amount, the strings and guidelines, or the beneficiaries.

Medicaid has thirteen area offices that serve as local liaisons to providers and recipients. The area offices handle claims resolution, training, transportation and manage Child Health Check-Up screenings on a local level.

Despite the difficulties that go along with reforming a federally-funded program, the state must do what it can to make cuts. In Tallahassee, some have suggested privatization, outsourcing Medicaid fulfillment to managed care companies, while others argue that privatization will result in compromised care for those who have the greatest need. When the budget tightens, generational conflicts emerge, pitting young against old and forcing the state to look to cut elsewhere in order to keep Medicaid afloat. Although eliminating fraud is far and away the most popular way to reduce costs, more drastic measures will undoubtedly be needed as federal health care reform and other factors continue to threaten the program's economic feasibility.

Education

Although education makes-up approximately half of the state's General Fund budget, it makes up a relatively smaller portion of the All Funds budget. As another major spending category, education is consistently the source of intense budgetary debates and generates vast media interest. There is constant tension between higher education and K-12 education, which is perceived as having a more widespread impact. The key questions surrounding K-12 education are how to improve the quality of education and how much, if at all, increasing spending helps further this aim. Some support incentivizing academic performance by instituting merit pay for teachers based upon standardized test scores (yet another subject of heated debate) and other metrics. Others, namely influential teachers' unions, vehemently argue that such measures would unfairly disadvantage teachers who confront factors outside of their control. Despite the fact that K-12 has traditionally won the political tug-of-war, Florida's business community warns that underfunding higher education will lead to diminished academic quality, high-achieving students leaving the state, a workforce less competitive in the global economy, and a not-so-bright future for the state's economy.

Criminal Justice and Corrections

Floridians have long debated whether the proper role of corrections is to punish or to rehabilitate inmates. Proponents of punishment argue the state should not spend to rehabilitate those with an outstanding debt to society. Proponents of rehabilitation argue that it makes practical sense to rehabilitate inmates, whose actions may have stemmed from a disadvantaged background, hopefully saving money in the long-run by preventing them from returning to corrections. However, as the budget tightens, focus shifts to the more immediate concern of how to pay for housing a large incarcerated population. Corrections may be the target of expensive lawsuits filed by politically powerful advocacy groups that

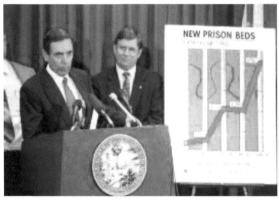

The need to build more prisons escalated after the legislature passed laws making it tougher for an inmate to get early release.

seek equitable treatment by investigating claims of racial and other injustices. Incidents of inhumane treatment, including brutality, can lead to federal court orders that dramatically affect the state's budget. Despite the relatively small share of total costs consumed by criminal justice and corrections, elected officials may pay a big price at the polls with just one high-profile case.

There is a lot of pressure on corrections officials to reduce the state's rapidly growing incarcerated population, especially nonviolent offenders, but this is easier said than done in a state plagued by larger-than-life criminal trials. Faced with intense pressure to cut costs, state leaders naturally look to privatization as a possible solution. At the same time, they are wary of the political fallout that can come when privatization efforts fail or lead to major lawsuits against the state for "cruel and unusual punishment." Even the traditional approach of simply building more prisons has come under attack because of the steep costs of borrowing money.[44]

Criminal justice and corrections is another functional area subject to generationally-based debates. Juvenile offenders who commit heinous acts raise the question of at what age do juveniles who commit adult crimes begin being prosecuted as such and at what cost. For aging inmates imprisoned for life, the rising costs of health care for them raises new questions about whether to release them when they are terminally ill.

Compared to corrections, law enforcement consumes a much smaller part of the state's Criminal Justice and Corrections budget. That is because law enforcement is a function primarily handled at the local level.

Transportation and the Environment

Transportation disputes center around how to connect the state's geographically dispersed metropolitan areas. Florida struggles with unique logistical challenges that arise from a large population of citizens and tourists that need to move efficiently throughout the oddly-shaped state. In addition to residents, Florida's businesses and the expanding number of tourists rely heavily on transportation infrastructure.[45] Infrastructure, which is vital to support growth, places a great deal of pressure on the state's finances.

Whether to accept federal assistance to help pay for public transportation, notably high-speed rail, is an ongoing debate. Some believe increasing public transit will alleviate problems, like congestion, while others believe the private sector would have already acted if there were enough demand. On another front, some say that regardless of demand, the state should accept the seemingly free federal money. Others are quick to remind the state that federally-assisted projects have a habit of backfiring, as federal priorities shift and states are left with no choice but to pick up the slack. There is a clear division between urban residents, who generally support spending on public transit, and rural residents, who are more in favor of spending on roads and bridges.

Environmental protection is also a top priority in a state that historically relies heavily on tourism and, until recently, population growth to fuel its economy. Florida's natural beauty is certainly among its greatest attractions. It also helps local governments establish a sense of community and maintain an image that communicates government's commitment to Floridians. Neglecting to properly care for the environment, which attracts not only tourists, but also new residents and relocating businesses, can exacerbate budgetary woes.

Administrative Expenses

The budget appropriates relatively little funding for administrative expenses. Among the public at-large, the term "administrative expenses" often conjures up images of bureaucrats spending wastefully. This image is attributable to a general lack of understanding of how these funds are used to benefit the public. Actually, these appropriations are used to implement, manage, and coordinate all of the state's programs. The state has more flexibility in how to use these funds than it does others, but that flexibility can be threatened when a poor economy imposes pressure to consolidate agencies.

Judiciary

The financial strains that the judicial branch faces may indicate more serious governmental issues. The court system struggled to keep pace as the state faced unprecedented foreclosures (See Figure 9-11.), in addition to the regular caseload, and little in the way of funding to hire more judges and court administrators. Besides confronting the normal competition for funding, the judicial branch also finds itself in a political predicament with the legislature. The courts, in an effort to preserve the checks and balances that are crucial to a functioning democracy, struggle to make objective rulings without putting their already inadequate funding at risk by upsetting the legislature, which would, in effect, be biting the hand that feeds.

Figure 9-9. During the Great Recession, Property Foreclosures Spiked and Were Slow to Come Down to Previous Levels

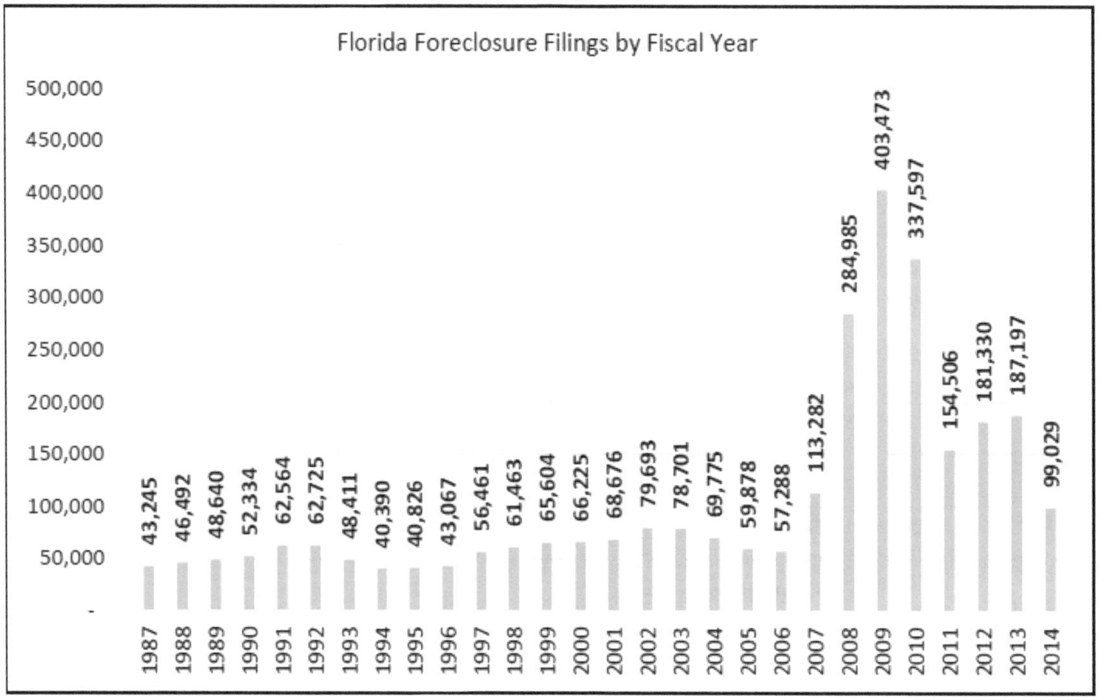

Source: "Florida: An Overview of Foreclosures," Office of Economic and Demographic Research (February 4, 2015). Available at http://edr.state.fl.us/Content/presentations/economic/FLOverviewofForeclosures_2-4-15.pdf.

The Most Essential Services to Keep if a Government Shutdown

For a short time in 2015, it looked as if there might be a shutdown of state government when the legislature had not passed a budget by the time the regular session ended. Perhaps as a way to "push" the Senate and the House into passing a budget in the special session, Governor Scott solicited from state agencies lists of essential services and obligations that would have to be met if there were a state government shutdown. The list he released to the public included programs and infrastructure that there were previous commitments and legal obligations in place to fund. Others listed were seen as "directly resulting in the loss of life" if not funded.[46] (See Table 9-2.) While the government ultimately did not shut down, the list forced lawmakers to see more vividly how legalities can dictate funding priorities.

Table 9-2. List of Critical Service Needs to Be Met Even If State Government is Shutdown

1. Fiscal Year 2014-2015 operating deficits in the Departments of Corrections, Juvenile Justice, Health, and Children and Families, and other funding shortfalls adopted by the most recent consensus estimating conferences.
2. Additional kindergarten through 12th grade students as determined by the April 13, 2015, enrollment conference with state funds maintained at the fiscal year 2014-15 level through the Florida Education Finance Program.
3. Medicaid expenditures based on the March 4, 2015, Social Services Estimating Conference.
4. Department of Transportation Work Program.
5. Economic development and housing programs at the fiscal year 2014-2015 funding level.
6. Minimum operating requirements necessary to continue emergency management and other current state services.
7. Fixed Capital Outlay for critical maintenance and repairs of state-owned and public school facilities.
8. Fixed Capital Outlay necessary to continue ongoing construction projects for special facilities.
9. Matching funds necessary for federally declared disasters and National Guard facilities.
10. Environmental initiatives consistent with Amendment One.
11. Actuarially-recommended rates for the Florida Retirement System.
12. Repayment of the final transfer to the Budget Stabilization Fund.
13. Other necessary technical adjustments that have no resulting policy implications."

Source: Steve Bousquet, "Gov. Rick Scott orders lists of critical state needs, hints at possible shutdown," *Miami Herald* (May 14, 2015).

State Always Looking for Ways to Control Spending

Because there are always more requests for funds than there are funds, the state is constantly searching for ways to cut costs and help control spending growth, usually by searching for more efficient and effective ways of providing public services. Over the years, the state's governors and legislators have turned to high-profile, high-powered commissions, task forces, and study groups made up of leaders from across the state to find ways to improve government operations. This approach began with the creation of the Tax and Budget Reform Commission (constitutionally mandated by Florida voters in 1988) and has continued over the years with Partners in Productivity, the Productivity Measurement and Quality Improvement Task Force, the Governor's Commission for Government by the People, the Commission on Accountability to the People, the Governor's Commission on Workers' Compensation Reform, the Study Committee on Public Records, and the Property Tax Reform Committee.

More recent cost saving task force efforts have focused on specific agencies and programs—increasing accessibility and efficiency in Florida elections, streamlining operations in the Florida State Parks, improving cost efficiencies in Florida's distance learning program, and improving transparency in the budget process, to name a few. Business-oriented groups like Florida TaxWatch and the James Madison Institute often conduct their analyses of state government programs and policies, then forward cost-saving recommendations to the governor and state legislators

Evaluation units have also been set up within government. In 1994, the legislature created the Office of Program Policy Analysis and Government Accountability (OPPAGA) to regularly examine how much programs cost and measure their efficiency and effectiveness. The agency conducts policy analyses and performance reviews and annually provides the legislature with recommendations that can save the state money or have other positive fiscal impacts. Recent reports have focused on the Florida Retirement System, the state's use of prison volunteers, Florida's biotechnology industry, and the state's nursing education programs.

Privatization is another cost-containment technique that has been used by state and local governments in Florida, albeit with mixed results. The most extensive and most controversial efforts at privatization have been promoted by the state's Department of Corrections as a way to save the state millions of dollars. In fact, Florida has been experimenting with private prisons for nearly 20 years, as the first private prison opened in 1995. Efforts to expand privatization in both the housing of and health care for inmates intensified during the Great Recession as a way to control rising costs. There have been other efforts to privatize services such as nursing and food services in the state's veterans' nursing homes and toll operations on the state's roads, to name a few.

As is often the case, privatization evokes strong opposition from public employees who worry about losing their jobs and their pensions. The battle lines are always the same: the state hoping to save money versus public employees hoping not to lose their jobs, and economists disagreeing with each other over whether such efforts do, in fact, save money.

BORROWING: TAPPING INTO RESERVES (SHORT TERM) AND SELLING BONDS (LONG TERM)

Borrowing remains a popular way of bridging the gap between insufficient current revenue and the revenue needed to fund capital projects, especially those related to education, transportation, and the environment. We can expect continued use of borrowing to meet growth- and security-driven infrastructure demands, especially for new schools, roads and turnpikes, airport and port security, and correctional facilities. Borrowing is also likely to continue for environmental-related needs, ranging from land purchases and environmental clean-ups to water resource protection. Borrowing can be in the short term or in the long term (usually for major infrastructure).

While Florida has borrowed a lot of money, particularly during the high growth years, and still has a lot of debt to repay (See Figure 9-12.), Florida's borrowing has not been as excessive or irresponsible as in some other states, like California. The Sunshine State's "conservative financial and budgeting practices, swift response to budget pressures, adequate reserves, moderate debt burden with clear guidelines, and a well-funded pension plan"[47] kept its credit rating from being lowered during much of the Great Recession. Although the state's economy is improving, the credit rating firms still watch it closely,[48] paying special attention to how well the state's pension system is funded.[49]

Types of Bonds: Full Faith and Credit (General Obligation) and Revenue

Governments borrow money by issuing *bonds*. A bond is a long-term promise by the borrower (bond issuer—the state) to the lender (bondholder—the investor) to pay back the face amount (principal) plus interest on a specific date.[50] As of 2014, the state's outstanding debt totaled $24.6 billion.[51] Over 83 percent of this debt is in the form of *full faith and credit bonds* (tax-supported *general obligation* bonds) which must be approved by Florida voters.

Education (PECO, lottery, university system improvements, community colleges) is the largest infrastructure program area funded by tax-supported debt, followed by Environmental programs (Preservation 2000/ Florida Forever, Everglades Restoration, Conservation and Recreation, Save Our Coast, Inland Protection), Transportation (right-of-way acquisition, state infrastructure bank, ports), and Appropriated debt for prisons, hospitals, charter schools, sports facilities, affordable housing, and other facilities. (See Figure 9-13.)

The remainder of the outstanding debt is in *revenue bonds* (self-supporting debt) that are repayable from funds derived directly from sources other than state tax revenues, usually from the revenues (fees, charges) generated by the project funded. These do not require voter approval. Self-supporting debt (revenue bonds) largely underwrites university auxiliary facilities like student housing (repaid by rents), water pollution control (partially repaid from fees charged for waste management or water bills), and toll facilities, roads, and bridges (repaid from toll revenue).

Figure 9-10. Total Debt Outstanding and General Fund Reserve Balance

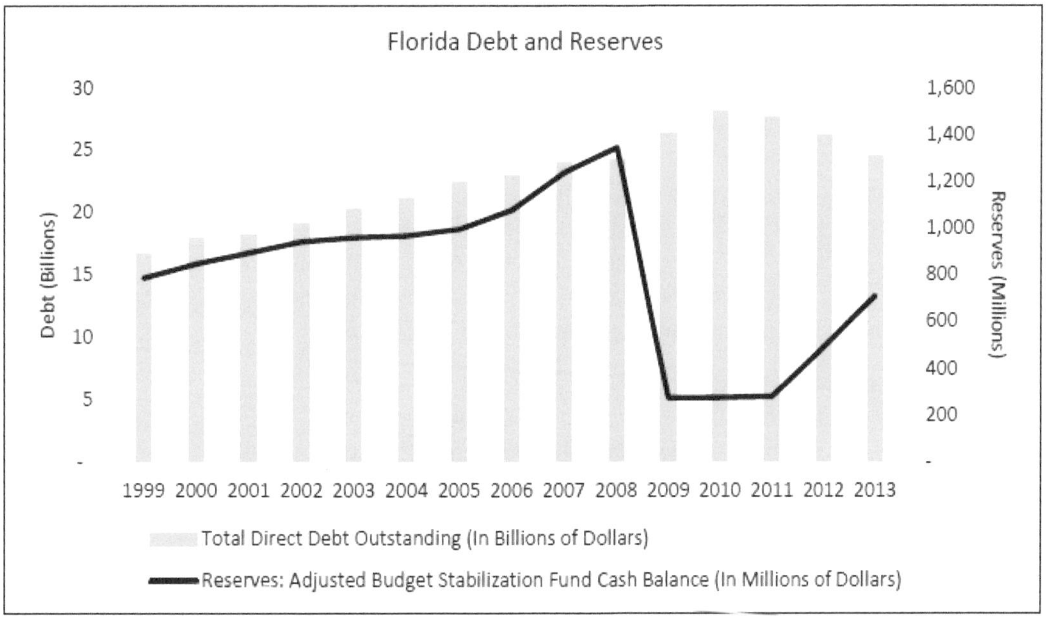

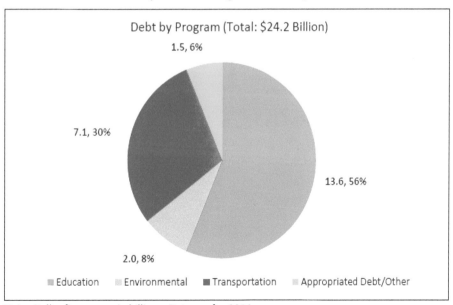

Source (Debt): Office of Economic & Demographic Research, *State of Florida Long-Range Financial Outlook, Fiscal Year 2015-16 through 2017-18*, 2014. Available at
http://www.edr.state.fl.us/Content/long-range-finacial-outlook/3-Year-Plan_Fall-2014_1516-1718.pdf.
Source (Reserves): The Florida Legislature, *2015 Florida Tax Handbook*.
Available at http://edr.state.fl.us/content/revenues/reports/tax-handbook/taxhandbook2015.pdf.

Figure 9-11. Infrastructure-Related Debt Outstanding by Program (General Obligation Bonds)

Note: Dollar figures are in billions. Data are for 2014.
Source: Division of Bond Finance, "State of Florida 2014 Debt Affordability Report," December 2014. Available at
https://www.sbafla.com/fsb/portals/bondfinance/DebtOverview/DAR2014.pdf.

Debt Limits and Restrictions

There are several restrictions on the state's ability to borrow money including how much can be borrowed (debt limit), what the money can be borrowed for, and the procedures for approving new debt. By law, the state's Division of Bond Finance must conduct an annual Debt Affordability Study to be used as a tool for measuring, monitoring, and repaying the state's debt.[52] Explicit rules govern the amount the state can borrow. For example, the amount borrowed through full faith and credit bonds may not exceed 50 percent of total state tax revenues for the two preceding fiscal years. In addition, Florida cannot borrow money for its operating budget (All Funds and General Revenue budgets), but rather only for long term infrastructure and land as described above. And finally, general obligations bonds can only be issued with the permission of voters. For example, if a school district wanted to issue general obligation bonds to build new schools, the voters in the school district would have to approve it in a referendum.

Florida Credit Rating

Higher credit ratings mean lower interest costs. In 2005, the state's full faith and credit bond rating was upgraded from AA+ to AAA, thereby saving the state millions in interest costs. Standard & Poor's (a credit rating agency) applauded the state for its "strong and conservative financial and budget management practices, coupled with substantial budget reserves and economic trends that have been among the strongest nationally."[53] The rating was also helped by voter approval of the Budget Stabilization Fund, which effectively forces the state to save money for emergencies, which can rarely be forecast.

A newly-emerged threat to Florida' good credit rating is the funding of government employee pensions. A host of circumstances (financial concerns, retiring Baby Boomers, increased life expectancies, rising health care costs, etc.) are making funding retirement benefits for public employees an increasingly challenging proposition. Florida's state and, especially its local governments, face concerns about huge pension obligations and health benefits. Reform efforts target policies that govern both the contribution and distribution sides of the issue.[54] If not successfully solved, this problem threatens Florida governments' financial integrity and, therefore, creditworthiness.

The Budget Stabilization Fund

Good financial principles call for putting some money aside in reserves for emergencies. In 1992, Florida voters approved a constitutional amendment creating the Budget Stabilization Fund. It was put on the ballot by the Taxation and Budget Reform Commission. The law requires that the emergency fund be funded at "not less than 5 percent of the previous year's General Revenue collections, but not more than 10 percent." When the economy sours, general revenue collections go down, thereby shrinking the amount of money available in the Reserve. (See Figure 9-22.) If monies are "borrowed" from the Fund, they must be put back into the fund by the legislature, beginning in the third year after the withdrawal. If the Fund dips too low, it may affect the state's credit rating, which would make it more expensive to borrow in the future. The costs of long-term borrowing, essential for major capital projects, would increase.

The Fund is primarily used to cover revenue shortfalls in the General Revenue Fund. However, the law does permit it to be used in emergencies as established by law. The Fund had to be tapped after 9/11 and again in the aftermath of major hurricanes, the Gulf oil spill, and the Great Recession.

CITIZENS GRADE THE STATE'S FINANCIAL MANAGEMENT AND THE TAXES PAID-SERVICES RECEIVED RATIO

In the years following the Great Recession, a majority of Floridians have viewed the state's management of its finances less than stellar, although their evaluations have improved slightly as the economy has gotten stronger. (See Figure 9-14.) So, too, have their assessments of taxes paid relative to quality of state services provided. The percentage of citizens saying their taxes were "much too high" relative to services received has been declining since 2011. (See Figure 9-15.) A majority now judges them to be "about right."

Figure 9-12. Citizen's Ratings of the State's Financial Management

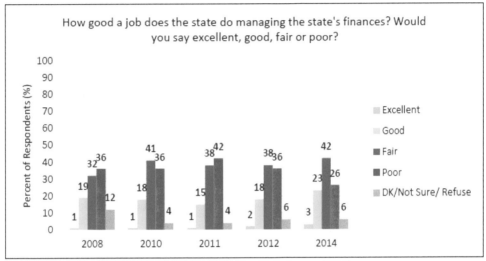

Source: University of South Florida-Nielsen Sunshine State Survey (2014).

Figure 9-13. Citizen Ratings: Taxes Paid Relative to Quality of State Services Provided

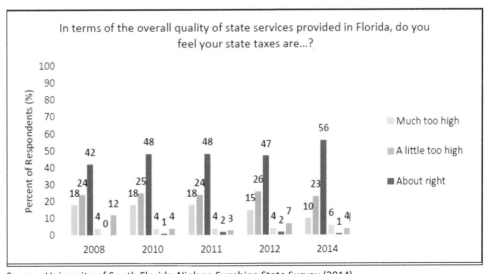

Source: University of South Florida-Nielsen Sunshine State Survey (2014).

LOOKING AHEAD: BUDGETARY CHALLENGES FACING FLORIDA

In the Sunshine State, it is always smart to look out for dark clouds, which may signal stormy weather ahead. While most economic forecasting firms and credit rating agencies continue to view Florida positively, some analysts are carefully tracking some potential problems. These include concerns about:

1. *Forecasting difficulties.* The state's constantly changing demographics and economic base can effectively alter budget priorities statewide and regionally. Anticipating costly federal mandates and lawsuits that create major revenue shortfalls is challenging. Unforeseen changes in the public's attitudes toward government may generate constitutional amendments that restrict a government's taxing, spending, and borrowing options.

2. *Cyber security breaches.* Surveys have shown Florida is vulnerable to cyber "warfare" that could do great damage to the state's public and private sector infrastructure.[55]

3. *Health care reform.* The fiscal consequences of revamping Medicaid and Medicare entitlement programs are not yet fully known. States and the federal government will continue to be at odds with one another over the structure and financing of these two popular programs.

4. *Pension reforms.* A number of Florida's local governments have grossly under-funded pension funds.[56] The question is what happens if their funds are depleted and they cannot meet their obligations to workers or retirees? Will the state's taxpayers at large have to pick up the tab?

5. *Population out-migration.* Will budgetary choices made by the state leaders negatively impact the quality of life that attracted persons to Florida to begin with and prompt out-migration of residents and businesses alike?

6. *Intergovernmental and interparty frictions.* Competition for funds and for political power can make a state more difficult to govern. Such fights tend to intensify when economies are weakened, creating a vicious downward spiral.

7. *Immigration reform.* Immigration is both an economic and a security issue that evokes considerable passion and activism. The economic fallout from protracted political and legal battles could be significant.

8. *Revenue diversification.* The state's heavy reliance on consumption-based taxes (primarily sales) makes it more vulnerable to swings in the economy than income-based taxes.

9. *Privatization and outsourcing.* Of interest is whether the state's pilot programs designed to test alternative service delivery methods of services can actually reduce costs without compromising quality.

10. *Transportation infrastructure.* Florida's geographically dispersed residents, businesses in a wide range of industries, and increasing number of visitors all strain the states' infrastructure amidst debate about whether the state should accept federal funding for transportation projects.

As this chapter has shown, reaching consensus on budgetary matters is extremely difficult in a fiscally-conservative state whose population is quite diverse, demographically and politically.

Building new infrastructure to accommodate growth
is very expensive. Governments often have to borrow
money by selling bonds to finance such endeavors.

ONLINE SOURCES FOR DATA AND INFORMATION UPDATES

The Bureau of Economic Analysis: Economy at a glance

BEBR provides a look into international, national, regional, and industrial economic accounts, as well as
statistics on GDP (real) and income.
http://bea.gov/newsreleases/glance.htm

Florida Office of Economic & Demographic Research

EDR produces objective information in support of the policy making process by the legislature. EDR is
primarily concerned with "forecasting economic and social trends that affect policy making, revenues,
and appropriations". Their data includes information on local option sales tax rates, total per capita state
appropriation, medicaid caseload and expenditures, Florida foreclosure filings by fiscal year, and Florida
debt and reserves.
http://edr.state.fl.us/Content/

Florida Office of Economic and Demographic Research: Long Term Revenue Analysis

The EDR is the research department of the Florida Legislature and is responsible for researching
economic and social trends and predictions, particularly those which affect policy making, revenues, and
appropriations. The "Long Term Revenue Analysis" page offers a look into state revenues, sources, and the
economic estimations for Florida and the U.S.
http://edr.state.fl.us/Content/conferences/longtermrevenue/2014longtermrevenueanalysis.pdf

Florida Office of Economic and Demographic Research: Long Range Financial Outlook

The "Long Range Financial Outlook" page features statistics and trends for the economy, income,
employment, population, job market, housing, homeownership, foreclosures, rentals, gas prices, and
general revenue adjustments.
*http://edr.state.fl.us/Content/presentations/long-range-financial-
outlook/3YearPlan_2015winterupdate.pdf*

Florida Office of Economic and Demographic Research: County Tax Rates

The "County Tax Rates" site has information on the different tax rates in Florida counties, including the current tax rates, county government levies, and school district levies.
http://edr.state.fl.us/Content/local-government/data/county-municipal/2015LDSSrates.pdf

Florida House of Representatives: General Appropriations Act

This site has a full text of the 2014 General Appropriations Act, and individual statistics for appropriated funds to each department.
http://www.myfloridahouse.gov/Sections/Documents/
loaddocaspx?PublicationType=Appropriations&CommitteeId=&Session=2014&DocumentType=Fiscal%20
Analysis%20In%20Brief&FileName=2014%20FAIB.PDF

Florida Tax Handbook

The tax handbook provides statutory and administering authority for all revenue sources and reviews tax collections. It also gives current revenue estimates and an analysis of alternative tax sources.
http://edr.state.fl.us/Content/revenues/reports/tax-handbook/index.cfm

Florida Division of Bond Finance

The Florida Division of Bond Finance is responsible for issuing and administering state bonds. This website includes an overview of Florida debt (by program), a Debt Affordability Report, bond programs, and bond program ratings.
https://www.sbafla.com/bondfinance/DebtOverview/tabid/1054/Default.aspx

Sunshine State Survey 2014

The SSS is an annual survey of Florida residents on different Florida Issues. The data is also cross referenced with age, race, income, gender, and party affiliation. The site has survey data archived since 2007. Specific data includes Florida opinions on the state managing finances, taxes paid relative to quality of state services provided and tax dollars spent wastefully (state v. local).
http://sunshinestatesurvey.org/

Chapter 10. Local Government in Florida

Florida has *lots* of local governments—more than 2,100 to be exact. (See Table 10-1.) They provide a wide range of services and programs—everything from schools, garbage collection, water, parks and recreation, sewers, and police and fire protection to election administration, public assistance, and mosquito control. Local politics is grassroots politics. People tend to get involved when something affects their own neighborhood or community, whether it is fighting to keep a sewage treatment plant *out* or to bring a new fire substation *in*. We refer to these two actions as NIMBY and GIMBY politics ("not in my back yard" or "get it in my back yard"). At the local level, it is the little things that matter most—the things that directly affect someone's daily quality of life. *Local politics is often said to be centered on "police, potholes, porno, property, pets, pollution, 'problem' neighbors, citizens' pocketbooks, and, of course, 'politicians.'"*[1]

Table 10-1. Number of Local Governments in Florida

Counties	Cities	School districts	Special districts	Total
67	411	67	1,647	2,193

Source: Compiled by the authors from data found online at Florida Association of Counties, Florida Office of Economic and Demographic Research and Florida Department of Economic Opportunity. Figures are as of 2014/2015.

Ironically, Floridians seem to know the least about how local governments function or even *which* local government is responsible for what. Voter turnout in local elections is often considerably lower than in a presidential or gubernatorial election for many reasons, one of which is citizens' lack of knowledge about local government. At the same time, Floridians, like Americans in general, rate the performance of local governments ahead of both the state (See Figure 10-1.) and national governments. They believe that local governments spend their tax dollars more wisely and more efficiently than either the federal or state government. Floridians also trust local governments the most to best respond to and meet their needs during emergency situations, most notably hurricanes.[2]

"THE BUCK STOPS HERE" AT THE LOCAL LEVEL

While it is true that local governments are perceived by taxpayers as giving them the most for their tax dollars, it is also true that when things start falling apart, local governments are much "easier to get to" via initiatives, referenda, protests, and boycotts than either the federal or state government. Florida's local governments are under a lot of pressure to resolve a wide range of problems, some of which are caused by rapid growth, others by a declining economy: the lack of affordable housing, traffic congestion, crumbling streets, inadequate water and sewer systems, poor families in need, crimes against tourists and the elderly, even lawsuits against cities and counties.

As they respond to problems in their own backyard, local governments must also pay close attention to what the Florida Legislature and the U.S. Congress propose that could have a major impact on local services, finances, and their jurisdiction. The Florida League of Cities, the Florida Association of Counties, the Florida School Boards Association, the Florida City and County Management Association, and the Florida Local Government Coalition have a strong presence in Tallahassee. Many of Florida's cities and counties even hire their own lobbyists to carefully monitor what's going on in Washington and Tallahassee, with an eye toward "bringing home the bacon"—getting grants for much needed local projects and services—or preventing the higher levels of government from preempting local authority.

Figure 10-1. Floridians Rate Local Governments Higher Than State Legislature and the Federal Government

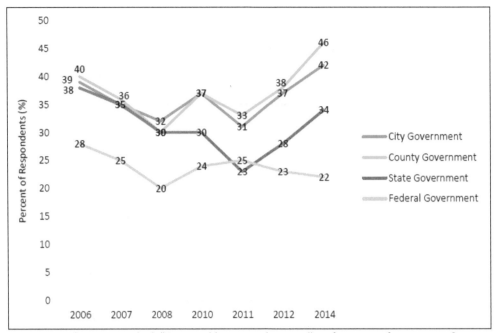

Note: Respondents were asked: "How would you rate the overall performance of government? Would you say that _____ consistently does an excellent, good, fair, or poor job of serving the public? Figures are for "excellent" + "good" responses.

Source: Leadership Florida Sunshine State Survey (2006-2008), Leadership Florida-Nielsen Company Sunshine State Survey (2010-2011), and University of South Florida-Nielsen Sunshine State Survey (2014).

"The buck stops here." That is certainly an apt description of how it is at the local government level. Counties, cities, and special districts are responsible for providing a wide range of services to Floridians and are truly the "first responders" in emergency situations.

Florida's local governments' expanding "first responder" role on the heels of several horrific hurricane seasons, the 9/11 terrorist attack, and the Gulf oil spill have placed additional fiscal and organizational pressures on them. The revamping of Florida's emergency management system has required local governments to re-examine their preparedness and their procedures for responding quickly to disasters. It has also forced local governments to improve their coordination and cooperation with each other through regional organizational structures. While Florida's emergency management system is considered one of the best in the nation, in part because of improved intergovernmental cooperation and new technology, working with other local governments can be a strain on the finances and employees of a city, county, or special district.[3] Yet, it is well understood that governmental responsiveness in times of crisis plays a critical role in how citizens judge their local governments.

Floridians trust their local governments more than the state or federal government when it comes to responding to them during emergency situations.

STRONG COMMUNITIES: KEY TO THE QUALITY OF LIFE IN FLORIDA

Florida's rankings as a great place to live are based on how well citizens like where they live, work, and play. If people feel good about the quality of life in their own community, they are far less likely to pack up and leave the state. Local governments play an important role in forging healthy relationships between the government, business, and not-for-profit sectors. It is not always easy. Governments must engage in both the provision of goods and services (its service function) and in managing conflict over public policies (its political function). The more socioeconomically and politically diverse a community, the more difficult it is to generate consensus and to create a sense of community.

Sense of Community

Citizen satisfaction with government is higher in places where community ties are stronger—where people have a sense of belonging and a feeling of efficacy and are proud to say they live there. Such feelings are strongest where friends and neighbors frequently interact with each other socially, volunteerism rates are high, communication channels between government and citizens are open, citizens are satisfied with local services, local governments cooperate with each other more than they conflict, and turnout in local elections is high.[4] Civic involvement is a real challenge, especially where there is an influx of new residents. In older, more established neighborhoods, neighbors often know each other, but in large new suburban developments, they do not.

Civic Activism

Building strong communities is not just about voting, although voting is important. Civic activism is also about caring for neighbors, participating in various types of community organizations and activities, and expressing one's opinions and policy preferences to public and private officials. Some Floridians are heavily engaged in volunteering, a product of the state's age makeup. Younger and older residents are the most likely to volunteer, younger because of school requirements, older because they have the time.

Civic involvement is essential because government cannot effectively provide all needed services, especially in communities where many residents oppose higher taxes. Civic engagement is also an important measure of how willing people are to invest their time and energy in their own neighborhood, whether it be participating in a neighborhood crime watch program, volunteering to tutor elementary kids who need help with reading, or engaging in a fundraising event to help the volunteer fire department.

Attending a local meeting or public hearing when an issue is being discussed that affects the community is another form of civic activism. While dealing with local government can be frustrating at times, it is still the most accessible level of government—a place where average citizens really can make a difference in the decision-making process. By attending public meetings and forums, citizens can better inform elected officials of their top policy priorities, criticize policies or public employee behavior, and band together with other like-minded citizens to force local officials to act on an issue they had been side-stepping. Research shows that citizens have the most impact if their opposition surprises officials, if the turnout of residents is very large, or if the elected officials are ambivalent on the issue.[5]

Increasingly, local governments are making it easier for citizens unable to attend formal meetings to interact with local officials. Interactive websites, telephone and online polls (citizen satisfaction surveys), government cable television, social media (Facebook, Twitter, YouTube) and even kiosks at malls have made it more convenient for citizens of all ages and educational levels to let public officials know what is on their minds.

The Most Active "Communities" within a Community

Activist interest groups differ in their level of involvement and their political clout from city to city and

county to county. Not all local governments have the same population, economic base, political makeup, or governing structure. (More will be said about local government structures later in the chapter.) In general, however, studies[6] have found that the most commonly active "interest communities" are:

- Civic associations
- Taxpayer groups
- Environmental and growth-management groups
- Neighborhood or homeowners associations
- Businesses—large and small
- Banks and financial institutions
- Contractors
- Real estate developers
- Media—newspapers, television, radio
- Religious/church groups
- Minorities—racial; ethnic; gay rights (LGBT); women
- Local government employees/public employee unions
- Professional associations
- Social service-oriented charities and not-for-profit agencies

The quality of life in local communities is often a good predictor of whether residents will choose to stay or leave Florida.

Rarely is an individual or group heavily involved in every single issue that emerges in a community. For example, religious groups are more likely to mobilize when a moral issue (location of bars or adult entertainment businesses) is being discussed by local government leaders. Neighborhood and homeowners associations become energized when a proposal before a county commission or city council threatens to devalue their property or poses a safety risk to their children (a zoning change; location of a halfway house).

A look at local headlines across Florida on a single day revealed issues ranging from a county commissioner indicted on bribery charges, use of red light cameras, the fatal shooting of a police officer, a drug sweep, discussions of watering rules during a drought, sinkholes, panhandling, the possible development of an old landfill, and rising unemployment rates, to a problem with underage drinking at a local fishing pier. Undoubtedly, each issue mobilized some groups to action more than others.

Neighborhood associations are active in local politics and will turn out
in mass if an issue promises to affect the quality of life where they live.

Local Actions (Inactions) Can Affect Citizen Out-Migration Decisions

How local officials deal with a specific issue or with problems in general can affect whether citizens choose to leave the community or the state. Consistently, throughout the Great Recession, about one in five Floridians mentioned thinking about moving on. Local governments—the frontlines of action—rushed to so something to stem the outward migration.

The biggest factor motivating residents to leave was the lack of jobs. (See Figure 10-2.) To keep businesses from closing, local officials in a number of cities and counties across the state passed ordinances granting them tax breaks, usually with the blessings of their constituents. These general purpose governments also reexamined rules and regulations (permitting, zoning) and licensing requirements that were perceived as hampering business formation (and job creation).

Figure 10-2. Reasons for Thinking About Leaving Florida Anchored in Local Community

Reason	Percent
Lack of Jobs	31
Quality of Life/ Want Change	17
Family, Health or Personal Situation	16
Cost of Living	15
Type of People Who Live Here	12
Elected Officials/Corruption	10
Prefer Cooler Climate	6
Too Crowded	6
Declining Property Values	4
High Taxes	4
Other/ Not Sure	4

Percent of Respondents (%)

Note: Respondents were asked, "If you are seriously considering moving out of the state of Florida, what is the reason?" Responses may not add to 100% due to rounding.
Source: The Leadership Florida-Nielsen Company Sunshine State Survey, 2011.

In high growth periods, the reasons for citizens deciding to move are often quite different—traffic congestion, noise, higher crime rates, crowded schools, rising rent and home prices resulting in the lack of affordable housing, and higher property taxes. In such times, local governments must respond as well.

Regardless of the economic situation, local governments are challenged to provide what citizens value most—a good quality of life.

Neighborhood Quality of Life Matters

Local government, business, and not-for-profit leaders closely track how Floridians feel about the future, particularly how the quality of life will be in their *own neighborhoods*—Do they feel things will get better, worse, or just stay the same over the next five years or so? Historically, a majority of Floridians do not anticipate much change in the quality of life in their own communities. (See Figure 10-3.) But attitudes often depend on the state of the economy. During the periods of economic decline, more residents tend to have dimmer views of how things will be in the future. As the economy improves, the percentage who see things looking better increases. Clearly, there is a link between the perceived quality of life at the community level and individuals' decisions to leave the state altogether.

Figure 10-3. Projected Quality of Life in One's Own Neighborhood Five Years From Now

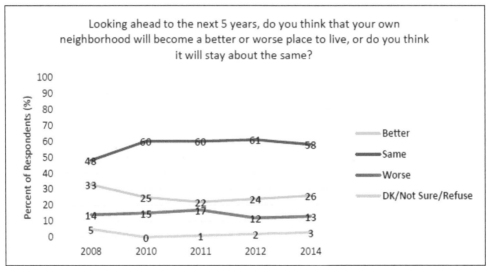

Note: Respondents were asked, "Looking ahead to the next 5 years, do you think that your neighborhood will become a better or worse place to live, or do you think it will stay about the same?" Responses may not add to 100% due to rounding.

Source: Leadership Florida Sunshine State Survey (2006-2008), Leadership Florida-Nielsen Company Sunshine State Survey (2010-2011), and University of South Florida-Nielsen Sunshine State Survey (2014).

"We're the Best": The Importance of Community Pride

Every city, county, and school district in Florida wants its residents to have pride in where they live, knowing that citizen satisfaction with the quality of life there can have major economic and political consequences. Communities try to brand themselves in a way that is appealing to both current residents and potential newcomers as great places to live and do business. Just a sampling of the bragging rights used by local governments in Florida includes the following: Sarasota County—the nation's best beaches according to "Dr. Beaches"; Palm Beach County—the most golf courses in the country; Marion County—horse capital of the world; Islamorada—sport fishing capital of the world; Tavares—"America's Seaplane City," Titusville—"Space City, USA," and Mount Dora—"Best Small Town to Visit." The number of small localities touting themselves as "the friendliest" is too numerous to count, as are the school districts that claim their students rank first. One of the most prestigious and competitive awards is the designation as an "All American City or County" by the National Civic League. It always makes news when a community lands atop a national or state list.

One of the most widely cited rankings of "great places to live" considers nine factors when it prepares its annual list: ambience, housing, the local economy, transportation, education, health care, crime, recreation, and climate.[7] Local governments that make it to any such list quickly begin promoting the ranking. Those that end up near the bottom often blame their shortcomings on their limited authority under Florida's Constitution, particularly restrictions on their ability to raise revenue.

Sarasota County beaches have been ranked as some of the best in the world—a fact that is used to promote the county as a great place to live and do business.

LOCAL GOVERNMENT IN THE FLORIDA CONSTITUTION

The Florida Constitution recognizes four types of local governments—counties, municipalities (cities), school districts, and special districts. Counties and cities are considered "general purpose" governments, while school districts and special districts are "special purpose" governments. In this chapter, we will describe each, although the primary focus will be on general purpose governments.

Understanding Structure: The Key to Holding Local Officials Accountable[8]
Most citizens see little need to understand the structure of the many different local governments that serve them. When there is a crisis or pressing need and citizens do not know whom to contact, it becomes quite apparent why it matters. *The bottom line is that one does not know whom to hold accountable for action—or inaction—unless he or she understands which official has the formal authority to deal with an issue or problem.*

As a citizen, one must know who hires and fires various types of local officials. Is it the voter (elected officials) or is it someone else (appointed officials), and, if so, who? It is equally important to know who has the major responsibility for preparing or drafting the budget and then approving it. No potholes will be filled, no school will be built, and no traffic light can be purchased and installed without funds being budgeted. Another key to understanding local government is determining the degree to which its structure provides for the separation of powers (checks and balances).

Unique Status of Local Governments
Local government is not mentioned in the U.S. Constitution. From a constitutional perspective, local governments are creatures of the *state*, subject to the obligations, privileges, powers, and restrictions that the state government imposes on them. Florida's Constitution specifies that all units of local government may be "created, abolished, or changed" by state law.

Dillon's Rule v. Home Rule
Dillon's Rule, the traditionally very restrictive interpretation of local governments' powers, prevents local governments from doing anything not specifically authorized by state laws. *Home rule*, in effect, reverses Dillon's Rule; it permits local governments to do anything not specifically prohibited. It frees cities and

counties from the need to seek state legislative approval for virtually everything they do and gives them more local control. In practice, *home rule* generally refers to the ability of local communities to adopt their own form of government, provide services, tax their residents, and exercise governmental powers that are not specifically denied them by state law.[9]

The Florida Constitution grants limited home rule powers to charter counties and municipalities:

> <u>Charter counties</u>: "all power of local self-government not inconsistent with general law."
> The procedures for becoming a home rule (charter) county are outlined in the *Florida Statutes*.
> (See Table 10-2 later in the chapter for a list of Florida's charter counties.)
> <u>Municipalities</u>: "any power for municipal purposes except as otherwise provided by law."

Generally, cities and counties in Florida can structure their governments as they see fit, choosing, for example, to employ city managers or county administrators to run their daily operations. They can decide to provide a wide range of public services, from traditional functions such as police and fire protection, sewage and sanitation, roads and streets, and parks and recreation, to mass transit, hospitals, airports, libraries, and community development.

General Laws and Special Laws

Counties and cities in Florida are subject to all *general laws* of the state—laws that do not specify a city or county by name but apply generally throughout the state. However, some general laws apply specifically to units of government by population size (*classification laws*) and may even pinpoint a particular city or county by specifying a size category that includes only one city or county.

Cities and counties are also subject to *special laws*—statutes that are drafted specifically naming a city or county. The Constitution states that special laws are subject to local referendum, "conditioned to become effective only upon approval by vote of the electors of the area affected" (Article III, Section 10). Special laws are usually introduced by the legislators representing the "affected" area. If these legislators are in agreement themselves, their special laws are usually enacted by the legislature with little or no debate.

The strengthening of home rule in Florida has reduced the number of special laws dealt with by the legislature.[10] It has also reduced the role of the state legislators in local government. Home rule means that city or county officials or local groups of citizens no longer need to petition their state legislators to undertake a new community service or activity. Nonetheless, state legislators continue to hold a reservoir of local power. Since state law supersedes city or county ordinances, legislators have the potential to reverse local actions. And, of course, legislators must be called upon when special laws are required by local governments.

Charters

All Florida cities and charter counties operate under a *charter*—a state grant of authority that sets forth governmental boundaries, powers and functions, structure and organization, methods of finance, and means of electing or appointing local officials. In other words, a charter may be thought of as a type of constitution; it must be approved, along with any amendments, by the voters. (See Figure 10-4 for an example of the contents of a county charter—Orange County.)

Cities and charter counties must adhere to each provision in their charter. Traditionally, changing or amending a charter required action by the state legislature. This action usually required a special act of the legislature and approval by the city's voters in a referendum. However, because of home rule, charter counties and cities can now amend their own charters, independent of the legislature, but any changes must be approved by the voters in a referendum election. The most common types of proposed changes have to do with duties of local officials, charter review ratification, charter language (usually getting rid of out-of-date language), and financial matters.

City councils and county commissions function as the legislative branches of their governments. County commissions may legislate for the entire county, including cities located within the county. City councils may legislate only within their own city boundaries. The Florida Constitution holds that a county ordinance in a non-charter county will not apply in a municipality if in conflict with a municipal ordinance and that, in a charter county, the charter will provide for resolution of such conflict. State laws, of course, apply in all cities and counties, and city and county officials, including city police and county sheriffs, must enforce them. Legislation passed by a city council or county commission is generally referred to an *ordinance*. It has the force of law within the city or county that enacts it.

County Government in Florida

Traditionally, county governments performed state-related functions as administrative subdivisions of the state.[11] The county courthouse was the local center of politics and government, and communities vied with each other to be the county seat. (See Appendix B for a list of county seats.) Today Florida has 67 counties. (See Figure 10-5.) Territorial Governor Andrew Jackson recognized Escambia and St. Johns as counties in 1821, making them the first two official counties in Florida. Over time, the Florida Legislature kept subdividing existing counties to create new ones. However, the Florida Legislature has not created a new county since 1925, when Martin, Indian River, Gulf, and Gilchrist became the 64th, 65th, 66th and 67th counties respectively.[12]

Three Key Structural Components of County Government[13]

A county government's structure includes the political institutions and processes created by the state to legally operate a county, the formal role and authority of the various county officials who must abide by those processes and operate within those institutions, and the methods used to select those officials.

The structure of county government determines the level of a county's independence from the state in making and implementing policy. The structure delineates who is responsible for making policy in a county (the legislative function) and who is responsible for overseeing the implementation of policy (the executive function). The structure also affects how well county residents are represented by their elected county officials, whether or not they are allowed to exercise local direct democracy (voting on initiatives, referenda, and recalls), the types of services provided by their county, and how efficiently those county services are delivered. In Florida, three basic structural decisions affect county government: (1) type of charter; (2) form of government; and (3) electoral districting plan.

Type of Charter

The first question is whether a county has decided to adopt a charter or not. Florida's 20 charter counties (home to 75 percent of the state's residents) have more freedom in making decisions than the 47 non-charter counties.[14] (See Table 10-3.) Charter status also affects the form of county government that can be chosen, the districting plan that can be chosen, and how the form and plan can be changed.

Figure 10-4. Orange County Charter

Source: Orange County Supervisor of Elections. Available at http://www.ocfelections.com/orangecountycharter.aspx.

Table 10-2. Florida's Charter Counties

Florida's 20 Charter Counties and Date Chartered			
Alachua	1987	Miami-Dade	1957
Brevard	1994	Orange	1986
Broward	1975	Osceola	1992
Charlotte	1986	Palm Beach	1985
Clay	1991	Pinellas	1980
Columbia	2002	Polk	1998
Duval	1967	Sarasota	1971
Hillsborough	1983	Seminole	1989
Lee	1996	Volusia	1971
Leon	2002	Wakulla	2008

Source: Florida Association of Counties. Available at http://www.fl-counties.com/about-floridas-counties/charter-county-information.

Table 10-3. Basic Differences between Charter and Non-Charter Counties

NON-CHARTER	CHARTER
Structure of county government specified in State Constitution and State Statutes. Only amending the State Constitution or State law can change structure.	Structure of county government specified in Charter as approved by the electorate. Structure can be tailored by the local electorate to meet the needs of the county.
Counties have powers of self-government as prescribed by the State Legislature.	Counties have all powers of self-government unless they are inconsistent with the Constitution or State law.
State Statutes do not provide for initiative or referendum, or recall of county officers.	County charter may provide for initiative, referendum and recall at the county level.
State Statutes do not require an Administrative Code.	County Charter can require an Administrative Code detailing all regulations, policies and procedures.
County cannot levy a utility tax in the unincorporated area.	County Charter can provide that a "municipal utility tax" is levied in the unincorporated area.
County ordinance will not apply in a municipality if in conflict with a municipal ordinance.	When there is a conflict between a county ordinance and a municipal ordinance the charter will provide for the resolution.

Source: Florida Association of Counties as supplemented by Aubrey Jewett.

Figure 10-5. Florida's 67 Counties

Source: U.S. Census Bureau, State and County Quick Facts, Florida Source.
Available at http://quickfacts.census.gov/qfd/maps/florida_map.html

Form of Government

The second decision is what form of government should be adopted to govern a county. Florida counties have three options: the traditional county commission used in some variation by 10 counties; the commission-administrator (or manager) used by 54 counties; and the commission-executive used by three counties. (See Figure 10-6 for examples of each form.) Two of the executive counties, Duval and Miami-Dade, have unique county structures: consolidated city-county government and federated government respectively.

All 67 counties have Boards of County Commissioners, and 66 have five elected constitutional officers. (Miami-Dade County appoints, rather than elects, all its constitutional officers.) The state's smaller, more rural counties are still governed by the *traditional commission structure* whereby the Board of County Commissioners has both legislative and executive duties. No single person is responsible for the administration of county functions.

The vast majority of Florida counties have adopted county governance structures that give major administrative—or executive—responsibilities to either a separately elected county mayor (*mayor-commission* or *council-county executive* form) or to a professional county manager (*commission-administrator*; also called the *commission-manager* form of government).

Figure 10-6. Three Forms of County Government

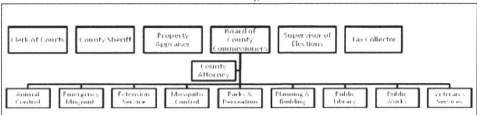

Traditional Commission Form of Government
Franklin County, Florida

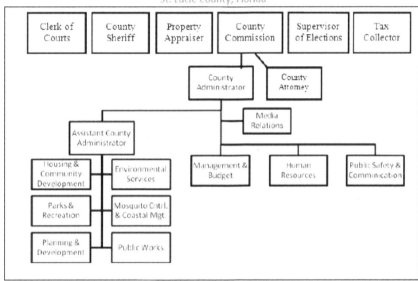

Commission-Administrator (Manager) Form of Government
St. Lucie County, Florida

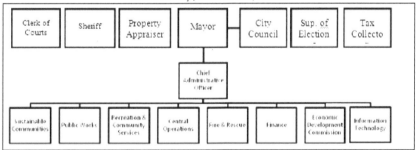

Council-County Executive (Mayor) Form of Government
Duval County / Jacksonville, Florida

Sources: Franklin County, St. Lucie County, Duval County websites; organizational chart designed by Aubrey Jewett.

A small number of charter counties have an elected county mayor—Duval, Miami-Dade, and Orange—while the majority of Florida counties (35 of 67)[15] have the commission-manager (or commission-administrator) structure. In a handful of counties, the county commissioners select one from among them to serve as mayor, who is mostly limited to presiding over commissions (traditional commission form) and is nowhere near as powerful as in the council-county executive form. In the commission-county executive form, the chief executive (county mayor) is separately elected by the voters.

The third decision is how to elect county commissioners and how many seats will be on the commission. There are three districting options: single-member districts, in operation in 20 counties; at-large, with residency requirement districts in place in 40 counties, and mixed (or combination) systems (some single-member district-based seats; some at-large residency district-based seats) found in the other 7 counties.[16] (See Figure 10-7.)

Figure 10-7. Three Methods Counties Use to Elect County Commissioners

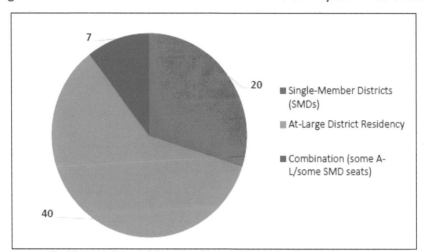

Source: Florida Association of Counties, "County Districting." Available at http://www.fl-counties.com/about-floridas-counties/county-districting.

The Florida Constitution spells out that in *non-charter* counties, county commissioners are to be elected using an *at-large, district residency system*. Specifically, the county is divided into equally populated, geographically defined districts. A candidate runs to represent the district in which he or she lives (e.g., District 1), but *all voters* in the county get to vote on who shall represent that district.

Charter counties may choose to have that same method (at-large, district residency) of electing their commissioners, but they may also elect commissioners from *single-member districts*. In a single-member district system, the county is carved into districts of equal population size, candidates file to represent the district in which they reside, and only residents of a district elect that district's commissioner. Charter counties may also choose to have a *combination, or mixed, system*—some commissioners elected at-large, some from single-member districts. (For example, Hillsborough County elects three commissioners at large and four from single-member districts.) Proponents of mixed systems promote them precisely because they allow some commissioners to bring a countywide perspective to matters before the Board of County Commissioners but allow other district-based commissioners to represent specific areas of the county.

County Commissions and Other Elected Officials

The traditional County Commission form of government has been in existence nationally since the late 19th century. It is characterized by two major features: (1) the existence of a plural executive (county constitutional officers plus the Board of County Commissioners) and (2) a legislative body (the Board of County Commissioners) that performs both legislative and executive functions. It is a system with *splintered executive authority* that was born in an era when the public greatly distrusted executive officials (the era of machine politics with its "big bosses" and corrupt local politicians). The system still exists in Florida, although it has been altered somewhat in recent years, as many of the state's counties have boomed and become much more heavily urbanized.

Florida counties are governed by elected Boards of County Commissioners. Even though it is a part-time position, many commissioners say it is more like a full-time job.

The form of county government organization in Florida has changed little in most Florida counties.[17] Under Florida's County Commission form of government, each county elects the following:

A Board of County Commissioners: Most boards are comprised of five or seven members (except for Broward, consolidated Duval-Jacksonville, and Miami-Dade counties). Commissioners are elected either from at-large residency-based districts, single-member districts, or a combination of both (mixed or combination electoral systems). Commissioners have four-year terms of office, term limits in some counties, and run in partisan elections (some charter counties have chosen non-partisan). Their terms are staggered so that not all are elected at the same time, providing for institutional memory.

Five Constitutional Officers: They are called constitutional officers because their duties are spelled out in the Florida Constitution—Article VIII, Section 1(d). They oversee specific executive and administrative functions in each county and are elected countywide. (The only exception is in Miami-Dade County where these officials are appointed by the county manager.) They are elected for four-year terms, run in partisan elections (some charter counties have chosen non-partisan), and most have term limits. (The Florida Supreme Court has ruled that voters in charter counties may impose term limits.) Their primary duties are as follows:

- Sheriff[18]—oversees law enforcement, public safety, and often corrections.
- Property appraiser—assesses the fair value of all property so that property taxes can be computed.
- Tax collector—receives property tax and other payments for both the county and the state.
- Supervisor of elections—registers voters and organizes all elections in the county.
- Clerk of the courts—maintains public records and is clerk to the county commission.
- *Two judicial branch officers*—While voters in every county elect these officials, they are actually part of the state judicial system and their budget comes from the state. (For a description of duties, see Chapter 8.)
- State attorney (elected countywide; partisan elections; four-year term; no term limits).
- Public defender (elected countywide; partisan elections, four-year term; no term limits).

More about Constitutional Officers

Each of the five constitutional officers administers his or her own office, although each must obtain budgets and facilities from the Board of County Commissioners. The sheriff usually submits the largest single budget request, covering countywide law enforcement and the operations of the county jail. It is not uncommon for sheriffs to press their county commissioners for sizeable budget increases, more deputies, and larger jails. County commissioners may risk appearing "soft on crime" if they continually oppose the sheriff's requests. However, if they do, and the sheriff believes it is insufficient, under *Florida Statutes*, the sheriff has the right to appeal the commission's budget decision to the state Administration Commission (governor and the Cabinet).[19]

County Functions

At one time, Florida counties limited themselves to law enforcement through the sheriff's office, road construction and maintenance, some public health and welfare duties, elections supervision, recording of deeds and other legal records, and appraisal of property and collection of property taxes. County courts were trial courts for the state's judicial system (see Chapter 8), and the county jail held pre-trial prisoners, as well as prisoners sentenced to less than one year. These were the traditional functions of rural counties in the United States.

Florida's counties continue to perform these traditional functions, but most now provide many additional urban services.[20] This is particularly true for counties with an administrator/elected mayor,[21] as well as Florida's 20 charter counties.[22] Operating under home rule, they may perform any functions and provide any services not denied them by state law. Roughly three-quarters of Florida's population resides in these charter counties. Today, most county governments in Florida engage in environmental protection, sewage and solid waste disposal, parks and recreation, fire-fighting and emergency medical services, planning and growth management, extended health services, cultural and library centers, airports, sports stadiums, and mass transit in addition to their traditional functions.[23] Figure 10-8 shows that counties spend the most money on public safety (police and fire protection), general government, transportation, and the physical environment.

Figure 10-8. Florida County Expenditures

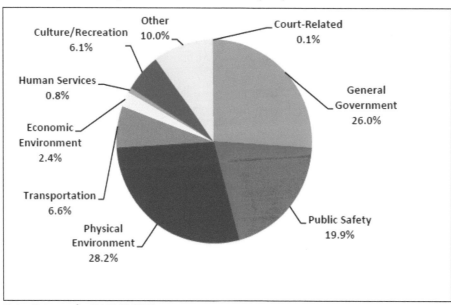

Note: Data are for FY 2012-2013.

Source: Florida Office of Economic and Demographic Research, "County Government Expenditures Reported by Account Code and Fund Type." Available at http://edr.state.fl.us/Content/local-government/data/revenues-expenditures/stwidefiscal.cfm.

CITY GOVERNMENT IN FLORIDA

Florida's city governments, officially "municipalities," operate under charters granted by the state. As noted earlier, under Florida's constitutional home rule provisions, Florida municipalities may "perform municipal functions and provide municipal services, and may exercise any power for municipal purposes except as otherwise provided by [state] law." County governments have jurisdiction over all territory outside city limits (*unincorporated areas*).

Florida has more than 400 cities. The two oldest cities are St. Augustine (which is also the oldest city in the United States) and Pensacola. Jacksonville is Florida's largest city because it consolidated its city and county (Duval) governments in 1967. The second largest city is Miami, followed by Tampa, St. Petersburg, Orlando, and Hialeah. (For a list of the 25 largest and 25 smallest cities, see Table 10-4.)

A State with Many Small Cities

Surprisingly, the nation's third largest state has no city with a population of one million or more. Florida consists of mostly smaller cities. Nearly half (47 percent) have a population of fewer than 5,000 people. Only six have a population of greater than 200,000. Believe it or not, there are several cities with 25 residents or fewer. (See Table 10-4.) The huge differences in the size of Florida's municipalities make it difficult for the legislature to craft one-size-fits-all laws.

The legislature does not have to wait until a new U.S. Census comes out (every 10 years) to get current population statistics. The Bureau of Economic and Business Research (BEBR) at the University of Florida releases new population estimates annually. Without these annual population projections, officials in this constantly changing state would be making policies based on highly questionable numbers.

Cities, Towns, Villages: All the Same under the Law

In Florida, new municipalities can officially call themselves a city, town, or village. By one count, out of more than 400 municipalities, there were 117 "towns," 15 "villages," and the rest "cities."[24] For example, we have the City of West Palm Beach, the Town of Otter Creek, and the Village of El Portal. Technically, they are the same under the law—incorporated municipalities. And by common practice, most people call all of them "cities."

Municipal Incorporation

Municipal incorporation is the process by which a city is formed. It is a fairly difficult and complex process.[25] While no new counties have been formed since the 1920s, new municipalities are constantly being created in Florida. Between 2000 and 2010, nine new cities were created, among them Miami Gardens, Doral, Southwest Ranches, Loxahatchee Groves, and Palmetto Bay.[26] Since 2010, only one new city has been created—Estero in Lee County (2014) although in 2015, the legislature approved giving the voters in Panacea (in Wakulla County) the opportunity to decide whether to incorporate the area.

Citizens may want to form a city for a number of reasons. One is that as an area becomes more densely populated, it may need sewer and water services or more police and fire protection than the county currently provides. Another reason for incorporation may be the desire for greater local control. Sometimes citizens simply want to have more of a say in governing themselves, particularly if they feel the county government is neglecting them or not sufficiently responsive to them.

Table 10-4. Florida's 25 Largest and 25 Smallest Municipalities

Largest Cities	2010 Pop.	Smallest Cities	2010 Pop.
Jacksonville city	846,421	Westville town	313
Miami city	428,107	St. Marks city	280
Tampa city	352,741	Jacob City	253
Orlando city	255,636	Raiford town	252
St. Petersburg city	252,372	Hillcrest Heights town	252
Hialeah city	230,544	Golf village	249
Tallahassee city	185,784	Ebro town	248
Fort Lauderdale city	171,544	Highland Park town	237
Port St. Lucie city	169,888	Campbellton town	227
Cape Coral city	163,599	Glen Ridge town	219
Pembroke Pines city	157,905	Noma town	200
Hollywood city	144,310	Layton city	186
Miramar city	127,432	Worthington Springs town	181
Gainesville city	125,661	Horseshoe Beach town	158
Coral Springs city	123,618	Cloud Lake town	133
Clearwater city	109,340	Otter Creek town	129
Miami Gardens city	108,160	Bascom town	124
Palm Bay city	105,815	Belleair Shore town	107
Pompano Beach city	104,662	Ocean Breeze city	95
West Palm Beach city	104,630	Indian Creek village	89
Lakeland city	100,728	Lazy Lake village	25
Davie town	95,505	Lake Buena Vista city	22
Miami Beach city	91,540	Bay Lake city	15
Sunrise city	88,033	Marineland town	6
Plantation city	86,782	Weeki Wachee city	5

Note: All are municipalities regardless of whether a city, town, or village. There is no legal difference between them.
Source: Office of Economic and Demographic Research, Population and Demographic Data, Florida Estimates of Population 2014. Available at: http://edr.state.fl.us/Content/population-demographics/data/

How to Become a City: Basic Requirements

Before an area can be considered for incorporation, it must meet five conditions. It must:

- Be compact and contiguous.
- Be large enough—at least 1,500 residents in small counties under 75,000 or 5,000 in counties over 75,000.
- Have an average population density of at least 1.5 persons per acre, unless there are extraordinary conditions.
- Be at least two miles from the boundaries of any existing municipality or have an extraordinary natural boundary.
- Have a proposed municipal charter that clearly defines who will have responsibility for legislative and executive functions.

Steps to Becoming Incorporated

Incorporation requires three steps.[27] First, a group of citizens or the county commission must propose a new charter that will govern the city, conduct a *feasibility study* to see if it makes sense to create a new municipality, and develop an interim service delivery proposal, complete with the estimated cost of the services. The *proposed charter* must address the proposed city's boundaries, the structure of government, administrative organization, elections, process for amending the charter, and finances.

Next, the local legislative delegation will have to *file a bill* in the legislature to incorporate the area. This is done through a special act that creates the new municipality and recognizes the proposed charter as the governing document of the new municipality. Normally legislators from other parts of the state defer to the wishes of the local delegation with the expectation that other members will show deference to them should they wish to file a special act for citizens in their parts of the state.

Finally, a *referendum* is held among the residents of the proposed city: if the majority votes in favor of incorporation and the new charter, then the new municipality is formed.[28]

Incorporated versus Unincorporated Areas

Florida's population is nearly evenly split between those living in an incorporated area (city) and those who live in an unincorporated area of the county. (See Figure 10-9.) Actually, many Floridians do not know whether they live in a city or in the unincorporated area of a county. The confusion often stems from the address system used by the U.S. Postal Service. For example, the University of Central Florida has an Orlando address but is actually eight miles outside the city limits of Orlando. Thus, residents who live near the campus actually live in unincorporated Orange County. They do not pay taxes to the City of Orlando, are not eligible to vote in City of Orlando elections, and do not receive city services. But they still think of themselves as residents of Orlando because their mailing address is Orlando.

Legally, people are city residents only if they live within the geographic boundaries of the city as defined in the charter. The confusion is one reason why turnout in local elections is often low.

Figure 10-9. Half of All Floridians Do Not Live in a City; They Live in an Unincorporated Area

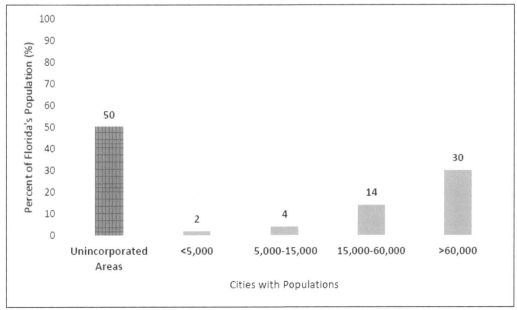

Source: Bureau of Economic and Business Research (UF) and the Florida League of Cities 2015

Municipal Functions

Florida's cities provide a wide range of functions and services, depending on their size and their citizens' preferences.[29] Almost all Florida cities provide traditional municipal functions—police and fire protection, street maintenance, water and sewage, solid waste disposal, and parks and recreation. Most of the state's larger cities also provide for environmental protection, mass transit, housing and community development, and planning and growth management.

Parks and recreation programs are popular in urban areas with lots of young families with children.

Some cities—Jacksonville, Orlando, Tallahassee—operate their own electric power companies. Some operate hospitals or contribute heavily to the operation of municipal hospitals. Some maintain libraries, theaters, art and cultural centers, golf courses and tennis courts, sports stadiums, and airports. In other cities, these activities may be contracted out to private businesses or nonprofit organizations or be provided by the private sector.

Figure 10-10 shows that the physical environment (water and sewer, electricity and gas, and solid waste) is, on average, the largest expenditure category for Florida cities, followed by general government,[30] public safety (police and fire protection), transportation (usually roads, bridges, and mass transportation), and culture and recreation (including libraries, golf courses, parks, and pools). City governments in Florida do not provide for education; education is a function of separate school districts. And most welfare services are provided through local and regional offices of the state's Department of Children and Families and the Department of Economic Opportunity. (See Chapter 11.)

Four Forms of City Government

Municipal governments in Florida take one of four forms—council manager, weak mayor-council, strong mayor-council, and commission—or a hybrid (combination of elements from other forms).[31] (See Figure 10-11.) They are similar (although not completely identical) to the forms existing at the county level.

Nearly two-thirds (63 percent) of Florida's cities have the *council-manager* form of government.[32] "This form is based on the business model of stockholders (voters) choosing a board of directors (council), which in turn appoints a professional chief executive officer (manager)."[33] As an appointed official, the manager, a full-time employee, serves at the pleasure of the elected commission. The manager is responsible for administering city services, executing the budget, and enforcing city ordinances in a professional, nonpartisan manner. It is also the manager's job to recommend policy and legislative options to the council, to propose the budget, and to hire and fire all staff. The council adopts policies and passes ordinances. The mayor, either chosen from among the council members or separately elected, may preside over city council meetings. But the manager is in effect the chief executive. Examples of cities using this form are Fort Lauderdale, Tallahassee, and Daytona Beach.

Figure 10-10. Florida Municipal Expenditures

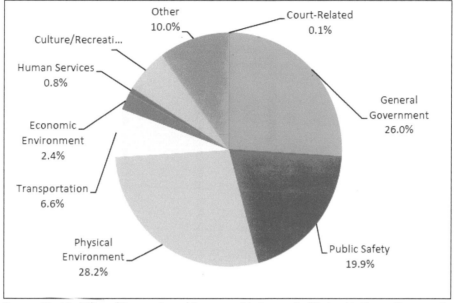

Source: Florida Office of Economic and Demographic Research, "Statewide Expenditures and Revenues Reported by Florida's Local Governments." Available at http://edr.state.fl.us/Content/local-government/data/revenues-expenditures/stwidefiscal.cfm. Data are for FY 2012-2013.

Figure 10-11. Forms of Government in Florida Cities

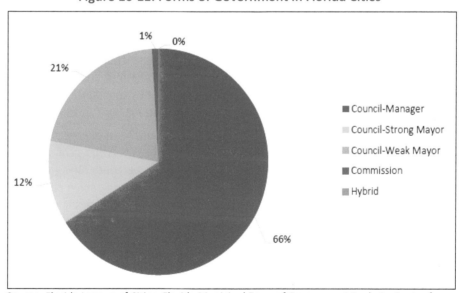

Source: Florida League of Cities, Florida Municipal Form of Government Analysis, Center for Municipal Research and Innovation, Florida League of Cities. Available at http://www.floridaleagueofcities.com/Assets/Files/2015MunicipalFormOfGovAnalysis.pdf, Data are for 2015.

Figure 10-12. Council-Manager Form Predominant Among All But the
Least Populous Florida Cities

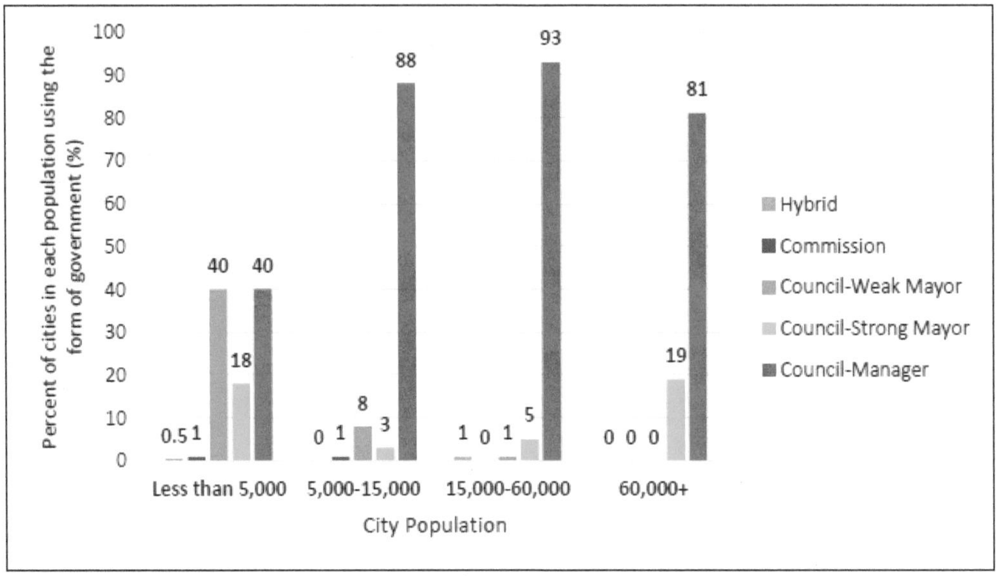

Note: The CityStats data base from which these figures were calculated does not include some cities
that failed to respond to the survey, including some large cities.
Source: Calculated from CityStats data base provided by the Center for Municipal Research and
Innovation, Florida League of Cities. Data are for 2014.

The second most common form, found in many smaller cities, is the *weak mayor-council* form. In this type of government, the council has the major responsibility for making policies, passing ordinances, and overseeing the operations of the city. It supervises department heads, approves the budget, monitors expenditures, and is responsible for planning—short- and long-term. The mayor has very little power. Frequently the position of mayor simply rotates among the members of the council. The mayor's main duties are to represent the city (a ceremonial function) and to preside over council meetings. Examples of cities with this type of governance are Bradenton Beach and Port St. Joe.

Larger cities in Florida are more likely to have a *strong mayor-council* form of government. Larger, more diverse cities have a greater need for a full-time mayor elected by the voters and a chief executive who can provide political leadership and has the power to act quickly in an emergency. Being mayor is a full-time job. The mayor appoints department heads, drafts the city's budget, and in some cities has veto power over council decisions. The council is the city's legislative body; it makes policies and passes ordinances. This form has a clear division between the executive and legislative branches—a system of checks and balances that the other forms do not have. (Figure 10-14 shows the organization of the strong mayor form of government in Tampa.) As a practical matter, however, even cities with the strong mayor form of government may hire professional administrators (chief administrative officers) to oversee day-to-day operations. Examples of strong-mayor governed municipalities are Jacksonville, Orlando, Tampa, and St. Petersburg.

Table 10-5. Four Forms of Municipal Government

Form of Government	Duties of the Mayor	Duties of the Council	Duties of the City Manager
Council-Manager • Most common form • Executive authority primarily is with professional manager • Legislative authority with council • Structured like a business corporation • Designed to separate policy making (council) from administration (manager)	• Sometimes filled by election, sometimes filled by council appointment • Presides over council meetings • Makes appointments to boards • Has little, if any, role in day-to-day municipal administration • Ceremonial head of city • Acts as ceremonial head of government at public functions	• Elected by voters • Adopts budget • Hires and fires manager	• Appointed by the majority of the council for an indefinite term and removable only by a majority of the council • Full-time; high salary • A professional administrator • Acts as chief executive • Fully responsible for municipal administration: supervises and coordinates the departments, appoints, and makes reports and recommendations to the council • Responsible for preparing a budget to present to the council, and responsible for the administration of the council-approved budget • Serves at the pleasure of the commission • Hires and fires department personnel
Weak Mayor-Council • No separation between legislative and executive branches • Typically found in small cities	• Is <u>not</u> directly elected as mayor • Selected by fellow council members to be mayor; usually rotated annually • Part-time position; low salary • Acts as ceremonial head of city government at public functions • Presides over council meetings • Does not hire and fire employees	• Directly elected by voters • Usually small group • Part-time; low salary • Prepares and adopts budget • Oversees spending • Initiates and adopts policies; passes ordinances • May not meet once a week • Hires and fires municipal employees	None in this form of government
Strong Mayor-Council • Separation of powers between legislative (council) and executive (mayor) branches • Usually in large cities that need executive who can act in a crisis • Clear lines of authority	• Directly elected by voters • Full-time; higher salary • Prepares budget • Makes appointments of department heads, boards and commission • Oversees departments • Acts as ceremonial head of city government at public functions • May have veto power over council legislation • Chief administrator • Supervises city departments	• Elected by voters • Higher salary • Adopts budget • Adopts policies and ordinances • Usually meets weekly	None in this form of government
Commission • Hardly used anymore • No separation of powers between legislative and executive branches • Executive authority rests with the council members as department heads • Legislative authority rests with commissioners acting collectively to enact legislation • Smaller cities	• Not directly elected • Part-time; low salary • Presides over commission meetings • Has no more power than fellow commissioners	• Usually small council Individually (Chief Executives): • Council members are heads of key departments (public safety, etc.) • Prepare budget for that department Collectively (Commission): • Pass budget • Make policies and pass ordinances • Directly responsible for operation of city departments and agencies	None in this form of government

Source: Created by authors.

Only a few cities have the *commission* form of government. Under this form, each member of the commission has formal executive and legislative roles. Commissioners are often elected to oversee specific functions (e.g., public safety commissioner, parks and recreation commissioner, public works commissioner, finance commissioner). In that capacity, they act individually as chief executives albeit over a specific function or service. But when they sit as the commission and act collectively to make policies and pass ordinances, they are serving as legislative officials. Obviously, one of the shortcomings of this form of government is the lack of checks and balances. An example of a municipality still using this form is the City of South Pasadena.

A few cities are more accurately described as having a *hybrid* form of government that incorporates elements of the other types. One example is the hybrid council manager-mayor form of government. The manager who is hired and fired by the council still functions as the chief executive, but the voters also separately elect a mayor. Another hybrid is the strong mayor-chief administrative officer (manager) combination mentioned above.

Size of City Councils or Commissions

The number of city council members or commissioners varies considerably. The size of a council may reflect the complexity of services provided, the council's workload, the diversity and size of the population, the political dynamics and the preferences of the city's voters, or a combination of these reasons.   Councils range in size from 3 to 19 (Jacksonville). (See Figure 10-13.) The two most common sizes are five members (68 percent) and six members (18 percent).[34] (The national average is 5.5.) The larger-sized councils are usually found in big cities, smaller councils in sparsely populated cities. St. Petersburg, with a population of more than a quarter of a million, is tied for the second most council members (9) after Jacksonville, population 846,421. Near the bottom of the list are Greenwood (population 675) and Highland Park (population 237), with four and three council members, respectively.

Figure 10-13. Size of City Councils/Commissions*

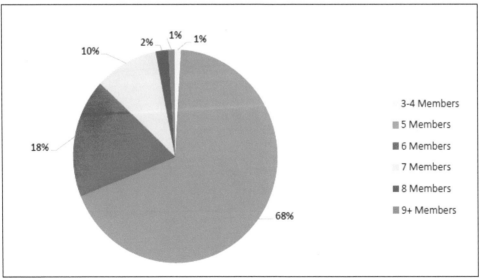

Note: *Some cities call their legislative bodies "councils", while others label them "commissions."
Source: Florida League of Cities, Center for Municipal Research & Innovation, "Florida Municipal Council Size
Analysis." Available at
http://www.floridaleagueofcities.com/Assets/Files/2015MunicipalCounSizeAnalysis.pdf, Data are for 2015.

Figure 10-14. City of Tampa Organizational Chart

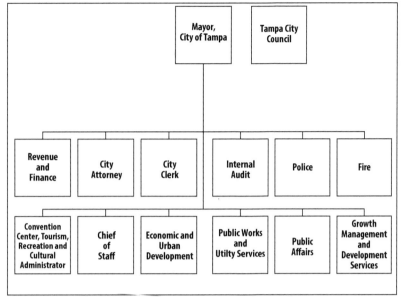

Note: The City of Tampa has a strong mayor-council form of government.
Source:City of Tampa. Available at http://www.tampagov.net/.

Municipal Elections: Nonpartisan

Most city elections in Florida are nonpartisan. Candidates do not run as Democrats or Republicans, nor is there a party label on the ballot. Indeed, it has been said, "There is no Republican or Democratic way to pave a street." In recent years, however, local politics has seen a growing incidence of party politics—where campaign literature is circulated identifying a candidate as a Democrat or a Republican. Such information is readily available via the county supervisor of elections voter registration lists, which are public records. Many good government groups strongly oppose this practice.

Electing City Council Members (or Commissioners)

Under Florida law, there is no legal difference between a council member and a commissioner. Cities have the option to call their legislative body a city council or a city commission. Municipalities can elect their council members in a variety of ways, but the most popular are the same as those used by counties: an at-large, district residency system; single-member districts; or a mixed, or combination, system. In racially and ethnically diverse cities, single-member districts and mixed systems are more common. They enhance the ability of minorities to get elected if a minority or ethnic group is of sufficient size, geographically concentrated, and politically cohesive.

Timing of Municipal Elections

Many Florida cities hold their elections at off-cycle times—in a year when there is no presidential or gubernatorial election or even in the spring. The reason is to enable voters (and the news media) to focus on *local* candidates and local issues.[35] Unfortunately, turnout in many of these off-cycle elections is low. Typical turnout rates for stand-alone municipal elections are in the 20-30 percent range. Ironically, more seats are often contested at the local than at the state legislative level. Local campaigns are often perceived as less expensive to run.

LOCAL ELECTED OFFICIALS: WHO RUNS, WHO WINS, AND WHY

Many who would like to run for public office ultimately decide against it, concluding, *"Who needs it?"* The "it" is the hassle of fundraising, the pain of enduring close and often negative media scrutiny of one's private life, and the humiliation of being regarded as "crooked" and/or "unethical" by many in the electorate, to name but a few reasons. In this era of cynicism, it comes as no surprise that many would-be candidates back away from running. Running for and holding office often takes a heavy toll on a person's time, family, finances, and privacy. Thankfully, plenty of willing candidates decide to run for local office in spite of the perceived hassles. It is a good thing. After all, the whole idea behind a democracy is allowing citizens to have a choice.

Why Citizens Run

Candidates offer themselves to the voters for a number of different reasons. Interviews with Florida local officials[36] reveal that some of the most common reasons for running are the following:

- **"Certain Issues Are Being Ignored by Current Officeholders."** The failure of government to address issues that an individual feels strongly about, especially if occurring over an extended period, often motivates someone to run.

- **"I Disagree With the Ideological Position of Sitting Officeholders."** When governing bodies are perceived as being too liberal or too conservative, persons who perceive themselves as middle-of-the-roaders or consensus-builders are the most likely to step up to the plate and run against incumbents perceived as ideologues.

- **"I Genuinely Love Politics."** Some candidates run because they simply enjoy politics. Many who run for this reason have grown up around politics. They have relatives who have held office, or they interned in a campaign or public official's office. These candidates are often drafted to run by family, friends, neighbors, and mentors. Surprisingly, women tend to cite this reason for running more than men candidates.

- **"It's An Opportunity to Give Something Back to My Community."** Often business or civic leaders who have benefited from the community's economy and/or its public services say they run for this reason. Typically, these are middle-to-older-age candidates. But wanting to give something back to the community is one of the two most common reasons why citizens run. (Issues being ignored is the most common reason.)

- **"I Was Drafted for My Experience/Leadership Skills."** Members of nonprofit, civic, neighborhood, and professional organizations often urge their strongest, most popular leaders to make the leap into the political fray. Studies have shown that these networks are particularly important to the success of first-time candidates. These networks are a source of volunteers, monetary contributions, and moral support.

- **"I Now Have the Time."** Retirees and stay-at-home mothers whose kids are grown and out of the house say that what finally allowed them to run was having the *time* to do so. National and statewide offices aside, insufficient time—more than insufficient funds—is the biggest deterrent to candidacies at the local level. (Unfortunately, the news media's coverage of fundraising in presidential and high profile congressional races creates the misperception that it takes millions to win *any* office, which is not true.) In addition, older candidates are more likely to say they have enough resources to live on apart from the office salary—which for many posts, especially in small cities, is not very high.

- **"I Ran Because No One Else Would."** Increasingly, citizens who seek office admit they do so somewhat reluctantly when "no one else would run." This tends to happen most in two situations: (1) when the partisan balance is one-sided; and (2) in low profile local races. The latter often used to be a major entry point for young persons interested in careers in politics. However, the growing disinterest of the young in political careers has meant that retirees have often had to step in to fill the candidate void.[37]

- **"We Need to Put More Women and Racial/Ethnic Minorities in Office."** Women and racial/ethnic minorities often run after being drafted by political parties, good government groups, and/or organizations representing women and minorities. A major intent of these candidacies is to diversify the profile of elected officials—to make them reflective of a community or state's demographics.

Candidates running for local office often choose to do so because of encouragement by friends and neighbors, family members, and local organizations in which they are active.

Salaries and Term Limits

Many local offices are perceived as more desirable to potential candidates than the state legislature. Local office salaries, particularly at the county level and in larger cities, are often higher than state legislative salaries, and, in the case of many county and city offices, there are no term limits. (See Table 10-6.) Plus, winning a local office means you do not have to leave home to go to Tallahassee for several months a year, which helps explain why women are more likely to seek local offices.

Diversity

Minorities have been most successful in running for local offices in more diverse, urbanized areas. A study by the Joint Center for Political and Economic Studies found that in the early 2000s, Florida had 24 black county commissioners, 5 other black county elected officials (e.g., county constitutional officers); 14 black mayors, and 120 black city council members.[38] An early study of Hispanics by the National Association of Latino Elected Officials (NALEO) identified 72 Hispanics who held local elected office in Florida.[39] Since those early studies, minority candidates' successes at the local level—counties, cities, school boards—have increased and will continue to do so as the state's population becomes more diverse. The memberships of both the Florida Black Caucus of Local Elected Officials (FBC-LEO) and the Hispanic Elected Local Officials (HELO) groups have grown significantly over the past decade as more minorities have been elected to office.

Isis Garcia-Martinez serves as President of the City Council of Hialeah, one of the state's largest municipalities.

Tallahassee Mayor Andrew Gillum is the past president of the Florida League of Cities.

Table 10-6. Local Government Salaries, Term of Office, and Term Limits

Elected Posts	Salary Range (FY 2014-15) $	Term of Office	Term Limits
Florida Legislature			
House	29,697*	2	Yes
Senate	29,697*	4	Yes
Counties			
County Commissioners	24,573-95,782	4	Most**
Constitutional Officers			
Tax Collector	93,305-182,218	4	Most**
Property Appraiser	93,305-182,218	4	Most**
Clerk of the Circuit Court	93,305-182,218	4	Most**
Supervisor of Elections	76,048-162,012	4	Most**
Sheriff	102,244-191,157	4	Most**
Municipalities			
Mayor	1-161,522[1]	varies	Some (26%)
Council Members	1-52,000[1]	varies	Some (25%)
School Districts			
School District Officials			
School Board	24,293-92,570	4	No
School Superintendent***	93,305-318,000	4	No

Notes:[1] The wide range of salaries of municipal officials is due to tremendous population size differences among the cities. Highest salaries (Orlando-council; Jacksonville-mayor).
*The President of the Senate and the Speaker of the House each get $41,181 annually.
**The Florida Supreme Court ruled that charter counties can impose term limits.
*** Some (41) superintendents are elected, others are appointed (26) by the School Board.
Sources: Legislature and County Officials – Office of Economic and Demographic Research, "Salaries of Florida's State Legislators" and "Salaries of Elected County Constitutional Officers and School District Officials." Municipal Officials – CityStats data base provided by the Center for Municipal Research and Innovation, Florida League of Cities. Data are for 2014. (Note: The CityStats data base does not include some cities that failed to respond to the survey, including some large cities.)

School Districts

Florida has the third largest public school system in the country, with more than 4,200 public schools (K-12), serving more than 2.7 million students[40] The school system is one of the state's biggest employers, and in some places across the state, it is the largest employer. (For more on K-12 Education see Chapter 11.)

School districts are a *special-purpose local government.* The state's 67 constitutionally created school districts share the same geographical boundaries as Florida's 67 counties, but the districts are separate governmental entities. Each school district has an elected school board that consists of five to nine members and a superintendent. The primary revenue sources for school districts are property taxes and money from the state.

School Boards

School board members run on a nonpartisan ballot and have staggered four-year terms. As with cities and counties, school boards differ on whether their members are elected from single-member districts, at-large residency-based districts, or a mixed (combination) type of district.

Minority and female representation levels are higher in larger school districts, which are typically more diverse. Several factors deter minorities from running for school board posts: income, time commitment required, and lack of experience in holding leadership posts. In some districts, at-large elections may make it more difficult as well. And running without a political party label (nonpartisan elections) may make it harder to raise funds.

Serving on a school board is a tough job, which ends up being nearly full-time, even though, formally, it is only a part-time position. Disgruntled parents, funding cuts from the federal and state governments, lawsuits, resistance to redrawing attendance districts, problems with bullying, hate crimes, child predators, standardized test scores, and even death threats, all make the job a difficult one. So does the fear of a natural disaster or a human-made form of terrorism, either of which can instantly create chaos. On the other hand, being on the school board can be rewarding. Studies show that those who serve on school boards are regarded by both teachers and school superintendents as being influential in the community in which they serve.[41]

School Superintendents

Only five states permit the election of school superintendents—Florida, Alabama, Kentucky, Maine, and Mississippi.[42] Of the state's 67 superintendents, 26 are appointed by their school boards and 41 are elected by their communities.[43] Some say the "traditional path to the superintendency—becoming a high school principal or central office business administrator—favors male candidates. Women are more likely to be elementary school principals or curriculum coordinators—jobs that are not considered stepping-stones to the superintendency."[44] Among Florida's superintendents, 18 (27 percent) are female. Six are minorities— three African Americans and three Hispanics. Five of the six are appointed, not elected, which is a similar pattern observed in other states.[45]

SPECIAL DISTRICT GOVERNMENTS

Special districts are "local units of special purpose governments, within limited geographical areas, which are utilized to manage, own, operate, construct, maintain, and finance basic capital infrastructure, facilities, and services."[46] They are usually created by general law, special act, local ordinance, inter-local agreement, or by rule of the governor and Cabinet.

Florida has thousands of special district governments, engaged in everything from public housing, airports, and soil and water conservation to mosquito control. Indeed, there are more special districts (including authorities) in the state than any other form of local government. As of 2015, there were about 1,647.[47] The number is constantly increasing. In fact, an average of 63 per year have been formed since 2000. The counties with the most special districts are among the state's largest counties (in descending order): Hillsborough (143), Miami-Dade (106), Broward (96), Lee (94), Palm Beach (94), and Manatee (71).

In spite of the fact that special districts are so plentiful and have budgets in the millions, most Floridians are unaware of them. The complexities of what they do and how they are governed and financed make it difficult for the average citizen to fully grasp how they operate and what a big role they play in the local government arena. Special districts are governments' best described as "hidden in plain sight."[48]

Table 10-7. Some Large Special District Governments in Florida

Bay County	Bay Medical Center
Brevard County	North Brevard Hospital District
Broward County	North Broward Hospital District
	Port Everglades Authority
	South Broward Hospital District
Hernando County	Southwest Florida Water Management District
Lee County	Lee Memorial Hospital District
Leon County	Florida Municipal Power Agency
Orange County	Orange County Housing Authority
	Reedy Creek Improvement District
Palm Beach County	Palm Beach County Health Care District
	Palm Beach County Housing Finance Authority
	South Florida Water Management District
Putnam County	St. Johns River Water Management District
Sarasota County	Sarasota County Public Hospital Board
Volusia County	Halifax Hospital Medical Center

Source: Calculated from Florida Department of Economic Opportunity: List of Special Districts. Available at https://dca.deo.myflorida.com/fhcd/sdip/OfficialListdeo/websitelist.cfm

Organization

The governing structure of special districts and authorities varies a great deal. Some elect their board members but most are governed by boards whose members are appointed by cities or counties in which the district or authority operates. Most boards, regardless of how selected, hire professional administrators or directors to supervise operations. For some of the larger special districts, with multi-million dollar budgets, the governor appoints the board and the board hires a professional administrator to execute the board's decisions—the five Florida Water Management Districts (see Chapter 12) operate under this arrangement as did the Florida Space Authority before it was converted to Space Florida.

Types of Special Districts

There are two types of special districts—dependent and independent. A *dependent special district* is governed by a board that is appointed by a single county or single municipality and its budget is approved by a single county or municipality as well. An *independent special district* is one that includes more than one county or has a board appointed or budget approved by more than one county or city. More than half (62 percent) of Florida's special districts are independent.

Most special districts in Florida have a single purpose. The five most popular functions of special districts (out of 70 functions) are the following:[49]

- Community development (592) often formed at the request of developers who need to fund new roads and sewer and water lines.
- Community redevelopment (216) to improve poor or declining neighborhoods.
- Housing authorities (91).
- Drainage and water control (86).
- Fire control and rescue (63).
- Soil and water conservation (63).

Other common functions of special districts include medical or hospital, neighborhood enhancement, airports, recreation facilities/programs, and ports.

Why Special Districts?

Several factors contribute to the popularity of special districts. First, they allow city and county governments to delegate direct responsibility for a particular function, such as community hospitals or public housing, to a separate entity. An authority or district can then collect its own revenues—federal grant money as well as rents, charges, and fees—and spend money and conduct operations without day-to-day supervision by city or county officials. Districts and authorities can usually float their own revenue bonds; this indebtedness is not counted against any city or county debt limits. Districts with taxing powers can add their bills to the property tax bills sent out each year by the county tax collector. This arrangement relieves county commissioners of the direct political responsibility for these added taxes. And, more important, perhaps, it enables the aggregate of local governments in an area to exceed the 10 mills tax cap imposed by the state Constitution on counties and municipalities.

Multi-County Districts

Multi-county special districts and authorities provide a partial solution to the funding and delivery of metropolitan-wide services. This advantage is particularly important when it comes to services like mass transit and water management, which are regional in nature. Without a special district that crosses county and city lines, it would be difficult for any single local government to provide regional mass transit services or to manage and protect Florida's water resources.[50]

The Central Florida Regional Transit Authority (LYNX) provides public transportation services for Orange, Seminole, and Osceola counties. Small portions of Lake, Polk, and Volusia counties are served as well.

Disney: Corporation or Government?

When Disney came to Florida in the 1960s, it "proposed one kind of development, which it used to gain special governmental powers, and then built something else."[51] Disney promised to build a theme park and EPCOT—an Experimental Prototype Community of Tomorrow—where people would actually live and work. With Disney promising to build a real city, the legislature agreed to create a two-tier system of government with two municipalities at one level and a special district at the other. The two cities are Bay Lake and Lake Buena Vista; the special district is the Reedy Creek Improvement District, controlled by the landowner—Disney. Reedy Creek provides "essential public services," such as roads (70 miles of roadway built and paid for), drainage, flood control, solid waste collection, wastewater treatment, pest control, fire protection (extensive use of smoke and heat detectors and sprinkler systems), emergency medical services, regulation of building codes (the EPCOT Building Codes under which Cinderella's Castle and the 18-story Geodesic Dome at EPCOT were built), and land planning within the district.[52]

Disney pays property taxes to Reedy Creek to fund its administrative operations. The only residents of the cities, Bay Lake and Lake Buena Vista, are loyal Disney employees (mostly management and retirees) living in company housing—tiny, gated mobile-home parks.[53] As of the 2010 Census, Bay Lake had just 47 residents and Lake Buena Vista had just 10. These residents hold elections to select a board and then the board turns over administrative responsibility to the Reedy Creek Improvement District. While Disney's arrangement may seem somewhat unusual, the creative use of special district governments is not.

GOVERNING METROPOLITAN AREAS

Florida is a metropolitan state. More than 96 percent of its people live in the state's 22 metropolitan statistical areas (MSAs). Each MSA, which is designated by the U.S. Census Bureau, is defined as a city of 50,000 or more people together with adjacent county populations with close ties to the city. Table 10-8 shows the 22 MSAs in Florida. Miami-Fort Lauderdale-West Palm Beach in South Florida is the largest MSA in Florida with more than five million residents. It spans three counties (Palm Beach, Broward, and Miami-Dade) and numerous large and small municipalities including Miami, Miami Beach, Fort Lauderdale, and West Palm Beach. Three other MSAs, Tampa, Orlando, and Jacksonville, all have more than one million residents and also encompass multiple counties and cities.

Metropolitan Fragmentation

People living in metropolitan areas, whether in the central city or in surrounding suburbs, depend on each other for employment, shopping, entertainment, hospital care, communication, and a host of other modern needs. Yet they are separated not only by location but often by race, ethnicity, and social class as well. Moreover, with multiple municipal governments, school districts, and special districts operating within a single metropolitan area, government itself has become fragmented. *Metropolitan fragmentation*—the existence of many local governments in a region—complicates the coordination of local services and often leads to competition between cities and between cities and counties.[54] Ironically, special districts are often created to help ease the problem of fragmentation—a situation in which more local governments are created to help remedy the problem of too many local governments in one area.

City-County Conflict

Disagreements between city and county governments over the performance of services, regulation of land use, growth management, annexation, and a variety of other matters is a frequent occurrence in Florida. Because the jurisdiction of county governments extends throughout the entire county, including its cities, a conflict of responsibilities is always possible. For example, the jurisdiction of the county sheriff's office extends to the whole county, even though a city police department provides for law enforcement within the city's boundaries. In counties with large cities, concerns over intergovernmental conflicts and disputes, overlapping and duplicating services, and diffusion of responsibility have inspired reformers to recommend city-county consolidation.

Consolidation

The Florida Constitution allows for the merger of local governments, including *city-county consolidation*, by special legislative act "if approved by vote of the electors of the county, or of the county and municipalities affected." Consolidation is intended to increase efficiency by creating one local government to replace two or more. Jacksonville and Duval County merged in 1967, following allegations of widespread corruption in the city government.[55] But consolidation proposals have been repeatedly rejected by voters elsewhere in the state.[56] Often incumbent officials and employees fear loss of their positions, racial minorities fear dilution of their power, and other voters fear larger, more expensive, and less responsive government. Even in Jacksonville, there has been little evidence that city-county consolidation has led to greater efficiency in government[57] or to a reduction in expenditures.[58]

Joint provision of services, often referred to as *"functional consolidation,"* is an increasingly—and more popular—type of consolidation. An example would be several local governments combining their Emergency Management Services (EMS) or crime lab operations.

Table 10-8. Florida's Metropolitan Areas (MSAs)

Rank by Size		Population
1	Miami-Fort Lauderdale-West Palm Beach	5,777,833
2	Tampa-St. Petersburg-Clearwater	2,889,440
3	Orlando-Kissimmee-Sanford	2,270,370
4	Jacksonville	1,397,224
5	North Port-Sarasota-Bradenton	726,685
6	Cape Coral-Fort Myers	653,485
7	Lakeland-Winter Haven	623,174
8	Deltona-Daytona Beach-Ormond Beach	602,972
9	Palm Bay-Melbourne-Titusville	552,427
10	Pensacola-Ferry Pass-Brent	463,692
11	Port St. Lucie	431,406
12	Tallahassee	375,270
13	Ocala	337,455
14	Naples-Immokalee-Marco Island	336,783
15	Gainesville	267,583
16	Crestview-Fort Walton Beach-Destin	250,459
17	Panama City	187,324
18	Punta Gorda	164,467
19	Sebastian-Vero Beach	140,955
20	Homosassa	140,798
21	The Villages	111,125
22	Sebring	99,918

Note: MSA= Metropolitan Statistical Area. Data are for 2014.

Source: Office of Economic and Demographic Research, "Population and Population Change for Metropolitan Statistical Areas in Florida." Available at http://edr.state.fl.us/Content/population-demographics/data/MSA-2014.pdf.

Federated Government

Another attempt to coordinate service delivery and mitigate the problems of metropolitan fragmentation is the creation of a federated local government. The Florida Constitution established home rule in 1956, and a special federated government was created in Dade County in 1957. (Dade County officially changed its name to Miami-Dade County in 1997.)

Unlike consolidation, federated government sets up a two-tier system of governance. The 35 municipalities in Miami-Dade make up the lower tier of government and provide police and fire protection, zoning and code enforcement, and other typical city services paid for by city taxes. The county is the higher tier of government and provides services that are more regional in nature such as emergency management, airport and seaport operations, public housing, health care, transportation, and environmental services that are funded by county taxes on all incorporated and unincorporated areas.[59] It is a confusing arrangement. While surveys have shown that Miami-Dade County residents would like to switch back to a more traditional county government structure, that is easier said than done. It would take a statewide constitutional amendment to undo what is already in the Florida Constitution, Article VIII, Section 11.

Annexation

Cities are created through the incorporation process but can add territory and grow through the process of annexation. Aggressive city governments in Florida often turn to annexation to resolve intergovernmental service problems and to add to their own property tax bases.

Annexation often pits city against city or city against county. For example, in the Tampa MSA, the cities of Largo and Pinellas Park aggressively fought each other over the right to annex portions of unincorporated Pinellas County that would give them access to waterfront property.[60] In the Orlando MSA, the City of Orlando's attempt to annex valuable property on International Drive in the tourist area was fought and eventually thwarted by Orange County. The county claimed that the city was seeking to annex only valuable territory, leaving Orange County saddled with considerably less tax revenue and more poor people to serve.

Annexation may be achieved by a special act of the legislature that specifies the area to be annexed to a particular city and the procedures to be followed. But more commonly annexation is achieved by a city through procedures set out by Florida's general law on annexation.

The Annexation Process

Chapter 171, Florida Statutes, allows for two primary methods of annexation: voluntary and involuntary. The most common type of annexation is *voluntary*. A city may annex by ordinance any area whose property owners submit a voluntary petition for annexation. For example, a developer might ask to have her property annexed so that city services like sewer and water could be used for a new shopping center. Sometimes, however, a city may turn down such a request, as did the Naples City Council when a homeowners association in the Brookside subdivision asked for the area to be annexed. The council concluded that "annexation would provide more benefits to Brookside residents than to the city in general" and noted that the reason the residents wanted to be annexed was that they would save 25 percent off their water bill." (That meant the city would lose those funds.)[61]

Involuntary annexation is also known as *annexation by referendum*. The process requires a majority vote in the city doing the annexing and in the area to be annexed. In this method, a municipality proposes to annex an area by adopting an annexation ordinance. The municipality might also allow city residents to vote on the annexation in a separate referendum. Either way, the approval of a majority of voters in the municipality is required.

It is usually easier to get a "Yes" vote out of city residents (who would like to share their tax burden with others) than out of residents in the area to be annexed (who may fear higher taxes or just prefer living in an unincorporated area). For example, a few years ago, 80 percent of voters living in an unincorporated area of Palm Beach County voted against a proposal that would have made them residents of the City of Tequesta. Thus, annexation campaigns by city governments focus more on convincing residents in the area to be annexed that the additional municipal services they will get—water and sewage, garbage collection, police and fire protection, and so forth—will be worth it. From local governments' perspectives (cities and counties), annexation is all about enhancing or protecting valuable tax dollars.

FINANCING LOCAL GOVERNMENT

Local economies are cyclical in nature. Just as with the State of Florida, local governments felt the bite of the Great Recession. In Florida, as across the United States, "Local governments [were] hit with a one-two punch."[62] State aid and local property taxes dropped simultaneously for the first time in more than three decades. At the same time, the demand for government services rose, driven by stubborn unemployment rates and foreclosures (residential and commercial). Calls for spending more on social services and economic development intensified in almost every Florida county and city.

The recession made local officials more aware of the importance of preparing for financial emergencies by regularly setting aside money in their annual budgets to fund reserves. More than half of Florida's cities now have written policy statements spelling out how reserves are to be created and how they can be spent.

By 2010, things had gotten better. After two years of economic decline, the state's economic growth rate turned positive as it did in some, although not all, of Florida's localities, many of which had expedited permitting to attract new businesses.

The economy is, indeed, cyclical, although the pace of recovery differs across jurisdictions.

Problems facing elected local officials in Florida are different when the economy is more robust. They feel squeezed between the demands of population growth in their communities and the limits the state places on their revenue-raising capabilities. The ability to freely make decisions on revenue is the one policy area to which local home rule has not been extended. City, county, school board, and special district officials regularly lobby in Tallahassee for greater revenue-raising authority, more state financial aid, and fewer state mandates that place added financial burdens on them.[63] Often they also press the legislature to remove the requirement for voter approval in a referendum for a tax increase, but without much success. Republicans in the Florida Legislature are not too keen on promoting tax increases at any level.

Revenue Reliance Patterns Vary by Type of Local Government

Florida's local governments vary in their revenue reliance patterns primarily for three reasons. First, the State of Florida does not permit all local governments to tap the same revenue sources at the same rate. Second, local governments have different functional responsibilities. Third, the socioeconomic and political makeup of Florida's communities varies considerably, thereby affecting revenue assessment and collection patterns and voter preferences.

Among Florida's general purpose local governments, **counties** are more dependent than the state's municipalities (cities, towns, villages) on *taxes* (property, local option, fuel, utility, insurance, communication, local sales, local business), *intergovernmental revenue* (federal and state grants, shared state tax revenue and from other local governments), and *other* sources (e.g., bonds, refinancing of bonds, inter-fund transfers). (See Figure 10-15.)

Cities rely more than counties on *permits, fees, and special assessments* (building permits, franchise fees, impact fees, local licenses), user *charges for services* (public safety, physical environment, transportation, economic environment, human services, culture/recreation, general government), and *miscellaneous revenues* (interest and other earnings, rents and royalties, sale of surplus property and materials, employee pension fund contributions, donations from private sources). (See Figure 10-15.) Many of the services municipalities deliver are more amenable to user fees and charges, including parks and recreation, water, sewers, solid waste collection, and utilities. In contrast, counties in Florida deliver a larger proportion of public-good services such as courts, corrections, roads, health, welfare, voter registration, and libraries, which are more heavily supported by tax revenue.

When local governments ask citizens to pay a higher local sales tax, it is important that they inform residents of the projects the monies will fund.

Figure 10-15. Sources of Revenue for Florida General Purpose Local Governments

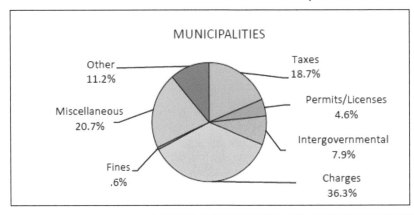

MUNICIPALITIES

Other 11.2%
Taxes 18.7%
Permits/Licenses 4.6%
Miscellaneous 20.7%
Intergovernmental 7.9%
Fines .6%
Charges 36.3%

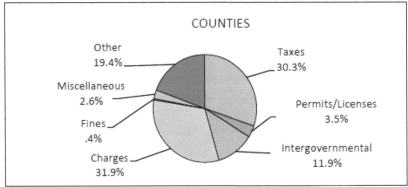

COUNTIES

Other 19.4%
Taxes 30.3%
Miscellaneous 2.6%
Permits/Licenses 3.5%
Fines .4%
Intergovernmental 11.9%
Charges 31.9%

Note: Data are for FY 2012-2013.
Source: "Statewide Expenditures and Revenues Reported by Florida's Local Governments,"
Florida Office of Economic and Demographic Research. Available at
http://edr.state.fl.us/Content/local-government/data/revenues-expenditures/stwidefiscal.cfm.

The revenue reliance patterns of Florida's special purpose local governments (school districts and special districts) are quite different from those of the state's general purpose (county, city) governments. Florida's **school districts** rely heavily on two major sources: state funding and local revenue. (See Figure 10-16.) The largest sources of state funding are from the Florida Education Finance Program (FEFP) and class size reduction operating funds. (See *2014-15 Funding for Florida School Districts* publication.[64]) By far the largest source of local revenue is the property tax, which accounts for more than 90 percent of all local revenue funds. School districts also have the option to impose a one-half-cent sales surtax (on top of regular sales tax) if voters in the district approve of it in a referendum. The sales tax proceeds must be used for fixed capital expenditures or fixed capital costs associated with the construction, reconstruction, or improvement of school facilities and campuses that have a useful life expectancy of five or more years, and any land acquisition, land improvement, design, and engineering costs associated with such facilities and campuses.[65] Fifteen counties now impose such a tax.[66]

Contrary to popular opinion, federal funds (direct and pass-through) make up a smaller portion of school district financing than monies from either the state or local governments. Other monies supporting schools come from sale of property, loss recoveries, and inter-fund transfers.

Figure 10-16. Major Revenue Sources for Florida School Districts

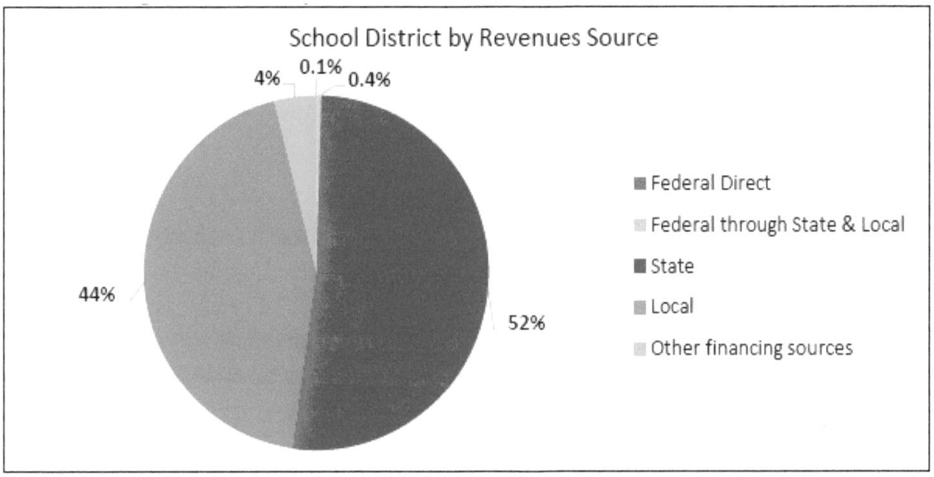

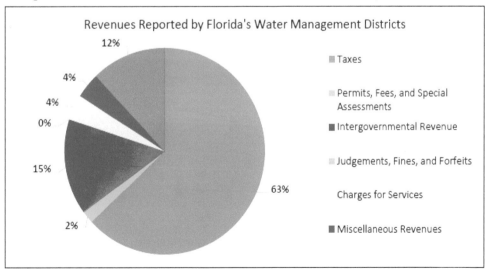

Source: Florida Department of Education Finance Data Base, "District Summary Budget: Estimated Revenues." Available at http://cdn.fldoe.org/core/fileparse.php/7507/urlt/d00budget1415.pdf.

Special districts have the statutory authority to generate revenue from property taxes, nonproperty taxes, fees, assessments, and bond sales. An examination of the revenue reliance patterns of Florida's five water districts (independent) shows that they get nearly half of their revenue from taxes—all from ad valorem (property) taxes. (See Figure 10-17.) Their intergovernmental revenue comes from federal and state grants, state shared revenues, grants from other local governments, and payments from other local governments in lieu of taxes. The bulk of their other-source revenue is generated from inter-fund transfers and the sale of capital assets. Other special districts, particularly those with more service-oriented functions, typically generate a higher percentage of their revenue from service charges and user fees and a lower share from property taxes, but, to date, data to document this has been sparse.

Figure 10-17. Revenue Sources of Florida's Five Water Management Districts

Source: Local Government Electronic Reporting (LOGER) data base, "Florida Water Management Districts Revenues," Florida Department of Financial Services' Bureau of Local Government, FY 2012-2013. Available at http://edr.state.fl.us/Content/local-government/data/revenues-expenditures/stwidefiscal.cfm.

In general, a majority of Floridians feel that their local taxes are "about right" relative to the quality of local services that are provided in their counties (from all governments). (See Figure 10-18.) However, more than one-third (38 percent) see them as either "much" or "a little" too high—a considerably larger proportion than those who see their taxes as either "much" or "a little" too low (6 percent). Local officials always have their eyes on the "much too high" trend line. A sharp uptick can create citizen-led tax revolts and spell incumbent defeat at the polls in the next election.

Revenue Legalities

Of the different types of taxes, the property tax is the most lucrative for many local governments.[67] It is known officially as the *ad valorem* tax because it is levied as a percentage of the assessed value of real property. Property tax rates are expressed as *mills*—dollars per $1,000 of assessed value of properties. The state also gives counties and cities the authority to raise revenues through several local option taxes (sales, gas) under certain conditions. In general, local option taxes may be limited to a certain type of local government or to a certain size jurisdiction or to a specific function. Local option taxes usually require voter approval. (See discussion of local option taxes in Chapter 9.)

Property Tax Assessments

County assessors are responsible for producing annual appraisals of all taxable real estate in their counties. But the Florida Constitution places a limit on annual increases on assessments. Assessed values of homes cannot be raised on current homeowners by more than three percent or the nation's inflation rate, whichever is less. However, new assessments at full value can be made of any property that changes ownership. This provision, passed as a constitutional initiative called Save Our Homes, protects long-held properties from reassessments that might result in major increases in tax bills. Predictably, it has generated claims of inequities, or unfairness, in the property tax from newcomers to Florida. The Great Recession also showed how vulnerable the tax is to economic downturns. The particularly dramatic fall in home values left many local governments with considerably smaller revenue intakes.

Figure 10-18. Voter Opinion: Local Taxes Relative to Quality of Local Services Provided Too High, Too Low, or About Right?

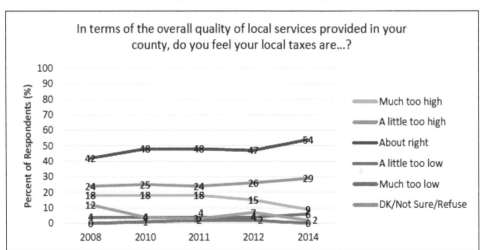

Source: "Leadership Florida Sunshine State Survey (2006-2008), Leadership Florida-Nielsen Company Sunshine State Survey (2010-2011), and University of South Florida-Nielsen Sunshine State Survey (2014)."

Property Tax Exemptions and Rate Differentials

Some properties are exempt from taxation, notably properties that are used for religious, charitable, educational, or other public purposes. *Property tax exemptions* for state or local government-owned buildings, parks, and recreation facilities, federal government offices, churches, and colleges and universities create special problems for cities, counties, and school districts with heavy concentrations of these untaxed facilities. For example, a considerably higher proportion of the land within the Tallahassee city limits is non-taxable than in many other Florida cities. (Tallahassee is home to many state office buildings, several large university campuses, and the headquarters of many charitable nonprofit groups.)

In addition to property tax exemptions, there are *property tax rate differentials*. Some types of property are taxed at lower rates than others—most often agricultural, commercial, or manufacturing. The most controversial are the tax breaks given to businesses or industries in an effort to induce them to locate in the community. But in places where jobs are scarce, there is considerable political pressure to grant these exemptions. At any rate, all these exemptions and rate differentials effectively reduce local government revenues.[68]

Every person who owns and resides on real property in Florida on January 1 and makes the property their permanent residence is eligible to receive a *homestead exemption* of up to $50,000. The first $25,000 applies to all property taxes, including school district taxes. The additional exemption up to $25,000, applies only to the assessed value between $50,000 and $75,000 and *does not extend to school taxes*.[69] This exemption benefits poor homeowners the most because $25,000 to $50,000 is a larger proportion of the value of their homes. On the other hand, the exemption negatively impacts the budgets of poorer rural counties and school districts the most, because it effectively takes away tax revenue that the local governments could have raised to support their operations, although the revenue losses would be less for the school districts than for the counties.

Setting Millage Rates

Property tax rates—millage rates—are set by city councils, county commissions, school boards, and the boards of those special districts with taxing authority. At budget time, these elected officials are responsible for estimating the financial needs of their governments, reviewing the total assessed value of property within their jurisdiction (provided by the property appraiser), and then determining a tax rate that raises sufficient revenue to meet financial needs. Thus, an individual property owner's total tax bill is a function of both the assessor's valuation of the property, exemptions given the property owner (like homestead exemption), and the total millage rates levied by county, city, school district, and special district officials.

TAXING AUTHORITY	MILLAGE RATE (DOLLARS PER $1,000 OF TAXABLE VALUE)	ASSESSED VALUE	EXEMPTION ($)	TAXABLE VALUE	TAXES LEVIED
		AD VALOREM TAXES			
COUNTY	4.8751	330,985	50,000	280,985	1,369.83
SCHOOL	7.8010	330,985	25,000	305,985	2,386.99
CITY OVIEDO	4.8626	330,985	50,000	280,985	1,366.32
SJWM	0.4158	330,985	50,000	280,985	116.83
COUNTY BONDS	0.1700	330,985	50,000	280,985	47.77
OVIEDO BONDS	0.2910	330,985	50,000	280,985	81.77
TOTAL MILLAGE	18.4155	TOTAL AD VALOREM TAXES			$5,369.51

An example of a property tax bill for a Seminole County home eligible for the homestead exemption. Exemptions are subtracted from assessed values to get taxable values. Taxable values are multiplied by millage rates to get the taxes levied.

Property Tax Limits

The Florida Constitution places a 10 mill cap ($10 of each $1,000 of assessed value) on property tax rates that can be levied by cities, counties, and school districts. But the combined city, county, school district, and special district rates on the taxpayer's bill can add up to more than 30 mills.

School districts must set their millage rates at a minimum level set by the state known as "required local effort" (on average, a little over 5 mills) as a condition of receiving full state educational aid. Most school districts also set a discretionary rate of 2-3 mills on top of the required amount.

Currently, most cities and counties are keeping their rates around 7 mills. But some of the state's smaller, poorer counties are either already or nearly capped out at their maximum millage rate. Rising property taxes can mobilize voters to pressure elected officials to order cuts in the millage rate. That is what happened in 2011 when the state legislature required the water management districts to roll back their property taxes by 30 percent, causing them to reduce their millage rates by a similar amount.

Charges and User Fees

Public reluctance to raise property taxes or approve local sales taxes has forced cities, counties, and special districts to resort to a wide variety of charges and user fees. In recent years, charges and user fees have been the most rapidly growing source of local revenue. Cities can levy charges on a wide variety of services—sewer and water, garbage collection, parks and recreation, and utilities, including the electric utilities. Counties rely somewhat less on charges and fees, but many fast growing counties impose impact fees on new construction when the economy is strong. Special districts are often created to undertake a particular function such as hospital care or public housing that relies primarily on charges, rents, and fees.

Impact fees, which can amount to thousands of dollars per building permit, are "charges imposed by local governments against new development to provide for capital facilities' costs made necessary by population growth. Rather than imposing the costs of these additional capital facilities upon the general public, impact fees shift the expense burden to newcomers."[70] During the Great Recession, many counties eliminated or reduced their impact fees as a way to attract and retain more businesses. But as the economy has recovered, more local governments are raising impact fees to cover the costs of needed infrastructure expansion related to growth.

State Aid

City, county, and school officials regularly lobby in Tallahassee for more state financial aid. State aid can come in the form of grant money or shared revenues. Florida cities and counties receive a specified share of all gasoline taxes, cigarette taxes, pari-mutuel betting taxes, and a few other excise taxes collected by the state. The sharing formulas for these various taxes are partly incorporated into the Constitution and partly set forth by law.[71] But these formulas are frequently the subject of dispute among the state, counties, and cities.

State Mandates

Local officials often complain about state laws that impose burdens on cities and counties but fail to provide financial assistance to deal with these burdens. The Florida League of Cities and the Florida Association of Counties have long opposed *unfunded mandates*. In 1990, they succeeded in winning voter approval for a constitutional amendment limiting unfunded mandates—"laws requiring counties or municipalities to spend funds or take action requiring the expenditure of funds"—unless approved by a two-thirds vote of both houses of the legislature. But local officials still complain that state laws, rules, and regulations continue to create many unfunded mandates.[72] State officials sometimes respond by pointing out that most local governments have not fully used their legal capacity to tax. That is, most local governments do not impose the full 10-mill property tax allowed by the state and do not impose the full amount of local option sales taxes allowable under the law. But local government officials counter with the argument that proposals to do that would be political suicide.

Local Government Employee Pension Funds

Florida has 491 local government pension plans—all monitored by the Florida Department of Management Services (DMS). The rising costs of employee benefits have been a source of financial stress to many of the state's local governments—a pattern observed across the United States.

A major study of Florida's municipal pension plans by the LeRoy Collins Institute found that just one-third earn an A or B grade—a figure that has been slipping, even as the economy has improved.[73] The same study detailed what will happen if so many public pension funds remain underfunded and/or poorly managed. It would:

- Require more budget resources.
- Crowd out spending on other services.
- May lead to increased tax burdens.
- Provoke divisive political conditions.
- Often prompt benefit reductions for public workers.
- Push the costs of accrued pension benefits onto future taxpayers.
- Signal credit risks to financial stakeholders, such as credit rating agencies and bond investors, who may raise borrowing costs for public infrastructure investments like city buildings, municipal roads and water systems.

In a step toward controlling the escalation of employee benefit (police, fire) costs, in 2015, the legislature passed and the governor signed a bill aimed at shoring up the finances of local police and firefighter pensions, based on (FDMS)[74] recommendations. The law "essentially repeals existing restrictions on how insurance premium taxes are spent, so long as local government and unions can come to agreement... if there is no agreement, the taxes will be sifted through a complex formula detailing how much should be spent on existing benefits and how much should be given to workers in a separate retirement account."[75] More basically, the law somewhat redefined pension benefits and altered a state funding source (insurance premium tax) shared with local governments and earmarked for police and firefighter pensions. It also increased minimum accrual rates and put a cap on overtime hours for calculating police benefits.[76] But that was just a first step toward relieving what is a growing fiscal headache for local government officials, a number of which disagreed with the FDMS recommendations.

The Troubled Jacksonville Police and Fire Pension Fund

To understand the severity of the public pension fund issue, one need look no further than to Jacksonville. In a particularly dire situation, Jacksonville's Police and Fire Pension Fund, with more than $1.6 billion in unfunded liabilities, was a key issue in the city's 2015 mayoral race. Despite the growth in unfunded liability that began in 2001, the city continued to cut taxes, and the pension fund took hits from a litany of other factors, including longer retirements and, since 2006, steady growth in benefits due to automatic cost-of-living adjustments (increases) that, unlike other benefit programs like Social Security, rise consistently even during economic recession.[77]

Jacksonville Police and Fire Pension benefits have doubled since 1999, a growth rate much faster than that of police and fire salaries (active employees).[78] While police and fire department unions cite the nature of their positions (inherent risk, physical demands, etc.) as rationale against pension reductions, it is clear that the recent trend is unsustainable. On the other side, proponents of pension reductions assert that lower benefits will not substantially hamper recruiting.

Initial reform efforts in Jacksonville were denied because they did not go far enough,[79] and a task force assigned to review the problem pushed for a balanced solution, in which both sides (the city/fund and police/fire unions) make sacrifices.[80] The inflow of money to the fund will likely increase as the economy recovers, but, if left unchecked, benefits will continue to expand.

Local Government Employee Retirement Health Benefits

Another financial problem facing local governments is retiree health-benefit liabilities. A Collins Institute analysis refers to "commitments to subsidize health care insurance premiums for retired workers" as "ticking time bombs."[81] The institute report concludes that this subsidy practice is nearly as big a looming fiscal crisis as local government pension liabilities. Health benefit programs are even less adequately funded. "Few Florida local governments have set aside [enough] funds to cover the promises they have made to their employees to provide health benefit subsidies during their retirement." Rather, most have chosen to pass the cost of retiree health benefits that have already been earned onto future taxpayers. That means unless action is taken, this practice will cause even more fiscal problems down the road as large numbers of Baby Boomers reach retirement age and are eligible for these benefits. But putting more money into retirement funds means less money will be available for current day operations—and that can create lots of political headaches for local elected officials, especially when local news stories call attention to how much money is being spent on retirees relative to current service and infrastructure needs.

Borrowing Patterns of Local Governments

Even during the Great Recession, most of the state's local governments maintained their good credit ratings, although a few dropped a few notches. Protecting one's bond rating is a high priority, which is why many jurisdictions purchase insurance to protect their borrowing. "Reneging on obligations to bondholders has traditionally been a last resort for struggling localities, in part because of the associated costs—penalties, fees, and potentially higher borrowing costs in the future."[82] Officials at the state level also closely monitor local borrowing, tracking back to the City of Miami's near fiscal collapse in 1996 and 1997, following widespread corruption involving elected officials and city financial managers.

Most local governments borrow to finance major long-term capital infrastructure projects including police and fire stations, emergency operations centers, airports, hospitals, water and sewer systems, roads and bridges, sports complexes, and convention centers, to name a few. The repayment of borrowed funds (principal plus interest) is spread out over time. This explains why in nearly every year, the amount borrowed (debt issued) is usually considerably more than the amount paid off (debt retired), although the sharp drop in interest rates during the Great Recession prompted a number of local governments to retire more debt than they borrowed.

Good credit ratings mean lower interest costs, which can save a local government millions of dollars over the life of the debt. When deciding which credit rating to give a local government, the bond rating firms consider (1) debt management using key financial ratios such as debt per capita, (2) administrative and management quality of the local government, (3) financial performance—revenue and expenditure trends, (4) a jurisdiction's economic outlook, based on its tax base, income, population, employment and other factors, and (5) its service base, which affects its ability to raise revenue from constituents and users.[83]

Sixty percent of Florida's local governments have good credit ratings—AAA or AA.[84] But like any other aspect of finance, a downturn in a local economy or a slower than anticipated economic recovery in a major sector can result in a downgraded bond rating. For example, in one six-month period in 2013, half of the 16 downgrades made by Moody's Investors Service were on housing-related bonds, most of which were held by local housing financing authorities in areas of the state with higher-than-average unemployment rates.

Looking ahead, employee pension and retiree health care benefit liabilities (both underfunded) will continue to put fiscal pressure on a number of Florida's local governments and be a major concern of credit rating firms. Although a rare practice, local governments may just have to call it quits and dissolve themselves.

Dissolution

Sometimes cities just cannot sustain themselves either financially or politically and need to "disincorporate." Actually the proper term is *"dissolution,"* which is "the dissolving of the corporate status of a municipality." The two procedures for dissolution are spelled out in the Florida Statutes, Title XII, 165.051:

"The charter of any existing municipality may be revoked and the municipal corporation dissolved by either:

a) A special act of the legislature; or

b) An ordinance of the governing body of the municipality, approved by a vote of the qualified voters."

For a city to dissolve, the county in which it is located or a nearby city must be able to provide services to the area. In addition, the dissolution must provide a fair way for employees who will lose their jobs to get their pensions and for the debt of the dissolving city to be paid (Section 165.061 (3), Florida Statutes).

Dissolution happens infrequently and for a variety of reasons. (See Table 10-9.) When citizens propose it, such as happened in Port Richey in 2006, it almost always tracks back to double taxation. Port Richey residents pushing for dissolution said they were "fed up with being taxed twice [property taxes], by the county and the city" and that "it costs more to live inside the city than it does outside it, and we don't get any better services."[85] (The proposal appeared on the ballot several times but never passed. In 2009 a majority of those elected to the city council by Port Richey voters opposed dissolution of the city.) The most recent dissolution occurred in the city of Islandia (an island in Miami-Dade County) simply because there were no longer any registered voters living on the island to elect governing officials.

Table 10-9. Dissolutions Since Passage of Home Rule Law in 1973

City	County	Year Dissolved	Notes
Bayview	Bay	1977	
Munson Island	Monroe	1977	
Painters Hill	Flagler	1981	
North Key Largo Beach	Monroe	1982/1983	
Hacienda Village	Broward	1984	Transferred assets and obligations to Town of Davie by Special Act
Pennsuco	Dade	1986	
Ward Ridge	Gulf	1987	Former city limits annexed by Port St. Joe
Golfview	Palm Beach	1998	Special Act; Area was sold to airport for new runway
Cedar Grove	Bay	2008	By vote of citizens
Islandia	Miami-Dade	2012	By County Commission because there were no registered voters living on the island; population had dwindled to fewer than five; no election had been held since 1990 (inactive during the ensuing years)

Source: Liane Schrader, "Incorporations and Dissolutions," Florida League of Cities. Accessed May 23, 2015 at http://www.floridaleagueofcities.com/ResearchMaterial.aspx?CNID=13139.

Privatization and Contracting Out

Sometimes the answer to better, cheaper, and more efficient service delivery for a local government may be to turn a specific activity completely over to the private sector (e.g., let private trash collectors offer garbage pickup to local residents).[86] Other times, it may be better to contract for the service from private businesses, nonprofits (especially for social services), or from other governments better positioned to provide the service (e.g., a small locality "buying" library services for their residents from a larger city or county). (See Figure 10-19.)

Governmental decisions to privatize (get out of a service or activity altogether) or contract out are almost always controversial. Such decisions generate considerable political heat from government employees who fear losing their jobs or pensions. Whether such decisions actually save the government money in the long term generates lots of debate. But fiscal realities in the short term remain the number one reason for privatizing and contracting out. Fiscal uncertainties in general are a perennial problem facing local officials throughout the state.

Local governments, hoping to save money, may contract out services to private or nonprofit firms. Such decisions can create controversy if it affects government employees who fear losing their pensions.

Figure 10-19. Florida Cities Frequently Contract Out Public Safety Services

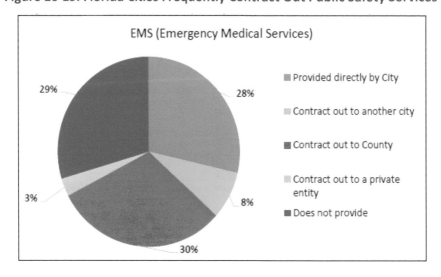

EMS (Emergency Medical Services)

- Provided directly by City: 28%
- Contract out to another city: 8%
- Contract out to County: 30%
- Contract out to a private entity: 3%
- Does not provide: 29%

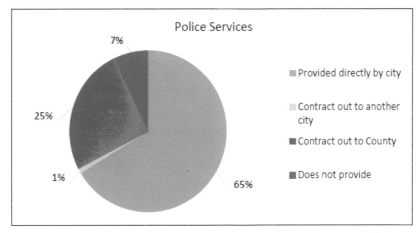

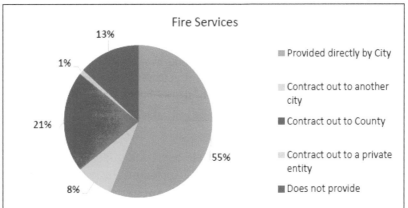

Source: Florida League of Cities Center for Municipal Research & Innovation, *2014 State of the Cities*. Available at http://www.floridaleagueofcities.com/Assets/Files/2014StateoftheCities.pdf.

BIG CHALLENGES AHEAD FOR LOCAL GOVERNMENTS: THE "NEW NORMAL"

The challenges faced by Florida's local governments are reflected in an announcement of a Florida City-County Management Association (FCCMA)/Alliance for Innovation conference that was recently sent to local officials across the state. Officials were encouraged to attend the "Transforming Local Government" workshop because *"This time of change demands new ideas and approaches to address the 'new normal.'"*

The "new normal" means that local officials must do more with less, refocus priorities, and become more collaborative.[87] Yet, while the conditions under which one must govern have changed, the overriding goal of local officials has not. It is still to "Seek new and innovative ways to connect people, information, and ideas [to create] the best communities in which to live, grow, work, play, and prosper."[88] It remains a formidable challenge, made considerably more difficult by *uncertainties* about the nature and magnitude of change. Common concerns include the following:

- *Fear of Loss of Local Control.* Local officials constantly worry about the state or the federal government putting more legal constraints on local officials' governing authority or imposing mandates that create fiscal nightmares in an era of uncertainty.
- *Unforeseen Disasters—Natural and Human-Made.* Florida's vulnerability to both types of emergencies is high. Local governments bear the brunt of such disasters in their role as first responders, and their

economies take the biggest direct hit. Natural resource shortages (e.g., water) are another potential form of disaster that threatens localities.

- *Population Shifts & Resulting Tensions*. In- and out-migration of residents directly impacts local government budgets, necessitating reprioritization and better conflict management. When the population composition shifts, generational and multi-cultural tensions rise.

- *Economic Uncertainties & Liabilities.* Economic ups and downs are creating considerable fiscal stress. Shrinking revenues (from federal and state aid) are forcing some localities to delay needed infrastructure repairs and to revamp employee benefits— creating considerable anxieties about liabilities on both fronts.

- *Growing Political Pressures*. Hostility toward government is on the upswing. Increasingly, even in nonpartisan settings, fierce partisanship has become a reality. The highly political process of redistricting (when it occurs) changes the political landscapes of many communities, but the direction of the change is difficult to project.

- *Technologically Based Challenges*. Changes in technology, particularly in the ways citizens get their information, have prompted local governments to revamp their whole communication systems. Citizens expect information to be available faster, more efficiently and effectively, and more extensively. Localities are under considerable pressure to respond, well aware that citizens' standard criteria for judging responsiveness and accountability have toughened. Increased demands for better online access have created new problems for localities. Costs associated with cyber security can be steep—both financially and politically. The latter battle can pit advocates for transparency against those insisting on privacy of individual records kept by government agencies and departments.

While this is hardly an exhaustive list of future challenges, it certainly shows the complexities, as well as the urgencies, that Florida's local governments face.

The wish lists of local government officials are long: fewer state mandates, more money for capital projects (particularly in high-growth areas), more unrestricted revenue sources, regulatory relief, fewer restrictions on inter-local agreements, more local control over growth management plans, and better funded employee pension and retiree health care benefit plans.

The Florida League of Cities conference theme captures the goal of *all* local governments—community building.

ONLINE SOURCES FOR DATA AND INFORMATION UPDATES

Florida Association of Counties

This is the official website for the Florida Association of Counties, a forum for Florida counties to discuss leadership and plans, with information on county statistics, districting, charter counties, election, methods used to elect county commissioners, and county ordinances.
http://fl-counties.com/

Florida League of Cities: Publications and Resources

Florida League of Cities acts as a voice for local government and municipalities and releases statistical data on Florida cities, as well as proposals for local governments. "Publications and Resources" provides data from publications such as Quality Cities magazine, State of the Cities Report, and the Center for Municipal Research featuring CityStats data.
http://www.floridaleagueofcities.com/Publications.aspx?CNID=182

Florida Municipal Electric Association: Municipal Owned Utilities

This page has data on the different utility sources for Florida regions and municipalities.
http://www.psc.state.fl.us/utilities/electricgas/statistics/statistics-2014.pdf

Florida School Board Association

The FSBA is the group in charge of connecting each of Florida's school boards and offers basic information on the Florida school system, school districts, and superintendents.
http://www.fsba.org/

Florida Association of District School Superintendents

The Association of Superintendents, responsible for connecting each of Florida's superintendents, gives information on Florida's superintendents, methods of appointment, district academic plans, economic plans, and budgeting.
http://www.fadss.org/superintendents.aspx

Florida Department of Economic Opportunity: Special Districts

The Department of Economic Opportunity is in charge of advancing Florida's economic development, as well as administering state and federal plans programs and initiatives. The "Special Districts" page provides an introduction to the districts and funding data.
http://www.floridajobs.org/community-planning-and-development/special-districts/special-district-accountability-program

Florida Office of Economic and Demographic Research: Local Government

The FEDR provides objective information to support the legislature's policy making process. EDR is primarily concerned with "forecasting economic and social trends that affect policy making, revenues, and appropriations." The FEDR website provides annual reports on development, taxes, and salaries of local government, as well as data on county expenditures, large and small municipalities, municipal expenditures, metropolitan areas, and sources of revenue for general purpose local governments.
http://edr.state.fl.us/Content/local-government/index.cfm

Florida Office of Economic and Demographic Research: Population

The "Population" page has data on current and projected populations in Florida, trends, and the characteristics of the population.
http://edr.state.fl.us/Content/population-demographics/data/

Sunshine State Survey: Results

The Sunshine State Survey polls Florida residents for their opinions on national and local issues, and includes statistics on the respondent's age, race, gender, party affiliation, employment, etc. The survey has data available from 2006 to 2014 (excluding 2013). Specific data can be found on trust in government leaders, the most important issue facing Florida, opinions on taxing and spending (tax revenue, least fair revenue source, and budget), issue stances, biggest divide for public officials, and the most important leadership quality.
http://sunshinestatesurvey.org/results/

Chapter 11. Public Policy: Education, Social Welfare, and Health Care

Floridians believe strongly in education, social welfare, and health care. They favor helping people who may not always be able to help themselves—the young, the poor, the sick, the disabled, and the elderly. While there is a fairly strong consensus on the need to educate, assist, and treat Floridians of all ages, there is often disagreement over how best to lend a helping hand. What works, and what does not? Who should be helped and under what conditions? Should government be the exclusive provider of these "social goods" programs, or can the private and nonprofit sectors be just as effective at running them? Who should pay for these programs—the federal, state, or local government? Working out the details of providing education, social welfare, and health care can be very politically and economically difficult in a state as large and diverse as Florida. Often, citizens have little knowledge of exactly which government or agency is fiscally and administratively responsible for these programs or how much is spent on them. Education and health/welfare are the most expensive items in Florida's budget (see Chapter 9).

PUBLIC OPINION ON K-12 EDUCATION

Education is, perhaps, the most important responsibility of state and local governments in the United States. Florida is responsible for the schooling of almost three million school age children. Historically, Florida's public schools have come under heavy criticism for failing to meet their responsibilities to these students. Florida's public schools are often accused of tolerating mediocrity, allowing dropout rates to soar, allowing achievement test scores to decline or, at best, slowly inch up, and failing to prepare students for meaningful employment. However, reforms over the past two decades have helped to improve K-12 education in the state.

Floridians consistently rank education as one of the state's most pressing problems. But surveys reveal the public does not have an accurate picture of this complex policy issue.

For years, the state's population explosion and the growing number of children and young adults put a lot of pressure on Florida's educational system. It is not surprising that, over time, the governor, the legislature, and the voters have implemented a series of educational reforms for both the K-12 system and the university system. All Floridians have opinions about education, including its importance, quality, funding, spending, and priorities, yet they do have some misconceptions about its structure and costs.

Importance and Quality

Over the past 20 years, education has often been listed as the most important problem facing Florida (see Chapter 3). From 2001 to 2006, it was listed as *the* most important problem. Since the downturn in the economy, jobs have been the first-ranked concern, but education was still the second-ranked problem in 2014.[1] Floridians tend to be rather split in the quality ratings to their local schools. (See Figure 11-1.) About 48 percent of Floridians rate the quality of education in their local public school as either "excellent" or "good," while 47 percent rate it "fair" or "poor." There were some differences in responses to that question among subgroups. Perhaps not surprisingly, people with children attending public schools were more likely to rate their local public schools as good or excellent, while people who homeschooled or had their child in private school were more likely to give their local public schools a poor rating.

Figure 11-1. Floridians Rate the Quality of Their Local Public School

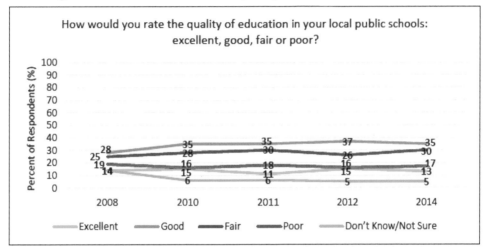

Source: "Leadership Florida Sunshine State Survey (2006-2008), Leadership Florida-Nielsen Company Sunshine State Survey (2010-2012), and University of South Florida-Nielsen Sunshine State Survey (2014).

On a separate question asking Floridians to evaluate how well the *state* provides a good public education (as opposed to their own local school), respondents' ratings were slightly lower—43 percent "good" or "excellent," 35 percent only "fair," and 18 percent "poor." Specifically related to how well Florida's education system prepares students for a complex global economy, a majority (64 percent) thinks the system is at least moderately successful. (See Figure 11-2.)

Amount and Effectiveness of Spending

Another survey looks at Floridians' views concerning the effectiveness and amount of spending on K-12 public schools.[2] A majority gives public school officials positive marks for spending educational funds in an *effective* manner (57 percent somewhat or very effective), although they do not believe enough is spent on education (58 percent say spending is too low). It is on the spending side that Floridians are the most misinformed. For example, a majority believes that Florida does not spend enough on education, yet, when asked how much *should* be spent per pupil, the amount they cite is well *below* how much Florida actually spends. One survey of Floridians found that 50 percent of the respondents recommended spending an amount that was less than what Florida actually spent on education which was between $7,000 and $8,000. (See Figure 11-3.)[3] These misconceptions persist in spite of a state law that requires Florida school districts to send parents an annual financial report, detailing actual revenues and expenditures.

Figure 11-2. How Prepared Are Florida Students for Complex Global Economy?

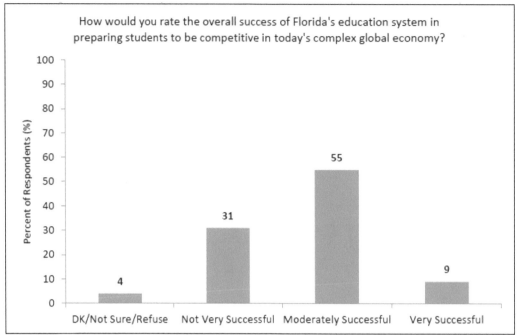

Source: University of South Florida-Nielsen Sunshine State Survey (2014).

Figure 11-3. Floridians Do Not Have an Accurate View of Per Pupil Education Spending

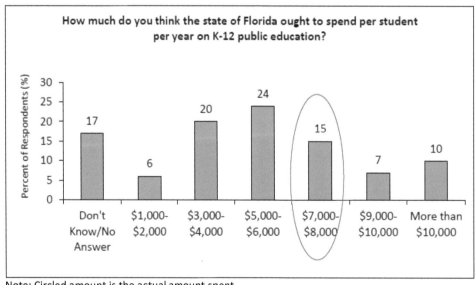

Note: Circled amount is the actual amount spent.

Source: Statewide telephone survey of a random sample of 1,200 Floridians conducted December 9, 2005-January 8, 2006 for the James Madison Institute, the Collins Center for Public Policy, and the Milton & Rose D. Friedman Foundation, January 24, 2006, margin of error less than 3 percent.

Priorities and Improvements

Floridians have fairly strong opinions on what should be the top priorities of public schools and what improvements should be made first. (See Figure 11-4.) Their top priorities are increasing teacher pay, requiring more accountability, improving discipline, raising standards and test scores, and reducing class size. When specifically asked whether rewarding good teachers with financial incentives or getting rid of ineffective teachers should be done first to improve public schools, 52 percent of Floridians support getting rid of ineffective teachers. Forty percent prefer rewarding good teachers with financial incentives.[4] Despite national news stories of tragic events like mass shootings, school safety remains near the bottom of the list of priorities, with 60 percent rating school safety as good or excellent. (See Figure 11-5.)

Figure 11-4. Floridians's Top Priorities for Local Public School System

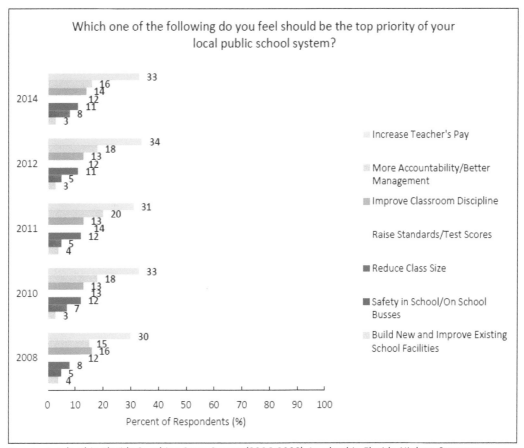

Source: Leadership Florida Sunshine State Survey (2006-2008), Leadership Florida-Nielsen Company Sunshine State Survey (2010-2012), and University of South Florida-Nielsen Sunshine State Survey (2014).

Figure 11-5. Most Floridians Rate School Safety as Good or Excellent

How good a job does the state do securing the safety of children at school?

Percent of Respondents (%)

DK/Not Sure/Refuse	Poor	Fair	Good	Excellent
5	11	24	49	11

Source: University of South Florida-Nielsen Sunshine State Survey (2014).

EDUCATIONAL NEEDS AND RESOURCES

Florida's population growth has outpaced that of the nation over the past few decades, and so has its growth in school-age population and public school enrollments. There are about 3.1 million children attending K-12 school in Florida: 2.7 million in public school (87 percent), 325,000 (10.5 percent) in private school, and 77,000 (2.5 percent) home schooled.[5]

Despite the historic growth in population and enrollments, Florida typically has one of the smallest (bottom 10) proportions of school-age population of any state in the nation (15.1 percent, compared to the national average of 17 percent[6]), primarily because of the state's relatively larger Baby Boomer and senior populations. But, in sheer numbers (rather than percents), Florida's student population is quite large. After the economic slowdown began, student population leveled off and, in some districts, even declined. However, as the economy has rebounded, the school population has increased again. Fluctuations in the economy make it difficult to accurately project the number of students.

Young mothers are very supportive of reading programs for their pre-school children.

Educational Spending

For years, the prevailing attitude has been that more money is the answer to Florida's education-related problems. The underlying assumption is that funding shortfalls are to blame for most of the school system's inadequacies. At budget time, there are perennial conflicts over which part of the educational system is most needing—or deserving—of additional funding. A recent study of educational funding in Florida describes the propensity of everyone in the system to think they deserve more funding:

"If a school district is doing well, more money should be directed there to reward good performance. If a school system is failing, more money should be directed there to help it improve. If federal or state mandates require that all students be taught by a qualified teacher or graduate with a basic set of knowledge, more money should accompany those mandates. If traditional public schools have to compete with charter schools, they will need more money to do so. If the government wants to try a voucher program, public schools should get more money for their cooperation."[7]

Overall, Florida spends about $22.4 billion for elementary and secondary education. If one adds in the costs of building new schools and the interest on money borrowed by school districts to build those schools, the figure is over $25.3 billion.[8]

According to the U.S. Census, Florida's per pupil spending is well below the national average (about $2,000 below), ranking it 42nd out of 50 states.[9] Florida has often been in the bottom 10 in such rankings, leading to pressure from the public to increase spending. Florida's reported per-pupil spending had to be cut by about $570 dollars for 2011-2012, reducing it from $6,900 to $6,300.[10] Governor Scott and the legislature have increased funding since that time, and the Governor proposed increasing per pupil funding to record amounts (approximately $7,200 per pupil) for 2015-2016. Since other states are also increasing funding, it is unlikely that Florida will move up very much in the state rankings.

In 2002, Florida voters approved a constitutional amendment to require the state to offer voluntary universal pre-kindergarten education.

Florida teachers' salaries, the largest portion of educational expenditures, are below the national average. Florida's average teacher salary is about $47,780, in comparison to the national average of $56,610. This places Florida at approximately 39th among the 50 states,[11] although there is considerable variation in teacher pay across the state's 67 school districts. Larger school districts usually pay more, but the cost of living in urban areas is generally higher.

School Financing

Public schools in Florida are financed by local property taxes levied by school districts, state aid given to local districts, and federal aid. Overall, the breakdown of which level of government pays is as follows: state government—45 percent; local school districts—45 percent; the federal government—10 percent.[12] Local school districts are authorized to levy a maximum 10 mills property tax. School districts must set their millage rates at a minimum level set by the state known as "required local effort" (on average a little over 5 mills), as a condition of receiving full state educational aid. Most school districts also set a discretionary rate of 2-3 mills on top of the required amount. State aid is provided through the Florida Education Finance Program (FEFP). These FEFP funds are allocated to local districts on a formula based on full-time equivalent enrollment (FTE), modified by an equalization calculation of the assessed valuation of property per FTE available to the local school district. This means that state aid is greater to school districts that have less valuable taxable property per pupil. This equalization of state aid across districts assures greater uniformity of resources across poor and affluent school districts.

There are still big differences in per pupil spending (as much as $1,000 dollars) among Florida school districts. And while some of that difference still represents real inequality between students in rich and poor districts, a good portion of the gap represents the higher cost of providing education in expensive counties. Areas with a higher cost of living have to spend more to buy land for schools, construct those schools, and pay higher teacher salaries to enable them to live in the district.

Lottery Funds

There are a lot of misunderstandings about how much of the total cost of public education in Florida is funded by the lottery. (See Chapter 9.) State law mandates that some one third of the funds generated by the lottery be earmarked to "educational enhancement," but funds generated by the lottery only cover about five percent of the total cost of education in Florida. To make matters worse, many citizens wrongly believe that the public schools are deriving huge revenues from the lottery and do not need any additional education funds. Lottery proceeds help fund the popular Bright Futures program (created in 1997) that provides tuition scholarships to Florida high school students to attend Florida public universities, although not at the level initially projected. Figure 11-6 shows how Florida Lottery profits are distributed through the Educational Enhancement Trust Fund.

Figure 11-6. Lottery: Educational Enhancement Trust Fund Appropriation

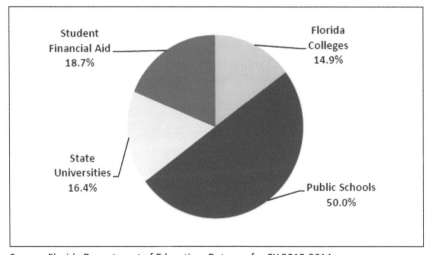

Source: Florida Department of Education. Data are for FY 2013-2014.
Available at http://www.fldoe.org/core/fileparse.php/7507/urlt/Lotbook.pdf.

EDUCATIONAL PERFORMANCE

Parents and citizen groups frequently urge the schools to get "back to basics," to concentrate greater attention on teaching the "three R's-readin', 'ritin', and 'rithmetic." The reform movement was given impetus by a 1983 report of the National Commission on Excellence in Education entitled *A Nation at Risk*, which concluded, "If an unfriendly foreign power had attempted to impose on America the mediocre educational performance that exists today, we might well have viewed it as an act of war."[13] Some educational progress has been made nationwide over the last decade. SAT scores have ended their long decline and dropout rates are lower.[14]

Historically, Florida schools have ranked at or near the bottom of most measures of educational performance. The rankings certainly explain why the public is alarmed about education and why politicians at all levels address the issue in their campaigns. Although Florida's rankings have improved with the implementation of some major educational reforms, the state still ranks low in both graduation rate and average SAT scores. While there should be no glossing over of Florida's rankings, there are some legitimate debates over the credibility of some of the traditional educational performance indicators themselves. But the reality is that ratings and grades have become an integral part of education funding.

On one recent "report card," Florida's K-12 education system earned a "C" grade (73.4 percent) for overall quality among states; the national average was 74.3 percent. The Sunshine State scored best (A-) in equity of student achievement, meaning there is a relatively small achievement gap between students of different backgrounds, and equity of school finance. The state's worst grade (F) was on spending for K-12 schools. Florida's schools are quite underfunded compared to most states. The good news is that the funding gap between rich and poor districts within the state is relatively small.[15]

The Graduation and Dropout Rates

High school graduation and dropout rates are important measures of a school system's performance and both can be calculated in various ways. The graduation rate is often measured as the percent of students that successfully complete high school in four years with a regular diploma. The dropout rate is usually based on the percentage of students that stop attending in a single year.[16]

The national graduation rate is around 80 percent, indicating that about 20 percent of ninth-graders do not graduate four years later. Only 76 percent of Florida's students graduate on time, placing it in the bottom 10 among the 50 states and below the national average.[17] As with most states, the graduation rate is lower among Hispanics, blacks, poor students, and disabled students. Florida has typically scored lower than most states on graduation rates, although there has been some progress over time due in part to reforms put in place under Governor Bush (discussed below).[18] The national dropout rate is about 3.3 percent, while in Florida it is 2.1 percent. The dropout rate has also been slowly improving.

SAT Scores

Over 70 percent of Florida's high school graduates take the national SAT Reasoning Test. For many years, average SAT scores throughout the United States and in Florida were declining. Nationally, they fell from a combined score of 1059 in 1967 to 994 in 1981.[19] Critics of public education frequently cited these declining scores as evidence of the failure of schools to teach basic reading and mathematical skills. But much of the decline could be attributed to more students taking the test. These new test takers had not aspired to go to college in the past and their scores were lower than those of the previously smaller group of college-bound SAT test-takers.

Educational reforms stressing basic skills and standardized testing appear to have resulted in a slight increase in SAT scores in recent years, although Florida's scores are still below the national average. The 2014 national average SAT score in critical reading and math was 1010 (497 in reading and 513 in math). In 2014, Florida's average score was 976 (491 reading and 485 math)—45th out of the 50 states and down slightly from the beginning of the decade.[20] It is true that states with a larger number of students taking the SAT usually have lower average SAT scores than do other states. While Florida is one of the states with a large number of test-takers, it still ranks lower than other states where at least 40 percent of the students take the SAT. (See Figure 11-7.) One of the reasons is that Florida also has a higher percentage of minority students and students for whom English is a second language. Research has shown that for a variety of reasons, these students do not perform as well on standardized tests as white students, although the racial gap is narrowing in Florida in response to a wide variety of reforms that have been implemented (discussed below).

Figure 11-7. Average SAT Scores for States with More Than 40% of Students Taking the SAT

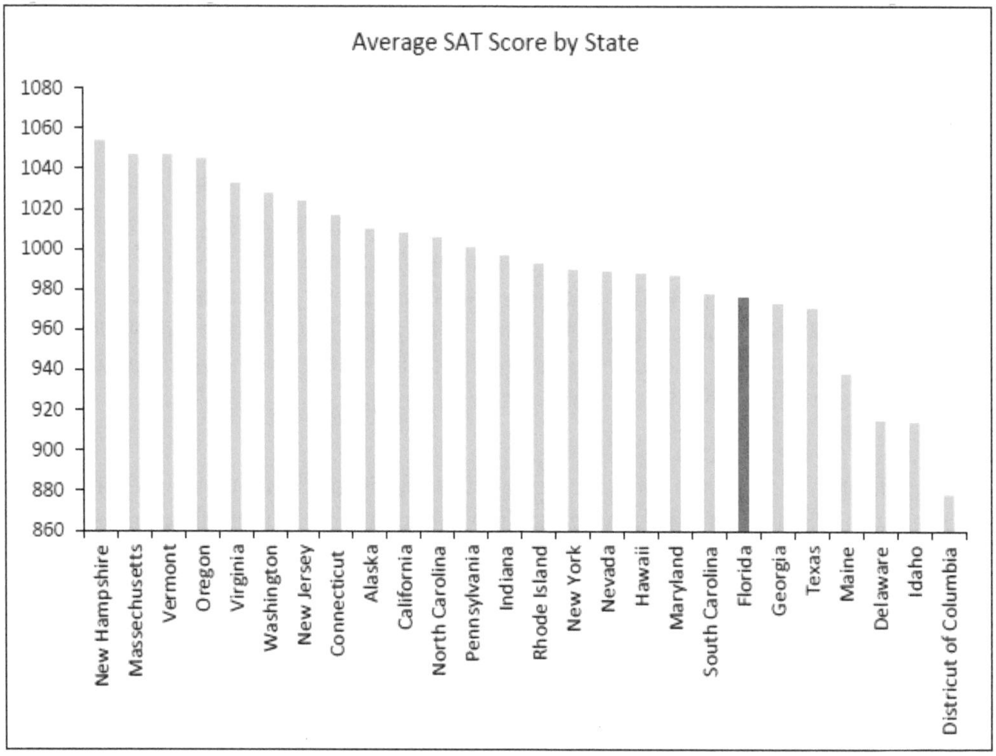

Source: College Board, SAT Scores by State, 2014. Combined Reading and Math Score. Data are for 2013-14.

EDUCATION REFORM

How can the quality of education in Florida be improved? Systematic research over the last two decades has made it clear that money alone does not guarantee good educational performance. The early landmark work of sociologist James Coleman, *Equality of Educational Opportunity* (popularly known as the Coleman Report), showed that per-pupil expenditures, teachers' salaries, classroom size, facilities, and materials were unrelated to student achievement.[21] Student success is more closely tied to the home environment than to the schools. However, Coleman and others later showed that student achievement levels are higher in schools in which there is a high expectation for achievement, an orderly and disciplined learning environment, an emphasis on basic skills, frequent monitoring of student progress, and teacher-parent interaction, and agreement on values and norms.[22]

The National Commission on Excellence in Education also made a series of recommendations to the states to improve public schools: greater use of standardized tests to monitor student achievement; a high school curriculum of four years of English and three years of mathematics; language study beginning in the elementary grades; more homework, reliable grades, and promotion standards; and performance-based rewards for teachers. Both the federal government and Florida have instituted major reforms to try and increase student education performance. In 1999, Florida passed a comprehensive education reform bill instituting Jeb Bush's A+ Education plan. And, in 2001, the U.S. Congress passed George W. Bush's No Child Left Behind Act. In 2002, Florida voters also approved constitutional amendments to require the state to offer voluntary universal pre-kindergarten education and to reduce class sizes at all grade levels. Florida officials have also sought to certify teacher competency, end tenure, and establish merit pay. High school students now face more curriculum choices, evolving standardized tests, and tougher graduation standards. Parents and students now have many more educational choices including magnet schools, virtual school, and charter schools. And, for disabled or poor students, there are two voucher programs that may be selected.

The A+ Education Plan and Its Evolution

The A+ Education Plan is based on three principles: setting high standards for student performance, measuring and publicly reporting on that performance, and providing state assistance, rewards, and sanctions. The A+ Plan for Education required testing of students in grades 3 through 11 in reading, writing, math and science on the Florida Comprehensive Assessment Test (FCAT). Students are assessed in part on these test scores. Annually, all public schools are graded (A, B, C, D, or F) based upon the performance and progress of students on the FCAT. Schools that improve a letter grade or receive an "A" are eligible for School Recognition funds of $100 per student. These funds can be used as bonuses for teachers, enhancements to the school, or incentives for students. Schools that need improvement also receive additional support and assistance. In fact, "F" schools get on average $1,000 more per student than "A" schools.[23] The FCAT 2.0 replaced the original FCAT and was used to measure student achievement of the *Next Generation Sunshine State Standards* (NGSSS) in reading, mathematics, science, and civics. These Sunshine State Standards set goals and objectives for learning for the various grade levels and academic classes.

Evaluating the A+ Plan

Critics attack the A+ plan and the FCAT for a variety of reasons. They worry about the over-reliance on a single test. They believe that it puts too much pressure on students and that it causes teachers to "teach to the test" at the expense of critical thinking and creative activities. Critics also worry that it causes schools to cut back on art, music, physical education and recess to provide more time to practice for the FCAT. Critics also do not think it is fair to judge teachers and rate schools based on the results of the test. They point out that teachers and schools do not have control over the socioeconomic status, intelligence, and motivation of their students or over the level of parental involvement. On the other hand, student FCAT scores in reading, writing, and math have increased over time for students of all races. And just as importantly, the test score gap between minority students and white students has begun to shrink. For a number of years, all average scores were rising, but scores for Hispanic and black students were rising faster than for white students. However, more recently, gains have leveled off for all groups.[24]

Common Core and the Florida Skills Assessment

Starting in 2015, the FCAT has been replaced by the Florida Skills Assessment (FSA) test. This test is keyed to the new Florida Standards which are, in turn, based on the Common Core State Standards. Common Core was developed by the Council of Chief State School Officers and the National Governor's Association for State Practices. The Common Core sets a national standard to replace what had been a wide variety of state standards, although each state may tweak the standards to better fit its needs. In addition to being more uniform, the standards are also more rigorous. The standards are voluntary, but some 42 states have adopted them. The Florida Standards replace the NGSSS and have new grade specific standards for each subject.

The Florida Skills Assessment test differs from the FCAT in a number of ways, but the most important differences are that it is perceived to be a harder test both in terms of subject matter and the types of questions asked. There are more critical thinking, analytic, and essay questions and fewer multiple choice questions. The test is taken online by all but the younger students. Common Core and the FSA reforms, while newer, have come under the same criticisms as the older A+ Plan and the FCAT.

Many conservatives dislike Common Core for two main reasons. First, they view it is as national standards being imposed on the states. Second, they dislike some of the specific standards. Conservatives are not the only ones complaining about Common Core. Many Florida parents and teachers have criticized the higher standards and harder questions on the FSA, along with the troubled roll out of the new exams. Embarrassing to the state Department of Education, there were numerous software and hardware problems that delayed test administration and, in some cases, interrupted exams in progress. Some parents have joined a group to fight Common Core (Florida Parents Against Common Core), while others have joined an "opt out" movement and refused to have their children take the exam.

No Child Left Behind

In 2001, Congress passed the No Child Left Behind Act. In many ways this is a federal version of what Florida adopted with its A+ Education Plan. Under the Act, the initial goal was that states were to improve student performance so that all children reached a proficient academic level by 2013-14. That goal was not met. It is still a work in progress. Schools must meet adequate yearly progress based on reading and math test scores. The law requires a focus on scores for a number of groups, including students from certain minority groups, with disabilities, with limited English proficiency, and from low income households. At least 95 percent of each subgroup must take the test. If even one subgroup fails the test, then the entire school fails if the school has at least 30 students in the subgroup. Schools that fail two years in a row and that receive Federal Title I funds (money for schools with a large number of students in poverty) face a variety of sanctions.

While there are many similarities, and Florida's FCAT (and now FSA) has generally been used to comply with the No Child Left Behind requirements, the standards used to interpret the results are much more rigid under the federal guidelines. For instance, one year, 90 percent of Florida schools missed the federal criteria, including 78 percent of schools ranked "A" under the state accountability system.[25] Florida and many other states have asked for more flexibility in the guidelines from the U.S. Department of Education.

Meanwhile, Congress has been working on a major overhaul of No Child Left Behind that would still require annual testing but would lessen the impact of scores by letting states decide whether to use them to evaluate teachers and how to sanction schools that do not make adequate yearly progress.[26]

Constitutional Reforms: Pre-K

In 2002, Florida voters approved two constitutional initiatives that have greatly impacted K-12 education. By a wide margin, voters approved universal voluntary pre-kindergarten education, requiring the state to provide a high quality pre-kindergarten opportunity to any four-year-old child in Florida. The goal of the program is to ensure that every young child receives some basic skills before starting kindergarten. Without the program,

Students at Lomax Elementary School in Tampa, Florida had a chance to ask the U.S. Secretary of Education questions about the No Child Left Behind law.

children of poor families who could not afford private Pre-K would be at a large disadvantage on their first day in elementary school. The legislature implemented the law in 2005. It offers school systems two options: a school-year program consisting of 540 instructional hours or a summer program consisting of 300 instructional hours. Voluntary Pre-K programs may be offered by public, private, and religious schools. Critics contend that the legislature should have provided more money for the program, required teachers to be trained in early childhood learning, and provided funding for full day Pre-K for a standard school year. But supporters firmly believe the program is working, particularly in areas where extreme poverty and low educational levels are present.

Constitutional Reforms: Class Size

In 2002, Florida voters more narrowly approved a constitutional amendment to reduce core class sizes in K-12 grades to a certain level by 2010. The theory behind reducing the size of classes is that teachers will have more time for individualized instruction and students will be more likely to stay on task. While the evidence for academic improvement based on class size is mixed unless the classes are quite small, there is some evidence that younger students do benefit from modest class size reductions.

Under the new law, the maximum number of students assigned to each teacher who is teaching in a public school classroom for grades Pre-K through grade 3 is 18 students, 22 students for grades 4-8, and 25 students in grades 9-12. The amendment required the state to begin providing funds in 2003-04 to reduce the average number of students per class by two students a year until the target goal was reached in 2010 which it was not. Florida was able to achieve the initial reductions in class size without new taxes partly because of a strong economy and partly because schools used existing space more efficiently. However, when the economic slowdown hit, legislators worried that they could not afford to pay for additional teachers and classroom space. So, in 2010, they proposed a constitutional amendment that would add some flexibility to the class size amendment. While the measure received a majority of the vote, it did not receive the required 60 percent to pass. Legislators then went in a different direction and passed a law declaring that a large number of classes were no longer "core" classes (for example, Advanced Placement courses), and, thus, not subject to the class size cap.

Pupil-Teacher Ratio

Whether the class size amendment has directly improved student learning is still up for debate. What is clear is that Florida's pupil-teacher ratio—the number of public elementary and secondary pupils divided by the number of classroom teachers—has been reduced because of the class size amendment. Before the amendment went into effect, Florida's pupil-teacher ratio was well above the national average. After it was implemented, the state's pupil-teacher ratio (14.2) dropped below the national average (15.4), as reported by the National Center for Educational Statistics. However, after legislative changes created more non-core classes, Florida's pupil-teacher ratio has crept back up to about average (16.0 for the Sunshine State; 15.9 for all states).[27]

Teacher Competence, Tenure, and Merit Pay

Florida's Department of Education (DOE) has tried to improve recruitment and retention of qualified teachers. However, the number of education majors graduating from the state's universities each year continues to be less than half the number of the annual vacancies. This shortfall necessitates heavy recruitment of out-of-state teachers. There is also unsettling evidence that the average quality of people recruited to the teaching profession is less than desirable. For example, average combined SAT scores of prospective education majors are 50 to 60 points lower than other college-bound students' scores.[28] To be fully certified as a teacher, the DOE requires a passing score on a professional skills test, a basic skills test, and a test on the subject matter that will be taught. Florida has also developed an alternative certification program to allow qualified subject-matter experts who were not education majors in college to teach in the schools. The program was seen as a way to address the teacher shortage problem and to bring teachers with practical experience in their subject into the classroom.

It may be harder to get rid of bad teachers than it is to hire good ones. Tenure protections ensure that teachers are given a renewable annual contract after a probationary period (often three years) and make it very difficult to get rid of low performing teachers. The Florida Legislature abolished tenure for Florida public school teachers starting with those hired for the 2011 school year. Teachers hired prior to this were allowed to keep their tenure. Over half (52 percent) of Floridians see getting rid of ineffective teachers as the first step toward improving education. However, they are divided on whether tenure for public school teachers should be eliminated.[29]

DOE conducts many training programs, summer institutes, and awards programs. But it is difficult to identify good teaching. College credits or years of experience are not the same as performing well in the classroom. So evaluating good teaching is critical but difficult. In most instances, teachers receive across-the-board raises, based on the union-negotiated contract and their years of service. The Florida Legislature has passed some types of merit-based rewards for teaching in the past, but they were difficult to administer and were not implemented successfully.[30] In 2011, the legislature passed a merit pay bill linking teacher evaluations and raises in part to their students' performance on standardized tests like the FCAT. One year earlier, teachers had lobbied hard against this legislation and were successful in convincing Governor Crist (R) to veto it. But the next year brought in a new governor, Rick Scott (R), who was quite willing to sign the bill once the legislature approved it and sent it his way. At the time, polls showed voters disapproved (57 - 39 percent) of the new merit pay law, but that did not stop the Governor.[31] After a union lawsuit against merit pay was dismissed, merit pay plans went into effect for all new teachers starting with the 2014-15 school year (although some school districts put it in place earlier). It is still quite controversial and intensely disliked by many teachers.

Critics of merit pay argue that it is unfair to evaluate and pay teachers on their students' performance, especially since teachers have little control over the intelligence, motivation, attendance, effort, and parental support of their students. Proponents of merit pay respond that teachers are hired to teach students and that their student's performance on tests is a legitimate way to see if students actually learned something from the teachers.

High School Curricula, End of Course Exams, and Graduation

In 2006, Governor Bush introduced his A++ Plan, which was approved by the state legislature. Its goal was to transform middle schools and high schools by instituting a stiffer academic curriculum for all secondary students, including encouraging students to choose a major. (A list of majors was actually approved but then eliminated by the legislature before students could enroll in them after negative feedback from a lot of constituents.) High school students are now required to take End of Course (EOC) exams in addition to the FSA. The Florida EOC Assessments are tests designed to measure student achievement for specific high-school level courses including Algebra I, Geometry I, Biology I, U.S. History, and Civics. The tests are mandated to be 30 percent of the student's final grade for the course. Because of the need to establish test validity and concerns over the difficulty of the new tests, the state said that EOC exams for math will not count towards final student grades in 2015 and gave school districts the option to decide how to use the EOC exams in other courses. Further, because of parental protests, the governor and legislature have begun to scale back some of the annual testing requirements (reducing slightly the number of required tests and capping the amount of time that can be spent on standardized tests).

Florida has also increased standards for graduation and created different levels of diplomas. The requirements keep getting steeper in terms of the number and difficulty of required classes goes. Further, students must pass the FSA (or achieve a high enough score on another standardized test) in order to graduate with a regular diploma. Florida high school students entering 9th grade have many options for graduation including the 24 credit program, the 18 credit Academically Challenging Curricula to Enhance Learning (ACCEL), the International Baccalaureate program, and the Advanced International Certificate of Education (AICE) curriculum. High performing students may also earn the scholar designation or merit designation on their diploma.

School Choice

A national movement to reform public education advocates parental choice among schools and promotes autonomy and competition among schools.[32] *School choice* means providing parents with educational options for their children, rather than simply assigning a child to a certain public school, based on where the child lives.

Florida permits an expanding range of school choices. For instance, a number of districts allow students to go to another public school outside their attendance zone if there is room at the new school. All Florida students can choose virtual school, and almost all districts have magnet schools and charter schools. And there are even two limited voucher programs that allow some poor or disabled students to attend private school.

Magnet and Virtual Schools

Two popular forms of public school choice in Florida are magnet schools and virtual schools. Magnet schools specialize in particular curricula, such as computer technology, visual and performing arts, foreign languages, science, or college prep. Magnet schools are open to all district students but may have limited admission based on a student's grades and talent. Originally, magnet schools began when schools were searching for ways to end school desegregation by creating schools that were not limited to students living in a particular area. Most of Florida's large school districts in urban areas have a number of magnet high schools.

The Florida Virtual School (FLVS) founded in 1997, was the country's first statewide Internet-based public high school. In 2000, the Florida Legislature established FLVS as an independent educational entity with a gubernatorially-appointed board. FLVS is part of the Florida public education system and serves students in all 67 Florida districts. FLVS offers more than 120 courses—including core subjects, world languages, electives, honors, and numerous Advanced Placement courses. FLVS courses are accepted for credit and are transferable. FLVS has nearly 2,000 staff members who reside throughout Florida and beyond. All FLVS teachers possess a valid Florida teaching certificate and are certified specifically in the subject they teach. FLVS currently serves about 200,000 students (up from 10,000 in the first year of operation in 2001). Enrollment is open to public, private, and home school students. FLVS graduated its first high school class in 2013. Beginning in 2011, all high school students are now required to take at least one online course to meet graduation requirements.[33] FLVS is the only public school with funding tied directly to student performance.

Charter Schools

Charter schools are "non-profit 501(c)(3) organizations that have a contract or charter to provide the same educational services to students as district public schools."[34] In 1996, the Florida Legislature authorized school districts to establish charter schools, and five schools formed the first year. Today, there are more than 650 charter schools in Florida with about 250,000 students. Community educational groups may petition their school district to grant them a "charter" to establish their own school. They receive waivers from many state and school district regulations to enable them to be more innovative. In exchange for this flexibility, they promise to show evidence of specific student achievement. If school districts reject a charter school application, the rejection can be appealed to the State Board of Education. Some appeals have been successful and others not. Florida charter schools receive public funding (although less per pupil than regular public schools), are generally open to any student in

FLORIDA'S
CHARTER
Schools

the district, and are evaluated using the same standards and procedures as public schools. Charter school students must take the same standardized tests as other public school students, and charter schools receive letter grades like other public schools.

Teachers unions and school boards have tended to fight the charter school movement. In spite of their efforts, the number of charter schools has climbed rather rapidly. Supporters believe they provide needed choices for students and, through competition for students, put pressure on the regular public schools to improve. Opponents, including some teachers, believe that charter schools siphon off money from the regular public schools, have little oversight, often provide a substandard learning experience, and sometimes have financial, organizational, or educational problems that cause them to shut down with little notice, often disrupting their students' school year.

Florida charter school students generally outperform students in traditional public school.[35] Charter school students on average score higher on standardized tests, have a smaller achievement gap between minority and white students, and are more likely to make learning gains. Supporters point to this data to suggest that charter schools do a better job than traditional public schools. Opponents say the difference is largely attributable to the fact that better students with involved parents are more likely to leave traditional public schools and attend charter schools.

Educational Vouchers

An even more controversial version of parental choice involves educational vouchers that would be given to parents to spend at any school they choose, public or private. The idea is that state governments would redeem the vouchers submitted by schools by paying specified amounts. All public and private schools would compete equally for students, and state education funds would flow to those schools that enrolled more students. Competition would encourage all schools to satisfy parental demands for excellence. Racial, religious, or ethnic discrimination would be strictly prohibited in any private or public school receiving vouchers. Providing vouchers for private school education would be most effective for children from poor or disadvantaged homes. These children currently do not have the same options as children from more affluent homes. They cannot afford to move to more expensive neighborhoods with better public schools or pay for private school tuition. Governor Rick Scott is a supporter of educational vouchers and would like to expand voucher programs in Florida. Such programs are highly controversial and, when proposed, tend to generate lawsuits by groups fervently opposed to them.

Voucher Opponents

There is strong opposition to the voucher idea. The most vocal opposition comes from professional school administrators and state educational agencies. They argue that giving parents the right to move their children from school to school disrupts educational planning and threatens the viability of schools that are perceived as inferior. It may lead to a stratification of schools into popular schools that would attract the best students and less popular schools that would be left with the task of educating students whose parents were unaware or uninterested in their children's education. Other opponents of choice plans fear that public education might be undermined if the choice available to parents includes the option of sending their children to private, church-related schools. Public education groups are fearful that vouchers will divert public money from public to private schools. They also complain that private schools accepting vouchers are not held to the same accountability standards as public schools.

Opportunity Scholarships

The voucher debate has been heated and ongoing in Florida for a number of years. While Florida does not have a statewide voucher system, it has had three smaller programs that involve vouchers. Under the original A+ Education Plan, students who were in a school that received a failing grade in more than two out of four years were eligible to receive a voucher (Opportunity Scholarship) to pay their tuition at a private school. But in January, 2006, the Florida Supreme Court ruled that the Opportunity Scholarships— vouchers—were unconstitutional because they violated Article IX, Section 1(a) of the Florida Constitution that requires the state to operate a "uniform, efficient, safe, secure, and high quality system of free public schools." Specifically, the Florida Supreme Court held that the Opportunity Scholarship Program "diverts public dollars into separate private systems parallel to and in competition with the free public schools" and that this diversion "also funds private schools that are not 'uniform' when compared with each other or the public system."[36]

The Court allowed the 763 students receiving Opportunity Scholarships to finish the school year. At the time, more than 90 percent of the 763 students participating in the program were minorities. After the ruling, the governor urged the legislature to put a constitutional amendment on the ballot so that Florida voters could decide whether they wanted vouchers, but that did not happen. Polls at the time suggested Floridians were evenly divided on vouchers with 48 percent supporting them and 45 percent opposing them.[37] The Florida Supreme Court intentionally ruled very narrowly in the voucher case, stating that the ruling did not necessarily affect the state's two other voucher programs.

Voucher Program: McKay Scholarships

The John M. McKay Scholarships for Students with Disabilities Program provides scholarships that allow parents to choose the best academic environment for their disabled children.[38] Since its inception in 2001, the number of scholarship recipients has grown to over 28,000 students in 1,250 private schools. Currently, total annual funding is almost $184 million dollars with scholarships ranging from $4,500 to over $19,000 with a $7,300 average. Eligible students include those with disabilities who have an Individualized Education Plan, and who were enrolled and reported for funding by a Florida school district the year prior to applying for a scholarship.

The John M. McKay Scholarships for Students with Disabilities Program allows parents to choose the best academic environment for their disabled child.

Voucher Program: Florida Tax Credit Scholarships

The other voucher program is the Florida Tax Credit Scholarship Program.[39] The law provides for state tax credits for contributions to nonprofit scholarship funding organizations, called SFOs. (Currently there are two of them.) The SFOs then award scholarships to eligible children of families that have limited financial resources. In 2009-10 about 29,000 students received scholarships and attended private schools. Five years later, the program had doubled in size to almost 60,000 students. Minority students applied for and received most of the scholarships (less than 25 percent went to white students). In 2014-2015, the total maximum amount to be distributed was $357 million and each scholarship was worth $5,272 for private school tuition and fees. A record 1,500 schools participated—71 percent religious and 29 percent non-religious.

The law imposes stricter accountability requirements on Florida private schools that accept these funds, although critics say they still are not as stringent as those placed on the state's public schools. As the program rapidly expanded, the teacher's union filed a lawsuit to declare the program unconstitutional. However the circuit court dismissed the case saying the union had no standing to sue since the program was funded by tax credits, which are not considered public funds or legislative appropriations. The union did not appeal the verdict.[40]

GOVERNING FLORIDA'S SCHOOLS

The governance of Florida's school system has undergone some major changes, thanks to several constitutional amendments approved by the state's voters. But even the "new and improved" structure can be very confusing. One board governs the state's K-12 schools and community colleges, and a separate board governs the public universities. At the local level, some school districts elect their school superintendents, while others appoint them. Some elect their school board members at-large from residency districts, others by single-member district. (See Chapter 10.) The education system remains fairly splintered to the average observer. However, the new system has greatly enhanced the governor's control over education.[41]

The Old System

Until 2002, formal authority over Florida's educational system rested with the state Board of Education under Florida's unique Cabinet system. The governor and all members of the elected six-member Cabinet (secretary of state, attorney general, treasurer and insurance commissioner, comptroller, commissioner of agriculture, and commissioner of education) served as the State Board of Education. This board usually deferred to the recommendations of the Commissioner of Education when educational matters came before it. (See Chapter 7.) The education commissioner supervised the entire system of public education in the state—elementary and secondary education, vocational adult and community education, blind services, community colleges, and State University System. In addition, there were separate boards with members appointed by the governor charged with making policy in their individual areas, including a Board of Regents for the state university system and a Board of Community Colleges. And there were/are 67 school boards, each with the authority to oversee the day-to-day operations of K-12 education in their district. Power and accountability for education under this system were widely diffused, although, in the minds of most voters, the governor was responsible for education.

Restructuring Education

In 1998, the Constitutional Revision Commission suggested, and voters approved, a restructuring of the education system. The *elected* Commissioner of Education was abolished along with several other statewide elected offices. (See Chapter 7.) The new, smaller three-person Cabinet and governor no longer act as the Board of Education. The governor was given authority to appoint the members of the State Board of Education and the Board was given the authority to appoint the Commissioner of Education. Subsequently, in accordance with the constitutional changes, the legislature changed state law to create a new system designed to be a *"seamless K-20 system"* with authority flowing from the governor to the appointed State Board of Education and appointed Commissioner of Education. The Board of Regents and the Board of Community Colleges were abolished, and, in their place, separate Boards of Trustees (largely appointed by the governor) were established for each state university and community college. All of these changes officially went into effect at the beginning of 2003 with the expiration of the term of the last elected Commissioner of Education and re-election of Governor Jeb Bush. The end result was to give far more power over, and accountability for, education to the governor in line with the expectations already held by most Floridians.

Creation of the Board of Governors

A number of people, including many university professors and administrators and U.S. Senator Bob Graham, worried that the new system would not work well for the state university system. They feared that each university and its Boards of Trustees would be in competition for programs and resources from the legislature in the absence of a statewide board to oversee and make policy recommendations for the system as a whole. In 2002, Senator Graham put his considerable political weight behind a citizen initiative that called for the creation of a new separate Board of Governors, in addition to the separate universities' Boards of Trustees. The constitutional amendment passed, thereby creating the Board of Governors to be appointed by the governor.

Initially, the Board of Governors did very little since it was appointed by Governor Bush who had opposed the idea because he believed it would dilute authority by adding another layer of governance. However, in 2006, following a lawsuit and judicial ratification of an agreement between the Board of Governors, State Board of Education, and the citizens group that brought the lawsuit, the role of the Board of Governors was clarified. In short, the Florida Constitution vests full authority over the state university system with the Board of Governors, while the State Board of Education has authority over the K-12 system and the community colleges. Figure 11-8 outlines the current organization of education in Florida.

Figure 11-8. Education Organization in Florida

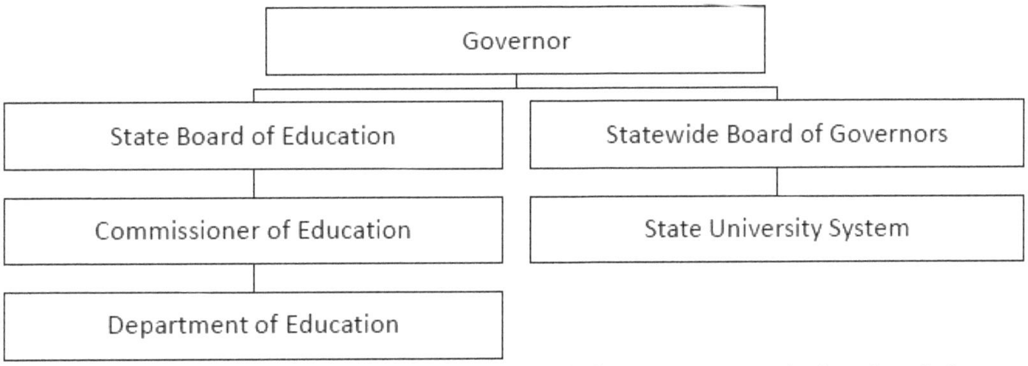

Note: The structure of educational governance has changed a lot in recent years. The State Board of Education oversees K-12 and the state college system. The Board of Governors oversees the state university system. This organizational structure gives Florida's governor a lot more authority over education than did the old system.

Source: Created by the authors.

State Board of Education

According to Article IX, Section 2 of the Florida Constitution, the State Board of Education consists of seven members appointed by the governor to staggered four-year terms, subject to confirmation by the Senate. Members serve without compensation. Florida law says that the State Board of Education is the chief implementing and coordinating body of public education in Florida, which shall focus on high-level policy decisions. It has authority to adopt rules to implement laws passed by the legislature designed to improve the K-12 education system and the community college system.

State law establishes more than 50 specific duties for the State Board of Education. But in brief, it must adopt educational objectives and plans to improve and develop education, supervise the Department of Education, and suggest budgets to the legislature. As a practical matter, the Board of Education can and does delegate its general powers to the Commissioner of Education or the directors of the divisions within the Department of Education.

Commissioner of Education

The Florida Constitution establishes that the Commissioner of Education is appointed by the State Board of Education. According to the Florida Statutes, the Commissioner of Education is the chief educational officer of the state, and is responsible for giving full assistance to the State Board of Education in enforcing compliance with the mission and goals of the Florida education system. While state law lays out a number of specific responsibilities, the main tasks are to give advice and counsel to the State Board of Education on all matters pertaining to education; to recommend to the State Board of Education actions and policies including annual budget recommendations; and to execute or provide for the execution of acts and policies as are approved.

Department of Education

The Commissioner of Education oversees the day-to-day operation of the Department of Education. The Department of Education has over 2,000 employees located in one of the newer state office buildings in Tallahassee. The Department is divided into several major areas: Public Schools; Florida Colleges; Career and Adult Education; Workforce Development; Accountability, Research, and Measurement; Technology and Innovation; Finance and Operations; Vocational Rehabilitation; and Blind Services.

Local School Boards

Florida is one of only two states that establishes school boards in its state Constitution. Most others do so by statutes. Florida's 67 school districts are governed by elected boards whose members are chosen in nonpartisan elections for staggered terms.[42] Twenty-one elect their school board members from single-member districts; 43 from at-large residency districts, and 3 use a combination of single member and at-large.[43] (See Chapter 10.) Most school boards have five members, but the larger urban districts have seven or even nine-member boards. While these boards have official responsibility for the operation of the state's elementary and secondary schools, their authority is heavily circumscribed by state laws and regulations issued by the state Department of Education. Their ability to determine school tax rates is limited by both minimum and maximum millage rates. Their control over classroom hours, number of days of instruction, curriculum content, teacher certifications, minimum competence testing, compulsory attendance, and many other matters is determined by state law and DOE regulations.

Much of the time in school board meetings is taken up by the task of interpreting and complying with state laws and regulations. However, some of the most contentious issues that come before local school boards involve redistricting (re-drawing school boundary lines), student discipline, dress codes, gifted programs (everyone thinks their child is "gifted"), bullying, and, lately, improper teacher-student relationships. Discussions of any of these issues usually generate large turnouts of parents and garner lots of media attention.

Challenges Faced by School Boards

Local control of schools by democratically-elected citizen boards remains an article of faith in America. It was the original concept in American public educational development in the 19th century. Yet as educational issues became more complex, the knowledge of citizen boards seemed insufficient to cope with the problems of modern school district administration—multi-million-dollar building programs, curricular innovations, collective bargaining with teachers' unions, special educational programs for handicapped and exceptional students, vocational training, and the intractable problems of race and ethnicity in the schools.

School board members from across Florida meet annually to discuss the problems facing their local school districts.

Over the years, democratically-elected citizen boards have had to increasingly turn to professional educators for guidance, posing a central dilemma in school governance: Should schools be governed by the local citizenry through their elected representatives, or should most policy questions be decided by professional educators based on their technical competence? On average, citizens think their schools boards are doing a pretty good job overall, with 45 percent ranking them as "good" or "excellent," 29 percent as "fair," but only 16 percent as "poor."[44]

School Superintendents

School district superintendents are responsible for the management of the public schools—hiring and supervising teachers and principals, planning and organizing the schools, preparing budgets and over-seeing expenditures, and recommending policy to the board. They are expected to bring professional expertise to the schools. Generally, candidates for the post stress their educational experience and credentials. The majority holds advanced degrees in education and have themselves served as teachers.

School superintendents have three major responsibilities. First, they set the agenda for school board decisions. Most agenda items are placed there by the superintendent. Second, they make policy recommendations. Most agenda items will carry a recommendation. Third, they implement board decisions. In performing these responsibilities, superintendents are expected to provide strong leadership—advocating policy changes and selling the programs to the community.

Selection of Superintendents

In most (41) of Florida's school districts, the superintendent is directly elected by the voters via partisan elections for four-year terms (no term limits). However, in 26 large urban districts superintendents are appointed by their school boards.[45] Arguments over whether superintendents should be elected or appointed follow familiar fault lines. Professional educators argue for the appointment, contending that it brings more expertise to the post, helps avoid partisan politics, and allows board members to scrutinize the professional qualifications of applicants. But many citizens argue that direct election of superintendents ensures greater responsiveness to the needs and concerns of the voters. The superintendent is a policy leader more than an administrator, and hence should be held directly accountable to the electorate.

The fact that many of Florida's school superintendents are elected rather than appointed by their school boards increases the potential for conflict over school policy. Both the superintendent and the board can claim to represent the citizenry. The board may overrule an elected superintendent but cannot dismiss one. Only the voters can do that.

Teachers and Administrators

Florida public schools have more than 317,000 full time employees: 60 percent (191,000) are teachers, 4 percent (12,000) are administrators, and 36 percent (114,000) are support staff. Florida's administrator-to-teacher ratio (1:16) is higher than the national average (1:11). Among instructional staff, about 60 percent hold bachelor's degrees, 35 percent hold master's degrees, and the remaining 5 percent hold doctorates or specialist degrees. About 70 percent of Florida teachers are white, 14 percent are black, and 13 percent are Hispanic.[46]

The Florida Education Association

The FEA is the largest union and association in the state based on its 140,000+ members. It was created from a merger of two different teacher groups who fought for control throughout the 1990s. The FEA maintains a large staff to assist affiliates in each school district in collective bargaining and contract negotiation, recruiting new members throughout the state, and lobbying both the Department of Education and the state legislature. (See Chapter 5.) The FEA and its affiliated political action committees (PACs) are major campaign contributors in state elections; virtually all of their contributions go to Democratic candidates. The FEA is regularly at odds with the Republican-controlled legislature that, in 2011, sought to pass a bill barring the state from collecting union dues from the paychecks of teachers. This bill was widely denounced by the FEA as a somewhat blatant attempt at "union busting." Floridians at-large were somewhat divided on the issue; 47 percent opposed it, while 43 percent favored the legislation.[47] The attempt to make it more difficult to collect union dues, along with the ending of tenure and the passing of merit pay, made the 2011 session one of the worst in Florida history for the teachers union. More recently, the FEA has fought with the legislature and governor to increase education spending, continue (rather than abolish) the Florida Retirement System, and impose a moratorium on the use of the new Common Core standards and FSA tests to evaluate teachers and students.

School Politics

Usually, only a small proportion of a community's voters appear interested in school politics. It is estimated that, on average, less than one-third of the eligible voters turn out for school board elections. Voter turnout for school bond and tax referenda is not much higher. Some studies have found that the larger the voter turnout in a school bond referendum, the more likely the defeat of the spending proposal. However, other studies have challenged this "rule of thumb" because older voters are more likely to make up a larger portion of low-turnout-election voters. Seniors do not always support school tax or bond proposals, primarily because they have little faith in school districts' ability to spend new money effectively.[48] Increasingly, school board elections in Florida are less about money and more about what is being taught in the classroom (morals, individual rights, patriotism) and children's safety at school and on busses.

HIGHER EDUCATION IN FLORIDA

Over one million Floridians are enrolled in institutions of higher education in the state. Over 80 percent of these students are enrolled in public institutions—the 12 campuses of the State University System and the 28 campuses of the state college system. (See Table 11-2.) As stated above, while the state Board of Education and the Commissioner of Education have overall responsibility for K-12 education and the state college system, the State University System has a separate governing structure with a Board of Governors overseeing the individual Boards of Trustees for each university. Floridians hope that higher education leaders address the serious situations facing college graduates, including the inability to find a job due to economic circumstances, lack of skills, or generational biases, all while trying to repay student debt. (See Figure 11-9.)

The New Florida State College System (The Old Community College System)

The 2008 Florida Legislature created the Florida College System—formerly known as the Florida Community College and Workforce Education System. With the passage of Ch. 2008-52, Laws of Florida, the 28 community colleges in Florida were provided the option to begin offering selected bachelor's degree programs. This change in the laws governing community colleges enabled many rural or ambitious community colleges to begin offering four-year degree programs. While still governed by local boards, the colleges and technical centers are coordinated under the jurisdiction of the State Board of Education. Administratively, the Chancellor of the Florida College System is the chief executive officer of the system, reporting to the Commissioner of Education who serves as the chief executive officer of Florida's K-20 Education System. Policies of Florida's College System are generated from activities of the State Board of Education and authorized by the Florida Legislature. The system is designed to provide a college facility within commuting distance of 99 percent of the state's population. Each college district in the system includes at least one county. Some even serve up to a five-county area. The board of trustees for each college appoints the president and oversees local operations.

Governor Charlie Crist signs the bill creating the Florida College System in 2008. The legislation enabled the state's 28 community colleges to begin offering selected bachelor's degree programs.

Figure 11-9. Employability, Student Debt among Most Serious Challenges Facing Graduates

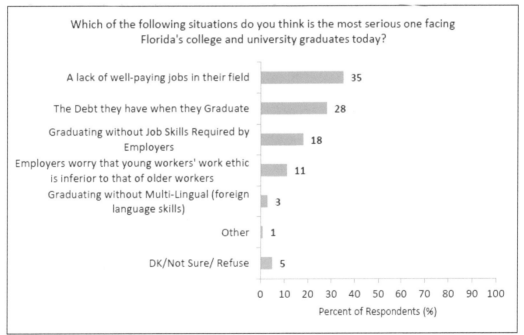

Source: University of South Florida-Nielsen Sunshine State Survey (2014).

Twenty-three of the 28 former community colleges are now state colleges. In most ways this change has made little impact on these schools. All remain open-door institutions, meaning they provide open enrollment to all students who meet minimum admission requirements (a high school diploma or the equivalent GED). While the former community colleges are permitted to award four-year degrees, for the most part, these state colleges remain focused on their community college missions—to provide two-year degree programs (Associate in Arts and Associate in Science programs). However, after the number of baccalaureate programs grew to 170 by 2014, the legislature passed a law putting a moratorium on new proposals for one year to ensure that these new programs did not overlap or compete with the university system and to ensure that the state colleges were still fulfilling their core mission.

The Florida College Responsibilities

The Florida colleges have diverse responsibilities. All provide the first two years of a baccalaureate degree program, while many have adopted or developed limited four-year program options. Any high school graduate may enroll in a Florida state college or community college. Upon successful completion of the two-year Associate of Arts degree at a Florida college, students are guaranteed an opportunity to transfer to an institution in the State University System with junior standing. The legislature has mandated that all universities accept full transfer of credit for Florida college academic work within the state. Over one-half of all juniors at state universities are community college transfers. The Florida state colleges and community colleges are also responsible for providing a large number of technical and vocational courses and programs, often developed to serve the needs of the local economy. These colleges also provide a great variety of courses in adult and continuing education, again with a special focus on programs serving local needs.

State University System

The State University System (SUS) is governed by a single Board of Governors consisting of 17 members: 14 appointed by the governor and confirmed by the Florida Senate, serving staggered seven-year terms. The commissioner of education, the chair of the Advisory Council of Faculty Senates, and the president of the Florida Student Association are also members. The Board of Governors employs a chancellor, who is the chief operating officer of the SUS. The chancellor oversees the SUS staff in Tallahassee. According to an agreement ratified by a state circuit court judge, the Board of Governors has the authority to:[49]

- Grant four-year degrees at state universities.
- Establish new colleges and universities, not including community colleges.
- Set tuition and fees for state universities (although the legislature has a role as well).
- Select the chancellor of the state university system and define the position's duties.
- Create the selection process and approve the appointment of university presidents.

About 65 percent of Florida's college bound high school graduates attend a state or community college, 32 percent enter one of the public universities, and the rest go to private institutions or technical centers.[50] Florida is one of the few states that automatically awards two years of credit toward the baccalaureate degree at its state universities to Associate of Arts degree recipients from state and community colleges.

Boards of Trustees

The Florida Constitution also gives the Board of Governors the right to establish the powers and duties of the local Boards of Trustees. Each university has a local Board of Trustees of 13 members consisting of 6 appointed by the governor and 5 citizens appointed by those 6 board members. The chair of the faculty senate and the president of the student body are also members. Appointed members are confirmed by the Florida Senate and serve staggered five-year terms. Generally, a Board of Trustees is responsible for setting policy for its university, hiring the university president, and overseeing and evaluating the performance of the president.

Table 11-1. Florida's Colleges and Universities

Colleges	State University System	Private Institutions
Broward College	Florida A&M University	Adventist University of Health Sciences
College of Central Florida	Florida Atlantic University	Ave Maria University
Chipola College	Florida Gulf Coast University	Barry University
Daytona State College	Florida International University	Beacon College
Eastern Florida State College	Florida Polytechnic University	Bethune-Cookman University
Edison State College	Florida State University	Clearwater Christian College
Florida State College at Jacksonville	New College of Florida	Eckerd College
Florida Keys Community College	University of Central Florida	Edward Waters College
Gulf Coast State College	University of Florida	Embry-Riddle Aeronautical University
Hillsborough Community College	University of North Florida	Everglades University
Indian River State College	University of South Florida	Flagler College
Florida Gateway College	University of West Florida	Florida College
Lake-Sumter State College		Florida Institute of Technology
Miami-Dade College		Florida Memorial University
North Florida Community College		Florida Southern College
Northwest Florida College		Hodges University
Palm Beach State College		Jacksonville University
Pasco-Hernando Community College		Keyser University
Pensacola State College		Lynn University
Polk State College		Nova Southeastern University
St. Johns River State College		Palm Beach
St. Petersburg College		Ringling College of Art and Design
Santa Fe College		Rollins College
Seminole State College		St. Leo University
South Florida State College		Southeastern University
State College of Florida		St. Thomas University
Tallahassee Community College		Stetson University
Valencia College		The University of Tampa
		University of Miami
		Warner University
		Webber International University

Source: Florida Department of Education: Florida Colleges Annual Report 2014; Florida Board of Governor: 2014-2015 Fact Books; Independent Colleges and Universities of Florida: Institutions.

Selection of Educational Leaders

Political connections can weigh heavily in the selection of chancellors, regents, and university presidents in Florida. A former chancellor, Charles Reed, served as Governor Bob Graham's chief of staff prior to appointment. Former Florida State University President "Sandy" D'Alemberte served as Speaker of the Florida House of Representatives, as did former FSU President T.K. Wetherell and current FSU President John Thrasher. Former University of South Florida President Betty Castor served as Commissioner of Education, actually stepping "down" to assume the presidency of that university. Former Florida Atlantic University President Frank Brogan was the former Commissioner of Education, then Lt. Governor under Jeb Bush. He went on to become the Chancellor of the State University System. Mark Rosenberg was Chancellor of the State University System before taking over as president at Florida International University and University of North Florida President John Delaney was previously Mayor of Jacksonville.

Politics and Institutional Proliferation

Higher education in Florida has been intensely political. Sectional politics and the increase in urban representation in the state legislature in the 1960s led to demands for new universities in the state's major population centers. Even with the addition of new universities, Florida is still last among the states in the number of public universities per capita (with only 12 universities serving nearly 19 million people).

The University of South Florida in Tampa, Florida Atlantic University in Boca Raton, and Florida International University in Miami were all established as comprehensive universities. The University of Central Florida near Orlando, University of West Florida in Pensacola, and the University of North Florida in Jacksonville were originally established as upper division (junior-senior) institutions to accept community college transfers. Florida International University today serves a predominately Hispanic student population while Florida A&M is the traditional school of choice for many black students. Florida Gulf Coast University, serves the rapidly growing Southwest Florida areas around Naples and Fort Myers. The University of Florida and Florida State University have the most extensive offerings of graduate programs, although the newer universities are expanding their graduate programs each year. New College is the state's public, but small, liberal arts college. The newest university, Florida Polytechnic in Lakeland, which focuses on applied science, technology, engineering and math, broke away from USF and began operating as a stand-alone school with an inaugural class of students in 2014. Virtually all of these state universities have multiple campuses, many of which were opened to satisfy the demands of nearby county residents and their legislators for "next door" service. Today nearly every student in the state lives within fifty miles of a state university.

Funding and Quality

Florida's funding for higher education expenditures per capita, per $1,000 of personal income, and per student is among the lowest of the 50 states. Its total per student funding (from legislative appropriations and student tuition) is *the* lowest of the 50 states. State support for the universities peaked in 2008 but fell dramatically during the Great Recession. Five years later, per student funding (measured in constant 2014 dollars) was still 20 percent less than it had been.[51]

The legislature and governor have announced goals to increase funds for the state universities. They have also tied some additional funding to performance. Each university (and the SUS as a whole) must now include in their annual accountability reports their progress towards reaching 10 goals (graduation rate, degrees awarded, median wages of graduates, etc.) Universities that meet or exceed most of the goals will receive additional funding.[52]

Many fruitless efforts have been made to rationalize the 12-campus system and determine appropriate non-duplicative roles for each institution. The scattering of scarce resources has prevented the state's "Very Active" research universities (University of Florida, Florida State University, the University of South Florida, and the University of Central Florida) from achieving true national rankings. Nearly every university now wants medical and

Florida A & M University (FAMU) has produced many of the state's minority political leaders.

law schools. Most recently, UCF and FIU got medical schools and FAMU had its law school reinstated. Professional schools stretch a university's resources and drain funds from other programs, often creating tensions on campus.

Overall, Floridians rate the quality of higher education in Florida's state colleges and universities very highly—71 percent as "good" or "excellent."[53] (See Figure 11-10). Part of the explanation is that admission to state universities has gotten very competitive. For example, the profile for an entering freshman at the University of Central Florida is an average GPA of 3.9 and an average SAT score of 1,257. Of the 34,000 who applied only 15,300 were accepted and 6,300 enrolled. Floridians generally feel that admission standards are about right (52 percent) with 23 percent saying they are "too hard" and 11 percent saying they are "too easy."[54] (See Figure 11-11).

Figure 11-10. Quality Rating of Higher Education in Florida

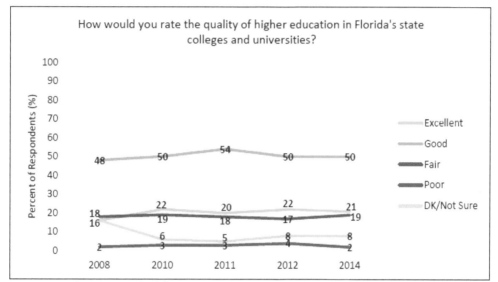

Note: Respondents were asked, "How would you rate the quality of Florida's State Colleges and Universities?"

Source: Leadership Florida Sunshine State Survey (2006-2008), Leadership Florida-Nielsen Company Sunshine State Survey (2010-2012), and University of South Florida-Nielsen Sunshine State Survey (2014).

Florida's graduation rate is higher than the national average and ranks among the top 10 states.[55] (Florida has gradually moved up in the rankings over time.) It is taking longer for students to graduate. Nationally, 33.3 percent of those who graduate from four-year colleges do it in four years, 57.6 percent in six years. Comparable figures for Florida college graduates are 38.7 percent and 64.4 percent respectively. The reasons for not finishing very quickly or dropping out altogether are largely academic, financial, and personal.

Graduation rates are lower for minority students and those from low-income families, but Florida's black and Hispanic students graduate from college at a higher rate than their peers in other states. The Sunshine State's above-average ranking is particularly impressive given Florida's very diverse student population.

Figure 11-11. Most Feel College and University Admissions Standards Are Appropriate

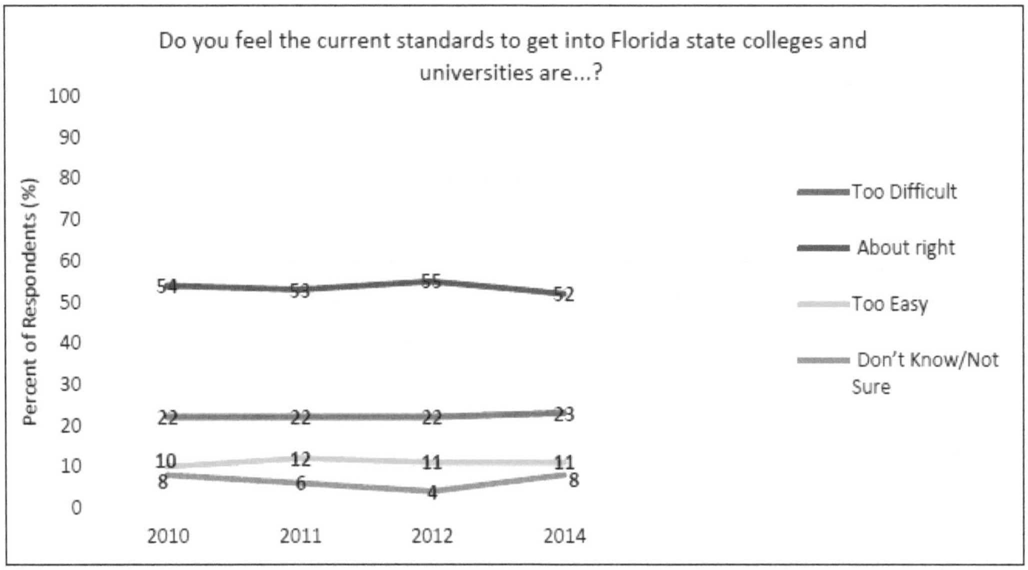

Do you feel the current standards to get into Florida state colleges and universities are...?

Source: Leadership Florida Sunshine State Survey (2006-2008), Leadership Florida-Nielsen Company Sunshine State Survey (2010-2012), and University of South Florida-Nielsen Sunshine State Survey (2014).

Tuition: Comparatively Low, but Rising

Tuition costs per student in Florida's university and community college systems are among the lowest (48th) in the nation. Most students think their tuition covers the total cost of higher education. Actually, it never has, but it covers more today than in the past. Prior to the Great Recession, when the economy was doing well, the state was generating more revenue, and legislative appropriations to universities were higher. During these boom years, student tuition accounted for less than 20 percent of the funds needed to pay for higher education. Taxpayers, plus auxiliary and research enterprises on the campuses, paid the rest. But as a consequence of tuition hikes of 50 percent during the recession and a slower-than-expected economic recovery from the recession, student tuition now accounts for over 35 percent of the requisite funds supporting higher education.[56]

Despite the fact that tuition rates for Florida colleges and universities are so low relative to other states, Floridians still feel they are "too high" (about 57 percent) with 28 percent saying they are "about right" and only 3 percent saying they are "too low."[57] (See Figure 11-12.) One reason so many people may think tuition is too high is because of the large tuition increases that were imposed for several years running. The bad economy caused the legislature to cut funding for higher education, and, in an attempt to maintain quality, the legislature allowed differential tuition increases. Universities were granted the authority to raise their tuition by a *maximum* of 15 percent each year. For example, if the legislature imposed a 7 percent increase, then universities could choose to increase their tuition by up to 8 percent more, thereby reaching the 15 percent maximum. The law further stated that tuition could be raised by up to 15 percent a year until such time as tuition in Florida reached the national average public university tuition rate. Not surprisingly, the differential tuition law was quite unpopular and prompted plenty of public backlash against it. After several years of intense criticism, many universities instituted a temporary tuition freeze, and the governor and legislature significantly limited differential tuition. Only the University of Florida and Florida State University now have permission to use it. These universities cannot impose any tuition hike in excess of 6 percent and can do so only if they meet certain performance guidelines.

Figure 11-12. Most Floridians Feel Tuition is Too High; Very Few Say Too Low

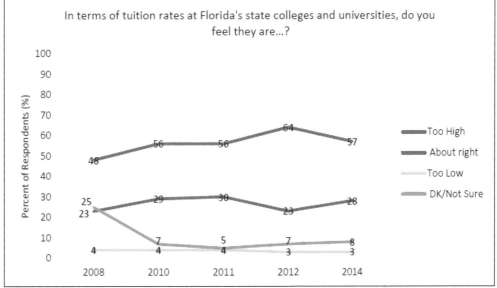

Source: Leadership Florida Sunshine State Survey (2006-2008), Leadership Florida-Nielsen Company Sunshine State Survey (2010-2012), and University of South Florida-Nielsen Sunshine State Survey (2014).

Bright Futures and Florida Prepaid

To help students afford college and to encourage smart high school students to stay in Florida for their higher education, the legislature created the Bright Futures program funded with lottery dollars.[58] Originally, Bright Futures Scholarships paid either 100 percent (Florida Academic Scholars) or 75 percent (Florida Medallion Scholars) of tuition at a Florida college or university depending on the award.[59]

To be eligible, students have to get good grades in high school, score reasonably well on the SAT, and perform a certain amount of volunteer service. More than 700,000 Florida high school students have received a Bright Futures Scholarship since the program began.[60]

As more students received awards and as tuition rates rose, the program became unsustainable. As a result, the legislature was forced to increase standards for eligibility and reduce awards substantially. As an example, Florida Medallion Scholars have to score a 1,170 or higher on the SAT (up from 980 in 2011-2012). And rather than pay a fixed 75 percent, the awards are fixed dollar amounts that cover less than 75 percent.[61] The increase in standards has reduced the number of student qualifying for Bright

Eligibility standards for the popular scholarship program have been raised and stipends reduced somewhat as a way to help balance the state's budget.

Futures substantially (particularly poor and minority students), re-igniting a debate over whether the awards should be needs-based rather than exclusively merit-based.

In addition to relying on the Bright Futures program, many Florida parents and grandparents have participated in the Florida Prepaid College Plan to help their children and grandchildren afford to go to college. Since its inception in 1987, over 1.6 million plans have been sold in the state, allowing parents to lock in tuition, fees, and dormitory housing at today's prices.[62] For several years during the Great Recession, Florida Prepaid had to increase costs substantially just to cover the large increases in Florida tuition that were expected over the next decade. However, with tuition increases now capped to more reasonable levels, the plans have dropped in price, although they are still less affordable than they once were. The price drop resulted in big refund checks to those who had over-paid. These checks arrived right before the 2014 gubernatorial election and were accompanied by a nice letter from the governor—up for re-election!

Affordability versus Quality (Tuition Increases vs. Lower Student-Faculty Ratios)

Is there a tradeoff between the affordability of Florida public universities and the quality of higher education as measured by the student-faculty ratio? Most students and many parents would argue that raising tuition does more harm than good by putting higher education out of reach of some students—the exact opposite of what should be the primary goal of higher education. Many professors and college administrators are more likely to favor tuition hikes. They strongly believe that the quality of higher education suffers when limited resources result in higher and higher student-faculty ratios. (The student-faculty ratio in Florida public universities is the highest among the 50 states and is on the rise.[63])

Proponents of strengthening Florida's higher education system say it will keep more talent in the state—talent that is critical to helping the state meet the medical needs of an aging population.

THE ENTITLEMENT SOCIETY

Florida's official poverty rate is above the national average. More than 3 million Floridians (16 percent) live in poverty. The federal government's *official poverty line* is the annual cash income required to maintain a relatively decent standard of living. Over the past several decades, between 10-15 percent of the United States' population had incomes below the poverty. Since the Great Recession, the poverty rate has hovered around 15 percent. Most Americans would agree that these people need help.

When most Americans think of social welfare programs, they think of poor people. However, most social welfare spending in America, including the largest programs—Social Security and Medicare—do *not* go to the poor. The major beneficiaries of social welfare spending in the United States are seniors who spend a disproportionately high amount of their income in the local economy. Florida's local governments benefit greatly from the senior entitlement dollars that work their way into local restaurants, pharmacies, and grocery stores.

Entitlements and Public Assistance

Today, nearly one-third of the population of the United States, and possibly more in Florida, is "entitled" to some form of government benefit. (See Table 11-2.) *Entitlements* are government benefits for which Congress has set eligibility criteria by law—age, retirement, disability, unemployment, and income or "means." Federal entitlements to Social Security (primarily cash payments to seniors) and Medicare (health coverage for seniors) are determined by age, not income or poverty. Entitlement to unemployment compensation benefits is determined by employment status, not poverty. These social insurance entitlements are non-means-tested; they may be claimed by persons regardless of their income or wealth. These programs account for the largest number of recipients of government benefits. In contrast, public assistance programs (including cash welfare assistance, Medicaid, and food stamps) are *means-tested*: benefits are limited to low-income recipients. Since many programs overlap, with individuals receiving more than one type of entitlement benefit, it is not really possible to know exactly the total number of people receiving government assistance. But it is clear that government entitlements go to a very large segment of our society.

Table 11-2. Major Social Insurance and Public Assistance Programs in Florida

SOCIAL INSURANCE PROGRAMS	Recipients in Florida (in 1,000s)
Social Security (federal)	4,115
Retirement	3,070
Survivors	379
Disabled	666
Medicare (federal)	3,621
Unemployment Compensation (federal/state)	226
Workers' Compensation (state)	50
PUBLIC ASSISTANCE PROGRAMS	
Temporary Assistance to Needy Families (TANF) (state)	87
Supplemental Security Income (SSI) (federal)	548
Medicaid & Children's Health Insurance Program (CHIP) (federal/state)	3,427
Federal Supplemental Nutrition Assistance Program* (SNAP) (federal/state)	3,526
Women, Infant and Children (WIC) (federal)	479
School Lunch (federal)	1,687
School Breakfast (federal)	799

Source: Social Security Administration; Centers for Medicare and Medicaid Services; U.S. Department of Labor; Florida Division of Workers Compensation; Medicaid.gov; U.S. Department of Agriculture[64]

Senior Politics

Florida has the highest percent of residents over the age of 65 of any state, making it no surprise that the Sunshine State has the largest number of Social Security and Medicare recipients of any state. Over 4.1 million Floridians (approximately 25 percent of the voting age population), receive Social Security benefits (See Table 11-3.) and/or Medicare. Most Floridians rate the state's provision of health care for seniors as "fair" or "good." The percent giving the state a "poor" rating of poor has steadily declined since 2008. (See Figure 11-13.)

In the past, these two programs (Social Security and Medicare) used to be referred to as the "third rail" of Florida politics: "Touch it and you die!"[65] That is still true to a certain extent, although more recent surveys of Florida seniors have found higher levels of support for making changes to Social Security and Medicare than in the past for the sake of their children and grandchildren. Part of the reason for the shift may also be that Florida's senior population is healthier, wealthier, younger, and better educated than it used to be. (And, as noted in Chapter 4, the senior vote is less solidly Democratic than it used to be with the younger-old replacing the oldest-old FDR generation that was so heavily dependent upon Social Security.) What has not changed is the attention politicians from both parties bestow on Florida's seniors, knowing full well that seniors are high turnout voters.[66]

Figure 11-13. Proportion Rating Health Care for Seniors as Poor Steadily Declining

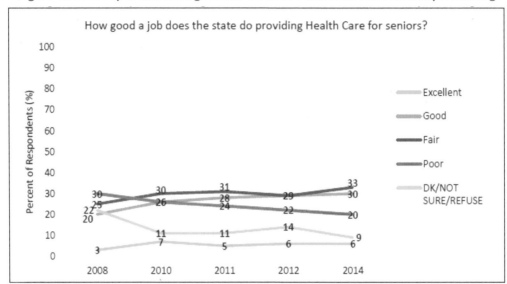

Source: Leadership Florida Sunshine State Survey (2006-2008), Leadership Florida-Nielsen Company Sunshine State Survey (2010-2012), and University of South Florida-Nielsen Sunshine State Survey (2014).

POVERTY IN FLORIDA

Public assistance programs for the poor are much more vulnerable politically than programs for the aged. The percentage of Floridians living below the poverty line has increased from 12.5 percent in 2005 to 16.3 percent. Florida's poverty rate—slightly higher than the national rate—reflects the state's higher unemployment and home foreclosure rates.[67]

Extreme poverty leads some to a life of crime.

Family Status and Poverty

Poverty in Florida and elsewhere in the nation is greatest among *families* headed by single women. Over 30 percent of these families fall below the poverty line. (See Table 11-3.)

Women and their children constitute around two-thirds of all *persons* living in poverty. Poverty rates for children age 17 or younger are much higher than those for adults—over 20 percent for both Florida and the nation. Clearly, poverty is closely related to family structure. Today, the disintegration of the traditional two-parent, two wage-earner family is the single most influential factor contributing to poverty.

Race, Poverty, and Gender

African Americans and Hispanics experience poverty in much greater proportions than do whites. The state's minority poverty rate is more the double that of whites. (For African Americans, it is triple.) While the gap between minorities and whites in Florida is still quite large, it has narrowed somewhat. Within the minority community, poverty is highest among black and Hispanic single mothers.

Table 11-3. Who Are the Poor?

Percentages Living Below the Poverty Line		
	Florida (%)	U.S. (%)
Total Population	16.3	15.4
Family Status		
Married couple	8.1	7.2
Families with female heads	31.0	33.3
Race/Ethnicity		
Whites	11.3	10.6
Blacks	28.2	27.1
Hispanics	21.3	24.7
Age		
Over age 65	10.1	9.4
Under age 18	23.6	21.6

Source: U.S. Bureau of the Census, *American Community Survey 5 year Estimates 2009-2013.* Selected Characteristics of People at Specified Levels of Poverty in the Past 12 Months.

Age and Affluence

Despite the popularity of the phrase "the poor and the aged," the aged actually experience less poverty than the non-aged. Florida enjoys a larger inflow of Social Security funds than any other state. Moreover, on average, the state's seniors are much wealthier than the rest of the population. They are more likely to own their own homes outright, with mortgages paid off. Medicare, another wholly federal entitlement program, pays a large portion of their medical expenses. With fewer expenses, the aged, even those with small incomes, experience poverty in a fashion different from that experienced by young mothers with children. The real fiscal stress on seniors comes when they are no longer able to drive or live by themselves. Just because people are living longer does not mean their quality of life stays the same in the elder years.

SOCIAL WELFARE SERVICES

The increased demand for social services like welfare, public and affordable housing, and food assistance fluctuates with the economy. Demand is highest when the economy is weak and unemployment rates are high. Over the years, an explosion in demand for social welfare services has prompted the state to "reorganize and reform" the service delivery system.

The notion of an umbrella organization—formerly the Florida Department of Health and Rehabilitative Services (HRS)—consolidating all of the state's social services, was widely applauded in 1969 when it was first introduced. People in need, no doubt, benefit from a single effective intake and referral system—a place where families, women, children, aged, abused, poor, disabled, homeless, and virtually anyone in need can go to seek help. Most people do not know what programs they qualify for or what benefits they are entitled to. But the creation of a single large bureaucracy, one that spent more money than any other agency except the Department of Education, offered an inviting target for the various interests it was designed to serve—the health care industry and the elderly. Demands for change ensued.

The health care industry—health insurance companies, HMOs, nursing homes, pharmacies—successfully lobbied for the creation of a separate Health Care Administration that would concentrate on the Medicaid program. The powerful AARP and its vocal elderly voters demanded and got a separate Department of Elder Affairs. And welfare reform in Florida, which actually predated congressional passage of welfare reform in 1996, led to a reorganized Department of Children and Families.

Welfare Cash Assistance

In 1996, Congress passed a welfare reform bill that "devolved" responsibility for welfare cash assistance from the federal government to the states. It replaced a 60-year-old federal entitlement program—Aid to Families with Dependent Children (AFDC) with a block grant to the states—Temporary Assistance to Needy Families (TANF). Some 10 years later, the TANF program was extended with some changes. The new law puts more pressure on states to "require poor parents to engage in work-related activities if they want to receive government aid." The new law, part of the federal Deficit Reduction Act of 2005, gave the federal government more authority over state-funded welfare programs than it previously had under the 1996 Act. The program is administered by the U.S. Department of Health and Human Services Administration for Children and Families (ACF).

The goals of the welfare reform legislation are to:

- Help more welfare recipients achieve independence through work.
- Increase the welfare-to-wok resources available for families.
- Protect children and strengthen families.
- Empower states to seek new and innovative solutions to help welfare recipients achieve independence.

The Act specifies more stringent work and eligibility requirements and penalizes states whose welfare programs do not meet them:[68]

- *Work requirements.* Requires 50 percent of single-parent families and 90 percent of two-parent families to work in federally-approved activities. States are penalized for failing to meet these requirements.
- *Eligibility requirement.* Most benefits can only be provided to: 1) citizens; or 2) non-citizens who are considered "qualified immigrants" and either have been in the U.S. for more than five years or meet certain exceptions to the five-year bar.
- *Federal funding.* Establishes a penalty of up to 5 percent of a state's block grant if a state does not implement HHS regulations dealing with procedures and internal controls.

Welfare Reform in Florida

The federal government's initial 1996 welfare reform law, Temporary Assistance to Needy Families, handed over cash welfare assistance to the states. In October 1996, Florida enacted the Work and Gain Economic Self-Sufficiency (WAGES) Act. The Act was developed to implement the requirements of TANF and to emphasize work, self-sufficiency, and personal responsibility, as well as time-limited assistance. In October of 2000, the Florida Legislature substantially redefined Florida's welfare delivery system by replacing the former WAGES program with the Welfare Transition (WT) program.[69] This legislation also consolidated and streamlined the state workforce and TANF programs under one board, Workforce Florida, Inc. (now CareerSource Florida). The new law created the Agency for Workforce Innovation (which subsequently was merged with two other agencies to form the Department of Economic Opportunity), which provides administrative and program guidance for workforce programs. Currently workforce, welfare, and employment services are delivered by the 24 Regional Workforce Boards (RWBS) via the local One-Stop Career Centers.

The goal of Florida's WT program is to emphasize work, self-sufficiency, and personal responsibility, as well as to enable welfare recipients to move from welfare to work. To accomplish this goal, Florida has developed a stronger support structure to deliver needed services. This structure includes the following programs and services: child care and transportation assistance; substance abuse and mental health treatment; child support enforcement programs; diversion programs to reduce domestic violence and child abuse; diversions to prevent families from going on welfare; relocation assistance; severance payments; and job training and employment programs.

How Welfare Transition Works

Under the WT program, a welfare applicant is no longer entitled to a government check just because she or he is poor. (More than two-thirds of welfare recipients are mothers and their children.) Upon initial application for cash assistance (which can be done online), the applicant will be referred to a local One Stop Career Center, which will help the person create a job résumé, learn interviewing techniques, and apply for jobs. If no work can be found, the individual will begin to receive benefits and the clock begins to tick on the two-year limit for cash assistance. He or she may be asked to work up to 20 hours a week in a community service job. The disabled and elderly are exempt from the time limits, as are teenage mothers who live with a parent and attend school.

Evaluating Welfare Reform

Florida actually started a welfare reform program several years before the passage of the TANF program in 1996 and welfare rolls began to drop in the state in 1994. Figure 11-14 shows the dramatic decline in Florida's welfare rolls following implementation of reforms. In the five years following the passage of WAGES in 1996, welfare rolls plummeted from about 201,000 to about 58,000—a decline of about 71 percent. The drop is even more impressive when considering that the state population increased by millions of people over that time-span. After that sharp decline, the number of welfare cases remained fairly steady at about 58,000 for several years before climbing back up to 100,000 by 2010. Since then, welfare caseloads have begun to decline again, as the economy has begun to recover and more jobs have been created.

Explaining Trends in TANF Recipients

The big decline in welfare recipients in the 1990s and early 2000s is primarily attributed to two factors. First, Florida's booming economy made jobs plentiful—unemployment in the state dipped to around three percent by 2006. Second, with new time limits in place, many former recipients chose to work rather than to use up their benefits, leaving them with nothing to fall back on in the event of another serious downturn in the economy. The increase in TANF recipients between 2006 and 2010 was a result of the poor economy that thrust more Floridians into poverty. The slow reduction in TANF rolls since 2010, in contrast, is a result of the recovering economy.

One of the goals of the TANF program is to work with families to help them become self-sufficient. It includes assistance to needy families so that the children can be cared for in their own home.

Whether measured by reductions in the number of people on welfare or the percent of Florida's population on welfare, the TANF program in Florida (implemented through WAGES, then WT) has been quite successful. But there are some recipients who simply will never find work. Even with low unemployment, some people may lose, or have a hard time finding, a job and may end up temporarily on assistance. Second, some of those still on public assistance suffer from mental impairment, physical disabilities or addictions. These persons make up a core group of the welfare caseload that is unlikely to ever get off the roll permanently.

Figure 11-14. TANF Total Number of Recipients in Florida

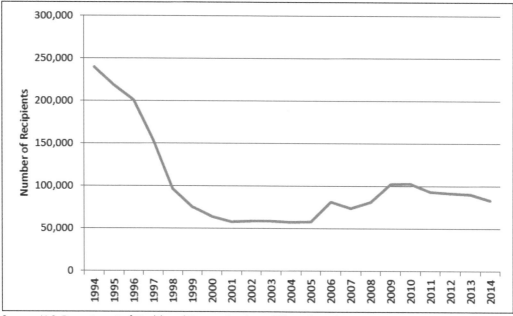

Source: U.S. Department of Health and Human Services, Office of Family Assistance. Available at http://www.acf.hhs.gov/programs/ofa/resource/caseload-data-2014. Figures are for July of each year.

Critics of Welfare Reform

Critics of Florida's welfare program make several points. First, a mother with children who receives cash benefits and food stamps is still only at about one-third of the federal poverty level.[70] Second, the types of jobs that are available to most WT participants tend to be low paying and without much chance for advancement. The Florida economy relies heavily on services—tourist attractions, hotels and motels, restaurants, hospitals, and nursing homes—that generate many unskilled, low-paying, entry-level jobs. The availability of these jobs may help the state in its efforts to put welfare recipients to work, but again most of these workers will still be living in poverty. Third, as discussed above, some long-term welfare recipients have physical disabilities, chronic illnesses, learning or emotional problems, or drug or alcohol problems that limit their employability. The TANF program acknowledges that some Americans may never be self-sufficient through a provision that exempts up to 20 percent of a state's welfare caseload from time limit requirements. However, once again, most of these persons will remain well below the poverty line even with state assistance. Finally, as Florida's economy slowed, unemployment rates rose substantially, almost doubling the number of people receiving TANF. If the economic problems had persisted, residents could have found themselves time-limited off welfare at the very time when there were no jobs available.

Food Assistance

The Supplemental Nutrition Assistance Program or SNAP (the official name for the former Food Stamps program) continues to be a federal entitlement, although administration of the program is in the hands of the states. Food stamps of¬fices are located in every county in Florida. However, states are permitted to align their food stamp eligibility with eligibility for the Temporary Assistance to Needy Families. To qualify, a family must make no more than 130 percent over the federal poverty line (as of 2015, about $31,000 for a family of four). Maximum monthly benefits for a family of four are $649.[71] Because of the bad economy, more than 3.5 million Floridians received Food Stamps in 2015—almost triple the amount in 2007. The relatively weak economic recovery has not been enough to spur a significant decline in SNAP recipients. Many Florida children also receive food assistance through the Federal School Lunch (1.7 million) or School Breakfast (800,000) programs. (See Table 11-2 above.)

HEALTH CARE PROGRAMS AND ISSUES

Floridians of all ages are concerned about rising health care costs, the quality of care, and the lack of coverage because the state has one of the highest percentages of residents and children without insurance. State and local governments are alarmed as well because they become the "safety nets" for those unable to afford coverage for themselves or their children.

The federal government plays a major role in funding and structuring health care programs. Medicaid is one of the fastest growing entitlement programs in the U.S. and one of the most expensive. It is jointly funded by the federal government and the state. Florida also gets funding from the national government to provide health insurance to children of the working poor who are not eligible for Medicaid coverage. The most controversial federal program was created by the Patient Protection and Affordable Care Act (also called the Affordable Care Act or "Obamacare"). Florida's Republican leaders have strongly opposed Obamacare.

Patient Protection and Affordable Care Act: "Obamacare" and Florida

The Affordable Health Care Act ("Obamacare") became law in 2010 with the goals of expanding health insurance coverage, increasing the quality of health insurance, and controlling the increasing costs of health insurance. It requires most Americans to obtain and maintain health insurance or pay a tax penalty (the individual mandate) and requires medium and large businesses to provide health coverage to their employees or pay a large fine (the employer mandate). The ACA encourages states to set up health care exchanges so that people can compare and buy health insurance online. There are large subsidies available to help lower income people make the purchase.

The Affordable Care Act also encourages states to expand Medicaid to cover the working poor who do not currently qualify for it and who do not make enough to qualify for a subsidy to buy insurance on the exchange. The federal government promises to pay all costs of the expansion for the first three years and then 90 percent thereafter. Obamacare also offers a variety of new benefits and protections, such as allowing children to stay on their parents' health plan until they turn 26, prohibiting insurance companies from charging more or denying coverage for preexisting conditions, ending life-time and annual insurance payout limits, and making sure that all health plans provide a certain level of benefits.

To date, Obamacare has never been supported by a majority of Americans or Floridians (although that may change over time). Republicans in particular are generally opposed to it, and Florida Republicans have been at the forefront of the fight against it. Attorney General Pam Bondi was a party to the original federal lawsuit against Obamacare. (In 2012, the U.S. Supreme Court declared most of Obamacare including the individual mandate constitutional, although they did stop the federal government from "blackmailing" states to expand Medicaid.) Governor Scott opposed Medicaid expansion, then said he would support it while running for re-election, then opposed it once back in office. The Republican House is adamantly opposed to Medicaid expansion, while the Florida Senate would like to take the federal money and use it to allow the working poor to purchase health insurance rather than participate in Medicaid. The Republican legislature and governor have refused to set up a state-run health insurance marketplace, and, instead, Floridians use an exchange run by the federal government. (There is a lawsuit pending that seeks to deny subsidies to people who buy insurance on a federally run exchange.) Most Republicans do not like the individual or business mandates contained in Obamacare, think that Medicaid is an expensive way to deliver bad health care, and do not trust the federal government to keep its promise to pay the ongoing increased costs of an expanded Medicaid.

Florida Democrats, some Republican state senators from urban areas, and health care providers favor expanding Medicaid (or at least using Medicaid dollars to expand private insurance). Many support expansion because they believe health care is a right and expansion will provide insurance to the working poor who are not currently eligible for Medicaid and otherwise cannot afford to purchase it. Supporters also believe that Florida should take advantage of the federal money being offered for expansion. They point out that Florida residents pay national taxes and are losing out on a chance to see some of their federal tax dollars come back to the state. And finally, advocates claim that expanding Medicaid will actually be cheaper than having the state taxpayers reimburse hospitals for treating the uninsured. (Florida hospitals are particularly worried that other federal programs that provide reimbursement for treating the poor are being cut back or eliminated. They fear hospitals will have to reduce care to the poor (or lose money) unless Medicaid funds are accepted.

Despite public, legislative, and executive opposition, Obamacare has been successful in increasing the number of people with health insurance, especially in the Sunshine State. Florida had more people sign up for health insurance through the federally run exchange than any other state during the 2015 sign up period (1.6 million over three months) and had the second highest number (almost 1 million) sign up during the initial 2014 sign up period. If the *King v Burwell* lawsuit is successful in denying subsidies to purchases made on the federal exchanges, it is estimated that 1.25 million Floridians will lose their subsidy and that many of them will not be able to purchase insurance without it. Marketplace premiums in Florida rose in 2015 by seven percent with an average monthly premium for a 40 year old non-smoker ranging from $303 for a bronze plan to $487 for a platinum plan.[72] Already, there has been a noticeable decline in the number of people who initially purchased an ACA-subsidized health care plan due to high deductibles. Republican lawmakers who vehemently oppose Obamacare will bear the heavy burden of finding funding for Floridians who lose their health care insurance.

Medicaid

Unlike Medicare, which provides health insurance for all seniors, Medicaid is a means-tested welfare program designed for needy people. It is funded by both the federal and state government but run primarily by the state following rules set by Congress. Medicaid services are available to people receiving Temporary Assistance to Needy Families and Supplemental Security Income, as well as to other low-income children, the elderly and disabled, low-income pregnant women, and children in foster care. The plight of the disabled is often in the minds of Floridians, who get constant reminders of them from news stories featuring disabled veterans and the elderly. (Figure 11-16 shows that more than half [51 percent] of Floridians feel the state does only a fair or poor job assisting disabled people.)

Medicaid pays the doctor, hospital, or other health bills as long as treatment is medically necessary. It can also pay for lab tests, prescriptions, eyeglasses, hearing aids, dentures, podiatry care, transportation, mental health services, and nursing care in a nursing home if these services are necessary for treatment.

The Agency for Health Care Administration (AHCA) is in charge of Florida's Medicaid program.[73] The number of Medicaid recipients has grown substantially. It actually doubled between 1999 and 2011, when caseloads hit almost 3,000,000. (See Figure 11-15.) The number of Floridians receiving Medicaid sharply increased during the Great Recession when lots of people lost their jobs and health care benefits. There could be another spike in the Medicaid rolls should the Florida Legislature decide to expand Medicaid and extend it to those who make 138 percent over the poverty level, although that seems unlikely at this point.

Figure 11-15. Florida Medicaid Caseloads

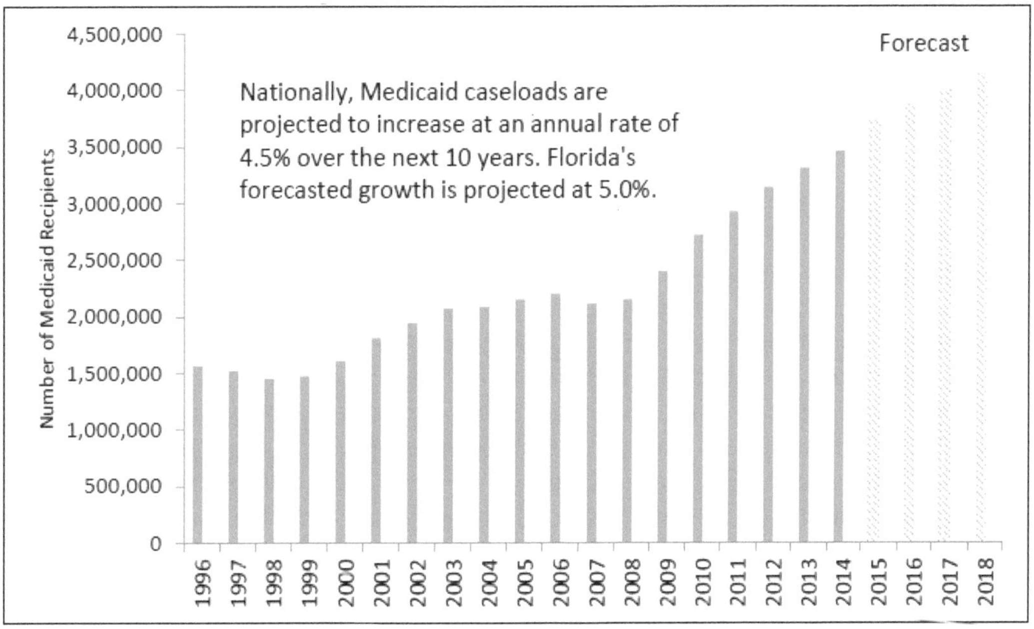

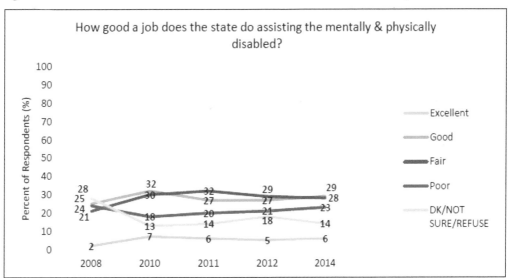

Source: The Florida Legislature Office of Economic and Demographic Research.

Figure 11-16. More than Half Rate State's Assistance of Disabled People as Fair or Poor

Source: "Leadership Florida Sunshine State Survey (2006-2008), Leadership Florida-Nielsen Company Sunshine State Survey (2010-2012), and University of South Florida-Nielsen Sunshine State Survey (2014).

Medicaid Spending

Between rising caseloads and health care cost inflation, Medicaid spending has exploded. (See Chapter 9.) From the mid-1980s to the mid-1990s, Medicaid expenditures in Florida grew from roughly $1 billion to $7 billion in federal and state money combined. Since then, Medicaid spending has continued to skyrocket. In 2014-15, Florida budgeted $23 billion dollars for Medicaid.[74] Approximately 59 percent of this money (called Title XIX funding) came from the federal government, leaving the state to pay 41 percent of the costs.[75] Despite this favorable sharing arrangement, Medicaid has grown so rapidly that it dominates the state's social service spending. Medicaid expenses have exploded as the number of poor families with children has grown and as more of the state's senior citizens have had to enter nursing homes. (Medicare only covers 60 days of nursing home care.) Nursing home care is very expensive, averaging from $7,000 to $8,000 per month. Many nursing home patients quickly use up their own savings or transfer them to others to become eligible for Medicaid. Florida Medicaid spending is expected to grow by about six to eight percent a year through 2020.[76]

Medicaid Reform in Florida

Even prior to the Great Recession of 2007, Medicaid costs had been rising by 14 percent a year in a number of states. Florida reacted to these escalating costs by successfully petitioning the federal government to allow the state to enact some of the most sweeping Medicaid reforms in the U.S. In 2005, Florida received a waiver from the federal government to turn its Medicaid program into a "defined contribution plan" as a pilot program in several counties[77] For each beneficiary, Florida pays a monthly premium to a private HMO plan which is chosen by the recipient and the HMO plan then pays doctors and hospitals. (In many states under regular Medicaid, the state would pay health care providers directly.) Insurance plans are allowed to limit "the amount, duration and scope" of services. A peer reviewed evaluation of the pilot program concluded that it gave patients more access to specialists, reduced unneeded emergency room use, provided better health improvement gains, and controlled costs.[78]

The program is being expanded into all counties now that the Obama administration gave its approval. The state projects that the defined contribution plan will save almost $2 billion dollars over three years.[79] Critics complain that any cost savings will come at the expense of quality of care.[80] While this may bring some cost predictability, the cost savings will not affect the underlying long-term demographics. As more Floridians enter the ranks of the population over 80 years of age, more will become increasingly dependent upon Medicaid to pay for nursing home care. When asked, Floridians thought that reducing Medicaid fraud and waste would be the best way to control Medicaid costs (66 percent)—only 1 percent thought that benefits should be cut to recipients.[81] One legislative agency has estimated that fraud, waste and abuse in Florida's Medicaid program averages about 12.5 percent of all billings.[82]

Children and the Working Poor

Florida is among the four states with the highest percent of children without health care coverage. The state has begun to make some progress in reducing the number of kids without coverage, but it is a constant battle given the ongoing population growth in the state. Almost half (45 percent) of Floridians think the state is doing an "excellent" or "good" job providing health care to children.[83] (See Figure 11-17). The positive rating may be at least partially a product of there being fewer children without health care coverage now than four years prior (12 percent compared to 17 percent).

Overall, Florida has the third highest number of residents without health insurance in the country (20 percent).[84] The largest group without health coverage continues to be the **working poor**. Middle income and wealthier individuals usually receive health insurance through their jobs or can afford to purchase it privately and the very poor are eligible for the various government programs. Floridians who work in low paying jobs that provide no health insurance often slip through the public safety net. It is this group that would have the most to gain if Florida expands Medicaid (or implements an alternative plan) to provide coverage to people earning between 100 percent and 138 percent above the poverty line.

The children of the working poor are eligible for some federally-funded programs. One is the Children's Health Insurance Program (CHIP). It helps provide coverage for uninsured poor children not eligible for Medicaid. Florida KidCare is comprised of several health insurance plans that are funded by CHIP money (also called Title XXI funding). Florida KidCare programs include MEDIKIDS for children ages 1 to 4, Healthy

Kids for children ages 5 to 18, and Children's Medical Services Network (CMSN) for kids with special health care needs.[85] The KidCare program checks Medicaid eligibility for all children who apply.

Figure 11-17. Nearly Half Rate Provision of Health Care for Young Children as Good or Excellent

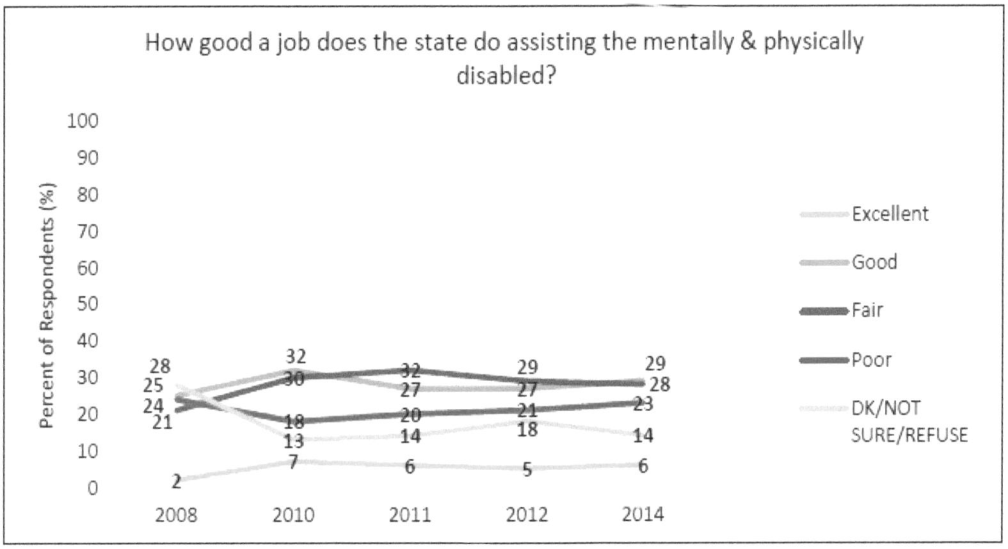

Source: Leadership Florida Sunshine State Survey (2006-2008), Leadership Florida-Nielsen Company Sunshine State Survey (2010-2012), and University of South Florida-Nielsen Sunshine State Survey (2014).

Child Support Enforcement

The Child Support Enforcement Program is a federal/state program. Federal regulations dictate major features of the program, funding amounts, and evaluation standards for state programs. The funding for the enforcement program comes from federal money and from child support collected by the state. In Florida, the program is run by the Department of Revenue. The program locates parents who owe financial support for their children, establishes paternity and support orders, enforces support orders, and collects and distributes support payments. This program is available to all custodial parents (including cases in which the parent owing support lives out of state), caretakers, or caretaker relatives of a dependent child when they are the custodian of a child who is not receiving public assistance. Non-custodial parents may apply for and receive child support services as well. By law, Florida guidelines for child support must take into consideration all income and earnings of both parents and the children's health care needs. Each year the Child Support Program in Florida helps about one million children and collects over a billion dollars in child support.[86]

Abuse Registry

The Florida Abuse Registry receives complaints alleging abuse, neglect, or exploitation of children and elderly or disabled persons 24 hours a day, 7 days a week. Many victims do not receive help because they are not reported to the system. These abused and neglected children span all ages, races, religions, and socio-economic backgrounds. Child maltreatment includes actions that result in imminent risk of serious harm, death, serious physical or emotional harm, sexual abuse or exploitation of a child under age 18 by a parent or caretaker. When parents either cannot or will not protect their children, the Department of Children and Families steps in to help by providing a full spectrum of services, from parenting classes and respite care to transportation and child care. The goal of the Department is to keep children safe in their own families when possible. About 200,000 cases of child abuse, abandonment, or neglect are investigated each year in Florida.[87]

Domestic Violence

Domestic violence is a serious public health problem in the U.S. and in Florida. Each year in Florida over 100,000 cases of domestic violence are reported to the police (although most cases of domestic violence go unreported) and over 60,000 arrests are made.[88] Domestic violence is "a pattern of controlling behaviors—violence or threats of violence—that one person uses to establish power over an intimate partner in order to control that partner's actions and activities."[89] While men are sometimes victims of domestic violence (1 in 7 will experience domestic violence in their lifetime), the victims are most often women (1 in 4) and their children.

The Florida Coalition Against Domestic Violence is the coordinating body for the 42 certified domestic violence shelters around the state. Most large counties have their own shelters, while small rural counties often share a facility. For instance, SafeHouse of Seminole County provides a 24-hour crisis hotline, counseling, safety planning, support groups, court advocacy, supervised visitation, and emergency shelter. SafeHouse also provides domestic violence education to teach teens about healthy relationships, to provide parents the tools to talk with their children about dating abuse, and to help businesses become safer violence-free workplaces.[90]

Domestic violence is a serious problem in Florida. One in three U.S. teens experiences abuse in a relationship. SafeHouse of Seminole County conducts domestic violence prevention education for teens, parents, and workplaces.

County Public Health Services

Public health services in Florida are offered through each of the 67 county health departments. Some services are free; others require a small charge. County health units provide free immunizations required by law for children entering schools, along with flu shots and vaccinations. They test for communicable diseases like venereal disease and other sexually transmissible diseases (STDs). Pregnant women and their small children can receive many services from the county health unit beginning with prenatal care. Other areas of service include restaurant inspections, investigation of animal bites, permits for septic tank installations, drinking water analysis, certified copies of vital records, mosquito control, regulation of the commercial pest control industry, and regulation of various health and environmental professions.

Challenges

Education, welfare, and health care are the most expensive and, arguably, the most important services provided by Florida state and local governments. Florida's population growth, diversity, and preference for low taxes make the provision of these essential services quite challenging. When there is an economic downturn, the challenge becomes even greater.

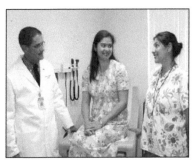

Florida's age, race/ethnicity, and income diversity means that the health care issues that must be addressed by the state and its localities vary considerably.

ONLINE SOURCES FOR DATA AND INFORMATION UPDATES

Florida Department of Education

The DOE manages education standards and funding for all school districts in the state. FLDOE.org has information on academics (Florida Standards, materials, subject areas, STEM education), data on school quality and opportunities, teaching resources and certifications, data on school grades and graduation rates, and school finance reports for school districts.
http://www.fldoe.org/

U.S. Census Bureau-Education

The Census Bureau is charged with conducting the U.S. Census every 10 years, as well as other annual surveys in order to properly allocate funds and make planning decision. The Census Bureau has data on educational attainment, school enrollment, public school system finances, school districts, and education services. Some of the data has been compiled in publications and infographics on specific topics
http://www.census.gov/topics/education.html

College Board-Data

CollegeBoard.org is home to the AP, PSAT, and SAT programs and basic information about each. Included for each test are results by state, and surveys.
http://research.collegeboard.org/data

Florida School Boards Association

The FSBA connects all of the school boards to provide a forum for discussion, research, and basic information about the districts. FSBA.org has publications and information about their goals, legislative sessions on education, districts and superintendents, and recent changes or news.
http://www.fsba.org/

Sunshine State Survey: Results

The Sunshine State Survey polls Florida residents for their opinions on national and local issues, and includes statistics on the respondent's age, race, gender, party affiliation, employment, etc. The survey has data available from 2006 to 2014 (excluding 2013). Specific data can be found on trust in government leaders, the most important issue facing Florida, opinions on taxing and spending (tax revenue, least fair revenue source, budget), issue stances, biggest divide for public officials, and the most important leadership quality.
http://sunshinestatesurvey.org/results/

Medicare

Medicare.com has basic information about Medicare, costs, funding, and statistical data on enrollment in the U.S. and the states.
https://medicare.com/

Medicaid

This is the official site of Medicaid in the U.S., which has basic information about Medicaid, eligibility, the Affordable Care Act, and data on Medicaid by population, state, and topic.
http://www.medicaid.gov/index.html

Florida Office of Economic and Demographic Research-Social Services

The EDR is the research body of the Florida Legislature, responsible for forecasting economic and social trends, particularly those that "affect policy making, revenues, and appropriations". Social Services research has data and presentations on education assessments, funding and enrollment, and Medicaid assessments including Kidcare and TANF.
http://edr.state.fl.us/Content/presentations/index.cfm#social-services

U.S. Department of Health and Human Services

This is the official home of HHS, and the department has programs such as Insurance programs, TANF, Head Start, and resources for child care, child support, public safety and emergency preparedness. This source also has information on health and poverty data.
http://www.hhs.gov/programs/research/index.html

Chapter 12. Public Policy: The Environment, Growth Management, Economic Development, and Transportation

Millions of people have moved to Florida during the last several decades. Millions more are projected to choose the Sunshine State as their home in the coming decades, although the growth rate is not expected to be as high as in the past. Florida's environment is a powerful magnet, drawing new residents and vast numbers of tourists from all over the world. The state's warm winters and sunny climate, the beautiful beaches and parks, the natural wonders, like the Florida Everglades and Florida Keys, and its unique wildlife are treasures worth protecting. The paradox is that Florida's environment attracts so many people that Florida's environment is in danger.

Rapid population growth creates real pressures on the environment. Protecting the quality and quantity of clean water, clean air, and natural land are big challenges in the face of high levels of in-migration. Large influxes of newcomers cause additional stress on wildlife, as their natural habitats are destroyed or polluted. High growth threatens the very survival of some animal and plant species.

To its credit, Florida has tried to protect its environment. It has traditionally been very progressive in passing laws to clean up and manage water resources, conserve natural land, restore habitats, like wetlands, and protect wildlife. Most Floridians consider themselves to be friends of the environment, at least to some degree. And most politicians describe themselves as concerned about conservation.

Florida tried to manage growth with the passage of the comprehensive Growth Management Act in 1985. But growth management is easier said than done; growth management efforts have not always gone as planned.[1] Politicians have struggled to find ways to pay for and manage new growth that are acceptable to the public. Florida is a state whose citizens like low taxes, property rights, and economic growth—and this political environment also attracts new residents. So, while there is general support for the environment, there is less support for specific laws or regulations that might cost more money, cause people to lose their jobs, constrain people's right to use their property as they wish, or result in a less favorable business climate.

Florida's policymakers, like its citizens, believe two of the state's higher priorities are to protect the environment and to ensure the livelihood (economy and jobs) of Floridians. Often, the two goals conflict with each other, creating intense political debates. The debates differ depending upon whether the state is in a high growth period or an economic slowdown. Slow population growth and a weak economy have most Floridians worried about jobs, and the emphasis swings back toward economic development. Instead of worrying about managing growth, many lawmakers are more concerned about encouraging growth— how to bring new businesses into state and keep existing ones in place. The tax incentives used to do so are often seen as undesirable during periods of high growth.

Regardless of whether the state is in a high growth or low growth period, transportation of people, goods, and services is vital to its economy. To many citizens the transportation system is a measure of the quality of life in the area in which they live, just as is the environment. Major battles ensue when some citizens see transportation plans as threatening the fragile environment.

ENVIRONMENTAL ACTORS AND REGULATION

Environmental policymaking involves key actors and agencies at the federal, state, and local levels. The officials at different levels often work in harmony; at other times, they get in each other's way. Turf battles in the environmental protection arena are not uncommon.

Federal Agencies

The federal government has played a key role in protecting the environment, beginning with the creation of the Environmental Protection Agency (EPA) in 1970. The EPA's main mission is to protect human health and the environment.[2] The EPA is specifically responsible for making and enforcing regulations aimed at eliminating water and air pollution, managing solid waste, and controlling radiation and hazardous and toxic substances. The EPA also provides financial assistance to state environmental programs, performs environmental research, and provides environmental education. The U.S. Fish and Wildlife Service enforces federal wildlife laws, protects endangered species, manages migratory birds, restores nationally significant fisheries, and conserves and restores wildlife habitat, such as wetlands.[3] And the National Park Service is responsible for maintaining and operating the many national parks throughout the country. Florida has 12 national parks.

National Environmental Regulations

Florida's state and local governments must comply with a mountain of federal environmental regulations that have been passed, amended, and extended since 1970. The Clean Air Act authorizes the EPA to identify dangerous air pollutants and take steps to reduce emissions. The Clean Water Act regulates the discharge of pollutants into water and sets water quality standards for contaminants in surface water. The act also allows the EPA to regulate wetlands. The Endangered Species Act authorizes the U.S. Fish and Wildlife Service to designate endangered species for federal protection and to regulate activities in their critical habitats; more than 1,000 species are listed. The Resource Conservation and Recovery Act authorizes the EPA to oversee solid waste disposal, including regulating landfills, incinerators, and recycling programs. And the Comprehensive Environmental Response Act has established a Superfund for cleaning up old hazardous waste sites around the country.

State Agencies

In Florida several agencies are charged with protecting the environment and conserving natural resources. The Florida Department of Environmental Protection protects, conserves, and manages Florida's natural resources and enforces the state's environmental laws. It also manages Florida's state park system, conserves environmentally sensitive land, and restores waterways. The Florida Fish and Wildlife Conservation Commission manages fish and wildlife resources to preserve their long-term well-being for the benefit of the people. Through its law enforcement division, the commission ensures compliance with fishing and hunting regulations, enforces state and federal laws that protect threatened and endangered species, and enforces laws dealing with commercial trade of wildlife and wildlife products. Among its many duties, the Florida Department of Agriculture and Consumer Affairs helps conserve and protect the state's agricultural and natural resources by

Florida has twice been honored as having the nation's best state park service. Florida has more than 150 state parks.

working to prevent wildfires, promoting environmentally safe agricultural practices, and managing public lands.

State Environmental Regulations

Florida's political leaders have enacted many state environmental regulations.[4] Virtually every governor in the modern era has initiated, renewed, or expanded environmental legislation. (See Chapter 7.) Claude Kirk helped to create the Water Pollution Control Commission and a state wilderness system. Reubin Askew signed off on four major comprehensive land and water management acts. Bob Graham created programs designed to save rivers, coasts, and the Everglades. Graham also signed the Wetlands Protection Act and the landmark Growth Management Act of 1985 (see the second half of this chapter). Bob Martinez signed into law the Surface Water Management Act and Preservation 2000 to expand the purchase of public lands. Lawton Chiles helped build a coalition of federal and state agencies, private programs, and money sources to begin restoration of the Everglades.

Jeb Bush pushed through a $1 billion successor to Florida's land preservation program that became known as Florida Forever. In 2000, he signed the state's Everglades Restoration Investment Act, committing Florida to half of the $8 billion cost of restoration. As the Everglades legislation moved through Congress, Governor Bush lobbied effectively to ensure its passage,[5] although securing adequate funding from Congress for the restoration has continued to be a struggle. Charlie Crist became the first governor to put an emphasis on combating global warming by hosting a high profile conference and establishing goals for state carbon emission control and green energy production.

Rick Scott initially looked like he might prove an exception to Florida's "green governors." His first term agenda focused almost exclusively on creating jobs, rather than environmental concerns, reflecting the status of the economy and citizen priorities at the time. Environmentalists worried that Scott's efforts to make Florida more business friendly by rolling back, or eliminating, regulations and taxes would permanently put environmental issues on the back burner. They were particularly upset by his major cuts to the Florida Forever fund—a choice he said was dictated by the state's budget shortfall. In Scott's State of the State address at the start of his second term, he expressed a strong commitment to protect the Everglades, protect land for the Florida panther, and invest more in land and water programs. Environmentalists were hopeful, but the tension between them, the governor, and the Florida Legislature soon erupted the interpretation and implementation of a constitutional amendment (Amendment 1—Land and Water Conservation) approved by 75 percent of Floridians in 2014.

A Constitutional Amendment Evokes Intensely Different Interpretations

The outrage over Amendment 1 stemmed from different readings of what the amendment actually required. A number of environmentalists favored using all the funds for *land acquisition* and spending more than the required minimum (33 percent). They were incensed when the legislature did not appropriate funds to purchase environmentally sensitive lands, such as tropical hardwood hammocks in the Keys, ranchlands inhabited by Florida panthers, and a large parcel of land owned by U.S. Sugar Corp. The most anger came from the state's failure to buy the U.S. Sugar Corp property, where a large reservoir could be built south of Lake Okeechobee to hold water taken out of Lake Okeechobee, treat it, then deliver it back to the Everglades to help "recharge the water supply and make the Everglades wetter."[6] Environmentalists accused legislators of defying the will of the people and diverting Amendment 1 funds to other uses.

Legislative leaders at the time defended their decision to spend more of the funds on other conservation efforts related to restoring, improving, and managing conservation lands, including some of the day-to-day operations of several state agencies.[7] A spokesperson for the Speaker of the House articulated the rationale for the legislature's spending decision: "The Speaker does not believe we should purchase land just for the sake of purchasing land. Buying up land we cannot care for that falls into disrepair or becomes a breeding ground for harmful invasive species is not a legacy he is interested in leaving. Instead, we should make sure we can maintain the 5.3 million acres of conservation lands we already own. We believe land should be purchased for strategic reasons, such as wildlife corridors and connecting existing state lands."[8] One senator's reaction to environmentalists' demand for the Everglades-related land purchase was this: "Voters all over Florida didn't support Amendment 1 for the purpose of preserving one isolated area of the state. We have to evaluate and prioritize the usage and management of all of Florida's water supply, not any one region."[9]

The actual wording of the amendment at the heart of the controversy stated that the funds could be used to finance or refinance the acquisition *and improvement* of land, water areas, and relative property interests. (See full text on the petition that was used to get the amendment on the ballot—Figure 12-1.) It also only stated that no less than 33 percent of the net documentary tax revenue be put in the Land Acquisition Trust Fund. It did not state how much more, if any, would have to be appropriated. Even the Ballot Summary clearly said that the funds could be used to acquire, *restore, improve,* and *manage* conservation lands including wetlands and forests; fish and wildlife habitat; lands protecting water resources and drinking water sources, including the Everglades, and the water quality of rivers, lakes, and streams; beaches and shores; outdoor recreational lands; working farms and ranches; and historic or geologic sites, by dedicating 33 percent of net revenues from the existing excise tax on documents for 20 years. But few voters really read an amendment's ballot summary. What is clear is that the term "environment" means different things to different people.

Public Opinion: Biggest Environmental Problems Facing Florida

Many Floridians worry about the environment.[10] Over the years, many Floridians have cited an environmental-related issue (pollution, diminishing natural resources, population growth, over-development, crowded roads and schools) as the "most important problem facing Florida". (See Chapter 3.) A survey taken shortly before the 2007 economic downturn reported that 60 percent wanted to see more funding for "programs to protect the environment." That support level had been fairly steady for more than a decade.

As Florida has grown, the number of environmental issues of concern to Floridians has expanded. (See Figure 12-2.) A re-classification of the specific responses to the question "What is the biggest environmental problem facing Florida today?" (See Figure 12-3.) into broader categories show water-related concerns top the list.

Water—39 percent

Quality; shortage; Everglades; erosion of coastlines/beaches, protection of state's springs.

Pollution—19 percent

Air pollution, litter/trash/not recycling; brownfields—polluted and abandoned areas; pollution in general; lack of alternative energy sources.

Government and Political—8 percent

Overdevelopment, overpopulation; government regulation; politicians/special interests; resource management.

Potential Disasters—Human or Nature-Driven—7 percent

Oil drilling offshore; climate change/global warming; storms/weather.

Food Production—2 percent

Chemicals used in food production; pests harming Florida's agricultural industry.

Another five percent cited a wide range of other issues. Almost one-fifth (18 percent) did not answer the question. The "no answer" response was most common among poorer, less educated, and less mobile Floridians—more limited in their awareness of environmental challenges facing the state today.

Environmental concerns reflect regional patterns. For example, water issues, with the exception of the Everglades, are most often cited by residents of Southwest Florida and those living in the I-4 Corridor (Tampa and Orlando media markets). The Everglades is of greatest concern to southeast area residents. Pollution citations are also highest among respondents living in the Miami and Palm Beach markets.

Figure 12-1. Amendment 1 (Water and Land Conservation) Is More Complex than Its Title

CONSTITUTIONAL AMENDMENT PETITION FORM

- *All information on this form, including your signature, becomes a public record upon receipt by the Supervisor of Elections.*
- *Under Florida law, it is a first degree misdemeanor, punishable as provided in s. 775.082 or s. 775.083, Florida Statutes, to knowingly sign more than one petition for a candidate, a minor political party, or an issue. [Section 104.185, Florida Statutes]*
- *If all requested information on this form is not completed, the form will not be valid.*

Your Name: ______________________________

(Please print name as it appears on your Voter Information Card)

Your Residential Street Address: ______________________________

City: ______________ Zip: ______________ County: ______________

Voter Registration Number: ______________ (or) Date of Birth ____ / ____ / ____

I am a registered voter of Florida and hereby petition the Secretary of State to place the following proposed amendment to the Florida Constitution on the ballot in the general election:

BALLOT TITLE: **Water and Land Conservation - Dedicates funds to acquire and restore Florida conservation and recreation lands**

BALLOT SUMMARY: Funds the Land Acquisition Trust Fund to acquire, restore, improve, and manage conservation lands including wetlands and forests; fish and wildlife habitat; lands protecting water resources and drinking water sources, including the Everglades, and the water quality of rivers, lakes, and streams; beaches and shores; outdoor recreational lands; working farms and ranches; and historic or geologic sites, by dedicating 33 percent of net revenues from the existing excise tax on documents for 20 years.

ARTICLE AND SECTION BEING CREATED OR AMENDED: Add a new Section 28 to Article X

FULL TEXT OF THE PROPOSED AMENDMENT:

SECTION 28. Land Acquisition Trust Fund.--

a) Effective on July 1 of the year following passage of this amendment by the voters, and for a period of 20 years after that effective date, the Land Acquisition Trust Fund shall receive no less than 33 percent of net revenues derived from the existing excise tax on documents, as defined in the statutes in effect on January 1, 2012, as amended from time to time, or any successor or replacement tax, after the Department of Revenue first deducts a service charge to pay the costs of the collection and enforcement of the excise tax on documents.

b) Funds in the Land Acquisition Trust Fund shall be expended only for the following purposes:

1) As provided by law, to finance or refinance: the acquisition and improvement of land, water areas, and related property interests, including conservation easements, and resources for conservation lands including wetlands, forests, and fish and wildlife habitat; wildlife management areas; lands that protect water resources and drinking water sources, including lands protecting the water quality and quantity of rivers, lakes, streams, springsheds, and lands providing recharge for groundwater and aquifer systems; lands in the Everglades Agricultural Area and the Everglades Protection Area, as defined in Article II, Section 7(b); beaches and shores; outdoor recreation lands, including recreational trails, parks, and urban open space; rural landscapes; working farms and ranches; historic or geologic sites; together with management, restoration of natural systems, and the enhancement of public access or recreational enjoyment of conservation lands.

2) To pay the debt service on bonds issued pursuant to Article VII, Section 11(e).

c) The moneys deposited into the Land Acquisition Trust Fund, as defined by the statutes in effect on January 1, 2012, shall not be or become commingled with the General Revenue Fund of the state.

Date: ______________________ ✱ ______________________

Date of Signature *Signature of Registered Voter*

Note: Few Floridians will ever read the full text of a proposed amendment before voting on it. Most just look at the Title although some will read the Ballot Summary, the language of which is often confusing.

Source: Florida Division of Elections. Available at http://dos.elections.myflorida.com/initiatives/initdetail.asp?account=59894&seqnum=1.

Environmental issues in general, however, are important to Florida voters throughout the state. Most politicians in the state, regardless of political party, must be pro-environment if they want to get elected and re-elected. Of course, it is not always that simple, particularly in tough economic times. Then, environmental concerns clash with economic concerns and no-growthers battle with pro-growthers. When the economy is bad, the public and lawmakers are much more likely to emphasize job creation at the expense of the environment. But when the economy recovers, public opinion usually reverts to a more balanced position.

Figure 12-2. Floridians Cite a Wide Range of Environmental Problems Facing the State

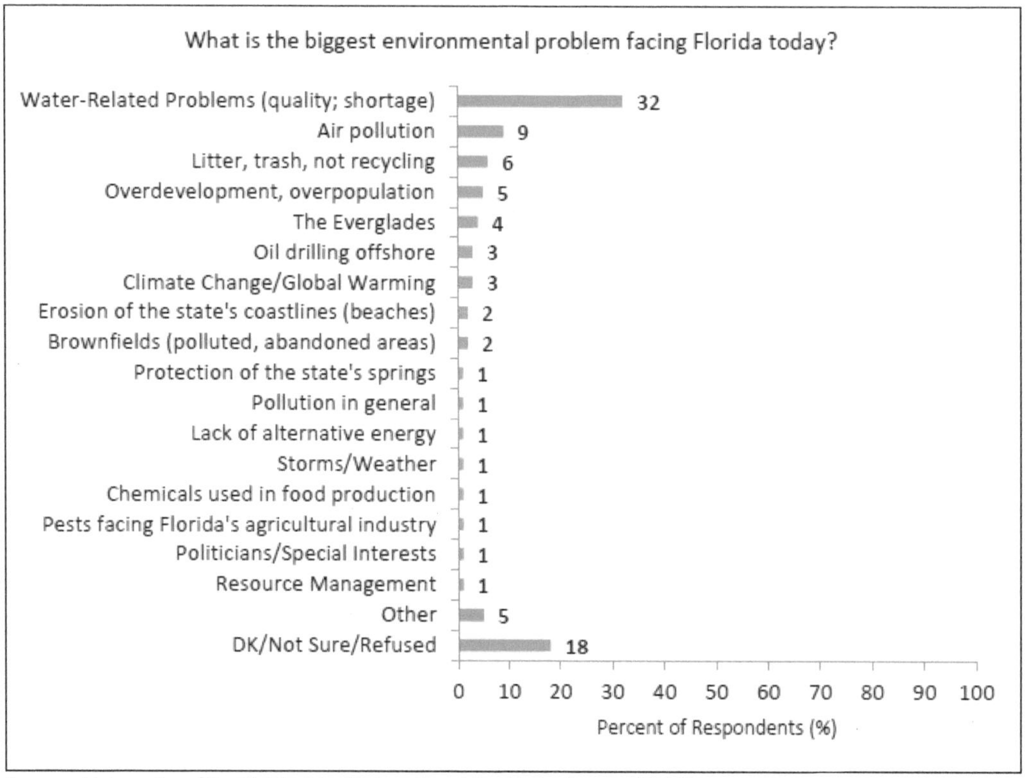

What is the biggest environmental problem facing Florida today?

Category	Percent
Water-Related Problems (quality; shortage)	32
Air pollution	9
Litter, trash, not recycling	6
Overdevelopment, overpopulation	5
The Everglades	4
Oil drilling offshore	3
Climate Change/Global Warming	3
Erosion of the state's coastlines (beaches)	2
Brownfields (polluted, abandoned areas)	2
Protection of the state's springs	1
Pollution in general	1
Lack of alternative energy	1
Storms/Weather	1
Chemicals used in food production	1
Pests facing Florida's agricultural industry	1
Politicians/Special Interests	1
Resource Management	1
Other	5
DK/Not Sure/Refused	18

Percent of Respondents (%)

Source: University of South Florida-Nielsen Sunshine State Survey (2014).

Swings in policy priorities are reflected in the state's three major growth management acts—1985, 2011, and 2015. (These are discussed later in the chapter.) The swings are observable in Floridians' judgments about how well the state is protecting the environment. The percent saying the state was doing a "Good" or "Excellent" job was the lowest in 2014 when the state's economy was stronger than at any time during or after the Great Recession. (See Figure 12-3.)

Interest Groups

Floridians often support national and state environmental groups through membership and donations. These groups can range from Florida-specific groups like the Florida Panther Society, Florida Native Plant Society, Friends of the Everglades, and the Florida Conservation Coalition (water) to state chapters of large national organizations, like the Sierra Club-Florida Chapter and Audubon of Florida.[11] The 40,000-member Save the Manatee Club was founded by former Governor Bob Graham and singer Jimmy Buffet in 1981 to encourage the public to get involved in protecting the endangered manatee.[12] The Florida Audubon Society was founded in 1900 in Maitland as a branch of the National Audubon Society and today has 40,000 members and 44 chapters around the state, dedicated to conserving and restoring natural ecosystems to protect birds and other wildlife.[13]

Figure 12-3. Criticism of State's Protection of Environment Higher When Economy Is Stronger

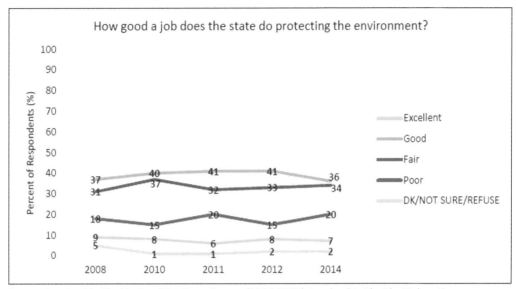

Source: Leadership Florida Sunshine State Survey (2006-2008), Leadership Florida-Nielsen Company Sunshine State Survey (2010-2011), and University of South Florida-Nielsen Sunshine State Survey (2014).

The Florida Chapter of the Nature Conservancy seeks to preserve the plants, animals, and natural communities that represent the diversity of life in Florida by protecting the lands and waters they need to survive. To date, they have preserved more than a million acres in Florida.[14] The Florida League of Conservation Voters (FLCV) is the nonpartisan advocacy and educational arm of the environmental and conservation movement in Florida governed by more than 100 environmental activists from around the state. The FLCV produces an annual environmental scorecard, grading Florida legislators based on their environmental votes, and they also endorse pro-environment candidates for office.[15] The powerful 1000 Friends of Florida group lobbies for smarter growth management, conservation of water and other natural resources, and environmentally friendly transportation.[16]

Florida's water resources are continually monitored by environmental groups.

Other entities are more focused on environmental justice. The Center for Environmental Equity and Justice at Florida A & M University identifies and addresses whether an environmental policy has a disproportionately negative impact on minorities and the poor.

MANAGING FLORIDA'S WATER RESOURCES

Florida is surrounded on three sides by water, is usually blessed with plenty of rainfall, sits atop two large aquifers, and has numerous lakes, springs, and streams. So, why is water an issue in Florida? Despite the abundance of water, Florida's booming population growth threatens to cause severe problems with both water supply and water quality.

Water Supply and Use

Floridians use more than 15 billion gallons of water per day: 8.6 billion gallons of saline water—almost all for power generation—and 6.4 billion gallons of fresh water.[17] Floridians also use 659 million gallons of reclaimed wastewater per day.

Ground water (water taken from underground) accounts for 65 percent of fresh water withdrawals, and surface water (like lakes and rivers) withdrawals account for the rest. Ninety-two percent of Florida residents rely on ground water for their drinking water needs, with fresh surface water providing drinking water for the remaining 8 percent. About 62 percent of the ground water comes from the Floridan aquifer present throughout most of the state. (See Figure 12-4 for a graphic view of how the Floridan aquifer is refilled.)

As Figure 12-5 shows, public supply accounts for 48 percent of fresh ground water use, and agricultural self-supply accounts for 34 percent. Agricultural self-supply is the largest category for fresh surface water use at 51 percent, followed by public supply, recreational landscape irrigation, and commercial use. Power generation accounts for nearly all (99.8 percent) of saline water withdrawals.

Figure 12-4. How the Expansive Floridan Aquifer Is Filled

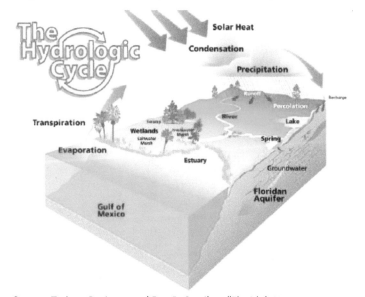

Source: Tatiana Borisova and Roy R. Carriker, "Florida's Water Resources," University of Florida Institute of Food & Agricultural Sciences (IFAS) Extension. Available at https://edis.ifas.ufl.edu/LyraEDISServlet?command=getImage Detail&image_soid=FIGURE%201&document_soid=FE757&document_ version=58885.

Figure 12-5. Florida's Fresh Ground and Surface Water Use by Source

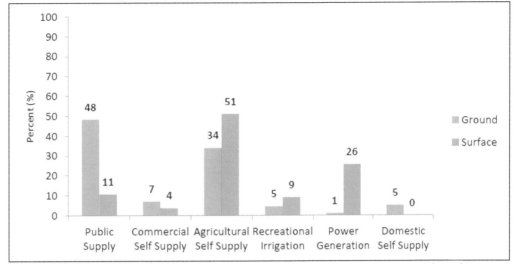

Source: Richard L. Marella, *Water Withdrawals, Use, and Trends in Florida, 2010.* U.S. Geological Survey Scientific Investigations Report 2014-5088. Available at http://pubs.usgs.gov/sir/2014/5088/.

Water Quantity and Quality

The water quantity problem in Florida can be described with a simple equation: more people equals more water usage! Floridians drink, bathe, flush, soak their grass, grow their crops, and generate power with water. The good news is that Florida, surrounded on three sides by water and averaging 54 inches[18] of rain a year, is not going to run out of water. The bad news is that it may cost Floridians a lot more money to get drinkable water. The Floridan Aquifer is a large, naturally occurring, underground reservoir of water found under much of the peninsula. For generations, it has been a plentiful, cheap, and reasonably clean supply of water, requiring little in the way of processing before use. As millions of residents have moved to Florida, the aquifer has not been able to replenish itself with rain as fast as it is drained. Residents are quite literally sucking the water out of the ground faster than nature can refill its "storage tank."

Compounding the problem is that the influx of millions of people and the homes, businesses, and roads built to accommodate them often cover up recharge areas where rain water used to soak through the ground into the aquifer. Coastal areas face the additional danger of salt water intrusion into the aquifer; as the water table is lowered, water with high saline content from the ocean or gulf may begin to contaminate the aquifer.

The other serious water quality problem is pollution. Pollution discharge from factories, oil and chemical spills, untreated sewage from failing septic tanks, and fertilizer runoff from farms, golf courses, and suburban lawns all threaten to contaminate the aquifer. These discharges have already polluted many surface water sources—rivers and lakes. And, of course, polluted surface water hurts more than just people. Florida wildlife suffers as well. For example, heavy fertilizer runoff into lakes causes excessive plant growth. The plants use up most of the oxygen in the water. Many fish die and then birds and other animals that rely on the fish for food are harmed.

Water Management Strategies

What strategies can be used to help resolve the water quantity and quality problems in Florida? Three general strategies have been used: conservation, protection, and new source utilization. Conservation is encouraged by Florida's state and local governments and by the national government. Laws have been passed mandating low-flow showerheads and toilets. Public relations campaigns have encouraged people to turn off the spigot while brushing their teeth and to use native plants in the garden that require less water. Regulations have been passed to limit lawn watering to one or two days a week and even prohibit it in some areas during a severe drought. After being processed, reclaimed water is re-piped to sprinkler systems for agricultural or industrial use or for lawn watering. Federal and state laws protect water resources by controlling or eliminating water pollution before it happens and cleaning up polluted waterways afterward. It is not uncommon for state and federal officials to fight over which standards should apply.

New sources of water have also been tapped. For instance, in Tampa, the water company has built and uses a desalination plant to provide about 25 million gallons of drinking water per day.[19] Another innovative way of tapping into new water sources is Aquifer Storage and Recovery (ASR)—a mechanism for storing water underground through an injection well to be withdrawn later through the same well. Typically, water is stored during times of excess supply to be used later when supplies are limited.[20] Of course, neither of these strategies is without drawbacks: Desalination is costly, and injection poses the possibility of aquifer contamination. Aside from these strategies, a number of areas that currently rely on the aquifer are seeking permits to tap into lakes and rivers. This is causing environmentalists to worry about the effect of lowering water levels on plants and wildlife, and residents downstream (like Jacksonville) worry about people upstream (like Seminole County) using up "their" water (the St. Johns River).[21]

Water Management Districts

Florida established five water management districts with the passage of the Water Resources Act in 1972. In 1976, Florida voters gave the districts the authority to levy property taxes to fund their operations. These five districts are regional in scope, with natural boundaries set by watershed areas. (See Figure 12-6.) The water management districts are responsible for flood control, ensuring adequate water supply, protecting water quality, and protecting natural ecosystems. The governing boards of the various districts are appointed by the governor and approved by the Florida Senate. Each board sets policy and hires a director to run day-to-day operations. Water management districts engage in a variety of specific activities. For example, the South Florida Water Management District operates 1,900 miles of canals and levees to alleviate flooding, oversees restoration efforts for the Everglades, helps restore estuaries, lakes and wetlands, plans for emergency management for floods or droughts, monitors the environmental quality of water, acquires land and wetlands to preserve water resources, issues permits for surface and ground water use, and, most importantly, manages water supplies.[22] Inter-district squabbles frequently surface during major droughts.

As water districts became more powerful, complaints about them from developers and homeowners escalated. The major criticisms were the districts' ever-expanding regulations and their excessively high tax rates. In his first year in office, Governor Scott successfully pushed the legislature to cut water management district tax rates by some 25 percent. This was consistent with his overall push to reduce government, cut regulations, and lower taxes. Critics worry that reduced revenues will impede the districts' ability to do their job effectively.[23] They are also worried that Governor Scott has stacked the water management districts with pro-development allies and forced the resignation of senior staffers.[24]

CONSERVING FLORIDA'S UPLANDS, WETLANDS, AND COASTAL AREAS

The destruction of natural habitats, wetlands, and pristine coastal areas in Florida continues to be a serious problem, as more people move into the state and development extends outward from large urban areas and inward from the heavily urbanized coastal areas. (Sixty percent of Florida's residents live within 10 miles of the coast. Three-fourths of all Floridians live in a coastal county.[25])

Figure 12-6. Florida's Five Water Management Districts

Source: St. Johns River Water Management District, Available at http://sjr.state.fl.us/.

Habitat Destruction

Sprawl—Florida's dominant development pattern—is extremely harmful to many native Florida species of plants and animals because of the loss of their natural habitat. The destruction of wetlands—marshy areas with water at the surface or with water saturated soil—is especially harmful to the ecosystem. These swamps help filter out pollutants, provide flood control and coastal protection during hurricanes, and act as a transition between drier uplands and wetter aquatic habitats. Ecologists estimate that about one-half of Florida was wetland before European settlement and that about one-half of Florida's original wetlands have been destroyed or significantly altered.[26] The draining, filling, and pollution of the Everglades over the decades by agriculture, private development, and government flood control has been particularly harmful.

The Florida Division of Forestry's mission is to protect and maintain the biological diversity of the ecosystems found in the state forests.

Land Conservation

Significant losses of habitat have created a sense of urgency and prompted Florida to engage in the nation's most ambitious program for acquiring environmentally sensitive lands, beginning in the late 1960's and early 1970s. In 1980, Florida started CARL (Conservation and Recreational Lands). By 1990, the program had expended some $2 billion to purchase 1 million acres of land. Florida then established the Preservation 2000 program to replace CARL. Preservation 2000 was a 10-year program that raised $3 billion (more than the U.S. government was spending nationwide for similar purposes) to protect more than 1.75 million acres of lands.[27] In 2000, the legislature passed Florida Forever as the successor program to Preservation 2000. Florida Forever has already saved more than a million acres of Florida since its inception. Unfortunately, with the bad economy and tight state budgets, legislators significantly reduced funding for the program for several years in a row, starting in 2009. That, in turn, pushed environmentalists into a successful petition drive that placed the Conservation Amendment on the ballot for voter approval in 2014. It passed.

In addition to land buying, Florida has 3 national and 37 state forests. The Apalachicola, Osceola, and Ocala national forests total about 1.1 million acres; the state forests cover about 1 million more. A major part of the mission of the Florida Division of Forestry is to "protect and maintain the biological diversity of the many ecosystems found in and around the state forests."[28] Florida also has an aggressive plan to protect and restore wetlands around the state, including the Everglades. Much of the land that has been purchased by the state is wetland habitat.[29]

Protecting Wetlands

A marshy area must first be officially delineated as a wetland to be protected by federal and state laws—a process that can be long and drawn out because of opposition from developers and land owners. Florida has adopted a policy of no net loss of officially designated wetlands. To ensure "no net loss," several strategies are used: restoration, creation, enhancement, reallocation, and mitigation. *Restoration* is returning a wetland that has been altered back into a wetland. *Creation* is developing a new wetland in an area that was not previously a wetland. *Enhancement* is making a positive improvement to a wetland area. *Reallocation* is transforming an existing wetland into a different kind of wetland. Because of growth pressures, the state still issues permits to developers, allowing the destruction of wetlands. *Mitigation* is the strategy often used by developers to comply with the "no net loss" doctrine. It requires a developer to restore or create new wetland areas in amounts equal to the wetlands that are destroyed. Environmentalists strongly oppose mitigation on the grounds that human-made wetlands rarely approximate what was destroyed because wetlands are ecologically complex, take many years to establish, and appear in many variations.

The River of Grass

In 1947, author Marjory Stoneman Douglas wrote the classic *The Everglades: River of Grass*, describing the Everglades as a unique natural treasure found nowhere else in the world: "The miracle of the light pours over the green and brown expanse of saw grass and of water, shining and slow-moving below, the grass and water that is the meaning and the central fact of the Everglades of Florida. It is a river of grass."[30] Water flows through the Everglades in a southwesterly direction into the Florida Bay. Because the area is covered with tall grass, often making it hard to see the water, "river of grass" is an apt description. Ironically, in 1948, just one year after publication of the classic work, Congress directed the U.S. Army Corps of Engineers to undertake a project that essentially drained much of the marsh to prevent flooding, irrigate farm lands, and provide drinking water to facilitate new development. Since then, the altered water flow has eaten away half of the Everglades, and water quality has been compromised.

Left: The Everglades, a "River of Grass." Right: A Florida panther

Restoring the Everglades

Over time, attitudes about the Everglades have changed. Most people now regard the Everglades as a natural treasure and crucial habitat. Fifty years after Congress directed the destruction of the Everglades, the State of Florida and the national government developed the Comprehensive Everglades Restoration Plan (CERP) and agreed to split the $8 billion cost. The CERP is designed to restore natural flows of water, water quality, and more natural hydro-periods and create a sustainable South Florida by restoring the ecosystem, ensuring clean and reliable water supplies, and providing flood protection.[31] The U.S. Army Corps of Engineers, in partnership with the South Florida Water Management District, is responsible for implementing the plan over three decades. The plan is to capture most of the 1.7 billion gallons of water that drain daily from the Everglades and then store it in surface and underground storage areas until it is needed. The timing and distribution of water to the ecosystem will be modified to more closely approximate pre-drainage patterns. To improve the quality of water discharged into the natural system, wetlands-based storm water treatment areas will be built. To help return the area to its more natural state, approximately 240 miles of internal levees and canals will be removed. About 80 percent of the new water obtained will be used to benefit the environment, and 20 percent will benefit urban and agricultural users. Funding the restoration continues to remain a challenge for both the state and federal government. There is never enough money.

Coastal Challenges

Florida has some of the best beaches in the world. A number of its beaches have topped the annual national "Best Beaches List" (you can win only once). Numerous others have been ranked in the top 10.[32] Florida beaches are important for recreation, ecology, and the economy. But the beaches and coastal areas in Florida face several serious challenges—pollution, Red Tide, erosion, the invasion of lionfish (they hurt the state's fishing and seafood industries by eating food sources of snook, mullet, and grouper), and possible drilling for oil and gas in the Gulf and in the waters off the Keys. (See Up-Close: Oil Drilling off the Florida Coast).

Since 2002, under the Healthy Beaches Program, all 34 coastal Florida counties conduct weekly tests of their beach water to analyze it for harmful bacteria.[33] In just one year, Florida beaches around the state failed the state health standard more than a thousand times because of high levels of bacteria in the water.[34] To address these water quality problems, state and local officials have encouraged a reduction in the use of fertilizers and pesticides near the coast, toughened pollution standards, and invested heavily in better sewage treatment and storm water management.

Up-Close: Oil Drilling off the Florida Coast

One of the challenges facing Florida's coastal regions is the possibility of oil drilling in the Gulf of Mexico or the Atlantic. Oil and gas drilling off the coast of Florida is a political tug-of-war between the federal and state governments, environmentalists, energy companies, and consumers.

The Ban on Drilling

Oil drilling off Florida's coast in federal waters is prohibited by the national government, and drilling in Florida territorial waters up to 10 miles from shore is prohibited by the state. But both bans are subject to change by Congress and the state legislature respectively. Despite the ban, numerous leases to drill in the Gulf have been issued in the past. Every time gas prices rise, so do pressures to allow drilling. For years, most Florida lawmakers and the public opposed drilling near Florida's coast. Floridians worried that an oil spill near Florida would do immeasurable harm to beaches and wildlife and decimate the tourism and fishing industry. However, whenever gas prices have risen dramatically, some policymakers have called for increasing domestic production of oil. Public opinion in Florida has tended to favor expansion of drilling during those times. (See Chapter 3 for a closer look at public opinion concerning oil drilling.)

When gas prices go up, support for oil drilling off the coast of Florida also goes up.

Proposals to Lift the Ban

When gas prices skyrocketed in 2008, Congress, the president, and the state legislature began to seriously consider lifting the ban on drilling in return for Florida receiving a share of the profits from oil production. In late spring 2008, Governor Crist, who was being considered for a Republican vice presidential nomination, publically changed his position and began to support presidential nominee John McCain's idea of allowing oil drilling off the coast to help bring down gas prices. In spring 2009, conservative GOP Florida House Speaker-elect Dean Cannon proposed that the legislature lift the ban on oil drilling between 3-10 miles off Florida's coast as a way to bring in $1 billion dollars a year in royalties to the state and to create thousands of jobs. And in March 2010, even progressive Democratic President Obama announced his plan to expand oil and gas drilling offshore in the Atlantic and Gulf of Mexico off of Florida's coast.

The BP Deepwater Horizon Oil Spill

The situation changed dramatically, however, when the BP Deepwater Horizon oil rig exploded and began leaking oil a mile deep in the Gulf of Mexico on April 20, 2010. The oil continued to gush for about 12 weeks as the depth of the well head made repairs excruciatingly slow and difficult. BP was finally able to cap the well on July 15, 2010. Estimates vary, but perhaps up to 5 million barrels of oil leaked into the Gulf and onto the shores of several states. BP spent billions of dollars on the cleanup and compensation of those who suffered economic loss from the spill. BP deployed oil booms to contain the spill, sprayed chemical dispersants to break it up, and relied on natural microbes to digest it. The wind, warm weather and currents also help mitigate much direct damage to Florida. Except for Pensacola, Florida beaches largely escaped oil damage. However, the perception of tourists, based on non-stop media coverage, was that Florida beaches were covered with oil. Consequently, all the coastal communities suffered enormous economic damage as large numbers of tourists stayed away from the Sunshine State. The Gulf fishing industries also endured economic anguish. BP paid millions to the Gulf states including $25 million to Florida to help compensate for these types of economic hardships.

The Future of Oil Drilling

A year later, the oil spill was largely forgotten as tourism and fishing rebounded and the Gulf ecosystem seemed in surprisingly good shape considering the size and scope of the original disaster. The public and lawmakers again began to consder drilling.

But regardless of what Congress and Florida legislators decide, oil drilling still may occur near Florida's coast. The Florida Keys could be in danger should Cuba go through with its plan to lease drilling rights off its coast to China or other countries. That drilling would easily be within 60 miles of Florida and could potentially be less than 10 miles from the Florida Keys. Those concerns have been somewhat set aside and replaced with renewed fears of lawmakers approving oil drilling. This fear came on the heels of the federal government's plans to grant more oil leases in the Gulf of Mexico and Atlantic regions. New concerns also stem from legislation proposed by a few Congress members from oil producing states that would allow oil rigs as close as 50 miles from Florida's Gulf Coast as opposed to the 125-mile buffer zone that is currently in place.[35]

Red Tides are caused by algae blooms, releasing dangerous neurotoxins that are lethal to fish. They cause a burning sensation in a person's eyes and nose and a dry choking cough. Red Tides have occurred naturally in the Gulf of Mexico for hundreds of years, but scientists are investigating whether pollution and the warming of the Gulf contribute to an increase in Red Tide.[36] At any rate, they pose a serious threat to tourism. Dead fish on the beach smell!

Beach erosion is another threat to the Florida environment. About 400 miles of Florida's 825 miles of sandy beaches are suffering from critical erosion.[37] While some of this erosion is natural, a significant amount is due to construction and maintenance of navigational inlets, which are important to the economy. Both the state and federal government help fund and oversee beach nourishment (pumping sand back onto the beach from offshore). The problem is another example of just how closely the environment and the economy interact with each other.

Threats to the environment and the economy in coastal areas can also come from fresh water and interstate legal squabbles. Such has been the case with the large lucrative oyster industry in Apalachicola Bay. Harvests dropped from more than three million pounds of oyster meat annually to one million in a year's time, prompting the National Oceanic and Atmospheric Administration to declare it a fishery disaster.[38] A big part of the problem is the lack of sufficient fresh water flowing downstream in the Apalachicola River from Georgia to Apalachicola Bay. Florida and Alabama have been engaged in a long legal battle in federal court against Georgia for siphoning off water to meet the drinking water demands of a growing population in Atlanta.[39] It will be up to the U.S. Supreme Court to resolve.

PROTECTING FLORIDA'S WILDLIFE

Florida's wildlife—whether measured in numbers or species—is being threatened by the state's changing demographics and land use patterns. The term "wildlife" includes "all living organisms out of the direct control of [humans], including undomesticated or cultivated plants and animals."[40] Endangered species acts, passed by both the federal and Florida governments in the 1970s, are critical to both the protection and restoration of vanishing animals and plants. One national study ranked the Florida Keys and parts of the Panhandle as "among the most vulnerable places in the nation for wildlife in danger of disappearing."[41]

Threatened and Endangered Species

The U.S. Fish and Wildlife Service defines a *threatened* species as one that is likely to become endangered if it is not protected. An *endangered* species is one that is in immediate danger of becoming extinct (no longer living on earth) and needs protection to survive. In order to receive protection under these laws, an animal (or plant) must be officially listed. Florida has 70 species of wildlife on the threatened or endangered species lists of the U.S. Fish and Wildlife Service and National Marine Fisheries Service. (See Table 12-1.) Listed animals include *fish* (sturgeon and darter), *amphibians* (salamanders and frogs), *reptiles* (crocodiles, snakes, and turtles), *birds* (terns, egrets, and herons), *mammals* (panthers, manatees, mice, and whales), and various *invertebrates* (coral, crayfish, butterflies, and mussels).

Florida creates a separate list, which has all the animals on the federal list and 61 additional ones.[42] The additional animals are listed as either *threatened* or as *"species of special concern"* to designate species whose numbers could drop significantly if not managed and protected. Once placed on the federal or state list, a species enjoys special protection until its numbers recover sufficiently, at which time they can be de-listed (removed from protection) or down-listed (classification changed from endangered to threatened). A number of animals have been removed from federal protection over the years, including the bald eagle in 2007. In 2011, the Florida Fish and Wildlife Conservation Commission voted to remove 16 more animals from the state list in the following year, including the alligator snapping turtle and the Florida black bear, because their numbers had recovered sufficiently to put them out of danger. Of course, new species are sometimes added to the lists as well.

To protect plants, Florida has established a conservation program whose goal is "to restore and maintain existing populations of listed plants on public lands and on private lands managed for conservation purposes."[43] The state has 59 plants on the federal endangered list. They include the fragrant prickly apple and the four-petal pawpaw. The State lists of plants, which are designated endangered, threatened, and commercially exploited, are administered and maintained by the Florida Department of Agriculture and Consumer Services.[44]

Species Decline, Species Protection

The population of animal species may decline for four major reasons: natural causes, overhunting, habitat loss, and the introduction of exotic animals. Extinction is a natural process, and as the fossil record shows, numerous species became extinct before people were involved. Most of the animals that became extinct in the last 400 years, however, were lost primarily due to human activity. Overhunting is a direct way that humans depopulate an animal species. When an animal is placed on the endangered species list, it receives protection from hunters. In some cases, no hunting of the animal is allowed and in other cases, a special permit is required to "take" an animal.

The destruction of critical habitat is more indirect, but over time it can have the same catastrophic results. The habitats of listed animals receive special protection, and much of Florida's effort to preserve habitat through various land buying programs (discussed above) is aimed at areas critical to the survival of threatened and endangered species.

Table 12-1. Florida's Endangered (E) and Threatened (T) Species, Federal List*

Status	Common Name	Status	Common Name	Status	Common Name
T	Bankclimber, Purple	E	Mouse, St. Andrew Beach	T	Snake, Eastern Indigo
E	Bat, Indiana	E	Panther, Florida	E	Sparrow, Cape Sable Seaside
E	Bat, Gray	E	Pigtoe, Oval	E	Sparrow, FL Grasshopper
E	Beetle, American Burying	T	Plover, Piping	E	Stork, Wood
E	Butterfly, Miami Blue	E	Pocketbook, Shinyrayed	E	Sturgeon, Atlantic
T	Caracara, Audubon's Crested	E	Rabbit, Lower Keys Marsh	T	Sturgeon, Gulf
T	Coral, Elkhorn	E	Rice Rat (Lower FL Keys)	E	Sturgeon, Shortnose
T	Coral, Staghorn	T	Salamander, Frosted Flatwoods	T	Tern, Roseate
E	Crocodile, American	E	Salamander, Reticulated Flatwoods	E	Three-Ridge, Fat
E	Curlew, Eskimo	E	Sawfish, Smalltooth	E	Vole, Florida Salt Marsh
T	Darter, Okaloosa	T	Scrub-Jay, Florida	E	Warbler, Bachman's
E	Deer, Key	E	Sea Turtle, Green (FL, Mexico Nesting Pops.)	E	Warbler, Kirland's
E	Kite, Everglade Snail	T	Sea Turtle, Green (Except Where Endangered)	E	Whale, Finback
E	Manatee, West Indian	E	Sea Turtle, Hawksbill	E	Whale, Humpback
E	Moccasinshell, Gulf	E	Sea Turtle, Kemp's Ridley	E	Whale, Right
E	Moccasinshell, Ochlockonee	E	Sea Turtle, Leatherback	E	Whale, Sei
E	Mouse, Anastasia Island	T	Sea Turtle, Loggerhead	E	Whale, Sperm
E	Mouse, Choctawhatchee	E	Seal, Caribbean Monk	E	Wolf, Gray
E	Mouse, Key Largo Cotton	T	Shrimp, Squirrel Chimney	E	Wolf, Red
E	Mouse, Perdido Key Beach	T	Skink, Bluetail Mole	E	Woodpecker, ivory-billed
T	Mouse, Southeastern Beach	T	Skink, Sand	E	Woodpecker, Red-Cockaded
E	Mouse, St. Andrew Beach	T	Slabshell, Chipola	E	Woodrat, Key Largo
E	Panther, Florida	T	Snail, Stock Island Tree		
E	Pigtoe, Oval	T	Snake, Atlantic Salt Marsh		

Note: *Does not include Whooping Cranes, which are an experimental population in Florida, or the American Alligator, which is listed only for its similarity in appearance to the endangered American Crocodile.

Source: Florida Fish and Wildlife Conservation Commission, "Florida's Endangered and Threatened Species." Available at http://myfwc.com/media/1515251/Threatened_Endangered_Species.pdf. Data are as of January 2013.

Protecting Manatees, Panthers, Sea Turtles, and Other Species

The West Indian **manatee**, often referred to as the "sea cow," is one of the most popular endangered species in Florida due to the efforts of the Save the Manatee Club. Manatees are mammals with no natural predators. They graze on aquatic plants in warm, slow moving rivers, bays, and canals. In addition to federal protections, the Florida Manatee Sanctuary Act makes it illegal to "to annoy, molest, harass, or disturb any manatee."[45] The leading cause of death for manatees is collision with water craft as manatees move slowly and often float near the surface. Manatee conservation efforts are centered in 13 counties where 80 percent of manatee deaths occur. Most of these counties have implemented speed limits for motorboats and developed detailed protection plans. Protection efforts may be paying off. Annual counts by the Florida Fish and Wildlife Conservation Commission show the manatees now number more than 6,000. The U.S. Fish and Wildlife Service has agreed to consider moving the manatee from endangered to threatened, but that will take years of biological reviews.[46]

The **Florida panther** is also popular with Floridians. The panther's status is much more precarious than is the manatee's, however.[47] Viewed as a threat to humans and livestock, the panther was hunted to near extinction throughout the Southeastern United States in the 1950s. More recently, its habitat has shrunk significantly due to development. Now on the list of endangered species, the panther is relatively safe from hunters. The panther's habitat has been expanded somewhat via the 700,000 acres in South Florida in national and state parks and the Florida Panther National Wildlife Refuge and there has been discussion of reintroducing the panther to North Florida. The panther population dropped to a low of 30-50 animals by the early 1990s and the species was facing imminent demise due to inbreeding since the panther had become isolated in South Florida. A program to introduce eight female Texas cougars to the South Florida panther population proved successful in increasing the number of animals to 50-70 and in diversifying the gene pool.

Among the top selling specialty license plates in Florida are Protect the Panther, Save the Manatee and Protect Wild Dolphins. Some of the proceeds from the sale of the plates are donated to government agencies and private groups that seek to protect these animals. For more on specialty license plate sales visit http://www.flhsmv.gov/specialtytags/tagsales.pdf.

More than 90 percent of **sea turtle** nesting in North America takes place in Florida. Many tourists visit Florida just to watch them nest and hatch. Five different types of sea turtles are threatened or endangered here: Green, Hawksbill, Kemp's Ridley, Leatherback, and Loggerhead. Many factors are leading to the decline of the world's sea turtle species, including death and injury in fishing nets (U.S. shrimp nets now must use Turtle Excluder Devices), destruction of habitats, ocean pollution, and exploitation for shells, meat, and eggs. In addition to federal protections, Florida passed the Marine Turtle Protection Act to protect turtles and their nesting habitats. Efforts to protect Florida's sea turtles have focused on land purchases and beach nourishment to ensure adequate habitat for nesting. Turtle nesting areas have been closed off to cars, people, and construction in certain beach areas. Inland lights near marine turtle nesting areas have been dimmed or covered to avoid confusing newborn turtles that are normally drawn to the sea, and safety, by moonlight reflecting off the ocean or gulf.

The **alligator** is no longer on the endangered species list but remains in a special category (threatened) on the federal and Florida lists because of its similarity in looks to the crocodile, which are far fewer in number. (Officials fear that hunters will accidentally kill crocodiles if they remove all restrictions from alligators.) To control the growing alligator population—estimated at 1.3 million—the Florida Fish and Wildlife Conservation Commission issues harvesting permits to individuals and alligator farms. Nuisance alligators, those that present a threat to people, pets, or property, are harvested by licensed trappers. Sometimes the complaints are more of a life-threatening nature. While deaths are still rare (about 30 suspected and 20 confirmed since 1948), the number of people attacked or killed in Florida by alligators is increasing. Alligators, like other wildlife, are being squeezed out of their natural habitats by humans and thus have more frequent contact with them.

In 2006, the U.S. Postal Service created the Southern Florida Wetland stamp pane depicting beautiful images of 21 plants and animals found in the Everglades. The purpose was to raise awareness of the diverse species inhabiting the world's largest subtropical marshland. Included in the pane are endangered species such as the American crocodile, Florida panther, and Cape Sable seaside sparrow.

Non-Native Animal and Plant Species: Threats to Environment & Economy

Florida has more non-native plants and animals than any other big state. This description pretty much describes the situation: "Burmese pythons. Cuban tree frogs. Nile monitor lizards. Giant African land snails. Just as humans from all corners of the globe flock to Florida, so, too, do creatures of every conceivable classification: mammals, fish, reptiles, mollusks, even microbes."[48] Not all become established or invasive, but those that do can be very destructive.

Human introduction of exotic plants and animals can cause grave harm to the environment, especially in Florida.[49] Non-native species usually lack natural enemies in their new habitat and often grow at an alarming rate. Exotic animals may either compete with native animals for food or prey directly on them. Exotic animals may also spread diseases to which the native population has little immunity and may inter-breed leading to the extinction of native species through hybridization. Exotic plants often squeeze out existing native plants and can come to dominate an entire ecosystem. For example, the Melaleuca plant (nicknamed the "paperbark tree") has spread outward from South Florida at the rate of 35 acres per day, replacing most native plants and creating a poor habitat for native species. At least 20 Florida species are endangered because of competition from introduced species.

The estimated 100,000-plus Burmese pythons in the Everglades have greatly altered the ecosystem by devouring everything from raccoons, opossums, bobcats, and deer to great blue herons and wood storks.[50] Some mammal species in the Everglades National Park have declined by more than 90 percent. So alarming is this problem that the Florida Fish and Wildlife Conservation Commission ultimately created a Python Removal Program allowing properly trained and permitted people to remove Burmese pythons and other non-native reptiles from state lands.[51]

While most Floridians favor wildlife protection, 62 percent admit they are "either not knowledgeable or only slightly knowledgeable on the invasive species topic, with many suggesting they don't know what types of invasive species are living in Florida or what they can do to prevent invasive species from entering the state."[52]

Non-Native Insect Threatens State's $10.8 Billion Dollar Citrus Industry

More than half of Florida's citrus trees are infected with what is called "citrus greening"—also known as "huanglongbing." The culprit is a tiny but lethal insect—the Asian citrus psyllid—thought to have come into Florida through the Port of Miami. It has already wreaked havoc on one of the state's signature industries. The nearly invisible pest infects citrus trees "producing misshapen, unmarketable and bitter fruit and over time, inhibits the tree's ability to produce fruit at all."[53] It eventually weakens the trees and kills them usually within three to five years. Already it has led to losses of nearly $4 billion in revenue and more than 6,600 Florida jobs in just the orange juice production part of the citrus industry.[54] No cure has yet been found in spite of millions of dollars spent on research by both the federal and state governments. This is a vivid example of how "importing" a non-native species can have dire economic consequences.

Florida: A Haven for Exotic Pets

Since colonization, thousands of non-native species have been introduced to Florida. One-fourth of all Florida flora and fauna is estimated to be non-native; millions of acres are dominated by introduced species. Why? Because Florida is geographically isolated, has a sub-tropical climate and large areas of human-produced habitats, is a hub for international trade and tourism, and is a center for trade in exotic pets. Indeed, many of the well-known non-native species in Florida were brought in as exotic pets and then released by their owners: pythons that have become a top predator in the Everglades,[55] spade toads in South Florida that grow to the size of a football, and 3-foot black spinytail iguanas that have overrun parts of Southeast and Southwest Florida. Boca Grande on Gasparilla Island has even created a special taxing district to raise money to fight the invading iguanas!

Combating Exotics

Florida has employed several strategies to stop the destruction caused by non-native species, but none to date have proved particularly effective. First, while some laws forbid the importation of harmful non-native species from overseas, only a few species are actually listed as harmful, and many are smuggled in undetected by customs. Plus, harmful non-native species are imported to Florida from other states but receive almost no scrutiny.

Second, total eradication is difficult and even controversial because eradication methods can often destroy many native species. For example, early attempts to destroy the fire ant in Florida in the 1950s resulted in poisoning of many native insects, birds, and animals.

The third strategy, limiting a non-native species through chemical control (pesticides), mechanical control (hand or machine weeding), or biological control (the introduction of a predator from the exotic's natural

Melaleuca, or paperbark trees, have taken over huge areas of Florida's Everglades. They are also known as "marsh burglars."

habitat) can, ironically, evoke protests from environmentalists. In the future, should citrus be genetically modified to safeguard it against greening, it is likely to "disgust anti-GMO [Genetically Modified Organism] activists."[56]

The environment vs. economic schism was even evident when the state Fish and Wildlife Conservation Commission proposed the banning of further imports of the lionfish that is believed to have been brought into Florida from the Indian and Pacific oceans to sell for use in home and restaurant aquariums. The ban was strongly supported by environmentalists but opposed by ornamental fish wholesale companies. The owner of such a company said, "an import ban would unfairly harm her company and others, since it would apply to all 10 species of lionfish, rather than the two species that have established themselves in Florida waters."[57] In her opinion, the fish most likely arrived "in ballast water discharged by ships" rather than via the aquarium trade. The state did impose the ban, which went into effect on August 1, 2014. Even bigger battles lie ahead over environmental issues characterized by deep ideological divides.

Big Battles Ahead: Climate Change, Rising Sea Levels, Action Plans

Scientific evidence shows that the earth has been warming rapidly for over a century (with particularly hot periods in the past 30 years) which is melting ice sheets and glaciers. The melt is causing a rise in sea level (an extraordinarily important issue for the low-lying state of Florida). Some 97 percent of the world's climate scientists agree that these climate changes are largely caused by human activity.[58] These same climate scientists agree that the main cause of this warming is the "greenhouse effect" where an increasing amount of greenhouse gasses (like carbon dioxide and methane) released by human activity since the Industrial Revolution, are building up in the atmosphere which traps an increasing amount of heat radiating from Earth towards space. An extensive National Climate Change Assessment[59] conducted by the U.S. Global Change Research Program has concluded: "Many independent lines of evidence demonstrate that the world is warming and that *human activity is the primary cause*" (emphasis added). While there is a large amount of scientific consensus, there is far less political agreement on the causes, the importance, or what to do about global climate change.

For instance, when asked whether climate change is human-made, a Florida Congress member replied: "The climate has changed since Earth was created. Why did the dinosaurs go extinct? Were there men that were causing [it]? Were there cars running around at that point that were causing global warming? No." He went on to argue the causality debate was far from over: "For us to say that it is a settled argument right now... is a foolish argument to make, because there are scientists on both sides of the issue that say that it's not settled."[60] Governor Scott and his administration came under national scrutiny when former Florida Department of Environmental Protection employees claimed an unwritten policy had banned state workers from even using the terms "climate change" or "global warming."[61] Scott denied the charge, but then soon after his emergency management chief refused to utter the words "climate change" under direct questioning by several senators at a Florida legislative subcommittee hearing (much to their amusement).[62]

The sharp divide on climate change falls along partisan lines—Democrats solidly line up on the side of human causality, independents lean toward the Democratic-held view, and Republicans are on the side of natural climate cycles. On the more general question of "How serious is climate change for Florida?" 71 percent of Democrats say "very serious" compared to 44 percent of independents and 26 percent of

Republicans. (The survey was sponsored by the Natural Resources Defense Council.) Similar partisan fault lines appear when respondents were asked if Florida has done enough to prepare for climate change or whether state officials should be doing more. Democrats (79 percent) and independents (62 percent) believe state officials should be doing more, compared to 40 percent of the Republicans surveyed.[63] The National Climate Change Assessment study found that in Florida, *local* governments were being far more proactive in preparing for the potential consequences of climate change than the state, which is not surprising given that Republicans are in control of state government. It also reflects the fact that some localities have already observed the impacts of climate change in their own backyards.

The blueprint for discussions of climate change is the extensive National Climate Change Assessment. It spells out in great detail Florida's key vulnerabilities—rising sea levels, extreme heat events, hurricanes, and decreased water availability. Each has the potential to have a devastating impact on the public's health, as well as the state's population growth and the economy:[64]

- **Rising sea levels** pose widespread and continuing threats to both natural and built environments and to the regional economy. Roads, railways, ports, airports, oil and gas facilities, and water supplies are vulnerable to the impacts of sea level rise. Miami and Tampa were singled out as the most at risk. Add to that the state's property and flood insurance industries. A number of local governments in coastal areas have begun to prepare for rising sea levels. Key West has added pumps, constructed a fire station at a higher elevation, and rebuilt portions of the island's seawall. Miami Beach has begun shoring up its storm drainage system and elevating roads and sidewalks.[65]

- **Increasing temperatures** and the associated increase in frequency, intensity, and duration of extreme heat events will affect public health, natural and built environments, energy, agriculture, and forestry. Children, the elderly, the sick, and the poor are especially vulnerable. Evidence is mounting that harm to the nation will increase substantially in the future unless global emissions of heat-trapping gases are greatly reduced. (The search for alternative energy sources is seen as imperative. A number of environmental groups are heavily promoting solar energy. On the Solar Energy Industries Association listing of states' potential for solar power generation, Florida ranks third.[66])

- **Decreased water availability,** exacerbated by population growth and land-use change, will continue to increase competition for water and affect the economy and unique ecosystems. Fresh water supplies from rivers, streams, and ground water sources near the coast are at risk from accelerated salt water intrusion due to higher sea levels. Porous aquifers in some areas make them particularly vulnerable to salt water intrusion. Continued urban development and increases in irrigated agriculture will increase water demand, while higher temperatures will increase evaporative losses. All of these factors will combine to reduce the availability of water.

- **More extreme weather events, wildfires, and diseases transmitted by insects, food, and water** threaten human health and well-being. Key weather and climate drivers of health impacts include increasingly frequent, intense, and longer-lasting extreme heat, which worsens drought, wildfire, and air pollution risks; increasingly frequent extreme precipitation, intense storms, and changes in precipitation patterns that can lead to flooding, drought, and ecosystem changes; and rising sea levels that intensify coastal flooding and storm surge, causing injuries, deaths, stress due to evacuations, and water quality impacts, among other effects on public health.

The potential consequences of inattention to the climate change-induced problems spelled out in the national report have alarmed many people. But the reality is that while the majority of Floridians believe that human-made global climate change is occurring, little consensus exists among Floridians about how important the problem is now, how long it will really be before the projected impacts actually occur, how to pay for it all, and which level(s) of government should be in charge of climate change policymaking.

For many local officials, the complexities and difficulties of dealing with climate change challenges are already crystal clear—"procrastination, disputes over property rights, and long battles over changing zoning and building codes to prohibit building in areas that can't be protected."[67] With the environment, as with most problems in Florida, there is simply no one-size-fits-all pattern—or solution. What is certain is that the decisions that will ultimately be made will directly impact the state's vital agriculture, water, energy, and transportation sectors, which, in turn, will affect population and economic growth rates.

RAPID GROWTH AND SLOW GROWTH IN FLORIDA: DIFFERENT DYNAMICS

Floridians' attitudes toward growth largely depend on the rate of growth overall. Rapid population growth has been a double-edged sword. Over the past half century, it created economic growth and jobs and expanded the state's tax base. At the same time, it put intense fiscal and political pressures on the state and local governments to deal with the challenges that stemmed from growth: crowded schools, clogged roads, and environmental stress.

When growth rates are high, Floridians worry about quality of life issues, think government needs to do a better job managing growth, assume that growth will continue, and give the government good marks for job creation. When the population growth rates decline, a different set of pressures come to bear as governments deal with the consequences of an economic slowdown, high unemployment, and a declining tax base. Citizens worry much more about creating jobs than about growth management, and if economic recovery lags, citizens will judge local officials more harshly.

Regardless of the growth rate at the time, Florida's growth has always been uneven. Some areas of the state have grown, or will grow, faster than other areas; the opposite is true as well. Attitudes on growth, and political tensions over growth, also vary significantly depending on where in the state a person lives and how long they have lived in Florida.

Affordable housing, traffic congestion, and commercial development pose challenges to Florida's governments during high growth periods.

Growth Issues Provoke Serious Political Conflicts

People who move to Florida tend to quickly adopt a "close the door behind me" anti-growth attitude once they get here. Old-timers resent the influx of newcomers who change the character of the place they have long called "home." That is why growth management issues often pit old-timers against newcomers and pro-growth proponents against those with an anti-growth/anti-developer sentiment. But in no-growth areas, voters become angry at elected officials who prove to be ineffective at promoting economic development and fail to bring new jobs to the area.

At the state level, legislators often vehemently disagree on growth management policy proposals, depending upon whether they represent high-growth districts or low-growth districts. Legislators from areas that are not growing and desperately need more jobs tend to favor economic development policies that offer tax incentives to businesses to locate there (a pro-growth position). Lawmakers from high-growth areas where there are water shortages, congested roads, and angry constituents may be more likely to have different (anti-growth) policy perspectives.

Intense Budget Pressures at Both the State and Local Levels

At the state level, legislators grapple with how to balance the budgetary needs of faster growing parts of the state and the poorer, more rural counties whose economies are not expanding as rapidly. At the local level, growth forces cities, counties, school districts, and special districts to spend proportionately more on capital, or infrastructure-related projects (new or expanded streets, sewers, water systems, police and fire substations, schools) than low- or no-growth localities that can budget a greater portion for services and programs. One study of local elections in Florida found that infrastructure-related budgetary decisions are often the reason incumbents are defeated when they run for re-election.[68] Infrastructure issues can spell defeat for elected officials in both high- and low-growth communities, but for different reasons.

Variation in Population Mobility Patterns Creates Uneven Growth

Florida's population is projected to grow in each of the next three decades. (See Chapter 1.) Some counties can expect higher growth rates than others. The "in-filling" trend that began in the late 1990s will likely continue. The state's interior counties will grow faster than the coastal counties that are already densely populated. Lower taxes, more pristine environments, and lower housing costs in these areas are attracting new residents who are coming from other states, other countries, and other Florida counties. Residents who live in congested areas are increasingly choosing to move to less crowded parts of the state. For others, interior county locations are perceived as safer from the direct hit of hurricanes. The bottom line is that growth pressures will not ease up in Florida for quite some time. That means battles over the environment, growth management, economic development, and transportation policies will continue. All involve serious debates over land use.

LAND USE AT THE HEART OF THE GROWTH MANAGEMENT BATTLE

Power in local communities in Florida and the United States centers on the control of land use. Land is a scarce and valuable resource. Historically, its use was determined by private owners responding principally to free-market economic forces—putting their land to its most productive use. But over time, land use decisions in Florida and elsewhere in the United States have been placed more in the hands of local governments than with private property owners. Local governments respond to both economic and political forces in determining how land within their communities is to be used. With the passage of the 1985 Growth Management Act, the state went one step further and took much of the control over land use away from the local governments and gave it to regional bodies and the state.

In 2011 (a slower economy) Governor Scott and the Republican legislature, seeking to reduce regulations and encourage growth, abolished many of the important restrictions that the Growth Management Act had previously placed on local governments, thereby greatly alarming the state's environmental community.

Four years later, in an effort to speed up the state's economic recovery rate, the Republican governor and legislature greatly reduced the role of regional bodies in reviewing proposals for large developments, and lessened the input of local governments into those decisions. The 2015 Act alarmed both environmentalists and local governments; each feared the consequences of uncontrolled growth.

Florida's Growth Management Act of 1985

Florida's 1985 Growth Management Act placed the state and its cities and counties at the national forefront of government efforts to take control of land use. It authorized the state to draw up a comprehensive plan and mandated that all cities and counties draw up comprehensive plans consistent with the state plan. All plans were required to include controls on local land use and development. Authority was given

to the Department of Community Affairs (now the Department of Economic Opportunity) to approve or disapprove of city and county plans. Disapproval could result in the loss of substantial state funding for local governments. City and county plans with "greater than local" impact were also subject to special reviews over developments of regional impact (DRI) and areas of critical state concern (ACSCs).[69] All plans had to incorporate land use controls and include sections on environmental, transportation, housing, education, and historic preservation. The plans had to be drawn to combat urban sprawl and encourage "compact urban development."

Supporters of passage of the Growth Management Act of 1985 saw it as a way to limit further urban sprawl.

The Concurrency Requirement

The most controversial element of the state's Growth Management Act was the concurrency requirement. It mandated that cities and counties establish *levels of service* for transportation, education, water and sewers, solid waste disposal, and other services. Once a level of service was set, it was unlawful for a city or county to allow any residential or commercial or industrial development that would lower the established level of service. For example, if a desired level of service for a particular highway was set at so many vehicles per lane, and a proposed development along that highway would create a traffic load in excess of the set limit, the development had to be rejected unless the developer were to pay for adding lanes to the road. Public facilities had to precede or be built *concurrently* with new developments they served. In 2005, the Florida Legislature added water and schools to the list of services that fall under the concurrency requirement. Because local government could set low levels of service standards, however, concurrency often managed growth better on paper than in real life.

Impact Fees

The Growth Management Act also authorized cities and counties to impose impact fees on builders and developers. These impact fees were supposed to pay for the new public infrastructure—roads, sewers, sewage disposal plants, police and firefighting facilities, schools, and so forth—needed to service a new development. (See Figure 12-7.) Impact fees were calculated differently from one locality to another. Some high-growth counties heavily relied on them to pay for growth; some slow-growth counties did not use impact fees at all, believing they would make it more difficult to entice firms to do business there. Impact fees "vary extensively depending on local costs, capacity needs, resources and the local government's determination to charge the full cost of the fee's earmarked purposes."[70] One of the most difficult tasks was generating credible estimates on what the overall costs of a new development would be to local governments. This uncertainty also made it hard to know whether the costs would be covered by the property taxes that the development would ultimately generate. Many builders and developers referred to impact fees as "legalized extortion"—demands by local officials for money as a condition of granting approval. During the boom times, it was not uncommon for impact fees to add as much as $10,000 or more to the cost of a new single family home and as much as $100,000 or more to a new commercial building.

During the 2007 recession, a number of local governments reduced or eliminated impact fees in an effort to retain and attract more businesses, especially when neighboring jurisdictions had already done so. Florida courts have ruled that impact fees cannot be greater than the costs incurred by a government to serve the new development and that such fees must be spent for the "substantial benefit" of the new residents. For instance, the builder of a senior-only community cannot be forced to pay impact fees for schools since no children will live in the development.

Figure 12-7. Categories of Impact Fees Used by Florida Cities and Counties

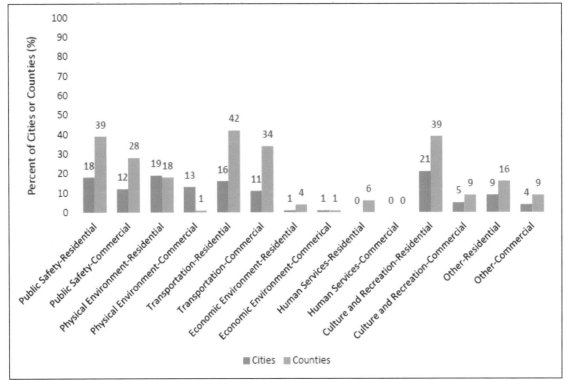

Source: Florida Department of Financial Services. Data are for fiscal year ending September 30, 2012.

Major Changes: The Growth Management Act 2011

The Florida Legislature has tinkered with the Growth Management Act over the years but managed only to anger the environmentalists, who were convinced the act was not effective in limiting urban sprawl, *and* the business community who believed it hurt the economy by artificially driving up construction costs and creating an affordable housing problem. In the midst of an economic slowdown, Governor Scott and the Republican legislature came down firmly on the side of the builders and developers and made a number of sweeping changes to the Growth Management Act. Supporters of growth management and the environment labeled the changes a "disaster for Florida." They predicted local governments would give in to short-term pressures for growth without worrying about the impact on basic services in the future.

Under the new law, the governor and legislature created a new Department of Economic Opportunity that absorbed and replaced the Department of Community Affairs, along with several other executive agencies. Second, the number of planners and assistants who review local plans was cut in half—from

61 to 32. Third, the state can reject a proposed change to a local long-term comprehensive growth plan only if the plan will have a negative impact on "important state resources and facilities" (which was left undefined in the legislation). Fourth, developers are no longer required to meet concurrency standards. Instead, local governments are responsible for controlling the impact of growth. And fifth, the law makes it more difficult for residents to stop proposed changes to a local growth plan by shifting the burden of proof to the citizens who file legal challenges.

Overall the changes to the Growth Management Act put growth management decisions squarely back under local control. While the law still allows local use of impact fees as a way to pay for growth, many local governments have chosen instead to reduce or eliminate these fees in an attempt to spur more local development.

The 2015 Growth Management Law

The movement that began in the last decade away from the state's historically strong growth management policies was punctuated by the 2015 growth management law. The law further scaled back review requirements, which the conservative legislature and governor saw as procedural impediments to the planning and development of large scale projects (economic development and job creation). The bill includes provisions that do the following:

- Replace the Development of Regional Impact program with the state coordinated review process.
- Clarify that amendments to sector plans must go through state coordinated review.
- Modify the sector planning process.
- Create the connected-city corridor pilot program in Pasco County.
- Eliminate one of Florida's 11 regional planning councils and limit the duties of the remaining planning councils.
- Exempt small local governments that use less than one percent of a public water utility's total permitted allocation from having to amend its comprehensive plan in response to an updated regional water supply plan.

Other parts of the law affect the statutory authority of Regional Planning Councils (reduced), concurrency and impact fees (capped for certain functions), protection of private property rights (required to be part of a local government's comprehensive plan), and definition of a blighted area (expanded) for purposes related to the Community Redevelopment Act.

Most notably, the law centralized growth management functions by eliminating the special approval process for a proposed Development of Regional Impact (DRI) and replacing it with the state coordinated review process. Florida law defines a DRI as "any development which, because of its character, magnitude, or location, would have a substantial effect upon the health, safety, or welfare of citizens of more than one county." The old review process was a joint effort between Florida's 11 Regional Planning Councils, the state Department of Economic Opportunity, other state agencies, and local governments.

The bill's supporters claimed that the old DRI review process, which was created in different circumstances, was no longer effective, was clearly too cumbersome, and restricted growth. In addition, it was asserted that the old process encouraged bad development by incentivizing developers to structure large projects into smaller pieces to come under the DRI threshold. The bill's proponents explained that much of the DRI review process was duplicated in the local government comprehensive planning process, which includes coordination among local governments.[71]

Opponents, while acknowledging a need for change, argued that the solution was not to scrap the 45-year-old process, but rather to streamline it and improve provisions for neighborly cooperation among local governments. They warned that the state coordinated review process significantly limits the ability of government to make objections when reviewing development plans. Supporters refuted this, claiming that, under the new rules, local governments can still review projects and use other tools at their disposal to influence development and that at least RCPs can still review comprehensive plans.[72]

Florida's local governments were among those opposing this centralization of authority that represented a shift away from home rule.[73] Among local governments' top concerns was that the new law failed to adequately provide for coordination among neighboring local governments when developments have extra-jurisdictional impact, like traffic congestion due to construction of a large outlet mall, something that was addressed in the old process.

Some argued that, while Florida's growth management laws had flaws, leaders ignored more measured alternatives, including encouraging more responsible use of natural resources and empowering cities to develop adequate public transit options.[74] They cautioned that, as Florida continues to grow, drastic changes in growth management may lead to history repeating itself. If the 2015 changes turn out to be short-sighted overreactions to a down economy, Florida may encounter some of the same problems (pollution, congestion, overcrowding, and crime) that led to bipartisan support for more intensive growth management in the 1980s.[75]

Reaction to Changes Paying for Growth

During periods of rapid growth, politicians get mixed signals from the public on how to pay for that growth. Surveys often show taxpayer unwillingness to fork out more money to help relieve some of the growth-related pressures and staunch opposition to any attempts to raise local property taxes. The few revenue sources that look more favorable all have a similar attribute—to the taxpayer, it looks like someone else will be paying. In other words, attitudes toward raising more monies to pay for growth-impacted infrastructure needs reflect a "YPNM" syndrome—"you pay, not me." A perfect example can be seen in the results of a countywide citizens opinion survey taken in Polk County during a high growth period. Polk County residents were opposed to using the property tax to pay for growth, preferring revenue solutions more likely to be paid by someone else: higher taxes in unincorporated areas—where many newcomers settle, impact fees (paid by developers), and permitting fees (paid by builders).

Developer Agreements

Often conflicts between local governments and developers are settled through developer agreements—contracts that specify the details of the proposed development. Occasionally lawsuits or the threat of lawsuits by developers force municipalities into such agreements. The municipality benefits by being able to specify the details of a project. The developer benefits by obtaining a legally binding contract that cannot be changed later by the municipality as the project proceeds to completion.

Community Redevelopment Agencies (CRAs)

In 1969, the Florida Legislature passed a law enabling local governments to set up a Community Redevelopment Agency (CRA) for the purpose of either eliminating and preventing the development of slums and blighted areas or providing affordable housing. A CRA's "statutory job is to leverage public dollars, in a transparent and fully accountable manner, with private sector investment to improve blighted areas."[76] In other words, the law requires public-private partnerships. With a CRA, a local government can create redevelopment districts and use a special kind of financing: Tax Increment Financing (TIFs),[77] along with the federal Community Development Block Grant and State Housing Initiative Partnership funds, among others, to fund the redevelopment of properties in those districts.[78] Hundreds of CRAs are now in place across the state.

"Smart" or "No-Growth" Politics

Passage of the Growth Management Act in 1985, particularly its concurrency requirement, was a major victory for opponents of uncontrolled growth in the state. Opposition to growth is generally concentrated among well-educated, upper-middle-class, older residents who own their own homes and whose income does not directly depend upon the economic health of the community. Unrestricted growth threatens the aesthetic preferences of these upper-middle-class homeowners. It brings congestion, noise, pollution, ugly factories, cheap commercial outlets, hamburger stands, fried chicken franchises, and "undesirable" residents. College and university faculty are fertile grounds for anti-growth movements. In fact, academics have cleverly given the label "smart growth" to these efforts, effectively labeling alternative viewpoints as "dumb growth."

Homeowners, especially seniors living on Social Security and retirement income, often oppose development. They fear that nearby development will increase their property tax assessments and taxes, as well as add to congestion, noise, and inconvenience. Hence, it is in the economic interest of homeowners to oppose further development.

The traditional community power structure tends to support growth. Real estate developers, builders, mortgage bankers, and retail merchants generally seek to encourage economic development. Occasionally larger, better-financed developers may support costly and cumbersome planning restrictions as a means of forcing smaller developers out of the local real estate market. Other times, residents may use the tools of direct democracy (amendments, referenda) to fight developers and restrict development.

Neighborhood Associations and NIMBYs

Neighborhood associations are found almost everywhere in Florida, and nearly every new development has one. They are formed to help keep up the property values of a community through a series of regulations. Neighborhood associations oppose any new developments that might reduce their property values, such as unwanted traffic, "undesirable" businesses or residents, or less open space. Even people who would otherwise support new commercial or housing developments or new public facilities may voice the protest, "Not in my back yard!" earning them the NIMBY label.

NIMBYs can be the noisiest of protest groups. They are the homeowners and voters who are most directly affected by a private or public project. They can organize, sue, petition, and demonstrate to block projects. Virtually every project inspires NIMBY opposition, especially waste disposal sites, incinerators, highways, prisons, mental health facilities, low-income public housing projects, power plants, pipelines, and factories.

Restricting Growth

Political cleavages in many Florida cities and counties occur along the fault line of growth, pitting no-growthers against builders, developers, business owners, and real estate interests. The Growth Management Act, with its concurrency requirement, also placed a powerful weapon in the hands of no-growthers. But city and county governments may restrict growth in a variety of ways, including zoning laws, subdivision restrictions, utility regulations, building permits, environmental regulations, and even municipal land purchases. Local governments use zoning restrictions to designate a particular use for land like agricultural, residential, commercial, or industrial. Zoning laws can rule out multifamily dwellings or specify only large expensive lot sizes for homes. They can also exclude heavy industrial development or restrict strip commercial development along highways. Opposition to street widening, road building, or tree cutting can slow or halt development. Public utilities needed for development—water lines, sewage disposal, fire houses, and so on—can be postponed indefinitely. High development fees, utility hookup charges, or building permit costs can all be used to discourage growth. Environmental controls are another effective tool that can be used to halt development.

Environmental Regulations

Local governments in Florida have increasingly turned to environmental laws and regulations to assert control over community development. Local ordinances may designate certain places as "areas of critical concern" in an effort to slow or halt development. These may be swamps, forests, waterfront, or wildlife habitats, or even historic, scenic, or archeological sites. "Critical" may also refer to flood plains or steep hillsides or any other land on which governments wish to halt construction. Designation of such areas is usually very subjective.

Cities and counties are increasingly requiring developers to prepare *environmental impact statements*—assessments of the environmental consequences of proposed construction or land use changes. These statements are usually prepared by professional consultants at added cost to builders and developers, who, in turn, pass the costs on to home buyers.

In most cities and counties, enforcement of environmental regulations is the responsibility of separate environmental departments. This means that landowners and developers usually have to deal with two separate bureaucracies—planning departments and environmental departments.

Using Direct Democracy to Halt Growth

One way residents can fight local development interests and their allies in local government is through direct democracy. The Hometown Democracy initiative was a prime example—although ultimately one that failed. The purpose was to amend Article II, Section 7 of the Florida Constitution to require voter approval of a local land-use comprehensive plan and any amendments to it. The leaders of the movement felt that local governments were too quick to approve changes requested by developers and that local citizens should have the final say on growth plan changes. The group's first effort, which easily got enough signatures, was removed from the ballot by the Florida Supreme Court in 2005 because the proposed ballot summary did not explain the chief purpose of the proposed amendment.[79] In response, the group started over. It revamped the amendment ballot summary and gathered new signatures. The Florida Supreme Court approved the newly written amendment (Amendment 4) for placement on the 2010 ballot.

Predictably, the Hometown Democracy initiative was vehemently opposed by Florida's local governments, as well as the business, real estate, and development communities. These groups raised and spent an enormous sum of money on television and radio ads urging voters to vote "No." It worked. Amendment 4 was easily defeated. Voters were convinced that Hometown Democracy would curtail economic development and make it more difficult to create new jobs. Ironically, had the amendment gone on the ballot during the boom times, when citizens were complaining about uncontrolled growth, it likely would have passed.

THE POLITICS OF ECONOMIC DEVELOPMENT

Most residents expect their state and local governments to be proactive in securing economic development, although they often differ on which paths to follow. A number of approaches are commonly used to promote economic development at the state and local levels.

Economic Development Approaches

In Florida, economic development commonly uses one of four approaches: investing in infrastructure and human capital; creating a business friendly environment with low taxes, limited government regulations, and a quality workforce; providing specific incentives like cash payments or tax breaks for new business to move or existing business to stay and expand; and marketing the state and its localities to attract more visitors, tourists, and conventions.

It is important to note that economic development efforts often involve both the state (which sets tax laws and offers fiscal incentives and technical assistance) and its local governments. The state's Department of Economic Opportunity coordinates services and programs related to economic development, workforce development, community planning, and affordable housing. Enterprise Florida, a public-private partnership, is the state's primary organization for economic development and leader of efforts to recruit and expand businesses. It also works with local communities to create site inventories to include in its online buildings and site data base.

One popular approach is to **focus on building infrastructure, improving the education system, and providing opportunities for local workers to be retrained.** Roads, mass transit, seaports, airports, power plants, cell phone towers, water and sewage treatment facilities all make it possible for businesses to form, succeed, and expand. In metropolitan areas, investment in libraries, sports stadiums, arenas, and performing arts centers can help lure businesses whose upper management and owners are also looking for cultural amenities. And states or localities that invest in education can offer a better educated, more skilled workforce to businesses or corporations interested in relocating. Obviously, each of these approaches costs a lot of money, which is difficult in areas where low taxes are a higher priority.

One popular economic development approach is to make major infrastructure-related improvements, such as a solar energy-producing plant, that will appeal to business owners and investors.

Other economic development proponents prefer to **attract business by creating a business friendly climate with low taxes and few regulations.** Florida stacks up better here because of its low tax burden and less regulatory-intensive environment. In a five year period, Florida's ranking as a business friendly state by *Chief Executive* magazine rose from the sixth most business friendly to third, then to second.[80] The improved ranking was due to stronger support for tax and regulatory relief at the state level, from the governor and the GOP-controlled legislature. Governor Scott took office promising to make Florida the number one business friendly state in the country.

A third economic development approach focuses on **attracting specific businesses by offering direct incentives to them, such as tax breaks or cash payments or training.** Florida offers a number of different types of incentives: (1) to targeted industries (tax refunds, capital investment tax credits, high impact performance grants; (2) for workforce training (for new industries coming in and to retrain employees at existing industries; (3) funding of transportation infrastructure (the Economic Development Trust Fund to alleviate transportation problems that adversely impact a company's location or expansion decision, goes to local government); (4) for special opportunities (for rural areas, urban areas, enterprise zones, and brownfield redevelopment.)[81] Critics of the incentive approach call it corporate welfare and see it as unfair to businesses that must compete without getting special incentives. Floridians have generally been supportive of these efforts, however, although their preference for offering more help to new than existing businesses varies with the status of the economy. The Sunshine State Surveys show that when the economy is bad, a higher percentage favors more efforts to attract new businesses and jobs than on keeping local businesses. (See Figure 12-8.) But when the economy is stronger, the support for the two approaches is almost equal.

Figure 12-8. Citizen Preferences for State Economic Development Agency Efforts

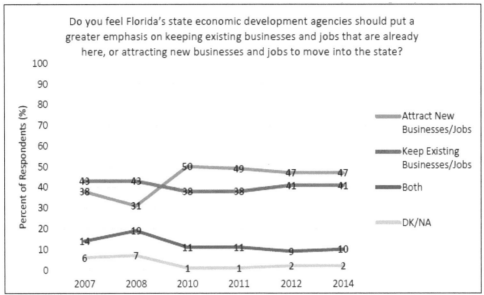

Source: "Leadership Florida Sunshine State Survey (2006-2008), Leadership Florida-Nielsen Company Sunshine State Survey (2010-2011), and University of South Florida-Nielsen Sunshine State Survey (2014)."

Florida and many local governments have used the tax breaks/tax incentives/cash payments approach to some success. For example, the state and some local governments have combined efforts and spent a lot of money on subsidies to lure biomedical firms to Florida including the following:[82]

- Burnham Institute, which received $300 million for a promise of 300 jobs in Orlando.
- Scripps Research Institute, which received $510 million for a promise of 2,800 jobs in Palm Beach.
- Max Planck Institute, which received $190 million for a promise of 189 jobs in Jupiter.
- Torrey Pines Institute, which received $86.5 million for a promise of 150 jobs in Port St. Lucie.

Not all deals go through, however. And some deals do not generate as many jobs as anticipated, which can cause an outcry among the citizenry. Unmet promises were one of the reasons that the state revised its policies regarding financial incentives. The head of Enterprise Florida said, "In weighing the value of incentives we must ask what government is doing to ensure that companies deliver on their promises when signing an incentive agreement. Incentives are performance-based, meaning companies must create and retain jobs before receiving funds."[83]

A fourth economic development approach employed by Florida is **heavily promoting (marketing) the state nationally and internationally to attract more conventions, tourists, and visitors.** Visit Florida is the state's official tourism marketing corporation with a mission to promote travel and drive visitation to and within the state. As the state's number one industry, tourism is responsible for welcoming nearly 100 million visitors each year, who spend more than $80 million, generate nearly one-fourth of the state's sales tax revenue, and employ more than a million Floridians. At the same time, groups like Florida TaxWatch have pointed out the strains that visitors can put on existing infrastructure—the state's roadways, airports, and cruise ports—and warned that if the state does not address infrastructure development needs, it could ultimately have a negative impact on Florida's multi-billion dollar tourism industry.[84]

Visit Florida receives millions of dollars in state funding ($74 million in FY 2014) and also solicits private matching funds ($120 million in one recent year). For every dollar spent on tourism marketing, Visit Florida generates more than $300 in tourism spending.[85]

Promoting the assets of local communities is just as important. A study conducted for the National League of Cities Center for Research and Innovation concluded that "Companies move to municipalities, not states. [Local] officials must play a critical role in attracting business investment, jobs, and a strong tax base."[86] The National League of Cities has laid out six things *local* officials need to do to attract (and keep) businesses[87]:

- Have streamlined and transparent regulations.
- Be honest about timelines.
- Make sure development services and permitting staff cooperate with the economic development staff.
- Have existing businesses communicate the merits of your community to prospective businesses.
- Stress the qualities of the local workforce. No amount of incentives can make up for the lack of readily available talent.
- Remember that quality of life in the community is important. Companies want to locate in a place where their employees want to live.

The tendency is for companies to choose a big city location. But as noted in the "Open for Business" article in the Florida League of Cities' *Quality Cities* publication, "small and mid-sized cities can compete by touting the strengths of their particular labor forces and taking a more regional approach to marketing. Smaller cities should also form tight partnerships with community organizations that have the same goals."[88] Partnerships with their county governments are also helpful.

The Local Growth Machine

Builders, developers, business, and real estate interests have maintained a lot of influence with local officials. Occasionally, these business-oriented groups have succeeded in ousting no-growth council members and commissioners in hard-fought elections. These interests have been labeled the "growth machine" because they actively promote community growth and business activity and because they receive direct financial benefit from increased growth.[89] Often they control the local chamber of commerce and junior chamber of commerce ("Jaycees").

Developers, builders, contractors, and other businesses doing business with local governments are a major source of campaign contributions for local office seekers. Developers of residential, commercial, and industrial property must work closely with city government officials to coordinate the provision of public services, especially streets, sewage, water, and electricity. They must also satisfy city officials regarding planning and zoning regulations, building codes, fire and safety laws, and environmental regulations. Many localities have adopted business-friendly policies that help expedite some of these processes. (See Figure 12-9.)

Citizens are more prone to view economic development negatively during a high growth period—as a "pro-developer" policy—but positively during an economic slowdown—as a "pro-jobs" policy.

Figure 12-9. Infographic Branding Florida as a Great Place to Do Business

Note: This infographic is designed to brand Florida as a business friendly state.
Source: "Why Florida? Fast Facts," Enterprise Florida. Available at http://www.
enterpriseflorida.com/wp-content/uploads/why-florida-fast-facts.pdf.

Successful Economic Development Involves Partnerships

In the end, successful economic development efforts involve state-local, inter-local, and public-private partnerships. A good example is the decision by a huge Japanese tech company to select Fort Lauderdale for its new software division (Sato Global Solutions)—its first global headquarters outside Japan. The president and chief executive of the company said it had also considered Chicago, Dallas, New York, and the Silicon Valley but chose South Florida because the area was less expensive, state and local governments were business-friendly and offered incentives, and its central location in South Florida could draw software engineers and other professionals all the way from West Palm Beach to Miami. The building's high-ceiling seventh floor could be turned in to a loft-like space that would help motivate creative employees and encourage them to stay.[90] Another plus of the location was its access to public transportation.

The company had been courted by the Greater Fort Lauderdale Alliance—the primary economic development organization for Greater Fort Lauderdale/Broward County. The president of the Alliance acknowledged the group had been and is still actively engaged in attracting IT corporations as a way to expand the area's economic brand beyond tourism: "We really want to build our brand on the technology side. We already have the brand on the fun side." The Alliance's members include business, government (county and city), academics, and community leaders. Their focus is on creating, attracting, expanding, and retaining high-wage jobs and capital investment in high value targeted industries, developing more vibrant communities, and improving the quality of life for the area's citizens.[91]

Figure 12-10. Florida Cities' Use of Economic Development Incentives

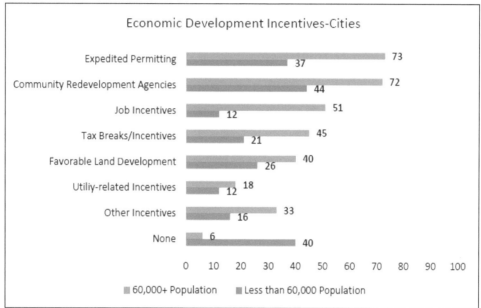

Source: Florida League of Cities, "2014 State of the Cities." Available at http://www.floridaleagueofcities.com/Assets/Files/2014StateoftheCities.pdf.

Constitutional Concerns: The Takings Clause

How far can government go in regulating the use of property without depriving individuals of their property rights? The Fifth Amendment to the U.S. Constitution states clearly: "nor shall private property be taken for public use, without just compensation." Taking land for highways, streets, and public buildings, even when the owners do not wish to sell, is known as the power of *eminent domain*. To exercise this power, a city or state must go to court and show that the land is needed for a legitimate public purpose. The court will then establish a fair price, "just compensation," based on testimony from the owner, the city or state, and impartial appraisers. This Takings Clause of the U.S. Constitution protects American citizens from arbitrary government seizure of their land.

But what if a government does not literally "take" ownership of the property but instead restricts the owner's use of it through regulation? Zoning ordinances, subdivision restrictions, environmental regulations, and building and housing codes may reduce the value of the property to the owner. Should the owner be compensated for loss of uses?

Owners of property have never been entitled to any compensation for obeying laws or ordinances with a clear public purpose, and local governments are not required to compensate owners for lost value as a result of zoning regulations. Yet it is still argued that some planning and zoning provisions, especially those designed for beauty and aesthetics, have no relation to public health, safety, and welfare (a police power that governments can legitimately regulate). They simply assert somebody's taste over that of their neighbor. But in 1954, the U.S. Supreme Court upheld a broad interpretation of the police power: "It is within the power of the legislature to determine that the community should be beautiful as well as healthy, spacious as well as clean, well-balanced as well as carefully patrolled."[92] So it is difficult to challenge the constitutionality of planning and zoning as a "taking" of private property without compensation.

Takings: When Cities Go Too Far

The U.S. Supreme Court has also held that a regulation that denies a property owner all economically beneficial use of land (for example, a state coastal zone management regulation preventing any construction on a beach lot) was a "taking" that required just compensation to the owner in order to be constitutional.[93] The Takings Clause of the Constitution's Fifth Amendment was designed to protect private property from unjust taking by government. Its purpose is "to bar Government from forcing some people alone to bear public burdens which, in all fairness and justice, should be borne by the public as a whole."[94] If a community wants open spaces, wildlife preserves, environmental havens, historic buildings, or other amenities, these should be paid for by all of the citizens of the community. All citizens should share in the costs of providing community amenities, not just the owners of particular properties.

The question remains, however, how far can government go in regulating land use without compensating property owners? Depriving landowners of all beneficial uses of their land without compensation is clearly unconstitutional. But what if the use of their land is devalued by 50 percent or 25 percent? Are governments constitutionally required to compensate them in proportion to their losses? In the past, federal courts have ruled that "mere diminution" in the value of property is not a "taking" within the meaning of the Fifth Amendment and hence does not require government to compensate landowners. In recent years, however, both Congress and the federal courts, as well as some states, have reconsidered how far government can go in depriving property owners of valued uses of their land. Increasingly, regulatory devaluations of 50 percent or more are becoming highly suspect, and property owners have a reasonable chance of recovering compensation from the government.

Local builders, developers, business owners, and real estate firms are almost guaranteed to attend any local Planning Commission meeting where there is discussion of major changes in local land use patterns.

The Backlash Against the U.S. Supreme Court's Kelo Ruling

Another constitutional question that arises is just what is public use? The Supreme Court has upheld a broad interpretation of public use going well beyond the traditionally accepted idea of public projects like highways or public buildings. In its highly controversial 5-4 ruling in the *Kelo* v. *New London* (2005) case, the U.S. Supreme Court ruled that "public use" included the ability of a local government to take a person's property and give it to another person for private development if that private development would provide a public benefit. For example, if an area of modest homes brought in only modest property tax revenues, the local government would be within its rights to take the property and turn it over to a private developer who might then build a shopping mall or office complex that would provide much greater tax revenue to be used for "the public good." The Supreme Court pointed out that states could regulate their local governments to limit this practice. Consequently, many states, including Florida, have passed their own laws limiting local governments' use of eminent domain and protecting private property owners. To take private property in Florida, any government entity must need it for a public purpose and "it must meet the SCALE criteria: It must enhance safety, be cost-effective, have no alternative, fit with long-range planning and be mindful of environmental concerns."[95] In 2006, Floridians overwhelmingly voted to put such a restriction in the Constitution itself with a 69 percent "Yes" vote.

Property Rights Controversies Are Ongoing

In 2015, a case before the Florida Supreme Court involved a dispute about whether Jacksonville should have to compensate owners of a riverfront lot who claimed their property's value dropped when the local government built a fire station adjacent to it. At the heart of the case was a state law known as the Bert J. Harris, Jr. Private Property Rights Protection Act, which says property owners are entitled to relief when government agencies take actions that "inordinately burden" use of a property. In this case, the landowners had purchased an undeveloped riverfront lot anticipating that it could be used as a luxury home site. But before that happened, Jacksonville rezoned a lot adjoining it and built a 13,000-square-foot fire station. The landowners claimed the station greatly reduced the value of their property by making it unmarketable as a luxury home site.[96] Regardless of how the Court rules, property rights will continue to be on the front burner in Florida as environmental issues escalate.

In looking ahead, one analyst has predicted that "Florida's future will be defined by a noisy, contentious public debate [between environmentalists, developers, private landowners, and local governments] over taxes, zoning, public works projects, and *property rights*."[97] (emphasis added)

Growth and land use issues are, in a nutshell, a microcosm of state and local politics. They affect every other issue in the state, from schools to transportation.

MOVING PEOPLE AND CARGO IN FLORIDA

The need to move the state's large and growing population, rising visitor counts, and an increasingly diverse set of industries makes transportation policy vital to Florida. The state's geographic characteristics, including its strategic location and long coastline, offer great trade advantages and present significant challenges to those in government who are tasked with managing the state's complex transportation infrastructure and preventing congestion on main roads, at airports, and around cruise ports. Funding is also a huge challenge. Florida's transportation system operates at a deficit and requires constant borrowing of funds to pay for road and bridge project obligation.[98] At one time, the federal government supported more than half of Florida's transportation projects—a figure that has dropped to 26 percent. (See Figure 12-11.) More fuel-efficient cars and the public's opposition to higher gas taxes have greatly reduced the federal Highway Trust Fund.

Responsibility for funding and managing transportation is split amongst federal, state, and local governments. Government goes even further to help Floridians move by providing public transit options (including commuter rail) and to help businesses trade by planning intermodal transportation centers in key locations. Florida's roads, railways, seaports (bustling with both cruise passengers and cargo), waterways, aviation, and evolving spaceports are increasingly busy, some at record-breaking levels.

Poorly designed or implemented transportation systems put the economy and environment at risk. Transportation infrastructure that does not have the capacity to efficiently handle the movement of growing volumes of people and goods serves as a limiting factor on growth.[99] Inadequate systems lead to reduced quality of life for residents, less enjoyable vacations for tourists (Florida tourism depends on repeat visitors), and more costly trade for a wide range of industries. The Florida Department of Transportation (F-DOT), regularly engages in quality assessments of the state's transportation system.

Figure 12-11. State's Transportation System Funding: Heavy Reliance on Borrowing (Bonds)

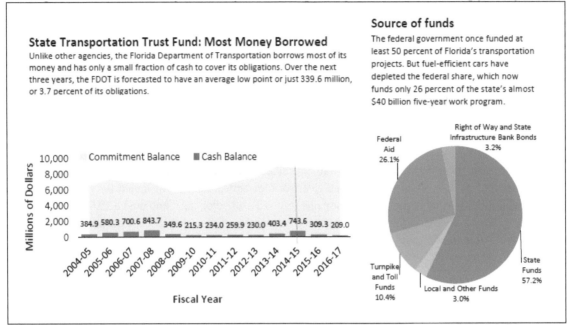

Source: Florida Transportation Commission, "Review of the Department of Transportation Tentative Work Program FY 2014/15 Through 2019/19," March 4, 2014. Available at http://www.ftc.state.fl.us/documents/presentations/FinalFTCPresentation3-4-14.pdf.

Table 12-2. FDOT's Performance Highlights, Goals, and Core Measures

Performance Highlights	Our Goals	Core Measure Highlights
Safety	Providing a safe and secure transportation system for all users	Fatalities and Serious Injuries
Maintenance	Proactively maintaining and operating Florida's transportation system	Pavement Condition, Bridge, Condition, Maintenance, Transit
Mobility	Improving mobility and connectivity for people and freight	Travel Quantity, Travel Quality, Accessibility, Utilization
Economy	Investing in transportation to support a prosperous globally competitive economy	Return on Investment, Projects On-Time, Projects Within Budget
Environment	Making transportation decisions that support communities and promote responsible environmental stewardship	Air Quality

Source: Florida Department of Transportation (FDOT) (March 12, 2015). Available at http://www.dot.state.fl.us/agencyresources/performance.shtm.

Government's Role in Transportation

How Transportation Is Supported

Transportation is a responsibility shared by all levels of government. (See Table 12-3.) From an owner/operator standpoint, roads are divided among federal, state, and local governments. Public transit, seaports, and airports are primarily local functions. Railways are run by the private sector with exceptions, including commuter rail. Waterways are shared by federal and state governments. Spaceports are governed by special districts.

Support for transportation systems is more complicated than direct owner/operator relationships.[100] For example, while FDOT is responsible for the State Highway System, the department also assists owners/operators of other transportation networks covering all modes.[101] FDOT's Strategic Intermodal System plan was adopted in 2005 to prioritize funding for transportation projects of statewide and interregional importance. Plans detailed unfunded transportation needs that, by 2030, would amount to billions of dollars in multi-modal transportation projects, mostly highways.

Table 12-3. Florida's Transportation System

Component	Owner/Operator	All Major Facilities	Strategic Intermodal System (FDOT has the lead role)
State Highways	State of Florida	12,099 centerline miles 6,783 bridges	4,425 centerline miles
Non-State Roads	Federal government and others	2,315 centerline miles 290 bridges	
	Local governments	107,674 centerline miles 5,091 bridges	48 centerline miles
Public Transit	Local governments Transit agencies	30 urban transit systems 23 rural transit systems 6 fixed guideway systems*	2 commuter rail systems (Tri-Rail, SunRail)
Rail	Private sector**	2,753 railway miles 143 miles state owned	2,063 miles of rail corridors 12 freight terminals 22 interregional passenger stations/hubs
Seaports	Local agencies	15 seaports	12 seaports
Waterways	Federal and state governments	3,475 miles of shipping, intra-coastal and inland routes	1,938 miles of waterway corridors
Aviation	Local agencies	780 airports***	17 commercial 2 general aviation reliever
Spaceports	Special district	2 spaceports 10 launch facilities	2 spaceports

Notes:*Tri-Rail, SunRail, Metrorail, Metromover, Skyway Express, and TECO Line Streetcar
**With exception of state-owned 81-mile Southeast Florida Rail Corridor (SFRC) and 62-mile Central Florida Rail Corridor
***129 public use (19 commercial and 110 general aviation) and 651 private use
Source: Florida Department of Transportation (FDOT) (February 23, 2015). Available at http://www.dot.state.fl.us/intermodal/system/.

Costs and Benefits of Public Transit

Local government plays a more direct role in providing transportation through public transit options, including para-transit in compliance with Americans With Disabilities Act (ADA) and state rules. The Florida Public Transportation Association, a group of 37 member agencies with $1 billion in operating budgets, reports that annual ridership is around 270 million with an average fare of $0.97.[102] The fare-box recovery ratio, or the operating costs covered by rider-paid fares, is about 26 percent.

Proponents of public transit cite economic and environmental benefits enjoyed by both riders and non-riders. Public transit leads to higher real estate values, employs drivers and maintenance workers, and provides alternatives for commuters. It also reduces pollution, and air quality is important to residents and tourists. Public transit promises to reduce congestion in Florida's most densely populated cities in the face of capacity challenges presented by a growing economy. Floridians are fairly critical in their assessments of how good a job the state does in providing for adequate public transportation. Just 35 percent see it as "good" or "excellent" while 60 percent rate it as "fair" or "poor." (See Figure 12-12.)

Figure 12-12. Floridians Split on Public Transportation

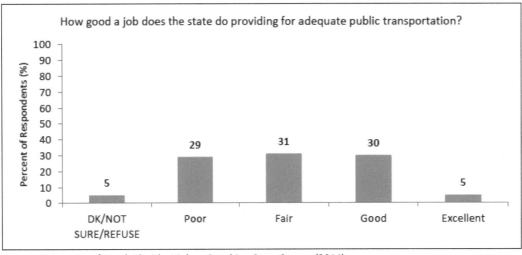

Source: University of South Florida-Nielsen Sunshine State Survey (2014).

Commuter rail has emerged as a possible solution to some of the state's transportation challenges. Florida's most used system, Tri-Rail, runs along the coast from Miami Dade, across Broward, and through much of Palm Beach County.[103] In Central Florida, SunRail began service in 2014. Phase I consists of 32 miles of railway connecting 12 stations, and Phase II will extend the track further north and south to more than 61 total miles with five new stations.[104] SunRail is the result of a public-private partnership, with hundreds of millions of dollars in public funding for construction and operations. Funding has come from the state, federal government (50 percent of funding for Phase I), the four counties reached by the rail, and the City of Orlando.

Another passenger rail system, All Aboard Florida, will connect Miami, Fort Lauderdale, West Palm Beach, and Orlando (and SunRail with Tri-Rail). All Aboard Florida, a project by Florida East Coast Industries (FECI), will be the first privately owned, operated, and maintained passenger railroad in the United States in the past 50 years.[105] There's no doubt that the route is heavily trafficked, with Florida East Coast Industries estimating 50 million travel, mostly by car, between Miami and Orlando annually.[106] The question is whether the benefits outweigh the costs to local communities and future expenses necessary for maintenance and operations.[107] Phase I consists of 66.5 miles from Miami to West Palm Beach and is scheduled to begin service in 2016—an ambitious goal in light of rising opposition. Not all Floridians are in favor of commuter rail projects, however. Commuter rail has always been the subject of heated political debate

While commuter rail projects offer jobs and economic growth, an enhanced tourism experience, and more efficient transportation for residents and business travelers, opponents of commuter rail in Florida warn of drawbacks. Among the top concerns are falling property values (noise, for example) and, consequently, reduced property tax revenues, congestion around crossings (including emergency first-responders waiting at crossings), and, perhaps most controversial, the need for future public funding to build crossings, quiet zones, and operate and maintain the commuter rail systems.

Passenger rail has been the subject of heated political debate, and in 2011 Governor Scott rejected $2.4 billion in federal funds for a high-speed railway connecting Orlando and Tampa. (See Chapter 9.) There's no doubt that the route is heavily trafficked, with Florida East Coast Industries estimating 50 million travel, mostly by car, between Miami and Orlando annually.[108] The question is whether the benefits outweigh the costs to local communities and future expenses necessary for maintenance and operations.[109]

Figure 12-13. Proposed All Aboard Florida Routes

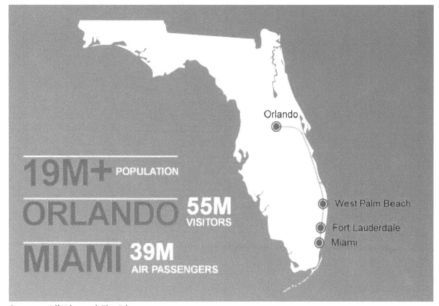

Source: All Aboard Florida.
http://www.ftc.state.fl.us/documents/presentations/13-01%20All%20Aboard%20
Florida%20general%20revised.pdf

Intermodal Logistics Centers

Florida's Strategic Intermodal System (SIS), a network of high-priority systems, designates three types of facilities: transportation hubs (ports and terminals), interregional corridors, and intermodal connectors, which link hubs, corridors, and military installations.[110] The third item, the intermodal logistics center (ILC), has been a focus of planning efforts by the state and private companies. Since development of the SIS, several other events have further grown logistics in Florida.[111] ILCs in Florida move people in addition to cargo, and they even incorporate spaceports.[112] (See Figure 12-14.)

Connecting Modes of Transport

Roads: State, Federal, and Local

Roads are arguably the most critical piece of the Florida transportation system. In addition to the large and growing population of residents who use roads to commute to work, visitors arriving by both land and air use roads to experience all that the state has to offer. When combined with mounting pressures placed on roads by growing trade, most of which travels to final destinations via truck, these demands are straining infrastructure that has largely struggled to keep pace. This is especially true in the state's urban areas, like Miami, where the effects of congestion have been particularly painful.[113] (See Table 12-4.) The fact that many of these urban areas are also tourist hot-spots compounds the problem. Despite congestion and other problems, the public's perception of the Florida roads and bridges is relatively positive with more than half (55 percent) of survey respondents rating the state's provision of roads and bridges as "good" or "excellent." (See Figure 12-15.)

Naturally, the huge number of vehicles traveling Florida's roads requires that government pay special attention to controlling the flow of traffic and the safety of drivers and passengers. In 2013, Florida was home to 15.4 million licensed drivers, and traffic enforcement issued more than 3.9 million tickets, 22 percent of which was by Florida Highway Patrol.[114] One goal of issuing tickets is to reduce accidents, especially fatalities. Also in 2013, 316,943 crashes occurred in Florida with 2,402 fatalities. Of the fatalities, 56 percent involved at least suspected influence of alcohol, and nearly half (46 percent) involved motorcycle, pedestrian, and bicycle fatalities. Non-car fatalities are common in part due to tourism and year-round warm weather.

Figure 12-14. Diagram of an Intermodal Logistics Center with State Funding Rates

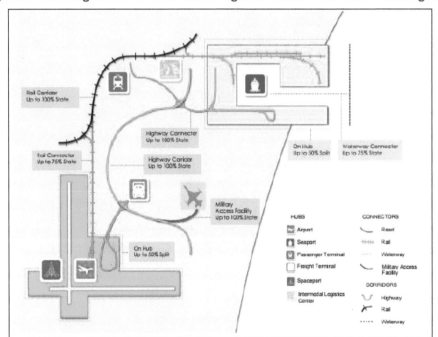

Source: "ILC Support Opportunities," Florida Department of Transportation (following FY 2013/2014). Available at http://www.dot.state.fl.us/planning/systems/programs/mspi/pdf/ILCSupportOppsFinal.pdf.

Taxis and Ridesharing

A relatively new concern that extends beyond the scope of transportation is how government will handle ridesharing services, like Lyft and, notably Uber. Debate ensues when these services defend their status as Silicon Valley tech companies that do nothing more than connect riders and drivers, whom the companies label as independent contractors that are beyond company control.[115] These companies, some of which have deep pockets, are a prime target for criticism.[116] Licensed cab drivers argue that Uber and other rideshare drivers have an unfair advantage because they are not currently subject to the same burdensome regulation. Local governments complain that Uber and Lyft do not have the legally required license and permits and have safety issues. The new ride-sharing companies are also facing pressure from former employees seeking benefits, riders pursuing civil cases after injury, and even the disabled community for alleged mistreatment. This will likely continue to be an issue as lines continue to blur between tech companies and cab service and between independent contractors and employees.[117]

Table 12-4. Most Congested Corridors in U.S.: Ranking of Florida Corridors

Rank	City	Road(s)	From	To
28	Miami	Dolphin Expy WB	12th Ave	FL-959/Red Rd
49	Miami	Palmetto Expy SB	58th St	25th St
113	Tampa	I-275 SB	I-4	US-92/Dale Mabry Hwy/Exit 23
143	Orlando	I-4 EB	FL-423/S John Young Pkwy/Exit 32	FL-423/Lee Rd/Exit 46
215	Miami	Palmetto Expy NB	FL-874	US-27/Okeechobee Rd
216	Miami	FL-821 NB	120th St/Exit 19	US-41/8th St/SW 25th Ter/Exit 25

Source: 2013 Full Year Scorecard Analysis, INRIX. Available at http://inrix.com/worst-corridors/.

Figure 12-15. Public's Perception of Florida's Provision of Roads and Bridges

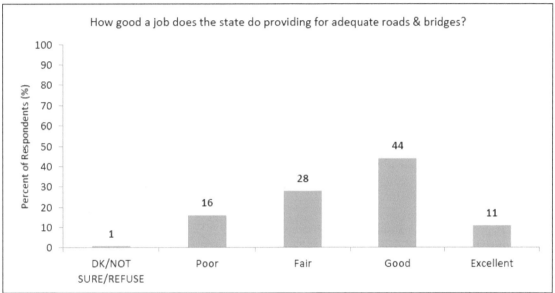

Source: University of South Florida-Nielsen Sunshine State Survey (2014).

World-Class Cruise Industry Shares Waterways

Florida is home to some of the busiest cruise ports in the world. Miami, Port Everglades, and Port Canaveral (rapid growth in recent years) are the three busiest cruise ports in the United States, and Tampa is ranked seventh. (See Figure 12-16.) Growth in the cruise industry is likely to continue with the possibility of cruising to Cuba, which recently opened itself to tourists, and even Asia, where cruising is growing in popularity.[118]

Florida's seaports move cruise passengers and, increasingly (by tonnage) cargo. Tampa and Jacksonville, the two busiest ports by trade tonnage, are projected to see growth with the completion of the Panama Canal expansion project. The expansion (expected completion 2016) is likely to have a significant impact on global trade as it opens the Eastern United States to more, larger (post-Panamax) cruise and cargo ships from Asia and other Pacific ports. The prospect of acute increases in port traffic (See Figure 12-17.), including larger vessels, has prompted Miami, Jacksonville, and other ports on the East Coast of the United States to make big investments in port infrastructure.[119] However, some warn that the impact may be overstated.[120]

Florida is also home to a significant part of America's Intracoastal Waterway, "...a network of canals, inlets, bays and rivers that runs the length of the Eastern Seaboard from Norfolk, Virginia, to the Florida Keys, and along the Gulf of Mexico from Apalachee Bay to Brownsville, Texas."[121] The waterway, which stretches more than 3,000 miles, provides a route for barges and small personal vessels that is more hospitable than the sometimes rough waves of the ocean. The waterway is also connected to inland waterways.

Figure 12-16. Florida Leader in Cruise Embarkations with Port Canaveral Growing Rapidly

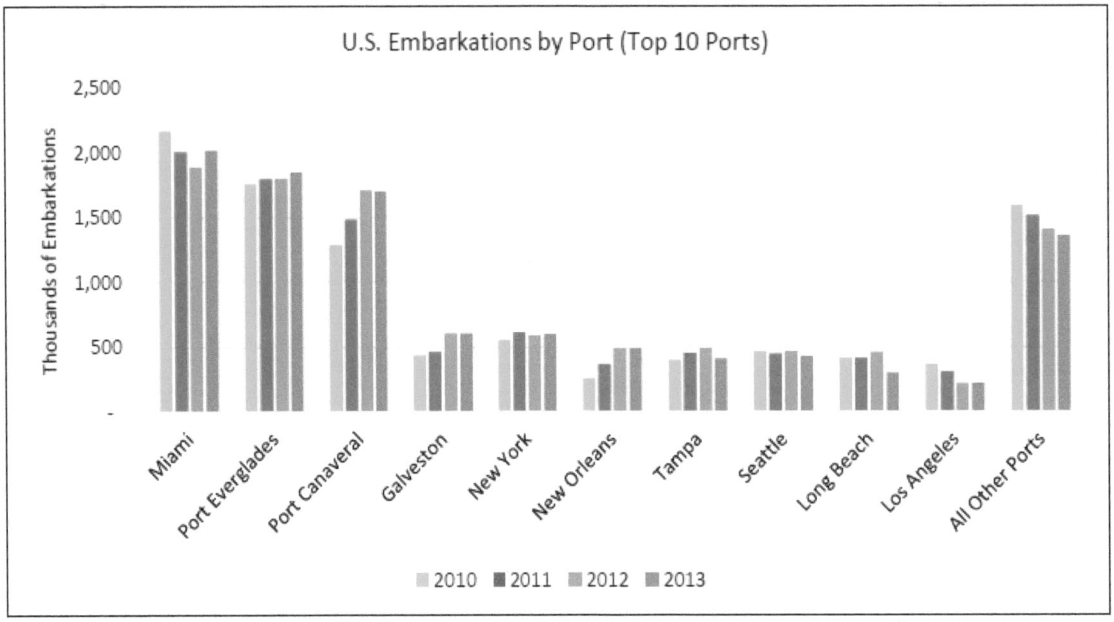

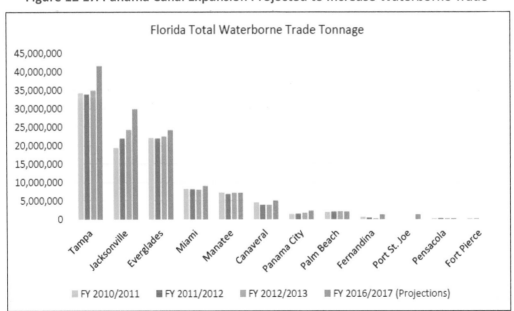

Source: "The Contribution of the North American Cruise Industry to the U.S. Economy in 2013," U.S. Cruise Ports and BREA (September 2014). Available at http://www.cruising.org/sites/default/files/pressroom/US-Economic-Impact-Study-2013Final_20140909.pdf.

Figure 12-17. Panama Canal Expansion Projected to Increase Waterborne Trade

Note: No cargo reported or projected for ports of Citrus, Key West, or St. Petersburg at time of publication.
Source: Individual seaports reported data to Florida Ports Council. Available at http://static.flaports.org/Exh-26.pdf.

Gateways to Tourism and Space

Air travel is vital to Florida's tourism industry and economy. Florida has 19 major commercial airports including four among the 30 busiest in the country: Miami, Orlando, Fort Lauderdale and Tampa.[122] Half of all visitors to the state arrive by plane each year and many companies ship freight by air (Florida ranks 4th among states in total air cargo tonnage).[123] As the entry point for many visitors, airports have the potential of restricting traffic if congestion leads to bottlenecks. The Federal Aviation Administration anticipates that congestion issues at FLL (Fort Lauderdale/Hollywood International) can be avoided if improvements, notably to runways, are made as planned.[124] The FAA also predicts congestion by 2020 at MIA (Miami International) and by 2030 at MCO (Orlando International) and TPA (Tampa International).

Most Florida major commercial airports are owned and operated by local governments (often counties such as Miami-Dade or Broward, or special districts like the Greater Orlando or Hillsborough County Aviation Authority). The airports are funded primarily by passenger fees, rental fees, and charges.

Airports also have to cope with challenges related to relationships with the federal government, including funding and implementing systems to address federal security mandates (Transportation Security Administration, or TSA). Florida airports also have to fight the public misconception that the state government is to blame for delays for international travelers. While most pass through customs in a timely fashion, peak wait times can be exorbitant.[125] In reality, federal U.S. Customs and Border Protection has the most control over wait times.

Florida plays a major role in the most modern transportation mode, space travel. Florida's spaceport system consists of five distinct components: spaceports (launch and re-entry), control centers and airspace (coordination centers), launch vehicles and spacecraft, payload processing facilities (for cargo), and intermodal connections. (See "Intermodal Logistics Centers" above.[126]) The state has two spaceports, Cape Canaveral and the recently licensed Cecil Spaceport. Florida has great history in space travel, and strategic planning is vital in order to compete in the growing market for public and private space travel.

Transportation in Florida is special in many ways. The state presents unique geographic, demographic, economic, and environmental advantages, as well as uncommon challenges to government at all levels. Perhaps most unique about transportation in Florida is that it is so closely intertwined with employment, tourism, and other activities that are essential to the livelihood of Floridians.

Florida is endowed with natural beauty that attracts visitors from around the world, and the state's environment is vital to the quality of life for much of Florida's expanding population. Public policy is needed to attract and retain people and companies (economic development), keep up with increasing demands on transportation and other infrastructure, and even directly or indirectly manage growth (except during economic downturns, when priorities shift to reducing regulation). The geographic, environmental, and demographic characteristics that make Florida unique also challenge leaders at all levels of government throughout the state to keep Florida a great place to work, play, and visit.

ONLINE SOURCES FOR DATA AND INFORMATION UPDATES

U.S. Fish and Wildlife Service

U.S. Fish and Wildlife Service is responsible for conserving, protecting, and enhancing the habitats of wildlife in the U.S. The service provides an index of its national programs, conservation efforts, endangered species, invasive species, environmental contaminants, grants, national wildlife refuges, hunting and permits requirements, and information on wind energy and climate change.
http://www.fws.gov/#

Florida Fish and Wildlife

Florida Fish and Wildlife is in charge of managing Florida's wildlife resources. This site provides Florida-specific information on fishing, hunting, boating, licenses and permits, wildlife viewing, wildlife habitats, research, education, and conservation.
http://myfwc.com/

National Park Service

The NPS manages all national parks, many national monuments, and other conservation or historical sites. The NPS offers information on national parks across the U.S., as well as information on the history of the parks service and environmental issues, such as climate change, biological, and geological resources.
http://www.nature.nps.gov/

Environmental Protection Agency: Laws and Regulations

The EPA protects human health and the environment through regulatory efforts. Regulatory information is available by topic, like acid rain and climate change, and by industry sector, such as agriculture or automotive. The site also has summaries and enforcement records of laws, including the Clean Air Act, the Clean Water Act, and the Endangered Species Act.
http://www2.epa.gov/laws-regulations

Florida Department of Environmental Protection

The DEP is responsible for environmental protection regulations and plans in the state of Florida. This website has information on regulatory programs, land and recreation, water policy, and ecosystem restoration. The site also has publications and reports on each of its regulatory sectors, including state lands, air, beached and coastal systems, springs, and wastewater.
http://www.dep.state.fl.us/

Florida Transportation Commission-Presentations

The FTC acts as a citizen's oversight board on Transportation throughout the state of Florida, offering leadership and guidance. The "Presentations" page has data published by the FTC on topics, such as All Aboard Florida, freight transport, vehicle transport, fuel taxes and user fees, the Department of Transportation, and future transportation plans and projections.
http://www.ftc.state.fl.us/presentations.shtm

Enterprise Florida: Data

Enterprise Florida releases data on Florida communities, industries, trade, economy, and accolades, as well as international trade. Specific data includes information on corporate headquarters, major employers, and economic regions in Florida.
http://www.enterpriseflorida.com/data-center/

Florida League of Cities: Publications and Resources

Florida League of Cities acts as a voice for local government and municipalities, and releases statistical data on Florida cities as well as proposals for local governments. Among the publications are Quality Cities magazine, State of the Cities Report, and the Center for Municipal Research featuring CityStats data.
http://www.floridaleagueofcities.com/Publications.aspx?CNID=182

Florida Redevelopment Association

The FRA, an organization dedicated to assisting community revitalization efforts, offers information on community redevelopment agencies and publications describing the fiscal impacts of community redevelopment agencies and grants to communities.
http://redevelopment.net/

Florida Department of Community Affairs

The Department of Community Affairs puts together information for communities to improve their workforce, local businesses, and local redevelopment. This site has information and publications to help manage growth at the local level, including grant programs, neighborhood stabilization, and disaster recovery.
http://www.floridajobs.org/community-planning-and-development

Sunshine State Survey: Results

The Sunshine State Survey polls Florida residents for their opinions on national and local issues, and includes statistics on the respondent's age, race, gender, party affiliation, employment, etc. The survey has data available from 2006 to 2014 (excluding 2013). Specific data can be found on trust in government leaders, the most important issue facing Florida, opinions on taxing and spending (tax revenue, least fair revenue source, and budget), issue stances, biggest divide for public officials, and the most important leadership quality.
http://sunshinestatesurvey.org/results/

Florida Department of Transportation

The FDOT is in charge of planning and developing safe transportation around the state and provides information about FDOT's basic functions, maps of counties, districts, and state highways, and data on traffic and bridges. FDOT offers information on active construction projects, future project development and public outreach, and long-term plans.
http://www.dot.state.fl.us/agencyresources/mapsanddata.shtm

All Aboard Florida

All Aboard Florida is the group responsible for planning a railway between Orlando and Miami. This website has information about the rail system's plans, route, projected economic impact, and construction costs.
http://www.allaboardflorida.com/

Appendices

APPENDIX A: PROPOSED AMENDMENTS TO FLORIDA'S CONSTITUTION

Year	Type*	Short Title (Amendments in Italics Did Not Pass)	Yes	No
1982	L	Searches and Seizures	63.5	36.5
	L	Pretrial Release and Detention	60.6	39.4
1984	L	Exemption Of Homestead and Personal Property From Forced Sale	79.0	21.0
	L	Disbursement of State Funds	72.8	27.2
	L	Procedures of Judicial Nominating Commissions	82.2	17.8
	L	*Speech Or Debate Privilege*	33.4	66.6
	L	Election Of County Commissioners By Single Member District	64.3	35.7
	L	Eligibility To Be A County Court Judge	75.4	24.6
	L	Bonds For State Capital Projects	65.4	34.6
	L	Public Education Capital Outlay Bonds - PECO	76.6	23.4
1986	L	Statewide Prosecutor	72.8	27.2
	I	*Casino Gambling*	31.7	68.3
	L	*Homestead Tax Exemption*	35.5	64.5
	L	Supreme Court Initiative On Proposed Initiatives	72.4	36.4
	I	State Operated Lotteries	63.6	36.4
1988	L	Impeachment Of County Court Judges	72.3	27.7
	L	Rights Of Victims Crimes	90.2	9.8
	L	Assessment Of High Water Recharge Lands	67.1	32.9
	L	Bonds For State Roads Or For Constructing Bridges	57.2	42.8
	L	Property Tax Exemption For Widowers	85.2	14.8
	L	Taxation And Budget Reform Commission	57.8	42.2
	L	*Terms Of Office For Trial Court Judges*	37.9	62.1
	L	Civil Traffic Hearing Officers	70.5	29.5
	L	Departments Of Veterans Affairs And Elderly Affairs	69.0	31.0
	I	*Limitation Of Non-Economic Damages In Civil Actions*	43.4	56.6
	I	English Is The Official Language Of Florida	83.9	16.1
1990	L	Regular Legislative Session	83.6	16.4
	L	Three Day Waiting Period For Handgun Purchases	84.5	15.5
	L	Laws Affecting Local Governmental Expenditures Or Revenue	64.0	36.0
	L	Open Government	87.7	12.3
1992	L	Emergency Suspension Or Delay Of General Election	71.6	28.4
	L	Access To Public Records And Meetings	83.0	17.0
	L	Historic Preservation Ad Valorem Tax Exemption	62.4	37.6
	TBRC	State Budgeting, Planning, And Appropriations Processes	82.7	17.3
	TBRC	Taxpayers' Bill Of Rights	90.0	10.0
	TBRC	*Authorize Local Government To Levy 1 Cent Tax With Voter Approval*	40.0	60.0
	TBRC	Bonds For The Construction Of Educational Facilities	67.9	32.1
	I	Limited Political Terms In Certain Elective Offices	76.8	23.2
	I	Homestead Valuation Limitation	53.6	46.4
1994	L	Start Of Regular Session Of The Legislature	74.0	26.0
	L	Limitations On State Revenue Collection	59.4	40.6
	I	Limiting Marine Net Fishing	71.7	28.3
	I	Initiatives Limiting Government Revenue May Cover Multiple Subjects	58.1	41.9
	I	*Limited Casinos*	38.0	62.0
1996	I	Tax Limitation	69.3	30.7
	L	Constitution Revision Commission	61.4	38.6
	L	Judiciary	74.9	25.1
	I	*Fee On Everglades Sugar Production*	45.6	54.4
	I	Responsibility For Paying Costs Of Water Pollution	68.1	31.9
	I	Everglades Trust Fund	57.3	42.7
1998	L	Historic Property Tax Exemption And Assessment	54.5	45.5
	L	Preservation Of The Death Penalty; Interpretation Of Cruel And Unusual	72.8	27.2
	L	Additional Homestead Exemption	68.5	31.5
	L	Recording Of Instruments In Branch Offices	74.1	25.9

	CRC	Creation Of Fish And Wildlife Conservation Commission	72.3	27.7
	CRC	Public Education Of Children	71.0	29.0
	CRC	Local Option For Selection Of Judges And Funding Of State Courts	56.9	43.1
	CRC	Restructuring The State Cabinet	55.5	44.5
	CRC	Basic Rights	66.3	33.7
	CRC	*Local And Municipality Property Tax Exemptions*	49.8	50.2
	CRC	Ballot Access, Public Campaign Financing, And Election Process Revisions	64.1	35.9
	CRC	Firearms Purchases: Local Option Criminal History Records/Waiting Period	72.0	28.0
	CRC	Miscellaneous Matters And Technical Revisions	55.0	45.0
2000	I	Florida Transportation Initiative For Statewide High Speed Rail	52.7	47.3
	CRC**	*Shall Circuit Court Judges Be Selected By Merit System?*	32.0	68.0
	CRC**	*Shall County Court Judges Be Selected By Merit System?*	26.0	74.0
2002	L	Amending Article I, Section 17 Of The State Constitution	69.7	30.3
	L	Economic Impact Statements For Proposed Constitutional Amendments	78.0	22.0
	L	*Authorizing Amendments To Miami-Dade County Home Rule Charter*	47.8	52.2
	L	Public Records Or Meetings Exemptions; Two-Thirds Vote Required	76.6	23.4
	I	Protection From 2nd-Hand Smoke By Prohibiting Workplace Smoking	71.0	29.0
	L	Exemption For Construction Of Living Quarters For Parents/Grandparents	67.3	32.7
	I	Voluntary Universal Pre-Kindergarten Education	59.2	40.8
	I	Florida's Amendment To Reduce Class Size	52.4	47.6
	I	Animal Cruelty Amendment: Limiting Confinement Of Pregnant Pigs	54.8	45.2
	I	Local Trustees & Statewide Board To Manage Florida's University System	60.5	39.5
2004	L	Parental Notification Of A Minor's Termination Of Pregnancy	64.7	35.3
	L	Constitutional Amendment Proposed By Initiative	68.4	31.6
	I	The Medical Liability Claimant's Compensation Amendment	63.6	36.4
	I	Miami-Dade & Broward Voters May Approve Slots In Pari-mutuel Facilities	50.8	49.2
	I	Florida Minimum Wage Increased to $6.15 per hour & Indexed to Inflation	71.3	28.7
	I	Repeal Of The High Speed Rail Amendment	63.7	36.3
	I	Patients' Right To Know About Adverse Medical Incidents	81.2	18.8
	I	Public Protection From Repeated Medical Malpractice	71.1	28.9
2006	L	State Planning and Budget Process (Limit Use of Non-recurring Revenue)	59.8	40.2
	L	Requiring Broader Public Support For Constitutional Amendments (60%)	57.8	42.2
	I	Protection From Addiction, Disease & Health Hazards Of Using Tobacco	60.9	39.1
	L	Increase Additional Homestead Exemption to $50k for Poor Seniors	76.4	23.6
	L	Permanently Disabled Veterans' Discount On Homestead Ad Valorem Tax	77.8	22.2
	L	Eminent Domain: Prohibits Transfer of Private Property to Private Entity	69.0	31.0
2008	L	Increase Property Tax Exemptions; Limitations on Property Tax Assessment (Voted on during Pres. Primary)	64.0	36.0
	L	*Declaration Of Rights (Repeal of Property Restrictions on non-citizens)*	47.9	52.1
	I	Florida Marriage Protection Amendment	61.9	38.1
	TBRC	Changes And Improvements Not Affecting The Assessed Value Of Residential Real Property	60.5	39.5
	TBRC	Property Tax Exemption Of Perpetually Conserved Land; Classification And Assessment Of Land Used For Conservation	68.6	31.4
	TBRC	Assessment Of Working Waterfront Property Based Upon Current Use	70.6	29.4
	TBRC	*Local Option Community College Funding*	43.5	56.5
2010	L	Repeal Of Public Campaign Financing Requirement	52.5	47.5
	L	Homestead Ad Valorem Tax Credit For Deployed Military Personnel	77.8	22.2
	I	*Referenda Required For Adoption And Amendment Of Local Government Comprehensive Land Use Plans.*	32.9	67.1
	I	Standards For Legislature To Follow In Legislative Redistricting	62.6	37.4
	I	Standards For Legislature To Follow In Congressional Redistricting	62.9	37.1
	L	*Revision Relaxing The Class Size Requirements For Public Schools*	54.5	45.5
	L	Balancing The Federal Budget (A Nonbinding Referendum - not a Constitutional Amendment)	71.9	28.1
2012	L	*Prohibit Laws Compelling Purchase of Health Care Coverage*	48.5	51.5
	L	Homestead Property Tax Discount for Veterans Disabled Due to Combat Injury	63.3	36.7
	L	*Replace Revenue Limitation Based on Income Growth with One Based on Inflation and Population Change*	42.4	57.6
	L	*Property Tax Limitations: Property Value Decline; Non-Homestead Assessment*	43.2	56.8
	L	*Allow Legislature to Repeal Rules of State Court with Majority Vote; Require Senate Confirmation of Florida Supreme Court Justices*	37.0	63.0
	L	*Prohibition on Public Funding of Abortions; FL Constitution May Not Create Broader Rights to Abortion than the U.S. Constitution*	44.9%	55.1%

	L	*Religious Freedom: Repeal Prohibition of Using State Funds Directly or Indirectly On Sectarian Institutions*	44.5	55.5
	L	Homestead Property Tax Exemption For Surviving Spouse of Military Veteran or First Responder	61.7%	38.3%
	L	*Tax Exemption for Tangible Personal Property Valued at $25,000-$50,000*	45.5	54.5
	L	Additional Homestead Exemption: Low Income Seniors Who Maintain Long-Term Residency	61.3	38.7
	L	*Appointment of Student Body President to Board of Governors*	41.5	58.5
2014	I	Water and Land Conservation: Dedicated Funds to Acquire & Restore	75.0	25.0
	I	*Use of Medical Marijuana for Certain Medical Conditions*	57.6	42.4
	L	*Prospective Appointment of Certain Judicial Vacancies*	47.9	52.1

*Type (How Proposed): I = Initiative, L = Legislature, TBRC = Taxation and Budget Reform Commission, CRC = Constitutional Revision Commission

**In 1998, voters approved an amendment to allow each county and circuit to vote on changing their method of judicial selection from partisan election to merit selection. The proposals were then defeated in each county and circuit in 2000. The vote percentage is the statewide average for county and circuit.

APPENDIX B: FLORIDA COUNTY SEATS, DATE FOUNDED, AND SQUARE MILEAGE

County	County Seat	Date Founded	Square Miles
Alachua County	Gainesville	1824	874
Baker County	Macclenny	1861	585
Bay County	Panama City	1913	764
Bradford County	Starke	1858	293
Brevard County	Titusville	1844	1,018
Broward County	Fort Lauderdale	1915	1,209
Calhoun County	Blountstown	1838	567
Charlotte County	Punta Gorda	1921	694
Citrus County	Inverness	1887	584
Clay County	Green Cove Springs	1858	601
Collier County	Naples	1923	2,026
Columbia County	Lake City	1832	797
DeSoto County	Arcadia	1887	637
Dixie County	Cross City	1921	704
Duval County/City of Jacksonville	Jacksonville	1822	774
Escambia County	Pensacola	1822	664
Flagler County	Bunnell	1917	485
Franklin County	Apalachicola	1832	534
Gadsden County	Quincy	1823	516
Gilchrist County	Trenton	1925	349
Glades County	Moore Haven	1921	774
Gulf County	Port Saint Joe	1925	565
Hamilton County	Jasper	1827	515
Hardee County	Wauchula	1921	637
Hendry County	La Belle	1923	1,153
Hernando County	Brooksville	1843	478
Highlands County	Sebring	1921	1,028
Hillsborough County	Tampa	1834	1,051
Holmes County	Bonifay	1848	482
Indian River County	Vero Beach	1925	503
Jackson County	Marianna	1822	916
Jefferson County	Monticello	1827	598
Lafayette County	Mayo	1856	543
Lake County	Tavares	1887	953
Lee County	Fort Myers	1887	804
Leon County	Tallahassee	1824	667
Levy County	Bronson	1845	1,118
Liberty County	Bristol	1855	836
Madison County	Madison	1827	692
Manatee County	Bradenton	1855	741
Marion County	Ocala	1844	1,579
Martin County	Stuart	1925	556
Miami-Dade County	Miami	1836	1,945
Monroe County	Key West	1823	997
Nassau County	Fernandina Beach	1824	652
Okaloosa County	Crestview	1915	936
Okeechobee County	Okeechobee	1917	774
Orange County	Orlando	1824	908
Osceola County	Kissimmee	1887	1,322
Palm Beach County	West Palm Beach	1909	2,034
Pasco County	Dade City	1887	745
Pinellas County	Clearwater	1911	280
Polk County	Bartow	1861	1,875
Putnam County	Palatka	1849	722
Santa Rosa County	Milton	1842	1,016

Sarasota County	Sarasota	1921	572
Seminole County	Sanford	1913	308
St. Johns County	Saint Augustine	1822	609
St. Lucie County	Fort Pierce	1844	572
Sumter County	Bushnell	1853	546
Suwannee County	Live Oak	1858	688
Taylor County	Perry	1856	1,042
Union County	Lake Butler	1921	240
Volusia County	De Land	1854	1,106
Wakulla County	Crawfordville	1843	607
Walton County	Defuniak Springs	1824	1,058
Washington County	Chipley	1825	580

Source: National Association of Counties, online at
http://www.naco.org/Template.cfm?Section=Find_a_County&Template=/
cffiles/counties/state.cfm&statecode=fl. Accessed August 10, 2006.

Notes

CHAPTER 1

[1] David R. Colburn, From *Yellow Dog Democrats to Red State Republicans: Florida and Its Politics Since 1940*. Gainesville, FL: University Press of Florida, 2007: 4. The quote about Florida being the "real deal" was made by Dan Rather, former CBS Evening News anchor during the 2000 election.

[2] Estimate by Stefan Rayer, population program director of the Bureau of Economic and Business Research at the University of Florida in Mike Schneider, Associated Press, "Florida Now No. 3 State in Population," accessed March 27, 2015.

[3] Susan A. MacManus, "Florida: The South's Premier Battleground State," *American Review of Politics* 26 (Summer 2005): 155-184.

[4] Data are from politicalmoneyline.com, March 1, 2005.

[5] MacManus, "Florida: The South's Premier Battleground State."

[6] See David R. Colburn and Lance deHaven-Smith, *Florida's Megatrends: Critical Issues in Florida*. Gainesville, FL: University Press, 2002.

[7] Tom Fiedler, "A Sense of Rootlessness," in *The Florida Handbook*, 1997-1998, ed. Allen Morris. Tallahassee, FL: Peninsular Press, 1997, p. 557.

[8] Lance deHaven Smith, *The Florida Voter*. Tallahassee, FL: Florida Institute of Government, 1995, p. 3.

[9] Sourced: Mike Schneider, Associated Press, "10 Important Events in Fla. in the 21st Century," *The Tampa Tribune*, January 3, 2014; Kate Gibson, "The 9 Fastest-Growing Metro Areas in the U.S.," CBS News, March 26, 2015; The Associated Press, "Six of Fastest-Growing Cities Are in Florida," Gainesville Sun, March 26, 2015.

[10] See Gary R. Mormino, *Land of Sunshine, State of Dreams: A Social History of Modern Florida*. Gainesville, FL: University Press of Florida, 2005.

[11] See David R. Colburn, "Florida Politics in the 20th Century," in *The New History of Florida*, ed. Michael Gannon. Gainesville, FL: University of Florida Press, 1996.

[12] Bureau of Economic and Business Research, *Florida Population: Census Summary 2010*. Gainesville, FL: University of Florida, April 2011.

[13] Palmetto Bay, Miami Lakes, Miami Gardens, Doral, Cutler Bay, West Park, Southwest Ranches, Grant-Valkaria, Loxahatchee Groves. Bureau of Economic and Business Research, "Florida Population: Census Summary 2010." Available at http://www.bebr.ufl.edu/sites/default/files/population/Census_Summary_2010.pdf.

[14] Stanley K. Smith, Scott Cody, and Stefan Rayer, "Revised Annual Population Estimates for Florida and Its Counties, 2000-2010, With Components of Growth," Gainesville, FL: Bureau of Economic and Business Research, University of Florida, Special Population Reports, Number 7, May 2011: 2.

[15] Mark Vitner and Joe Seydl, "Florida Economic Outlook: February 2011," Wells Fargo Securities, February 14, 2011. Available at www.wellsfargo.com/research.

[16] "Florida's Population Center Migrates Through History," Gainesville, FL: Bureau of Economic and Business Research, University of Florida, accessed April 2015.

[17] Office of Economic & Demographic Research, The Florida Legislature, "Population and Population Change for Metropolitan Statistical Areas in Florida—2014 estimate. Accessed May 5, 2015 at http://edr.state.fl.us/Content/population-demographics/data/MSA-2014.pdf.

[18] Susan A. MacManus, "It's All About Jobs: What the Term *Economic Development* Means to Floridians in Tough Economic Times," column posted on sayfiereview.com, September 28, 2009.

[19] Susan A. MacManus, *Florida's Minority Trailblazers*. Gainesville, FL: University Press of Florida (forthcoming 2016).

[20] Ronald Brownstein, "The States That Will Pick the President: The Sunbelt," *National Journal*, February 4, 2015.

[21] Kevin A. Hill, Susan A. MacManus, and Dario Moreno, eds. *Florida Politics: Ten Media Markets, One Powerful State*. Tallahassee, FL: John Scott Dailey Florida Institute of Government, Florida State University, 2004.

[22] See Andrea Greenbaum, ed., *Jews of South Florida*. Waltham, MA: Brandeis University Press, 2005.

[23] Drew Desilver, "The Politics of American Generations: How Age Affects Attitudes and Voting Behavior," Pew Research Center, July 9, 2014.

[24] Presidents at the time members of that generation turned 18 years of age.

[25] Desilver, op.cit.; Kenwood Hearing Center, "Communicating Across Generations," November 14, 2014; available at http://www.kenhear.com/communicating-across-generations.; Jill Novak, "The Six Living Generations in America," MarketingTeacher.com, May, 2014.

[26] Thom File, "Young-Adult Voting: An Analysis of Presidential Elections, 1964-2012," U.S. Census Bureau, April 2014. Accessed May 5, 2015 at https://www.census.gov/prod/2014pubs/p20-573.pdf.

[27] Susan A. MacManus, *Targeting Senior Voters: Campaign Outreach to Elders and Others With Special Needs*. Boulder, CO: Rowman & Littlefield, 2000.

[28] CNN. Available at http://www.cnn.com/ELECTION/2004/pages/results/states/FL/P/00/epolls.0.html; http://www.cnn.com/ELECTION/2008/results/individual/#FLP00.

[29] Walter A. Rosenbaum and James W. Button, "Is There a Gray Peril? Retirement Politics in Florida," *Gerontologist* 29 (1995): 301.

[30] Pew Forum on Religion and Public Life, "U.S. Religious Landscape Study," national survey conducted May 8-August 13, 2007. Available at http://religions.pewforum.org/maps.

[31] Mark S. Krzos and Denes Husty III, "Asians Flock to SW Florida," Fort Myers *News-Press*, April 3, 2011.

[32] Asian American Federation of Florida, "AAFF." Available at http://asianamericanfederation.org.

[33] Toluse Olorunnipa, "South Florida Leading National Census Trend," *The Miami Herald*, March 18, 2011.

[34] Immigration Policy Center, "New Americans in the Sunshine State," July 2010. Available at www.immigrationpolicy.org/just-facts/new-americans-sunshine-state-0.

[35] NALEO Educational Fund, "2010 Census Profiles: Florida." Available at http://www.naleo.org/downloads/FL_Census_2010_Profile_fin03-11.pdf.

[36] Pew Research Center, "The 2010 Congressional Reapportionment and Latinos," January 5, 2011. Available at http://pewresearch.org/pubs/1845/2010-congrssional-reapportionment-hispanics.

[37] *Smith v. Allwright*, 321 US 649 (1944).

[38] *Brown v Board of Education of Topeka Kansas*, 347 US 483 (1954).

[39] In 2015, 17 percent of Florida's legislators were African American compared to 16 percent of Florida's population.

[40] The three districts drawn in 1992 to enhance the opportunity for black representation in Congress were Florida's Third, Seventeenth, and Twenty-third Districts. The Third District stretched from Jacksonville to Orlando in an effort to incorporate black communities in Northeast and Central Florida. After the U.S. Supreme Court ordered the redrawing of its lines in 1996, the district became less than 50 percent black, but African-American Congresswoman Corrine Brown still retained her seat. Florida's Seventeenth District, which was represented by African-American Carrie Meek, included most of Miami-Dade County's black communities, including Liberty City. Florida's lengthy Twenty-third District combined black neighborhoods from northern Miami-Dade County, through Fort Lauderdale, to West Palm Beach. It was represented by the controversial Alcee Hastings, who as a federal judge, was impeached by the U.S. House of Representatives and convicted by the U.S. Senate in 1988. (Hastings' rebuttal is that he was acquitted of wrongdoing in a criminal trial.)

[41] For a detailed analysis of the 2012 redistricting process and its impacts, see Seth C. McKee, *Jigsaw Puzzle Politics in the Sunshine State*, Gainesville, FL: University Press of Florida (forthcoming 2015).

[42] For a good summary of the congressional map controversies prior to the 2015 Florida Supreme Court's ruling on plaintiffs' request to adopt an alternative congressional redistricting map, see Mary Ellen Klas, "Florida Supreme Court Hears One More Challenge to Congressional District Maps," *Tampa Bay Times*, March 4, 2014.

[43] See Mary Mederios Kent, "Immigration and America's Black Population," *Population Bulletin* 62 (December 2007), p. 8.

[44] Cedric Audebert, "Residential Patterns and Political Empowerment Among Jamaicans and Haitians in the U.S. Metropolis: The Role of Ethnicity in New York and South Florida," *Human Architecture: Journal of the Sociology of Self-Knowledge*, 7 (Fall, 2009): 53-68.

[45] See Kent, op. cit.

[46] Audebert, op. cit., p. 54.

[47] Chiamaka Nwosu and Jeanne Batalova, "Haitian Immigrants in the United States: Migration Policy Institute, May 29, 2014. Data are from the U.S. Census American Community Surveys, 2008-2012.

[48] José Patiño Girona, "More Haitians Make Tampa Bay Their Home." *Tampa Tribune*, October 26, 2016.

[49] Audebert, op. cit.

[50] Audebert, op. cit., p. 64.

[51] "Where Jamaicans Live." Available at www. Jamaicans.com/jamaicansoverseas/Miami/whrewelive.htm; also see Audebert, op. cit.

[52] Maxine D. Jones, Larry E. Rivers, David R. Colburn, R. Thomas Dye, and William W. Rogers, *A Documented History of the Incident Which Occurred at Rosewood, Florida in 1923: A Report Submitted to the Florida Board of Regents. Tallahassee*, FL: Florida State Archives, December 1993.

[53] As featured in Rosewood, the motion picture released by Warner Brothers, produced and directed by John Singleton, starring Jon Voight.

[54] NALEO, March 18, 2011, op. cit.

[55] NALEO Educational Fund, "2010 Census Profiles: Florida." Available at http://www.naleo.org/downloads/FL_Census_2010_Profile_fin03-11.pdf.

[56] Mike Schneider and Laura Wides-Munoz, "Central Fla. Hispanic Population Surging," The Associated Press, May 2, 2011. Available at http://www.bradenton.com/2011/05/02/3157936/central-fla-hispanic-population.html.

[57] In 2006, African Americans comprised 14 percent of the Florida electorate; Hispanics, 11 percent. The higher black turnout was a function of an African American on the ballot (the running mate of Democratic gubernatorial candidate Jim Davis) and growing animosity toward Republican President George W. Bush.

[58] Dario Moreno, "Broward Hispanic Poll," May 16, 2010.

[59] Ibid.

[60] Jose E. Serrano, "Hispanic Americans in Congress, 1822-1995." Available at www.loc.gov/rr/hispanic/congress/introduction.html.

[61] In 2010, Lincoln Diaz-Balart decided not to run again. His brother Mario ran from Lincoln's old district. David Riviera was elected to Mario's old seat. All are Cuban-American Republicans.

[62] NALEO Educational Fund, "A Profile of Latino Elected Officials in the United States and Their Progress Since 1996." Available at http://www.naleo.org/downloads/DirecSummary2010B.pdf.

[63] Cubans can be denied entry to the United States and returned to Cuba if intercepted at sea before stepping foot on U.S. soil.

[64] Broward, Hardee, Hendry, Hillsborough, Miami-Dade, Orange, Lee, Osceola, Palm Beach, and Polk counties.

[65] John F. Stack, Christopher L. Warren, and Dario A. Moreno, "Politics and the Challenge of Ethnicity," in *Government and Politics in Florida*, 2nd edition, ed. Robert J. Huckshorn. Gainesville, FL: University Press of Florida, 1998.

[66] Christopher L. Warren, "Hispanic Incorporation and Structural Reform in Miami," in *Racial Politics in American Cities* 2nd edition, ed. Rufus P. Browning, Dale Rogers Marshall, and David Tabb. New York: Longman, 1997.

[67] Elie Mambou, "South Africans and Mexicans in Florida: Intergroup Conflict," *Journal of Black Studies*, March 2011.

[68] Carl L. Bankston III, "Cubans and African Americans," *African American History*. Salem Press, August 2005. Also see Marvin Dunn, *Black Miami in the Twentieth Century*. Gainesville: University Press of Florida, 1997.

[69] G. Scott Thomas, *The United States of Suburbia*. Amherst, NY: Prometheus, 1998.

[70] For an excellent overview of interracial political conflict at the local level, see Rodney E. Hero and Robert R. Preuhs, *Black-Latino Relations in U.S. National Politics*, New York: Cambridge University Press, 2013.

[71] James G. Gimpel and Frank Morris, "Immigration, Intergroup Conflict, and the Erosion of African American Political Power in the 21st Century," Center for Immigration Studies, February 2007. Available at www.cis.org/AfricanAmericanPoliticalPower-Immigration.

[72] Stefan Rayer, "Asians in Florida," Bureau of Economic and Business Research, University of Florida, n.d. Accessed May 7, 2015 at https://www.bebr.ufl.edu/articles/population-studies/asians-florida.

[73] Wendell Cox, "Asians: America's Fastest Growing Minority," newgeography.com, January 12, 2015. Available at http://www.newgeography.com/content/004825-asians-americas-fastest-growing-minority.

[74] Tim Mak, "Asian-Americans Are The New Florida," *The Daily Beast*, January 8. 2015. Available at http://www.thedailybeast.com/articles/2015/01/08/asian-americans-are-the-new-florida.html.

[75] Asian Women in Business, "Florida." Accessed May 7, 2015, at http://www.awib.org/index.cfm?fuseaction=page.viewPage&pageID=837&nodeID=1.

[76] United States Census Bureau, *The 2011 Statistical Abstract*, "State Rankings" http://www.census.gov/compendia/statab/2011/ranks/rank13.html

[77] "The Seminole Tribe," *Sun-Sentinel*. Available at http://www.sun-sentinel.com/topic/social-issues/minority-groups/the-seminole-tribe-ORCUL000056-topic.html.

[78] For a more detailed account of the history, culture, and government of the Seminole and Miccosukee tribes from their own perspective, see www.semtribe.com/.

[79] The Seminole Tribe. Available at http://www.semtribe.com/Government/.

[80] The Miccosukee Tribe. Accessed May 7, 2015 at www.miccosukee.com/tribe.

[81] See Harry A. Kersey, Jr. *An Assumption of Sovereignty: Social and Political Transformation Among the Florida Seminoles*, 1953-1979. Lincoln, NE: University of Nebraska Press, 1996.

[82] "NCAA Bans Indian Mascots during Postseason," Associated Press, August 5, 2005. Available at http://usatoday30.usatoday.com/sports/college/2005-08-05-indian-mascots-ruling_x.htm.

[83] Steve Wieberg, "NCAA Allowing Florida State to Use Its Seminole Mascot" *USA Today*, August 23, 2005. Available at http://usatoday30.usatoday.com/sports/college/2005-08-23-fsu-mascot-approved_x.htm.

[84] Frank Newport and Gary J. Gates, "San Francisco Metro Area Ranks Highest in LGBT Percentage," March 20, 2015. Data were from Gallup Daily tracking interviews conducted between June 2012 and December 2014. Available at http://www.gallup.com/poll/182051/san-francisco-metro-area-ranks-highest-lgbt-percentage.aspx.

[85] Diane C. Lade, "Wilton Manors: A Perfect 100 in Best Gay Cities Ranking," *Sun Sentinel*, November 29, 2014.

[86] Equality Means Business, "The Link Between Economic Competitiveness and Workplace Equal Opportunity in Florida," March, 2015. Available at https://drive.google.com/file/d/0B53y9MHaclfrM3AtNWxJenp2aVk/view.

[87] Aaron Mesmer, "St. Pete Council Swears in 2 Openly Gay Members," myfoxtampabay.com, February 28, 2014.

[88] Denis Dyson, "LGB or T? Learn How to Run for Office," *Gay Politics*, January 20, 2010. Available at https://www.victoryfund.org/our-story/gaypolitics/2010/01/20/lgb-or-t-learn-how-to-run-for-office-and-win/.

[89] Equality Florida Action Network, Inc. Available at http://www.eqfl.org/Safe_Schools.

[90] Enterprise Florida, "Why Florida?" (2015). Available at http://www.enterpriseflorida.com/wp-content/uploads/why-florida-fast-facts.pdf.

[91] U.S. Chamber of Commerce, Bureau of Economic Analysis, accessed May 2015.

[92] Linares, Jennifer, "Florida TaxWatch Economic Commentary," Florida TaxWatch. (April 2015). Available at http://www.floridataxwatch.org/resources/pdf/Apr15ECFINAL.pdf.

[93] Florida TaxWatch, "Investing in Tourism: Analyzing the Economic Impact of Expanding Florida Tourism" (Jan. 2013). Available at http://floridataxwatch.org/resources/pdf/2013TourismFINAL.pdf.

[94] Florida Citrus Mutual, "Citrus Industry History" (2012). Available at http://www.flcitrusmutual.com/citrus-101/citrushistory.aspx.

[95] Jeff Harrington, "Florida economy growing in the 'right' way, economist says," *Tampa Bay Times* (Nov. 19, 2015). Available at http://www.tampabay.com/news/business/economicdevelopment/report-shows-florida-economy-growing-in-the-right-way/2207134.

[96] Scott Drenkard and Joseph Henchman, "2015 State Business Tax Climate Index," Tax Foundation (Oct. 28, 2014). Available at http://taxfoundation.org/article/2015-state-business-tax-climate-index.

[97] Michael Pollick, "Florida leading way in recovery," *Herald-Tribune* (May 2, 2015). Available at http://www.heraldtribune.com/article/20150502/ARTICLE/305029997?p=1&tc=pg.

CHAPTER 2

[1] Susan A. MacManus, "Implementing Florida's Constitutional Amendments: Truth and Consequences," *The Journal of the James Madison Institute* 31 (Spring 2005): 39-51.

[2] Florida Statutes are available online at the Florida legislature's website, www.leg.state.fl.us.

[3] The Florida Administrative Code is available online at https://www.flrules.org/.

[4] Many county and city codes for Florida and other states can be found at https://www.municode.com/ on the Municipal Code Corporation website.

[5] Florida Cases, in *Southern Reporter*, 2nd Series. St. Paul, MN: West Publishing Co., 1997. Decisions made by the Florida Supreme Court since 1995 are available online at www.flcourts.org/ and at websites run by both the University of Florida College of Law and Florida State University College of Law.

[6] http://www.wfsu.org/gavel2gavel/index.php: This link provides access to oral argument archives in front of the Florida Supreme Court.

[7] See https://www.floridamemory.com/collections/constitution/ to view Florida's early constitutions online. Print versions of the texts of the Constitutions of 1838, 1861, 1865 and 1868 may be found in *Florida Statutes* 1941, Volume 3, labeled "Useful and Helpful Matter." The 1885 Constitution as amended can be found in various editions of *The Florida Handbook* prior to 1965-1966. A fairly detailed summary of the first five Florida Constitutions can be found in The Florida Handbook 1999-2000, ed. Allen Morris. Tallahassee, FL: Peninsular Press, 1999, pp. 673-676

[8] From Associated Press, "Florida Bill Passes on Autopsy Photos," *Los Angeles Times*, March 30, 2001. Available at http://articles.latimes.com/2001/mar/30/sports/sp-44558.

[9] See the July 1, 2003 disposition from the Supreme Court of Florida referencing SC02-1635 (Lower Tribunal No. 5D01-2419) *Campus Communications Inc. v Teresa Earnhardt et. al.*

[10] The full updated text of the Florida Constitution is available online at http://www.leg.state.fl.us/Statutes/Index.cfm?Mode=Constitution&Submenu=3&Tab=statutes.

[11] MacManus, "Implementing Florida's Constitutional Amendments."

[12] The Constitutional Revision Commission will meet next in 2017 and then the Tax and Budget Reform Commission will meet in 2027.

[13] The original version stated that the proposal was "consistent with the U.S. Constitution" while the reworded version that appeared on the ballot stated that the proposal would be in effect "except as required by the First Amendment to the U.S. Constitution." See the letter from Florida Attorney General Pam Bondi to the Secretary of State at http://election.dos.state.fl.us/initiatives/pdf/2012Amd_ReligiousFreedom_ATGLetter.pdf.

[14] For instance in 2005, the Division of Elections rejected a petition pertaining to redistricting because the ballot summary was several words over the seventy-five word limit.

[15] See Robert A. Kurfirst "The Second Time Around: Florida's Constitutional Revision Commission Meets with Success," *Political Chronicle* 12 (Spring 2000): 4-14.

[16] Susan A. MacManus, "Major Tax Reform Via State Constitutional Revision: A Tough Sell in Today's Antigovernment Environment." *Madison Review* 3 (Fall, 1997): 22-27.

[17] The U.S. Supreme Court held that a state may not prohibit financial payments for the circulation of petitions in Meger v Grant, 486 U.S. 414 (1988).

[18] For an excellent historical overview of special interest group use of the initiative process, see Daniel A. Smith, "Special Interests and Direct Democracy: An Historical Glance," in M. Dane Waters, ed., *The Battle Over Citizen Lawmaking.* Durham, NC: Carolina Academic Press, 2001.

[19] Arguments for and against the initiative process in Florida can be found in *Madison Review* 2, no. 4 (Summer 1997), published by the James Madison Institute, Tallahassee.

[20] Susan A. MacManus (with Kristine Zooberg and Andrew Quecan), "Education Matters! Informing Voters About Impending Constitutional Amendments," *The Journal of the James Madison Institute,* Fall 2006

[21] Mark Pritchett and Bob McClure, "Poll Shows Public Distrust of Amendment Process," *The Journal of the James Madison Institute* 30 (Winter 2005): 4-6, 11.

[22] Information for this section comes from MacManus, "Implementing Florida's Constitutional Amendments," p. 42.

CHAPTER 3

[1] Scott Keeter, "Ask the Expert," Pew Research Center Publications, December 9, 2010. Available at http://pewresearch.org/pubs/1770/ask-the-expert-pew-research-center.

[2] Robert Weissberg, "Why Policymakers Should Ignore Public Opinion Polls," *Policy Analysis,* May 29, 2001.

[3] Mark Blumenthal, "So What 'Is' A Push Poll?" Pollster.com, August 22, 2006. Available at http://www.pollster.com/blogs/so_what_is_a_push_poll.html

[4] The Florida Annual Policy Survey reports, data, and codebooks are available at http://survey.coss.fsu.edu/FAPS/. The survey was discontinued for financial reasons.

[5] Gallup Opinion Polls; See Arthur H. Miller, "Confidence in Government During the 1980s," *American Politics Quarterly* 19 (April 1991): 147-73.

[6] In FAPS surveys, the question was "What is the most important *problem* facing the state of Florida today?"

[7] Discussion is based on a question asked in the 2010 Leadership Florida/Nielsen Sunshine State Survey: "If the State Legislature has to reduce current spending levels to help balance the state budget, which of the following service areas would you recommend be reduced first?" See third edition of *Politics in Florida.*

[8] Susan A. MacManus, *Young v. Old: Generational Combat in the 21st Century.* Boulder, CO: Westview Press, 1996.

[9] Florida Division of Emergency Management, State Emergency Response Team (SERT). 2007. Long-Range Program Plan, FY2008-09 through 2012-13.

[10] Florida Division of Emergency Management, *State of Florida Comprehensive Emergency Management Plan,* February 2004: 8.

[11] Susan A. MacManus, "Florida: The South's Premier Battleground State," *American Review of Politics* 26 (Summer 2005): 155-184.

[12] John Pacenti, "Fracking Bill Passes Florida House Over Fierce Democratic Opposition," *Palm Beach Post,* April 27, 2015.

[13] Florida Statutes, Chapter 776, Section 13.

[14] Ashley Portero, "Florida's 'Stand Your Ground' Law: 5 Things to Know," *International Business Times,* March 21, 2012.

[15] Ibid.

[16] "Are 'Stand Your Ground' Laws a Good Idea?" Debate Club, *US News & World Report,* n.d. Accessed May 12, 2015 at http://www.usnews.com/debate-club/are-stand-your-ground-laws-a-good-idea.

[17] Available at http://www.sptimes.com/2004/03/08/State/Floridians_oppose_gay.shtml.

[18] Public Policy Polling, "FL's Scott Would Get Trounced by Sink in Re-Do Election," March 29, 2011. Available at www.publicpolicypolling.com/pdf/PPP_Release_FL_032913.pdf.

[19] StateImpact Florida, "Your Essential Guide to the Core," National Public Radio, accessed May 11, 2015 at http://stateimpact.npr.org/florida/tag/common-core/.

[20] Blake Neff, "People Like Common Core, as Long as It Isn't Called That," Daily Caller News Foundation, March 31, 2015. The poll testing different wording was conducted by Louisiana State University.

[21] Leslie Portal, "Common Core: Parents More Negative, Teachers Mixed, Polls Show," *Orlando Sentinel,* October 29, 2014; John O'Connor, "Poll Finds Support for Common Core Declining Among Republicans and Teachers," WLRN (NPR), August 19, 2014.

[22] Scott Clement and Emma Brown, "Poll: Widespread Misperceptions About the Common Core Standards," *The Washington Post,* February 20, 2015.

[23] "Florida Gambling Laws," Findlaw.com. Accessed May 15, 2015 at statelaws.findlaw.com/florida-law/florida-gambling-laws.html.

[24] Florida Chamber of Commerce, "Florida Chamber's Mark Wilson Testifies Against Expansion of Gambling; Urges Lawmakers to Stay Focused on High-Wage, High-Skill Jobs," News Release, March 26, 2015.

CHAPTER 4

[1] Justin Sayfie, "SayfieReview.com/AIF/Zogby: Florida Divided," December 19, 2009.
Available at http://aif.com/information/2009/sn091216.html.

[2] For fascinating descriptions of these times, see Frederick B. Karl, *The 57 Club: My Four Decades in Florida Politics*. Gainesville, FL: University Press of Florida,2010; *Buddy MacKay, How Florida Happened: The Political Education of Buddy MacKay*. Gainesville, FL: University Press of Florida, 2010.

[3] See Tom R. Wagy, *Governor LeRoy Collins: Spokesman of the New South*. Tuscaloosa, AL: The University of Alabama Press, 1985. Also see Martin A. Dyckman, A Floridian of His Century: The Courage of Governor LeRoy Collins. Gainesville, FL: University Press of Florida, 2006.

[4] See Martin A. Dyckman, *Reubin O'D. Askew and the Golden Age of Florida Politics*. Gainesville, FL: University Press of Florida, 2011.

[5] Stephen C. Craig, "Elections and Partisan Change," in *Government and Politics in Florida*, 2nd Edition. Robert J. Huckshorn, Ed. Gainesville, FL: University Press of Florida, 1998.

[6] Aubrey W. Jewett, "Partisan Change in Southern Legislatures," *Legislative Studies Quarterly* 26 (August 2001): 457-486.

[7] Charles D. Hadley and Lewis Bowman, Eds. *Southern State Party Organizations and Activists*. Westport CT: Praeger, 1995.

[8] Stephanie Maier, "The Battle for America 2010: Party Time in Florida," September 6, 2010. Available at http://pjmedia.com/blog/the-battle-for-america-2010-party-time-in-florida/.

[9] Susan A. MacManus, "Florida: A Plummeting Economy, Tea Parties, and Palin Give GOP a Clean Sweep," in Charles S. Bullock III, Ed., *Key States, High Stakes: Sarah Palin, The Tea Party, and the 2010 Elections,*" Boulder, CO: Rowman & Littlefield, 2011.

[10] The actual application to the Florida Division of Elections in the office of the Florida Secretary of State was dated July 29, 2009, but was rejected due to some inconsistencies in the wording of the party's constitution. The party was officially recognized as a minor political party on August 14, 2009. However, it was not until early November 2009 that the new party got much news coverage.

[11] For an example of this line of thinking, see "Phony Registered Florida Tea Party?" posted on the Save America group's website on January 9, (2009 sic) 2010; www.changefor2012.com/2010/01/phony-florida-tea-party-part-ii; accessed December 18, 2010. This article articulated a commonly held belief among conservative grassroots supporters of the tea party movement in Central Florida that the ultra-liberal U.S. Congressman Alan Grayson (D) had ties to the Tea Party: "Fred O'Neil (sic) was a registered Democrat when he registered the Florida Tea Party. According to Tim McClellan, a political consultant, 'O'Neil is now trying to be passed off as a 'Reagan Democrat,' although he supported both Barack Obama and Alan Grayson in 2008." The article asked whether "Grayson [was] creating a political opportunity to exploit the real Tea Party Movement." Throughout the campaign, rumors persisted that Grayson was underwriting much of the Tea Party campaign activities. For a detailed discussion of the links between Grayson and the Tea Party, see Nathan L. Gonzales, "Link Between Grayson, Tea Party Questioned," *Roll Call*, June 22, 2010. http://www.rollcall.com/issues/55_151/-47556-1.html, accessed December 19, 2010. Also see Tony Pipitone, "Money Trail Links Grayson to Fla. Tea Party," WKMG-TV 6 Orlando, June 25, 2010; Mark Schlueb, "Tea Partyers Clash, Accuse Each Other of Intimidation," *Orlando Sentinel*, June 25, 2010.

[12] Michael Peltier, "Tea Party Less Successful Than Tea Party Movement," *News Service of Florida*, November 4, 2010.

[13] Tom Fiedler, "The Encore of 'Key Largo,'" in *Overtime: the Election 2000 Thriller*, Larry J. Sabato, Ed. (New York: Longman, 2002) pp. 1-14.

14 One idea of how to reform the universal primary is to move such an election to the general election—which would increase the number of persons choosing who will be the officeholder. However, such a proposal is likely to generate opposition from party activists.

[15] Susan A. MacManus and Mark S. Pritchett, "Florida's First Universal Primary Season: What Happened, Why and What Should Be Done?" *Political Chronicle* 14 (Spring 2002): 4-32.

[16] *Sun Sentinel* Editorial Board, "A Way to Fix Write-in Trickery," October 6, 2014.

[17] *Fort Lauderdale Sun-Sentinel*, "Florida Legislature Must Stop Bogus Write-in Mess, Open Primaries," reprinted in Bradenton Herald, November 28, 2014.

[18] The second (runoff) primary was permanently eliminated in 2005 before the 2006 elections. It had actually been suspended by the legislature before the 2002 and 2004 elections.

[19] Descriptions from the websites of the Collier and Pinellas County Supervisor of Elections websites. Available at http://www.votepinellas.com/index.php?id=34; http://dos.myflorida.com/elections/contacts/frequently-asked-questions/faq-elections/

[20] William March, "Florida Parties Move Presidential Primary," *The Tampa Tribune*, May 8, 2013.

[21] Section 99.012(3), Florida Statutes. For a good overview of the "resign-to-run" law, go to http://dos.myflorida.com/elections/contacts/frequently-asked-questions/faq-resign-to-run/.

[22] There is one situation in which a person can be a candidate for two separate offices on the same ballot and that can occur only in a party primary in a presidential election year. A person could be a candidate in a competitive party race to be a state party committeeman or woman and also seek another office for which there is competition within the party.

[23] Ibid.

[24] For a detailed account of the fraud, see Patricia Mazzei, "Ex-Aide to Miami Rep. Joe Garcia to Head to Jail in Absentee-Ballot Case," *Miami Herald*, October 20, 2013.

[25] Survey Research Laboratory of the Policy Sciences Center at Florida State University, *Florida Annual Policy Survey 2000*, available at http://survey.coss.fsu.edu/FAPS/; Leadership Florida Sunshine State Survey, 2011.

[26] See Florida Statute 101.043 "Identification required at the polls" for a detailed description.

[27] Section 101.043, F.S. If the picture identification does not contain a signature, you will be asked to provide an additional identification with your signature.

[28] United States Government Accountability Office, Report to Congressional Requesters, *Elections: Issues Related to State Voter Identification Laws*, September 2014. Available at http://www.gao.gov/assets/670/665966.pdf; Brennan Center for Justice, Research on Voter ID, October 16 2014. Available at http://www.brennancenter.org/analysis/research-and-publications-voter-id.

[29] This information is maintained by the U.S. Election Assistance Commission. For voter registration and turnout statistics for elections 1960-2002, see http://www.eac.gov/research/voter_registration_turnout_statistics_19602002.aspx. For information since 2002, see the Election Administration and Voting Survey, available at http://www.eac.gov/research/election_administration_and_voting_survey.aspx.

[30] National Conference of State Legislatures, "Absentee and Early Voting," February 11, 2015. Available at http://www.ncsl.org/research/elections-and-campaigns/absentee-and-early-voting.aspx.

[31] Aaron Deslatte, "Does Early Voting Raise Turnout?" *Orlando Sentinel*, May 1, 2011.

[32] Much of the following discussion about Florida election reforms is from Susan A. MacManus, "Implementing HAVA's Voter Education Requirement: A Crisis and a Federal Mandate Improve State-Local Cooperation in Florida," Publius 35 (Fall 2005): 537-558; Susan A. MacManus, "Goodbye Chads, Butterfly Ballots, Overvotes, & Recount Ruckuses! Election Reform in Florida: 2000-2003," in Daniel J. Palazzolo and James W. Ceaser, Eds., *Election Reform: Politics and Policy*. Lanham, MD: Lexington Books, 2004, pps. 37-58; and Susan A. MacManus, "Voter Education: The Key to Election Reform Success, Lessons From Florida," *University of Michigan Journal of Law Reform*, 36 (Spring 2003): 517-546.

[33] Anger at voters, local election officials, and poll workers was especially intense in Palm Beach, Miami-Dade, Broward, Duval, and Volusia counties. These counties were the primary focus of post-election litigation. Palm Beach County's Supervisor of Elections Theresa LePore, designer of the infamous butterfly ballot, became the symbol of county-level problems. At the state level, Democrats' anger was primarily directed at the Republican Secretary of State Katherine Harris for her rulings and eventual certification of the election results because Harris had served as co-chair of the Bush campaign. But Republicans were equally angered at actions by Attorney General Bob Butterworth (Democrat) who had served as co-chair of the Gore campaign. See The Political Staff of The Washington Post, *Deadlock: The Inside Story of America's Closest Election*. New York: Public Affairs, 2001; Correspondents of The New York Times, *36 Days: The Complete Chronicle of the 2000 Presidential Election Crisis*. New York: Times Books, 2001; Martin Merzer and the Staff of The Miami Herald, *The Miami Herald Report: Democracy Held Hostage*. New York: St. Martin's Press, 2001.

[34] A statewide public opinion survey of 600 adult Floridians, conducted April 3-8, 2001 by Schroth & Associates (a Washington D.C.-based firm) for two Florida think tanks—the Collins Center for Public Policy, Inc., and the James Madison Institute, margin of error +/- 4 percent, showed the depth of public support for reform. Eighty-one percent agreed that Florida's election system needed revamping. Three-fourths said it was "very important" for the state legislature to enact reforms before the 2002 election. Ninety-one percent of those surveyed strongly or somewhat favored better voter education for new registrants and better training of poll workers. See Susan A. MacManus, Dario Moreno, Richard Scher, and Henry Thomas, *Floridians Want Reform of the Election System...Now!* Tallahassee, FL: The Collins Center for Public Policy, Inc., and The James Madison Institute, April 16, 2001.

[35] Interview of Christy McCormick, Chair of the EAC, by Doug Chapin, "ElectionlineWeekly Q & A With New EAC Commissioners," May 8, 2015. Available at http://blog.lib.umn.edu/cspg/electionacademy/2015/05/electionlineweekly_qa_with_new.php.

[36] Steve Bousquet and Amy Sherman, "Florida Halts Purge of Noncitizens From Voter Rolls," *Tampa Bay Times*, March 27, 2014.

[37] Secretary of State Ken Detzner, "Recommendations for Increased Accessibility & Efficiency in Florida Elections," Florida Department of State, February 4, 2013: p. 6.

[38] Pew Charitable Trusts, "The Elections Performance Index 2012: The State of Election Administration & Prospects for the Future," April 7, 2014. Available at http://www.pewtrusts.org/en/research-and-analysis/reports/2014/04/07/the-elections-performance-index-2012

[39] Aaron Blake citing a study by the Brennan Center for Justice, "The Wait Times to Vote in Florida Are Horrendous," *The Washington Post*, September 15, 2014. Available at http://www.washingtonpost.com/blogs/the-fix/wp/2014/09/15/study-states-with-long-lines-are-failing-to-meet-their-own-election-day-requirements/.

[40] The original deadline was 2012.

[41] The Sentencing Project, "Felony Disenfranchisement Laws in the United States," March, 2011. Available at http://sentencingproject.org/doc/publications/fd_Felony%20Disenfranchisement%20Laws%20in%20the%20US.pdf.

[42] Florida Division of Elections, "Election Myths vs Facts." Accessed May 15, 2015 and available at http://election.dos.state.fl.us/mythsFacts.shtml.

[43] *Palm Beach Post* Editorial, "Most Provisional Ballots in County Are Not Counted," *Palm Beach Post*, September 27, 2014.

[44] There are numerous thorough accounts of the 2000 presidential election including two by the press: Political Staff of The Washington Post, *Deadlock: The Inside Story of America's Closest Election* (New York: Public Affairs, 2001) and Correspondents of The New York Times, *36 Days: The Complete Chronicle of the 2000 Presidential Election Crisis* (New York: Holt, 2001). A thorough academic look at the 2000 election can be found in Gerald M. Pomper, Ed., *The Election of 2000* (New York: Seven Bridges Press, 2001) with Chapter 6 on "The Presidential Election" covering Florida's role extensively. Another superior resource with thorough coverage of every aspect of the Florida election can be found in Larry J. Sabato, Ed., *Overtime: The Election 2000 Thriller* (New York: Longman, 2002). Finally, a brief yet highly detailed account designed for undergraduates is *Bush v. Gore: The Fracas over Florida* (New York: W. W. Norton, 2001).

[45] Diana Owen, "Media Mayhem: The Performance of the Press in Election 2000," in Overtime: *The Election 2000 Thriller*, Larry J. Sabato, Ed. (New York: Longman, 2002), pp. 123-156.

[46] See Opinions of the Supreme Court of Florida, SC00-2431 *Albert Gore, Jr., v. Katherine Harris*.

[47] Supreme Court's stay decision in *Bush v. Gore*, 121 S. Ct. 512 (2000).

[48] *George W. Bush et al., v. Albert Gore Jr.*, et al., 531 US 527, 530 (2000).

[49] See Martin Merzer, Ed., *The Miami Herald Report: Democracy Held Hostage*. New York: St. Martin's Press, 2001, for the results of the group led by the accounting firm of BDO Seidman and http://www.norc.org/Pages/default.aspx for the data and findings of the group led by the National Opinion Research Center.

[50] MacManus, "Florida: The South's Premier Battleground State."

[51] Susan A. MacManus and Andrew Quecan, "The Surrogate Campaign." Paper presented at the annual meeting of the Southwestern Political Science Association, 2006.

[52] Much of the discussion in this section is from Susan A. MacManus, "Presidential Election 2008: An Amazing Race, So What's Next?" In Larry J. Sabato, Ed., *The Year of Obama: How Barack Obama Won the White House*. New York: Longman, 2010, pp. 261-296.

[53] Susan Davis, "Obama's Caucus-State Magic," *The Wall Street Journal*, February 6, 2008.

[54] CNN, "If allowed, Florida, Michigan could tip nomination," March 6, 2008.

[55] RealClearPolitics, "Florida Democratic Primary," January 29, 2008.

[56] Much has been made about this being a Republican tactic. But Democratic and Republican legislators alike voted to move the primary date forward, and several Democratic leaders made public statements about the importance of Florida going earlier in the process. That said, the

calendar change was part of a larger election reform bill that included getting rid of touch screen voting machines—a high priority for Democratic legislators. See "Governor Crist Signs Legislation Creating Paper Trail for Florida Votes," http://www.votetrustusa.org/index.php?option=com_content&task=view&id=2458&Itemid=94.

[57] Dan Balz and Robert Barnes, "Economy Becomes New Proving Ground for McCain, Obama," *Washington Post*, September 16, 2008.

[58] PBS, "Social Web Sites Emerge as Way to Generate Supporters, Funds," July 17, 2007. Smith, Aaron and Lee Rainie, "The Internet and the 2008 Election," Pew Internet and American Life Project, June 15, 2008. Linnie Rawlinson, "Will the 2008 USA Election be Won on Facebook?" accessed December 4, 2008. Matthew Fraser and Soumitra Dutta, "Barack Obama and the Facebook Election," *U.S. News & World Report*, November 19, 2008.

[59] Tamara Lush, Associated Press, "FL Election Results 2012: Barack Obama Defeats Mitt Romney," November 10, 2012. Available at http://www.huffingtonpost.com/2012/11/10/fl-election-results-2012_n_2109753.html.

[60] Anthony Man, "All Roads to the White House Pass Through South Florida," *Sun Sentinel*, May 17, 2015. The reporter quotes Robin Rorapauh, a Democratic Party political consultant who has run a number of statewide campaigns in Florida.

[61] The 1876 governor's race during the Reconstruction era was slightly closer when Democrat George Drew beat Republican Marcellus Stearns 50.2 percent to 49.8 percent.

[62] The information in this paragraph is from Susan A. MacManus, "Florida Governor: Three Elections in One" in Larry J. Sabato, Ed. *Midterm Madness: The Elections of 2002*. Boulder, CO: Rowman & Littlefield, 2003, pp. 195-207.

[63] Much of the following discussion about the 2006 governor's race is from Susan A. MacManus, "Florida Governor & U.S. Senate Races: Split Decisions Give Both Parties Something to Cheer About," in Larry Sabato, Ed. The Six-Year Itch. Boulder, CO: Rowman & Littlefield, 2007.

[64] In black-majority precincts in Miami-Dade County, turnout averaged 33 percent compared with the county's 38 percent. In Broward County's black-majority precincts, turnout averaged just 34.5 percent, well below the county's 44 percent. See Linda Kleindienst, Jerry Milarsky, and Gregory Lewis, "Low Black-Voter Turnout Hurt Davis," *Orlando Sentinel*, November 11, 2006.

[65] Crist ran the most expensive campaign in the nation and outspent Davis by at least 3 to 1. See Linda Kleindienst, Jeremy Milarsky, and Gregory Lewis, "Low Black-Voter Turnout Hurt Davis," *Orlando Sentinel*, November 11, 2006.

66 Ibid.

[67] Crist, divorced and never remarried, was constantly plagued with questions and accusations about his sexual preference, but the topic never got massive coverage by the mainstream media.

[68] Susan A. MacManus, "Florida: A 'Red Tide' Beaches All Democrats Running Statewide: U.S. Senate & Gubernatorial Races Highly Nationalized," in Larry Sabato, Ed., *Pendulum Swing*. Boulder, CO: Rowman & Littlefield, 2011, pp. 217-238.

[69] Adam C. Smith, "A Wild Ride Nobody Envisioned," *St. Petersburg Times*, October 31, 2010.

[70] Lisa de Morase, "CNN Florida Governor's Race Debate: No Fan, Much Hot Air," *Deadline*, October 21, 2014. Available at http://deadline.com/2014/10/cnn-debate-fangate-charlie-crist-rick-scott-jake-tapper-853911/.

[71] George Bennett and John Kennedy, "How Did Scott Win? Call It the I-10 Strategy," *Palm Beach Post*, November 5, 2014.

[72] Information in this paragraph is from Robert Crew, Terri Susan Fine, and Susan MacManus," The 2004 Florida U.S. Senate Race: Full of 'Firsts.'" Article completed for a national research project tracking the impacts of campaign finance reform in election 2004.

[73] Illinois was the other; two African-American males competed for that seat.

[74] Richard E. Foglesong, *Immigrant Prince: Mel Martinez and the American Dream*. Gainesville, FL: University Press of Florida, 2011.

[75] Republican U.S. Senator Connie Mack III retired in 2000 after serving two terms.

[76] U.S. President/Florida exit poll survey conducted by Edison Media Research/Mitofsky International for the AP and television networks. Survey results were posted on CNN.com website. Available at http://www.cnn.com/ELECTION/2004/pages/results/states/FL/P/00/epolls.0.html

[77] Al-Arian was found not guilty on most charges by a federal jury in 2005, and the jury was hung on several other charges.

[78] See Barbara Liston, "Katherine Harris's Comedy of Errors," Time.com, September 2, 2006. Available at http://content.time.com/time/nation/article/0,8599,1531257,00.html.

[79] Much of the discussion in this section is from MacManus, "Florida: A 'Red Tide' Beaches All Democrats Running Statewide; U.S. Senate & Gubernatorial Races Highly Nationalized," pps. 217-238; MacManus, "Florida: A Plummeting Economy, Tea Parties, and Palin Give GOP A Clean Sweep."

[80] Prior to his running for the Senate, Meek had been a Florida Highway Patrol trooper before serving eight years in the state Legislature and three terms in Congress.

[81] John Fritze, "Kendrick Meek Wins Democratic Primary in Florida," *USA Today*, August 24, 2010. Greene spent more than $23 million of his own money; Meek spent just over $4.7 million, according to the article.

[82] Adam Smith, "A Wild Ride Nobody Envisioned," *St. Petersburg Times*, October 31, 2010.

[83] Estimates are from Chris Cillizza, "Senate Races in 2016 Look Poised to Set Spending Records," *The Washington Post*, April 19, 2015. Available at http://www.washingtonpost.com/politics/senate-races-in-2016-look-poised-to-set-spending-records/2015/04/19/105fa832-e6c5-11e4-9767-6276fc9b0ada_story.html.

[84] For a detailed description of the Florida Cabinet, see http://www.myflorida.com/myflorida/cabinet/..

[85] For historical overviews of redistricting in Florida, see articles in Susan A. MacManus, Ed., *Reapportionment and Representation in Florida: A Historical Collection*. Tampa, FL: Intrabay Innovation Institute, University of South Florida, 1991; and Susan A. MacManus, Ed., *Mapping Florida's Political Landscape: The Changing Art & Politics of Reapportionment and Redistricting*. Tallahassee, FL: Florida Institute of Government, 2002.

[86] Florida State University currently houses the Mildred and Claude Pepper Library and the Pepper Center for Aging.

[87] The Democratic loser in congressional District 13, Christine Jennings, contested the outcome of that race, claiming that the electronic touch screen machines were flawed. The House of Representatives delcared in early 2008 that Republican Vern Buchanan has rightfully won the election, see https://archive.is/tqPcO. Ms. Jennings challenged Buchanan again in the 2008 election and lost.

[88] This discussion is from MacManus, "Florida: A Plummeting Economy…"

[89] Tampa Bay Times, "Redistricting Florida," Available at http://www.tampabay.com/specials/2011/reports/redistricting/congress.shtml.

[90] Allysia Finley, "Behind the GOP Statehouse Juggernaut," *Wall Street Journal*, December 12, 2014.

[91] Scott Maxwell, "10 Lessons from Florida's 2014 Election Season," *Orlando Sentinel*, November 9, 2014.

[92] Amy Walter, "Democrats' Downballot Troubles," *The Cook Political Report*, December 3, 2014. Available at http://cookpolitical.com/story/8123.

[93] William Frey, senior fellow at the Brookings Institution quoted by Daniel J. McGraw, "The GOP is Dying Off. Literally," *Politico*, May 17, 2015. Available at http://www.politico.com/magazine/story/2015/05/the-gop-is-dying-off-literally-118035.html?hp=m1#.VVtC10bqWAo.

[94] William E. Gibson, "Florida's Close Elections Set Stage for 2016," *Sun Sentinel*, November 5, 2014.

CHAPTER 5

[1] "Florida's Establishment," *Florida Trend*, November 1969.

[2] Burdett A. Loomis and Allan J. Cigler "The Changing Nature of Interest Group Politics" in Burdett A. Loomis and Allan J. Cigler, eds. *Interest Group Politics*, 4th ed. Washington D.C.: CQ Press, 2002.

[3] Florida Annual Policy Survey, 1995. Florida State University Survey Research Lab.

[4] James Madison, Alexander Hamilton, and John Jay, *The Federalist Papers*, Number 10. New York: Mentor Books, 1961.

[5] To see the overall power of business groups across the states see the series of edited books by Ronald J. Hrebenar and Clive Thomas. These include *Interest Group Politics in the Southern States*. Tuscaloosa: University of Alabama Press, 1992; *Interest Group Politics in the Midwestern States*. Ames: Iowa State University Press, 1993; Interest *Group Politics in the Northeastern States*. University Park: Pennsylvania State University Press, 1993; and *Interest Group Politics in the American West*. Salt Lake City, University of Utah Press, 1987.

[6] Enterprise Florida, Florida's 2014 Florida International Business Highlights, Merchandise Trade, Florida-Origin Exports, & Foreign Direct Investment, April 2015. Available at http://www.enterpriseflorida.com/wp-content/uploads/report-florida-international-business-highlights.pdf.

[7] Paul Brace, *State Government and Economic Performance*. Baltimore: Johns Hopkins University Press, 1993.

[8] Statistics on tourism compiled by Visit Florida, the public – private partnership created by the legislature to promote tourism in Florida. http://www.visitflorida.org/about-us/tourism-fast-facts/.

[9] For a critical look at the power of Disney in Florida see Richard E. Foglesong, *Married to the Mouse*. New Haven: Yale University Press, 2001.

[10] Florida Agricultural Overview and Statistics, Florida Department of Agriculture and Consumer Services, http://www.freshfromflorida.com/Divisions-Offices/Marketing-and-Development/Education/For-Researchers/Florida-Agriculture-Overview-and-Statistics.

[11] Alexis de Tocqueville, *Democracy in America*, 1835. New York: Mentor Books, 1956.

[12] C. Wright Mills, The Power Elite. New York: Oxford University Press, 1956, p. 289.

[13] Hill, MacManus, and Moreno, eds. *Florida's Politics: Ten Media Markets, One Powerful State*.

[14] For a complete listing of media in Florida, see *Marth's Florida Guide* (published annually) by Suwannee River Press. Branford, Florida.

[15] Ibid.

[16] Data are for June 2015. Source: www.mondotimes.com/newspapers/usa/florida.html.

[17] Garry Boulard, "More News. Less Coverage," *State Legislatures* (June 1999): 14-18.

[18] Steven D. Stark, "Local News: The Biggest Scandal on TV," *Washington Monthly* (June 1997): 8-10.

[19] Lou Frey, Jr and Aubrey Jewett eds. *Political Rules of the Road*. New York: U.S. Association of Former Members of Congress and University Press of America, 2009.

[20] Lou Frey, Jr. "Dealing with the Press," in Lou Frey, Jr. and Michael T. Hayes eds. *Inside the House: Former Members Reveal How Congress Really Works*. New York: U.S. Association of Former Members of Congress and University Press of America, 2001, p. 233.

[21] According to the Florida Commission on Ethics, "Executive branch departments, state universities, community colleges, and water management districts are prohibited from using public funds to retain an executive branch (or legislative branch) lobbyist, although these agencies may use full-time employees as lobbyists [Sec.11.062, *Florida Statutes*]. Available at http://www.ethics.state.fl.us/ethics/lobbyist_info.html; accessed June 1, 2006.

[22] Clive S. Thomas and Ronald J. Hrebenar, "Who's Got Clout? Interest Group Power in the States," *State Legislatures* (April 1999): 30-34.

[23] Bureau of Labor Statistics are for 2014. Available at http://www.bls.gov/news.release/union2.t05.htm.

[24] Aubrey Jewett, "Workers' Compensation Reform in Florida: Why Did Two Innovative Return to Work Programs Fail?" *Policy Studies Review* 18 (Autumn 2001): 109-147.

[25] Suzanne Parker, "Interest Groups and Public Opinion," in Robert J. Huckshorn ed., *Government and Politics in Florida*, 2nd edition. Gainesville: University Press of Florida, 1998.

[26] Anne E. Kelly and Ella L. Taylor, "Florida: The Changing Patterns of Power" in Ronald J. Hrebenar and Clive S. Thomas eds. *Interest Group Politics in the Southern States*. Tuscaloosa: University of Alabama Press, 1992.

[27] Florida Chamber of Commerce. Available at http://www.flchamber.com/.

[28] Joint Rule One Lobbyist Registration and Compensation Reporting Act, CS for SCR 1869, passed by the Florida Legislature, 2006.

[29] Ibid.

[30] Lobbying statistics can be found at https://floridalobbyist.gov/.

[31] Online Sunshine, FAQs For Lobbyists Before The Florida Legislature, 2015, Available at http://www.leg.state.fl.us/cgi-bin/View_Page.pl?Tab=lobbyist&Submenu=1&File=faq_leg-2010.html&Directory=Lobbyist/&Location=app

[32] See Compensation Reports: Aggregate Totals at https://floridalobbyist.gov/CompensationReportSearch/CompAggregateTotals.

[33] Joni James and Steve Bousquet, "Lawmakers Ban Gifts From Lobbyists," *St. Petersburg Times*, December 9, 2005; available at www.sptimes.com/2005/12/09/news_pf/State/Lawmakers_ban_gifts_f.shtml.

[34] Ibid.

[35] Quotations from the *Tallahassee Democrat*, January 12, 1992.

[36] Ibid.

[37] Amy Keller, "Florida's Top Lobbying Firms," *Florida Trend*, March 15, 2013. Available at http://www.floridatrend.com/article/15382/floridas-top-lobbying-firms.

[38] Associated Press, "Fla. Gets Tough New Child-Sex Law," CBS News, May 2, 2005.

[39] http://www.followthemoney.org/database/state_overview.phtml?s=FL&y=2014 National Institute on Money and State Politics, Florida, 2014.

[40] According to data collected by the National Conference of State Legislatures. Available at www.ncsl.org.

[41] *Buckley v. Valeo*, 424 U.S. 1 (1976).

[42] *Davis v. Federal Election Commission*, 554 U.S. 724 (2008).

[43] *Citizens United v. Federal Election Commission*, 558 U.S. 08-205 (2010).

[44] *McCutcheon v. Federal Election Commission*, 572 U.S. ___ (2014); Aggregate donation limits had been established by the original FECA in the 1970s and modified by BCRA to place a $123,200 cap on contributions an individual could give to all federal candidates, parties and political action committees in a two-year election. With aggregate limits struck down, a person or PAC may now give the maximum legal amount to every candidate, political party and PAC if they wish.

[45] Until they were eliminated in 2013, Florida used to have a another type of political group called Committees of Continuing Existence (CCEs). There were even more CCEs (600) than there were PACs primarily because CCEs could take in unlimited sums of money and PACs were limited to $500 donations under the old rules. In addition most candidates were setting up CCEs because they could then spend the money on campaign related activities and even use CCE money as a "slush fund" to pay for expensive travel, hotels, and meals that otherwise would be prohibited by the ban on direct gifts from lobbyists to lawmakers.

[46] The number of political committees (including PACs, ECOs, IXOs, Party Committees, and Affiliated Party Committees) including names and amount of money raised by each for different time periods can be found at the Florida Division of Elections, Campaign Finance Database, at http://dos.elections.myflorida.com/campaign-finance/contributions/.

[47] See *Florida Statutes* Title IX Electors and Elections Chapters 102 and 106.

[48] Alan Rosenthal, *The Third House: Lobbyists and Lobbying in the States* 2nd edition. Washington DC: CQ Press, 2001. See especially Chapter 6 on "Building Relationships" and Chapter 7 on "Playing Politics." While the book covers lobbying behavior in all states, there are frequent references to Florida specifically.

[49] A notorious example of criminal behavior by elected officials occurred in Escambia County in 2002 when four of five commissioners were removed from office by the Governor and convicted of a variety of charges including extortion, bribery, money laundering, and receiving unlawful compensation or reward for official behavior. See "West Florida: Conservative Florida" by James Witt in *Florida Politics: Ten Media Markets, One Powerful State*, eds. Kevin Hill, Susan MacManus, and Dario Moreno, (Florida Institute of Government Press: Tallahassee, 2004).

[50] Florida Division of Elections, 2014 Public Campaign Financing Handbook.

[51] Public Campaign Finance, Matching Funds Distribution, Florida Division of Elections, http://dos.myflorida.com/elections/candidates-committees/campaign-finance/

[52] Robert Dreyfuss, "Reform Gets Rolling: Campaign Finance at the Grass Roots," *The American Prospect* (July/August 1999): 39-43.

[53] Aubrey Jewett, "The Changing Interest Group System in Florida," Political Chronicle 22 (Winter 2014): 8-32.

CHAPTER 6

[1] See Alan Rosenthal, *Heavy Lifting: The Job of the American Legislature*. Washington, D.C.:CQ Press, 2004. Chapter 2 discusses the importance of, and reasons for, constituency service.

[2] Sandra L. Myres, *One Man, One Vote*. Austin, TX: Steck-Vaughn, 1970.

[3] Hugh Douglas Price , "Florida: Politics and the 'Pork Choppers.'" In *The Politics of Reapportionment*, ed. Malcolm E. Jewell. Westport, CT: Greenwood Press, 1962.

[4] *Baker v Carr*, 369 U.S. 186 (1962). See also *Reynolds v Sims*, 377 U.S. 533 (1964) and *Wesberry v. Sanders*, 376 U.S. 1 (1964).

[5] Michael Maggioto et. al., "The Impact of Reapportionment on Public Policy," *American Politics Quarterly* 13 (January 1985): 101-21.

[6] MacManus, *Reapportionment and Representation in Florida: A Historical Collection*.

[7] Aubrey Jewett, "Republican Strength in a Southern Legislature: The Impact of One Person, One Vote Redistricting in Florida," *American Review of Politics*, 21 (Spring 2000): 1-18.

[8] Shelby County v. Holder, 570 U.S. ___ (2013). The ruling declared unconstitutional the outdated formula used to determine which jurisdictions were required to get preclearance. Congress could pass a law updating the formula and then some jurisdictions might be required to seek preclearance again.

[9] *Shaw v. Reno* 509 U.S. 630 (1993) and *Miller v Johnson* 515 U.S. 900 (1995).

[10] *Thornburg v. Gingles*, 478 U.S. 30 (1986).

[11] For a number of years after *Miller v Johnson* in 1995 no new significant Supreme Court cases emerged on the issue of racial gerrymandering. However in 2015 the Supreme Court ruled in an Alabama case that the legislature had relied too heavily on race when drawing districts after the 2010 census and continued to place too high a percentage of blacks into majority black districts. See *Alabama Legislative Black Caucus v. Alabama*, No. 13-895 and *Alabama Democratic Conference v. Alabama*, No. 13-1138, 575 U. S. ____ (2015).

[12] *Johnson v. DeGrandy* 512 US 997 (1994).

[13] For a thorough review of all issues affecting redistricting in Florida in 1992 through 2001 see MacManus ed., *Mapping Florida's Political Landscape*. Florida Institute of Government Press: Tallahassee, 2001.

[14] It was rejected for covering too many subjects (an independent redistricting commission and single-member-districts) and for calling the commission nonpartisan when it also required a certain number of Republican and Democrats on the commission.

[15] Susan A. MacManus, Joanna M. Cheshire, Tifini L. Hill, and Susan C. Schuler, "Redistricting in Florida, Loud Voices from the Grassroots," in Seth C. McKee, ed. *Jigsaw Puzzle Politics in the Sunshine State*, Gainesville, FL: University Press of Florida, 2015, pp. 126-162.

[16] For more details on the congressional redistricting process and results see Aubrey Jewett, "Fair" Districts in Florida: New Congressional Seats, New Constitutional Standards, Same Old Republican Advantage?" in William J. Miller and Jeremy D. Walling, eds. *The Political Battle Over Congressional Redistricting*, Lanham, MD: Lexington Books, 2013, pp. 111-136.

[17] Aubrey Jewett, "New Rules for an Old Florida Game: The 2012 Legislative and Congressional Redistricting Process," in Seth C. McKee, ed. *Jigsaw Puzzle Politics in the Sunshine State*, Gainesville, FL: University Press of Florida, 2015, pp. 41-76.

[18] Alan Rosenthal, "The Nature of Representation" in Florida House of Representatives and Collins Center for Public Policy, *The Legislature Project: Making Florida Democracy Work*. Tallahassee: Collins Center for Public Policy, 1995, p. 14.

[19] Independents have rarely won office in modern times. The last independent elected to the Florida Legislature was Lori Wilson from Cocoa Beach who served in the Senate from 1972 to 1978.

[20] The last blacks to serve in the state legislature before Mr. Kershaw were George Lewis and John Scott who were elected from Jacksonville in 1889.

[21] Susan A. MacManus and Amanda C. Chew, "Minority Path-Breakers in Florida Politics: First to Win Various Types of Elective Offices in the Sunshine State," paper presented at the annual meeting of the Florida Political Science Association, Pembroke Pines, FL, April 8, 2006.

[22] Florida Conference of Black State Legislators. Available at http://www.fcbsl.org/.

[23] Mary Herring, "Legislative Responsiveness to Black Constituencies," *Journal of Politics* 52 (August 1990): 740-58.

[24] Aubrey Jewett, "Party and Ideological Voting in the Florida Legislature," presented at the annual meeting of the Southern Political Science Association, Atlanta, GA, November 2000.

[25] Kevin Hill and Dario Moreno, "A Community or a Crowd: Racial Ethnic, and Regional Bloc Voting in the Florida House of Representatives, 1989-98" *Politics and Policy*, March. Members of the caucus supported liberal Democrat Tom Gustafson of Ft. Lauderdale for Speaker and were rewarded with Committee Chairmanships and millions of dollars for local projects in Miami.

[26] Center for American Women and Politics, Rutgers University, New Brunswick, NJ. Figures are for 2015. http://www.cawp.rutgers.edu/fast_facts/levels_of_office/documents/stleg.pdf.

[27] Virginia Shapiro, "Private Costs of Public Commitments: Family Roles versus Political Ambition," *American Journal of Political Science* 26 (May 1982): 265-79.

[28] Carol Nechemias, "Geographic Mobility and Women's Access to State Legislature," *Western Political Quarterly* 38 (March 1985): 119-31.

[29] Susan A. MacManus, "Women in State Legislative Office," *Political Chronicle* 6 (Winter/Spring 1994-1995): 10-18.

[30] Susan A. MacManus, "The Race to Put Women's Faces in High Places: Florida's Parties Keep Score in the Early 2000s," *The Florida Political Chronicle* 15 (Spring 2004): 19-38.

[31] Susan A. MacManus, Charles S. Bullock III, Karen Padgett, and Brittany Penberthy, "Women Winning At The Local Level: Are County & School Board Positions Becoming More Desirable & Plugging The Pipeline to Higher Office?" in Lois Duke Whitaker, ed. Women in Politics, 4th ed. (Prentice-Hall, 2006), pps. 117-136; Susan A. MacManus, "Women Follow Different Paths to the Florida Legislature: A Look at the Class of 2002-2004," *The Florida Political Chronicle* 16 (Spring 2005): 11-28.

[32] Quoted in the *Tampa Tribune*, July 27, 1987.

[33] Marianela Toledo, FloridaWatchdog.org. "Florida Lawmakers' Personal Wealth Keeps Growing," *Sunshine State News*, August 9, 2014. Available at http://www.sunshinestatenews.com/story/florida-lawmakers%E2%80%99-personal-wealth-keeps-growing.

[34] All statistics for occupation are for the 2015 legislative session.

[35] For an early study see Scot Schraufnagel and Karen Halperin, "Term Limits, Electoral Competition, and Representational Diversity: The Case of Florida," *State Politics and Policy Quarterly* 6 (Winter 2006): 448-462.

[36] Kathryn A. DePalo, *The Failure of Term Limits in Florida*, Gainesville, FL: University Press of Florida, 2015.

[37] House Speaker Peter Rudy Wallace commissioned the study *The Legislative Project: Making Florida Democracy Work* in 1995.

[38] Richard A. Clucas, "Principal-Agent Theory and the Power of State House Speakers," *Legislative Studies Quarterly*, 26 (2001):319-338. Pages 326-327 display the power rankings.

[39] Mary Ellen Klas, "GOP Infighting and the Partial-Blind Selection of Leaders Eight Years Out," *Miami Herald*, April 15, 2015. Available at http://miamiherald.typepad.com/nakedpolitics/2015/04/gop-infighting-and-the-partial-blind-selection-of-leaders-eight-years-out.html.

[40] Representative Tom Feeney, James Madison Institute Forum, January 30, 1997.

[41] Ibid.

[42] Aubrey Jewett, "Party and Ideology in a Southern State Legislature" presented at the annual meeting of the Southern Political Science Association, November 1995, Tampa, Florida.

[43] Steve Bousquet and Mary Ellen Klas, "Cracks Emerge in GOP's Big Tent in Tallahassee," Miami Herald, April 24, 2015. Available at http://www.miamiherald.com/news/politics-government/article19395666.html.

[44] Ibid.

[45] Scott Maxwell, "Taking Names: Rep. Mike Miller – a health care flip-flop?" *Orlando Sentinel*, April 27, 2015. Available at http://www.orlandosentinel.com/news/taking-names-scott-maxwell/os-rep-mike-miller-a-healthcare-flipflop-20150427-post.html

[46] For an excellent description of the committee system, see Eric Prier, *The Myth of Representation and the Florida Legislature: A House of Competing Loyalties*. Gainesville, FL: University of Florida Press, 2003.

[47] Rosenthal, "The Nature of Representation."

CHAPTER 7

[1] The possum festival has become a must-attend event for politicians since its inception in 1970. Politicians bid on possums, get their photos taken with the marsupials, and hope to get the rural Panhandle vote. It is held in Wausau, Florida, near Chipley.

[2] Only Mississippi, South Carolina, Texas, and North Dakota ranked below Florida. Joseph A. Schlesinger, "The Politics of the Executive," in Herbert Jacob and Kenneth N. Vines, *Politics in the American States*. New York: Little, Brown, & Co., 1965, pp. 207-237.

[3] Ferguson, Margaret. 2013. "Governors and the Executive Branch." In *Politics in the American States*, edited by Virginia Gray, Russell L. Hanson, and Thad Kousser. 208-250. Los Angeles: Sage/CQ Press. Pages 225-226 contain the comparison chart of formal powers.

[4] Technically it is correct to say the "governor and the Cabinet" since the constitution makes clear that the Cabinet is made up of the three other statewide elected officials (See Florida Constitution Article IV Section 4). However, as a practical matter many people simply say the "Cabinet" when referring to the governor and the other statewide elected officials when they are making collective decisions.

[5] Alan Ehrenhalt, "Electoral Overload," Governing (August 2001): 7.

[6] See Matthew T. Corrigan, *Conservative Hurricane: How Jeb Bush Remade Florida*. Gainesville, FL: University Press of Florida, 2014.

[7] The Florida Constitution in Article IV, Section 4 defines the Cabinet as "Composed of an attorney general, a chief financial officer, and a commissioner of agriculture."

[8] There are certain gubernatorial appointments (and removals) that require Senate confirmation or the approval of the Cabinet.

[9] The Department of Economic Opportunity began in October 2011 and replaced the Department of Community Affairs which used to oversees local governments and growth management.

[10] Cabinet meeting dates, agendas, transcripts and live broadcasts are available at http://www.myflorida.com/myflorida/cabinet/.

[11] Kathleen Murphy, "Lt. Govs More Than Spare Tires Study Shows," in Thad Beyle ed., *State and Local Government 2002-2003*. Washington, D.C.: CQ Press, 2002.

[12] Index of informal powers developed by political scientist Thad Beyle. Archived rankings are available at https://web.archive.org/web/20131228030443/http://www.unc.edu/~beyle/gubnewpwr.html.

[13] An archive of previous executive orders is available is available at the State Library online at http://edocs.dlis.state.fl.us/fldocs/governor/orders/index.htm.

[14] Executive orders for the current governor can be found at http://www.flgov.com/media-center/executive-orders/.

[15] For an excellent analysis of the governor's suspension powers, see Frederick B. Karl, *The Power to Suspend: An Important Process For Fighting Corruption in Public Office*. Tallahassee, FL: The Florida Senate, February 2006.

[16] Ibid.

[17] James Witt, "West Florida: Pensacola to Fort Walton Beach" in Hill, MacManus and Moreno eds. *Florida Politics: Ten Media Markets, One Powerful State*, p. 106.

[18] Paradise Afshar, "Appeals Court Rules That Pizzi Is the Rightful Mayor of Miami Lakes," *Miami Herald*, April 24, 2015.

[19] Karl, *The Power to Suspend*.

[20] Julie Mason, "Jeb Bush Silent on Political Future," *Houston Chronicle*, June 4, 2006.

[21] Crist line item vetoed $91 million in proposed spending that the legislature tried to make in a January 2009 special session called to bring the mid-year budget into balance and then vetoed a proposed 2 percent pay cut to state employees (equal to about $30 million) in the 2009 regular session. Thus the net line item veto savings for his term is actually a little less than $1 billion.

[22] Joni James, Alex Leary, and Janet Zink, "Veto Ax Lands on Dreams for River," *St. Petersburg Times*, May 26, 2006.

[23] Richard S. Conley and Richard K. Scher, "'I Did It My Way': Governor Jeb Bush and the Line Item Veto in Florida," paper presented at the Citadel Symposium on Southern Politics, March 7-8, 2002.

[24] A federal judge ruled the law banning partial birth abortion unconstitutional. In 2000, the legislature passed a similar ban that was signed by Jeb Bush. A similar federal law was passed and eventually upheld by the U.S. Supreme Court in 2007.

[25] See U.S. Census, Foreign Trade, State Exports and Imports for Florida 2015, available at https://www.census.gov/foreign-trade/statistics/state/data/index.html

[26] Enterprise Florida, Inc. (EFI) is the public-private partnership responsible for leading Florida's statewide economic development efforts. The organization's mission is to diversify Florida's economy and create better paying jobs for its citizens by supporting, attracting and helping to create businesses in innovative, high-growth industries. Available at http://www.enterpriseflorida.com/about-efi/.

[27] Governor's Office of Tourism. Trade, & Economic Development, "Consular Corps," Available at http://www.flgov.com/governor%E2%80%99s-office-of-tourism-trade-and-economic-development/.

[28] Compiled by Thomas A. Watson, "International Trade and Florida: Examining the Governor's Role," Honors Thesis, University of South Florida, 2006

[29] Megan O'Matz, "Governor Crist and Entourage Traveled Across In Style across Europe As Business and Taxpayers Footed the Bill," *South Florida Sun Sentinel*, December 7, 2008.

[30] See Kevin Gale, "Governor Scott Pushes International Trade," *South Florida Business Journal*, January 11, 2011.

[31] Matt Dixon, "Gov. Rick Scott's Choice to Lead Florida Republican Party Loses," Naples Daily News, January 17, 2015.

[32] Of course, President Bush's very poor response to Hurricane Katrina in Louisiana and Mississippi in 2005 reversed the high marks he had previously received for hurricane responsiveness, while his brother Jeb's remained high.

[33] See Paul Quinlan, "In Florida's Senate Race, Crist's Fortunes Fall with End of Oil Spill," *New York Times*, September 16, 2010.

[34] See Martin A. Dyckman, *Floridian of His Century: The Courage of Governor LeRoy Collins*. Gainesville, FL: University Press of Florida, 2006.

[35] For excellent biographies, see Thomas R. Wagy, *Governor LeRoy Collins of Florida, Spokesman of the New South*. University of Alabama Press: Tuscaloosa, 1985; Dyckman, Floridian of His Century.

[36] *Baker v. Carr*, 369 U.S. 186 (1962); *Reynolds v. Sims*, 377 U.S. 533 (1964).

[37] *Brown v. Board of Education of Topeka Kansas*, 347 U.S. 483 (1954).

[38] Allen Morris and Joan Perry Morris, *The Florida Handbook 2003-2004*. Tallahassee, FL: The Peninsular Publishing Company, 2003, p. 324.

[39] For an interesting biography of Kirk and his time as governor see Edmund Kallina, *Claude Kirk and the Politics of Confrontation*. Gainesville: University Press of Florida, 1993.

[40] Martin A. Dyckman, *Reubin O'D. Askew and the Golden Age of Florida Politics*. Gainesville, FL: University Press of Florida, 2011.

[41] See S.V. Date, *Quite Passion: A Biography of Bob Graham*, New York: Tarcher, 2004 for a look at the Bob Grahams time as governor and senator.

[42] *Florida Tax Handbook*. Tallahassee: Florida Legislature, 1996.

[43] Morris and Morris, *The Florida Handbook 2003-2004*.

[44] See John Dos Passos, *Walkin' Lawton*. Cocoa, FL: Florida Historical Society Press, 2012 for a biography of Chiles' time as a senator and governor.

[45] Governor Lawton Chiles, Second Inaugural Address, January 1995.

[46] See Buddy MacKay and Rick Edmonds, *How Florida Happened: The Political Education of Buddy MacKay*. Gainesville, FL: University of Florida Press, 2010 for a look at the political career of Buddy MacKay and of Lawton Chile's time as governor.

[47] For a negative view of Jeb Bush's time as governor see S. V. Date, *Jeb: America's Next Bush*, New York: Tarcher, 2007. For a detailed look at Jeb Bush policies see Robert Crew, *Jeb Bush: Aggressive Conservatism in Florida*, Lanham, MD: University Press of America, 2009. For

an argument that Bush made a powerful lasting change in Florida politics see Matthew T. Corrigan, *Conservative Hurricane: How Jeb Bush Remade Florida*, Gainesville: University Press of Florida, 2014.

[48] Fred Barnes, "Governor in Chief: Jeb Bush's Remarkable Eight Years of Achievement in Florida," *The Weekly Standard* 11 (37) (June 12, 2006).

[49] www.charliecrist.com, accessed December 11, 2006.

CHAPTER 8

[1] B.K. Roberts, "The Judicial System," in Allen Morris and Joan Perry Morris eds. *The Florida Handbook, 2005-2006*. Tallahassee: The Peninsular Publishing Company, 2005.

[2] Thomas R. Dye and Susan A. MacManus, *Politics in States and Communities*, 12th ed. Upper Saddle River, NJ: Prentice Hall, 2007.

[3] The Florida Constitution establishes a mandatory retirement age for Justices that occurs on or after their 70th birthdays. The exact date of retirement depends upon when the 70th birthday occurs. If it occurs during the first half of a Justice's six-year term, then the mandatory retirement age is the same as the birthday. If the 70th birthday occurs in the second half of a Justice's six-year term, then the Justice can remain in office until the full term expires.

[4] National Center for State Courts, Judicial Salary Tracker (data for January 1, 2015), available at http://www.ncsc.org/salarytracker.

[5] Carol M. Bast, *Florida Courts*, 4th ed. Upper Saddle River, NJ: Prentice Hall, 2005.

[6] A felony "is punishable by death or imprisonment. A felony is classified as capital felony, a life felony, a felony of the first degree, a felony of the second degree, and a felony of the third degree, depending on the severity" of the crime. Definitions are from Bast, *Florida Courts*, p. 17.

[7] Definitions are from Bast, *Florida Courts*.

[8] A misdemeanor is "punishable by imprisonment in a county correctional facility for not more than a year. A misdemeanor is classified as a misdemeanor of the first degree and a misdemeanor of the second degree, depending on the severity. Definitions are from Bast, *Florida Courts*, p. 17.

[9] Bast, *Florida Courts*, p. 1.

[10] The Florida Bar Roster Report (as of 05/01/2015), available at https://www.floridabar.org/tfb/flabarwe.nsf/ f6301f4d554d40a385256a4f006e6566/47fc0a8f415a11d285256b2f006ccb83?OpenDocument#Frequently%20Asked%20Questions%20 About.

[11] Bast, *Florida Courts*, p. 7.

[12] Bast, *Florida Courts*, pp. 7-8.

[13] James P.Wenzel, Shaun Bowler, and David J. Lanoue, "The Sources of Public Confidence in State Courts," American Politics Research 31 (March 2003): 191-211.

[14] See Opinions of the Supreme Court of Florida, SC09-565 Robert J. Pleus Jr. v Charles J. Crist Jr.

[15] Drew Noble Lanier, "Florida," In *Legal Systems of the World: A Political, Social and Cultural Encyclopedia*, ed. Herbert M. Kritzer, Santa Barbara, CA: ABC-CLIO, 2002. See the JQC website for more recent disciplinary cases. Available at http://www.floridasupremecourt.org/pub_info/jqc.shtml.

[16] See "A History of the Clerk's Office" found at the web site of the Leon County Clerk of Courts https://cvweb.clerk.leon.fl.us/public/login.asp?action=iframe&whichpage=announcement_details.asp%3Fid%3D282

[17] See The Florida Bar, *About the Bar, Frequently Asked Questions*. Available at http://www.floridabar.org/.

[18] Bast, *Florida Courts*, p. 17.

[19] See "AIF Applauds Passage of Tort Reform Legislation," Capital Soup, May 4, 2011. Available at http://capitalsoup.com/2011/05/04/aif-applauds-passage-of-tort-reform-legislation/.

[20] See Drew Noble Lanier and Roger Handberg, "In the Eye of the Hurricane: Florida Courts, Judicial Independence, and Politics," *Fordham Urban Law Journal* 29 (February 2002): 1029-1052.

[21] See Martin Dyckman, *A Most Disorderly Court: Scandal and Reform in the Florida Judiciary*. Gainesville, FL: University Press of Florida, 2008.

[22] Roger Handberg and Mark Lawhorn, "The Courts: Powerful but Obscure," in Robert Huckshorn ed. *Government and Politics in Florida*, 2nd ed. Gainesville: University of Florida Press, 1998.

[23] Susan A. MacManus, "Florida Women Slowly Narrowing the Gender Gap on the Bench," sayfiereview.com, July 13, 2006.

[24] Steve Bousquet, "Florida Gov. Rick Scott Appointing Fewer Black Judges than Predecessors," Tampa Bay Times, September 14, 2014.

[25] The opinion can be found at http://www.supremecourt.gov/opinions/14pdf/13-1499_d18e.pdf.

[26] See Mark S. Hurwitz and Drew Noble Lanier, "Diversity in State and Federal Appellate Courts: Change and Continuity Across 20 Years," *The Justice System Journal* (Vol. 29, No. 1 2008): 47-70.

[27] Statistics for minorities and women come from Malia Reddick, Michael J. Nelson, and Rachel Paine Caufield, "Racial and Gender Diversity on State Courts: An AJS Study," *The Judges Journal* 48, (3) (Summer 2009).

[28] State rankings are taken from the American Bar Association, "National Database on Judicial Diversity in State Courts. Available at http://apps.americanbar.org/abanet/jd/display/national.cfm.

[29] MacManus, "Florida Women Slowly Narrowing the Gender Gap on the Bench."

[30] The statistics in this section come from Florida Department of Law Enforcement, *Crime in Florida 2013*. Available at http://www.fdle.state.fl.us/Content/getdoc/7d48bbb5-9a13-43b2-9b80-cdc900b08652/Proportion.aspx.

[31] Florida Department of Juvenile Justice 2013-2014 Delinquency Profile.

[32] Ian Cummings, "Juvenile Justice? Bill Touts New Way," Herald-Tribune (March 31, 2015). Available at http://politics.heraldtribune. com/2015/03/31/justice-for-juveniles-house-bill-touts-a-new-way/.

[33] CS/SN 378-Juvenile Justice. Available at https://www.flsenate.gov/Committees/BillSummaries/2015/html/902.

[34] *District of Columbia v. Heller*, 554 U.S. 570 (2008) and McDonald v. Chicago, 561 U.S. ___, 130 S.Ct. 3020 (2010).

[35] Florida Department of Agriculture and Consumer Services, Division of Licensing, Number of Licenses by Type, April 30, 2015, available at http://www.freshfromflorida.com/content/download/7471/118627/Number_of_Licensees_By_Type.pdf.

[36] Michael Auslen, "Florida Gov. Rick Scott signs 44 bills into law, including concealed carry, body camera legislation," Bradenton Herald (May 21, 2015). Available at http://www.bradenton.com/2015/05/21/5810931_florida-gov-rick-scott-signs-44.html?rh=1.

[37] See Susan Taylor Martin, Kris Hundley, and Connie Humburg, "Race Plays a Complex Role in Florida's 'Stand Your Ground' Law," Tampa Bay Times, June 2, 2012. The Tampa Bay Times continues to update the database used for the analysis and it can be found at http://www.tampabay.com/stand-your-ground-law/fatal-cases.

[38] See "Best States for Gun Owners 2014" at http://www.gunsandammo.com/network-topics/culture-politics-network/best-states-for-gun-owners-2014/.

[39] Associated Press, "Federal Court Upholds FLA.'s Docs vs. Glocks Law," Politico, July, 26, 2014. http://www.politico.com/story/2014/07/federal-court-upholds-florida-docs-vs-glocks-law-109403.html.

[40] "Governor Rick Scott signs 27 bills into law," Associated Press (May 14, 2015). Available at http://www.mynews13.com/content/news/cfnews13/news/article.html/content/news/articles/bn9/2015/5/14/scott_new_laws.html.

[41] "Is 'revenge porn' getting out of control?" Palm Beach Post (May 9, 2015). Available at http://opinionzone.blog.palmbeachpost.com/2015/05/09/is-revenge-porn-getting-out-of-control/.

[42] An important exception to state law that prohibits recording without consent and the use of such recordings as evidence in court cases also became law in 2015. HB 7001 allows minors to make record incidents of sexual and other physical abuse without consent. This is especially important because victims are often reluctant to report these crimes due to fear of not being believed. "Scott signs law to allow secret recordings in sex abuse cases," Orlando Sentinel (May 22, 2015). Available at http://www.orlandosentinel.com/news/politics/political-pulse/os-scott-signs-law-to-allow-secret-recordings-in-sex-abuse-cases-20150522-post.html.

[43] Brett Clarkson, "Florida is a 'hub' for human traffickers, attorney general says," Sun Sentinel (September 23, 2012). Available at http://articles.sun-sentinel.com/2012-09-23/news/fl-human-trafficking-pam-bondi-20120921_1_human-attorney-general-pam-bondi-south-florida.

[44] Frances Robles, "Questionable Florida police shootings triple in past 15 years," Miami Herald (May 31, 2015). Available at http://www.miamiherald.com/news/local/crime/article22738308.html.

[45] Michael Auslen, "Florida Senate considers shielding video from police body cameras," Tampa Bay Times (April 13, 2015). Available at http://www.tampabay.com/news/politics/stateroundup/florida-senate-considers-shielding-video-from-police-body-cameras/2225346.

[46] Brian Ballou, "Broward judges toss 24,000 red-light camera tickets totaling millions," South Florida Sun-Sentinel. Available at http://www.sun-sentinel.com/local/broward/fl-red-light-cameras-court 20150316-story.html.

[47] Lisa Huriash, "Tamarac pulls plug on red light cameras," Sun Sentinel (June 1, 2015). Available at http://www.sun-sentinel.com/local/broward/fl-tamarac-red-light-cameras-20150601-story.html.

[48] Perry Chiaramonte, "'War on Police': Line-of-Duty Deaths Rise Amid Racially-Charged Rhetoric, Anti-Cop Climate," Fox News, May 17, 2015. Available at http://www.foxnews.com/us/2015/05/17/war-on-police-line-duty-deaths-rise-amid-racially-charged-rhetoric-anti-cop/.

[49] The statistics in this section can be found at the Florida Department of Corrections, Annual Report 2012-2013, available at http://www.dc.state.fl.us/pub/annual/1213/AnnualReport-1213.pdf.

[50] Editorial Board, "Reforming Our Prisons," The Miami Herald, May 13, 2015. Available at http://www.miamiherald.com/opinion/editorials/article20783670.html.

[51] Executive Order 15-102. Available at http://www.dc.state.fl.us/secretary/press/2015/EO15-102.pdf.

[52] "Florida's Aging Prisoner Problem," Florida TaxWatch (September 2014). Available at http://www.floridataxwatch.org/resources/pdf/ElderlyParoleFINAL.pdf.

[53] "Prisoners in 2013," U.S. Department of Justice, available at http://www.bjs.gov/content/pub/pdf/p13.pdf.

[54] "Frequently Asked Questions Regarding Parole," Florida Department of Corrections, June 2011. Available at http://www.dc.state.fl.us/oth/inmates/parole.html.

[55] Prison Policy Initiative, data from Bureau of Justice Statistics, Corrections Statistical Analysis Tool. Available at http://www.prisonpolicy.org/profiles/FL.html.

[56] See Brown v Plata, 563 U.S. (2011) where the U.S. Supreme Court required California to release thousands of prisoners because it ruled that severe prison overcrowding was cruel and unusual punishment.

[57] See the 2010 Florida Department of Corrections report "Doing Time." Available at http://www.dc.state.fl.us/pub/timeserv/doing/index.html.

[58] Associated Press, "Court Lets 3 Strikes Law Stand, St. Petersburg Times (October 1, 2004). http://www.sptimes.com/2004/10/01/State/Court_lets_3_strikes_.shtml

[59] See the Florida Department of Corrections , "10-20-Life, 2005" Available at http://www.dc.state.fl.us/pub/10-20-life/.

[60] See University of Florida News, "UF Study Shows Florida's 3-Strikes Law Fails to Curb Crime," January 10, 2006. Available at http://news.ufl.edu/2006/01/10/three-strikes-law/.

[61] Florida Department of Corrections, 2013-2014 Agency Statistics, available at http://www.dc.state.fl.us/pub/annual/1314/stats/csp_pop_quarter.html.

[62] Florida Parole Commission, 2013 Annual Report, available at https://www.fcor.state.fl.us/docs/reports/FCORannualreport201213.pdf

[63] "Doing Time," Florida Department of Corrections (January 2014), available at http://www.dc.state.fl.us/pub/timeserv/doing/.

[64] John Dilulio, "Punishing Smarter," Brookings Review (Summer 1989): 8-12.

[65] See the Florida Department of Correction Annual Report FY 2012-2013, available at http://www.dc.state.fl.us/pub/annual/1213/AnnualReport-1213.pdf.

[66] William J. Bennett, John Dilulio, and John P. Waters, Body Count. New York: Simon and Schuster, 1996, p.119.

[67] Available at http://www.floridataxwatch.org/resources/pdf/ElderlyParoleFINAL.pdf.

[68] Florida TaxWatch Center for Smart Justice, "Over-Criminalization in Florida," April 2014. Available at http://floridataxwatch.org/resources/pdf/ThirdDegreeFINAL.pdf.

[69] See Bill Cotterill, "Prison System Hopes Privatization Cheaper," Florida Today, May 22, 2011.

[70] See Florida Office of Program Policy Analysis and Government Accountability. Available at http://www.oppaga.state.fl.us/Default.aspx.

[71] Sascha Cordner, "Even With Scott's Executive Order, Prison Reform Bills Still In The Works for 2016," WFSU, May 15, 2015. Available at http://news.wfsu.org/post/even-scotts-executive-order-prison-reform-bills-still-works-2016

[72] Death Penalty Information Center, "Facts About the Death Penalty," (May 29, 2015), available at http://www.deathpenaltyinfo.org/documents/FactSheet.pdf.

[73] *Profitt v. Florida*, 428, U.S. 242 (1976).

[74] Steven C. Tauber, "Capital Punishment Decision Making on the Supreme Court of Florida," *Politics & Policy* 30 (December 2002): 680-699.

[75] See "Government Program Summary: Capital Collateral Regional Counsels (Death Penalty Appeals)," Florida Legislature's Office of Program Policy Analysis and Government Accountability, May 4, 2010. Available at http://www.oppaga.state.fl.us/profiles/1025/.

[76] *Facts about the Death Penalty*, Death Penalty Information Center (2015). Available at http://www.deathpenaltyinfo.org/documents/FactSheet.pdf.

[77] Death Row Roster, Florida Department of Corrections. Available at http://www.dc.state.fl.us/activeinmates/deathrowroster.asp.

[78] The execution of Angel Diaz was so badly botched that it prompted then-Governor Jeb Bush to temporarily suspend executions so the state's lethal injection procedure could be reviewed. See Ben Crair, "Photos from a Botched Lethal Injection: An Exclusive Look at What Happens When an Execution Goes Badly," New Republic, May 29, 2014. Available at http://www.newrepublic.com/article/117898/lethal-injection-photos-angel-diazs-botched-execution-florida.

[79] Tierney Sneed, "Lethal Injection Case Splits Supreme Court," *US News & World Report*, April 29, 2015. Available at http://www.usnews.com/news/articles/2015/04/29/lethal-injection-case-splits-supreme-court.

[80] Andrew Welsh-Huggins, "Pharmaceutical Company Demands States Return Supplies of Drugs Obtained for Lethal Injection," US News & World Report, May 6, 2015. Available at http://www.usnews.com/news/business/articles/2015/05/06/pharmaceutical-firm-wants-lethal-injection-drugs-returned.

[81] FBI, Uniform Crime Reports, "Crime in the United States 2013," available at http://www.fbi.gov/about-us/cjis/ucr/crime-in-the-u.s/2013/crime-in-the-u.s.-2013/tables/table-77/table_77_full_time_law_enforcement_employess_by_state_2013.xls.

CHAPTER 9

[1] Katie Sanders, "Rick Scott Says Next Year's Record Tax Collections Result of 'Conservative, Pro-Growth' Policies," PolitiFact.com, September 6, 2013. Available at http://www.politifact.com/florida/statements/2013/sep/06/rick-scott/rick-scott-says-next-years-record-tax-collections-/.

[2] John Pamer, "Guest Column: Florida's Rick Scott Not Governing a Popularity Contest: He's Trying to Strengthen the State Financially," *TCPalm*, June 9, 2011. Available at http://www.tcpalm.com/news/2011/jun/09/john-pamer-floridas-rick-scott-not-governing-a/?partner=RSS.

[3] The Leadership Florida Nielsen Company Sunshine State Survey, 2011.

[4] Steve Bousquet, "Florida Lawmakers Aim to Avoid Pitfalls of Past, Troubled Special Sessions," *Tampa Bay Times*, May 8, 2015.

[5] Institute on Taxation and Economic Policy, "Who Pays? A Distributional Analysis of the Tax Systems in All Fifty States (5th ed.), January 14, 2015. Available at http://www.itep.org/whopays.

[6] For data on general revenues, including sales tax receipts, refer to the Office of Economic & Demographic Research's "Long-Term Revenue Analysis," available at http://edr.state.fl.us/Content/revenues/index.cfm.

[7] *Florida Tax Handbook*, Office of Economic & Demographic Research (2015). Available at http://edr.state.fl.us/content/revenues/reports/tax-handbook/.

[8] The sales tax base also includes some other goods and services in addition to those mentioned here, a list of which is available in the tax handbook.

[9] *How Florida Compares*, Florida TaxWatch (2015). Available at http://www.floridataxwatch.org/resources/pdf/2015_HFCTaxes_Final.pdf.

[10] The Tax Foundation. Available at http://taxfoundation.org/article/state-sales-gasoline-cigarette-and-alcohol-tax-rates.

[11] Ibid.

[12] Calculated as percent of total taxes. Data are from U.S. Census Bureau, 2010.

[13] Tax Foundation Facts & Figures 2015: How Does Your Sate Compare? Available at http://taxfoundation.org/sites/taxfoundation.org/files/docs/Fact%26Figures_15_web_2.pdf

[14] Adam Smith, "Anti-Internet Group Poll: Fla. Voters Don't Want Internet Sales Tax," *Tampa Bay Times*, September 22, 2014.

[15] "Florida State & Local Taxes in 2015," Institute on Taxation and Economic Policy, 2015, available at http://www.itep.org/whopays/states/florida.php

[16] Source: Visit Florida, "About VISIT FLORIDA, Florida's Official Travel Planning Website." Available at http://origin.www.visitflorida.com/en-us/about-visit-florida.html.

[17] *Who Pays: A Distributional Analysis of the Tax Systems of All 50 States*, Institute on Taxation and Economic Policy, 2015. Available at http://www.itep.org/whopays/full_report.php.

[18] Bill Kaczor, "Corporate Tax Repeal Stirs up Memories," *Tallahassee Democrat*, June 13, 2011.

[19] *How Florida Compares*, Florida TaxWatch (2015). http://www.floridataxwatch.org/resources/pdf/2015_HFCTaxes_Final.pdf.

[20] For an overview of the arguments against the intangibles tax, see Randall G. Holcombe, "Now Is The Time to Repeal Florida's Intangibles Tax," *Point of View*, The James Madison Institute, Tallahassee, FL: January 18, 2005.

[21] James L. Rosica, "Lower Auto Registration Fees Go Into Effect Next Week," *The Tampa Tribune*, August 27, 2014.

[22] Susan A. MacManus, "The Widening Gap Between Florida's Public Schools and Their Communities: Taxes and a Changing Age Profile." Tallahassee: James Madison Institute, 1995.

[23] The source of information in this section is Office of Economic and Demographic Research, The Florida Legislature, *Review of Federal Funding to Florida in Fiscal Year 2010*, February 2012. Available at http://edr.state.fl.us/Content/local-government/reports/fedfunds10.pdf.

[24] The Florida Legislature. *2015 Florida Tax Handbook*, p. 121. Available at http://edr.state.fl.us/content/revenues/reports/tax-handbook/taxhandbook2015.pdf.

[25] U.S. Census Bureau, *Federal Aid to States For Fiscal Year 2009*, August 2010. Available at http://www.census.gov/prod/2010pubs/fas-09.pdf.

[26] Janet Zink, "Florida Gov. Rick Scott Rejects Funding for High-Speed Rail," *The St. Petersburg Times*, February 16, 2011. Available at http://www.tampabay.com/news/localgovernment/gov-rick-scott-rejects-funding-for-high-speed-rail/1151937.

[27] The Florida Legislature. *2011 Florida Tax Handbook*, p. 111. Available at http://edr.state.fl.us/Content/revenues/reports/tax-handbook/taxhandbook2010.pdf.

[28] "Florida Bright Futures Student Counts and Total Costs," Florida Bright Futures Scholarship Program (2014). Available at http://www.floridastudentfinancialaid.org/ssfad/PDF/BFstats/BFReportsA.pdf.

[29] For an excellent history of the lottery, see Florida Department of Education, " 2014-15 Education Appropriations Funded by the Florida Enhancement (Lottery) Trust Fund," October, 2014; Available at http://www.fldoe.org/core/fileparse.php/7507/urlt/Lotbook.pdf.

[30] The Florida Legislature. *2015 Florida Tax Handbook*, p. 124. Available at http://edr.state.fl.us/content/revenues/reports/tax-handbook/taxhandbook2015.pdf.

[31] Scott Travis, "Bright Futures Scholarship Program Faces $100 Million Funding Cut," *Sun Sentinel*, February 28, 2011. Available at http://articles.sun-sentinel.com/2011-02-28/news/fl-bright-futures-20110227_1_bright-futures-state-universities-scholarship-requirements.

[32] The discussion on the use of the lottery as an economic stimulus is from Susan A. MacManus, "The Lottery as an Economic Stimulus Tool: The Case of Florida," in Howard A. Frank, ed. *Handbook of Public Financial Management*. New York: Taylor & Francis Books, Inc., 2006, pps. 237-264.

[33] The Florida Legislature. *2015 Florida Tax Handbook*, FY 2014-2015. Available at http://edr.state.fl.us/content/revenues/reports/tax-handbook/taxhandbook2015.pdf.

[34] See Brad Goldstein and Jeff Testerman, "In Seminole Gambling, a Few are Big Winners," *St. Petersburg Times*, 2006. Available at www.sptimes.com/News2/seminolegambling/dayone/main.html; Jerry W. Jackson, "New Casinos Raise the Stakes in Florida," *Orlando Sentinel*, June 30, 2002, H1.

[35] See Alan Meister, *Casino City 2009-2010 Indian Gaming Industry Report*, Casino City, Inc., 2010. Available at http://www.casinocitytimes.com/news/article/casino-city-releases-2009-2010-indian-gaming-industry-report-191882.

[36] Jon Burstein, "Seminoles Snap Up Hard Rock Empire," *South Florida Sun-Sentinel*, December 8, 2006. Available at http://articles.sun-sentinel.com/2006-12-08/news/0612071251_1_seminole-hard-rock-morgans-hotel-group-rank-group-plc.

[37] *Seminole Tribe v. Florida*, 517 US 44 (1996).

[38] News Service of Florida, "Crist Quietly Signs Seminole Gaming Compact," *The Jacksonville Observer*, April 29, 2010. Available at http://www.jaxobserver.com/2010/04/29/crist-quietly-signs-seminole-gaming-compact/.

[39] Dara Kam, "Crist, Seminole Tribe Sign Gambling Deal That Seems to Offer Winning Hand to Lawmakers," *The Palm Beach Post*, April 7, 2010. Available at http://www.palmbeachpost.com/news/state/crist-seminole-tribe-sign-gambling-deal-that-seems-531295.html.

[40] News Service of Florida, "Florida House Keeps Guns, Ammo in Proposed Sales Tax Holiday," April 1, 2015.

[41] For detailed information on key budget drivers, refer to *State of Florida Long-Range Financial Outlook* (fall 2014), available at http://www.edr.state.fl.us/Content/long-range-finacial-outlook/3-Year-Plan_Fall-2014_1516-1718.pdf.

[42] Florida's Water and Land Legacy, "About the Amendment 1 Campaign," 2014. Available at http://floridawaterlandlegacy.org/sections/page/about.

[43] Associated Press, April 28, 2015.

[44] Collins Center for Public Policy,/Florida TaxWatch Special Report, "A Billion Dollars and Growing: Why Prison Bonding is Tougher on Florida's Taxpayers Than on Crime," April 2011. Available at http://www.floridataxwatch.org/resources/pdf/04062011ABillionDollarsGrowingWhyPrisonBondingTougherFloridasTaxpayersThanCrime.pdf.

[45] Making Room for 100 Million Visitors: An analysis of Florida's transportation infrastructure and its relationship to Florida's vital tourism industry, Florida TaxWatch (April 2015). Available at http://www.floridataxwatch.org/resources/pdf/tourisminfrastructureFINAL.pdf.

[46] Michael Aislen, "No Teacher Pay, Private Prison Monitoring if Government Shuts Down," *Tampa Bay Times*, May 19, 2015.

[47] The Division of Bond Finance, "State of Florida 2010 Debt Affordability Report," December 2010. Available at https://www.sbafla.com/fsb/portals/bondfinance/archive/DAR_DebtAffordabilityReportArchive/DAR2010.pdf.

[48] "S & P Downgrades Florida's Financial Outlook to 'Negative,'" *St. Petersburg Times*, January 19, 2009. Available at http://www.tampabay.com/news/business/realestate/article968862.ece.

[49] *Long-Range Financial Outlook*, Office of Economic and Demographic Research (multiple years). Available at http://www.edr.state.fl.us/Content/long-range-finacial-outlook/index.cfm.

[50] John L. Mikesell, *Fiscal Administration*, 6th ed. Belmont, CA: Thomson Wadsworth, 2003, p. 543.

[51] Division of Bond Finance, "State of Florida 2014 Debt Affordability Report," December 2014. Available at https://www.sbafla.com/fsb/portals/bondfinance/DebtOverview/DAR2014.pdf.

[52] This law (215.98, *Florida Statutes*) was passed in 2001. Source: Preliminary Official Statement Dated March 1, 2005 for State of Florida Full Faith and Credit State Board of Education Public Education Capital Outlay Refunding Bonds, 2005 Series C, p. A-20.

[53] Standard & Poor's Public Finance, RatingsDirect, February 25, 2005.

[54] Dr. Carol Weissert, "Hidden and In Plain Sight: Florida Local Governments and Retirement Benefits," *The Journal of the James Madison Institute* (Spring 2015). Available at http://www.jamesmadison.org/wp-content/uploads/Retirement-Benefits-JMI-Journal-Spring-2015-7.pdf.

[55] Susan A. MacManus, Kiki Caruson, and Brian McPhee, "Cybersecurity Policy-Making at the Local Government Level: An Analysis of Threats, Preparedness, and Bureaucratic Roadblocks to Success," Paper presented at the annual meeting of the Midwest Political Science Association, Chicago, IL, April, 2011.

[56] Randall G. Holcombe, "Protecting Florida's Cities Through Pension Reform," The James Madison Institute Backgrounder, January 2011. Available at http://www.jamesmadison.org/wp-content/uploads/pdf/materials/Backgrounder_PensionLiabilities_HolcombeJan11.pdf; The LeRoy Collins Institute, *Tough Choices Facing Florida's Government: Trouble Ahead: Florida Local Governments and Retirement Obligations*, February 2011. Available at http://collinsinstitute.fsu.edu/files/ToughChoiceTroubleAheadReport.pdf.

CHAPTER 10

[1] Thomas R. Dye and Susan A. MacManus, *Politics in States and Communities*, 12th Ed. Upper Saddle River, NJ: Prentice Hall, 2007.

[2] A poll of 800 registered voters taken right after the 2005 hurricane season, with its four major storms, found that 63 percent of the respondents felt more confident about their local government's overall responsibilities after seeing how they responded during the hurricane season. Florida League Cities, "Florida Mayors Forge New Leadership Voice," May 29, 2006.

[3] For analyses of intergovernmental cooperation on emergency management issues, see Kiki Caruson and Susan A. MacManus, "Mandates and Management Challenges in the Trenches: An Intergovernmental Perspective of Homeland Security," Public Administration Review, July 2006.

[4] See David Jacobson, *Place and Belonging in America*. Baltimore, MD: Johns Hopkins University Press, 2001.

[5] Brian Adams, "Public Meetings and the Democratic Process," *Public Administration Review*, January/February 2004. Reprinted in Bruce Stinebrickner, Ed., *Annual Editions*: State and Local Government, 12th Edition. Dubuque, IA: McGraw-Hill/Dushkin, 2005, pp.70-79.

[6] Christopher A. Cooper, Anthony J. Nownes, and Steven Roberts, "Perceptions of Power: Interest Groups in Local Politics," *State and Local Government Review*, 37 (3): (2005).

[7] David Savageau, *Places Rated Almanac*, 7th Ed. Washington, DC: Places Rated Books, 2007.

[8] Much of this discussion is from Thomas R. Dye and Susan A. MacManus, Politics in States and Communities, 14th Ed. Upper Saddle River, NJ: Pearson Prentice Hall, 2011.

[9] For a time after the adoption of the Constitution of 1968, courts continued to define these powers in a restrictive manner. Indeed, only 19 counties are "charter" counties; most counties remain "unchartered" counties that can exercise powers only "as provided by general or special law." But the Florida Legislature reinforced home rule in several important acts in the 1970s. Nine Non-charter counties have come to exercise just about the same powers as charter counties. More important, all cities and counties came to exercise considerable home rule. See *Florida Handbook*, 1995-96, pp. 104,116.

[10] Allen Morris, *Florida Handbook*, 1995-96. Tallahassee, FL: Peninsular Publishing, 1995, pp. 104, 116.

[11] For an excellent overview of local government in Florida, see John Wesley White, "Local Government," in Allen Morris and Joan Perry Morris, Eds., *The Florida Handbook 2003-2004*. Tallahassee: The Peninsular Publishing Company, 2003, pp. 226-235.

[12] Florida Department of Education, *Florida City and County Government: A Condensed Reference Version*. Tallahassee, FL: 1991; pp.19-24.

[13] Much of this discussion is from Aubrey Jewett, "County Government Structure in Florida" in Florida Association of Counties, *Florida County Government Guide*. Tallahassee, FL: 2010; pp. 7-26.

[14] Current information on the structure of all Florida counties was compiled by the author from a survey of the websites of the Florida Association of Counties, the Municipal Code Corporation, and the 67 individual counties in Florida. Follow-up phone calls and e-mails were also made to a number of counties where web-data was unavailable or unclear.

[15] Florida City and County Management Association, "Florida Manager Quick Facts," 2011. Available at http://fccma.org/manager-facts/.

[16] For a list of the counties using each districting system, see Florida Association of Counties, "County Districting." Accessed May 23, 2015 at http://www.fl-counties.com/about-floridas-counties/county-districting.

[17] See the Florida Association of Counties at http://www.fl-counties.com/.

[18] Miami-Dade County is the only county without an elective sheriff or an agency titled "Sheriff's Office." Instead the equivalent agency is known as the Miami-Dade Police Department, and its leader is known as the Metropolitan Sheriff and Director of the Miami-Dade Police Department.

[19] Pursuant to Section 129.03, *Florida Statutes*, on or before June 1 of each year, sheriffs are required to submit a tentative budget to the board of county commissioners for the operation of the sheriff's office for the ensuing fiscal year. Along with the tentative budget, Section 30.49, *Florida Statutes*, requires the sheriff to submit a sworn certificate that the proposed expenditures are "reasonable and necessary for the proper and efficient operation of the office for the ensuing year." The board of commissioners is to review the budget request and may require changes made as it deems necessary. Section 30.49, *Florida Statutes*, allows the sheriff, within 30 days, to file an appeal to the Administration Commission regarding the approved budget. The Executive Office of the Governor is required to provide a budget hearing to allow both parties to present their case. Upon the findings and recommendations of the Executive Office of the Governor, the Administration Commission may amend the budget if it finds that any aspect of the budget is unreasonable. The budget as approved, amended or changed by the Administration Commission is final.

[20] See J. Edwin Benton, *Counties as Services Delivery Agents: Changing Expectations and Roles*. Westport, CT: Praeger, 2002; J. Edwin Benton, "Providing Services to Local Government Citizens in Florida: The Role of Counties, Municipalities, and Special Districts," Florida Political Chronicle 18 (2006).

[21] See J. Edwin Benton and Donald C. Menzel, "County Services and Practices: The Case of Florida," *State and Local Government Review* 23 (Spring, 1991): 69-75,

[22] See J. Edwin Benton, "The Impact of Structural Reform on County Government Service Delivery," *Social Science Quarterly* 84 (December 2003): 858-74.

[23] See J. Edwin Benton and Donald C. Menzel, "County Services: The Emergence of Full-Service Governments," in David R. Berman, Ed., *County Governments in an Era of Change*. New York: Greenwood Press, 1993, pp. 53-69.

[24] Calculated from Florida Department of State, Division of Library & Information Services, "Florida Cities: U.S. Census." Available at http://dos.myflorida.com/library-archives/.

[25] For an excellent description of the incorporation (and dissolution) process, see Liane Schrader, "Municipal Incorporations & Dissolutions," Center for Municipal Research and Innovation, Florida League of Cities. Available at http://www.floridaleagueofcities.com/ResearchMaterial.aspx?CNID=13139.

[26] The other newly formed cities are Grant-Valkaria, West Park, Cutler Bay, and Miami Lakes. Office of Economic and Demographic Research, "2010 Census Data." Available at http://edr.state.fl.us/Content/population-demographics/2010-census/data/index.cfm.

[27] Florida League of Cities, "Incorporation, Merger and Dissolution." 2008. Available at http://www.floridaleagueofcities.com/ResourceDocuments/incorporation,%20mergers%20and%20dissolution.pdf.

[28] A referendum is not required by law, but the legislature has required one for all new incorporations for some time.

[29] See the Florida Local Government Financial Report (various years) compiled by the Florida Department of Financial Services at http://www.myfloridacfo.com/Division/AA/LocalGovernments/default.htm. Also, see Benton, "Providing Services to Local Government Citizens in Florida."

[30] General government expenditures include those for the legislative, executive, and judicial branches, financial management, legal counsel, planning, non-court information systems, debt service payments, pension benefits payments, and other non-court related expenses. Source: Local Government Electronic Reporting system, "Expenditure Account Codes for 2014." Available at https://apps.fldfs.com/LocalGov/Reports/.

[31] For an excellent overview of the forms of municipal government in Florida, see Florida League of Cities, "Getting to Know Your Florida Cities: Chapter 1: What Is a City in Florida." Available at http://www.floridaleagueofcities.com/.

[32] Florida City and County Management Association, "Florida Manager Quick Facts," 2011. Available at http://fccma.org/manager-facts/.

[33] Florida League of Cities, "Responsibilities and Roles of Mayors and Councilmembers (Commissioners) in Florida," Accessed May 23, 2015 at http://www.floridaleagueofcities.com/News.aspx?CNID=4376.

[34] National League of Cities, "City Councils," Accessed May 24, 2015 at
http://www.nlc.org/build-skills-and-networks/resources/cities-101/city-officials/city-councils.

[35] Susan A. MacManus, "The Resurgent City Councils," in Paul R. Brace and Ronald E. Weber, Eds., *Change and Continuity in American State and Local Politics*. New York: Chatham House Publishers, 1999, pp. 166-193.

[36] Susan A. MacManus, "Commissioners Views on Elective Office: Why They Run But Others Don't," *Florida Counties* (January/February 1997): 6-10; Susan A. MacManus, "Running for Office: Why Take the Plunge?" *Florida's Counties* (March/April 2004): 16-17.

[37] Susan A. MacManus, "Seniors in City Hall: Causes and Consequences of the Graying of City Councils," *Social Science Quarterly* 79 (September, 1998): 620-633.

[38] David A. Bositis, *Black Elected Officials: A Statistical Summary 2001* (Washington, DC: Joint Center for Political and Economic Studies, 2003).

[39] National Association of Latino Elected Officials, press release, "2004 Primary Election Profile: Florida Primary: March 9, 2004." Available at http://www.naleo.org/.

[40] Florida School Boards Association, "Education Fast Facts—2010-2011." Available at www.fasb.org. Ranking of state is from National Education Association (2012 figure) available at http://www.nea.org/assets/docs/NEA-Rankings-and-Estimates-2013-2014.pdf. School enrollment figures are for 2013-14—Florida Department of Education "Florida Student Enrollments," https://edstats.fldoe.org/.

[41] Albert Nylander,"National Superintendent Survey 2008" and "National Teacher Survey on School Boards 2009." Superintendent Survey available at http://www.oldham.kyschools.us/files/reports/National_Surveys/National%20Teacher%20Survey%20on%20School%20Boards%202009%20Final%20Results.pdf; National Teacher Survey on School Boards available at http://www.oldham.kyschools.us/files/reports/National_Surveys/National%20Teacher%20Survey%20on%20School%20Boards%202009%20Final%20Results.pdf.

[42] Education Commission of the States, "Local Superintendents" (2013). Available at http://mb2.ecs.org/reports/Report.aspx?id=171.

[43] Calculated from data provided by the Florida Association of District School Superintendents, 2015. Available at http://www.fadss.org/membership/superintendents

[44] Kathleen Vail, "The Changing Faces of Education," *American School Board Journal* 188 (December): 39-42.

[45] Calculated from data provided by the Florida Association of District School Superintendents, 2015. Available at http://www.fadss.org/membership/superintendents.

[46] Office of the Governor, State of Florida, "2012. Executive Order Number 12-10 Review of Special Districts," January 11, 2012. Accessed at http://www.flgov.com/wp-content/uploads/2012/01/EO-12-10.pdf.

[47] See the "Special District Accountability Program" maintained by the Florida Department of Economic Opportunity at https://dca.deo.myflorida.com/fhcd/sdip/OfficialListdeo/.

[48] Carol Weissert, "Hidden in Plain Sight: Florida's Special Districts," Tallahassee, FL: LeRoy Collins Institute, Florida State University, July, 2014. For detailed analyses of the state's special districts, see other Collins Institute studies—Robert Eger and Joe Vonasek, "Piecing Together the Governing Puzzle: An Exploration of Florida's Special Districts," September 2014; Ken van Assenderp, "Florida DCCs: Financial and Accountability Issues," July, 2014. All studies available at http://collinsinstitute.fsu.edu.

[49] See the Special District Basics provided by the Florida Department of Economic Opportunity at http://floridajobs.org/docs/default-source/2015-community-development/community-assistance/sdap/specialdistrictpresentation.pdf?sfvrsn=2.

[50] All five water management districts have websites that provide detailed information. See, for instance, the South Florida Water Management District at http://www.sfwmd.gov/portal/page/portal/sfwmdmain/home%20page.

[51] See Richard E. Foglesong, "When Disney Came to Town," *The Washington Post Magazine*, May 15, 1994. Reprinted in *The Politics of Urban America: A Reader*, Dennis R. Judd and Paul P. Kantor, Eds. Boston: Allyn and Bacon, 1998, pp. 238-241, quote on 238. See also Richard E. Foglesong, *Married to the Mouse*. New Haven: Yale University Press, 2001.

[52] See the Reedy Creek Improvement District's "About RCID" at http://www.rcid.org/About.aspx.

[53] Sandra Pedicini, "Walt Disney World's City Residents Help Keep Resort Running," Orlando Sentinel, May 22, 2015. Available at http://www.orlandosentinel.com/business/tourism/os-disney-cities-20150522-story.html.

[54] See G. Ross Stephens and Nelson Wikstrom, *Metropolitan Government and Governance*. New York: Oxford University Press, 2000.

[55] For a good description, see James B. Crooks, *Jacksonville: The Consolidation Story, from Civil Rights to the Jaguars*. Gainesville, FL: University Press of Florida, 2004.

[56] Areas that have rejected city-county consolidation include Tampa-Hillsborough in 1967, 1970, and 1972; Pensacola-Escambia in 1970; Fort Pierce-St. Lucie in 1972; Tallahassee-Leon in 1973, 1976, and 1993; Gainesville-Alachua in 1975, 1976, and 1990; and Okeechobee City and County in 1979 and 1989.

[57] Bert Swanson, "Jacksonville: Consolidation and Regional Governance" in H.V. Savitch and Ronald K. Vogel, Eds., *Regional Politics: American in a Post-City Age* Thousand Oaks, CA: Sage Publications, 1996.

[58] See J. Edwin Benton and Darwin B. Gamble, "City/County Consolidation and Economies of Scale: Evidence from a Time-Series Analysis in Jacksonville, Florida," *Social Science Quarterly* 65 (March 1985): 190-98.

[59] See http://miamidade.gov/wps/portal/Main/government. For an early look at the establishment of federated government in Miami-Dade, see Edward Sofen, *The Miami Metropolitan Experience* (Garden City, NY: Anchor Books, 1966).

[60] Rob Gurwitt, "Not So Smart Growth," *Governing*, October 2000.

[61] Aisling Swift, "Naples Rejects Brookside's Request to be Annexed," *Naples Daily News*, May 7, 2015.

[62] Pew American Cities Project, "The Local Squeeze: Falling Revenues and Growing Demand for Services Challenge Cities, Counties, and School Districts." Washington DC: Pew Charitable Trusts, June 2012, p. 1.

[63] It is important to note that Home Rule powers for municipalities do not extend to fiscal Home Rule because the state reserves all taxing authority to itself. The Florida League of Cities, "A Quick Review," 2011. Available at www.floridaleagueofcities.com/Resources.aspx?CNID=878.

[64] Florida Department of Education, "2014-15 Funding for Florida School Districts: Statistical Report." Available at http://www.fldoe.org/core/fileparse.php/5423/urlt/Fefpdist.pdf.

[65] Florida House of Representatives, "School Capital Outlay Surtax (Half-cent Sales Tax), Education Fact Sheet 2010-11, http://www.myfloridahouse.gov/FileStores/Web/HouseContent/Approved/Web%20Site/education_fact_sheets/2011/documents/2010-11%20School%20Capital%20Outlay%20Surtax%20%28half-cent%20sales%20tax%29.3.pdf.

[66] Florida Revenue Estimating Conference, *2015 Florida Tax Handbook*. Available at http://edr.state.fl.us/content/revenues/reports/tax-handbook/taxhandbook2015.pdf, p. 238.

[67] For an excellent overview of the local property tax, see *Quality Cities*, March/April 2015. Available at http://publications.flcities.com/qc/201503/#?page=38.

[68] See Sarah M. Bleakley, "Florida's Property Tax—A Review of Its Inequities and Proposals for Change," a white paper prepared for the Florida City and County Management Association, March 2006.

[69] See the Florida Department of Revenue at http://dor.myflorida.com/dor/property/taxpayers/exemptions.html.

[70] The Florida Legislature's Office of Economic and Demographic Research, *2014 Local Government Financial Information Handbook*, December 2014. Available at http://edr.state.fl.us/Content/local-government/reports/lgfih14.pdf.

[71] See Florida Revenue Estimating Conference, *2015 Florida Tax Handbook* for detailed description of the different tax formulas. Available at http://edr.state.fl.us/content/revenues/reports/tax-handbook/taxhandbook2015.pdf.

[72] For historical overviews of mandates and their perceived impacts at the local level, see Susan A. MacManus, "'Mad' About Mandates: The Issue of Who Should Pay for What Resurfaces," *Publius* 21 (Summer, 1991): 59-75; Susan A. MacManus, Mark S. Pritchett, and Uri J. Fisher, "Amendments, Mandates, and Money: Challenges Facing Florida Counties," *Florida Counties* 5 (September/October, 2001): 18-19.

[73] LeRoy Collins Institute, "Tough Choices Facing Florida's Governments: Report Card Update: Florida Municipal Pension Plans," September 2014. http://collinsinstitute.fsu.edu/sites/collinsinstitute.fsu.edu/files/Tough%20Choices%20Report%20Card%20Update%20SEP%202014_1.pdf.

[74] The Florida Senate, "CS/SB 172—Local Government Pension Reform."Available at http://www.flsenate.gov/Committees/BillSummaries/2015/html/1054

[75] *News Service of Florida*, "Scott Signs Reform of Local Pensions," May 21, 2015.

[76] John Kennedy, "44 Bills Signed by Scott Affect Guns, Muni Pensions, Distilleries," *Palm Beach Post*, May 21, 2015. Available at http://www.palmbeachpost.com/news/news/state-regional-govt-politics/44-bills-signed-by-scott-affect-guns-muni-pensions/nmLwQ/.

[77] David Bauerlein, "Times-Union Investigation: Jacksonville Pension Crisis," *The Florida Times-Union*. Available at http://jacksonville.com/files/interactives/pensions/.

[78] Ibid.

[79] Stephanie Brown, "Police and Fire pension reform proposal fails at Jacksonville City Council," WOKV (March 25, 2015). Available at http://www.actionnewsjax.com/news/news/local/police-and-fire-pension-reform-proposal-fails-jack/nkfcR/.

[80] Jim Piggott, "Police, firefighters pension becomes political issue," WJXT – Jacksonville (March 27, 2015). Available at http://www.news4jax.com/news/police-firefighters-pension-becomes-political-issue/32052790.

[81] LeRoy Collins Institute, "Beyond Pensions: Florida Local Governments and Retiree Health Benefits," February 2015. Available at http://collinsinstitute.fsu.edu/sites/collinsinstitute.fsu.edu/files/Tough%20Choices%20-%20Beyond%20Pensions-OPEBs%20Feb%202015.pdf.

[82] Pew American Cities Project. 2012. *The Local Squeeze: Falling Revenues and Growing Demand for Services Challenge Cities, Counties, and School Districts*. Washington, DC: Pew Charitable Trusts, June; Accessed at http://www.pewstates.org/uploadedFiles/PCS_Assets/2012/Pew_Cities_Local%20Squeeze_report.pdf.

[83] Alan Probst, "Bonds & Bond Ratings: Financial Management Series Number 12," University of Wisconsin-Extension's Local Government Center, 2013. Accessed at lgc.uwex.edu/Finance/FM12Bond.ppt.

[84] MuncipalBonds.com. 2013. "Florida Moody's Research Reports" (March 13 to September 5, 2013); Accessed at lorida.municipalbonds.com/bonds/moodys_reports?filter_moodys_report=florida&keywords=&submit.x=14&submit.y=12&submit=Search.

[85] Christian M. Wade, "Little City, Big Rift," *The Tampa Tribune*, February 28, 2006.

[86] For a study of the motivations for county governments in Florida to award franchises or contract out for services, see J. Edwin Benton and Donald C. Menzel, "Contracting and Franchising County Services in Florida," *Urban Affairs Quarterly* 27 (March 1992): 436-56.

[87] Announcement of the "Transforming Local Government/FCCMA 2011 Conference." Available at http://tlgconference.org/..

[88] Ibid.

CHAPTER 11

[1] University of South Florida-Nielsen Sunshine State Survey (2014) available at http://sunshinestatesurvey.org/data/data-release1.pdf.

[2] Statewide telephone survey of a random sample of 1,200 Floridians conducted December 9, 2005-January 8, 2006 for the James Madison Institute, The Collins Center for Public Policy, Inc., and the Milton & Rose D. Friedman Foundation, January 24, 2006, margin of error less than 3 percent.

[3] Figures reflect spending on operations, capital outlay, and interest on debt. Greg Forster, "Florida's Opinion on K-12 Public Education Spending," Report prepared for The James Madison Institute, Collins Center for Public Policy, and Milton & Rose D. Friedman Foundation, January 24, 2006; Susan Aud, "Florida's Public Education Spending," study released jointly by the Milton & Rose D. Friedman Foundation, The James Madison Institute, and the Collins Center for Public Policy, January 2006.

[4] Leadership Florida Nielsen Company Sunshine State Survey (2010-2011)

[5] Figures compiled from the Florida Department of Education School Choice Facts and Figures website including Home Education Fast Facts and Program Statistics and Private School Annual Reports. Available at http://www.fldoe.org/schools/school-choice/facts-figures.stml.

[6] U.S. Census, State and County Quick Facts, Florida, 2015 available at http://quickfacts.census.gov/qfd/states/12000.html

[7] Aud, "Florida's Public Education Spending," p. 10.

[8] Florida Department of Education, "Financial Profiles of Florida School Districts, 2012-2013 Data Statistical Report," January 2014, available at http://www.fldoe.org/core/fileparse.php/7506/urlt/0084484-12-13profiles.pdf. Per pupil spending can be calculated in various ways and most states calculate it differently than the U.S. Census. But the U.S. Census figures are considered a reliable basis for comparison.

9 Mark Dixon, "Public Education Finances: 2012," United States Census Bureau, May 2014 available at
http://www2.census.gov/govs/school/12f33pub.pdf

10 See "Per-Student Funding Dropping $572 or 8%," *FlaglerLive*, May 9, 2011. Available at
http://flaglerlive.com/21826/florida-per-student-funding/comment-page-1.

11 See "Average Salary of Public School Teachers," Rankings and Estimates, National Education Association, March 2015 available at
https://www.nea.org/assets/docs/NEA_Rankings_And_Estimates-2015-03-11a.pdf.

12 Aud, "Florida's Public Education Spending," p. 12.

13 National Commission on Excellence in Education, *A Nation at Risk*. Washington, D.C.: Government Printing Office, 1983.

14 See Thomas R. Dye, *Understanding Public Policy*, 9th ed. Upper Saddle River, N.J.: Prentice Hall, 1998, pp. 425-28.

15 Quality Counts 2015: State Report Cards, Education Week, available at
http://www.edweek.org/ew/qc/2015/2015-state-report-cards-map.html?intc=EW-QC15-LFTNAV.

16 The statistics for this section come from Marie C. Stetser and Robert Stillwell, "Public High School Four-Year On-Time Graduation Rates and Event Dropout Rates: School Years 2010-11 and 2011-12," National Center for Education Statistics, April 2014 available at
http://nces.ed.gov/pubs2014/2014391.pdf.

17 Education Week, *Diplomas Count 2015*, available at http://www.edweek.org/ew/dc/, See in particular Graduation Rats by State, Student Group.

18 Allison Nielsen, "Florida High School Graduation Rate Leaps 5 Points," *Sunshine State News*, June 5, 2015, available at
http://www.sunshinestatenews.com/story/floridas-high-school-graduation-rate-leaps-five-points

19 See the College Board web site for "Table 2: Mean SAT Scores of College Bound Seniors, 1967-2005"
http://www.collegeboard.com/prod_downloads/about/news_info/cbsenior/yr2005/table2-mean-SAT-scores.pdf.

20 The College Board, "State Profile Report: Florida, 2014. Available at
https://secure-media.collegeboard.org/digitalServices/pdf/sat/FL_14_03_03_01.pdf.

21 James S. Coleman, *Equality of Educational Opportunity*. Washington, D.C.: Government Printing Office, 1996.

22 James S. Coleman et al., *High School Achievement*. New York: Basic Books, 1982.

23 Foundation for Florida's Future, "School Grade FAQs." Available at
http://www.afloridapromise.org/Images/FCAT%20Results%20Graphics/SchoolGradesFAQs.pdf.

24 Florida Department of Education. Available at http://fcat.fldoe.org/mediapacket/2010/pdf/FCATMediaP2010.pdf.

25 Scott Young, "The Challenges of NCLB," *State Legislatures*, December 2003.

26 Eric Westervelt, "Senators Try To Revise No Child Left Behind – A Few Years Behind," NPR, April 13, 2015. Available at
http://www.npr.org/sections/ed/2015/04/13/398804901/senators-try-to-revise-no-child-left-behind-a-few-years-behind.

27 See "Students Enrolled per Teacher in Public K-12 Schools," Rankings and Estimates, National Education Association, March 2015 available at https://www.nea.org/assets/docs/NEA_Rankings_And_Estimates-2015-03-11a.pdf.

28 The College Board, "Table 5, Intended Majors" in *2005 College Bound Seniors, Total Group Profile Report*, available at
http://www.collegeboard.com/prod_downloads/about/news_info/cbsenior/yr2005/2005-college-bound-seniors.pdf.

29 See Quinnipiac University, "Florida Voters Turn Thumbs Down On Gov. Scott, Quinnipiac University Poll Finds; Voters Back Drug Tests For State Workers Almost 4-1," April 6, 2011. Available at http://www.quinnipiac.edu/x1297.xml?ReleaseID=1583.

30 Howard Troxler, "Changing the Way We Pay Teachers," *St. Petersburg Times*, June 4, 2006.

31 Quinnipiac University, "Florida Voters Turn Thumbs Down On Gov. Scott, Quinnipiac University Poll Finds; Voters Back Drug Tests For State Workers Almost 4-1."

32 See John E. Chubb and Terry M. Moe, *Politics, Markets and America's Schools*. Washington, D.C.: Brookings Institution, 1990.

33 Florida Virtual School Legislative Report 2013-2014 available at
http://www.flvs.net/areas/aboutus/Documents/Legislative-Report-2013-14.pdf.

34 This quote and other basic information about charters schools in this section comes from Florida Charter Schools. "What is a Charter School," Florida Consortium of Public Charter Schools, June 2015. Available at
http://floridacharterschools.org/schools/what_is_a_charter_school/.

35 Florida Department of Education, "Student Achievement in Florida's Charter Schools: A Comparison of the Performance of Charter School Students with Traditional Public School Students" available at
https://www.floridaschoolchoice.org/PDF/Charter_Student_Achievement_2013.pdf

36 *Bush v. Holmes*. 2006. 919 So. 2d 392 (Fla.).

37 See Florida Annual Policy Survey. Available at http://coss.fsu.edu/srl/content/florida-annual-policy-survey-faps.

38 "McKay Scholarship Program," Florida Department of Education, November 2014. Available at
http://www.fldoe.org/core/fileparse.php/5606/urlt/Fast_Facts_McKay.pdf.

39 "FTC Scholarship Program," Florida Department of Education. November 2014. Available at
http://www.fldoe.org/core/fileparse.php/5606/urlt/Fast_Facts_FTC.pdf.

40 Lynn Hatter, "Judge Dismisses School Choice Voucher Lawsuit," WFSU, May 18, 2015 available at
http://news.wfsu.org/post/judge-dismisses-school-choice-voucher-lawsuit. The union may appeal the decision.

41 See Susan A. MacManus and Carolyn D. Herrington, *Continuity and Accountability in a Changing Political Environment: Ramifications for Educational Policy Making*. Jacksonville, FL: Florida Institute of Education at the University of North Florida. FIE Policy Brief 2, June 2005.

42 Until a constitutional amendment was approved in 1998, school board candidates ran in partisan races.

43 Available at http://www.fsba.org/wp-content/uploads/2014/06/School-Board-Fast-Facts.pdf

44 University of South Florida-Nielsen Sunshine State Survey (2014). Available at http://sunshinestatesurvey.org/results/.

45 Available at http://www.fsba.org/wp-content/uploads/2014/06/School-Board-Fast-Facts.pdf

46 PK-12 Public School Data Publications and Reports: Staff 2014-2015, Florida Department of Education. Available at
http://www.fldoe.org/accountability/data-sys/edu-info-accountability-services/pk-12-public-school-data-pubs-reports/staff.stml

47 Quinnipiac University. Available at http://www.quinnipiac.edu/x1284.xml?ReleaseID=1583&What=&strArea=;&strTime=0. Floridians did support by 74-22 percent the idea of requiring unions to get member permission before using dues payments for political purposes.

[48] Susan A. MacManus, "Selling School Taxes to a Generationally-Diverse Electorate: Some Lessons From Florida Referenda," *Government Finance Review* 13 (April, 1997): 17-22.

[49] Karen Fischer, "Court Ratifies Florida Governing Board's Authority but Leaves a Key Dispute Unresolved," *The Chronicle of Higher Education*, March 21, 2006. Available at http://chronicle.com.

[50] Available at https://www.floridacollegesystem.com/sites/www/Uploads/Publications/2014_FCS_Annual_Report.pdf.

[51] State Higher Education Finance (SHEF): FY 2014, State Higher Education Executive Officers Association (SHEEO), available at http://www.sheeo.org/sites/default/files/project-files/SHEF%20FY%202014-20150410.pdf.

[52] See for instance "2013-14 System Accountability Report," State University System of Florida, Board of Governor, available at http://www.flbog.edu/about/_doc/budget/ar_2013-14/2013_14_System_Accountability_Report_Summary_REVISED_FINAL.pdf. Each university report can be found at http://www.flbog.edu/resources/publications/2013-14_accountability.php.

[53] Leadership Florida Nielsen Company Sunshine State Survey, 2014. Available at sunshinestatesurvey.org/results.

[54] Ibid.

[55] "College Completion: Who Graduates from College, Who Doesn't and Why it Matters," The Chronicle of Higher Education, available at http://collegecompletion.chronicle.com/state/#state=fl&sector=public_four.

[56] State Higher Education Finance (SHEF): FY 2014, State Higher Education Executive Officers Association (SHEEO), available at http://www.sheeo.org/sites/default/files/project-files/SHEF%20FY%202014-20150410.pdf.

[57] Leadership Florida Nielsen Company Sunshine State Survey, 2014

[58] For more details on the Bright Futures Program, see Florida Department of Education. Available at http://www.floridastudentfinancialaid.org/ssfad/bf/.

[59] There is also a Florida Gold Seal Vocational Scholars program.

[60] See Florida Lottery, *Florida Bright Futures Scholarship Program*. Available at http://www.flalottery.com/brightFutures.do.

[61] For more information about Bright Futures eligibility and award amounts, see Florida Department of Education, "Bright Futures Student Handbook." Available at http://www.floridastudentfinancialaid.org/ssfad/bf/.

[62] See http://www.myfloridaprepaid.com/who-we-are/.

[63] See National Center for Education Statistics, *Digest of Education Statistics*, Table 314.50. Available at http://nces.ed.gov/programs/digest/d13/tables/dt13_314.50.asp.

[64] The specific sources for information in the table can be found at: Social Security Administration, OASDI Beneficiaries by State and County 2013. Available at http://www.ssa.gov/policy/docs/statcomps/oasdi_sc/2013/fl.pdf; Centers for Medicare and Medicaid Services, Medicare and Medicaid Statistical Supplement, http://www.cms.gov/Research-Statistics-Data-and-Systems/Statistics-Trends-and-Reports/MedicareMedicaidStatSupp/2013.html; U.S. Department of Labor, Employment and Training Financial Data Handbook 394 Report, http://workforcesecurity.doleta.gov/unemploy/hb394.asp; Florida Division of Workers' Compensation, Workers Compensation Claims Statistics, http://www.myfloridacfo.com/wcapps/claims_research/stats_search.asp; Social Security Administration, SSI Recipients by State and County 2013, http://www.ssa.gov/policy/docs/statcomps/ssi_sc/; Medicaid.gov, State Medicaid and Chip Profiles, http://www.medicaid.gov/Medicaid-CHIP-Program-Information/By-State/By-State.html; USDA Food and Nutrition Service, Data and Statistics, Program Data SNAP, WIC & Child Nutrition , http://www.fns.usda.gov/data-and-statistics.

[65] The "third rail" adage refers to subway and metro rail systems where there are the two rails that a train's wheels roll on and a "third rail" with high voltage electricity that powers the train and would be lethal if touched.

[66] Susan A. MacManus, *Targeting Senior Voters*. Boulder, CO: Rowman & Littlefield, 2000.

[67] U.S. Census Bureau, *American Community Survey 2013*.

[68] For a detailed analysis of the Act, see "Implementing the TANF Changes in the Deficit Reduction Act: 'Win-Win' Solutions for Families and States," report prepared by the Center on Budget and Policy Priorities and the Center for Law and Social Policy, May 9, 2006.

[69] Information on Welfare Transition program comes from the Florida Department of Economic Opportunity website at http://www.floridajobs.org/office-directory/division-of-workforce-services/workforce-programs/welfare-transition-program.

[70] See "Florida's Children 2006" published by the Child Welfare League of America at http://www.cwla.org/advocacy/statefactsheets/2006/florida.htm.

[71] USDA Food and Nutrition Service, Supplemental Nutrition Assistance Program (SNAP) Eligibility, http://www.fns.usda.gov/snap/eligibility. Florida eligibility requirements are available at http://www.myflfamilies.com/service-programs/access-florida-food-medical-assistance-cash/food-assistance-and-suncap.

[72] Louise Norris, "Florida Health Insurance Exchange / Marketplace," healthinsurance.org, June 2, 2015, available at http://www.healthinsurance.org/florida-state-health-insurance-exchange/

[73] Florida Agency for Health Care Administration, *About Us*. Available at http://www.fdhc.state.fl.us/Medicaid/index.shtml.

[74] See The Florida Legislature Office of Economic and Demographic Research, "Social Services Estimating Conference Medicaid Caseload and Expenditure," December, 2014 Available at http://www.edr.state.fl.us/content/conferences/medicaid/archives/141212medicaid.pdf

[75] See Florida KidCare Coordinating Council, 2014 Report and Recommendations. Available at http://www.floridakidcare.org/council/wp-content/uploads/2014/08/2014_Annual_Report.pdf.

[76] See The Florida Legislature Office of Economic and Demographic Research, "Social Services Estimating Conference Long Term Medicaid Services and Expenditures Forecast." Available at http://www.edr.state.fl.us/content/conferences/medicaid/medltexp.pdf.

[77] Robert Pear, "U.S. Gives Florida a Sweeping Right to Curb Medicaid," *New York Times*, October 20, 2005. http://www.nytimes.com/2005/10/20/us/us-gives-florida-a-sweeping-right-to-curb-medicaid.html.

[78] Michael Bond and Emily Patch, "Florida''s Market-based Reform Demonstration: Cost and Quality Issues," *Journal of Applied Business and Economics*: 16 (6) 2014. Available at http://www.na-businesspress.com/JABE/BondM_Web16_6_.pdf.

[79] Available at http://www.politifact.com/florida/promises/scott-o-meter/promise/602/reform-medicaid-with-a-federal-waiver/

[80] See N.C. Aizenman, "Fla. Pilot Program to Cut Medicaid Costs Raises New Questions," *Washington Post*, May 11, 2011. http://www.washingtonpost.com/national/florida-adopts-new-medicaid-plan-to-cut-costs/2011/05/06/AFTByItG_story.html.

[81] Leadership Florida Nielsen Company Sunshine State Survey for data from 2010 to 2011.

[82] See Kimberly Morrison, "Florida Medicaid Reports $56 Million in Fraud," *Jacksonville Business Journal*, January 16, 2009.

83 University of South Florida-Nielsen Sunshine State Survey (2014).

84 Jessica C. Smith and Carla Medalia, "Health Insurance Coverage in the United States: 2013," U.S. Census Bureau, September 2014, available at https://www.census.gov/content/dam/Census/library/publications/2014/demo/p60-250.pdf.

85 See Florida KidCare. Available at http://www.floridakidcare.org.

86 Florida Department of Revenue, Child Support, available at http://dor.myflorida.com/childsupport/Pages/default.aspx.

87 See Department of Children and Family Services, Child Welfare, FY 2014-15. Available at http://www.dcf.state.fl.us/general-information/quick-facts/cw/.

88 Florida Department of Law Enforcement, UCR Domestic Violence Data, "Statewide Domestic Violence Victim Totals by Offense, 1992-2014." Available at https://www.fdle.state.fl.us/Content/FSAC/Menu/Data---Statistics-%281%29/UCR-Domestic-Violence-Data.aspx.

89 Florida Coalition Against Domestic Violence, "What is Domestic Violence?" Available at http://www.fcadv.org/about/what-is-domestic-violence.

90 SafeHouse of Seminole County, available at http://safehouseofseminole.org/. See http://www.fcadv.org/centers/local-centers for a list of all 42 Domestic Violence Shelters in Florida.

CHAPTER 12

1 See Gary Mattson, *Small Towns, Sprawl, and the Politics of Policy Choices: The Florida Experience*. New York: University Press of America, 2003; In-Sung Kang, *Politics, Institutions, and the Implementation of Growth Management Policy in Florida Cities*. ProQuest/UMI, 2006.

2 For more information about the U.S. Environmental Protection Agency see http://www.epa.gov/.

3 For more information about the U.S. Fish and Wildlife Service see http://www.fws.gov/.

4 Much of the information in this section for the governors preceding Jeb Bush comes from "Governing Florida," *The Daytona Beach News-Journal*, April 2, 2006, Section B.

5 Mark R. Howard, "Jeb's Legacy," *Florida Trend*, March 2006. Available online at http://www.floridatrend.com/issue/default.asp?a=5773&s=1&d=3/1/2006.

6 Audubon Executive Director Eric Draper quoted by Jim Turner, "Environmentalists Continue Push for Everglades Reservoir," News Service of Florida, May 27, 2015. Available at http://news.wgcu.org/post/environmentalists-continue-push-everglades-reservoir.

7 Lizette Alvarez, "Florida Legislature Has Its Own Ideas for Voter-Approved Conservation Fund," *New York Times*, April 25, 2015. Available at http://www.nytimes.com/2015/04/26/us/florida-legislature-has-its-own-ideas-for-voter-approved-conservation-fund.html?_r=0.

8 David Fleshler, "Environmental Land Money Diverted by Legislature,'" *Sun Sentinel*, May 9, 2015. Available at http://www.sun-sentinel.com/news/florida/fl-amendment-one-20150507-story.html.

9 Wilton Simpson, "Column: A Water Policy for All of Florida," *Tampa Bay Times*, May 5, 2015. Available at http://www.tampabay.com/opinion/columns/column/2228369

10 Florida Annual Policy Survey 2003-2004, Florida State University Survey Research Lab, http://coss.fsu.edu/srl/content/florida-annual-policy-survey-faps.

11 For a list of the many environmental groups operating in Florida, see Eco-USA. Available at http://www.eco-usa.net/orgs/fl.shtml.

12 For more information about the Save the Manatee Club see http://www.savethemanatee.org/.

13 For more information about the Audubon Society of Florida see http://www.audubonofflorida.org/.

14 For more information about the Florida Chapter of the Nature Conservancy see http://www.nature.org/wherewework/northamerica/states/florida/.

15 For more information about the Florida League of Conservation Voters see http://www.flcv.com/.

16 For more information about the 1000 Friends of Florida see http://www.1000friendsofflorida.org/.

17 Water usage statistics come from Richard L. Marella, *Water Withdrawals, Use, and Trends in Florida, 2010: U.S. Geological Survey Scientific Investigations Report 2014-5088*. Available at http://pubs.usgs.gov/sir/2014/5088.

18 Tatiana Borisova and Roy R. Carriker, "Florida's Water Resources," University of Florida Institute of Food & Agricultural Sciences (IFAS) Extension. Available at https://edis.ifas.ufl.edu/fe757.

19 For more details on the desalination plant, see Tampa Bay Water. Available at http://www.tampabaywater.org/.

20 For more information on the underground injection control program, see Florida Department of Environmental Protection, *Underground Injection Control Program*. Available at http://www.dep.state.fl.us/water/uic/index.htm.

21 See Pat Hatfield, "Judge Sides with Seminole County on Tapping St. Johns River," *West Volusia Beacon*, January 14, 2009. http://www.beacononlinenews.com/news/daily/1415.

22 See the South Florida Water Management District, "What We Do" at http://www.sfwmd.gov/portal/page/portal/common/newsr/history_summit.pdf.

23 See John Kennedy, "Budget Negotiators OK Water Management District Tax Cuts Sought by Scott," *Palm Beach Post*, May 1, 2011. http://www.postonpolitics.com/2011/05/budget-negotiators-ok-water-management-district-tax-cuts-sought-by-scott/.

24 See "Tallahassee Muddles Water Management," *Daytona Beach News Journal*, May 16, 2015. Available at http//www.news-journalonline.com/article/20150516/OPINION/150519628/-1/archive?p=1&tc=pg.

25 Laura Parker, "Treading Water," *National Geographic*, February 2015. Available at https://books.nationalgeographic.com/2015/02/climate-change-economics/parker-text

26 See "Wetlands" at http://aquat1.ifas.ufl.edu/guide/wetlands.html at the University of Florida.

27 See Florida Department of Environmental Protection, "Preservation 2000." Available at http://www.dep.state.fl.us/lands/acquisition/p2000/.

28 See Florida Forest Service, "State Forests in Florida." Available at http://www.fl-dof.com/state_forests/index.html.

29 See the Florida Wetlands Information Center at the Florida Department of Environmental Protection at http://www.dep.state.fl.us/water/wetlands/fwric/index.htm.

30 Marjory Stoneman Douglas, *The Everglades: River of Grass*. New York: Rinehart, 1947. Quote on page 1. See chapter 1 for a thorough description of the Everglades at the midpoint of the 20th century.

31 The details found in this section provided by the official site for the Everglades Restoration Plan. Available at http://www.evergladesrestoration.gov/.

32 The Best Beaches list is updated and maintained by Dr. Stephen Leatherman at http://www.drbeach.org/.

[33] To see the results from weekly testing conducted at beaches in every coastal Florida county see http://www.floridahealth.gov/environmental-health/beach-water-quality/.

[34] Ludmilla Lelis, "Surf's Up – So is the Risk," *Orlando Sentinel*, May 29, 2006.

[35] William E. Gibson, "Pressure Mounts to Drill for Oil Near Florida Shores," *Sun Sentinel*, May 28, 2015. Available at http://www.sun-sentinel.com/news/florida/fl-oil-drilling-pressure-mounts-20150531-story.html.

[36] See "General Information About Red Tide" posted at the Mote Marine Laboratory at https://mote.org/news/florida-red-tide.

[37] "Beach Erosion and Control Program," Florida Department of Environmental Protection, June 15, 2011. Available at http://www.dep.state.fl.us/beaches/programs/becp/index.htm

[38] Kevin Derby and Nancy Smith, "Florida Delegation Stands Fast Behind Graham's Bill to Save Oyster Industry," *Sunshine State News*, May 26, 2015. Also see Melissa Nelson-Gabriel, "Dwindling Oyster Supply Threatens Florida Town's economy," Associated Press, April 5, 2015.

[39] Margie Menzel, "Florida Water Fight With Georgia Could be Delayed," News Service of Florida, September 24, 2014. The case is now scheduled to be settled by the U.S. Supreme Court, most likely in 2016. Available at http://www.newsherald.com/news/government/florida-water-fight-with-georgia-could-be-delayed-1.378481.

[40] Greg Yarrow, "Wildlife and Wildlife Management," Forestry and Natural Resources, Fact Sheet 36, Clemson University Extension, May 2009. Available at https://www.clemson.edu/extension/natural_resources/wildlife/publications/pdfs/fs36_wildlife_and_wildlife_management.pdf.

[41] Jenny Staletovich, "Study Ranks Florida Among Top Places Where Rare Wildlife Not Being Protected," *Miami Herald*, April 6, 2015. Study cited appeared in the Proceedings of the National Academy of Sciences, 2015. The Florida Panhandle and Keys ranked five and six on the list of regions for concern. Available at http://www.miamiherald.com/news/local/environment/article17547776.html.

[42] Florida Fish and Wildlife Commission, *Florida's Endangered and Threatened Species*. May, 2015. Available at http://myfwc.com/media/1515251/Threatened_Endangered_Species.pdf.

[43] "Florida Statewide Endangered and Threatened Plant Conservation Program," http://www.freshfromflorida.com/Divisions-Offices/Florida-Forest-Service/Our-Forests/Forest-Health/Florida-Statewide-Endangered-and-Threatened-Plant-Conservation-Program.

[44] This list of plants can be obtained at http://www.freshfromflorida.com/Divisions-Offices/Florida-Forest-Service/Our-Forests/Forest-Health/Florida-Statewide-Endangered-and-Threatened-Plant-Conservation-Program/Florida-s-Federally-Listed-Plant-Species.

[45] For more information about the manatee see http://myfwc.com/manatee/.

[46] Chad Gillis, "Record 6,063 Manatees County by Biologists," Fort Myers News-Press, March 18, 2015. Available at http://www.news-press.com/story/news/2015/03/17/record-manatees-counted-biologists/24894601/.

[47] For more information about the Florida panther see http://www.floridapanthernet.org/.

[48] David Breen, "On Foot, Wing or Claw, Invasive Species Make Way to Florida," *Orlando Sentinel*, March 15, 2014. Available at http://staugustine.com/news/florida-news/2014-03-15/foot-wing-or-claw-invasive-species-make-way-florida.

[49] See Trade and Environment Data (TED) Case Study 462, "Non-Indigenous Species Threaten the Habitat Of Florida's Flora And Fauna," available at http://www1.american.edu/ted/florida.htm. The information on exotics in this chapter comes primarily from this report.

[50] Oscar Corral, "The Python Invasion: Documentary Gives Glimpse of Invasive Reptiles Threatening the Everglades," *Miami Herald*, April 20, 2014. Available at http://www.miamiherald.com/news/local/environment/article1963154.html. Also see Nancy Smith, "We're Saving the Everglades for...the Pythons?" *Sunshine State News*, May 27, 2014 Available at http://www.sunshinestatenews.com/story/were-saving-everglades-pythons.

[51] For a description of the Python Removal Program, go to http://myfwc.com/license/wildlife/nonnative-species/python-permit-program/.

[52] Press Release, University of Florida, "Floridians Passionate About, But Puzzled by, Endangered and Invasive Species, Survey Finds," August 18 2014. Survey was conducted by UF/IFAS Center for Public Issues Education. Available at http://news.ufl.edu/archive/2014/08/floridians-passionate-about-but-puzzled-by-endangered-and-invasive-species-survey-finds.html.

[53] Nancy Smith, "Florida Oranges, State Symbol, Remain in Life-Death Struggle," *Sunshine State News*, April 19, 2014. Available at http://www.sunshinestatenews.com/story/florida-oranges-state-symbol-remain-life-death-struggle.

[54] Kevin Derby, "Florida TaxWatch Looks at How Citrus Greening Has Hurt Florida," *Sunshine State News*, May 21, 2015. Available at http://drawnlines.com/florida-taxwatch-looks-at-how-citrus-greening-has-hurt-florida/.

[55] Even alligators are not necessarily safe from exotics: a 13 foot python exploded after trying to digest a six foot alligator in the Everglades in October 2005. Type the words "python versus alligator" into a search engine to see the grisly results.

[56] Phil Latzman "Citrus Industry Really Being Squeezed in Florida," *Sun Sentinel*, March 5, 2015. Available at http://www.sun-sentinel.com/opinion/commentary/fl-plcol-oped0305-20150304-column.html.

[57] David Flesher, "State Considers Lionfish Ban," *Sun Sentinel*, April 15, 2015. The ban was imposed and took effect on August 1, 2014.

[58] NASA, "Climate Change: How do we know?" Available at http://climate.nasa.gov/evidence/.

[59] U.S. Global Change Research Program, *National Climate Assessment* 2014. Available at http://nca2014.globalchange.gov/report.

[60] U.S. Rep. Jeff Miller (a Republican from the Panhandle) interview on MSNBC by host Richard Lui. Reported by Catherine Thompson, "GOP Congressman: 'Foolish' To Think Humans Can Cause Climate Change," *Talking Points Memo* (TPM), June 9, 2014. Available at http://talkingpointsmemo.com/livewire/jeff-miller-human-activity-climate-change-foolish. Also see JD Sullivan, "Congressman Miller Asks 'Then Why Did the Dinosaurs Go Extinct'" Available at http://greenactionnews.net. June 9, 2014

[61] Terrence McCoy, "Threatened by Climate Change, Florida Reportedly Bans Term 'Climate Change,'" *The Washington Post*, March, 9 2015. Available at http://www.washingtonpost.com/news/morning-mix/wp/2015/03/09/florida-state-most-affected-by-climate-change-reportedly-bans-term-climate-change/

[62] Tim Elfrink, "Video, Watch Scott's Disaster Chief Refuse to Say "Climate Change" in Hearing," *Miami New Times*, March 20, 2015. Available at http://www.miaminewtimes.com/news/video-watch-scotts-disaster-chief-refuse-to-say-climate-change-in-hearing-7548413.

[63] SurveyUSA News Poll #21478 of 1,005 Floridians likely to vote in the November 2014 election conducted July 14-17, 2014.The poll was sponsored by the Natural Resources Defense Council. Available at http://www.surveyusa.com/client/PollPrint.aspx?g=861ac6ca-f6c2-437c-a6a8-489d3a8bc0e1&d=0.

[64] U.S. Global Change Research Program, *National Climate Assessment* 2014. Available at http://nca2014.globalchange.gov/report.

[65] Laura Parker, "Climate Change Economics: Treading Water," *National Geographic*, February, 2015. Available at http://ngm.nationalgeographic.com/2015/02/climate-change-economics/parker-text.

66 Ivan Penn, "Utilities Change Their Tune on Solar Power," *Tampa Bay Times*, May 29, 2015.

67 Laura Parker, "Climate Change Economics: Treading Water," *National Geographic*, February, 2015. Available at http://ngm.nationalgeographic.com/2015/02/climate-change-economics/parker-text.

68 Susan A. MacManus, "'Bricks and Mortar' Politics: How Infrastructure Decisions Defeat Incumbents," *Public Budgeting & Finance* 24 (Spring 2004): 96-112.

69 As of 2006, only four Areas of Critical State Concern had been identified: Big Cypress Swamp; the Green Swamp; the Apalachicola Bay; and the Florida Keys.

70 Florida Impact Fee Review Task Force, "Final Report and Recommendations: A Report to the Governor, President of the Senate, and Speaker of the House of Representatives," February 1, 2006.

71 Dan DeWitt, "Tampa Bay legislator pushes overhaul of growth management laws," (March 7, 2015). Available at http://www.tampabay.com/news/growth/tampa-bay-legislator-pushes-overhaul-of-growth-management-laws/2220396.

72 Thomas O. Ingram and Valerie J. Hubbard, "Major Revision to Development of Regional Impact Review Process Passed by 2015 Florida Legislature; Awaits Action By Governor," (May 11, 2015). Available at https://www.akerman.com/documents/res.asp?id=2282.

73 Eric Poole, "Growth Management," Florida Association of Counties. Available at http://www.fl-counties.com/advocacy/fac-policy-action-center/growth-management.

74 Editorial, "Need to manage growth evident as Florida passes New York," *The Tampa Tribune* (January 5, 2014). Available at http://tbo.com/list/news-opinion-editorials/need-to-manage-growth-evident-as-florida-passes-new-york-20140105/.

75 Ibid.

76 Carol Westmoreland, "Why Do Community Redevelopment Agencies Succeed?" Quality Cities, March/April 2014. Available at http://publications.flcities.com/qc/201403/. 77 Tax increment financing works as follows: "when a redevelopment area is established, the current assessed values of the property within the project area are designated as the base year value. Tax increment comes from the increased value of property, not from an increase in tax rates. Any increases in property values as assessed because of change in ownership or new construction will increase tax revenue generated by the property. This increase in tax revenue is the tax increment that goes to the CRA." Gainesville Community Redevelopment Agency, "Redevelopment: What it is and How it Works." Available at http://www.gainesvillecra.com/about_redev.php; accessed June 10, 2015.

78 For an excellent overview, see "Redevelopment Agency FAQs," City of Palm Bay, Florida; http://www.palmbayflorida.org/government/ departments/bayfront-community-redevelopment-district/frequently-asked-questions; accessed June 10, 2015.

79 Supreme Court of Florida, Advisory Opinion to the Attorney General RE: Referenda Required for Adoption and Amendment of Local Government Comprehensive Land Use Plans," March 17, 2005, p. 17.

80 "2015 Best and Worst States for Business," *Chief Executive Magazine*, May 15, 2015. Available at http://chiefexecutive.net/best-worst-states-for-business.

81 For a detailed description of each type of incentive, see Enterprise Florida, "Incentives." Available at http://www.enterpriseflorida.com/ why-florida/business-climate/incentives/. Also see Florida Department of Revenue, Tax Incentives. Available at http://dor.myflorida.com/ dor/taxes/tax_incentives.html. Florida Department of Environmental Protection, "Brownfields." Available at http://www.dep.state.fl.us/ waste/categories/brownfields/default.htm. Florida Department of Economic Opportunity, "Florida Enterprise Zone Program Annual Report (November 1, 2014)." Available at http://www.enterpriseflorida.com/wp-content/uploads/Report-Florida-Enterprise-Zone-Program-Annual.pdf.

82 See http://www.siteselection.com/ssinsider/incentive/ti0801.htm.

83 Bill Johnson, "Column: Financial Incentives Help Florida Attract Jobs," *Tampa Bay Times*, May 25, 2015. Available at http://www.tampabay.com/opinion/columns/column-financial-incentives-help-florida-attract-jobs/2231028. Also see Valerie Garman, "Gaetz: Florida Changing Its Approach to Attract New Businesses," The *News Herald*, July 15, 2014. Available at http://www.newsherald.com/news/business/gaetz-florida-changing-its-approach-to-attract-new-businesses-1.346410.

84 Valerie Garman, "Study: Investment Key For Tourism Growth in Florida," *Panama City News Herald*, May 7, 2015.

85 Visit Florida, "About VISIT FLORIDA, Florida's Official Travel Planning Website." Available at http://www.visitflorida.com/en-us/about-visit-florida.html. Data are for 2013. State funding (2014) from http://www.wtxl.com/news/visit-florida-given-record-setting-million-budget/article_8db25006-d441-11e3-8142-0017a43b2370.html.

86 Erika D. Peterman, "Open for Business: Sowing the Seeds of Economic Development," *Quality Cities* November/December 2014, p. 23.

87 National League of Cities' Cities Speak blog, "How Do I Attract Businesses to My Community?" December 3, 2012. Available at http://citiesspeak.org/2012/12/03/how-do-i-attract-businesses-to-my-community/.

88 Peterman, "Open for Business," p. 25.

89 See Harvey Molotch, "The City as a Growth Machine," *American Journal of Sociology*, 82: no. 2 (1976): 309-331.

90 Doreen Hemlock, "Japanese Tech Giant Plans Global Hub in South Florida," *Sun Sentinel*, May 28, 2015. Available at http://www.pressreader.com/usa/sun-sentinel-broward-edition/20150528/281513634752316/TextView.

91 Greater Fort Lauderdale Alliance, "About the Alliance." Available at http://www.gflalliance.org/aboutus/about-the-alliance/

92 *Berman v Parker*, 348 U.S. 26 (1954).

93 *Lucas v South Carolina Coastal Council*, 112 S. Ct. 2886 (1992).

94 *Dolan v City of Tigard*, 527 U.S. 883 (1994).

95 Wayne Washington, "Eminent Domain: Costly, Time-Consuming, Crucial Part of County Work," *Palm Beach Post*, May 7, 2015. Available at http://m.palmbeachpost.com/news/news/local-govt-politics/eminent-domain-costly-time-consuming-crucial-part-/nmBXX/.

96 This discussion is from the News Service of Florida, "Supreme Court to Take Up Property Rights Right," May 26, 2015. Available at http://www.news4jax.com/news/supreme-court-to-take-up-property-rights-fight/33222470.

97 Laura Parker, "Climate Change Economics: Treading Water," *National Geographic Magazine*, February 2015. Available at http://ngm.nationalgeographic.com/2015/02/climate-change-economics/parker-text.

98 Michael Van Sickler, "Gov. Rick Scott, State DOT Reject Talk of Gas Tax Increase Despite Transportation Deficit," *Tampa Bay Times*, March 20, 2015. Available at http://www.tampabay.com/news/transportation/gov-rick-scott-and-dot-reject-talk-of-gas-tax-increase-despite/2222135.

[99] *Making Room for 100 Million Visitors*, Florida TaxWatch (April 2015). Available at http://www.floridataxwatch.org/resources/pdf/tourisminfrastructureFINAL.pdf.

[100] For a visual representation of the complexity of transportation funding sources and just their primary uses, see Figure 4 in "Florida's Transportation Tax Sources: A Primer," FDOT (January 2014). Available at http://www.dot.state.fl.us/officeofcomptroller/pdf/GAO/RevManagement/Tax%20Primer%202014%20JAN.pdf.

[101] "Transportation Infrastructure Investment Will Stimulate Florida's Sluggish Economy and Increase Productivity," Florida TaxWatch (April 2008). Available at http://www.floridataxwatch.org/resources/pdf/042008TransportationimpactStudy.pdf.

[102] "Florida Transit Quick Facts," Florida Public Transportation Association. Available at http://www.floridatransit.org/aboutus.html.

[103] http:///.tri-rail.com/

[104] "The Rise of Commuter Rails in Florida," Florida TaxWatch (May 2014). Available at http://floridataxwatch.org/resources/pdf/May14ECFINAL.pdf.

[105] Ibid.

[106] "All Aboard Florida Rail Line Leases Final Piece Of Route Between Miami To Orlando," Reuters (2013). Available at http://www.huffingtonpost.com/2013/10/03/all-aboard-florida_n_4040567.html.

[107] "Work begins — finally — on Miami-to-Orlando fast train," Miami Herald (August 25, 2014). Available at http://www.miamiherald.com/news/business/article1981627.html.

[108] "All Aboard Florida Rail Line Leases Final Piece Of Route Between Miami To Orlando," Reuters (2013). Available at http://www.huffingtonpost.com/2013/10/03/all-aboard-florida_n_4040567.html.

[109] "Work begins — finally — on Miami-to-Orlando fast train," Miami Herald (August 25, 2014). Available at http://www.miamiherald.com/news/business/article1981627.html.

[110] "Florida's Strategic Intermodal System," FDOT (September 2014). Available at http://www.dot.state.fl.us/planning/sis/Strategicplan/brochure.pdf.

[111] In 2011, Enterprise Florida's recognition of logistics as a target industry; in 2011, the creation of the Office of Freight, Logistics and Passenger Operations within FDOT; and, in 2012, HB599 (development of the Freight Mobility and Trade Plan to facilitate trade and increase ILCs, manufacturing, and use of alternative energy). See next endnote for source.

[112] "Florida's Transportation System Is Adding More Intermodal Components," Florida TaxWatch (October 2014). Available at http://floridataxwatch.org/resources/pdf/Oct14ECFINAL.pdf.

[113] Nicholas Nehamas, "Traffic jamming up the local economy," Miami Herald. Available at http://digital.olivesoftware.com/Olive/ODE/MiamiHerald/LandingPage/LandingPage.aspx?href=VE1ILzIwMTUvMDUvMTg.&pageno=MQ..&entity=QXIyRTI.&view=ZW50aXR5.

[114] "Florida Department of Highway Safety and Motor Vehicles By the Numbers In 2013," FLHSMV. Available at http://www.flhsmv.gov/html/factsfigures/tei2013.pdf.

[115] Robert Wood, "Florida Says Uber Drivers Are Employees, But FedEx, Other Cases Promise Long Battle," Forbes (May 26, 2015). Available at http://www.forbes.com/sites/robertwood/2015/05/26/florida-says-uber-drivers-are-employees-but-fedex-other-cases-promise-long-battle/.

[116] Brittany Wallman, "Uber: 'We cannot operate' under new Broward law," Sun Sentinel (April 29, 2015). Available at http://www.sun-sentinel.com/local/broward/fl-uber-law-vote-20150428-story.html.

[117] Michael Austen, "Florida House, Senate far from compromise on Uber regulation," (April 23, 2015). Available at http://www.tampabay.com/news/politics/stateroundup/florida-house-senate-far-from-compromise-on-uber-regulation/2226806.

[118] "Florida is the World's Port of Call", Florida TaxWatch (April 2015). Available at http://www.floridataxwatch.org/resources/pdf/Apr15ECFINAL.pdf.

[119] Mimi Whitefield, "Miami is betting big that expansion of Panama Canal will bring in megaships," Miami Herald (September 2014). Available at http://www.miamiherald.com/news/business/biz-monday/article2197067.html.

[120] Some analysts assert that, even after the expansion, it will still be more cost effective for Chinese exporters to ship to ports on the West Coast of the United States and move the freight to its final destination by land. See Mark Koba, "Panama Canal expansion boom might sail past U.S. ports," CNBC (October 28, 2013). Available at http://www.cnbc.com/id/101140505.

[121] "About the Intracoastal Waterway," USA Today (accessed May 2015). Available at http://traveltips.usatoday.com/intracoastal-waterway-103173.html.

[122] See "Data and Statistics," Federal Aviation Administration, http://www.faa.gov/airports/

[123] Florida Airport Fast Facts, March 2015, Florida Airports Council. Available at http://www.floridaairports.org/members/files/2015%20FDOT%20FL%20Airport%20FastFacts.pdf

[124] "FACT3: Airport Capacity Needs in the National Airspace System," Federal Aviation Administration (January 2015). Available at http://www.faa.gov/airports/planning_capacity/media/FACT3-Airport-Capacity-Needs-in-the-NAS.pdf.

[125] "Making Room for 100 Million Visitors," Florida TaxWatch (April 2015). Available at http://www.floridataxwatch.org/resources/pdf/tourisminfrastructureFINAL.pdf.

[126] "Florida Spaceport System Plan 2013," Space Florida. Available at http://www.spaceflorida.gov/docs/spaceport-ops/florida-spaceport-systems-plan-2013_final.pdf.

Photo Credits

For page with multiple photos, photos are listed left to right and top to bottom.

(Page) Source

Chapter 1
(2) Sarasota County
(3) Susan A. MacManus
(7) Polk County
(10) Sarasota County
(12) Florida Memory Project,
http://www.floridamemory.com/PhotographicCollection/
(15) Susan A. MacManus
(15) Sarasota County
(22) Susan A. MacManus
(26) Florida Memory Project, www.floridamemory.com
(27) Susan A. MacManus
(27) Susan A. MacManus
(28) Susan A. MacManus
(36) The Seminole Tribe,
htttp://www.semtribe.com/TourismAndEnterprises/
(37) CBS Interactive,
http://seminolescstv.com/trads/fsu-trads-osceola.html
(39) The Memory Project, www.floridamemory.com
(40) Sarasota County

Chapter 2
(50) The Memory Project, www.floridamemory.com
(50) The Florida Memory Project, State Library and Archives of Florida, www.floridamemory.com
(53) Sarasota County
(54) The Memory Project, www.floridamemory.com
(55) Florida Division of Elections,
http://election.dos.state.fl.us/laws/AdoptedRules.pdf
(58) Susan A. MacManus
(61) Susan A. MacManus
(63) Susan A. MacManus
(65) Susan A. MacManus
(66) Susan A. MacManus

Chapter 3
(68) Sarasota County
(71) Susan A. MacManus
(73) Susan A. MacManus
(75) Susan A. MacManus
(79) University of Florida Levin College of Law,
http://www.law.ufl.edu/uflaw/09spring/web-extras/commencement-2009
(80) Sarasota County
(80) Sarasota County
(87) Polk County
(87) Polk County
(88) Polk County***
(90) Polk County
(90) Sarasota County

Chapter 4
(92) Florida Memory Project, http://www.floridamemory.com/PhotographicCollection
(94) Susan A. MacManus
(97) WFLA-TV (Tampa) and The Tampa Tribune
(98) Susan A. MacManus
(100) Kevin Hettinger
(109) Susan A. MacManus
(110) Susan A. MacManus
(110) The Memory Project, www.floridamemory.com
(118) Susan A. MacManus
(118) Susan A. MacManus
(120) Susan A. MacManus
(120) Susan A. MacManus
(124) The Memory Project, www.floridamemory.com
(126) The Memory Project, www.floridamemory.com
(126) The Memory Project, www.floridamemory.com
(127) The Memory Project, www.floridamemory.com
(129) The Memory Project, www.floridamemory.com
(130) Susan A. MacManus
(132) Susan A. MacManus (REPEAT)
(132) Susan A. MacManus
(132) Susan A. MacManus
(135) The Memory Project, www.floridamemory.com
(136) The Memory Project, www.floridamemory.com
(136) The Memory Project, www.floridamemory.com
(137) United States Senate, www.senate.gov
(138) Susan A. MacManus
(138) Susan A. MacManus
(139) Susan A. MacManus
(140) Susan A. MacManus
(141) The Memory Project, www.floridamemory.com
(145) Susan A. MacManus

Chapter 5
(150) Susan A. MacManus
(150) Sarasota County
(154) Susan A. MacManus
(154) Sarasota County
(156) Susan A. MacManus
(156) Susan A. MacManus
(161) Susan A. MacManus
(162) The Memory Project, www.floridamemory.com
(165) Susan A. MacManus
(165) Susan A. MacManus
(168) Susan A. MacManus
(169) Susan A. MacManus
(173) Susan A. MacManus
(176) The Memory Project, www.floridamemory.com

Chapter 6

(179) Susan A. MacManus
(183) Susan A. MacManus
(184) The Memory Project, www.floridamemory.com
(186) Susan A. MacManus
(186) Susan A. MacManus
(192) The Memory Project, www.floridamemory.com
(197) The Arthenia Joyner Campaign
(201) Florida House of Representatives,
http://www.myfloridahouse.gov
(201) Florida Senate, http://www.flsenate.gov
(202) The Memory Project, www.floridamemory.com
(203) The Memory Project, www.floridamemory.com
(207) The Memory Project, www.floridamemory.com
(207) Florida House of Representatives,
http://www.myfloridahouse.gov
(208) Florida Archives Collection,
http://fpc.dos.state.fl.us/prints/pr11150.jpg

Chapter 7

(210) Susan A. MacManus
(212) The Memory Project, www.floridamemory.com
(213) Susan A. MacManus
(216) State of Florida,
http://www.myflorida.com/myflorida/cabinet/index-html
(219) Floridians for Better Transportation,
http://www.bettertransporation.org/images/toni_jennings.jpg
(219) State of Florida, http://www.flgov.com/
(219) State of Florida,
http://www.flgov.com/meet-the-lt-governor/
(226) State of Florida http://www.flgov.com
(227) Special Collections Department,
University of South Florida
(227) The Curator of the Mansion
(228) The Memory Project, www.floridamemory.com
(229) The Lou Frey Institute
(229) Bright House Networks,
http://www.baynews9.com/images/news/2005/10/21/martinez/jpg
(229) University of Central Florida
(230) Susan A. MacManus
(230) Susan A. MacManus
(231) The Florida Governors' Portraits collection
(232) The Florida Governors' Portraits collection
(232) The Florida Governors' Portraits collection
(233) Museum of Florida History
(233) Museum of Florida History
(234) Museum of Florida History
(236) Museum of Florida History
(237) The Florida Governors' Portraits collection
(238) The Memory Project, www.floridamemory.com
(238) The Museum of Florida History,
http://www.museumoffloridahistory.com/resources/collections/governors/about.cfm?id=50
(240) The Florida Governors' Portraits collection
(241) Office of the Governor,
www.flgov.com/meet-governor-scott

(244) Susan A. MacManus
(244) Susan A. MacManus

Chapter 8

(246) Susan A. MacManus
(247) Kevin Hettinger
(247) Kevin Hettinger
(251) Ninth Judicial Court Circuit, http://www.ninthcircuit.org/programs-services/court-interpreter/index.shtml
(252) The Thirteenth Judicial Circuit, http://www.fljud13.org/info_jury1.htm
(255) University of Florida, http://pested.ifas.ufl.edu/newsletters/2011-02/courts.html
(258) The Bernie Silver Campaign
(259) Florida Supreme Court, http://www.floridasupremecourt.org/justices/index.shtml
(260) The Memory Project, www.floridamemory.org
(272) FL Department of Corrections
(272) FL Department of Corrections
(273) FL Department of Corrections
(273) FL Department of Corrections
(274) The Memory Project, www.floridamemory.com
(276) Susan A. MacManus

Chapter 9

(282) Sarasota County
(287) Sarasota County
(289) Polk County
(290) The Memory Project, www.floridamemory.com
(291) The Florida Lottery
(292) Collier County Public Schools, www.collier.k12.fl.us/bch/images/FrontBig.jpg
(292) Visit Florida, http://www.visitflorida.com/
(293) Hard Rock Café International, Inc., http://news.hardrockhotels.com/post/2008/12/01/Fre-concert-at-seminole-hard-rock-tampa-during-Charliepalooza-2008!.aspx
(296) The Memory Project, www.floridamemory.com
(301) HP Enterprise Services, http://portal.flmmis.com/flpublic/Provider_AreaOffices/tabid/37/Default.aspx
(302) The Memory Project, www.floridamemory.com
(311) Polk County

Chapter 10

(314) Polk County
(314) Federal Highway Administration, http://www.tfhrc.gov/pubrds/05nov/05.htm
(315) Polk County
(315) Polk County
(316) Susan A. MacManus
(317) Sarasota County
(319) Sarasota County
(327) Sarasota County
(332) Sarasota County
(339) Susan A. MacManus

(339) City of Hialeah
(339) City of Tallahassee
(343) Zimek Technologies, IP, LLC.,
http://www.zimek.com.news09.asp
(347) Sarasota County
(351) Aubrey Jewett
(356) Polk County
(356) Polk County
(356) Polk County
(358) Florida League of Cities, Inc.,
http://www.floridaleagueofcities.com/News.aspx?C
NID=1377

Chapter 11
(360) Polk County
(360) Polk County
(364) Sarasota County
(365) Polk County
(370) U.S. Department of Education,
www.ed.gov/news/photos/2002/0807/edlite-0807_2.html
(373) State of Florida,
http://www.doh.state.fl.us.chdlee/schoolhealth/ind
ex.html
(375) The Chase Academy, Inc.,
http://www.tcaofvolusia.org/mckay.html
(378) www.ThomasTalksonCitrusSchools.com
(381) The Memory Project, www.floridamemory.com
(384) Florida Agricultural And Mechanical University,
http://www.famu.edu/index.cfm?a=headlines(p
=display&news=1763
(387) Pinellas County Schools
(388) University of Florida,
http://news.health.ufl.edu/2010/11735/college-of-med
icine/com-celebrates-50th-commencement/

(390) Polk County
(393) TANF.us, http://www.tanf.us/florida.html
(400) Courtesy of Aubrey Jewett
(401) Sarasota County
(401) Sarasota County
(401) Sarasota County
(401) Sarasota County

Chapter 12
(404) FL Department of Environmental Protection,
http://www.dep.state.fl.us/parks/OPG/baldpoint/
photos/BAP-October2004(2).jpg
(409) Sarasota County
(413)Florida Forestry Association, http://www.
floridaforest.org/advertising.php
(415) U.S. Department of the Interior, http://pubs.
usgs.fov/fs/2004/3095/fig1.jpg
(415) National Parks Service, http://www.nps.gov/
bicy/forteachers/curriculum-and-materials.htm
(416) Sarasota County
(420) Florida Division of Motor Vehicles
(421) U.S. Postal Service, http://www.usps.com/
communications/news/stamps/2006/sr06_044.htm
(423) United States Department of Agriculture, www.
ars.usda.gov/is/kids/insects/story2/insectstory.htm
(425) Sarasota County
(425) Sarasota County
(427) Sarasota County
(433) Sarasota County
(438) Sarasota County

Index

492   Politics in Florida

Wallace, George, 135

Walls, Josiah T., 21

Wasserman-Schultz, Debbie, 144

Water and Land Conservation Amendment, 158, 300

Watergate, 58, 73, 75, 124, 146

Weak mayor-council, 332, 334

Webster, Daniel, 144

Welfare (Program, Transition), iii, viii, 36, 176, 181, 219, 222, 239, 242, 298, 328, 332, 347, 360, 388, 389, 391, 392, 393, 394, 396, 401, 429, 433, 437, 475, 476

West , Allen, 21, 23, 144, 145

Wetherell, T.K., 383

Wexler, Robert, 144

Wildlife, 36, 214, 403, 404, 406, 409, 411, 412, 416, 417, 418, 421, 422, 432, 438, 447, 448, 477

Wilson, Frederica, 23, 144

World Fuel Services, 150

Wyllie, Adrian, 98, 132

Young, Bill, 142

YPNM syndrome, 430

Zapata, J. C., 30

Zimmerman, George, 5, 84, 266

CPSIA information can be obtained
at www.ICGtesting.com
Printed in the USA
BVHW021936270120
570429BV00011B/84

* 9 7 8 1 6 1 4 9 3 3 8 1 6 *